Prentice Hall

GENERAL
SCIENCE
A Voyage of Exploration

Prentice Hall

GENERAL SCIENCE
A Voyage of Exploration

Dean Hurd

Physical Science Instructor
Carlsbad High School
Carlsbad, California

Charles William McLaughlin

Chemistry Instructor
Central High School
St. Joseph, Missouri

Susan M. Johnson

Associate Professor of Biology
Ball State University
Muncie, Indiana

Edward Benjamin Snyder

Earth Science Instructor
Yorktown High School
Yorktown Heights, New York

George F. Matthias

Earth Science Instructor
Croton-Harmon High School
Croton-on-Hudson, New York

Jill D. Wright

Professor of Science Education
University of Tennessee
Knoxville, Tennessee

 Prentice Hall, Englewood Cliffs, New Jersey 07632

Prentice Hall General Science Program

Student Text and Annotated Teacher's Edition

Laboratory Manual and Annotated Teacher's Edition

Teacher's Resource Book

General Science Color Transparencies

General Science Courseware

Other programs in this series

Prentice Hall General Science *A Voyage of Adventure* © 1989

Prentice Hall General Science *A Voyage of Discovery* © 1989

General Science Reviewers

John K. Bennett
Science Specialist
State Department of Tennessee
Cookeville, Tennessee

Sue Teachey Bowden
Department of Science Education
East Carolina University
Greenville, North Carolina

Edith H. Gladden
Curriculum Specialist
Division of Science Education
Philadelphia, Pennsylvania

Gordon Neal Hopp
Carmel Junior High School
Carmel, Indiana

Stanley Mulak
Science Supervisor
Springfield School District
Springfield, Massachusetts

Richard Myers
Science Instructor
Cleveland High School
Portland, Oregon

Reading Consultant

Patricia N. Schwab
Chairman, Department of Education
Guilford College
Greensboro, North Carolina

ISBN 0-13-704629-4

10 9 8 7 6 5 4 3 2 1

Prentice-Hall of Australia, Pty. Ltd., Sydney
Prentice-Hall Canada Inc., Toronto
Prentice-Hall Hispanoamericana, S.A., Mexico
Prentice-Hall of India Private Ltd., New Delhi
Prentice-Hall International (UK) Ltd., London
Prentice-Hall of Japan, Inc., Tokyo
Prentice-Hall of Southeast Asia Pte. Ltd., Singapore
Editora Prentice-Hall do Brasil Ltda., Rio de Janeiro

Prentice Hall
A Division of Simon & Schuster
Englewood Cliffs, New Jersey 07632

Photograph credits begin on page 576

Cover Photographs

The three main branches of science studied in a General Science course are illustrated on the cover. The top photograph, representing Physical Science, shows a magnetic cube levitating above a superconductive material. *(Bill Pierce, Sygma)* The photograph on the left, representing Life Science, is of a leopard staring directly ahead through the jungle underbrush. *(Kenneth W. Fink, Bruce Coleman)* The photograph on the right, representing Earth Science, shows eroded sea stacks near the ocean shoreline. *(Omni Photo Communications)*

Back Cover Photographs

Top left, P. Runyon/*The Image Bank;* top center, NASA; top right, © Michael Melford/*Wheeler Pictures;* bottom left, Herman Kokojan/*Black Star;* bottom center, Barbara Laing/*Picture Group;* bottom right, Bill Wood/*Bruce Coleman.*

Contents

UNIT ONE
Forms of Energy   10–161

CHAPTER 1
Exploring Energy   12–31
1-1 What Is Science?   14
1-2 Scientific Measurements   19
1-3 Tools of a Scientist   23
1-4 Safety in the Science Laboratory   26

CHAPTER 2
Heat Energy   32–51
2-1 Molecules and Motion   34
2-2 Temperature and Heat   37
2-3 Heating and Refrigeration Methods   44

CHAPTER 3
Electricity and Magnetism   52–83
3-1 Electric Charge   54
3-2 Static Electricity   60
3-3 The Flow of Electricity   63
3-4 Electric Circuits   67
3-5 Magnetism   71
3-6 Magnetism from Electricity   74
3-7 Electricity from Magnetism   76

CHAPTER 4
Sound   84–107
4-1 Sound Waves   86
4-2 Characteristics of Waves   91
4-3 Properties of Sound   93
4-4 Wave Interactions   98

CHAPTER **5**

Light 108–135

5-1 What Is Light? 110
5-2 Sources of Light 116
5-3 Reflection 119
5-4 Refraction 123
5-5 The Color of Light 127
5-6 Light and Technology 129

CHAPTER **6**

Nuclear Energy 136–153

6-1 The Structure of the Atom 138
6-2 Transmutation of Elements 142
6-3 Nuclear Power 146

SCIENCE GAZETTE 154–161

Stephen Hawking—
    Changing Our View of the Universe 154
How Practical Is Flower Power? 156
The Green People of Solaron 159

UNIT TWO
Science and Technology 162–275

CHAPTER **7**

Energy Resources 164–185

7-1 Fuels and Their Use 166
7-2 Solar Energy 170
7-3 Wind and Water 174
7-4 Nuclear Power 178
7-5 Energy: Today and Tomorrow 180

CHAPTER **8**

Chemical Technology 186–203

8-1 Fuels from Petroleum 188
8-2 Petroleum Products 190
8-3 Health Chemistry 195

CHAPTER **9**

Space Technology 204–227

9-1 Rocketry 206
9-2 Artificial Satellites 211
9-3 People in Space 215
9-4 Deep Space Probes 220
9-5 Space Technology Spinoffs 222

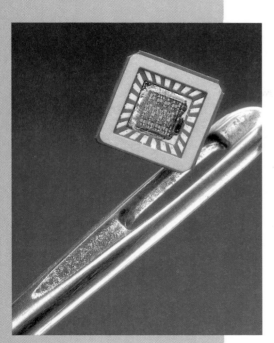

CHAPTER **10**

The Computer Revolution 228–247

10-1 Computer Technology 230
10-2 Computer Operation 234
10-3 Computer Applications 238

CHAPTER **11**

Pollution 248–267

11-1 Pollution—What Is It? 250
11-2 Water Pollution 251
11-3 Air Pollution 257
11-4 Land Pollution 261

SCIENCE GAZETTE 268–275

Jerrold Petrofsky and His Walking Machine 268
Is the Space Program a Good Buy? 270
Sailing to the Stars 273

UNIT THREE

Oceanography 276–335

CHAPTER **12**

Currents and Waves 278–293

12-1 Ocean Waves 280
12-2 Ocean Currents 286

CHAPTER **13**

The Ocean Floor 294–311

13-1 Continental Margins 296
13-2 Deep-Sea Basins 300

CHAPTER **14**

Ocean Life 312–327

14-1 Life in the Ocean Zones 314
14-2 Life Around Deep-Sea Vents 322

SCIENCE GAZETTE 328–335

*Robert Ballard and the Search
   for the* Titanic 328
Are We Destroying the Greatest Creatures of the Sea? 330
Cities Under the Sea 333

UNIT FOUR
Weather and Climate   336–403

CHAPTER 15
The Atmosphere   338–351
15-1 The Origin of the Earth's Atmosphere   340
15-2 The Present Atmosphere   343

CHAPTER 16
Weather   352–377
16-1 Forces That Shape Weather   354
16-2 Heating the Earth   355
16-3 Atmospheric Pressure   358
16-4 Winds   359
16-5 Moisture in the Air   364
16-6 Weather Patterns   369

CHAPTER 17
Climate   378–395
17-1 The Nature of Climate   380
17-2 Climate Regions of the United States   385
17-3 Changes in Climate   390

SCIENCE GAZETTE   396–403
Joanne Simpson's Stormy Struggle   396
Skyfire and Stormfury: Missions Impossible?   398
Tomorrow's Climate: The Heat's On!   401

UNIT FIVE
Heredity and Adaptation   404–491

CHAPTER 18
Genetics   406–425
18-1 History of Genetics   408
18-2 Modern Genetics   417

CHAPTER 19
Human Genetics   426–443
19-1 Inheritance in Humans   428
19-2 New Developments in Human Genetics   436

CHAPTER 20
Changes in Living Things Over Time   444–465
20-1 Change Over Time   446
20-2 Natural Selection   453
20-3 Migration and Isolation   458
20-4 Change: Rapid or Slow?   460

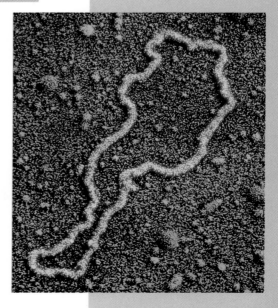

CHAPTER 21
Human History 466–483
21-1 The Search for Human Ancestors 468
21-2 The First Humans 471
21-3 The Wise Humans 476

SCIENCE GAZETTE 484–491
Barbara McClintock: She Discovered "Jumping" Genes 484
Are We Speeding Up Extinction? 486
Evolution on Vivarium 489

UNIT SIX
Ecology 492–557

CHAPTER 22
Biomes 494–515
22-1 Biogeography 496
22-2 The Tundra 500
22-3 Forests 502
22-4 Grasslands 508
22-5 Deserts 510

CHAPTER 23
Pathways in Nature 516–531
23-1 Rhythms and Cycles 518
23-2 Chemical Cycles 521
23-3 Ecological Succession 526

CHAPTER 24
Conservation of Natural Resources 532–549
24-1 Nonliving Resources 534
24-2 Living Resources 538

SCIENCE GAZETTE 550–557
Agent "X"—Animal Smugglers Beware! 550
People vs. Wildlife—Can Both Be Winners? 552
What Will Become of Africa's Animals? 555

For Further Reading 558

Appendix A The Metric System 560

Glossary 561

Index 569

Forms of Energy

With a loud pop, the gas burner bursts into flames. The flames lick at the air as a crowd of excited people watch from a distance. Invisible to the people, tiny bits of matter in the heated air begin to move faster and faster. The space between the bits of matter grows larger and larger. The heated air rises upward toward an opening in a splendidly decorated nylon bag.

Soon the bag is full of hot air. Gently the bag lifts off the ground, carrying with it a smiling man in a basket. Within minutes, a dozen similar vehicles have soared into the sky. The hot-air-balloon race is on. Although the racers may know little about what makes a hot-air balloon go up, such knowledge could turn defeat into victory for them. The secret lies in a mysterious transformation—the turning of energy locked up in a cool gas into fiery heat.

CHAPTERS

1 Exploring Energy

2 Heat Energy

3 Electricity and Magnetism

4 Sound

5 Light

6 Nuclear Energy

Relying on energy to get up, up, and away

1 Exploring Energy

CHAPTER SECTIONS

1-1 What Is Science?
1-2 Scientific Measurements
1-3 Tools of a Scientist
1-4 Safety in the Science Laboratory

CHAPTER OBJECTIVES

After completing this chapter, you will be able to:

1-1 Describe the various steps in the scientific method.

1-1 Compare a variable and a control.

1-1 Identify the main branches of science.

1-2 Compare the various units of length, mass, volume, and temperature in the metric system.

1-2 Describe the system of measurement used by scientists.

1-3 Describe the importance of tools in scientific studies.

1-4 Apply safety procedures in the classroom laboratory.

Jagged strokes of lightning pierce the dark, icy sky. Each blinding bolt brings fear to a small band of people who huddle just inside the mouth of a damp cave. The sounds of booming thunder grow nearer and nearer as the full fury of the storm breaks upon the cave. Suddenly, a streak of lightning knifes into the trunk of a nearby tree, setting it ablaze. Then, as quickly as the storm arose, it is gone.

One by one, the people edge out of the cave. All that remains to remind them of the storm is the fallen tree, which still burns in the cold night. Shivering, the people draw closer to the burning tree. Its warmth is as welcome as the lightning was feared. Some of the people recognize a connection between the lightning and the flames. But none understands the nature of this connection. Thousands of years will pass before people learn the secrets of these awesome forms of energy—and how to tame them.

At first, that learning will be as simple as making fire and cooking food. Later, people called scientists will probe deeper into the mysteries of energy. They will point to unsolved puzzles and suggest possible solutions. Experiments of many kinds will be performed. As each experiment yields knowledge, scientists will follow a new path in their unending journey of discovery.

Nature's awesome display of energy

1-1 What Is Science?

The universe around you and inside of you is really a collection of countless mysteries. It is the job of scientists to solve those mysteries. And, like any good detective, a scientist uses special methods to find truths about nature.

These truths are called facts. An example of a fact is that the sun is a source of light and heat. But science is more than a list of facts. Jules Henri Poincaré, a famous nineteenth-century French scientist who charted the motions of planets, put it this way: "Science is built up with facts, as a house is with stones. But a collection of facts is no more a science than a heap of stones is a house."

So scientists do more than just seek facts. Using the facts they have learned, scientists propose explanations for the events they observe. Then they perform experiments to test their explanations.

After a study of facts, observations, and experiments, scientists may develop a **theory.** A theory is the most logical explanation for events that occur in nature. Once a theory has been proposed, it must be tested over and over again. If the theory is tested many times and is generally accepted as true, scientists may call it a **law.** However, both theories and laws may change as a result of future observations and experiments.

Figure 1-1 *It is a fact that water freezes into ice at a certain temperature. A theory would explain why salt water freezes at a lower temperature than fresh water.*

The Scientific Method

In order to solve a problem, scientists use the **scientific method.** The scientific method is a systematic approach to problem solving. **The basic steps in the scientific method are**

Stating the problem

Gathering information on the problem

Forming a hypothesis

Performing experiments to test the hypothesis

Recording and analyzing data

Stating a conclusion

The following example shows how the scientific method was used to solve a problem. As you will see, the steps of the scientific method often overlap.

Stating the Problem

Bundled up in warm clothing, heads bent into the wind, the two friends walked along the beach. Drifts of snow rose against the slats of a fence that in the summer held back dunes of sand. Beyond the fence, a row of beach houses drew the attention of the friends.

There, from the roofs of the houses, hung glistening strips of ice. Only yesterday these beautiful icicles had been a mass of melting snow. Throughout the night, the melted snow had continued to drip, freezing into lovely shapes.

Near the ocean's edge, the friends spied a small pool of sea water. Surprisingly, it was not frozen as were the icicles on the roofs. What could be the reason for this curious situation?

Without realizing it, the friends had taken an important step in a scientific method. They had recognized a scientific *problem*. A scientist might state the problem another way: What causes fresh water to freeze at a higher temperature than sea water?

Figure 1-2 *Although water on the trees freezes into the familiar forms of icicles, sea water remains a liquid.*

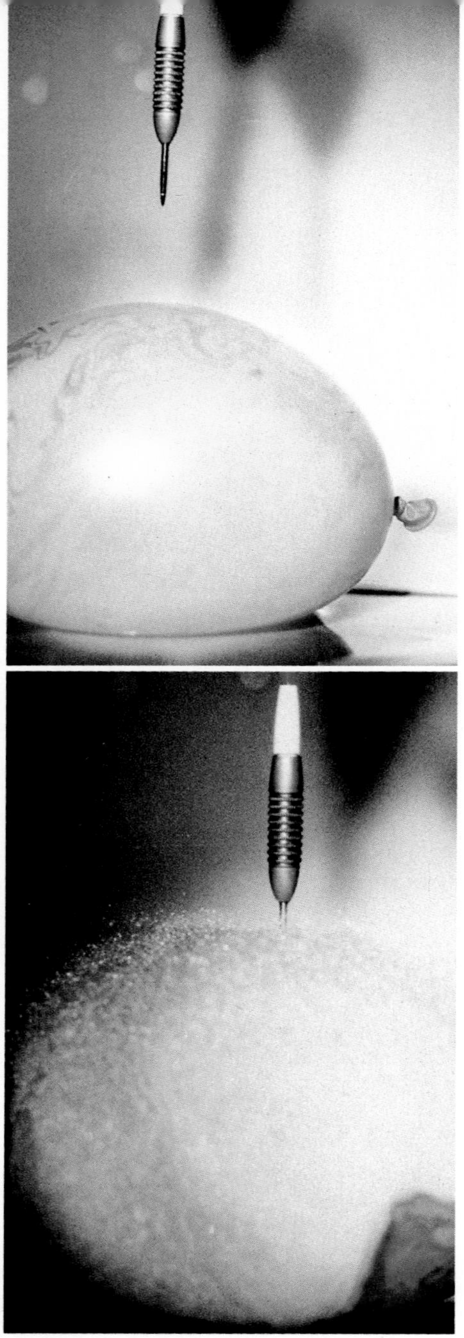

Gathering Information on the Problem

A scientist might begin to solve the problem by gathering *information*. The scientist would first find out how the sea water in the pool differs from the fresh water on the roof. This information might include the following facts: The pool of sea water rests on sand, while the fresh water drips along a tar roof. The sea water is exposed to the cold air for less time than the fresh water. The sea water is saltier than the fresh water.

Forming a Hypothesis

Using this information, the scientist then suggests a possible solution to the problem. A proposed solution to a scientific problem is called a **hypothesis** (high-PAH-thuh-sis). A hypothesis almost always follows the gathering of information about a problem. But sometimes a hypothesis is a sudden idea that springs from a new and original way of looking at a problem.

Among the hypotheses that might be suggested as solutions to the problem described above is this: Because fresh water does not contain salt, it freezes at a higher temperature than sea water.

Experimenting

In science, evidence must be found that either supports a hypothesis or does not support it. That is, a hypothesis must be tested to show whether or not it is correct. Such testing is usually done by performing one or more *experiments*.

Experiments are performed according to specific rules. By following these rules, scientists can be confident that the evidence they uncover will *clearly* support or not support a hypothesis. For the problem of the sea water and fresh water, a scientist would have to design an experiment that ruled out every factor *but* salt as the cause of the different freezing points.

Let's see how a scientist would actually do this. First, the scientist would put equal amounts of fresh water into two identical containers. Then the scientist

Figure 1-3 *It has long been a theory that a liquid does not retain its shape when removed from its container. However, scientists were forced to change this theory after observing the photographs you see here. The photograph on the bottom shows that the water in the balloon retained its balloon shape for 12 to 13 milliseconds after the balloon had been burst by a dart.*

would add salt to only one of the containers. The salt is the **variable,** or the factor being tested. In any experiment, only one variable can be tested at a time. In this way, the scientist can be fairly certain that the results of the experiment are caused by one and only one factor—the salt. To eliminate the possibility of hidden, unknown variables, the scientist would run a **control** experiment. A control experiment is set up exactly like the one that contains the variable. The only difference is that the control experiment does not contain the variable.

In this experiment, the scientist uses two containers of the same size with equal amounts of water. The water in both containers is at the same temperature. The containers will be placed side by side in the freezing compartment of a refrigerator and checked every five minutes. *But only one will have salt in it.*

Recording and Analyzing Data

To determine whether salt affects the freezing temperature of water, a scientist must observe the experiment and write down important information. Recorded observations and measurements are called **data.** In this experiment, data would include the time intervals at which the containers were observed, the temperatures of the water at each interval, and whether it was frozen or not.

From this experiment, the scientist would find that the temperatures in both containers fall at the same rate. But the fresh water freezes at a higher temperature than the salt water.

Stating a Conclusion

If the friends had followed the same steps as the scientist, they would now be ready to state a conclusion. Their conclusion would be this: When salt is dissolved in water, the freezing temperature of the water goes down. For this reason, fresh water freezes at a higher temperature than does sea water.

Why does this happen? This question sounds very much like the beginning of a new problem. It often happens in science that the solution of one problem leads to yet another problem. Thus the cycle of discovery goes on and on.

Branches of Science

Science is divided into many branches depending upon the subject matter. Each branch is made up of a small or large topic in science. There are three main branches of science.

Physical science Physical science is the study of matter and energy. Some physical scientists explore what substances are made of and how they change and combine. This branch of physical science is called **chemistry.** Other physical scientists study forms of energy such as heat and light. This study is the branch of physical science called **physics.**

Earth science Earth science is the study of Earth and its rocks, oceans, volcanoes, earthquakes, atmosphere, weather, and other features. Usually, the earth sciences also include **astronomy.** Astronomers explore nature beyond Earth. They study such objects as stars, planets, and moons.

Life science Life science deals with living things and their parts and actions. Smaller branches of life science include **zoology,** the study of animals, and **botany,** the study of plants.

Figure 1-5 *One branch of physical science is called chemistry. Chemists study the physical and chemical changes that occur when a candle burns.*

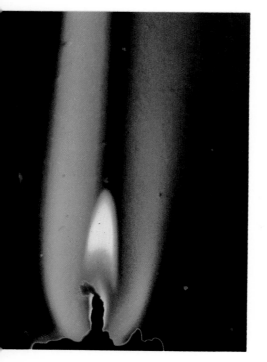

SECTION REVIEW

1. What is a hypothesis?
2. What are the three main branches of science?
3. Explain why an experiment should have only one variable.

Figure 1-6 *The water spout* (left) *is the result of temperature and pressure changes in the air and ocean, and is studied as part of earth science. Zoology, the study of animals such as this two-toed tree sloth* (right), *is a branch of life science.*

1-2 Scientific Measurements

You have read that experiments are a necessary part of the scientific method and that experiments involve measurements. It is important that measurements be accurate and easily communicated to other people. Therefore, a system of measurement having standard units must be used. You can imagine the confusion that would result if measurements were made without reference to standard units. For example, when asked how long it took an object to move a certain distance, a scientist might reply with the number five. It would be up to the listener to decide whether this meant five seconds, five minutes, five years, or the time it takes for the heart to beat five times!

The system of measurement used by scientists in all countries of the world is the metric system. The **metric system** is a decimal system. It is based

COMMONLY USED METRIC UNITS

Length

Length is the distance from one point to another.

A meter is slightly longer than a yard.

1 meter (m) = 100 centimeters (cm)

1 meter = 1000 millimeters (mm)

1 meter = 1,000,000 micrometers (μm)

1 meter = 1,000,000,000 nanometers (nm)

1 meter = 10,000,000,000 angstroms (Å)

1000 meters = 1 kilometer (km)

Mass

Mass is the amount of matter in an object.

A gram has a mass equal to about one paper clip.

1 kilogram (kg) = 1000 grams (g)

1 gram = 1000 milligrams (mg)

1000 kilograms = 1 metric ton (t)

Volume

Volume is the amount of space an object takes up.

A liter is slightly larger than a quart.

1 liter (L) = 1000 milliliters (mL) or 1000 cubic centimeters (cm³)

Temperature

Temperature is the measure of hotness or coldness in degrees Celsius (°C).

0°C = freezing point of water

100°C = boiling point of water

Figure 1-7 *The metric system is easy to use because it is based on units of ten. How many grams are in one kilogram?*

on the number ten and multiples of ten, such as 100 and 1000. The metric system is also called the International System of Measurement, or SI.

Length

The basic unit of length in the metric system is the **meter**. A meter (m) is equal to 39.4 inches. Most adults are between 1½ and 2 meters tall. A new pencil is too small to be measured in meters. It is measured in centimeters instead. One centimeter (cm) is ¹⁄₁₀₀ of a meter. There are 100 centimeters in a meter. A new pencil is about 19 centimeters long. An even smaller division of the meter is the millimeter. The prefix *milli-* means ¹⁄₁₀₀₀. One millimeter (mm) is ¹⁄₁₀₀₀ of a meter. There are 1000 millimeters in a meter. And there are 10 millimeters in a centimeter.

The millimeter is too large to use when describing the size of atoms, the building blocks of matter. These particles are measured in angstroms. One angstrom is one ten-billionth of a meter.

It would take an average person about 10 minutes to walk a distance of 1000 meters, or one kilometer. The prefix *kilo-* means 1000. A kilometer (km) is equal to 1000 meters, or about the length of five city blocks.

Activity

Quick Change

Use your knowledge of the metric system to make the following conversions.
Do not write in this book.

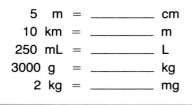

5	m	=	_____ cm
10	km	=	_____ m
250	mL	=	_____ L
3000	g	=	_____ kg
2	kg	=	_____ mg

Volume

The amount of space an object takes up is called its volume. The **liter** is the basic unit of volume in the metric system. A liter (L) is slightly larger than a quart. To express volumes smaller than a liter, milliliters (mL) are used. Remember that the prefix *milli-* means ¹⁄₁₀₀₀. There are 1000 milliliters in a liter. An ordinary drinking glass holds about 200 milliliters of liquid. Another convenient unit of volume is the cubic centimeter (cm³). One cubic centimeter is exactly equal to a milliliter. How many cubic centimeters are there in one liter?

Mass and Weight

The **kilogram** is the basic unit of mass in the metric system. **Mass** is a measure of the amount of matter in an object. From your experience, you know that there is more matter in an automobile than in a toy wagon. Therefore, an automobile has more mass than a wagon. One kilogram (kg) equals

Figure 1-8 *Scientists use many tools to study their world. A metric ruler (top, left)* measures length. A *graduated cylinder (top, right) helps measure the volume of liquids. A triple-beam balance (bottom, left)* may be used to *measure mass. And a Celsius thermometer is used to measure temperature.*

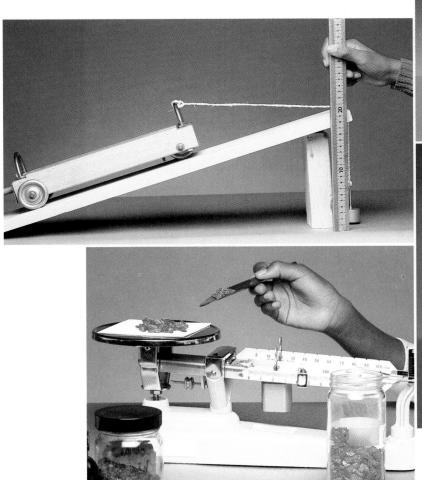

slightly more than two pounds. The mass of an average person is measured in kilograms. But to measure the mass of a nickel, grams (g) are used. There are 1000 grams in a kilogram. A nickel has a mass of about 5 grams. Objects with even smaller masses are measured in milligrams (mg). Each milligram is $\frac{1}{1000}$ of a gram. Thus 1000 milligrams equal a gram. How many milligrams are in a kilogram?

Mass is not the same as **weight.** Weight is a measure of the attraction between two objects due to **gravity.** All objects exert a force of gravity on each other. The strength of the force is determined by the mass of the objects and the distance between them. You may not be aware of it, but the gravity of your body pulls the earth toward you. At the same time, the gravity of the earth pulls you toward its center. Your mass, however, is much smaller than the mass of the earth. As a result, the force of gravity you exert is very small compared to that of the earth. You remain on the surface of the earth because of the force of the earth's gravity. And your weight is a measure of this force. As the distance between objects increases, the force of gravity between them decreases. Thus you would weigh less on the top of a mountain than at sea level, since on a mountaintop you are farther away from the center of the earth.

It may be apparent to you now that mass is a constant and weight is not. Weight can change. For example, a person who has a certain weight on the earth would weigh much less on the moon. This is because the gravity of the moon is about one-sixth the gravity of the earth. Can you explain why this same person would weigh about two and one-half times more on Jupiter? The mass of the person, however, does not change. It is the same on the moon, Earth, or Jupiter.

DENSITY The measurement of the amount of mass in a given volume of an object is called its **density.** Density is defined as the mass per unit volume of a substance. The following formula shows the relationship between density, mass, and volume:

$$\text{density} = \frac{\text{mass}}{\text{volume}}$$

Activity

Using the Metric System

Here are some measurements you can make about yourself and your surroundings. Use the metric units of length, mass, volume, and temperature. Use a metric ruler or tape, a measuring cup, and a thermometer. Record your observations in chart form.

Make the following measurements about yourself:

height

arm length

waist size

body temperature

volume of milk you drink in a day

Make the following measurements about your surroundings:

outdoor temperature

automobile speed limit

distance to school

ingredients in your favorite brownie recipe

An object with a mass of 10 grams and a volume of 5 milliliters has a density of 2 grams per milliliter, or 2 g/mL. Since the density of water is 1 g/mL, this object is more dense than water and would sink. The density of wood is less than 1 g/mL, as shown by the fact that wood floats in water. Density is an important quantity because it allows scientists to identify and compare objects.

Temperature

In the metric system, temperature is measured on the **Celsius** scale. On this temperature scale, water freezes at 0° C and boils at 100° C. This is not an accident. The metric system of temperature was set up in such a way that there are exactly 100 degrees between the freezing point and the boiling point of water. Thus, each Celsius degree represents $\frac{1}{100}$ of this range. Normal body temperature is 37° C. Comfortable room temperature is about 21° C.

SECTION REVIEW

1. What are the basic units of length, volume, and mass in the metric system?
2. What is the difference between mass and weight?
3. In the metric system, on what scale is temperature measured? What are its fixed points?
4. What is density? Why is it an important scientific measurement?

Figure 1-9 *To increase her density so that she can sink to the cold depths of the sea bottom, this scuba diver wears a belt of lead weights.*

1-3 Tools of a Scientist

Scientists use a variety of tools: Some of these tools are used for making measurements, others are used for carrying out experiments. Beakers, flasks, and test tubes are familiar scientific tools. So are electric meters and Geiger counters, which are more complex tools.

Scientists choose the tools most appropriate for solving a problem. Not all these tools are used only by scientists, however. For example, scientists use pencils and paper to record data, just as you do!

Career: *Scientific Editor*

A group of scientists at a large research laboratory have found a new way to make hydrogen fuel. Sunlight is used to break up water into hydrogen and oxygen. The new method promises to be an important source of energy.

The staff of a popular science magazine agree that this development will be of interest to their readers. Choosing topics for scientific articles is part of the job of **science editors.** Science editors must also select the writers who prepare the stories, and then review those stories. This may involve rewriting, correcting errors, and preparing the material for printing. The editors may also select drawings, photos, or charts to be included with the story.

Editorial opportunities are available with book, magazine, and newspaper publishers and with broadcasting companies. To learn more about a career in science editing, write to The Newspaper Fund, Inc., P.O. Box 300, Princeton, NJ 08540.

You can get an idea of the kinds of tools scientists use by examining three common, but very different, scientific instruments.

Spectroscope

You may not know it, but white light is actually made up of many different colors. A **spectroscope** (SPEK-truh-skohp) is a device that breaks up light into its particular colors. The band of colors that is produced is called a **spectrum.** When certain substances give off energy, they often do it in the form of light. This light is separated into a characteristic spectrum as it passes through a spectroscope. A substance's spectrum is like a fingerprint of that substance. Thus the spectrum of a substance helps scientists identify the substance. Using a spectroscope, scientists once discovered a new substance. The substance, called helium, was first discovered as being a part of the sun. Later, helium was found on the earth.

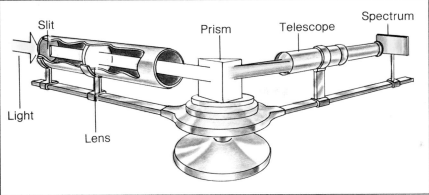

Figure 1-10 *A spectroscope (left) is used to analyze light. As light passes through the lens and prism, it forms a spectrum of rainbow colors (right).*

Laser

Besides being broken up, light can also be concentrated by a tool called a **laser.** A laser produces a narrow beam of light. Laser beams can be used to burn through metal, weld materials, send information, or perform delicate surgery.

Electron Microscope

For hundreds of years, scientists have been able to view tiny objects by using an instrument called a **microscope.** An optical microscope uses a beam of light and a system of lenses to produce an image of

Figure 1-11 *Lasers are used in a variety of ways—from illuminating a stage to cutting and welding metal.*

Figure 1-12 *Modern microscopes have been able to take pictures of individual atoms. This photograph is the first ever taken of an atom and its bonds. A bond is the way different atoms are chemically joined together. The bright round objects are single atoms. The fuzzy areas between atoms represent the bonds.*

an object that can be enlarged up to about 2000 times. But an optical microscope is not useful for viewing very small objects, such as viruses.

If, instead of light, a beam of tiny, fast-moving particles called electrons is used, objects can be magnified more than five million times. The device that does this is the **electron microscope.** Through the electron microscope, scientists are able to see objects as small as atoms, which are the tiny particles that make up matter. By carefully viewing individual atoms, no bigger than one angstrom in diameter, scientists are improving their basic understanding of the nature of matter.

SECTION REVIEW

1. What is a spectroscope and how is it used?
2. Name two other tools of a scientist and briefly explain their uses.

1-4 Safety in the Science Laboratory

When working in the laboratory, scientists know that it is very important to follow safety procedures. All of the work you will do in the laboratory this year will include experiments that have been done over and over again. When done properly, the experiments are interesting and safe. However, if they are done improperly, accidents can occur. How can you avoid such problems?

First and foremost, always follow your teacher's directions or the directions in your textbook exactly as stated. Never try anything on your own without asking your teacher first. And when you are not sure what you should do, always ask first. As you read the laboratory activities in the textbook, you will see safety alert symbols next to certain procedures that require special safety care. Look at Figure 1-13 to learn the meanings of the safety symbols and the important safety rules you should follow. Read each rule carefully. If you do not understand a rule, ask your teacher to explain it.

LABORATORY SAFETY: RULES AND SYMBOLS

Glassware Safety

1. Whenever you see this symbol, you will know that you are working with glassware that can be easily broken. Take particular care to handle such glassware safely. And never use broken glassware.
2. Never heat glassware that is not thoroughly dry. Never pick up any glassware unless you are sure it is not hot. If it is hot, use heat-resistant gloves.
3. Always clean glassware thoroughly before putting it away.

Fire Safety

1. Whenever you see this symbol, you will know that you are working with fire. Never use any source of fire without wearing safety goggles.
2. Never heat anything—particularly chemicals—unless instructed to do so.
3. Never heat anything in a closed container.
4. Never reach across a flame.
5. Always use a clamp, tongs, or heat-resistant gloves to handle hot objects.
6. Always maintain a clean work area, particularly when using a flame.

Heat Safety

Whenever you see this symbol, you will know that you should put on heat-resistant gloves to avoid burning your hands.

Chemical Safety

1. Whenever you see this symbol, you will know that you are working with chemicals that could be hazardous.
2. Never smell any chemical directly from its container. Always use your hand to waft some of the odors from the top of the container towards your nose—and only when instructed to do so.
3. Never mix chemicals unless instructed to do so.
4. Never touch or taste any chemical unless instructed to do so.
5. Keep all lids closed when chemicals are not in use. Dispose of all chemicals as instructed by your teacher.

6. Rinse any chemicals, particularly acids, off your skin and clothes with water immediately. Then notify your teacher.

Eye and Face Safety

1. Whenever you see this symbol, you will know that you are performing an experiment in which you must take precautions to protect your eyes and face by wearing safety goggles.
2. Always point a test tube or bottle that is being heated away from you and others. Chemicals can splash or boil out of the heated test tube.

Sharp Instrument Safety

1. Whenever you see this symbol, you will know that you are working with a sharp instrument.
2. Always use single-edged razors; double-edged razors are too dangerous.
3. Handle any sharp instrument with extreme care. Never cut any material towards you; always cut away from you.
4. Notify your teacher immediately if you are cut in the lab.

Electrical Safety

1. Whenever you see this symbol, you will know that you are using electricity in the laboratory.
2. Never use long extension cords to plug in an electrical device. Do not plug too many different appliances into one socket or you may overload the socket and cause a fire.
3. Never touch an electrical appliance or outlet with wet hands.

Animal Safety

1. Whenever you see this symbol, you will know that you are working with live animals.
2. Do not cause pain, discomfort, or injury to an animal.
3. Follow your teacher's directions when handling animals. Wash your hands thoroughly after handling animals or their cages.

SECTION REVIEW

1. What is the most important general rule to keep in mind whenever you work in the laboratory?
2. Suppose your teacher asked you to boil some water in a test tube. What precautions would you take so that this activity would be done safely?
3. Why is laboratory experimentation an important part of the scientific method?

Figure 1-13 *You should become familiar with these safety rules and symbols because you will see them in the laboratory activities in this textbook. What is the symbol for special safety precautions you should take when using a sharp instrument?*

LABORATORY ACTIVITY

Uncertainty of Measurements

Purpose

In this activity, you will determine how accurately matter can be measured.

Materials *(per station)*

Station 1: meterstick

Station 2: metric ruler
regular object

Station 3: graduated cylinder
beaker with colored liquid

Station 4: triple-beam balance
small pebble

Station 5: graduated cylinder
beaker of water
irregular object

Station 6: Celsius thermometer
beaker with ice and water
paper towel

Procedure

1. Station 1: Use the meterstick to measure the length and width of the desk or lab table. If the table is irregular, measure the shortest width and the longest length. Express your measurements in centimeters.
2. Station 2: Use the metric ruler to find the volume of the regular object. Express the volume in cubic centimeters.
3. Station 3: Use the graduated cylinder to find the volume of the colored liquid in the beaker. Then pour the liquid back into the beaker. Express your measurement in milliliters.
4. Station 4: Place the pebble on the pan of the triple-beam balance. Move the riders until the pointer is at zero. Record the mass of the pebble in grams. Remove the pebble and return all riders back to zero.
5. Station 5: Fill the graduated cylinder half full with water. Find the volume of the irregular object. Express the volume of the

object in cubic centimeters. Carefully remove the object from the graduated cylinder. Pour the water back into the beaker.
6. Station 6: Use the Celsius thermometer to find the temperature of the ice water. Record the temperature in degrees Celsius. Remove the thermometer and carefully dry it with a paper towel.

Observations and Conclusions

1. Your teacher will construct a large class data table for each of the work stations. Record the data from each group on the class data table.
2. Do all the class measurements have the exact same value for each station?
3. Which station had measurements that were most nearly alike? Explain why these measurements were so similar.
4. Which station had measurements that were most varied? Explain why these measurements were so varied.

SUMMARY

1-1 What Is Science?

■ A theory is the most logical explanation of events that occur in nature.

■ When a scientific theory has been tested many times and is accepted as true, scientists may call it a law.

■ The scientific method is a process used by scientists to discover facts about nature.

■ The basic steps of the scientific method are stating the problem, gathering information, forming a hypothesis, experimenting, recording and analyzing data, and stating a conclusion.

■ A variable is the one factor that is being tested in an experiment.

■ Scientists run an experimental setup and a control setup, or experiment without the variable, to make sure the results of the experiment were caused by the variable and not some hidden factor.

■ The three branches of science are physical science, earth science, and life science.

1-2 Scientific Measurements

■ The metric system is the system of measurement used in science.

■ The meter is the basic unit of length in the metric system.

■ The liter is the basic unit of volume in the metric system.

■ The kilogram is the basic unit of mass in the metric system.

■ Mass is a measure of the amount of matter in an object. Weight is a measure of the attraction between objects due to gravity.

■ Density is a measure of the amount of mass in a given volume of an object.

■ Temperature is measured on the Celsius scale, which has 100 degrees between the freezing point and the boiling point of water.

1-3 Tools of a Scientist

■ A spectroscope breaks up light into its particular colors.

■ A laser produces a kind of concentrated light that can be used to cut objects and to transmit messages.

■ The electron microscope helps scientists view tiny objects such as atoms.

1-4 Safety in the Science Laboratory

■ When working in the laboratory, it is important to take all necessary safety precautions. These include using safety equipment and following all instructions carefully.

■ If all safety rules are followed, the laboratory can be a safe and exciting place.

VOCABULARY

Define each term in a complete sentence.

astronomy	electron microscope	mass	spectroscope
botany	gravity	meter	spectrum
Celsius	hypothesis	metric system	theory
chemistry	kilogram	microscope	variable
control	laser	physics	weight
data	law	scientific method	zoology
density	liter		

CONTENT REVIEW: MULTIPLE CHOICE

Choose the letter of the answer that best completes each statement.

1. The branch of physical science that deals with different forms of energy is
   a. astronomy.   b. chemistry.
   c. physics.   d. botany.
2. The basic unit of volume in the metric system is the
   a. liter.   b. gram.
   c. meter.   d. kilogram.
3. One kilometer is equal to
   a 1000 meters.   b. 1/1000 meter.
   c. 100 meters.   d. 10 meters.
4. One milliliter is equal to
   a. 100 liters.   b. 1/100 liter.
   c. 1/1000 liter.   d. 1000 liters.
5. The meter is the basic unit of
   a. volume.   b. mass.
   c. length   d. density.
6. The basic unit of mass is the
   a. liter.   b. kilogram.
   c. gram.   d. meter.
7. The amount of mass in a given volume of an object is called
   a. gravity.   b. temperature.
   c. area.   d. density.
8. The boiling point of water is
   a. 32° C   b. 0° C   c. 100° C   d. 212° C
9. Light is broken up into its colors by a(n)
   a. spectroscope.   b. ammeter.
   c. laser.   d. triple-beam balance.
10. The safety precaution symbol you will see whenever you work with fire is
    a. a razor blade.   b. an electrical plug.
    c. safety goggles.   d. a flask.

CONTENT REVIEW: COMPLETION

Fill in the word or words that best complete each statement.

1. A suggested solution to a problem usually based on information related to the problem is called a(n) _____.
2. The factor being tested in an experiment is the _____.
3. The _____ system is the system of measurement used in science.
4. The prefix _____ means 1000.
5. One meter is equal to _____ millimeters.
6. One ten-billionth of a meter is called a(n) _____.
7. _____ is a measure of the amount of matter in an object.
8. Water freezes at _____° C.
9. A narrow beam of intense light is produced by a(n) _____.
10. A(n) _____ is the symbol for glassware safety.

CONTENT REVIEW: TRUE OR FALSE

Determine whether each statement is true or false. If it is true, write "true." If it is false, change the underlined word or words to make the statement true.

1. The process used by scientists to discover facts about their world is called the <u>scientific method</u>.
2. Recorded observations that often involve measurements are called <u>conclusions</u>.
3. The <u>control</u> experiment is the experiment without the variable.
4. The basic unit of length is the <u>kilogram</u>.
5. One cubic centimeter is exactly equal to a <u>liter</u>.
6. The force of attraction between objects is called <u>gravity</u>.
7. An object with a mass of 12 grams and a volume of 6 milliliters would have a density of <u>2 grams per milliliter</u>.
8. The boiling point of water is <u>37° C</u>.
9. A <u>telescope</u> is a device that breaks up light into its particular colors.
10. The device that enables scientists to see atoms is the <u>optical telescope</u>.

CONCEPT REVIEW: SKILL BUILDING

Use the skills you have developed in this chapter to complete each activity.

1. **Applying concepts** Determine which metric units you would use when measuring the following objects.
   a. the volume of a glass of milk
   b. the length of your textbook
   c. the mass of a compact car
   d. the temperature of a lake
   e. the mass of a pencil
   f. the height of a two-story house
   g. the density of a block of wood

2. **Making calculations** Convert each of the following.
   a. 50 km = _____ m
   b. 10 mL = _____ cm^3
   c. 5 kg = _____ mg
   d. 25,000 g = _____ kg
   e. 2.5 L = _____ mL

3. **Making inferences** How could you determine if an object will float in water without placing the object in water?

4. **Designing an experiment** Antifreeze is a substance people put into their car's radiator during hot summer months. Design an experiment to test if antifreeze has any effect on the boiling point of water. Make sure your experiment has a variable and a control.

CONCEPT REVIEW: ESSAY

Discuss each of the following in a brief paragraph.

1. Describe briefly the basic steps of the scientific method.
2. Compare mass and weight.
3. Describe how a spectroscope works and why it is an important device.
4. Why is it important that scientists all use the same system of measurement?
5. What role might luck or chance play in the advancement of science?
6. Compare a theory and a law.

2 Heat Energy

CHAPTER SECTIONS

2-1 Molecules and Motion

2-2 Temperature and Heat

2-3 Heating and Refrigeration Methods

CHAPTER OBJECTIVES

After completing this chapter, you will be able to:

2-1 Define heat.

2-1 Compare the three methods of heat transfer.

2-2 Compare kinetic and potential energy.

2-2 Relate heat energy and temperature to the motion of molecules.

2-2 Define specific heat.

2-2 Describe the law of conservation of energy.

2-3 Relate heat transfer and energy conversions to heating and cooling systems.

Lost in the snowy, lonely wilderness, a man wanders in search of warmth and shelter. He is rapidly losing his body heat to the colder surroundings. Although he is dressed in layers of thick clothing, he cannot conserve enough heat to keep his body functioning. He is slowly freezing to death. Somehow he must find a way to get warm. He knows he could burn wood to produce heat. But the snow and icy water have made it difficult to start a fire. His numb fingers and toes and an overwhelming feeling of tiredness can only mean time is running out.

This wonderful adventure story, called "To Build a Fire," was written by the American author Jack London. But it is more than just an exciting story of a man's struggle to survive. It is also a story about heat and the attempt to understand and control it. In this sense, it is a story about scientific knowledge.

An understanding of heat and the many roles it plays in the lives of real people is important to you too. Who knows? Some day such knowledge may even save your life. As for the man lost in the snow, you will have to read the original story to find out what happened to him!

Lost in the snowy wilderness

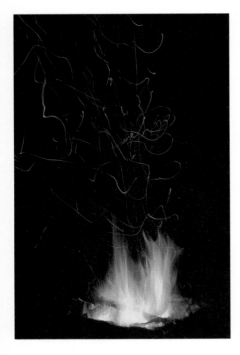

Figure 2-1 *At one time, people believed the heat from a fire was a substance called caloric. Heat is now known to be a form of energy related to the motion of molecules.*

Figure 2-2 *Heated molecules (right) move faster and are farther apart than cooler molecules (left).*

2-1   Molecules and Motion

For thousands of years, people have wondered about the nature of heat. Some eighteenth-century scientists proposed a theory that heat was actually a substance, which they called caloric. Invisible and weightless, caloric could flow from hotter objects to colder ones. Some of the properties of heat seemed to support this theory. For example, the heat from a flame will flow into an object such as a cold piece of metal.

Other scientists, however, did not accept the theory of caloric. Benjamin Thompson, an American better known as Count Rumford, was one of these scientists. In 1798, he used a scientific method to prove that heat was *not* a substance. It was the motion of matter, and not caloric, he suggested, that produced heat.

Forty years later, the British scientist James Prescott Joule performed a series of experiments that seemed to show that objects in motion did indeed produce heat. Furthermore, Joule found that the more motion there was, the more heat was produced. You are probably familiar with this effect, although you may not be aware of it. For example, have you ever rubbed your hands together to make them warm? Or perhaps hammered a nail and then noticed how hot it has gotten? In each case, motion produced heat.

By Joule's time, scientists already knew that energy must be used to produce motion. By putting this fact together with his observations, Joule concluded that heat is simply a form of energy.

Other scientists working at this time had correctly suggested that most kinds of matter are made up of tiny particles called **molecules.** So scientists concluded that heat was somehow related to the motion of molecules.

Heat Transfer

Heat energy does move from warmer objects to colder ones, of course. If you have ever touched the handle of an iron frying pan sitting over the flame of a stove, you have discovered this fact for yourself. The heat moves from the hot pan through the handle to your hand! An ice cube in a glass of warm water melts because heat in the water is transferred to the ice cube. The water does not cool because it has absorbed "coldness" from the ice, as some early scientists thought. It cools because it loses heat.

The movement of heat is called heat transfer. **There are three types of heat transfer: conduction, convection, and radiation.**

CONDUCTION In **conduction** (kuhn-DUHK-shuhn), heat is transferred through a substance, or from one substance to another, by the direct contact of one molecule with another. Warmer, more rapidly moving molecules strike other, more slowly moving ones. As the molecules collide, some of the energy of the warmer molecules is transferred to the cooler, more slowly moving molecules. Because these molecules now have more energy, they speed up. This process is repeated again and again. Heat transfer by conduction takes place in solids, liquids, and gases, since they all are made up of molecules.

Some substances transfer heat better and more rapidly than other substances. Such substances are said to be good heat conductors. Silver is one of the best conductors of heat. Copper is another very good conductor of heat. Why do you think the bottoms of many pots and pans are made of copper? Why should the handles be made of wood or plastic instead of iron or copper?

Figure 2-3 *Heat transfer by conduction involves the direct contact of molecules. As fast-moving warmer molecules collide with slow-moving cooler molecules, heat energy is transferred from the warmer to the cooler molecules.*

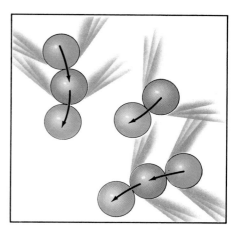

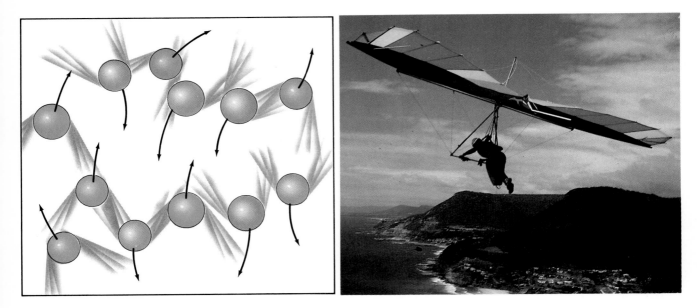

Figure 2-4 *Heat transfer by convection involves the motion of molecules in currents in liquids and gases. Heated molecules speed up and spread out, causing the warmer part of the liquid or gas to become less dense than the cooler part. The heated portion rises, creating currents that carry heat (left). Hang gliders rely on the updrafts formed by convection currents when warm air rises as cooler air sinks (right).*

CONVECTION In **convection** (kuhn-VEK-shuhn), molecules of liquids or gases move in currents, transferring heat as they move. When a liquid or a gas is heated, some of the molecules begin to move faster and farther apart. This results in a decrease in the density of that part of the liquid or gas. That is, the molecules are less closely packed. Because it is less dense than the surrounding liquid or gas, the heated portion rises, creating currents that carry heat.

Warm air near the surface of the earth tends to rise. As it moves up, it transfers heat. This is not because "heat rises," as many people think, but because the warm air is less dense than the cold air above it. The cold air tends to sink, just as a dense rock sinks in water. Hang-glider pilots often rely on updrafts of warm air to help keep them aloft. See Figure 2-4.

Figure 2-5 *Radiation is the transfer of heat energy in the form of invisible infrared rays. In this illustration, you can see how molecules (red) can give off infrared rays that travel through space and then are absorbed by other molecules (purple).*

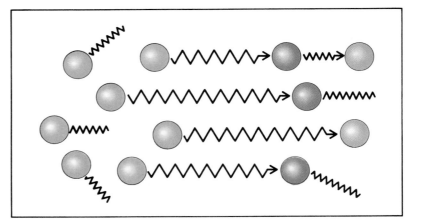

RADIATION When heat energy is transferred through space, **radiation** (ray-dee-AY-shuhn) is taking place. The heat energy is in the form of invisible light known as infrared. Heat from the sun reaches the earth by radiation.

SECTION REVIEW

1. What were the contributions of Count Rumford and James Prescott Joule to an understanding of the nature of heat?
2. What are molecules?
3. What are the three types of heat transfer? How does each work?

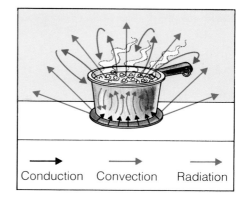

| Conduction | Convection | Radiation |

Figure 2-6 *The pot of boiling water illustrates the three methods of heat transfer—conduction (black arrows), convection (blue arrows), and radiation (red arrows).*

2-2 Temperature and Heat

Many people—perhaps even you—confuse heat with temperature. Though the two are related, they are not the same thing. In order to understand what they are, you will need to look more closely at how energy and the motion of molecules are related.

Kinetic Energy

Objects that are moving can do **work.** You may think of work as doing chores such as washing the car or raking leaves. Scientists, however, define work as a force acting on an object and causing it to move. A falling hammer, for example, can do the work of driving in a nail. Such work can be done because moving objects have energy. This energy of motion is called **kinetic energy.** The faster an object moves, the more kinetic energy it has. So a rapidly falling hammer can do more work than a slowly falling one. You may be familiar with this idea if you have ever played the hammer game at an amusement park. What counts is how fast you slam the hammer against the pad.

Molecules, like all objects, have kinetic energy because of their motion. **Temperature** is a measure of the average kinetic energy of molecules. The higher the temperature, the faster the molecules in a given

Figure 2-7 *This wrecking block has an enormous amount of kinetic energy.*

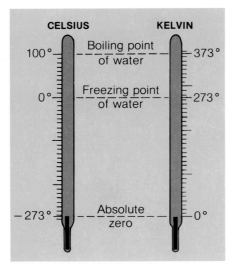

Figure 2-8 *A comparison of Celsius and Kelvin temperature scales*

Figure 2-9 *At a temperature of −195.8° C, nitrogen gas becomes a liquid. A banana dipped in liquid nitrogen becomes so frozen it can be used to hammer a nail into a block of wood.*

sample are moving, on the average. Likewise, a lower temperature indicates the molecules are moving more slowly. For example, the molecules in a pot of water at 90° C move more rapidly than those in a pot of water at 70° C.

Measuring Temperature

Have you ever touched an object that you thought was very cold but that a friend thought was only mildly cold? Not all people agree on how hot or cold things are. So a more accurate way of measuring temperature must be used. The **thermometer** is an instrument for measuring temperature. Most common thermometers contain a liquid, usually alcohol or mercury, in a very thin tube. Along the tube is a set of numerals, called a scale, that allows you to read the temperature. Remember, molecules in a heated gas or liquid move farther apart. So the warmer the liquid gets in a thermometer, the higher the liquid rises in the tube. The reverse happens as the liquid cools. The scale of a scientific thermometer shows the temperature in degrees Celsius. This is the metric unit most often used to measure temperature. Water freezes at 0° C and boils at 100° C.

Scientists sometimes use another metric temperature scale, the **Kelvin scale.** On this scale, temperatures are measured in units called kelvins (K). To convert Celsius degrees to Kelvin degrees, you simply add 273 to the Celsius temperature. For example, on the Kelvin scale water freezes at 273°K (273 + 0). Water boils at 373°K (273 + 100). The Kelvin scale is useful partly because its lowest value, 0°K (which equals −273° C), is actually the lowest temperature that anything can reach. This temperature is often called **absolute zero.** You may not have guessed that there is a lowest possible temperature. Recalling that temperature is a measure of the energy of motion of molecules, what do you think happens at absolute zero?

Thermal Expansion

Temperature affects the size of objects. Most objects expand, or get larger, when their temperature is raised. Remember, the higher the temperature,

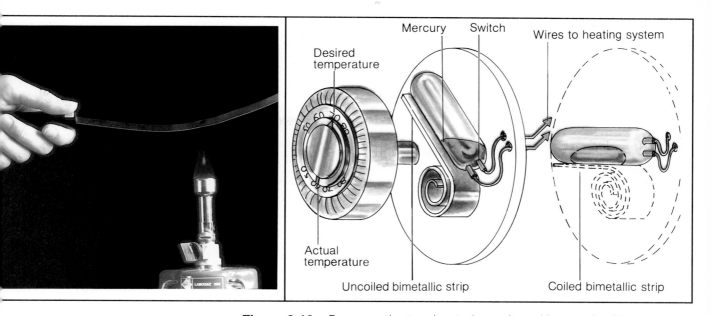

Figure 2-10 *Because the two heated metals making up the bimetallic strip expand at different rates, the strip bends (left). A bimetallic strip is an important part of a thermostat (right). When the temperature gets too cold, the bimetallic strip uncoils. This action causes a drop of mercury to close a switch and start the heating system. When the temperature reaches the desired level, the strip coils up, the mercury opens the switch, and the heat goes off.*

the greater the kinetic energy, and the faster and farther apart the molecules of a substance move. The mercury that is used in most thermometers expands in a regular way as the temperature increases. This permits you to measure temperature by reading the length of a column of mercury on a calibrated, or marked, scale of degrees.

Thermal, or heat, expansion must be considered when certain structures are designed. For example, sidewalks are laid out with slight spaces between the squares. This permits expansion in hot weather, which might otherwise cause buckling and cracking of the sidewalk.

Materials differ in how much they expand when heated. A **bimetallic strip** is a device that makes use of different rates of expansion of solids. Such a strip consists of two different metals joined together. When heated or cooled, one of the metals expands or contracts faster than the other, causing the strip to bend. The metal that expands more forms the outside of the curve of the bimetallic strip.

Bimetallic strips are used as switches in heat-control devices called **thermostats** (THER-muh-stats).

Investigating Molecular Motion

1. Fill one beaker about two-thirds full with water at or near room temperature.

2. Fill a second beaker about two-thirds full with water that has been chilled by ice for several minutes. Remove the ice cubes once the water is cold.

3. Fill a third beaker about two-thirds full with hot water.

4. Use a dropper to place one drop of dark food coloring on the surface of the water in each beaker. Do not stir.

5. Describe the changes you see in each beaker of water. Note how slowly or quickly the changes occur in each beaker.

Explain your observations in terms of the effect of heat on the motion of molecules.

Thermostats help control the temperature of an indoor area or of an appliance. They are used to turn on and off furnaces and air conditioners in buildings such as your home. They are also used in appliances such as refrigerators, ovens, and electric blankets. The bending and unbending of the bimetallic strip opens and closes an electric circuit that controls the heating or cooling device.

Do all substances expand when heated and contract when cooled? No. At certain temperatures, water is one of the few exceptions to this principle. It expands as it cools from liquid to solid; that is, as it turns to ice. Because of this expansion, the density of water decreases between 4° C and 0° C. The lowest density is reached at 0° C, the freezing point of water. Thus ice is less dense than liquid water and floats in it. What would be the effect on life on earth if ice were more dense than liquid water?

Measuring Heat

Heat energy is needed to produce changes in temperature, or changes in the motion of molecules. Temperature is a measurement of the motion of molecules.

Figure 2-11 *Foods have potential, or stored, energy. No matter how exotic the food, when it is "burned" in your body, this potential energy is released. The amount of energy a food can supply when burned is measured in Calories.*

Heat is measured in units called **calories.** One calorie is defined as the amount of heat needed to raise the temperature of one gram of liquid water one degree Celsius—for example, from 3° C to 4° C, or from 10° C to 11° C. Notice that the number of calories needed for a certain temperature change depends on the mass of the substance being heated. For example, it takes ten calories to raise the temperature of one gram of water ten degrees Celsius. If you had ten grams of water instead of one, the ten calories would raise the temperature only one degree Celsius.

The fact that heat and temperature are measured in different units shows that the two are not the same. Another indication that heat and temperature are different is that the *same* amount of heat produces *different* temperature changes in *different* substances. This is because some substances absorb heat energy better than other substances. Such substances require fewer calories to raise their temperatures one degree Celsius.

A measure of this heat-absorbing ability is called **specific heat.** The specific heat of a substance is the number of calories needed to raise the temperature of one gram of that substance one degree Celsius. Different substances have different specific heats. The specific heat of water has a value of 1. That of copper has a value of 0.093. Less that one tenth of a calorie would be needed to change the temperature of one gram of copper one degree Celsius.

Foods have a caloric value because when they are "burned," either inside or outside the body, they release heat energy. How much heat they give off is indicated by the number of calories they contain.

There is one big difference, however. Food calories are really kilocalories. One food calorie, written with a capital "C," is equal to 1000 of the calories just discussed. These calories are written with a small "c." The next time you go on a diet, tell people that you are watching your kilocalories!

Heat and Potential Energy

Heat is not an average quantity, as is temperature. Rather, heat depends upon the quantity of matter present. Five grams of water at 90° C has

TABLE OF SPECIFIC HEATS

Substance	Specific Heat (cal/g · C °)
Air	0.25
Aluminum	0.22
Copper	0.09
Glass	0.20
Ice (−20°C to 0°C)	0.50
Mercury	0.03
Ocean water	0.93
Water	1.00
Wood	0.42

Figure 2-12 *This table shows the specific heats of some common substances. According to this table, which heats up more quickly, aluminum or mercury?*

Food Calories

All foods have a caloric content. You might be very surprised to learn exactly what that value is for some common foods you eat regularly.

Use calorie counters, cookbooks, or the information provided on the food package to determine the caloric content. Put your information into chart form and keep it handy. Determine how many Calories you eat each day. Remember, the calories listed are really kilocalories.

more heat energy than one gram of water at the same temperature. This means that if it came in contact with your skin the five grams of water at 90° C would produce a more severe burn than the one gram of water at 90° C!

When does heat energy not cause a change in the temperature of a substance? The answer to this scientific riddle is very simple: when the heat energy is stored. Stored energy, in the form of heat or other kinds of energy, is called **potential energy.**

Think for a moment of a garden hose. When the tap is turned on, water flows out of the pipes, through the hose, and onto the lawn. The water has kinetic energy, or energy of motion. You know this because the water can do work. It can move tiny particles of soil, blades of grass, or leaves of plants. When the tap is turned off, the water remains in the pipes and does no work. However, it has the potential of doing work once it begins to move. So it has stored energy, or potential energy.

Potential heat energy is present in chemical substances such as fuels. This stored energy is released when the substances are burned. Foods also contain

Figure 2-13 *These marathon runners will rely on the potential energy of foods, especially sugars and starches. By "burning" the foods, potential energy is changed to kinetic energy, or energy of motion.*

Figure 2-14 *As the liquid fuel in the engines of the Space Shuttle is burned, chemical energy is changed to heat and light. In turn, the heat energy is changed to mechanical energy.*

potential heat energy. When sugars, for example, are burned in the body, heat needed to keep the body functioning is produced.

Energy in all forms can be changed from kinetic to potential energy and back again. The total amount of energy present never changes, however. The **law of conservation of energy** states this clearly. **According to the law of conservation of energy, energy can be neither created nor destroyed but can only change form.** Heat energy can be converted to other forms, such as mechanical energy or light energy. For example, in the engine of an automobile, the heat energy released by the burning fuel is changed to mechanical energy—the motion of pistons, gears, and wheels. In a fireworks display, the colors you see come from heat energy changing to light. Can you think of other energy conversions?

SECTION REVIEW

1. Compare kinetic energy and potential energy.
2. What is temperature? How is it measured?
3. What is heat? In what units is it measured?

2-3 Heating and Refrigeration Methods

Controlling the temperature of the environment is an important application of scientific knowledge about heat. Warming and cooling homes and workplaces involves designing and constructing various types of heating and refrigeration systems. **The methods used in all heating and cooling systems apply the knowledge of heat transfer and energy conversion.**

Figure 2-15 *HEATING SYSTEMS*

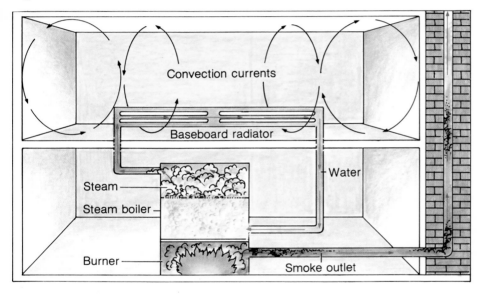

Steam Heat In a boiler above the furnace, water changes to steam. Steam has higher potential energy than liquid water. It stores more heat. The steam passes through pipes to radiators. Metal radiators have large surface areas that permit rapid heat transfer to the surrounding air. The heat transfer is by conduction and radiation. Heated air near the radiator rises in convection currents and circulates through the room. As the steam releases its stored energy in the form of heat, it cools and changes back to liquid water. The liquid water returns to the boiler, and the cycle begins again.

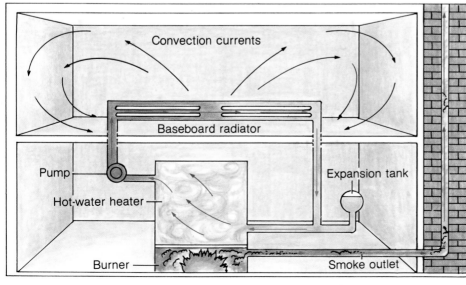

Hot Water Heat released by burning fuel or by electric coils in a furnace is absorbed by water in a boiler. The hot water is piped through the rooms, usually in radiators. Heat flows from the hot water to the cooler air in the room. As the air near the radiator warms and rises, convection currents are formed. The cooled water returns to the boiler, and the process begins anew.

Forced Air *Air is heated either by a furnace burning fuel or by an electric furnace. The hot air is then blown by fans through ducts in the rooms. Convection currents keep the warm air moving as it transfers its heat to the surrounding air.*

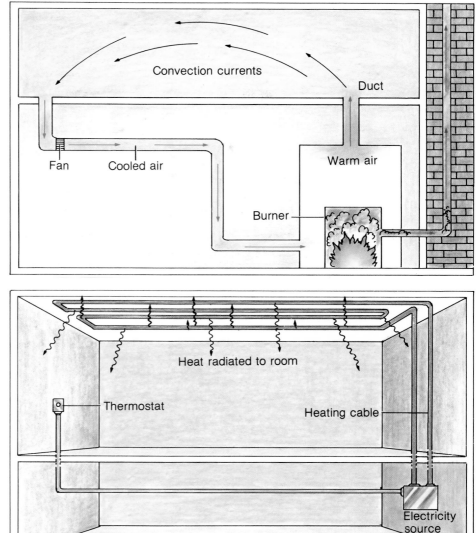

Convection currents

Duct

Fan

Cooled air

Warm air

Burner

Electric Heat *Cool air is brought into contact with hot coils or hot cables that have been placed within panels in ceilings or walls. In radiant heaters, electric energy is converted to invisible light energy, which then heats the rooms through radiation.*

Heat radiated to room

Thermostat

Heating cable

Electricity source

Insulation

To heat a room, heat must be transferred from a radiator, fireplace, or other device to the air in the room. What is more, this heat must be prevented from escaping, or being transferred, out of the room. **Insulation** reduces heat transfer that occurs by conduction. Insulating materials such as glass wool are poor conductors of heat. This is partly because small pockets of air are trapped in the glass wool. Air is a poor conductor of heat. Insulating materials are packed beneath roofs and in the outside walls of buildings. Double-pane window glass also is

Figure 2-16 *Invisible heat energy, or infrared energy, can be "seen" by using a device called a thermograph. This thermogram, or heat picture, reveals heat losses from several houses. Generally, the lighter and brighter the color, the greater the heat loss. A thermogram such as this can help homeowners better insulate their houses.*

useful in insulating a house. The air trapped between the panes does not conduct heat well. And the air space is so small that convection cannot take place either. You should remember that good insulation not only keeps heat in but also keeps heat out. So a well-insulated building remains cool in hot weather.

Career: *Air-Conditioning Mechanic*

HELP WANTED: AIR-CONDITIONING MECHANIC Must have completed four-year apprenticeship program supervised by air-conditioning contractor. Job involves installing a system in new shopping mall. Indoor and outdoor work.

People are always seeking ways to make the buildings in which they live, work, and play more comfortable. Today, air conditioning is used to control the environment in any enclosed area—from a home to a space capsule. Temperature can be maintained, humidity can be controlled, and air can be filtered and cleaned of pollutants. The people who install and service these air-conditioning systems are **air-conditioning mechanics.**

To install air-conditioning systems, mechanics must know how to assemble all the parts. To do this, they follow blueprints and design details. Then they connect the equipment to an electric power source, add refrigerant, and

check to see that the system works. A variety of tools, including hammers, wrenches, metal snips, drills, and torches, are used. Mechanics work in homes, office buildings, and factories.

If this career interests you, write to the Air-Conditioning and Refrigeration Institute, 1815 North Fort Myer Drive, Arlington, VA 22209.

Cooling Systems

Refrigeration systems are designed to cool buildings in hot weather and to preserve food. In refrigeration systems, electric energy is used to remove heat energy from a room, building, or other space, such as the inside of a refrigerator. The heat is conducted into the outside air by a liquid that is pumped through the refrigerator by an electric motor. You have probably noticed this when you have passed in front of the outside part of an air conditioner at work. A home refrigerator transfers the heat into the room. For this reason, you should never try to cool off the kitchen by opening the refrigerator door. This will only force the refrigerator to work harder to cool itself, releasing more heat back into the room.

Refrigerators and air conditioners contain coolant liquids such as Freon or ammonia. In the cooling process, these liquids are changed into gases. The process requires heat, just as heat is required to boil water, changing the liquid water into gaseous water. Where does the heat come from? It comes from the space near the cooling device—the inside of the refrigerator or the room.

This is not the end of the process, which must go on continuously to keep the space cool. A compressor pumps the hot gas back into a condenser, where the gas changes back to a liquid. As it does so, it gives off heat to the outside air. This is usually done by means of condenser coils that radiate the heat to the surrounding air. Such coils are often found on the back surfaces of refrigerators. Fans are sometimes used to help blow away the air that is heated by the coils, which can become rather warm. Therefore, you must be careful not to touch these coils. You might also warn other people not to touch the coils. It would probably be the first time that they would have been warned not to burn themselves on the refrigerator!

Figure 2-17 *Believe it or not, blocks of ice can be used to insulate a home, as this Eskimo of the Arctic Circle well knows. How is an igloo insulated?*

Figure 2-18 *In this diagram, you can see how all the parts of a refrigerator work to keep things cold.*

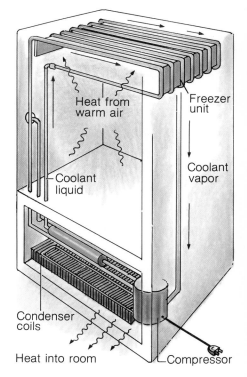

Heat from warm air

Freezer unit

Coolant vapor

Coolant liquid

Condenser coils

Heat into room

Compressor

SECTION REVIEW

1. What is the purpose of insulation?
2. How do double-pane windows insulate a house?
3. How does a refrigerator work?

LABORATORY ACTIVITY

Calibrating a Thermometer

Purpose

In this activity, you will mark off the freezing point and the boiling point of water on an uncalibrated thermometer.

Materials *(per group)*

Medium-sized beaker Unmarked
Glass-marking pencil   thermometer
Ice
Hot plate
Metric ruler

Procedure

1. Fill a medium-sized beaker to the halfway mark with ice and water.

2. Hold the unmarked thermometer in the beaker of ice and water. Do not let the thermometer touch the sides or bottom of the beaker.

3. Wait several minutes until the level of the liquid in the thermometer stops moving. Then mark the lowest point reached by the liquid in the thermometer. This is the zero point on the Celsius scale.

4. Gently heat the ice-water mixture on the hotplate, keeping the thermometer in the beaker. Again, do not let the thermometer touch the beaker. **CAUTION**: *Avoid touching the hotplate.*

5. During the time it takes for the ice to melt, observe the height of the liquid in the thermometer.

6. When all the ice is melted, continue heating the water.

7. When the liquid in the thermometer stops rising, mark on the thermometer the highest

Ice and water

Boiling water

point reached by the liquid. This temperature is 100° C.

8. Take the thermometer out of the beaker and allow it to cool. Using the ruler, divide the distance between the two marks into ten equal spaces. The first mark will represent 10° C, the second 20° C, and so on.

Observations and Conclusions

1. What happened to the level of the liquid in the thermometer in step 5? Why?

2. What is happening to the water at 100° C?

3. Use your thermometer to estimate the temperature of the room. Compare your results with those of other students.

CHAPTER REVIEW

SUMMARY

2-1 Molecules and Motion

- Heat is a form of energy related to the motion of molecules.
- Conduction is the transfer of heat by the direct contact of one molecule with another.
- Convection is the transfer of heat by molecules of liquids and gases moving in currents.
- Radiation is the transfer of heat through space in the form of infrared light.

2-2 Temperature and Heat

- Work is defined as a force acting on an object and causing it to move.
- Kinetic energy is energy of motion.
- Temperature is a measure of the average kinetic energy of molecules.
- A thermometer is the instrument used to measure temperature.
- The metric scales of temperature are the Celsius and Kelvin scales.
- Absolute zero is the lowest possible temperature.
- Most objects expand when heated.

- Water expands as it is cooled from 4° C to 0° C.
- A calorie, the unit used to measure heat, is the amount of heat needed to raise the temperature of one gram of liquid water one degree Celsius.
- Potential energy is stored energy.
- The specific heat of a substance is the number of calories needed to raise the temperature of one gram of that substance one degree Celsius.
- The law of conservation of energy states that energy can be neither created nor destroyed but can only be changed from one form to another.

2-3 Heating and Refrigeration Methods

- Common heating systems include steam heat, hot water, forced air, and electric heat.
- Insulation reduces heat transfer that occurs by conduction.
- Refrigerators and air conditioners contain liquid coolants that absorb heat from an area as they change from liquids to gases.

VOCABULARY

Define each term in a complete sentence.

absolute zero	insulation	molecules	temperature
bimetallic strip	Kelvin scale	potential energy	thermometer
calorie	kinetic energy	radiation	thermostat
conduction	law of conservation of energy	specific heat	work
convection			

CONTENT REVIEW: MULTIPLE CHOICE

Choose the letter of the answer that best completes each statement.

1. An early theory proposed that heat was an invisible, weightless substance called
   a. energy.   b. joules.   c. caloric.   d. absolute zero.

2. The transfer of heat by the direct contact of one molecule with another is
a. convection.   b. conduction.   c. radiation.   d. infrared.

3. Heat transfer through the movement of liquids or gases in currents is
a. convection.   b. conduction.   c. radiation.   d. infrared.

4. Heat that is radiated through space is in the form of
a. ultraviolet light.   b. sound.   c. convection currents.   d. infrared light.

5. A measure of the average kinetic energy of molecules is called
a. heat.   b. caloric.   c. temperature.   d. expansion.

6. On the Kelvin scale, the freezing point of water is
a. 0°.   b. 273°.   c. 212°.   d. 373°.

7. A device that makes use of the rates of expansion of substances is a(n)
a. thermometer.   b. bimetallic strip.   c. Kelvin.   d. insulator.

8. The number of calories needed to raise the temperature of one gram of a substance one degree Celsius is called its
a. specific heat.   b. potential energy only.
c. both kinetic and potential energy.   d. mechanical energy.

9. Heat energy involves
a. kinetic energy only.   b. potential energy only.
c. both kinetic and potential energy.   d. mechanical energy.

10. Heat transfer by conduction can be reduced with
a. insulation.   b. silver.
c. thermostats.   d. copper.

CONTENT REVIEW: COMPLETION

Fill in the word or words that best complete each statement.

1. Matter is made up of tiny particles called _____.

2. Heat transfer through space is called _____.

3. _____ energy refers to energy of motion.

4. The _____ is the instrument used for measuring temperature.

5. _____ is the lowest possible temperature.

6. Heat energy is measured in units called _____.

7. _____ energy refers to stored energy.

8. _____ degrees Kelvin is the boiling point of water.

9. The _____ states that energy can neither be created nor destroyed but can only be converted from one form to another.

10. _____ and _____ are coolant liquids often used in refrigerators and air conditioners.

CONTENT REVIEW: TRUE OR FALSE

Determine whether each statement is true or false. If it is true, write "true." If it is false, change the underlined word or words to make the statement true.

1. Heat is a form of <u>matter</u>.
2. Materials such as silver and copper are said to be good <u>insulators</u>.

3. Generally, when a liquid or gas is heated, its density <u>decreases</u>.

4. A force acting on an object and causing it to move is the definition of <u>temperature</u>.

5. As the speed of an object <u>increases</u>, its kinetic energy <u>decreases</u>.

6. Temperature is a measure of the <u>total</u> kinetic energy of molecules.

7. One Calorie is equal to <u>100</u> calories.

8. Most common thermometers contain either <u>water</u> or alcohol.

9. Devices that help control the temperature of an indoor area are <u>thermostats</u>.

10. In an automobile engine, <u>light</u> energy is converted into mechanical energy.

CONCEPT REVIEW: SKILL BUILDING

Use the skills you have developed in this chapter to complete each activity.

1. Making comparisons Compare the three methods of heat transfer in terms of how heat moves and in what kinds of substances the transfer takes place.

2. Applying concepts Explain why five grams of water at room temperature does not have "more temperature" than one gram of water at room temperature. Then explain why three grams of water at 50° C has more heat energy than one gram of water at 50° C.

3. Interpreting diagrams

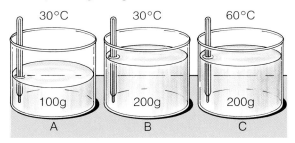

a. Which container(s) has(have) the greatest heat content?

b. In which containers is the motion of molecules the same?

c. Compare the molecular motion in containers a and C.

d. Compare the kinetic energy of containers A and B.

e. Which container needs the greatest number of calories to change the temperature by one Celsius degree?

4. Applying technology A thermos bottle keeps liquids hot or cold by preventing heat transfer. Study the illustration of a typical thermos bottle. In terms of preventing heat transfer, explain the importance of the vacuum, double-walled glass bottle, and air space. Use the terms convection and conduction in your answer.

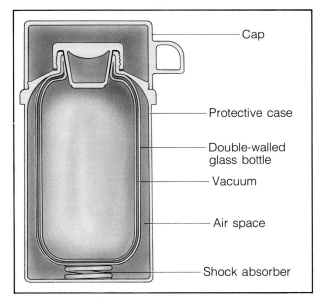

CONCEPT REVIEW: ESSAY

Discuss each of the following in a brief paragraph.

1. Explain the relationship among work, heat, and energy.

2. Describe how a bimetallic strip works.

3. Compare and contrast the four types of heating systems.

3 Electricity and Magnetism

CHAPTER SECTIONS

3-1 Electric Charge

3-2 Static Electricity

3-3 The Flow of Electricity

3-4 Electric Circuits

3-5 Magnetism

3-6 Magnetism from Electricity

3-7 Electricity from Magnetism

CHAPTER OBJECTIVES

After completing this chapter, you will be able to:

3-1 Explain how electric charge is related to atomic structure.

3-1 Compare the interactions of like and unlike charges.

3-2 Define static electricity.

3-3 State Ohm's law.

3-4 Describe an electric circuit and compare series and parallel circuits.

3-4 Identify electrical safety rules.

3-5 Relate magnetism to the attraction or repulsion of electrons.

3-6 Describe how an electric current gives rise to a magnetic field.

3-7 Describe how electric currents can be produced when a wire passes through a magnetic field.

You have probably seen monster movies, such as *Frankenstein* and *The Bride of Frankenstein*. These exciting movies often express people's hidden hopes and fears about a world in which scientific knowledge can be used for either good or evil. There is usually at least one scene in which the power of electricity is used to create life or to destroy it. Picture this: Early in the story, a crazed scientist uses lightning from an electric storm to bring to life a creature put together in the laboratory. By the end of the film, however, things have gone terribly wrong. The hero reaches for the big switch—the electric connection needed to blow up the crazed scientist and the monstrous creation. With them go the laboratory, the castle, and most of the mountain on which the castle stands!

For hundreds of years, many people have thought of electricity as a force that is in some way connected to the secret of life. Today scientists know a great deal about electricity and about magnetism, which is closely related to electricity. Scientists no longer think of electricity as a magical power or as the secret of life. But they do know that electricity plays an important role in the chemical activities that take place within living things. Today the many applications of electricity and magnetism, though not exactly life-giving in Dr. Frankenstein's sense, are at least making life easier and more comfortable.

Dr. Frankenstein at work

3-1 Electric Charge

"It made my hair stand on end!" Perhaps you are familiar with this expression, which is often used to describe a frightening or startling experience. According to biologists, it is possible for human hair to stand on end in moments of extreme fear. But there is another force that can make hair stand on end. You probably have experienced it on a cold, dry day when your hair seemed to "fly" all around as you tried to comb it.

What you experienced was electricity. Electricity may also give you a shock if you walk along a carpet and then touch a metal doorknob. Electricity enables you to rub a balloon on your sleeve and make it stick to the wall. And electricity produces the awesome flashes of lightning in the sky.

What is electricity? Where does it come from? How does it move? To answer these questions, you must first understand atoms and charges, which are both related to electricity.

Subatomic Particles and Electricity

All matter is made of **atoms.** An atom is the smallest particle of an element that has all the properties of that element. An element contains only one kind of atom. For example, carbon is made of only carbon atoms. Gold is made of only gold atoms.

Figure 3-1 *The metal sphere this girl is touching is part of a device called a Van de Graaff generator. This particular generator, located at the Ontario Science Center, produces charges of static electricity great enough to make the girl's hair stand on end.*

Atoms are made of even smaller particles called **subatomic particles.** These subatomic particles include **protons, neutrons,** and **electrons.**

Protons and neutrons are found in the **nucleus,** or center, of an atom. Protons and neutrons account for most of the mass of an atom. Whirling around the nucleus is a cloud of electrons. Electrons occupy different energy levels, depending upon their distance from the nucleus.

Both protons and electrons have a basic property called **electric charge.** However, the kind of charge is not the same for both particles. Protons have a positive charge, which is indicated by a plus symbol (+). Electrons have a negative charge, which is indicated by a minus symbol (−). Neutrons are neutral. Neutrons have no electric charge.

Charge and Force

When charged particles come near one another, they give rise to two different forces. A force is a pull or push on an object. A force can pull objects together or it can push objects apart.

A force that pulls objects together is a **force of attraction.** A force of attraction exists between oppositely charged particles. So negatively charged electrons are attracted to positively charged protons. This force of attraction holds the electrons in the electron cloud surrounding the nucleus.

A force that pushes objects apart is a **force of repulsion.** A force of repulsion exists between particles of the same charge. So negatively charged electrons repel one another, just as positively charged protons do. **Electric charges behave according to this simple rule: Like charges repel each other; unlike charges attract each other.**

From your experience, you know that when you sit on a chair, pick up a pen, or put on your jacket, you are not attracted or repelled by these objects. Although the protons and electrons in the atoms of these objects have electric charges, the objects themselves are neutral. Why?

The number of electrons in an atom is equal to the number of protons in that atom. So the total negative charge is equal to the total positive charge. The atom is neutral. It has no overall charge.

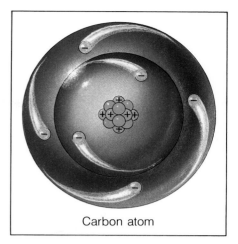

Carbon atom

Figure 3-2 *This atom of carbon shows the arrangement of the subatomic particles known as protons, neutrons, and electrons. Where is each particle found? What is the charge on each?*

Figure 3-3 *When charged particles come near each other, a force is produced. The force can be either a force of attraction or a force of repulsion. What is the rule of electric charges?*

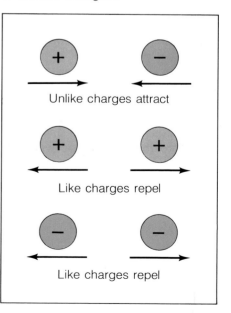

Unlike charges attract

Like charges repel

Like charges repel

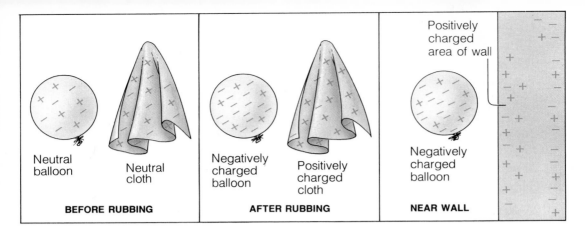

BEFORE RUBBING	AFTER RUBBING	NEAR WALL

Neutral balloon — Neutral cloth

Negatively charged balloon — Positively charged cloth

Positively charged area of wall — Negatively charged balloon

Figure 3-4 *Rubbing separates charges, giving the cloth a positive charge and the balloon a negative charge. When the negatively charged balloon is brought near the wall, it repels electrons in the wall. The nearby portion of the wall becomes positively charged. What happens next?*

Activity

Balloon Electricity

1. Blow up three or four medium-sized balloons.

2. Rub each balloon vigorously on a piece of cloth or article of clothing. Wool works especially well.

3. "Stick" each balloon on the wall. Note and record the day and time.

4. Every few hours, check the position of the balloons. Record the position as well as the day and time. If your balloons are very "sticky," you may have to extend your experiment overnight.

How long did the balloons stay attached to the wall? Why did the balloons eventually begin to slide and fall off the wall?

How, then, do objects such as balloons and strands of hair develop an electric charge if these objects are made of neutral atoms? The answer lies in the fact that electrons, unlike protons, are free to move. In certain materials, the negative electrons are only loosely held by the positive protons. These electrons can easily be separated from their atoms.

Rubbing separates charges on objects. When two objects are rubbed together, one object loses electrons while the other object gains these electrons. The object that gains electrons has an overall negative charge. The object that loses electrons has an overall positive charge. Remember that *only the electrons move,* not the protons. A neutral object develops an electric charge when it either gains or loses electrons.

If you rub a balloon against a piece of cloth, the cloth loses some electrons and the balloon gains these electrons. The balloon is no longer a neutral object. It is a negatively charged object because it has more electrons than protons. As the negatively charged balloon approaches the wall, it repels the electrons in the wall. The electrons in the area of the wall nearest the balloon move away, leaving that area of the wall positively charged. Using the rule of charges, can you explain why the balloon now sticks to the wall?

Electric Fields

If two charged particles come close to each other, they will experience a force. If the two particles are alike in charge, the force will be one of repulsion. If the two particles are opposite in charge, the force will be one of attraction. The repulsion and attraction of particles occurs because charged particles have **electric fields** around them.

An electric field is the region surrounding a charged particle in which an electric force affecting other charged particles is noticeable. The electric field is strongest near the charged particle. It is weakest far away from the charged particle. The strength of an electric field depends upon the distance from the charged particle. As the distance from a charged particle increases, the strength of the electric field decreases.

SECTION REVIEW

1. What are the charged particles in an atom?
2. What is the rule of electric charges?
3. How does an object develop an electric charge?
4. A positively charged particle is placed 1 centimeter from positively charged particle X. A negatively charged particle is placed 10 centimeters from particle X. Compare the forces experienced by both the positively charged particle and the negatively charged particle.

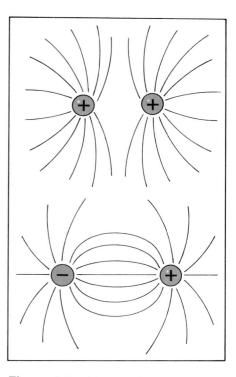

Figure 3-5 *Lines of force show the nature of the electric field surrounding two particles of the same charge* (top) *and two particles of opposite charge* (bottom).

3-2   Static Electricity

When you read that the loss or gain of electrons produces an electric charge and electricity, you may have noticed that the words *electron* and *electricity* are similar. This similarity is no accident. Electricity depends upon electrons. In fact, **electricity** can now be defined as the energy associated with electrons that have moved from one place to another.

You are probably most familiar with electricity that flows through electric wires. But the movement of electrons is not always a continuous flow through a wire. Sometimes electrons can move from one object to another and then remain at rest. This type of electricity is called **static electricity.** The word *static* means "not moving," or "stationary."

Static electricity is the buildup of electric charges on an object. The electric charges build up because electrons have moved from one object to another. However, once built up, the charges do not flow. They remain at rest.

Activity

Spark, Crackle, Move

You can observe the effects of static electricity by doing these activities.

1. Comb your hair several times in the same direction. Bring the comb near your hair but do not touch it.

2. Repeat step 1 but now bring the comb near a weak stream of water from a faucet.

3. In a darkened room, walk across a wool carpet and then touch the doorknob with a metal pen or rod.

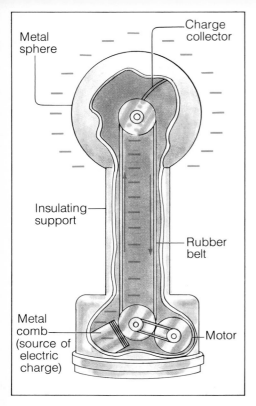

Figure 3-6 *A Van de Graaff generator produces static electricity by friction. Electrons supplied by a metal comb ride up a rubber belt to the top of the generator, are picked off by the charge collector, and transferred to the metal sphere. A large negative charge is built up and used to produce discharges of static electricity.*

Figure 3-7 *A metal rod can be charged negatively (left) or positively (right) by conduction.*

Methods of Charging

An object can become charged with static electricity in three ways: friction, conduction, and induction. Rubbing a balloon with a piece of cloth is an example of charging an object by friction. The motion of the cloth against the balloon causes charges on both objects to separate. Since the electrons in the cloth are more loosely held than the electrons in the balloon, electrons move from the cloth to the balloon. What is the resulting charge on the cloth? On the balloon?

If a hard rubber rod is rubbed with fur, friction separates charges on both the rod and the fur. Electrons are transferred from the fur to the rod. Because the rubber rod has gained electrons, it is negatively charged. The fur, which has lost electrons, is positively charged.

If a glass rod is rubbed with silk, electrons are transferred from the glass rod to the silk. The glass rod, which has lost electrons, is positively charged. What is the charge on the silk?

Charging by **conduction** involves the direct contact of objects. In conduction, electrons flow through one object to another object. Certain materials allow electrons to flow freely. Materials that permit electric charges to move easily are called **conductors.** Most metals are good conductors of electricity. Silver, copper, aluminum, and mercury are among the best conductors.

Materials that do not allow electrons to flow freely are called **insulators.** Insulators do not conduct electric charges well. Good insulators include

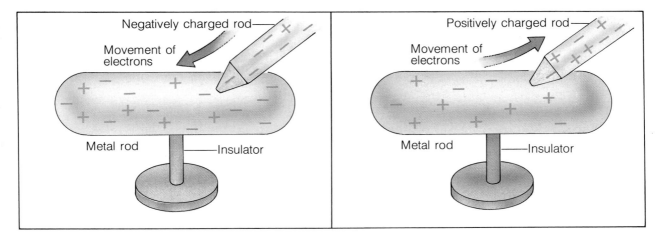

rubber, glass, wood, plastic, and air. The rubber tubing around an electric wire and the plastic handle on an electric power tool are examples of insulators. What do these insulators do?

An object can acquire a charge by **induction.** Induction involves a rearrangement of electric charges. For induction to occur, a neutral object need only come close to a charged object. No contact is necessary. For example, a negatively charged rubber rod can pick up tiny pieces of paper by induction. The electric charges in the paper are rearranged by the approach of the charged rubber rod. The electrons in the area of the paper nearest to the rod are repelled, leaving the positive charges near the rod. Because the positive charges are closer to the negative rod, the paper is attracted.

Figure 3-8 *Electric wires, often made of conductors such as copper, are covered by insulators such as rubber or plastic. Does an insulator conduct electricity?*

The Electroscope

An electric charge can be detected by an instrument called an **electroscope.** An electroscope consists of a metal rod with a knob at the top and a pair of thin metal leaves at the bottom. The rod is inserted in a one-hole rubber stopper, which fits into a flask. The flask contains the lower part of the rod and the metal leaves. See Figure 3-10 on page 60.

In an uncharged electroscope, the leaves hang straight down. When a charged object touches the metal knob, electric charges travel down the rod and into the leaves. The leaves spread apart, indicating the presence of an electric charge. Since the charge on both leaves is the same, the leaves repel each other and spread apart.

Figure 3-9 *A charged rod brought near a conductor induces an electric charge in the conductor. Using this figure and Figure 3-7, compare the charge given to the metal rod by each charged rod when done by conduction and by induction.*

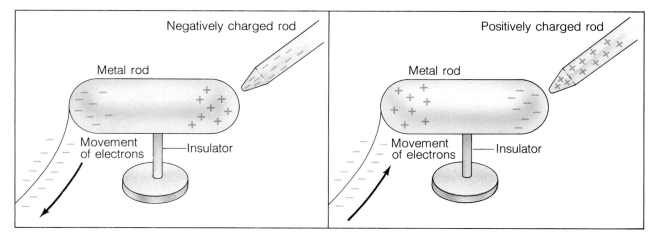

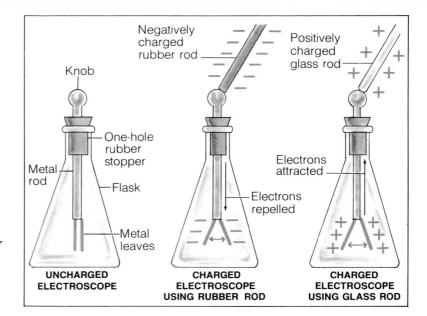

Figure 3-10 *An electroscope is used to detect electric charges. Why do the leaves in the electroscope move apart when either a negatively charged rubber rod or a positively charged glass rod makes contact?*

Figure 3-11 *The discharge of static electricity from one metal sphere to another can be seen as a spark.*

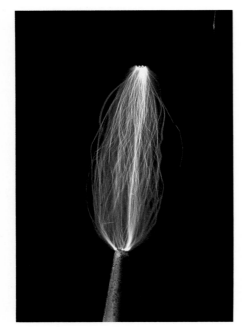

An electroscope can be charged by conduction. A charged object is brought in direct contact with the knob of the electroscope. For example, if a negatively charged rubber rod touches the knob, electrons from the charged rubber rod move to the knob of the electroscope and then down the metal rod to the thin metal leaves. The leaves gain a negative charge, repel each other, and spread apart.

If a positively charged glass rod touches the knob of the electroscope, free electrons in the leaves and metal rod are attracted by the glass rod. The metal rod and knob conduct these electrons out of the electroscope to the glass rod. The loss of electrons causes the leaves to become positively charged. They repel each other and spread apart.

Lightning

Electrons that move from one object to another and cause the buildup of charges at rest, or static electricity, eventually leave the object. Usually these extra electrons escape into the air. Sometimes they move onto another object. The charged object loses its static electricity and becomes neutral.

The loss of static electricity as electric charges move off an object is called **electric discharge.** Sometimes the discharge is slow and quiet. Sometimes it is very rapid and accompanied by a shock, a spark of light, or a crackle of noise.

One of the most dramatic examples of the discharge of static electricity is **lightning.** During a

Figure 3-12 *Lightning is a spectacular discharge of static electricity. Here lightning bolts light up the dome of the telescope at Kitt Peak National Observatory in Arizona.*

storm, particles contained in clouds are moved about by the wind. Charges become separated, and there are buildups of positive and negative charges. If a negatively charged cloud forms near the surface of the earth, objects on the earth become electrically charged by induction. Soon electrons are jumping from the cloud to the earth. The result of this transfer of electrons is a giant spark called lightning.

Lightning can also occur as electrons jump from cloud to cloud. As electrons jump through the air, intense light and heat are produced. The light is the bolt of lightning you see. The heat causes the air to expand suddenly. The rapid expansion of the air is the thunder you hear. Lightning contains dangerously high amounts of electric energy. An average lightning bolt transfers 6 billion billion electrons between a cloud and the earth.

One of the first people to understand lightning as a form of electricity was Benjamin Franklin. In the mid-1700s, Franklin performed experiments that provided evidence that lightning is a form of static electricity, that electricity moves quickly through certain materials, and that a pointed surface attracts electricity. Franklin suggested that pointed metal rods be placed above the roofs of buildings as protection from lightning. These rods were the first lightning rods. Luckily for Franklin, he put a lightning rod on his roof. Shortly afterward, lightning struck his home!

Lightning rods work according to a principle called grounding. A discharge of static electricity usually takes the shortest path from one object to

Activity

Observing Static Electricity

1. Place two books about 10 cm apart on a table.

2. Cut tiny paper dolls or some other object out of tissue paper and place them on the table between the books.

3. Place a 20- to 25-cm glass square on the books so that the glass covers the paper dolls.

4. Using a piece of silk, rub the glass vigorously. Observe what happens.

Using the rule of electric charges and your knowledge of static electricity, explain what you observed.

Figure 3-13 *Benjamin Franklin's famous experiments provided evidence that lightning is a form of static electricity that moves quickly through certain materials (top). Using these observations and the observation that pointed surfaces attract electricity, Franklin invented the lightning rod. Lightning rods attached to the tops of buildings provide a safe path for the lightning directly into the ground (bottom).*

another. So lightning rods are attached to the tops of buildings and a wire connects the lightning rod to the ground. When lightning strikes the rod, which is taller than the building, it travels through the rod and the wire harmlessly into the earth.

Unfortunately, other tall objects such as trees can also act as grounders. That is why it is not a good idea to stand near a tree during a lightning storm. Why do you think it is also not a good idea to stand in an open field during an electric storm?

Voltage: The Push of Electrons

It takes energy to move an object from one place to another. Even though electrons are very small, it still takes energy to move them. When you rub a balloon against your sleeve, you apply a force. This force moves electrons from the cloth to the balloon. You are able to apply this force because you have energy. The energy you expend goes to the electrons, which move. This energy is the "push" that makes electric charges move.

A measure of the energy available to move electrons is called **voltage.** Voltage is sometimes called potential difference. Voltage can be thought of as the "push" that makes electrons move. The higher the voltage, the more energy each electron carries. The more energy each electron carries, the more energy it can deliver, and the more work it can do.

Voltage is measured in units called **volts.** The symbol for volts is the letter "V." If you see the marking "10V," you know that it means ten volts. An instrument called a voltmeter is used to measure voltage.

SECTION REVIEW

1. What is static electricity?
2. What are the three ways in which an object can acquire an electric charge?
3. How can you tell if an object touching an electroscope is neutral or has a charge?
4. What is lightning?
5. What is voltage? In what units is it measured?
6. What would happen if a lightning rod were made of an insulator rather than a conductor?

3-3   The Flow of Electricity

Once electrons are pushed into moving, they can be made to continue flowing provided they have a path and a source. A wire made of a suitable conducting material forms the path. A device that pumps electrons from one object to another is the source. The electrons are ready to go!

Electric Current

The flow of electrons through a wire is called an **electric current.** So current simply means the number of electrons that pass a given point in a unit of time, or the electrons' rate of flow. The higher the electric current in a wire, the more electrons are passing through.

The symbol for current is the letter "I." And the unit in which current is expressed is the **ampere.** The ampere, or amp for short, is the amount of current that flows past a point per second. Scientists use instruments such as ammeters and galvanometers to measure current.

Resistance

You know that light bulbs give off light and heat. Have you ever wondered where the light and heat come from? They are not pouring into the bulb through the wires that lead from the wall. Rather, some of the electric energy passing through the filament of the bulb is converted into light and heat energy. The filament is a very thin piece of metal that resists, or opposes, the flow of electricity within it. Think of the traffic tie-up that results when a wide highway narrows at a certain point because of construction. The narrowed road resists the normal flow of cars. In much the same way, some materials resist the flow of electrons more than others.

Opposition to the flow of electricity is called **resistance.** The unit of resistance is the **ohm.** Different wires have different resistances. Copper wire has less resistance than iron wire. Copper is a good conductor; iron is a poor conductor. Nonconductors

Low Current and Low Voltage

Each electron carries little energy, and there are few electrons. Little total energy is delivered per second; power is low.

High Current and Low Voltage

Each electron carries little energy, but there are many electrons. Moderate total energy is delivered per second; power is moderate.

Low Current and High Voltage

Each electron carries much energy, but there are few electrons. Moderate total energy is delivered per second; power is moderate.

High Current and High Voltage

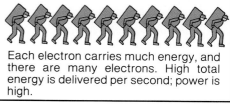

Each electron carries much energy, and there are many electrons. High total energy is delivered per second; power is high.

Figure 3-14 *Voltage is a measure of electron energy or "push." Current is a measure of the rate of electron flow through a conductor. In this figure, voltage is represented by the size of the load these workers carry. Current is represented by the number of workers.*

Figure 3-15 *As electrons pass through the thin filament of the bulb, they meet with resistance. This resistance converts some of the electric energy into light and heat energy.*

offer such great resistance that almost no current can flow. What is another name for nonconductors? For what purpose are nonconductors used in wiring?

An equation called Ohm's law relates electric current, voltage, and resistance. **Ohm's law states that the current in a wire (I) is equal to the voltage (V) divided by the resistance (R).**

$$\text{current} = \frac{\text{voltage}}{\text{resistance}}$$

or

$$I = \frac{V}{R} \qquad \text{amperes} = \frac{\text{volts}}{\text{ohms}}$$

If the resistance in a wire is 100 ohms and the voltage is 50 volts, the current is $50 \div 100 = 0.5$ ampere. You can rearrange the equation in order to calculate resistance or voltage. What is the resistance if V = 10 volts and I = 2 amperes?

Producing a Current

Remember how you produced a weak movement of electrons when you rubbed a balloon on your sleeve? The amount of electricity you produced was enough to make the balloon stick to the wall, but certainly not enough to be very useful as a source of electrons. If you want electricity to do work, you need a steady supply of electric current. To obtain this electric current, you can use **electrochemical cells.** An electrochemical cell is a cell in which chemical energy produced by a chemical reaction is changed into electric energy.

DRY CELLS One source of electricity is called the **dry cell.** Although this "electron pump" is called a dry cell, do not let its name fool you. A dry cell is not completely dry. It consists of a zinc can that contains a moist, pastelike mixture of chemicals. In the center of the zinc can is a solid carbon rod. A chemical reaction takes place between the zinc can and the paste, and the electrons are released. The post that picks up these electrons is called the **negative terminal.** This is logical, since electrons are negatively charged particles. The other post, which has a shortage of electrons, is called the **positive terminal.** The differ-

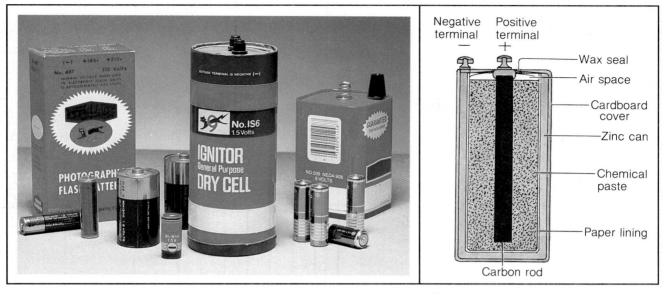

Figure 3-16 *Dry cells come in a variety of shapes and sizes specially suited for their uses* (left). *The basic design of most dry cells, however, is the same* (right).

ence in number of electrons between the two terminals creates the "pressure" that pumps the electrons. If a wire is connected to each terminal, the electrons will flow from the negative terminal through the wire and back to the positive terminal. As the chemical reaction continues, the returning electrons are pumped back to the negative terminal. In this way, the negative terminal keeps its negative charge, and electrons can move through the complete path for a long time.

Although the electrons in the dry cell are never used up, the chemicals eventually are. When the chemical reaction stops, electrons are no longer released. What do you think happens to the dry cell?

BATTERIES Sometimes more energy than one electrochemical cell can provide is needed. So two or more electrochemical cells are connected to increase the amount of electric energy. This arrangement is called a **battery.** Besides starting cars, can you think of other common uses for batteries? Do not be confused by simple dry cells, which are often labeled batteries.

Current Direction

Have you ever drawn a picture by following the dots? Each dot has a number, and you must follow these numbers in the correct order, always moving in the same direction. By contrast, drawing a picture

Activity

Ohm's Law

Complete the following chart.

I (amps)	V (volts)	R (ohms)
	12	75
15	240	
5.5		20
	6	25
5	110	

Figure 3-17 *On November 9, 1965, a major blackout plunged more than 200,000 square kilometers of the Northeast into total darkness! From New York to Canada, over 30 million people were without electricity to power lights, radios, TVs, appliances, elevators, and trains.*

without using dots might involve moving your pencil first in one direction and then in another, over and over again.

Electrons moving through a wire can do the same thing. They can move continuously in the same direction, or they can change direction back and forth over and over again.

DIRECT CURRENT When electrons always flow in the same direction, the current is called **direct current,** or DC. Electricity from dry cells and batteries is direct current.

ALTERNATING CURRENT When electrons move back and forth, reversing their direction regularly, the current is called **alternating current,** or AC. The electricity in your home is alternating current. In fact, the current in your home changes direction about 60 times every second. Direct current electricity serves many purposes. But to transport the huge amounts of electricity required to meet people's needs, alternating current must be used. You will learn how alternating current is produced later in this chapter when you read about generators.

Electric Power

You probably use the word "power" in a number of different senses—to mean strength, or force, or energy. To a scientist, power is the rate at which work is done or energy is used. **Electric power** is a measure of the rate at which electricity does work or provides energy.

Pick up a light bulb. Do you notice any words written on it? For example, you may see "60 watts" written on the bulb. **Watts** are the units in which electric power is measured. But to understand what that means and how power is measured, let's back up a few steps.

Electric power can be calculated by using the following equation:

$$\text{power} = \text{voltage} \times \text{current}$$

Or, put another way:

$$\text{watts} = \text{volts} \times \text{amps}$$

Now let's think back to that light bulb. The electricity in your home is 120 volts. The light bulb itself operates at 0.5 amp. Multiplying these two numbers gives the bulb's wattage, or 60 watts. The wattage tells you the power of the bulb. As you might expect, the higher the watts the brighter the bulb—and the more expensive to run.

To measure large quantities of power, such as the total used in your home per month, the kilowatt is used. The prefix *kilo-* means 1000. So one kilowatt is 1000 watts. What is the power, in watts, of a 0.2-kilowatt light bulb?

Figure 3-18 *Electricity for your home is purchased on the basis of the amount of energy used and the length of time it is used. Power companies install an electric meter in your home to record this usage in kilowatt hours. One kilowatt hour is the energy of 1000 watts supplied constantly for one hour.*

SECTION REVIEW

1. What is the unit in which current is expressed?
2. Name two types of electrochemical cells.
3. Give a formula for calculating electric power.
4. What is Ohm's law?

3-4 Electric Circuits

Try this if you can. Connect one wire from a terminal on a dry cell to a small flashlight bulb. Can you guess what will happen? If you said "nothing," you were right. Now connect another wire from the bulb to the other terminal on the dry cell. The light

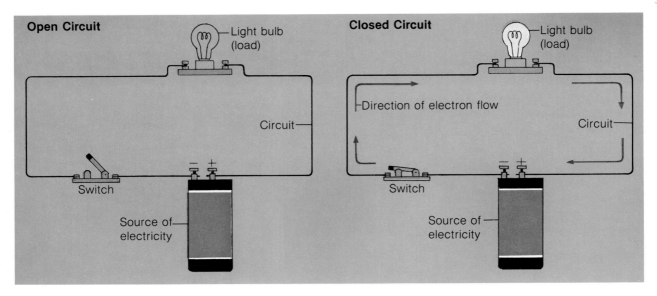

Open Circuit

Light bulb (load)

Circuit

Switch

Source of electricity

Closed Circuit

Light bulb (load)

Direction of electron flow

Circuit

Switch

Source of electricity

Figure 3-19 *No electricity can flow through an open circuit (left). When the switch is flipped on, the circuit is closed and the electrons have a complete path through which to flow (right).*

Figure 3-20 *Power lines bring electricity from a generating plant to your home. When severe weather conditions damage the lines, the flow of electricity is interrupted.*

goes on immediately. You have simply provided a path for the flow of electrons. You have made an **electric circuit.** If you remove one of the wires, the light goes out again. What does this tell you about the nature of an electric circuit? If you are still not sure, think of a word that sounds like "circuit" and means a round, closed loop. **An electric circuit provides a complete closed path or "circle" that must be present in order for electrons to flow.**

A simpler way of opening and closing an electric circuit is with a switch. If you connect a switch to your circuit, you can flip the switch on and off. When the switch is on, there is a closed path, or circuit, for the flow of electrons. When the switch is off, the path is broken. The electrons do not flow anymore. This is a very important rule to remember: *Electricity cannot flow through an open circuit. Electricity can flow only through a closed circuit.*

Every time you turn an appliance on or off, you are closing or opening a circuit. For example, when you turn on a light switch, you are actually causing a piece of metal to move in such a way that a circuit is completed. As a result, electricity can flow from the power line through the light bulb and back to the power line in a closed circuit.

Series and Parallel Circuits

Think for a moment about drawing a picture by following the dots. To get the right picture, you must follow the dots in order, passing through each dot as you do. This idea should help you better understand how electricity flows in a **series circuit.** In a series circuit, there is only one path for the electrons to take. See Figure 3-21. A disadvantage of a series circuit is that if there is a break anywhere in the circuit, the entire circuit is opened and no current can flow. Inexpensive holiday tree lights are often connected in series. What happens in such a circuit when a single bulb burns out? Why is this so?

Now imagine you are drawing a maze picture and not following the dots. In a maze, there are several paths for you to follow. You need not pass through every path along the way to get to the end. This idea is similar to how electricity flows in a **parallel circuit.** In a parallel circuit, there is more than one path the electrons can take. See Figure 3-21. If there is a break in one of the branches, electrons can still flow through the other branches. The electric outlets in your home are connected in parallel. If they were not, what would happen if even a single appliance were turned off?

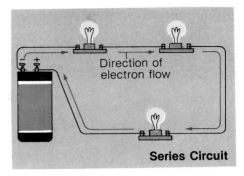
Direction of electron flow

Series Circuit

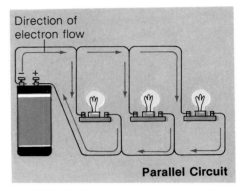
Direction of electron flow

Parallel Circuit

Figure 3-21 *A series circuit* (top) *provides only one path for the electrons to take. A parallel circuit* (bottom) *provides several paths.*

Figure 3-22 *Old types of tree lights used series circuits. Newer lights, like these, are connected in parallel. So if one bulb goes out, this lovely display will not go dark.*

Figure 3-23 *Remember to exercise care and good judgment when using electricity. Avoid unsafe conditions such as the ones shown here.*

Using Electricity Safely

"Don't put your fingers in an electric socket!" "Never stick a utensil in a toaster that is plugged in!" "Always repair worn wires!" Do these warnings sound familiar to you? If not, you should learn them, because they are good rules to follow in using electricity safely. Here are some other important rules.

1. **Never handle appliances when your hands are wet or when you are standing in water.** Water is a fairly good conductor of electricity. If you are wet, you may unwillingly become an alternate path for the flow of electricity!

2. **Never run wires under carpets.** Breaks or frays in the wires will not be easily noticed. These breaks cause short circuits. A short circuit represents a shorter and easier path for electron flow. It can be very dangerous because the electricity flowing through the break can cause shocks or fire.

3. **Never overload a circuit by connecting too many appliances to it.** Each electric circuit is designed to carry a certain amount of current safely. Overloading can cause a short circuit and a fire.

FUSES Your home has a great deal of electricity running through it. If too many appliances are all running at once or if the wires have become old and frayed, heat can build up in the wiring. The results can be dangerous. To protect against too much current flowing at once, your home may have **fuses** in a fuse box.

Inside each fuse is a thin strip of metal through which current flows. If the current becomes too

Activity

Electricity in Your Home

Ask an adult to open the fuse box or circuit breaker box in your home. Describe the appearance of the fuses or circuit breakers. What different areas of your home do they protect?

Examine the appliances in your home for their power rating. Make a chart of this information. What is the relationship between an appliance's power rating and the amount of heat it produces?

high, the strip of metal melts and breaks the flow of electricity. So a fuse is an emergency switch.

CIRCUIT BREAKERS Like fuses, **circuit breakers** protect a circuit from overloading with electricity. Modern circuit breakers have a switch that flips open when the current flow becomes too high. These circuit breakers can easily be reset and used again once the problem has been found and corrected. Circuit breakers are easier to use than fuses.

SECTION REVIEW

1. What is an electric circuit?
2. Compare a series circuit and a parallel circuit.
3. Does your home have circuit breakers or fuses? Explain how the device you have works.

3-5 Magnetism

More than 2000 years ago, in a part of Turkey known as Magnesia, the Greeks discovered a type of rock that could attract materials that contained iron. The Greeks called this rock magnetite. The Greeks also noticed that if a piece of magnetite was allowed to swing freely from a string, the same part of the rock would always face in the same direction. That direction was toward a certain northern star, called the leading star or lodestar. Thus magnetite also came to be known as lodestone.

In the twelfth century, the Chinese built the first compass to help them navigate. Like the Greeks before them, these early scientists were making use of **magnetism,** a property of certain materials. **Today scientists believe that magnetism is caused by a force of attraction or repulsion due to the arrangement of electrons in a material.**

You are probably familiar with magnetism and its various uses. Have you ever used a compass to find direction? Or held up messages on your refrigerator door with small magnets? Perhaps less familiar to you is the use of magnetism in devices such as motors, generators, telephones, and doorbells.

Figure 3-24 *Magnetite, or lodestone, is a natural magnet that was discovered by the Greeks more than 2000 years ago.*

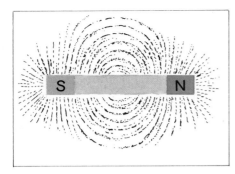

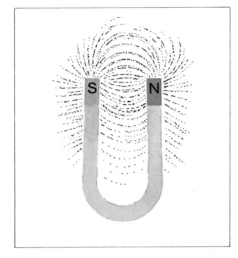

Figure 3-25 *Magnetic forces around a bar magnet* (top) *and a horseshoe magnet* (bottom) *can be seen by the attraction of iron filings. Notice how dense the iron filings are in the space between the north and south poles. What does this tell you about the strength of magnetic forces?*

Magnetic Forces

You read that moving electrons cause electric energy as well as exert electric forces. And electric forces in motion result in magnetic forces. Magnetic forces, like electric forces, involve attractions and repulsions. The magnetic forces are usually strongest at the two ends of the magnet. These ends are called **poles.** If a magnet is suspended horizontally and allowed to swing freely, one end of the magnet will always point toward the north. This end is called the **north magnetic pole.** The other end, which points toward the south, is the **south magnetic pole.** Perhaps this gives you some clue about how to build a compass.

When two magnets are brought near each other, they exert a force on each other. If the two north poles are brought close together, they will repel each other. So will the two south poles. However, if the north pole of one is brought near the south pole of the other, the poles will attract each other. Magnetic poles behave in the same way electric charges do. That is, *like poles repel each other and unlike poles attract each other.*

The attractive and repulsive forces of a magnet are not limited to the poles of the magnet, although they are strongest there. These forces are felt all around the magnet. The region in which magnetic forces can act is called a **magnetic field.** It may help you to think of a magnetic field as an area mapped out by magnetic lines of force. These lines of force

Figure 3-26 *Electromagnets placed on both the tracks and the train produce magnetic forces that enable this Japanese maglev train to reach speeds of up to 520 kilometers per hour.*

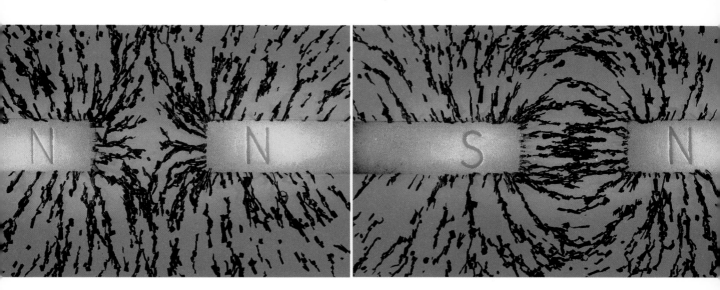

Figure 3-27 *The iron filings show that like poles of magnets repel each other* (left). *Unlike poles attract each other* (right).

can easily be demonstrated by sprinkling iron filings on a piece of cardboard placed on top of a magnet. Perhaps you have seen such patterns of lines of force. If not, why not try doing this demonstration yourself? Where would you expect the lines of force to be most numerous and closest together?

An Explanation of Magnetism

Think back for a moment to what you read about electrons. These negatively charged subatomic particles are found moving around the nucleus of an atom. As they revolve around the nucleus, they also spin on their own axes. As a result of this spinning, each electron becomes a tiny magnet itself.

When electrons are paired together, as they often are in atoms, their opposite spins cancel each other. No magnetism results. But some metals—iron, cobalt, and nickel, for example—contain atoms with unpaired electrons. Usually these unpaired electrons have a random arrangement. That is, they are not lined up in any one direction. Their magnetic fields extend in many different directions. See Figure 3-28. The force of magnetism is not felt, and the metal is unmagnetized. Now, if all these individual magnetic fields are arranged in the same direction—that is, all north poles facing one way, all south poles facing the other—the strength of the total magnetic field is greatly increased. See Figure 3-28. The metal is magnetized.

Figure 3-28 *In an unmagnetized substance, the individual magnetic fields extend in many different directions* (top). *When these magnetic fields are all arranged in the same direction, the substance becomes magnetized* (bottom).

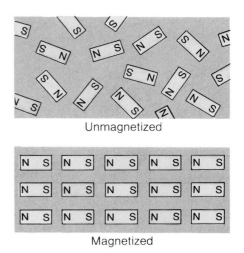

Unmagnetized

Magnetized

If a metal is magnetized when all the individual magnetic fields are lined up, how could this magnetism be destroyed? You are right if you suggested heating or hammering the metal. What effect do you think breaking the magnet into many pieces would have?

Types of Magnets

Some substances that occur in nature, such as lodestone, are already magnetized. They are called natural magnets. Other substances can be made into magnets by stroking them in the same direction several times with strong magnets. Such substances are easy to magnetize, but they also lose their magnetism very easily. Soft iron is an example of this type of magnet. Some substances are more difficult to magnetize. However, once magnetized they tend to stay that way. These substances are called permanent magnets. Alnico, which contains aluminum, nickel, and cobalt, is a very strong permanent magnet.

SECTION REVIEW

1. What causes a magnetic force?
2. What are the two ends of a magnet called?
3. What is the name for the region around a magnet in which its magnetic forces can act?

3-6   Magnetism from Electricity

Here is an interesting experiment for you to do. Bring a compass near a wire carrying an electric current. The best place to hold the compass is just above or below the wire, but parallel to it. Observe what happens to the compass needle when electricity is flowing through the wire and when it is not. What do you observe? Can you suggest a possible link between electricity and magnetism?

Magnetism is closely related to electricity because both involve the motions of electrons. In the nineteenth century, scientists discovered something quite remarkable. **An electric current flowing through a**

wire gives rise to a magnetic field surrounding the wire. Thus magnetism could be produced from electricity. Equally important was the discovery that a looped, or coiled, wire acted like a magnet when a current passed through it. The more coils the wire had, the greater the strength of the magnet. It then occurred to scientists that coiling a conductor around a piece of soft iron would produce an even more powerful magnet.

The relationship between electricity and magnetism is called **electromagnetism.** Many applications of electromagnetism are part of your daily life. Powerful temporary magnets called electromagnets can be made by wrapping a coil of wire around a soft iron core and passing a current through the wire. Electromagnets are used in telephones, telegraphs, washing machines, and doorbells. Electromagnets are used to lift heavy loads of iron or steel. One of the most important uses of electromagnets is in electric motors.

An electric motor is a device that converts electric energy into mechanical energy, or energy of motion. An electric motor contains a movable electromagnet and one or more fixed permanent magnets. Alternating current supplied to the movable electromagnet causes the poles to change constantly from north to south and back to north again as the current

Figure 3-29 *By coiling a current-carrying wire around a soft iron core, a simple electromagnet can be made* (left). *Large electromagnets used to lift heavy loads require more loops of wire and larger currents* (right).

Activity

Making an Electromagnet

Obtain a low-voltage dry cell, nail, and length of thin insulated wire.

1. Remove the insulation from the ends of the wire.

2. Wind the wire tightly around the nail so that you have at least 25 turns.

3. Connect each uninsulated end of the wire to a post on the dry cell.

4. Collect some lightweight metal objects. Touch the nail to each one. What happens?

switches direction. Thus a given end of the electromagnet will be attracted, then repelled, then attracted again to a pole of a fixed magnet. This shifting attraction causes the electromagnet to spin, and the mechanical energy of its motion can be used to turn a shaft and do work.

There are many types of electric motors. Each is designed for a particular use. However, they all operate on the principle of creating a magnetic field from an electric current. Can you think of some appliances that use electric motors?

SECTION REVIEW

1. Why is magnetism closely related to electricity?
2. What is the relationship between magnetism and electricity called?
3. How does an alternating-current electric motor work?

3-7 Electricity from Magnetism

If electricity produces magnetism, is the reverse possible? Can magnetism produce electricity? If you have a bicycle whose lights are powered by a generator, then you may know the answer to this question.

Suppose it is dark out, and to ride safely you need to turn on your bicycle lights. Reaching for the

Figure 3-30 *When a wire circuit is moved through a magnetic field, an electric current is produced in the wire. The current is alternating current because the lines of force are cut first in one direction* (left) *and then in the other* (right).

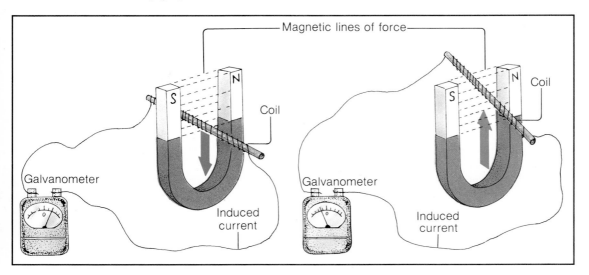

generator attached to the back wheel, you position the knob so that it touches the wheel. As you pedal away, the spinning wheel turns the generator knob, and the lights go on. How does this happen?

To understand what produces the electric current, you will have to think back to what you learned about magnetic lines of force. These imaginary lines map out the magnetic field of a magnet. **When a conducting wire cuts across magnetic lines of force, electrons flow through the wire, and current is produced.** Because the lines of force are cut first in one direction as the wire moves up and then in the other as the wire moves down, the electrons flow first one way and then the other. An alternating current results. The more lines of force that are cut, the greater the flow of electrons, or current.

It is not very convenient to move a wire up and down in a magnetic field. But if the wire is shaped into a loop and rotated in the magnetic field, electricity is produced more efficiently. This is exactly what an electric generator does. An electric generator converts mechanical energy into electric energy.

Career: *Electrician*

HELP WANTED: ELECTRICIAN Experienced electrician needed to maintain and repair communications equipment at recording and broadcasting studio. Must hold certificate showing completion of apprenticeship.

Since Benjamin Franklin first flew his kite during a thunderstorm in 1752, knowledge about and uses of electricity have increased tremendously. By 1861, electric wires were strung throughout the United States. In 1866, a telegraph cable was laid across the Atlantic Ocean floor, marking the beginning of communication across the seas. As the demand for electricity increased, the need for skilled electric workers, or **electricians**, increased.

Electricians know how to read blueprints, how to work safely with high electric voltages, and how to install, repair, and service complex electric equipment. Some electricians install the systems that guide missiles, submarines, and computers. Other electricians service jukeboxes, run lighting systems at ballparks, and control amusement rides. Electricians work in shipyards, on railroads, and in offices and homes. For more information about a career as an electrician, write to the International Brotherhood of Electrical Workers, 1125 Fifteenth Street N.W., Washington, DC 20005.

When you pedal your bike, you produce mechanical energy that turns the wheel. This makes the generator knob turn. The knob is connected to a shaft inside the generator. The shaft turns and thereby rotates the conducting wire loop. Magnetic lines of force are cut, and an electric current is produced.

Pedaling a bicycle produces enough mechanical energy to generate electricity for bicycle lights. But it certainly could not generate enough electricity to light your home and run your appliances. Or, for that matter, all the lights and appliances in homes in your town!

Large generators used in power plants produce enormous quantities of electricity. These generators get their mechanical energy from turbines. Turbines are wheels turned by the force of moving steam or water. As the turbine rotates, it turns the coiled wire in a magnetic field produced by a large, powerful magnet. As magnetic lines of force are cut, a current flows in the conducting wire.

The electricity produced by the generator is conducted in power lines that eventually reach your home. When you turn on a switch that completes a circuit in one of the parallel pathways, the electric energy becomes available to do the work you wish to do. This work might be to light a room, send electron beams to your television or computer screen, cook a steak, or warm or cool a room. The energy has completed its long journey from the power plant to your home.

Figure 3-31 *In the operation of a generator, water turns a turbine, which in turn moves large electromagnets encased in coils of insulated wire. As the electromagnets move, the coiled wire cuts magnetic lines of force. Current is produced in the wire and conducted through power lines that eventually reach homes and other buildings.*

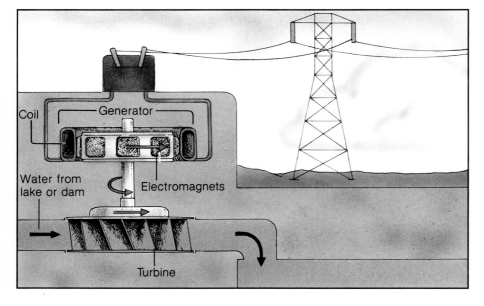

Coil

Generator

Water from lake or dam

Electromagnets

Turbine

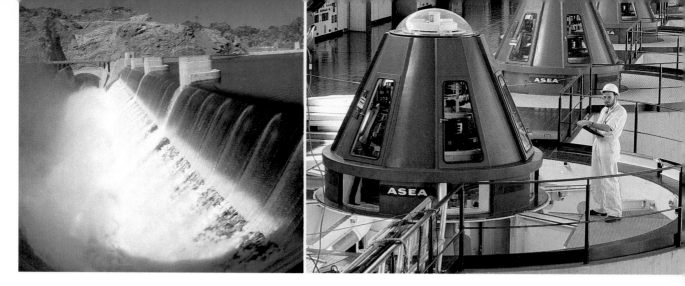

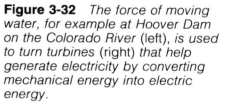

Now you know that electricity and magnetism do not involve magic at all. Whatever "magic" is involved lies in the creativity of those who have developed ways to make electricity serve people rather than harm them. You are way ahead of Dr. Frankenstein. With electricity you can enrich your life—without damaging your castle!

Figure 3-32 *The force of moving water, for example at Hoover Dam on the Colorado River (left), is used to turn turbines (right) that help generate electricity by converting mechanical energy into electric energy.*

Figure 3-33 *Electricity that makes your life easier and more enjoyable completes its journey from a power plant to your home through power lines such as these.*

SECTION REVIEW

1. How does magnetism produce electricity?
2. When a conducting wire cuts magnetic lines of force, is alternating current or direct current produced?
3. What energy conversions are involved in the operation of a generator?

LABORATORY ACTIVITY

Conductors and Insulators

Purpose

In this activity, you will test some common materials and determine which are electric conductors and which are insulators.

Materials (*per group*)

1.5-volt dry cell
1.5-volt lamp with base
3 connecting leads approximately 30 cm each with ends stripped back, exposing the last 2 cm of copper
Testing materials: penny (copper), dime (silver), paper, wax, glass, aluminum foil, plastic, paper clip (steel), wood, rubber, cloth, pencil lead (carbon)

Procedure

1. Your conductivity tester should be set up as shown in the illustration.
2. Keep the ends of the two test wires about 2 cm apart. Bring them into contact with each of the materials to be tested. Record your results (bright, dim, or no light) in a data table.
3. When you are finished, disconnect the wires from the dry cell.

Observations and Conclusions

1. Which of the materials you tested are good conductors of electricity?
2. Which of the materials you tested are electric insulators?
3. Are metals electric conductors or insulators?
4. Are nonmetals electric conductors or insulators?

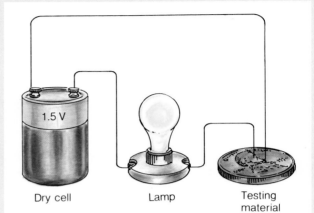

Dry cell   Lamp   Testing material

Material	Relative Brightness		
	Bright	**Dim**	**No Light**
Copper			
Silver			
Paper			
Wax			
Glass			
Aluminum foil			
Plastic			
Paper clip			
Wood			
Rubber			
Cloth			
Carbon			

CHAPTER REVIEW

SUMMARY

3-1 Electric Charge

- All matter is made up of atoms.

- A force that pulls oppositely charged objects together is a force of attraction. A force that pushes similarly charged objects apart is a force of repulsion.

3-2 Static Electricity

- The buildup of electric charge is called static electricity.

- Objects can be charged by friction, conduction, and induction.

- A measure of the energy available to move electrons is called voltage, which is measured in units called volts (V).

3-3 The Flow of Electricity

- Electric current is the number of electrons passing a given point during a unit of time. Current is measured in amperes.

- Resistance is the opposition to the flow of electricity and is measured in ohms.

- Ohm's law is $V = I \times R$.

- Electrochemical cells change chemical energy into electric energy.

- Electric power is measured in watts.

3-4 Electric Circuits

- A series circuit has only one path for the electrons to take. A parallel circuit has more than one path for the electrons to take.

3-5 Magnetism

- Like poles of magnets repel each other and unlike poles attract each other.

- The region in which magnets exert forces is called a magnetic field.

3-6 Magnetism from Electricity

- Electromagnetism is the relationship between electricity and magnetism.

3-7 Electricity from Magnetism

- An alternating electric current is produced in a wire if that wire cuts through the magnetic field of a magnet.

VOCABULARY

Define each term in a complete sentence.

alternating current	electric current	fuse	parallel circuit
ampere	electric discharge	induction	pole
atom	electric field	insulator	positive terminal
battery	electric power	lightning	proton
circuit breaker	electricity	magnetic field	resistance
conduction	electrochemical cell	magnetism	series circuit
conductor	electromagnetism	negative terminal	south magnetic pole
direct current	electron	neutron	static electricity
dry cell	electroscope	north magnetic pole	subatomic particle
electric charge	force of attraction	nucleus	volt
electric circuit	force of repulsion	ohm	voltage
			watt

CONTENT REVIEW: MULTIPLE CHOICE

Choose the letter of the answer that best completes each statement.

1. A subatomic particle that carries a negative electric charge is called a(n)
   a. neutron.   b. positron.   c. electron.   d. proton.
2. Electricity resulting from the buildup of electric charges is
   a. alternating current.   b. magnetism.
   c. electromagnetism.   d. static electricity.
3. As extra electrons on an electrically charged object leave, the object becomes
   a. rectified.   b. resistant.   c. charged.   d. discharged.
4. Which of the following is the best electric conductor?
   a. air   b. silver   c. glass   d. wood
5. The unit in which resistance is measured is the
   a. ohm.   b. watt.   c. ampere.   d. volt.
6. Which of the following equations represents Ohm's law?
   a. $V = I \times R$ b. $I = V \times R$
   c. $V = I \times P$ d. $P = V \times I$
7. A string of lights that goes out when one bulb burns out is connected
   a. indirectly.   b. in series.   c. in parallel.   d. in tandem.
8. Which of the following can be dangerous?
   a. running a wire over a carpet
   b. drying your hands before using a hair dryer
   c. sticking a fork in a plugged-in toaster
   d. none of these
9. Which substance is a natural magnet?
   a. copper   b. aluminum   c. lodestone   d. alnico
10. A wire coiled around a soft iron core forms a(n)
    a. dry cell.   b. electromagnet.   c. lightning rod.   d. series circuit.

CONTENT REVIEW: COMPLETION

Fill in the word or words that best complete each statement.

1. A positively charged proton will repel a(n) _____.
2. Whenever lightning occurs, there is a discharge of _____ electricity.
3. The flow of electrons through a wire is a(n) _____.
4. A shortage of electrons exists at the _____ terminal of a dry cell.
5. The rate at which work is done or energy is produced is called _____.
6. A 100-watt light bulb operates at 220 volts and about _____ amperes.
7. An electric current that completes a loop is called an electric _____.
8. A reusable device that protects against dangerous heat buildup in a circuit is a(n) _____.
9. The end of a magnet where magnetic force is strongest is a(n) _____.
10. Electric currents can be produced by cutting through the _____ of a magnet.

CONTENT REVIEW: TRUE OR FALSE

Determine whether each statement is true or false. If it is true, write "true." If it is false, change the underlined word or words to make the statement true.

1. Like charges <u>attract</u> each other; unlike charges repel each other.
2. A neutral object develops a negative charge when it <u>gains</u> electrons.
3. Charging by <u>conduction</u> involves a rearrangement of electric charges.
4. A measure of energy available to move electrons is called <u>friction</u>.
5. Materials that do not allow electrons to flow freely are called <u>insulators</u>.
6. Ohm's law states that the current in a wire is equal to resistance divided by voltage.
7. In a <u>series</u> circuit, electric appliances are on different branches of the circuit.
8. Rubber is a relatively <u>poor</u> conductor of electricity.
9. The region around a magnet in which magnetic forces can act is an <u>electric field</u>.
10. Generators obtain their mechanical energy from <u>turbines</u> powered by water or steam.

CONCEPT REVIEW: SKILL BUILDING

Use the skills you have developed in the chapter to complete each activity.

1. **Applying concepts** Provide an explanation for the following observations:
   a. Clothes dried in a dryer often stick together with "static cling."
   b. Never touch both terminals at the same time when working on a car battery.
   c. It is dangerous to use a 30-amp fuse in a circuit calling for a 15-amp fuse.

2. **Making calculations** A light bulb operates at 60 volts and 2 amps.
   a. What is the power of the light bulb?
   b. How much energy does the light bulb need, to operate for eight hours?
   c. What is the cost of operating the bulb for 8 hours at 7¢ per kilowatt-hour?

3. **Designing an experiment** A plastic ruler is rubbed with waxed paper. The ruler gains an unknown charge. Describe an experiment you could perform using an electroscope, a rubber rod, and a piece of fur to determine the charge on the ruler.

4. **Identifying relationships** Identify each of the following statements as being a characteristic of (a) a series circuit, (b) a parallel circuit, (c) both a series and a parallel circuit:
   a. $I = V/R$
   b. The total resistance in the circuit is the sum of the individual resistances.
   c. The total current in the circuit is the sum of the current in each resistance.
   d. The current in each part of the circuit is the same.
   e. A break in any part of the circuit causes the current to stop.

CONCEPT REVIEW: ESSAY

Discuss each of the following in a brief paragraph.

1. Discuss three safety rules to follow while using electricity.
2. Describe the three ways in which an object can be charged.
3. Compare an insulator and a conductor. How might each be used?

4 Sound

CHAPTER SECTIONS

4-1 Sound Waves
4-2 Characteristics of Waves
4-3 Properties of Sound
4-4 Wave Interactions

CHAPTER OBJECTIVES

*After completing this chapter,
you will be able to:*

4-1 Relate the motion of molecules to the production of sound.

4-1 Identify a sound wave as a series of periodic compressions and rarefactions.

4-2 Describe the amplitude, shape, wavelength, and frequency of a sound wave.

4-3 Relate pitch to the frequency of a sound wave.

4-3 Compare the amplitude of a sound wave and its intensity.

4-4 Describe the interactions of sound waves that produce resonance, sound quality, and interference.

4-4 Compare the characteristics of music and noise.

"Turn down the noise of that radio! I'm on the phone," you might shout at a friend.

"Stop shouting! I can't hear the music," might come the reply.

Clearly, one person's "noise" may be another person's music. It is largely a matter of opinion—or is it? Is there something about sounds that sets them apart from one another?

Scientists tell us there is. They use certain basic characteristics to describe sounds and the differences between them. Taken together, these characteristics are what make beautiful music and noise, pleasant sounds and unpleasant sounds, soothing sounds and painful ones.

After you have learned the secrets of sound, you may be able to startle a friend who is playing loud music by saying, "The intensity of those sound waves is too high, and their vibrations are too irregular. Please reduce the decibel level!"

A flutist producing pleasing music

4-1   Sound Waves

Learning about sound may be easier than you think. For sound involves two ideas you are already familiar with: motion and molecules. Perhaps you have never thought about sound in this way. You are used to sounds reaching your ears; you do not usually see anything moving. However, sound is a form of energy that causes molecules to move. The way that molecules move and transmit their energy is the same for all sounds—from whispers to wails, from squeaks to sonic booms.

Vibrations in a Medium

Have you ever made "music" with a rubber band? If you stretch a rubber band and then pluck it, you will hear a sound. You will also see the rubber band moving. If you listen and look carefully, you may even notice a relationship between the sound produced and the speed at which the rubber band moves. You will read more about that later.

Now try this. Place two fingers gently on your throat and speak or sing. Although you cannot see anything moving this time, you can feel some rapid movements, and you certainly hear sounds.

When a sound is produced, there is always motion involved. The motion is the rapid movement of molecules back and forth. **Sound is caused by the vibration of molecules of matter.** There can be no sound without vibrating molecules.

Figure 4-1 *Sound is a form of energy that causes molecules of a medium to vibrate back and forth, as you can clearly see from the splashes of water created by a vibrating tuning fork* (left). *If there are no molecules of a medium present, such as on the moon, there will be no sound. So astronaut Harrison Schmitt explores a lunar boulder in the silent world of the moon* (right).

Once a sound is produced, it travels away from its source. And if you are to hear it, the sound must reach your ears. You can probably guess that sound travels through air. Air, of course, is a gas. If you have ever been under water and heard a noise, you know that sound also travels through liquids. Any substance that transmits sound is called a **medium.** Gases and liquids are mediums of sound. What about solids? Since sound involves the vibration of molecules, you may have already figured out that sound travels through solids too. Solids, liquids, and gases are made up of molecules. What, then, do you think would happen if you and a friend tried to have a conversation on the moon?

Figure 4-2 *As the strings on this guitar are plucked, they begin to vibrate. The molecules of air around the strings also begin to vibrate. These vibrations reach your ears, and you hear sounds.*

Making Waves

When you pluck a rubber band, it begins to vibrate. Then the molecules of air surrounding the rubber band also begin to vibrate. Soon the vibrations reach your ears. You hear something, but you certainly do not feel a rush of air against your ear. Likewise, when you put your ear against a wall and someone taps another part of the wall, you hear the tapping without the wall moving to your ear! In both of the examples, the sound is transmitted through the medium *without* movement of the medium as a whole. In other words, energy is transmitted, but matter is not.

How, then, does the sound energy get from one place to another? Sounds are transmitted as **waves.** It may help if you think of an ocean wave moving toward shore. As the wave rushes to shore, the ocean water is moved up and down a great deal. Although it looks as if the water itself is going toward shore, it is not. Only the wave motion, and thus the energy of the wave, moves forward. This passage of wave energy through the medium causes the water to rise up and then fall down again. You can think of a wave, then, as a repeating series of disturbances that moves through a medium.

Now try to imagine that you can see the air molecules around the plucked rubber band. What does the vibration do to the molecules? As the band vibrates, it first moves forward. It pushes the molecules of the medium in front of it. So these

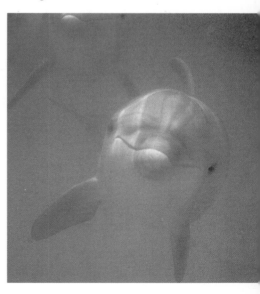

Figure 4-3 *In order for sounds to be transmitted, molecules of a medium must be present. Liquids are good mediums for sound transmittal. Dolphins can "talk" and "listen" to each other because sounds are easily transmitted through water.*

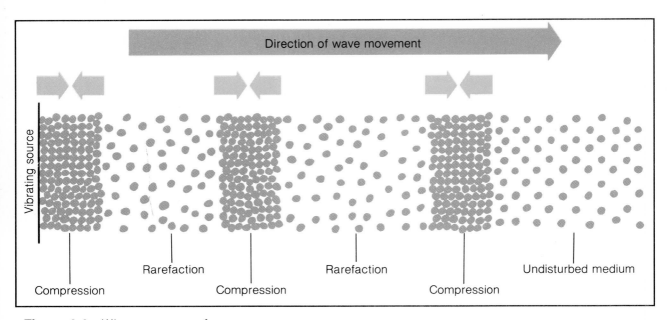

Direction of wave movement

Vibrating source

Compression · Rarefaction · Compression · Rarefaction · Compression · Undisturbed medium

Figure 4-4 *When a source of sound is set in motion, the molecules around it are first crowded together, causing a compression, and then spread out, causing a rarefaction. This periodic series of compressions and rarefactions moving through a medium is a sound wave.*

molecules crowd together, causing a **compression** (kuhm-PRESH-uhn). See Figure 4-4. Now the vibrating band moves backward, allowing the molecules of the medium to move back to fill the space. In this space, the molecules are more spread out. A space in which there are fewer molecules is called a **rarefaction** (rayr-uh-FAK-shuhn). See Figure 4-4. As the compressed molecules near the vibrating band move outward, they collide with the next layer of air molecules. These molecules also become compressed. The compressions move outward through the medium as each layer of molecules pushes the next layer. Rarefactions also move outward, as one layer of molecules after another moves back.

As the layers move back and forth throughout the medium, compressions and rarefactions develop and "move" through the medium in a regular, repeating way. As the string keeps vibrating back and forth, the molecules of air are compressed and rarefied over and over again. **The periodic series of compressions and rarefactions, or a sound wave, transmits energy through layers of vibrating molecules in a medium.**

Look again at Figure 4-4. You will notice that in **sound waves** the molecules of the medium move back and forth *parallel* to the direction in which the wave moves. Such waves are called **longitudinal** (lawn-juh-TOOD-uhn-uhl) **waves.**

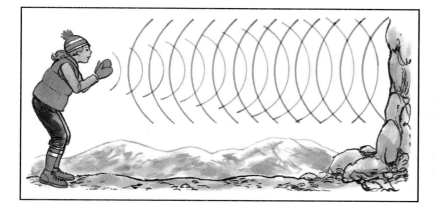

Figure 4-5 *When sound waves strike a hard surface, such as a brick wall or a mountainside, they are reflected, or bounced back. A reflected sound is called an echo. An echo has the same series of compressions and rarefactions as the original wave.*

The Best Medium

Now let's go back to the idea of sound traveling through a medium. Think of the wave as a series of compressions and rarefactions. Also think about the arrangement of molecules in solids, liquids, and gases. Can you come up with an idea about which medium is best for transmitting sound? If you said solids are the best, you are right. The molecules of solids are the most closely packed. Vibrations are most easily passed from one molecule to another in a solid. That is why you put your ear to a door to hear sounds on the other side. And that is why outlaws used to put an ear to the ground to listen for the hoofbeats of an approaching posse!

Since a sound wave is a series of compressions and rarefactions of molecules, solids that are elastic, or that return quickly to their original shape after being disturbed, are good carriers of sound. Sound travels quickly through highly elastic materials. Solids such as iron, nickel, and steel are good carriers of sound because they are very elastic. Lead, although it is also a solid, is not very elastic, so it is not as good at carrying sound as steel. What kinds of materials do you think should be used to build soundproof rooms?

Knowing that molecules are more closely packed in a liquid than in a gas, how do you think water and air compare as mediums for sound? Next time you are swimming with a friend, try this. Stand several meters away from your friend with your head above water. Have your friend tap two stones together above the water. Notice how well you hear the

Activity

Viewing Vibrations

Sound is caused by vibration. You can observe this by experimenting with a tuning fork.

1. Strike the prongs of a tuning fork with a pencil and then hold the fork close to your ear. Record your observations. What happens when you touch the prongs of the fork?

2. Next, strike the prongs of the tuning fork and place the ends of the prongs in a glass of water. What happens?

3. Tie a small piece of cork to a string and hold the string in one hand so the cork can swing freely. Strike the prongs of the tuning fork and hold one prong against the cork. Observe and record what happens.

Figure 4-6 *It is important that some places be as quiet as possible. A variety of soundproofing materials and methods, being tested here by sound technicians, prevent echoes and absorb sounds.*

sound. Then have your friend tap the stones together under water while you have your head under water. Which is the better medium, air or water?

Think back to your conversation on the moon. There is no air on the moon and, therefore, no air molecules. Without molecules to vibrate, there can be no sound, so you could not hear your friend's voice. Sound, then, cannot be produced in a vacuum, which is empty of all matter. You would not be able to hear sounds in outer space, either, since such regions are nearly perfect vacuums. The next time you see a science fiction movie in which explosions and collisions in space are accompanied by booming sound effects, you will know that this could not happen. The battle would go on in total silence!

The Speed of Sound

Snap your fingers, and you hear the sound almost instantly. The starting gun at a race is fired, and you hear it right away. From these and other experiences, you may think sound travels very fast—perhaps as fast as light. Actually, the speed of sound in air is about 340 meters per second. This is considerably slower than the speed of light, which is almost one million times as great as the speed of sound. A familiar illustration of the difference in speeds of sound and light is a thunder-and-lightning storm. The sound of thunder reaches you *after* the light from a flash of lightning—even though both are produced at the same time!

You can observe the relative slowness of sound yourself. Have a friend move about 100 meters away from you and clap his or her hands. You will notice a delay between the time you see the hands come together and the time you actually hear the sound. Perhaps you have noticed a similar example at a baseball game. As the batter connects with the pitch, you see the impact first and a moment later hear the crack of ball against bat.

Had this ball game taken place on a rather cold day, the delay in your hearing the sound after seeing the hit would have been greater than on a warm day. For one of the factors that affects the speed of sound is the temperature of the medium. Sound travels faster at high temperatures than at low ones.

Another factor that affects the speed of sound is the kind of medium through which it travels. Sound travels fastest in solids because the molecules are most closely packed. The next-best medium to a solid is a liquid, in which the molecules are moderately close together. In a gas, the molecules are the most loosely packed; sound travels most slowly through a gas.

SECTION REVIEW

1. Compare the speed of sound in the mediums of solid, liquid, gas.
2. Explain the difference between compressions and rarefactions in a wave.

4-2 Characteristics of Waves

Energy travels in waves—sound waves, light waves, radio waves, ocean waves. **All waves, regardless of their kind, share certain basic characteristics: amplitude, shape, wavelength, and frequency.** Figure 4-8 on page 92 illustrates these properties.

Like ocean waves, sound waves can be gentle or powerful; they can be tall or short; there can be large or small distances between the waves; and the waves can arrive in a regular pattern or in a random pattern.

SPEED OF SOUND

Substance	Speed (meters per second)
Rubber	60
Air at 0° C	331
Air at 25° C	346
Cork	500
Lead	1210
Water at 25° C	1498
Copper	3100
Brick	3650
Wood	3850
Glass	4540
Aluminum	5000
Iron	5103
Steel	5200
Stone	5971

Figure 4-7 *The speed of sound varies in different mediums. In which medium does sound travel the fastest? The slowest?*

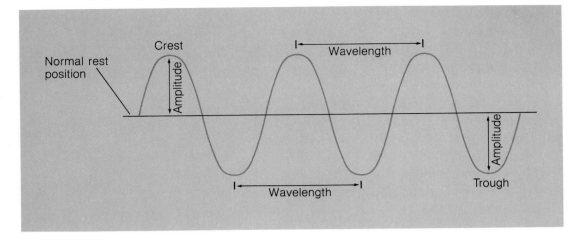

Figure 4-8 *Some of the basic characteristics of a wave—amplitude, wavelength, crests, and troughs—can be seen in this diagram.*

Amplitude

As a sound wave travels through a medium, the molecules of the medium begin to vibrate. They are moved from their rest position. The *maximum* distance the vibrating molecules are moved from their rest position is called the **amplitude** (AM-pli-tyood) of the wave. The amplitude of a wave indicates how much energy is used to produce the sound.

Shape

Think of the rest position of a molecule of a medium as a straight line. Now think of the forward vibrations as distances above the line, and the backward vibrations as distances below the line. One complete wave, then, has the shape you see in Figure 4-8: rest position up to high point, back through rest position to low point, and back to rest position.

The high point in a wave is called the **crest**. The low point is called the **trough** (trawf). The distance from rest position to crest, or rest position to trough, is the height of the wave. You now know that this height is also called amplitude.

Wavelength

If a wave has height, it also has length. The length of a wave is called its **wavelength.** A wavelength is the distance between the crests of two waves that are next to each other, or the troughs of two consecutive waves. In fact, you can measure wavelength from any point on a wave as long as you measure to the *same point* on the next wave.

Frequency

If you were sitting by the ocean and wanted to count waves, you might do so by locating a floating object and watching it bob up and down. For as each wave passed, the object would move up once and then down once. The number of bobs up or down would tell you how frequently the waves were moving toward the shore. The **frequency** (FREE-kwen-see) of any wave is the number of complete wave vibrations, or cycles, per unit time. Since each wave consists of both a crest (bob up) and a trough (bob down), you can think of frequency as the number of crests or troughs produced per unit time. See Figure 4-9.

Another way to think of frequency is as the number of compressions and rarefactions produced per unit time. If 100 complete cycles of compressions and rarefactions are carried by a layer of the medium in one second, the frequency of the sound wave is expressed as 100 cycles per second. The unit called the **hertz**, or Hz, is often used to express frequency. One hertz equals one cycle per second.

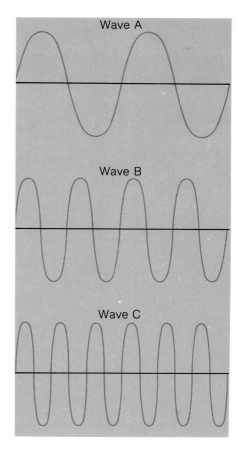

Figure 4-9 *The frequency of a wave is the number of complete wave vibrations per unit time. You can determine the frequency of these waves by counting crests or troughs. What is the frequency of each wave?*

SECTION REVIEW

1. Define the following wave characteristics: amplitude, crest, trough, wavelength.
2. What is wave frequency and how is it measured?

4-3 Properties of Sound

Many different sounds reach your ears every hour of every day. Some sounds are pleasant; some are unpleasant. You may call certain sounds music and other sounds noise. Sounds can be loud or soft, high or low. And a song played on a guitar usually sounds different from the same song played on a

Figure 4-10 *Bats use ultrasonic sounds, or sounds with frequencies higher than 20,000 hertz, to locate prey and to help them navigate.*

trumpet. There are many kinds of sounds, and each sound has its own special properties.

Pitch

Go ahead—sing the notes of the musical scale to yourself: do, re, mi, fa, sol, la, ti, do. What do you notice about each consecutive note? If you are singing the scale correctly, you should observe that the notes become higher and higher. The first "do" is a low note; the last "do" is a high note. Each note has its own **pitch**. The pitch of a sound is how high or low the sound is. Do not confuse high and low with loud and soft! You can demonstrate this difference to yourself by again singing the musical scale—both loudly and softly.

The pitch of a sound depends on how fast an object vibrates. Frequency is a measure of how fast an object vibrates. **The pitch of a sound depends on the frequency of the sound wave.**

Sound waves that have a high frequency are heard as sounds of high pitch. A piccolo produces high-pitched sounds. Sound waves that have a low frequency are heard as sounds of low pitch. A tuba produces low-pitched sounds. A high note sung by a soprano may have a frequency of 1000 hertz. A low note sung by a bass may have a frequency of about 70 hertz. Now think about the musical scale you just sang. The first "do" has a low pitch. The second "do" has a high pitch. What can you suggest about the frequency of each of these sounds?

The human ear can hear sounds that range from about 20 hertz to about 20,000 hertz. Sounds of higher frequency than 20,000 hertz are called

ultrasonic (uhl-truh-SAHN-ik) sounds. Although most people cannot hear ultrasonic sounds, many animals can. Dogs, for example, can hear sounds with frequencies up to 25,000 hertz. Bats actually produce ultrasonic sounds and then use their echoes to locate prey or to avoid bumping into objects. In this way, bats can fly about safely in the dark.

THE DOPPLER EFFECT Have you ever stood at a railroad crossing waiting for a train to pass? If so, you may have noticed something interesting about the sound of the train whistle as the train comes speeding by. The pitch of the sound becomes higher as the train approaches and gets lower as the train moves farther away.

Or perhaps you have been on a train as it passed through the railroad crossing and have heard the sound of the warning bells. As you approach the crossing, the pitch of the warning bells becomes higher. As you move away, the pitch gets lower. In either case, what you are observing is a change in the pitch of a sound due to the motion of either the sound source or the listener. This change in frequency and pitch is known as the **Doppler effect**.

The Doppler effect results from the fact that the approaching source generates compressions and rarefactions from points that become closer and closer to you. Waves reach you sooner than they would have if the source had been producing them from its original position. The wave cycles reach your ear more frequently as the source approaches. The sound waves are crowded closer together. You, the listener, hear sounds of increased frequency and thus higher pitch. As the source moves away, frequency and pitch decrease. The sound waves are now farther apart, and they reach you later than they would have if the source were not moving.

RADAR A police car with a radar device is probably a familiar sight to you. The device busily checks the speeds of cars passing along the road. This speed-checking ability is based on the Doppler effect.

Radar devices send out a continuous stream of waves. These waves vibrate at a known frequency. If the waves hit a stationary object, they bounce back at

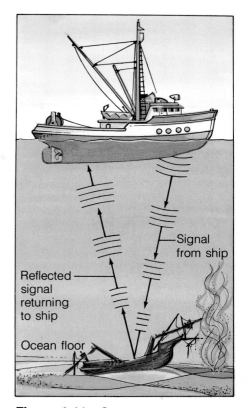

Figure 4-11 *Sonar is used to locate objects or determine distances under water. Sound waves given off by sonar instruments on the ship strike an object or the sea floor and bounce back. A receiver picks up the returning waves. Distances are calculated by knowing the speed of sound in the medium and the time it takes the sound to make a round trip.*

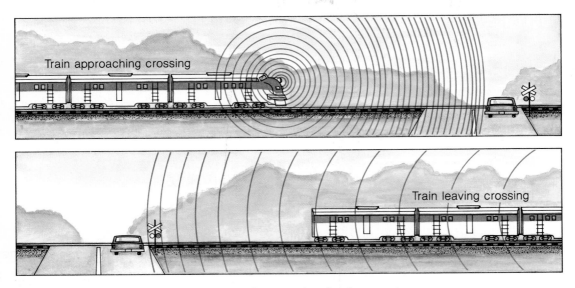

Figure 4-12 *As the train approaches the crossing* (top), *sound waves are crowded closer together and reach the listener's ears more frequently. So the sound has a higher pitch. As the train leaves the crossing* (bottom), *the sound waves are farther apart. Both frequency and pitch decrease. This is the Doppler effect.*

the same frequency. If the object is moving toward the radar receiver, however, the frequency of the echo waves is increased. And the faster the object is moving, the higher the wave frequency. Differences in frequency between the waves sent out and those bounced back are used to determine how fast the object is moving—and whether it is moving faster than the speed limit!

Intensity of Sound

How would you distinguish between the roar of a lion and the squeak of a mouse? Your first answer might be that a lion's roar is a low-pitched sound, while a mouse's squeak is high-pitched. And certainly you would note that a lion roars loudly and a mouse squeaks softly.

You already know that pitch is determined by frequency. What accounts for the loudness or softness of a sound? If a great deal of energy is used to produce a sound, the sound is loud, or has a high **intensity**. A nearby clap of thunder is a loud sound. A whisper is a soft sound. Not as much energy is used to produce a soft sound, or a sound of low intensity.

So the loudness of a sound is determined by the energy used to produce it. And energy moves molecules from their rest positions. Based on these facts, can you guess what characteristic of a wave determines loudness? You are right if you said amplitude. **The intensity of a sound depends upon the amplitude of the sound wave.** High-energy sound waves have a greater amplitude than low-energy sound waves.

Intensity is measured in units called **decibels**. A sound so soft that it can barely be heard has an intensity of about 0 decibels. A very loud sound, such as a clap of thunder, may have an intensity of about 120 decibels. Sounds with intensities greater than 120 decibels can cause pain in human beings. The intensity of a jet engine is about 170 decibels—a sound very painful to human ears. Music may be considered loud if its intensity reaches about 100 decibels, although an unwilling listener might think even 40 decibels was too loud!

INTENSITY OF SOUND

Sound	Decibels
Threshold of human hearing	0
Whisper	10–20
Very soft music	30
Classroom	35
Average home	40–50
Conversation	60–70
Loud music	90–100

Figure 4-13 *Decibel levels of some familiar sounds are shown in this table. What would you estimate is the decibel level in the room you are in right now?*

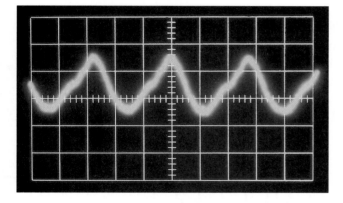

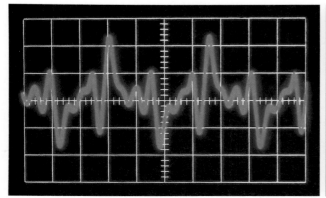 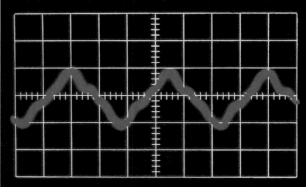

Figure 4-14 *An instrument called an oscilloscope converts sound waves into electric signals, which are displayed as a pattern of light on a screen. Here you see the pattern produced by a human voice (top), a harmonica (bottom, left), and a recorder (bottom, right) all sounding the same note. Notice that the pattern shows amplitude, wavelength, and frequency.*

1. Explain how frequency and pitch are related.
2. What is the Doppler effect?
3. What is sound intensity and how is it measured?

4-4   Wave Interactions

As you know, sound waves are energy waves that cause molecules in a medium to vibrate back and forth. But did you know that sound waves can interact? **The interactions of sound waves produce resonance, sound quality, and interference.**

Resonance

Objects that produce sounds do so because they vibrate. Each object has its own frequency of vibration, or **natural frequency**. For example, one object may have a natural frequency of 480 hertz, another object 600 hertz.

Sometimes an object vibrating at its natural frequency will cause a nearby object to start vibrating *if that object has the same natural frequency*. The second object picks up some of the vibration energy of the first object and vibrates "in sympathy" with it. This ability of an object to vibrate by absorbing energy of its own natural frequency is called **resonance**. A win-

Figure 4-15 *When one tuning fork is set in motion, it begins to vibrate at its natural frequency. These vibrations travel through the air and the wooden resonance box, which strengthens them. The tuning fork on the right will begin to vibrate "in sympathy" because it absorbs energy of its own natural frequency.*

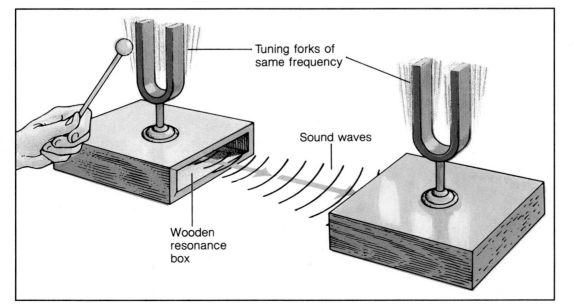

Tuning forks of same frequency

Sound waves

Wooden resonance box

dow may resonate to a loud noise outside. A vase resting on a radio may "ring" if a certain note is played. And a singer standing near a piano can make a piano string vibrate if she sings a note with the same frequency as the piano string.

Although you may not be aware of it, you are applying the idea of resonance every time you tune your radio to a particular station. Each radio station broadcasts at a specific frequency. When you "tune in" to your favorite station, you are matching the frequency of that station.

Making Music

Musical instruments produce sounds in different ways, depending upon the instrument. Percussion instruments, such as drums and cymbals, are set vibrating by being struck. In wind and brass instruments, such as flutes, clarinets, trumpets, and trombones, columns of air within the instrument are made to vibrate at various frequencies.

Activity

Making Music

The piano, guitar, and trombone are examples of the three different kinds of musical instruments. The piano is a percussion instrument; the guitar is a stringed instrument; and the trombone is a wind instrument. Each of these instruments produces sound vibrations in a different way.

Examine each instrument and describe how it works. A diagram would be helpful in explaining this information.

Career: *Sound Mixer*

HELP WANTED: SOUND MIXER To regulate sound levels and sound quality in recording studio. High school diploma and commercial radio operator's license required. Some training in operating electronic equipment needed. Experience in broadcasting desirable.

The scene is set for the train robbery. The television cameras carefully follow the bandits as they chase the speeding train, while a technician sits at a table busily turning knobs and dials. The technician adjusts several microphones so that the many sounds that will be heard are correctly balanced. The sounds of the bandits' voices, galloping hoofs, chugging train, and background music all have to be combined in the most striking and exciting way.

The technician who controls volume level and sound quality during a radio, television, or motion picture production is called a **sound mixer**. Sound mixers control the output of individual sources of sound so that a balance of music, dialogue, and sound effects is obtained.

Sound mixers also direct the installation of microphones and amplifiers. Using special testing equipment, they locate defects in the sound equipment and make repairs.

Anyone interested in a career as a sound mixer can obtain more information by writing to the Federal Communications Commission, 1919 M Street N.W., Washington, DC 20554.

Figure 4-16 *A stringed instrument, such as the one this Indonesian girl is playing* (top), *produces sound when the strings are set in motion by plucking or bowing. This traditional African drum* (bottom) *is a percussion instrument, which vibrates when struck.*

Plucking or rubbing across the string of a stringed instrument produces a regular vibration of the string back and forth. This is the way instruments such as the guitar, violin, and harp produce sounds. The vibration produced has a certain frequency, and thus a certain pitch. But you know from your experience that a guitar or violin produces a wide variety of pitches. How does this happen?

The pitch of a sound depends upon the speed of vibration. You can change this speed of vibration by changing the length, tightness, or thickness of the string.

The shorter a string is, the faster it vibrates and the higher its pitch. Thus the short strings of a violin or guitar produce higher notes than the long strings of a cello. The vibrating length of a string can be shortened by fingering along the string. This is what musicians do to produce the pitches they desire.

The more tension in a string, the higher the frequency and pitch. When musicians tune stringed instruments, they are either tightening or loosening the strings. If they tighten the strings, they get a higher-pitched sound. If they loosen the strings, they get a lower-pitched sound.

If you look closely at the strings of a piano or cello, you will notice that some strings are thicker than others. Thicker strings vibrate more slowly than thinner strings. Which strings produce sounds of high pitch? Of low pitch?

The Quality of Sound

You can easily recognize the sounds of different instruments even when the instruments are playing the same note. A note played on a trumpet is very different from the same note played on a flute! The instruments have different **quality**, or **timbre** (TAM-buhr). Although the pitches of the notes are the same, each instrument has its own special sound. You may be more familiar with another example of sound quality. When a friend calls to you, you can recognize the voice even if you cannot see the person. What gives voices, notes, and other sounds their timbre?

You have learned that when an object vibrates, it does so at a certain frequency. Actually, most objects

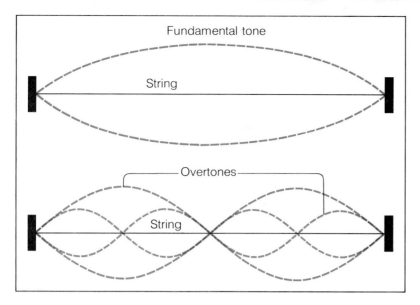

Figure 4-17 *A fundamental tone is produced when the whole string vibrates* (top). *When sections of the string vibrate faster and produce a higher pitch, these notes are called overtones* (bottom).

that produce sound *vibrate at more than one frequency at the same time.* Each frequency produces a sound with its own pitch. The blending of all the pitches gives the sound its quality.

To understand this better, let's look at a guitar string. When the *whole string* vibrates, the note produced is called the **fundamental tone.** It is the lowest-pitched tone the string can produce. See Figure 4-17. At the same time, sections of the string are vibrating faster and producing sounds of higher pitch. These notes are called **overtones.** Sounds always have a fundamental tone and one or more overtones. When the fundamental tone and overtones blend, they produce a sound that has a characteristic quality, or timbre. If the overtones produced by the trumpet and by the flute were removed, it would be impossible to distinguish between the two instruments. In fact, a violin, a clarinet, and your voice would all have the exact same sound quality.

Combining Sounds

Sound waves produced at the same time by different sources can interact with each other and produce various effects—from pleasing to annoying!

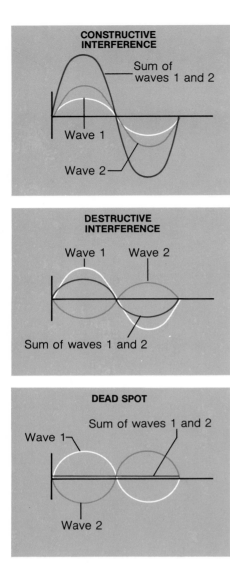

Figure 4-18 *When waves combine so that compressions of one wave meet compressions of the other, constructive interference results (top). The resulting sound has a greater intensity, or is louder. When compressions of one wave combine with rarefactions of the other, destructive interference results (center). The resulting sound is softer. Dead spots are produced when waves interfere destructively and cancel each other out (bottom).*

Sound waves produced at the same time can "add together" when compressions and rarefactions combine. Such combining is called **interference.**

CONSTRUCTIVE INTERFERENCE If the waves combine in such a way that compressions due to one wave meet compressions due to other waves, **constructive interference** results. See Figure 4-18. Because the waves match each other crest for crest, they are said to be in phase or in step. Constructive interference produces a sound that has greater intensity, or is louder.

DESTRUCTIVE INTERFERENCE If the waves combine in such a way that compressions due to one wave meet rarefactions due to other waves, then **destructive interference** results. See Figure 4-18. The total intensity of the sound is reduced. The sound is softer. In destructive interference, the sound waves are out of phase; the crest of one wave is opposite the trough of another wave. Actual "dead" spots in which no sound can be heard may result. Dead spots are especially troublesome in large halls that have hard surfaces that bounce sounds back into the room. These bounced-back sounds interfere destructively and cancel each other. Thus the shape, position, and materials of an auditorium must be carefully designed to eliminate interference problems and provide the best sound possible.

Music or Noise?

Would you consider the honk of a car horn noise or music? How about the squeak of chalk on a chalkboard? You probably agree that these sounds are noise, not music. But you would say that the sound of a symphony played by an orchestra or a song strummed by a guitarist is music.

You might think that the difference between noise and music is a matter of personal taste. Your music might be someone else's noise, and vice versa. But to a scientist there are several characteristics of music that set it apart from noise.

Music has a pleasing quality.

Music has a definite, identifiable pitch.

Music has a definite, repeated timing called rhythm.

The wave patterns shown in Figure 4-19 illustrate both music and noise. Can you identify each? Think about the sounds you hear in an average day and determine whether they are music or noise.

Noise Pollution

Noise is basically unwanted sound. Most people think of noise as an annoyance. But when noise reaches a level that causes pain or damages body parts, it becomes more than an annoyance. It becomes noise pollution. Loud street sounds, loud music at a concert, airport noise, and a wide variety of other loud noises are examples of noise pollution.

Noise pollution can have a serious effect on people's health. The stress from listening to loud noises can raise a person's blood pressure and cause nervous tension. Studies with guinea pigs exposed to loud noises over a prolonged period of time clearly show that noise can damage delicate tissues of the ear.

What can you do about noise pollution? In many countries, laws have been passed to prohibit noise pollution. People are not allowed to bring loud radios into public places. Of course, you don't have to wait for a law to follow this example. In your home, you can look for sources of noise pollution. Then you can determine which sources are within your control. You cannot stop a loud appliance in your kitchen, of course. But placing a rubber pad under the appliance will lessen its noise level. What other ways can you help prevent noise pollution?

SECTION REVIEW

1. What is natural frequency and how is it related to resonance?
2. In what three ways can the pitch of a sound produced by a string be changed?
3. How is sound quality produced?
4. What is wave interference? What are the two types of wave interference?
5. Compare music and noise.

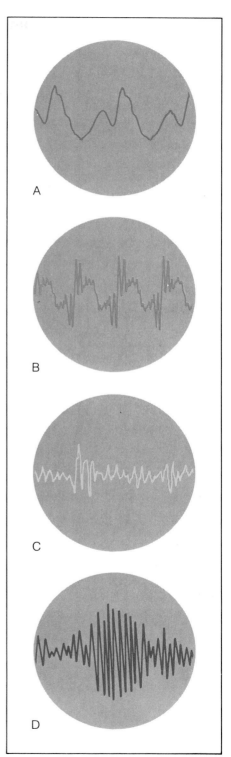

Figure 4-19 *These four wave patterns illustrate both music and noise. What distinguishes music from noise?*

A

B

C

D

LABORATORY ACTIVITY

Speed of Sound in Air

Purpose

In this activity, you will calculate the speed of sound in air.

Materials *(per group)*

1000-mL graduated cylinder
Hollow glass tubing, approximately
   2.5 cm × 45 cm
Tuning fork of known frequency
Meterstick
Water

Procedure 🔺

1. Fill the graduated cylinder with water to about 3 cm from the top.
2. Hold the hollow tubing in the water.
3. Strike the tuning fork against the heel of your shoe. Quickly place the fork just over the top of the hollow tube, as shown in the accompanying figure.
4. Move the hollow tube up and down until the *loudest* sound is heard. If there is more than one position in which the sound appears the loudest, choose the position in which the length of the tube above the water's surface is the shortest.
5. Record the length, L, of the air column to the nearest 0.1 cm.
6. Measure and record the inside diameter of the hollow tube to the nearest 0.1 cm.
7. Record the frequency of the tuning fork.

Observations and Conclusions

1. Calculate the wavelength of the tuning fork using the following formula:
   wavelength = (4 × L) + (1.6 × D)
      where L = length of the air column
             D = diameter of the tube

2. Calculate the speed of sound in air using the following formula:
   speed of sound = frequency ×
                      wavelength
3. The speed of sound in air is about 34,500 cm/sec. How close is your calculation to this value?
4. How do you account for differences between your calculated value and the given value?
5. If a tuning fork with a different frequency were used, would you expect a different value for the speed of sound? Explain your answer.
6. If this investigation were performed at a temperature of 5°C above or below the actual temperature, would the speed of sound be different? Explain your answer.

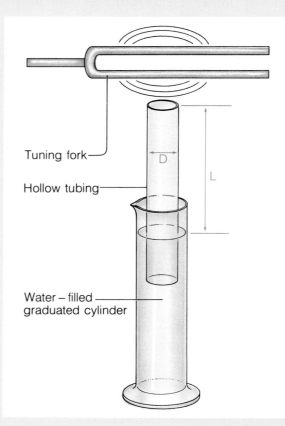

Tuning fork
Hollow tubing
Water – filled graduated cylinder

CHAPTER REVIEW

SUMMARY

4-1 Sound Waves

- Sound is caused by the vibration of molecules of matter.

- A substance that transmits sound is called a medium.

- Sound energy is transmitted as a periodic series of compressions and rarefactions.

- Sound is transmitted in longitudinal waves that can travel only in a solid, liquid, or gas.

- The speed of sound in air is 340 meters per second.

4-2 Characteristics of Waves

- The amplitude of a wave is the maximum distance the vibrating molecules are moved from their normal rest position.

- The distance between any point on a wave and the same point on the next wave is the wavelength.

- Frequency is the number of complete wave vibrations per unit time and is often measured in hertz, or cycles per second.

4-3 Properties of Sound

- Pitch—how high or low a sound is—depends on frequency of vibration.

- Ultrasonic sounds have frequencies above those that humans can hear.

- The Doppler effect is the apparent change in frequency and pitch due to the motion of either the sound source or the listener.

- Intensity is the loudness of a sound and is measured in decibels.

4-4 Wave Interactions

- Resonance is the ability of an object to vibrate by absorbing energy of its own natural frequency.

- Quality, or timbre, is produced by the blending of the fundamental tone with overtones.

- Sound waves can interfere, or combine, either constructively or destructively.

- Music, as opposed to noise, has a pleasing quality, definite pitch, and rhythm.

VOCABULARY

Define each term in a complete sentence.

amplitude	frequency	natural frequency	timbre
compression	fundamental tone	overtone	trough
constructive interference	hertz	pitch	ultrasonic
crest	intensity	quality	wave
decibel	interference	rarefaction	wavelength
destructive interference	longitudinal wave	resonance	
Doppler effect	medium	sound wave	

CONTENT REVIEW: MULTIPLE CHOICE

Choose the letter of the answer that best completes each statement.

1. There can be no sound transmitted through a
   a. solid. b. liquid. c. vacuum. d. gas.

2. The space in which vibrating molecules are pushed close together is a
   a. rarefaction.   b. compression.   c. trough.   d. dead spot.
3. The high point in a wave is called the
   a. crest.   b. trough.   c. wavelength.   d. amplitude.
4. The distance between two consecutive crests is called the
   a. amplitude.   b. height.   c. wavelength.   d. frequency.
5. A sound device used to measure the depths of oceans is called
   a. laser.   b. sonar.   c. radar.   d. pulsar.
6. The speed at which an object vibrates determines its
   a. amplitude.   b. loudness.   c. intensity.   d. pitch.
7. The loudness or softness of a sound is
   a. intensity.   b. quality.   c. pitch.   d. timbre.
8. A sound of 130 decibels would be
   a. harmless.   b. painful.   c. soft.   d. low.
9. The ability of an object to vibrate by absorbing energy of its own natural frequency is called
   a. timbre.   b. interference.   c. compression.   d. resonance.
10. The combining of sound waves produced at the same time is called
   a. resonance.   b. interference.   c. rhythm.   d. intensity.

CONTENT REVIEW: COMPLETION

Fill in the word or words that best complete each statement.

1. Sound is caused by the _____ of molecules of matter.

2. A repeating series of disturbances that moves through a substance is called a(n) _____.

3. _____ is the maximum distance the moving molecules are displaced from their rest position.

4. Frequency is often measured in cycles per second, or _____.

5. _____ sounds are sounds of frequencies greater than 20,000 cycles per second.

6. The _____ is the apparent change in the pitch of a sound due to the motion of the sound source or the listener.

7. _____ is the unit for measuring sound intensity.

8. The blending of the fundamental tone of an object with its overtones gives the sound its _____.

9. A sound of greater intensity can result from _____ interference.

10. A definite pitch and rhythm are characteristics of _____.

CONTENT REVIEW: TRUE OR FALSE

Determine whether each statement is true or false. If it is true, write "true." If it is false, change the underlined word or words to make the statement true.

1. A substance that transmits sound is called a <u>vacuum</u>.

2. Sound waves are <u>longitudinal</u> waves.

3. The speed of sound <u>decreases</u> as the temperature increases.

4. Sound travels <u>faster</u> in water than in air.

5. The low point in a wave is called the <u>crest</u>.

6. The pitch of a sound depends on the <u>frequency</u> of vibration.

7. A large amount of energy produces a sound of <u>low</u> intensity.
8. Actual dead spots in which no sound can be heard may result from <u>destructive interference</u>.
9. A string can be made to produce a higher pitched sound by <u>loosening</u> it.
10. <u>Noise</u> has a pleasing quality as well as a definite pitch.

CONCEPT REVIEW: SKILL BUILDING

Use the skills you have developed in the chapter to complete each activity.

1. **Making comparisons** List the following materials from best to worst as transmitters of sound: (a) iron, (b) oxygen gas, (c) soup.

2. **Making calculations** The speed of sound in air is 340 m/sec. If thunder is heard five seconds after a flash of lightning is seen, how far away is the lightning?

3. **Relating cause and effect** Assume you are standing still. As a car approaches you, its horn becomes stuck. Describe the sound of the horn as it approaches you and then as it passes you. Would the sound of the horn change if you were in the car?

4. **Applying concepts** A sonar device on the ocean surface sends sound waves to the ocean floor. If the sound waves take three seconds to reflect off an object on the ocean floor and return to the sonar device, what is the distance to the reflecting object? Assume the speed of sound in ocean water is 1530 m/sec.

5. **Making graphs** Plot a graph showing how the speed of sound in air varies with the temperature, using the following data:

Temperature °C	Speed m/sec
−10	325
0	331
10	337
20	343

6. **Interpreting graphs** From your graph in question 5, determine the speed of sound in air a. at 18°C b. at 25°C. By how much does the speed of sound change for a change in temperature of 1°C?

7. **Applying definitions** Overtones that sound well together are said to be in harmony. In order for sounds to be harmonic, their overtones must have frequencies that are whole-number multiples of the fundamental. Which of the following frequency combinations will produce harmonic sounds? What will the other combinations produce?
a. 256, 512, 768, 1024 Hz b. 128, 256, 1024 Hz c. 288, 520, 2048 Hz d. 128, 288, 480 Hz e. 512, 1024, 4096 Hz

CONCEPT REVIEW: ESSAY

Discuss each of the following in a brief paragraph.

1. Explain why a sound can be heard better when you are closer to the sound source.
2. Distinguish between a note sung by a soprano and one sung by a bass.
3. Describe how to make sounds of different pitches with a glass bottle and water.
4. Explain why your voice and those of your friends do not sound alike.
5. Suggest a reason for the presence of the wooden bridge between the strings of a violin and the body of the instrument.
6. It has been demonstrated that exposure to loud noises over long periods of time will damage a person's hearing. Discuss how you might go about avoiding this problem in your neighborhood.

5 Light

CHAPTER SECTIONS

5-1 What Is Light?
5-2 Sources of Light
5-3 Reflection
5-4 Refraction
5-5 The Color of Light
5-6 Light and Technology

CHAPTER OBJECTIVES

After completing this chapter, you will be able to:

5-1 Describe the electromagnetic spectrum.

5-1 Compare evidence for the particle theory of light and the wave theory of light.

5-2 Describe the types of light produced by luminous objects.

5-3 Relate the surface of an object to the kind of reflection it forms.

5-3 Compare plane, concave, and convex mirrors.

5-4 Compare refraction through a convex lens and a concave lens.

5-5 Describe the various interactions that can occur when light strikes an object.

5-6 Describe several new applications of light technology.

The light of a single lantern flickered from the steeple of the Old North Church in Boston on a night in April 1775. It signaled that the British army was about to attack the colonial forces at Lexington and Concord—and that the British soldiers would come "by land." That faint light was one of the most important messages in American history. But it was not the last of its kind.

Over one hundred years later, light was again serving American soldiers well. A device called a heliograph used mirrors to create flashes of reflected light. Short and long bursts of light, which represented the dots and dashes of the Morse code, were sent as messages from one army camp to another. Depending on the clearness of the sky, the length of uninterrupted sight, and the size of the mirrors, messages could be sent over distances as great as 48 kilometers. This was quite an achievement for an instrument that relied simply on the power of light.

Modern technology has brought communications techniques a long way since then. Yet light still serves as an important tool for transmitting messages of all kinds. A distance of 48 kilometers seems insignificant when compared with the experimental laser-light communication between the earth and orbiting spacecraft. Telephone and electronic signals are converted into light impulses and carried over long distances in special tubes called optical fibers. Your life is more convenient and enjoyable because of the many applications of light. No more need for lanterns atop church steeples!

Optical fibers—stars of light technology

Figure 5-1 *This beautiful fireworks display and the lights of the city skyline are two examples of visible light, which is only one of the many forms of light.*

5-1 What Is Light?

When you think of light, you probably think only of what you can see—visible light. Perhaps rainbows, movies, fireworks displays, and city skylines come to mind. You do not think of radio waves, microwaves, or X-rays as light because you cannot see them. Radio waves carry the sound signals you hear; microwaves can be used in ovens to cook food; and X-rays are used to take pictures of the inside of various objects and of humans. Yet these waves, in addition to infrared rays, ultraviolet rays, and gamma radiation, are indeed light—invisible light!

Light Energy

All forms of light, whether visible or invisible, begin in atoms. You may recall that tiny electrons move about the nucleus of an atom. Electrons carry a specific amount of energy. However, an electron can absorb more energy. Later, the electron may release the energy in a tiny packet called a **photon.** See Figure 5-2. The photon contains the exact amount of extra energy that the electron has absorbed—no more, no less.

Light is made up of these tiny packets of energy, or photons. In fact, you can think of light as a stream of photons. As you might expect, some photons contain more energy than others. The energy of a photon depends on how much energy the electron in an atom absorbs and then releases. The amount of energy in a photon helps determine the kind of light wave that is given off. For example, photons of visible light contain a moderate amount of energy. X-ray photons, on the other hand, contain a good deal more energy. They are high-energy photons. Radio waves do not contain as much energy as visible light. Radio waves are made up of low-energy photons.

Electromagnetic Waves

Now you know two differences between light waves: Some light waves are visible while others are not; and the photons of different forms of light waves contain different amounts of energy. However, all light waves also share many characteristics.

Light waves are **electromagnetic waves.** Unlike sound waves, electromagnetic waves do not need a medium, or substance, through which to travel. So electromagnetic waves can travel through the vacuum of space. Also, all electromagnetic waves travel at the same speed. In a vacuum, the speed of light is about 300,000 kilometers per second.

All light waves are **transverse waves.** This name describes how the wave energy moves in relation to the space through which it travels. You should remember that a sound wave was described as a longitudinal wave because the direction of wave energy is parallel to the movement of the molecules as they vibrate. Well, a light wave is a bit more difficult to describe because there are no moving molecules of matter, only moving photons of energy. These moving photons generate electric and magnetic fields.

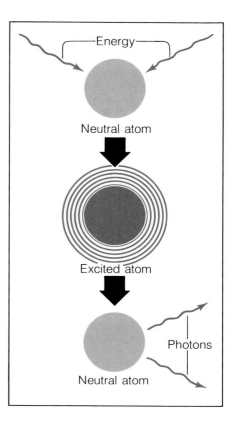

Figure 5-2 *As a neutral atom absorbs energy, it becomes excited. Some of its electrons capture the energy and then release it in tiny packets called photons.*

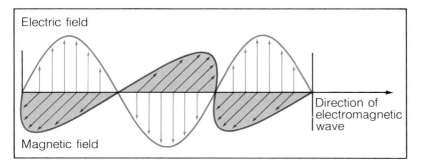

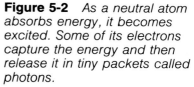

Figure 5-3 *In a transverse wave, the direction of the wave energy is at right angles to the electric and magnetic fields.*

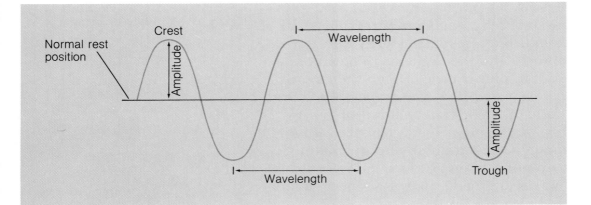

Figure 5-4 *A light wave has characteristic crests, troughs, wavelength, and amplitude.*

That is why light waves are called electromagnetic waves. In transverse waves, the wave energy is *at right angles* to these electric and magnetic fields.

You may understand the movement of light waves better if you think of a jump rope that you are holding at one end and a friend is holding at the other. If you move your hand up and down, you will produce up-and-down motions, or pulses, of the rope. The direction of wave energy is straight ahead, toward your friend. The pulses are up and down, or at right angles to the wave direction.

As with any wave, the "up" part of the electromagnetic wave is the crest; the "down" part is the trough. The maximum distance the wave travels from its normal rest position is the amplitude. And the distance between one point on a wave and the same point on the next wave is the wavelength. The number of waves passing a point in a given amount of time is the wave frequency. See Figure 5-4.

The Electromagnetic Spectrum

Scientists organize the different forms of light and their characteristics in the **electromagnetic spectrum.** Each kind of light in the electromagnetic spectrum has a particular frequency, wavelength, and photon energy. **The electromagnetic spectrum consists of radio waves, infrared rays, visible light, ultraviolet rays, X-rays, and gamma rays.**

Study the electromagnetic spectrum in Figure 5-5. You can see that the spectrum is arranged in order of increasing frequency, decreasing wavelength, and increasing photon energy. Which waves have the highest frequency? The lowest energy?

Activity

Shadows

A shadow is an area of darkness that is formed when an object blocks light from striking some surface. Often a shadow has two parts. When the light is completely blocked, the very dark umbra forms. The area outside the umbra receives some light and appears gray. This area is the penumbra.

With the sun or another light source behind you, observe your shadow or that of some other object. Identify the umbra and penumbra. Does the shadow change with the type of light source?

THE VISIBLE SPECTRUM   Look again at Figure 5-5. You will notice that only a small portion of the electromagnetic spectrum contains visible light—the light your eyes are sensitive to. Although you may think of most light as being white light, you can see that the visible spectrum is broken down into different colors. White light is made up of many different colors of light.

The visible spectrum contains light waves with frequencies between 400 trillion and 750 trillion hertz. These different frequencies of visible light correspond to the colors in white light: red, orange, yellow, green, blue, and violet. Color, then, depends on frequency. Within the visible spectrum, red has the lowest frequency. And red photons are the least energetic of visible light. As you go from red to violet, the frequency increases. What, then, must be true of the wavelengths of visible light? Of the wave energy?

THE INVISIBLE SPECTRUM   Look to the left of the color red on the spectrum. You will find light waves with a frequency slightly lower than that of red. These waves make up infrared light. You may be familiar with infrared light if you have ever had your dinner kept warm beneath a special lamp in a restaurant. You cannot see infrared rays, which are

Figure 5-5 *The various forms of light that make up the electromagnetic spectrum are arranged according to their increasing frequency and decreasing wavelength.*

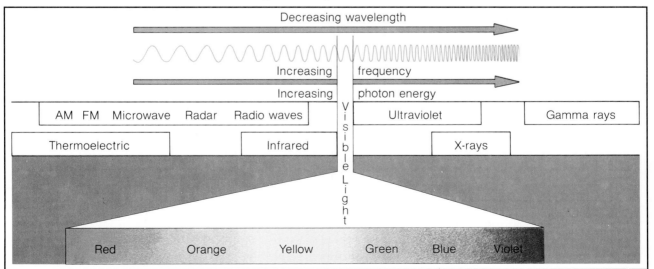

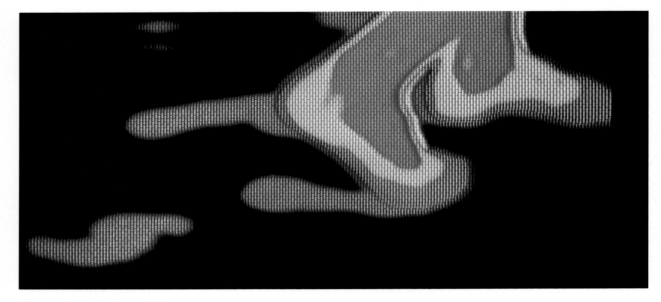

Figure 5-6 *Infrared light cannot be seen, but it can be detected as heat. This thermogram, or heat picture, shows the heat left by footprints. The brighter colors indicate areas of greater heat.*

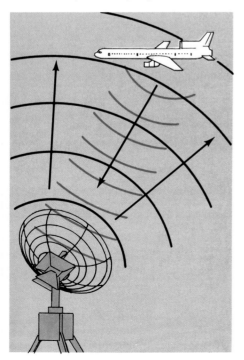

Figure 5-7 *Radar comes from the first letters of "Radio detecting and ranging." A radio transmitter sends out high-frequency waves that bounce off objects and return as "echoes" picked up by a receiver.*

given off by most objects, but you can feel them as heat. Hot objects produce more infrared rays than cold objects. And the hotter the object becomes, the greater the infrared radiation.

Beyond infrared radiation are the radio waves. Some of the lowest frequencies in radio waves are used for AM radio broadcasts. Higher-frequency radio waves are used in FM broadcasts. Even higher frequencies are used to transmit television signals through the air. Finally come the radio waves called microwaves and the radio waves used in radar.

Now look to the right of the color violet on the visible spectrum. Waves with a frequency slightly higher than that of violet light are called ultraviolet. These waves have a great deal of energy—enough to kill living things. Ultraviolet radiation is used to destroy bacteria and preserve food. Too much ultraviolet light can be harmful to people as well. Remember this the next time you go out to sunbathe. The ultraviolet rays from the sun may actually be burning your skin!

Beyond ultraviolet are waves of even higher frequencies and energy levels. First you will find X-rays. X-rays pass easily through many materials and can be used to take photographs of the insides of objects and people. Too much X-ray radiation, as you might expect, can be very harmful. After X-rays come gamma rays. Gamma rays are given off by certain radioactive elements. They, too, are very dangerous to living things.

Particle, Wave, or Both?

Throughout this chapter, you have read about the characteristics of light waves, such as frequency and wavelength. And, in fact, the "wave model" of light successfully explains most of the properties and behavior of light. However, in the early 1900s, scientists discovered something rather unusual about light. The scientists shone violet light onto the surface of certain metals. The energy carried by photons of violet light was absorbed by electrons in the atoms of the metal plate. This photon energy actually knocked electrons out of the atoms in the metal plate. In fact, enough electrons could be knocked off the metal plate to cause an electric current to flow. Since the experiment involved electrons and photons, this result came to be known as the **photoelectric effect.**

Next, the scientists repeated the experiment with red light. Nothing happened! No matter how long the red light was shone or how bright it was, no electrons were ever knocked out of the metal's atoms.

As you know, photons of red light have less energy than photons of violet light. However, if red light strikes a metal plate as a continuous wave, then eventually the electrons should "soak up" enough energy so that they can escape from their atoms. That does not happen. But suppose, in this case, light acts more like a stream of particles than like a wave. Then each individual red light photon, acting on its own, can never knock an electron from an atom. No single red light photon packs enough energy to do the job, no matter how long the light is on or how bright the light is. On the other hand, violet light photons carry more energy than red light photons. So a single violet light photon can knock an electron right out of its atom. In the photoelectric effect, it certainly appears as if light acts more like individual particles than a continuous wave!

The photoelectric effect can only be explained in terms of the particlelike nature of light. Yet most

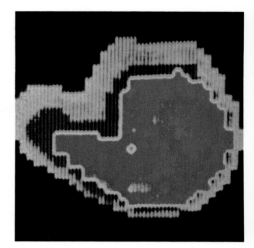

Figure 5-8 *This gamma camera image of the heart was produced when a patient was injected with a substance that gives off gamma rays.*

Figure 5-9 *The energy of individual photons of violet light can produce an electric current (top). The energy of individual photons of red light cannot (bottom).*

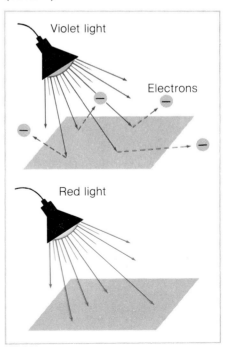

other aspects of the behavior of light require an explanation in terms of waves. Confused? Don't be. Scientists today describe light as both particlelike and wavelike, depending upon the situation. This is a good opportunity for you to remember that science is a way of explaining observations; it is not absolute knowledge.

SECTION REVIEW

1. List three properties of electromagnetic waves.
2. Compare the visible and invisible spectrum.
3. Explain why scientists describe light as both particlelike and wavelike.

5-2 Sources of Light

Have you ever done this? You go out on a beautiful day and notice how intensely the sun is shining. Later, you observe the moon shining brightly in the night sky. You know that both the sun and moon give off light. However, you might not know that each object gives off light in quite a different way.

Almost all of the natural light the earth receives comes from the sun. The sun and other objects that

Figure 5-10 *A flashlight is a luminous object because it gives off its own light. Illuminated objects are visible because of light bouncing from them.*

give off their own light are called **luminous** (LOO-muh-nuhs) objects. Stars, light bulbs, candles, and even fireflies are luminous objects.

Objects such as the moon can be seen because light shines on them and then bounces off. Objects that can be seen because of the light bouncing from them are called **illuminated** (i-LOO-muh-nayt-ed) objects. How would you describe this page? A lamp?

Producing Light

Luminous objects can produce incandescent light, fluorescent light, or neon light. Fluorescent and neon light are often called gas discharge light.

INCANDESCENT LIGHT   Certain objects can be heated until they glow, or give off light. **Incandescent** (in-kuhn-DES-uhnt) lights in your home produce light in this way. Inside a glass bulb is a thin wire filament made of the metal tungsten. Tungsten can be heated to over 2000° C without melting. When the light is switched on, electrons flow through the tungsten wire. Because the filament is thin, there is resistance to the electron flow. Electric resistance produces heat. Enough heat will cause the tungsten to glow as photons of visible light are emitted.

FLUORESCENT LIGHT   Some lamps produce light when they are cool, not hot. Instead of being used to build up heat, electrons are used to bombard molecules of a gas kept at low pressure in a tube. **Fluorescent** (floo-RES-uhnt) light is cool light that uses much less electricity than incandescent light.

Fluorescent tubes, usually long and narrow or circular in shape, contain mercury vapor and argon gas. When electricity flows through the tube, it causes the mercury vapor to give off ultraviolet light. You cannot see this ultraviolet light. So the inside of the tube is coated with special substances called **phosphors.** Phosphors absorb ultraviolet rays and change them into visible light. The color a fluorescent bulb produces depends on the phosphors used.

NEON LIGHT   Similar to fluorescent lights, **neon** lights produce light when electricity passes through

Figure 5-11 *An incandescent bulb produces light as electricity flows through the thin tungsten filament inside (top). Certain living organisms, such as glowworms, are bioluminescent. They can produce light through chemical reactions in their bodies (bottom).*

Figure 5-12 *This picture of a house is made by passing electricity through tubes filled with different gases under pressure. Neon gas produces red light. Mercury vapor produces greenish-blue light.*

Activity

Heat and Light

You can compare the amount of heat given off by incandescent and fluorescent lights.

1. Place a thermometer on a dinner plate.

2. Position an incandescent light bulb 10 cm above the thermometer.

3. Turn on the bulb. After about 5 minutes, record the temperature.

4. Repeat the procedure, but this time use a fluorescent bulb.

Which light source operates at a higher temperature? Why is this an advantage?

tubes filled with a gas under pressure. An electric discharge passing through neon gas causes it to give off red light. If other gases are added to neon, other colors are produced.

When Light Strikes

No matter what the source, whenever light strikes matter three things can happen. First, the light can be absorbed, or soaked up, by the object. Some objects absorb light better than others.

Some of the light that strikes an object bounces off it, or is reflected. Mirrors, ponds, the moon, and highly polished surfaces reflect light. You will read more about reflection in the next section of this chapter.

Finally, light can pass through, or be transmitted by, the matter it strikes. If the light is transmitted readily, the substance is said to be **transparent.** Objects seen through transparent substances are very clear. Glass, water, and air are transparent. Can you think of some other examples?

If you look through a piece of waxed paper or frosted glass, you can see light. But the object you see is unclear and lacks detail. A fuzzy view results because as the light is transmitted, it is also scattered. Substances that transmit light but no detail of that light are said to be **translucent** (trans-LOO-suhnt).

If you hold a block of wood or a piece of black paper up to a light, all the light is blocked. These substances are said to be **opaque** (oh-PAYK) because they do not transmit light. Think back to what can happen when light strikes matter. If opaque substances do not transmit light, what do they do with it? What opaque substances can you think of?

SECTION REVIEW

1. What is the difference between a luminous object and an illuminated object?
2. Distinguish among absorption, reflection, and transmission of light.
3. Explain transparent, translucent, and opaque.

Figure 5-13 *A translucent substance does not transmit light readily, so objects seen through it are unclear and lack detail. These flowers were photographed through a translucent screen.*

5-3   Reflection

Imagine you are warming up for a game of tennis by hitting the ball against a backboard or a smooth wall. Each time you swing, the ball hits the wall and bounces back. And each time it bounces back, you are in the right position to receive it. You know just about where the ball will land because it bounces back in a fairly regular way. But suppose the wall is not smooth. Rough cement, for instance, creates an uneven surface. When you swing, the ball hits the wall and takes a "crazy bounce." You don't know where to stand because you cannot predict

Figure 5-14 *The castle you see is actually an image of the real thing produced by light rays reflected from the surface of the water.*

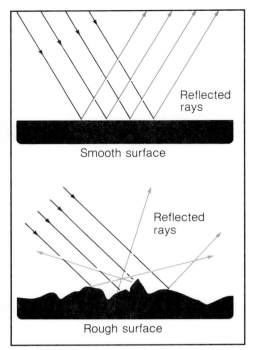

Figure 5-15 *Reflection from a smooth surface does not produce much scattering of light rays (top). Reflection from an uneven surface produces considerable scattering of light rays (bottom).*

Activity

Using a Plane Mirror

1. Stand 1 or 2 meters away from a full-length mirror. Have a friend or classmate place pieces of masking tape at the points on the mirror where you see the top of your head and your feet.

2. Compare the distance between the pieces of tape with your height.

3. Without changing the position of the mirror, move so that you are a distance of 4 or more meters from it. Does your image still fill the space between the tapes?

how the ball will bounce back. It has no regular pattern. Let's hope that your tennis game will be easier than this!

Light behaves in much the same way as the tennis ball. When light strikes a surface, whether smooth or rough, it can bounce back. This bouncing back of light is called **reflection** (re-FLEK-shuhn).

Kinds of Reflection

The type of surface the light strikes determines the kind of reflection that is formed. A mirror is a very smooth surface that reflects light from an object in a regular way. Because there is little scattering of the reflected light, the image formed is clearly defined and looks exactly like the object. This type of reflection is called **regular reflection.** It is similar to the tennis ball bouncing off the smooth wall.

When you look in a pool of water, you see an image of yourself that is not clearly defined. Instead, you look a bit "fuzzy," and your outline keeps changing. The surface of the water is not smooth. As the light is reflected from the uneven surface, it is scattered in many directions. A **diffuse** (di-FYOOS) **reflection** is the result.

Although diffuse reflections are not desirable for seeing your image, they are rather important. If the sun's rays were not scattered by reflecting off uneven surfaces and dust particles in the air, you would see only those objects which are in direct sunlight. Places in the shade of trees and buildings and in corners of rooms would be in darkness. In addition, the glare of the sunlight would be so strong that you would have difficulty seeing.

Mirrors

The most common reflecting surfaces are mirrors. A mirror is to light rays as the smooth wall is to your tennis ball. Any polished surface that reflects light and forms images can be used as a mirror.

PLANE MIRRORS A mirror with a perfectly flat surface is a **plane mirror.** Images formed by plane mirrors appear to be behind the mirror. You know, however, that this cannot be so, since the mirror is

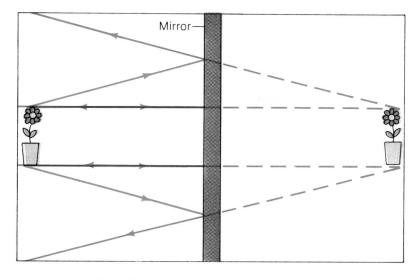

Mirror

Figure 5-16 *This diagram shows how an image is formed in a plane mirror. The reflected rays never really meet in front of the mirror. But if extended in back of the mirror, they come together and an image is formed.*

opaque and no light can pass through it. Figure 5-16 will help you understand how an image is formed in a plane mirror.

As you look at the figure, you should notice several things about the image. It is right-side-up, is the same size as the object, and appears to be as far in back of the mirror as the object is in front. There is one thing you cannot tell from the figure that you can, however, determine for yourself. Stand in front of a mirror and raise your *left* hand. Which hand of your image appears to be raised? If an object is moving right to left, how will it appear to move in a mirror?

CONCAVE MIRRORS   A mirror can be curved instead of flat. If the mirror surface curves *inward*, the mirror is called a **concave mirror.** Most images formed by concave mirrors are inverted, or upside-down. You can experiment with a concave mirror by looking at the inner surface of a shiny metal spoon. Move it back and forth and observe what happens to your image.

When light shines on a concave mirror, the light is reflected back through a point called the focal point. However, when a light source is placed exactly at the focal point of a concave mirror, something interesting happens. All the light waves are reflected back parallel to one another in a concentrated beam of light. See Figure 5-18 on page 122. If you open a flashlight, you will find a concave mirror behind the bulb. The bulb is placed at the focal point of the

Figure 5-17 *These people are using an optical instrument known as a periscope to see an event that is actually blocked from their view* (top). *Light enters at the top of the periscope, is reflected from one mirror to the other, and then to the viewer's eye* (bottom).

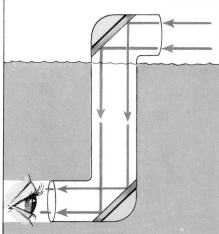

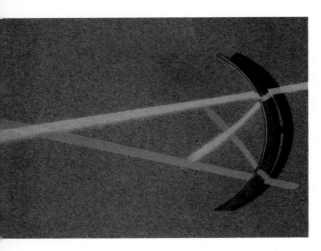

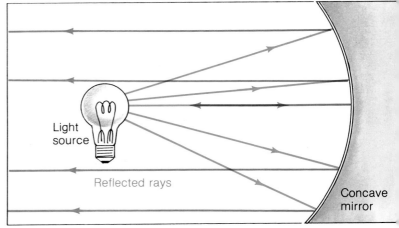

Figure 5-18 *A concave mirror reflects light rays so that they converge at a point called the focal point (left). If a light source is placed at the focal point, the reflected rays are all parallel to one another (right). No image is formed, but a concentrated beam of light is produced.*

mirror so that the reflected light forms a powerful beam. Concave mirrors are placed behind car headlights and are used in spotlights. They are also used in reflecting telescopes to gather light from space.

CONVEX MIRRORS If you turn the spoon over, you will notice that the mirror surface curves *outward*. A **convex mirror** has a reflecting surface that curves out like the surface of a ball. Reflected rays spread out from the surface of a convex mirror, as you can see in Figure 5-19. The image formed by a convex mirror is always right-side-up and smaller than the object. Like the image formed by a plane mirror, this image is located behind the mirror.

Convex mirrors have very large areas of reflection. For this reason, they are used in automobile side-view and rear-view mirrors. They are also used in stores to provide security guards with a wide view

Figure 5-19 *A convex mirror spreads out reflected light rays from its very large area of reflection.*

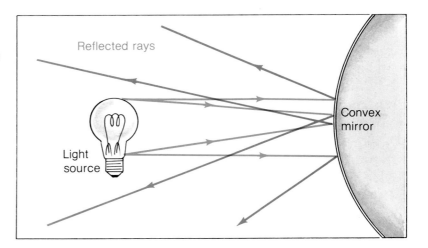

of the shopping area. However, convex mirrors give a distorted indication of distance. Objects appear to be farther away than they actually are. Why is this an important concern when using a car mirror?

SECTION REVIEW

1. Define reflection. What are the two kinds of reflection?
2. Name the three kinds of mirrors and tell how each is used.

5-4 Refraction

You can win the stuffed animal at the carnival if only you can throw the penny into the cup at the bottom of the fishbowl. It sounds easy, but it is actually rather difficult—unless you know that the bending of light makes the cup appear to be where it is not!

Light does not bend as it travels through a medium. It travels in straight lines. However, when light passes at an angle from one medium to another—air to water, glass to air, for example—it bends. This bending of light is called **refraction** (ri-FRAK-shuhn).

Refraction occurs because light moves at different speeds in different mediums. As it passes from one medium to another, it either speeds up or slows down. Because of refraction, a stick may look bent or broken when placed in a glass of water. If you are standing on the bank of a lake and you see a fish, it may appear closer to the surface than it actually is. And as if by magic, a coin out of your line of sight in the bottom of an empty cup may become visible when the cup is filled with water. Try it!

Bending and Separating

Have you ever seen a rainbow in a puddle of water or a drop of oil? Perhaps you have played with a triangular piece of glass that could form a rainbow from white light. How does this happen?

Activity

Making a Rainbow

This is an activity to do on a bright, sunny day just before the sun goes down.

Hook up a garden hose and walk with it to a sunny place in your yard. With the sun directly behind you, form a very fine spray of water in front of you. The spray should cover a large area. If you are situated properly, you will see a whole circle of rainbow near the boundary of the spray. Can you pick out all the colors of the visible spectrum and their order?

Figure 5-20 *As light passes at an angle from air to water, its speed changes. In this case, it slows down. The light is refracted, or bent, as a result.*

Figure 5-21 *A rainbow is formed when water droplets in the air act as tiny prisms. White light is refracted and separated into the six colors of the visible spectrum.*

Figure 5-22 *As white light passes through a prism, it is refracted. Since each frequency is bent a different amount, the white light breaks up into the colors of the visible spectrum.*

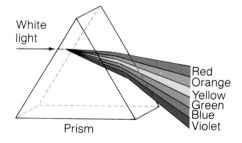

You learned that the visible spectrum is made up of the colors red, orange, yellow, green, blue, and violet. As white light passes from air into another medium, its speed changes and it is refracted. However, each frequency of the light is refracted a different amount. Violet, which has the highest frequency, is refracted the most. Red, with the lowest frequency, is refracted the least. The result is the separation of white light into the six colors of the spectrum, or a rainbow. Figure 5-22 shows how this bending and separating takes place.

The piece of glass that forms the spectrum is called a **prism** (PRIZ-'m). Notice that the light bends as it enters the prism and as it leaves it. The bending occurs as the light leaves the prism because the speed of light changes again as the light passes from glass back to air. At this point, which color is refracted the most? The least?

Lenses

Have you ever used a magnifying glass, a camera, or a microscope? If so, you were using a **lens** to form an image. A lens is any transparent material that refracts light. The light is said to be focused through the lens. Most lenses are made of glass or plastic and have either one or two curved surfaces. As the light rays pass through the lens, they are refracted so that they either come together or spread out.

124

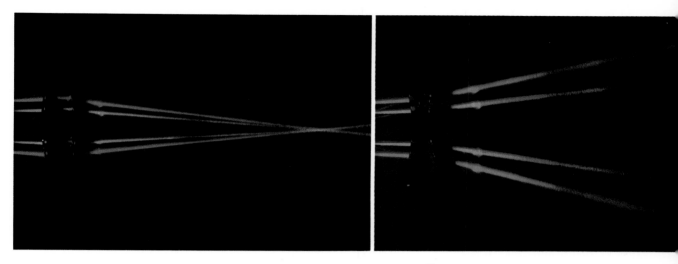

Figure 5-23 *A convex lens converges light rays* (left). *A concave lens spreads out light rays* (right).

CONVEX LENSES   Figure 5-23 shows a lens that is thicker at the center than at the edges. The rays of light are bent toward the center, the thickest part of the lens. The light rays come together, or converge. This type of lens is called a **convex lens.**

A convex lens can form different types of images when used in different instruments. Sometimes the image is upside-down and smaller, as in a camera or the lens of your eye. The image formed by the lens in a microscope or a slide projector is also upside-down, but it is larger than the object. How do you think a slide must be placed in a projector in order for the image to be right-side-up? Finally, a convex lens can form an image that is right-side-up and enlarged, as in a magnifying glass or binoculars.

CONCAVE LENSES   A lens that is thicker at the edges and thinner in the center bends light so that it spreads out, or diverges. This type of lens is called a **concave lens.** See Figure 5-23. All images produced by concave lenses are right-side-up and smaller than the object. Such lenses are most often used along with convex lenses to help form a sharper image.

How You See

You would not be learning about light now if you could not see the words printed on these pages. In fact, the process of refraction, which you just read about, is going on in your eyes at this very moment!

Figure 5-24 *These droplets of water act as convex lenses. Notice how they magnify the tiny veins in the leaf.*

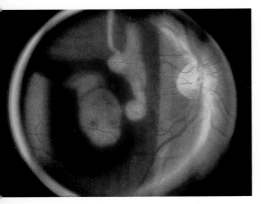

Figure 5-25 *You are looking at the image of a girl as it is formed on the retina of the eye. Remember that the image is upside down as a result of passing through the convex lens of the eye.*

Activity

Hole in Your Hand

Here is an optical illusion for you to try.

1. Roll a sheet of notebook paper into a tube and hold one end of it up to your right eye.

2. Place the side of your left hand against the tube with palm toward you at a distance of 15 centimeters from your eye.

3. Keep both eyes open and look at a distant object. Describe what you see.

Light enters the eye through an opening called the **pupil.** The colored area surrounding the pupil, called the **iris,** controls the amount of light that enters the pupil. A convex lens in the eye refracts the light and makes it converge on the **retina.** Muscles attached to the lens adjust its shape so that you can see objects both near and far away. How would you describe the image that is formed? Is it larger or smaller than the object? Upright or inverted?

The retina is made of light-sensitive nerves that transfer the image to the brain. The retina also contains nerve cells called rods, which are sensitive to light and dark. Other nerve cells called cones are responsible for your seeing colors. Without cones, you would see everything as black and white and shades of gray.

Ideally, the image formed by the lens should fall directly on the retina. In certain cases, the image falls in front of the retina or behind it. If the eyeball is too long, the image forms in front of the retina. A person has difficulty seeing objects at a distance but no trouble seeing objects nearby. This condition is called **nearsightedness.** A correcting lens would have to make the light rays diverge before they enter the eye. What kind of lens does this? Right, a concave lens. Figure 5-27 will help you understand this idea.

If the eyeball is too short, the image is focused behind the retina. The person can see distant objects clearly but has difficulty with nearby objects. This problem is called **farsightedness.** A convex lens, which makes light rays converge, is used to correct farsightedness. See Figure 5-27.

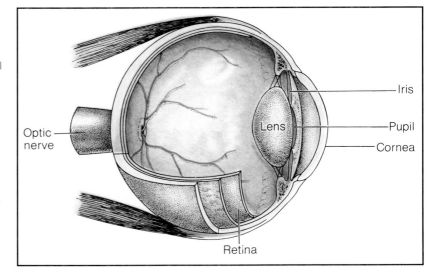

Figure 5-26 *The various parts of the eye all work together to enable you to see.*

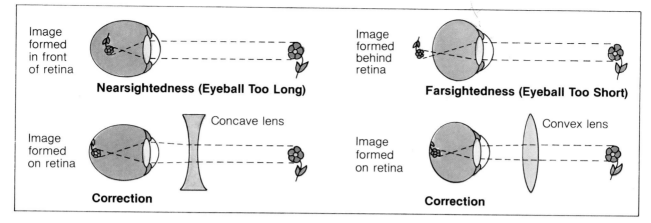

Figure 5-27 *Nearsightedness is corrected by using a concave lens. Farsightedness is corrected by using a convex lens.*

SECTION REVIEW

1. What causes light to be refracted?
2. Compare a convex lens and a concave lens.
3. What is nearsightedness? Farsightedness?

5-5   The Color of Light

Try to describe your clothes in detail without using colors. Pretty difficult, isn't it? Just look around. The world is full of colors. To understand why objects have color you must know what happens when light strikes an object. **When light strikes any form of matter, the light can be absorbed, reflected, or transmitted.**

The Color of Opaque Objects

An opaque object, an apple for example, does not allow any light to pass through it. The light falling on it is either absorbed or reflected. If the light is absorbed, can it reach your eyes? Obviously not. Only the light that is reflected reaches you. So the color of an opaque object is the color it reflects. A red apple reflects red and absorbs all other colors, while the green leaves on the stem reflect green.

Figure 5-28 *In white light, this apple appears red because it reflects red light (top). If only green light shines on it, the apple reflects no light. So it appears black (bottom).*

Figure 5-29 *The colors in these opaque sails are the colors of light that are reflected.*

Color and Absorption of Light

A dark object absorbs light rays, while a light object reflects them. The absorption of light rays increases the heat energy of the object. Dark objects should be warmer than light objects when exposed to a light source, and you can prove this yourself.

Obtain a small juice can and darken one half of the inside of the can by holding the flame of a lighted candle against it. **CAUTION:** *Be very careful when using a lighted candle.*

Using a little wax from the candle, coat one side each of two pennies and stick them to the outside of the can—one opposite the light side, the other opposite the dark side.

Now stand the lighted candle at the exact center of the can. Watch the coins. Which coin falls off first? Why?

Now think about an object that is white. White is the presence of all the colors of the spectrum. So what is being reflected from a white object? You are right if you said *all* the colors are reflected. No color is absorbed.

If all the colors are absorbed, then no color is reflected back to you. The object appears black. Black is the absence of color. Most objects reflect more than one color, however. These colors combine and produce a great variety of color mixtures such as aqua or brown.

The Color of Transparent Objects

Transparent objects allow light to pass through them. It is the color that is transmitted that reaches your eyes. The other colors are absorbed. So the color of a transparent object is the color of light it transmits. Red glass absorbs all colors but red, which it transmits. Green glass transmits only green light. Ordinary window glass transmits all colors and is said to be colorless. You should now be able to explain how the red and green colors on a traffic light are produced.

Figure 5-30 *At sunrise and sunset, the sun's rays must travel a greater distance through the atmosphere to reach you. More blue light is scattered, so the light that reaches you directly has more red in it.*

The Color of the Sky

"Why is the sky blue?" is not really a silly question. And there is a very good scientific answer. All the light in the sky comes from the sun. As the white light passes through the atmosphere, it is scattered by particles of dust in the air. Red and yellow light pass through the air directly, while blue light is scattered. It is the scattered blue light, then, that reaches your eyes, and you see the sky as blue.

SECTION REVIEW

1. What causes the color of an opaque object?
2. Why does white light passing through a green filter appear green?
3. Why does the sky often look blue?

5-6 Light and Technology

Anyone who has ever read a book on a dark winter day or enjoyed attending a baseball game at night knows the importance of being able to use and control light. Today, scientists have developed new and exciting ways to use light. **New developments in light technology include fiber optics, lasers, and holography.**

Fiber Optics

Imagine a doctor being able to see inside a patient's body without having to perform surgery! Advances in the field of **fiber optics** have made this possible. Fiber optics deals with the transfer of light through long, thin, flexible fibers of glass or plastic called optical fibers. An optical fiber, for example, can be inserted into a vein and threaded through the vein to the heart. A doctor can then photograph the heart to check for any problems.

In addition to instruments used in medicine, fiber-optic devices are used to transmit television programs and other video images. Some telephone

Career: *Holographic Technician*

HELP WANTED: HOLOGRAPHIC TECHNICIAN On-the-job training to assist in research laboratory for holography. High school diploma and two years of college math, physics, and chemistry required. Knowledge of photography and of general lab techniques desired.

The lines are long again at the supermarket checkout counter. The clerk runs the scanner over the bar code on a can of peas several times until the price appears on the register. The market manager, observing this time-consuming process, wonders about the efficiency of this new technology. As a result of some research, a new scanning system is ordered for the market. In the new system, a holographic lens replaces the glass lens used to focus a laser beam. It is the laser beam that reads the package bar codes. With the holographic system, the bar code is read the first time the scanner passes over it.

Holographic technicians work with laser beams in creating the holographic patterns that produce a three-dimensional image of an object. The technician's job involves caring for the

mirrors and lenses, operating the holographic equipment, and developing the resulting film.

Holographs are being used today in a variety of ways. Because they can test the ability of materials to withstand stress and vibration, they are important in testing artificial limb joints, automobile engines, and even guitars. The three-dimensional image they produce will find uses in the fields of medicine, computer technology, and communications. If you are interested in learning more about this exciting field, write to the Museum of Holography, 11 Mercer Street, New York, NY 10013.

130

systems now use fiber-optic transmission. You might wish to find out whether your telephone uses optical fibers.

Lasers

Unlike white light, which is a mixture of many frequencies, light from a **laser** is made up of only one frequency. Laser light is in phase. That is, the crests and troughs of each wave are lined up with the crests and troughs of all other waves. Light from a laser, then, travels in almost parallel lines with very little spreading. These characteristics make laser light extremely intense, concentrated, single-color light.

Lasers have uses in medicine, manufacturing, transportation, communication, and even earthquake prediction. You may soon be using lasers in video disks and computers, and possibly even in three-dimensional television!

Holography

A fiber-optic device can give doctors a photograph of the inside of a person's heart or stomach. A photograph, however, is two-dimensional. It would be more helpful if a three-dimensional image could be obtained. This capability may not be too far in the future as many new applications of **holography** are developed.

Holography is a technology that uses light to produce a three-dimensional image of a scene. This image is called a hologram. The image is so lifelike it seems as if you are looking at the real scene through a window. You can even look around nearby objects in the hologram to see in back of them!

Holograms have many possible uses. They can store a lot of information in a limited space, give details of structural flaws in automobile engines, display the interior of body organs, and observe crystal growth aboard the Space Shuttle.

SECTION REVIEW

1. List three uses of optical fibers.
2. What are three properties of laser light?
3. What is holography?

Figure 5-31 *These laser beams from atop the Empire State Building are made up of intense concentrated single-color light.*

Figure 5-32 *This hologram, or three-dimensional image of an object, was the first all-color hologram to be created. What kind of light is used in holography?*

LABORATORY ACTIVITY

Images from Reflected Light

Purpose

In this activity, you will observe a beam of light reflecting off several different surfaces.

Materials *(per group)*

Slide projector and slide
2 chalk erasers or dusty rag
Plane mirror
Aluminum foil
Assorted reflecting surfaces: plastic wrap, waxed paper, colored construction paper

Procedure

1. Put a slide in a slide projector. Turn on the projector and turn out the lights. Aim the projector at a 90-degree angle away from the screen.
2. Use a mirror to reflect the image onto the screen. Clap two chalkboard erasers together in front of the mirror. If you do not have erasers, shake a dusty rag. Observe the path of the beam and the image on the screen. Record your observations.
3. Carefully tear off a piece of aluminum foil without crinkling it. Place the aluminum foil over the mirror. The shiny side should be showing. Smooth out the foil and repeat step 2. Record your observations.
4. Remove the aluminum foil and crumple it into a ball. Uncrumple the foil and smooth it out on the mirror. Repeat step 2. Record your observations.
5. Repeat step 2 using plastic wrap, then waxed paper, and finally colored construction paper. Record your observations.

Observations and Conclusions

1. Which materials reflect light in a regular manner and which materials scatter light?
2. In order for a clear image to be produced, how must the rays of light be reflected?

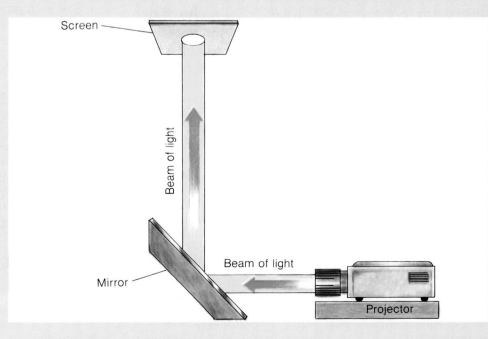

CHAPTER REVIEW

5-1 What Is Light?

■ The electromagnetic spectrum is an arrangement of different kinds of light waves in order of increasing frequency.

■ All light waves are transverse waves.

■ The visible spectrum consists of red, orange, yellow, green, blue, and violet.

■ The energy of light waves is contained in particlelike packages called photons.

5-2 Sources of Light

■ Luminous objects give off light. Illuminated objects bounce light off their surfaces.

■ Light passes through transparent objects, is scattered by translucent objects, and is absorbed by opaque objects.

5-3 Reflection

■ Reflection is the bouncing of light off a surface. Plane mirrors have flat surfaces, concave mirrors curve inward, and convex mirrors curve outward.

5-4 Refraction

■ Refraction is the bending of light as it passes from one medium to another.

■ A prism refracts light and separates it into the six colors of the visible spectrum.

■ A convex lens makes light rays converge. A concave lens makes light rays diverge.

5-5 The Color of Light

■ The color of an opaque object is the color of light reflected back to the human eye.

■ The color of a transparent object is the color of light that passes through the object.

5-6 Light and Technology

■ Fiber optics deals with the transfer of light through optical fibers.

■ Lasers produce extremely intense, concentrated, single-color light.

■ Holography uses laser light to produce a three-dimensional image of a scene.

VOCABULARY

Define each term in a complete sentence.

concave lens
concave mirror
convex lens
convex mirror
diffuse reflection
electromagnetic
   spectrum
electromagnetic
   wave
farsightedness
fiber optics
fluorescent
holography
illuminated

incandescent
iris
laser
lens
luminous
nearsightedness
neon
opaque
phosphor
photoelectric
   effect
photon
plane mirror
prism

pupil
reflection
refraction
regular reflection
retina
translucent
transparent
transverse wave

CONTENT REVIEW: MULTIPLE CHOICE

Choose the letter of the answer that best completes each statement.

1. All light waves
   a. are electromagnetic waves.   b. are transverse waves.
   c. travel at the same speed.   d. all of these.
2. The distance between one point on a wave and the same point on the next wave is called the
   a. amplitude.   b. crest.   c. trough.   d. wavelength.
3. Which color in the visible spectrum has the highest frequency?
   a. blue   b. red   c. violet   d. yellow
4. Lamps that produce light by heating tungsten metal until it glows are called
   a. incandescent lights.   b. fluorescent lights.   c. infrared lights.   d. neon lights.
5. Substances that do not transmit light are
   a. translucent.   b. illuminated.   c. opaque.   d. transparent.
6. A mirror with a surface that curves inward is called a
   a. concave mirror.   b. convex mirror.   c. regular mirror.   d. plane mirror.
7. A lens that is thinner in the center and diverges light is a
   a. transverse lens.   b. plane lens.   c. convex lens.   d. concave lens.
8. Cones are nerve cells in the eye that
   a. refract the incoming light.   b. control the amount of light getting in.
   c. allow you to see color.   d. reflect the incoming light.
9. What is the color of an object that reflects all colors of the spectrum?
   a. yellow   b. blue   c. black   d. white
10. Which of the following devices is used by doctors to see within a patient's body?
    a. prism   b. hologram   c. optical fiber   d. telescope

CONTENT REVIEW: COMPLETION

Fill in the word or words that best complete each statement.

1. The _____ is an arrangement of all the different kinds of light waves.
2. In certain metals, electrons may be knocked out of their atoms due to the absorption of light energy in a process called the _____.
3. Packages of energy given off as light are called _____.
4. Because stars and fireflies give off their own light, they are _____ objects.
5. In _____ lamps, electrons bombard mercury and argon gas molecules kept under pressure in a tube.
6. The bouncing back of light off a surface is called _____.
7. Although _____ mirrors give a distorted indication of distance, they are used in automobile side-view and rear-view mirrors because they have large areas of reflection.
8. _____ is the bending of light as it passes from one medium to another.
9. A(n) _____ is a transparent material that refracts and focuses light.
10. The color of an opaque object is the color that it _____.

CONTENT REVIEW: TRUE OR FALSE

Determine whether each statement is true or false. If it is true, write "true." If it is false, change the underlined word or words to make the statement true.

1. In light waves, the wave energy is <u>parallel</u> to the electric and magnetic fields.
2. The arrangement of types of light in the electromagnetic spectrum is in order of <u>decreasing frequency</u>.
3. Ultraviolet light waves have a <u>higher</u> frequency than infrared light waves.
4. Objects that can be seen because light bounces off them are called <u>luminous</u>.
5. Mirrors, ponds, and polished surfaces are examples of objects that <u>absorb</u> light.
6. Light reflected from an uneven surface results in a <u>diffuse reflection</u>.
7. If an object is moving to the left, in a mirror the object will appear to move to the <u>right</u>.
8. The piece of glass that separates <u>white</u> light into the colors of a rainbow is a <u>lens</u>.
9. A convex lens is used to correct a vision problem called <u>nearsightedness</u>.
10. The color of a <u>transparent</u> object is the color of light that the object transmits.

CONCEPT REVIEW: SKILL BUILDING

Use the skills you have developed in the chapter to complete each activity.

1. **Making comparisons** Compare the way in which light is produced in an incandescent bulb, a fluorescent bulb, and a neon bulb.
2. **Applying definitions** One example of a mirror is a still pool of water. Explain the difference in reflections and images produced from a still pool and a rippled pool.
3. **Applying concepts** Imagine you are building an incubator to keep chicken eggs warm. Would you use an incandescent or fluorescent bulb? Explain your answer.
4. **Relating concepts** Explain why the wave theory of light cannot explain the photoelectric effect.
5. **Interpreting data** Two electrons drop from a higher energy level to a lower energy level. The first electron releases twice as much energy as the second electron. Which electron emits the higher frequency photon? Explain your answer.
6. **Making predictions** A prism separates white light into the colors of the spectrum. Predict what would happen if a second prism were placed in the path of the separated colors. Use a diagram in your answer.

CONCEPT REVIEW: ESSAY

Discuss each of the following in a brief paragraph.

1. The technology is now available to place a series of mirrors in orbit. These mirrors would reflect light back to earth in order to illuminate major urban areas at night. Discuss the problems and the benefits that would result from such a project.
2. Some objects are given certain colors for reasons other than looks. Explain why roadways are usually black or gray, while clothing worn for sports such as tennis is often white.
3. The United States flag appears to be red, white, and blue. Explain what colors of light are reflected by each color of the flag. Then explain how the flag would appear if viewed through red glass.

6 Nuclear Energy

CHAPTER SECTIONS

6-1 The Structure of the Atom
6-2 Transmutation of Elements
6-3 Nuclear Power

CHAPTER OBJECTIVES

After completing this chapter,
you will be able to:

6-1 Identify the subatomic particles that make up the nucleus of an atom.

6-1 Describe the force that balances the electromagnetic force of repulsion and binds protons and neutrons in the atomic nucleus.

6-1 Compare the number of protons and neutrons in various isotopes.

6-2 Relate natural and artificial transmutation to changes in the nucleus of an atom.

6-2 Compare the three types of radioactive decay.

6-2 Define radioactivity.

6-3 Describe the process of nuclear fission.

6-3 Identify the parts of a nuclear reactor and the reactions taking place within it.

In an underground building, a group of scientists anxiously prepares to test a new design in particle accelerators. The accelerator, housed inside the same underground complex, contains a circular tunnel over 6.3 kilometers long. Over 1000 magnets lining the tunnel produce powerful magnetic fields. These magnetic fields will guide a beam of charged particles around and around over 200,000 times, so that the particles travel farther than the distance to the moon and back! With each circuit of the tunnel, the charged particles–in this case, protons—will gain energy and speed. When their energy level is just right and they are traveling at nearly the speed of light, they will be released down a long, straight track to collide with other charged particles or with entire atoms. The results of such collisions may give the scientists cause to celebrate.

Later, with the test completed, the scientists peer at a strange-looking "map" and smile. The "map" is actually a photograph of the interactions of the particles as they passed through a bubble chamber. The bubble chamber is filled with liquid hydrogen in which the tracks of particles are seen as trails of bubbles. After studying hundreds of thousands of photographs, the scientists declare the accelerator a success. Two high-speed protons have collided. New particles, never before seen, have appeared, if only for a fraction of a second. Yet even the brief existence of these tiny particles is a clue to the mysteries of the atom and the universe itself.

Mapping atomic particles

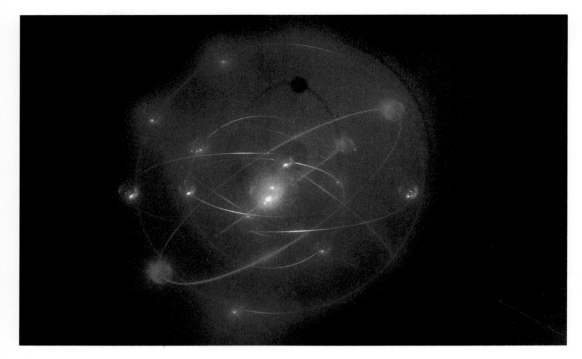

Figure 6-1 *This model of the atom shows the nucleus, with its protons and neutrons. The nucleus is surrounded by the electron cloud, which contains rapidly moving electrons.*

6-1 The Structure of the Atom

In Chapter 3, you learned that the atom is made up of a nucleus that contains protons and neutrons. These particles account for most of the mass of the atom. Whirling around the nucleus are electrons. For years, scientists believed that electrons moved about the nucleus in fixed orbits, much as the planets orbit the sun. Today scientists know that electrons do not revolve around the nucleus in regular paths. Instead, electrons are said to travel in a cloud-like region around the nucleus. This region is called an **electron cloud.**

Subatomic Particles

It would be nice if the parts of the atom could be limited to simply electrons, protons, and neutrons. But nature is often far from simple. Instruments like particle accelerators and bubble chambers have revealed to scientists a highly complex world within the nucleus of an atom. This world is filled with strange particles. Some are so short-lived that they exist for only millionths of a second. Others are so tiny, light, and full of energy that they pass through the earth without striking anything.

By now, scientists have discovered hundreds of subatomic nuclear particles. To bring some order to this collection of subatomic particles, scientists have proposed that all nuclear subatomic particles are made up of basic particles called **quarks** (kwahrks).

There are several different types of quarks. One group of three quarks will produce a neutron. Another group of three quarks will produce a proton. If protons are accelerated so that they collide with other particles, different groups of three quarks may form. Each different group will produce a different subatomic particle.

It is important for you to understand that a wide variety of subatomic particles exists in the atom. However, to learn about nuclear energy, you need to know about only the proton, neutron, and electron.

The Strong Force

You also learned in Chapter 3 that there is an electromagnetic force of repulsion between objects with the same charge. And you know that the protons clustered together in the nucleus all have a positive charge. So why don't the protons repel each other, causing all the atoms in the universe to explode? The answer lies in another force in the nucleus. **A force called the strong force can balance the electromagnetic force of repulsion between protons and thus hold the subatomic particles in the nucleus together.**

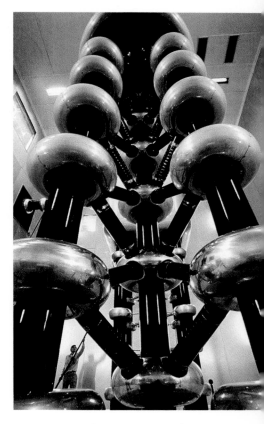

Figure 6-2 *This generator is one of four accelerators connected together to make the particle accelerator at Fermilab in Batavia, Illinois. Particle accelerators such as this one have revealed to scientists the highly complex world of subatomic particles.*

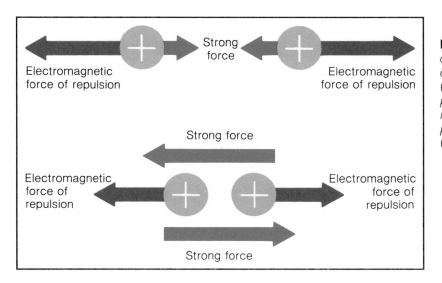

Figure 6-3 *The strong force opposes the electromagnetic force of repulsion between two protons (top). The strong force becomes powerful enough to overcome the repulsive force only when the protons are very close together (bottom).*

The **strong force,** which "glues" protons together in the nucleus, is not well understood. One thing that does seem certain is that the strong force works only when protons are very close together. However, to work against the force of repulsion and bind protons together in the nucleus takes an enormous amount of energy. This energy locked in the nucleus during the binding of protons is called **nuclear energy.** Perhaps it now occurs to you that if the nucleus can be broken apart, tremendous amounts of nuclear energy will be released. You will read more about nuclear energy and its uses later in this chapter.

Atomic Number

All atoms are made up of protons, electrons, and neutrons. And all protons are identical, as are all electrons and neutrons. How, then, can there be so many different kinds of atoms in the world? What makes an atom of hydrogen, the lightest element and a gas, so different from uranium, one of the heaviest elements and a solid? The answer must lie in the number of protons, electrons, or neutrons an atom has. But which particle is it? Let's try to figure it out.

Figure 6-4 *You can see a great variety of substances in this photo. These substances are made of elements that contain protons, electrons, and neutrons. However, all these elements are very different from one another. Why? Each element has a different number of protons in its nucleus.*

In Chapter 3, you learned that electrons can easily be rubbed off an object. Remember how the charged balloon stuck to the wall? Surely the balloon remained a balloon even after it lost electrons. So it is not the number of electrons that determines the kind of atom.

In Figure 6-5, you can see the atoms of boron and carbon. Count the number of neutrons in the boron atom. Then count the number in the carbon atom. Boron and carbon are different elements. Yet their atoms have the same number of neutrons. So the number of neutrons does not determine the kind of atom.

That leaves only one particle. You have probably concluded that protons make the difference, and you are right. What makes an atom of an element unique, or unlike an atom of any other element, is the number of protons in its nucleus. A hydrogen atom is different from a uranium atom because a hydrogen atom has 1 proton in its nucleus while a uranium atom has 92.

The number of protons in the nucleus of an atom is called the **atomic number.** The atomic number tells you how many protons an atom of an element has and what element it is. Hydrogen, with 1 proton, has an atomic number of 1. Only hydrogen atoms have 1 proton. Uranium, with 92 protons, has an atomic number of 92. Uranium is the only element whose atoms contain 92 protons. The atomic number of boron is 5. Its atoms have 5 protons. And carbon,

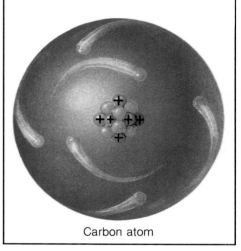

Boron atom

Carbon atom

Figure 6-5 *Each boron atom and carbon atom has six neutrons in its nucleus. Yet they are different elements. It is the number of protons in the nucleus that makes boron unlike carbon. How many protons does boron have? Carbon?*

Figure 6-6 *In this diagram, you see atoms of the elements hydrogen, oxygen, and lithium. What is the atomic number of each of these elements?*

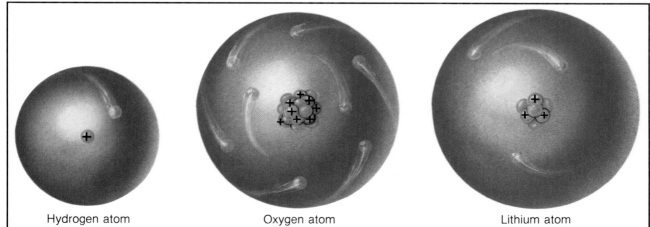

Hydrogen atom   Oxygen atom   Lithium atom

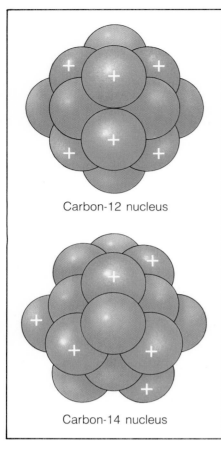

Figure 6-7 *Isotopes are atoms that have the same number of protons but different numbers of neutrons. Both these isotopes of carbon have 6 protons. But carbon-12 has 6 neutrons while carbon-14 has 8.*

with 6 protons, has an atomic number of 6. So even though atoms of boron and carbon have the same number of neutrons, they are different elements. Their numbers of protons are different.

Isotopes

The number of protons in atoms of the same element cannot vary. Carbon atoms would not be carbon atoms if they had 5 protons or 7 protons. Only 6 will do! Yet there are some carbon atoms that have 6 neutrons, while others have 8 neutrons. The difference in the number of neutrons affects the characteristics of the atom but not its identity. Both atoms are carbon because they both have 6 protons. Atoms that have the same number of protons but different numbers of neutrons are called **isotopes** (IGH-suh-tohps).

Isotopes are usually identified by their **mass number.** The mass number is the total number of neutrons and protons in the nucleus. For example, the mass number of the isotope of carbon that has 6 protons and 6 neutrons is 6 plus 6, or 12. This isotope of carbon is called carbon-12. It is the most common isotope of carbon. The mass number of the isotope of carbon that has 6 protons and 8 neutrons is 14. This isotope is called carbon-14.

SECTION REVIEW

1. Describe the structure of the atom. What is meant by the term "electron cloud"?
2. What is a quark?
3. Describe the strong force.
4. What is the atomic number of an element? The mass number?

6-2 Transmutation of Elements

The alchemists dreamed of turning metals such as iron and lead into gold. For more than 1700 years, these early scientists blended science and magic in pursuit of wealth, long life, and knowledge. Although they failed in their efforts to make gold

Figure 6-8 *Radioactive elements have nuclei that break apart spontaneously, giving off nuclear radiation. Such elements must be kept in shielded containers to prevent the release of radiation.*

from other elements, they did establish important experimental techniques. Chemists of the eighteenth and nineteenth centuries learned much from the work of the alchemists. And they, too, reached the conclusion that it was impossible for one element to change into another.

Science, however, is full of surprises. Modern chemists have succeeded in making some of the alchemists' dreams come true. In particle accelerators, for example, gold can be made from the elements lead and mercury. This "magic" is the result of **transmutation** (tranz-myoo-TAY-shuhn), a process in which the nucleus of an atom changes so that a new element is formed. **Transmutation, the change of one element into another as the result of nuclear changes, can occur naturally or by artificial means.**

Radioactive Decay

The subatomic particles in the nucleus of an atom are held together by the strong force. For some nuclei, such as those of carbon-12, the force is strong enough to keep the particles together permanently. Other nuclei, however, are unstable. The subatomic particles are not held together as strongly. So these nuclei tend to break apart and undergo natural transmutation. This spontaneous breakdown of an unstable atomic nucleus is called **radioactive decay.** Elements whose atoms undergo such decay are called **radioactive** elements.

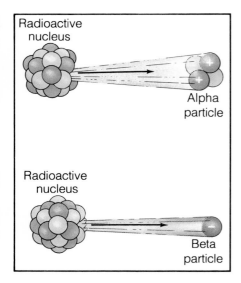

Figure 6-9 *In alpha decay (top), the nucleus of a radioactive element releases an alpha particle, which is two protons and two neutrons. During beta decay (bottom),* a negatively charged *electron is released.*

Figure 6-10 *Radioactive elements give off both particles and energy called radiation. These rectangular blocks containing radioactive cesium were the only source of illumination for this time-exposure photograph.*

Radioactive elements decay at a fixed rate called the **half-life.** The half-life of an element is the amount of time it takes for *half* the atoms in a sample to decay. For example, the half-life of carbon-14 is 5568 years. In 5568 years, half the atoms in a given sample of carbon-14 will have decayed to another element, nitrogen-14. In another 5568 years, half the remaining carbon-14 will have decayed. At this time, one-fourth, or one-half of one-half, of the original sample will be left. Half-lives vary greatly from element to element. For example, the half-life of rhodium-106 is only 30 seconds. But the half-life of uranium-238 is 4.5 billion years!

Radioactive decay releases both particles and energy that together are known as nuclear radiation. The type of decay is determined by the nature of the nuclear radiation.

ALPHA DECAY   In **alpha decay,** the nucleus of the radioactive atom releases 2 protons and 2 neutrons. These 4 particles are released together and are known as an alpha particle. An alpha particle is actually a helium nucleus—2 protons and 2 neutrons.

By giving off an alpha particle, an atom loses 2 protons. So alpha decay results in a new atom with an atomic number *two less* than the original. For example, an atom of the radioactive isotope uranium-238 has 92 protons. This atom undergoes alpha decay to become an atom of thorium, which has 90 protons.

BETA DECAY   An electron, which is a negatively charged particle, is released from the nucleus during **beta decay.** Perhaps you are wondering how an electron can be in the nucleus. After all, you learned that electrons are found in the electron cloud outside the nucleus. It is thought that each neutron in the nucleus is composed of a proton and an electron. During beta decay, the neutron breaks up. The proton stays in the nucleus, and the electron is released as a beta particle. Beta decay produces an element with the same mass number as the original atom but with an atomic number one higher than before. Thus carbon-14, with its 6 protons and 8 neutrons, undergoes beta decay to form nitrogen-14, which has 7 protons and 7 neutrons.

You just learned that uranium-238 undergoes alpha decay to form thorium. This thorium isotope is also radioactive, and it undergoes beta decay to form another radioactive element. You can see that one radioactive nucleus can transmute into another radioactive nucleus, which may also decay. In time, through a series of spontaneous alpha and beta decays, a stable nucleus is formed. For uranium-238, the decay chain ends with the formation of the stable nucleus of lead.

GAMMA DECAY Radioactive decay releases enormous amounts of energy stored in the nucleus. Often this energy is released in the form of gamma rays. You may recall from Chapter 5 that gamma rays are electromagnetic waves of very high frequency and energy. **Gamma decay,** the release of gamma rays, usually accompanies alpha and beta decay.

Artificial Transmutation

Radioactive decay is one type of **radioactivity.** Radioactivity is the release of energy and matter that results from changes in the nucleus of an atom. Radioactive decay occurs spontaneously. However, another type of radioactivity can be achieved artificially. Instruments that exceed the wildest imaginations of the alchemists now exist. In such instruments, artificial transmutation takes place,

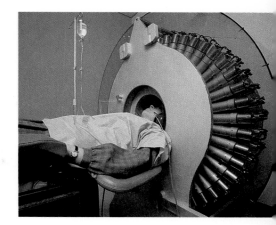

Figure 6-11 *In order to see inside the body, doctors use a variety of scanning devices, such as the PET scanner shown here. When certain radioactive isotopes are injected into the body, they interact with electrons to produce gamma radiation. This radiation produces a picture that is used to study the structure and behavior of body organs.*

Figure 6-12 *A Geiger counter detects and measures radioactivity (left). A spiderwort plant is nature's radiation detector (right). The stamens of the spiderwort flower are usually blue or blue-purple. In the presence of radiation, however, the stamens turn pink.*

Figure 6-13 *Artificial transmutation of elements is done in a particle accelerator such as the one at Fermilab in Illinois. This aerial view (left) shows the outline of the underground tunnel, which is more than 6.3 kilometers long. Protons traveling through long tubes (right) will reach a final speed greater than 99.999 percent of the speed of light!*

Figure 6-14 *Fission, or the splitting of an atomic nucleus, is the reaction that makes the atomic bomb possible.*

changing one kind of known element into another and also creating elements that never before existed on the earth.

One instrument in which artificial transmutation takes place is the particle accelerator. In a particle accelerator, atomic nuclei are bombarded with high-speed protons or neutrons. As the atomic nuclei are forced to absorb additional protons or neutrons, new elements are produced. Today, the dream of the alchemists has come true. Scientists can even change lead into gold!

SECTION REVIEW

1. What is the relationship between transmutation and radioactive decay?
2. Describe the three different types of radioactive decay.

6-3 Nuclear Power

You learned that when the protons in the nucleus of an atom are brought close enough, the strong force can exert its binding power. A huge quantity of energy is required to bring the protons close together. This energy is locked up inside the nucleus. Now if somehow the nucleus could be split apart, some of that nuclear energy would be released.

Fission

The possibility of splitting the nucleus intrigued scientists for many years. But their work was theoretical, not experimental. Then in 1938, the first **fission** (FISH-uhn) reaction was carried out. **Fission is the splitting of an atomic nucleus into two smaller nuclei of roughly equal mass.** Fission does not occur spontaneously; it must be made to take place.

In one typical fission reaction, a uranium-235 nucleus is bombarded by a neutron, or "nuclear bullet." Two smaller nuclei are produced, barium-141 and krypton-92. Do not confuse krypton with kryptonite, the substance fatal to Superman! Three neutrons are also released in this fission—the original "bullet" and two neutrons from the uranium nucleus. What happens to these neutrons?

Each neutron that is released is capable of splitting another uranium-235 nucleus, which will produce even more neutrons. These neutrons may then split even more uranium atoms. This continuous series of fission reactions is called a **chain reaction.**

Activity

A Domino Chain Reaction

Place one domino in the first row. Behind it place two dominoes, side by side. In the third row place four dominoes; in the fourth row, eight. Knock down the first domino and trace the path of domino collapse. Would the reaction be as fast if the fifteen dominoes were simply lined up one behind the other?

Figure 6-15 *In this diagram of a chain reaction, a uranium-235 nucleus is bombarded with a neutron. The nucleus breaks up, producing a nucleus of krypton-92 and one of barium-141. Large amounts of energy as well as two additional neutrons are released. Each neutron is capable of splitting another uranium-235 nucleus.*

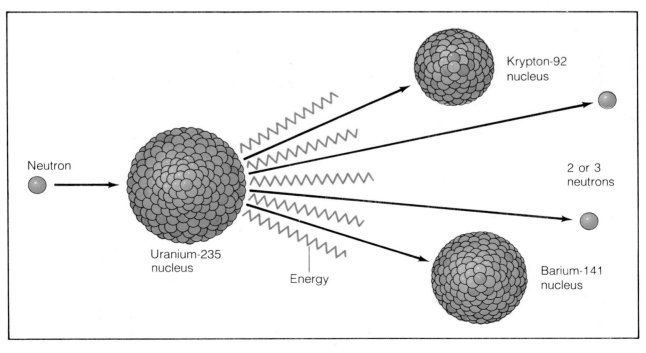

Isotopes

U-235 and U-238 are isotopes. They both have an atomic number of 92. How many protons does each have? How many neutrons?

Nuclear Reactor

The energy released during fission can be harnessed to do useful work. Fission reactions can be produced and carefully controlled in devices known as **nuclear reactors.**

NUCLEAR FUEL One of the most common nuclear fuels is uranium-235. Uranium-235 rods are placed in a nuclear reactor. When a neutron strikes a uranium atom, fission begins. If the uranium rods are placed at the proper distance from one another, a chain reaction will occur.

MODERATOR The neutrons released by the fission are moving rapidly. However, the uranium-235 cannot absorb fast-moving neutrons easily. So it is necessary to slow them down. A material that slows down neutrons in a nuclear reactor is known as a moderator. A form of water known as heavy water, D_2O, which is inexpensive and plentiful, is a good moderator.

Career: *Particle Physicist*

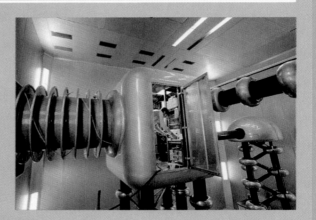

HELP WANTED: PARTICLE PHYSICIST Opportunity to engage in a challenging career in particle physics. Advanced degree in physics required. Research experience in particle physics preferred.

What do the words "charm," "strange," "beauty," and "truth" have in common? They are names scientists have given to tiny particles known as quarks. These particles are believed to be the subatomic bits of matter that make up protons and neutrons. Quarks are always found combined with other quarks. They seem to be bound to one another by forces produced by particles called gluons. Quarks, gluons, and other tiny subatomic particles are studied by scientists known as **particle physicists.**

Particle physicists do research into the structure of the atom and the relationship between matter and energy. By doing experiments and making observations, they hope to discover and isolate the basic particles of matter. Such a discovery would help them develop a theory that unites all the forces in the universe under one main force.

Particle physicists work in private industry, in government labs, in research centers, and in universities. For further information, write to the American Institute of Physics, 335 East Forty-fifth Street, New York, NY 10017.

CONTROL RODS Not only the speed but also the number of the neutrons must be regulated. If too many neutrons are produced and absorbed by uranium-235 nuclei, a runaway chain reaction will result. Energy will be released too quickly, and the reactor will get hotter and hotter. In fact, the core, or center, of the reactor may melt. A "meltdown" is a very dangerous event.

To control the neutron supply, rods of the metal cadmium are inserted in the reactor. These control rods "soak up" extra neutrons. To slow down or even stop the reaction, the control rods are inserted deeper into the reactor. To speed up a reaction going too slowly, the control rods are pulled out a bit.

In a power plant, the heat energy released from the fission is used to turn water into steam. The resulting steam can then be used to rotate turbines and generate electricity.

Nuclear Energy—A Potentially Destructive Force

The power within the atom can be used as the most destructive force ever developed. The same concepts involved in harnessing nuclear energy are also used to build atomic bombs and other atomic weapons. Such nuclear weapons, stockpiled in many parts of the world, have the capacity to destroy our planet.

Speaking of the United States and the Soviet Union and their nuclear missiles, President Reagan said at a news conference on September 17, 1985: ". . . there are already more than enough to blow both countries out of the world." At the same news conference, the President said that preventing a nuclear war was largely in the hands of these two great nuclear powers.

Preventing a nuclear war is one of the most pressing issues on Earth. A way must be found if we are to assure future generations that they will inherit a world safe from nuclear destruction.

SECTION REVIEW

1. What is fission?
2. What is meant by a chain reaction?
3. Discuss the use and importance of nuclear fuel, a moderator, and control rods in a nuclear reactor.

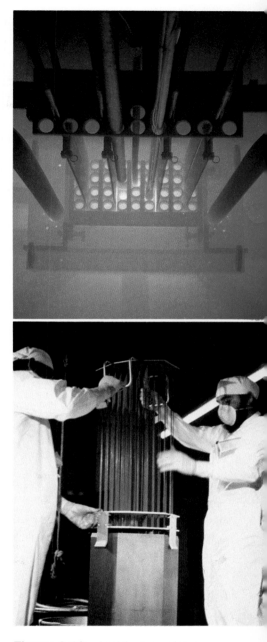

Figure 6-16 Inside a nuclear reactor, radioactive fuel rods give off energy that produces a blue glow in the water (top). Before being placed in the reactor, a bundle of uranium-containing fuel rods must be carefully checked (bottom).

LABORATORY ACTIVITY

The Half-life of a Sugar Cube

Purpose

In this activity, you will determine the half-life of a large sample of sugar cubes.

Materials (*per group*)

250 sugar cubes
Food coloring
Large bowl
Medicine dropper

Procedure

1. Place a small drop of food coloring on one side of each sugar cube.
2. Put all the sugar cubes in a bowl. Then dump them on the table. Move any cubes that are on top of other cubes. Be gentle with the cubes, since they are easily broken.
3. Remove all the sugar cubes that have the colored side facing up. If you have room on the table, arrange the sugar cubes you removed in a vertical column. Put the rest of the cubes back in the bowl.
4. Repeat step 3 several more times until five or fewer sugar cubes remain.
5. On a chart similar to the one shown, record the number of tosses (times you dumped the sugar cubes), the number of sugar cubes removed each time, and the number of sugar cubes remaining. For example, suppose after the first toss you removed 40 sugar cubes. The number of tosses would be 1, the number of cubes removed would be 40, and the number of cubes remaining would be 210 (250 − 40).

Observations and Conclusions

1. Make a full-page graph of tosses versus cubes remaining. Place the number of tosses on the horizontal (X) axis and the number of cubes remaining on the vertical (Y) axis. Start at zero tosses with all 250 cubes remaining.
2. Determine the half-life of the decaying sugar cubes in the following way. Find one-half of the original sugar cubes (125) on the vertical axis. Then move vertically down until you reach the horizontal axis. Your answers will be in tosses.
3. How many tosses are required to remove one-half of the sugar cubes? How many tosses are required to remove one-fourth of the sugar cubes?

Tosses	Sugar Cubes Removed	Sugar Cubes Remaining
0	0	250
1	40	210
2		
3		
4		
5		
6		
7		
8		
9		

CHAPTER REVIEW

SUMMARY

6-1 The Structure of the Atom

- An atom consists of a nucleus that contains protons and neutrons surrounded by an electron cloud.

- Scientists theorize that all subatomic particles are made up of different combinations of quarks.

- Protons, which normally repel one another, are bound together in the nucleus by the strong force.

- The energy locked within the nucleus during the binding of protons is called nuclear energy.

- The atomic number is the number of protons in the nucleus. Atoms of different elements have different atomic numbers.

- Isotopes are atoms of the same element that have the same number of protons but different numbers of neutrons.

- The total number of neutrons and protons in the nucleus is called the mass number. Isotopes are identified by their mass number.

6-2 Transmutation of Elements

- During radioactive decay, unstable nuclei spontaneously break down.

- The half-life is the amount of time it takes for half the atoms in a sample of a radioactive element to decay.

- During alpha decay, the nucleus of a radioactive atom releases two protons and two neutrons, or an alpha particle.

- During beta decay, a neutron breaks down into a proton and an electron. The electron is released from the nucleus as a beta particle.

- In a decay chain, a radioactive nucleus continues to transmute until a stable nucleus is formed.

- During gamma decay, which often accompanies alpha and beta decay, gamma rays are released.

- Radioactivity is the release of matter and energy that results from changes in the nucleus of an atom.

6-3 Nuclear Power

- Fission is the splitting of an atomic nucleus into two smaller nuclei of roughly equal mass.

- A continuous series of fission reactions is called a chain reaction.

- Uranium-235 rods are used as fuel in nuclear reactors.

- Heavy water is used as a moderator in nuclear reactors to slow down neutrons.

- In a nuclear reactor, control rods that soak up neutrons are used to speed up or slow down the reaction.

- In a power plant, the heat energy given off during fission reactions is used to generate electricity.

VOCABULARY

Define each term in a complete sentence.

alpha decay	**fission**	**nuclear energy**	**radioactivity**
atomic number	**gamma decay**	**nuclear reactor**	**strong force**
beta decay	**half-life**	**quark**	**transmutation**
chain reaction	**isotope**	**radioactive**	
electron cloud	**mass number**	**radioactive decay**	

CONTENT REVIEW: MULTIPLE CHOICE

Choose the letter of the answer that best completes each statement.

1. The force that binds protons together within a nucleus is called the
   a. electromagnetic force of repulsion.   b. subatomic force.
   c. strong force.   d. force of least resistance.
2. The subatomic particle that makes an atom of an element unique is the
   a. neutron.   b. proton.   c. electron.   d. quark.
3. The number of protons in the nucleus of an atom is called the
   a. atomic number.   b. mass number.   c. quark.   d. isotope.
4. The mass number of an atom is equal to the total number of
   a. electrons.   b. protons.
   c. neutrons and electrons.   d. neutrons and protons.
5. During natural transmutation, the nuclei of atoms undergo
   a. artificial transmutation.   b. radioactive decay.
   c. fission.   d. meltdown.
6. The amount of time it takes for half the atoms in a sample of a radioactive element to decay is called the
   a. isotope.   b. transmutation.   c. moderator.   d. half-life.
7. During which type of radioactive decay is an electron released from a nucleus?
   a. alpha decay   b. beta decay
   c. gamma decay   d. electron decay
8. The particle used to split the nucleus of a uranium atom in a fission reaction is the
   a. neutron.   b. proton.   c. electron.   d. quark.
9. The fuel used in a nuclear reactor is
   a. carbon-14.   b. thorium-234   c. uranium-235.   d. uranium-238.
10. If the number of neutrons in a fission reaction is not controlled, then
    a. a runaway chain reaction will result.   b. a meltdown may result.
    c. both a and b.   d. neither a, b, nor c.

CONTENT REVIEW: COMPLETION

Fill in the word or words that best complete each statement.

1. The _____ is the region around the nucleus in which electrons may be located.
2. Basic particles called _____ may make up all the other nuclear subatomic particles.
3. Energy released when the nucleus breaks apart is called _____.
4. The process by which the nucleus of an atom changes so that a new element forms is called _____.
5. _____ is the spontaneous breakdown of atomic nuclei.
6. _____ decay releases high-energy electromagnetic waves.
7. If a radioactive element has a half-life of 10.5 years, the fraction of a sample of that element that will remain after 21 years is _____.
8. _____ is the splitting of a nucleus into two smaller nuclei of roughly the same mass.

9. A continuous series of fission reactions is called a(n) _____.

10. A(n) _____ slows down the fast-moving neutrons in a nuclear reactor.

CONTENT REVIEW: TRUE OR FALSE

Determine whether each statement is true or false. If it is true, write "true." If it is false, change the underlined word or words to make the statement true.

1. Electrons whirl about the nuclei of atoms in fixed orbits.
2. The strong force within the nucleus binds the protons together.
3. Most of an atom's mass is made up of neutrons and electrons.
4. Atoms having the same number of protons but different numbers of neutrons are called isotopes.
5. The total number of neutrons and protons in the nucleus is the atomic number.
6. The half-life of an element is the amount of time needed for half the atoms in a sample to decay.
7. An atom loses two protons and two neutrons during beta decay.
8. Scientists can change one element into another by natural transmutation.
9. Elements heavier than uranium have been created in particle accelerators.
10. Controlled fission reactions can be produced in bubble chambers.

CONCEPT REVIEW: SKILL BUILDING

Use the skills you have developed in the chapter to complete each activity.

1. **Making comparisons** Compare the three types of radioactive decay.
2. **Making calculations** The half-life of cobalt-60 is 5.26 years. How many grams of a 40-gram sample of cobalt-60 remain after 10.52 years? After 15.78 years?
3. **Making comparisons** Compare artificial and natural transmutation.
4. **Applying concepts** Three atoms each contain 6 protons. Yet each atom has a different mass number. Explain how that can occur.
5. **Making graphs** Sodium-24 has a half-life of 15 hours. Make a graph to show what happens to a 100-gram sample of sodium-24 over a 5-day period. Hint: Plot the time along the horizontal axis and the mass along the vertical axis.
6. **Analyzing data** A skeleton of an ancient fish is found to contain one-eighth the amount of carbon-14 that it contained when it was alive. How old is the skeleton? Hint: Assume the half-life of carbon-14 is 5568 years.
7. **Making calculations** After 3200 years, 0.5 gram of a 2-gram sample of a radioactive element remains. What is its half-life?

CONCEPT REVIEW: ESSAY

Discuss each of the following in a brief paragraph.

1. Discuss the ways in which radiation is both harmful and helpful to human beings.
2. Describe two parts of a nuclear reactor that keep a chain reaction under control.

Adventures in Science

STEPHEN HAWKING: Changing Our View of the Universe

Scientists have long struggled to find the connection between two branches of physics. One of these branches deals with the forces that rule the world of atoms and subatomic particles. The other branch deals with gravity and its role in the universe of stars and galaxies. Physicist Stephen Hawking has set himself the task of discovering the connection. Leading theoretical physicists agree that if anyone can discover a unifying principle, it will certainly be this extraordinary scientist.

Dr. Hawking's goal, as he describes it, is simple. "It is complete understanding of the universe, why it is as it is and why it exists at all." In order to achieve such an understanding, Dr. Hawking seeks to "quantize gravity." Quantizing gravity means combining the laws of gravity and the laws of quantum mechanics into a single universal law. Dr. Hawking and other theoretical physicists believe that with such a law, the behavior of all matter in the universe, and the origin of the universe as well, could be explained.

Dr. Hawking's search for a unifying theory has led him to study one of science's greatest mysteries: black holes. A black hole is an incredibly dense region in space whose gravitational pull attracts all nearby objects, virtually "swallowing them up." A black hole is formed when a star uses up most of the nuclear fuel that has kept it burning. During most of its life as an ordinary star, its nuclear explosions exert enough outward force to balance the powerful inward force of gravity. But when the star's fuel is used up, the outward force ceases to exist. Gravity takes over and the star collapses into a tiny core of extremely dense material, possibly no bigger than the period at the end of this sentence.

Hawking has already proved that a black hole can emit a stream of electrons. Prior to this discovery, scientists believed that nothing, not even light, could escape from a black hole. So scientists have hailed Hawking's discovery as "one of the most beautiful in the history of physics."

Probing the mysteries of the universe is no ordinary feat. And Stephen Hawking is no ordinary man. Respected as one of the most brilliant physicists in the world, Hawking is also considered one of the most remarkable. For Dr. Hawking suffers from a serious disease of the nervous system that has confined him to a wheelchair, barely able to move or to speak. Although Dr. Hawking gives numerous presentations and publishes countless articles and papers, his addresses must be translated and his essays written down by other hands.

Hawking became ill during his first years at Cambridge University in England. The disease progressed quickly and left the young scholar quite despondent. He even considered giving up his research, as he thought he would not live long enough to receive his Ph.D. But in 1965, Hawking's life changed. He married Jane Wilde, a fellow student and language scholar. Suddenly life took on new meaning. "That was the turning point," he says. "It made me determined to live, and it was about that time that I began making professional progress." Hawking's health and spirits improved.

His studies continued and reached new heights of brilliance. Today, Dr. Hawking is professor of mathematics at Cambridge University and a husband and father who leads a full and active life.

Dr. Hawking believes that his illness has benefited his work. It has given him more time to think about physics. So although his body is failing him, his mind is free to soar. Considered to be one of the most brilliant physicists of all times, Dr. Hawking has taken some of the small steps that lead science to discovery and understanding. With time to ponder the questions of the universe, it is quite likely that Stephen Hawking will be successful in uniting the world of the tiniest particles with the world of stars and galaxies.

Stephen Hawking, shown here with his family, is Lucasian professor of mathematics at Cambridge University—a position once held by Isaac Newton. Hawking has received numerous prizes for his work.

HOW PRACTICAL IS FLOWER POWER?

Scientists are hard at work trying to find an energy substitute for oil, and it may be an ordinary green plant. But will the price be too high?

The day may come when the energy in plants will become a substitute for the energy in oil.

The sun rises on a summer day in the not-too-distant future. As its rays spread over the land, a farmer goes to work in his fields. His crop is almost ready for harvesting and will bring him a good price. What kind of crop is he growing? This farmer of the future is growing energy!

This may not seem like news to you. After all, some plants, such as trees, are already sources of energy. Trees are used as firewood. And when wood is burned, energy is released in the form of heat and light. Where does this energy come from? It comes from the sun!

Each green leaf in a plant uses energy from the sun—sunlight—to build chemical molecules of sugar. In the process, the sun's energy gets locked up in the sugar molecules and other plant substances. That energy is given off when a plant or its parts are burned.

The same thing happens when coal, oil, and natural gas are burned. These fuels were formed from decaying plants, and from animals that ate plants. Buried in the earth for millions of years, the remains of the plants and animals were converted by tremendous heat and pressure into the coal, oil, and gas of today. But only a small percent of the sun's energy originally absorbed by the plants stayed in these fuels. So the burning of fuels is not the most efficient way of getting at plant energy.

Fuel from Plants

Melvin Calvin, a Nobel Prize winning chemist at the University of California at Berkeley, has worked for years on finding a better way to recover the solar energy stored in plants. One way to get more energy out of plants is to take their chemicals and make them into high-energy fuels. One such fuel is alcohol. When burned, alcohol is a powerful fuel. Some high-powered race cars, for instance, run on pure alcohol.

Unfortunately, alcohol is not made directly by plants but from their sugar compounds. Sugar cane and cereal grains such as corn produce large amounts of sugars. Through a chemical process called fermentation, these sugars can be broken down into alcohol.

A mixture of gasoline and alcohol produces gasohol, which is sold as a substitute for gasoline at some filling stations. When gasohol was first marketed a few years ago, it was hailed as a solution to the energy crisis. But gasohol has never really become popular or practical. The following reasons highlight why "Flower Power" may not become a reality in the near future.

Energy to Make Energy

For one thing, a lot of energy is needed to make energy. Corn, for example, is a major source of gasohol. Yet, one scientist notes, "Corn grown in the U.S. requires a surprising amount of energy."

For example, corn plants need large amounts of fertilizer. And most of the fertilizers used for growing corn are made from oil. And, of course, it takes a lot of energy to get oil out of the ground and to move it to where it is used. Other ways that energy is used to produce corn are the burning of tractor fuel for planting, cultivation, and harvesting; the production of heat for grain drying; and, if irrigation is needed, energy to pump water.

Most of this energy comes from oil or natural gas. Moreover, converting the grain to

Substitutes for oil and gas are always being hunted. Corn, for example, is a source of alcohol, which is combined with gasoline to make the fuel gasohol. But growing and harvesting corn uses up a lot of fuel and energy—too much, maybe, to make gasohol a practical substitute for gasoline.

alcohol requires even more energy. Equally important, if land is used to produce fuel, how would the world's food supplies be affected? In other words, does it make sense to "farm" fuel? It makes sense only if no one goes without food and if the fuel is inexpensive. So far this does not seem to be the case.

However, scientists have come up with a possible way to get around the problem—farm plants that *directly* produce fuel. Oil from plants sounds impossible, doesn't it? But some plants produce hydrocarbons, which are the basic compounds in oil. Among these plants are the rubber tree and its relatives. Some of these plants resemble cacti. The hydrocarbons are in the milky sap of the plants. They might be used to produce inexpensive fuels. Melvin Calvin and other researchers have been trying to find a way to produce fuel from plants.

Calvin has also done research on the gopher plant, which grows in the western part of the United States. He and scientists working with him are growing gopher plants on experimental plots on Calvin's own ranch in California. They hope to determine the amount of hydrocarbons the gopher plants produce and the cost of making fuel from them.

Because gopher plants are wild and have not been cultivated before, little is known about methods of growing them and the conditions they require. The sap of the gopher plant, moreover, cannot be easily tapped like that of some of its relatives.

Perhaps the gopher plant will prove to be too difficult to grow. Or possibly the amount of hydrocarbons that can be gotten from it will not be large enough to make it a good fuel source. On the other hand, the gopher plant could turn out to be a substitute for an oil well. And if it is not, perhaps some other plant will be.

There may, of course, be other sources of inexpensive energy we should look to—solar energy, nuclear energy, old-fashioned coal, oil, and natural gas energy, and wind energy. But each has its problems. Can "Flower Power" compete with these energy sources? What do you think?

Melvin Calvin stands in a field of gopher plants at his ranch in California. Calvin and other scientists like him hope to use gopher plants, and other plants, as new sources of fuel. Will gopher plants help to replace oil wells? Some scientists think so.

The Green People of Solaron

Experiments being performed today may help to produce people that are like green plants.

The temperature outside the bubble is 100° C. The 30-hour day on the planet Solaron is only half over.

Solaron, which is in a galaxy 20 light-years from Earth, was colonized by 100 humans in the year 2186. Now, in the year 2215, the colony has a population of 2000.

These people can live here because the colony is covered by a huge plastic bubble. Inside the bubble are schools, stores, offices, and other buildings. The artificial atmosphere is made up of oxygen, carbon dioxide, nitrogen, and the other gases that make up Earth's atmosphere. Outside the bubble, there is no air. Except for a single bright sun that always shines, the sky is black. The hot surface of the planet is covered with red sand, rocks, and boulders.

Zara Starr looks out the window of her ninth-grade classroom. Through the window, she can see the clear plastic bubble that encloses her world. She can see the horizon far off in the distance, where the black sky meets the red soil.

Suddenly, the bell rings, and Zara and her twin brother Lars gather their books and walk quickly to their lockers. As they pass through the corridor, some new students, who have just arrived at the colony, gape at the Starr twins. The new students have never seen green people before. The twins ignore the stares of the new students. They don't mind being different. In fact, Zara and Lars are proud of being green. They are part of an important experiment that appears to be successful.

Green Is Good

Scientists on Earth wanted to know whether human skin cells could act like tiny plants by using the energy of sunlight to make glucose from carbon dioxide and water. This process called photosynthesis produces glucose, a sugar plants use as food. If human cells could make their own food, scientists thought,

colonists on planets such as Solaron would not have to grow so much food. With less need for grown food, the colonists on Solaron could have smaller farms. This would save precious space under the colony's bubble and conserve limited energy resources. Green people could help Solaron in another way, too. Oxygen is a by-product of photosynthesis. So human photosynthesis would be a source of oxygen. Green people would give off oxygen—just as green plants do—for other people to breathe.

To begin this great experiment, scientists first made copies of the genes that control the tiny, green food-making organs in plants. The techniques for gene copying, called genetic engineering, had been developed in the 1980s. At that time, scientists put the copies of these plant genes into special viruses. These viruses were similar to the viruses that cause the common cold. But researchers had changed the viruses slightly so that they would go only to skin cells after being injected into human volunteers. When the viruses reached the skin cells, the plant genes inside the viruses joined the human genes inside the skin cells. As the plant genes began to work inside the skin cells, the volunteers

slowly turned green. That was because the plant genes were making chlorophyll. Chlorophyll is the special green chemical that captures the energy of sunlight to use for photosynthesis. Because the sun shines all the time on Solaron, the green skin of the volunteers carries on photosynthesis every day.

Green people shed old, dead skin cells, just as other people do. And just like other people's, their bodies make new skin cells. Each new skin cell is an exact copy of the green parent cell. So green people never lose their color.

Because Zara, Lars, and their parents are green, they live in a special house with a clear plastic roof. Sunlight pours down through this roof and onto the members of the Starr family as they go about their chores.

When the Starrs wake up in the morning, they are never hungry, because their skin cells have made glucose during the night. Some of the glucose leaves the skin cells and is stored in the liver. When the body needs food during the day, the liver releases some of the stored glucose. So Zara and Lars never have to eat foods rich in sugar.

At lunch time, when their schoolmates are in the cafeteria, the Starr twins and other green students go to a special room called the solar room. It has a clear plastic ceiling that allows the students to get plenty of sunlight. The students read, talk, or just lie back and close their eyes, imagining they are relaxing on a beach on Earth. Meanwhile, their skin cells are storing the sun's energy.

The New Kids in Town

Most students are used to seeing green students sitting next to them in class. But today, all the students are staring at some new volunteers for the photosynthesis experiment. These new students have red skin. Scientists succeeded in putting a special pigment, a

colored chemical called anthocyanin, into skin cells, along with chlorophyll. In the leaves of plants and trees, anthocyanin pigments are different colors under different conditions. In the fall, when the green chlorophyll of leaves breaks down, the reds, blues, and purples of anthocyanins start to show. The leaves are said to "change color."

The new students have a red pigment in their skin cells that hides the green color of the chlorophyll. However, the chlorophyll still works as well as it does in green people. Scientists want to experiment with different skin colors. That way, volunteers could have a choice of what color they want to be. The scientists hope that being able to choose from among many colors will make more people volunteer for the experiment. Then there will be more people on Solaron making their own food and producing oxygen.

In a few days, no one will notice that the red people are different from anyone else. Everybody is too busy with schoolwork, dances, parties, sports, and families. After all, says one of the students, "It doesn't matter whether we're green or red. We're all just human."

Science and Technology

Below, the earth whirled by at more than 6 kilometers a second. Above, the Space Shuttle *Challenger* soared through the sky at 28,163 kilometers an hour. Suddenly, a figure floated out of the shuttle's cargo bay. For the first time, a person had become a human satellite.

The person was astronaut Bruce McCandless, whose voice crackled over the radio, "It's a heck of a big leap for me." A piece of space technology called the Manned Maneuvering Unit, or MMU, had made that leap possible.

Powered by a set of tiny jet thrusters, the device, which looked like a legless white aluminum chair, propelled McCandless more than 90 meters into space. One day, the same kind of flying backpack would help scientists, technicians, and construction workers build and repair structures far above the surface of the earth.

CHAPTERS

7   **Energy Resources**

8   **Chemical Technology**

9   **Space Technology**

10   **The Computer Revolution**

11   **Pollution**

Bruce McCandless—satellite!

7 Energy Resources

CHAPTER SECTIONS

7-1 Fuels and Their Use

7-2 Solar Energy

7-3 Wind and Water

7-4 Nuclear Power

7-5 Energy: Today and Tomorrow

CHAPTER OBJECTIVES

After completing this chapter, you will be able to:

7-1 Define combustion.

7-1 Describe the types of fossil fuels and their various uses.

7-2 Compare direct and indirect uses of solar energy.

7-2 Describe a typical solar heating system.

7-3 Discuss the types of locations in which wind generators can be used.

7-3 Relate hydroelectric power to the movement of water.

7-4 Compare nuclear fission and nuclear fusion.

7-5 Describe geothermal energy and its uses.

7-5 Discuss the need for all people to conserve energy and to use nonpolluting energy resources.

On July 4, 1876, Americans from many parts of the nation crowded into Philadelphia's Fairmount Park to celebrate the 100th birthday of the United States with a visit to the Centennial Exhibition. Dozens of different exhibits vied for the visitors' attention, but the biggest attraction was the Hall of Machinery. People waited on long lines to see the shape of things to come.

Within the immense hall, light from the flickering flames of numerous gas lamps gleamed off the world's biggest steam engine. Visitors marveled at it and at the other engines that were changing the United States from a farming nation into the world's leading industrial power.

In 1876, steam engines seemed to be the ultimate technological development. In mills and factories they were helping to produce more goods than could ever have been made with the energy of muscle, wind, or flowing water. Over land, steam engines were moving trainloads of people and goods at speeds never before dreamed of. And at sea, steam was rapidly replacing the use of wind and sail.

But the age of steam had its dark side. Engines were noisy and sometimes dangerous. They filled the air with soot and smoke. Many people hoped for a cleaner energy source.

Though overshadowed by the great steam engines, a new energy source was represented in the Hall of Machinery that day. A few small electric generators heralded a new age of technology. Electricity, produced by coal, oil, moving water and wind, the energy of the atom, and the sun, was soon to come.

A steam powered train in 1872

7-1 Fuels and Their Use

A gust of wind whistles through the cave and scatters a few glowing embers, producing cries of fear from a group of people in the cave. The cave dwellers scramble to scoop up each ember. One by one, the embers are placed within a circle of stones. Pieces of wood and dry grass are added to them. An old man pokes and puffs at the embers. The others wait in suspense.

At last a flame appears. Then another and another. There are gasps of relief. The fire has been saved!

Combustion

To cave people living about 20,000 years ago, a fire meant the difference between life and death. It not only provided warmth and the means to cook food but also helped ward off the dangers of the night. Scientists do not know exactly when people first learned to *start* fires. It is likely that long before they learned how to build fires on their own, cave dwellers used embers from fires started by nature. But how does nature start fires?

Figure 7-1 *Long before they knew how to start their own fires, early peoples learned to use fires started by volcanoes and lightning.*

Lightning is one major cause of nature's fires. When lightning strikes trees or dry grass, it can cause them to burst into flames. Sometimes natural gas and oil seep from the soil. Lightning or the heat of the sun's radiation can cause these substances to burn. And that can touch off a wider fire. Volcanic eruptions of red-hot lava are another way nature can touch off forest or grass fires.

Whether lightning or a volcano is the cause, when a substance is heated above a certain temperature, it combines with oxygen from the air. Heat and light are given off. This process, which you call burning, is also known as **combustion**.

The secret of combustion did not remain a mystery for long. At some point, primitive people learned how to produce combustion. Perhaps they used the sparks that were given off when two pieces of flint were struck together. Or they may have used the heat produced by friction when two pieces of wood were rapidly rubbed against each other.

The ability to start combustion freed people from the dangerous task of snatching embers from forest fires or the edges of volcanoes. Encouraged by their success, people began to put fire to more and more uses: to clear land, to bake clay pots, and to make tools, ornaments, and weapons out of metal. Mastery of combustion—the burning of fuels to produce heat and light—was an important step along the road to civilization.

Fueling the Fire

Since the first civilizing spark of combustion, people have learned how to harness other forms of energy. These forms have included animal muscle power, flowing and falling water, blowing wind, solar radiation, chemical reactions, and the splitting of atoms. But combustion was, and still is, the method most often used by people to produce energy.

For many centuries, the most commonly used fuel was **vegetation,** which includes wood, rushes, reeds, and dried grass and leaves. Now **fossil fuels** have largely replaced wood as a fuel for industrialized nations. **The three main fossil fuels are coal, oil, and natural gas.** How did fossil fuels form and why are they so useful?

Activity

Early Use of Fire

Using your imagination and the information provided in this chapter, prepare a colorful chart that shows how primitive people may have discovered fire and learned to start fires as they needed them.

Figure 7-2 *This chart shows the various uses of coal in the United States. What is most of the coal used for?*

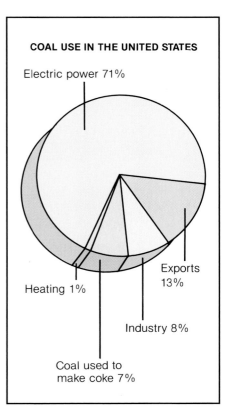

COAL USE IN THE UNITED STATES

Electric power 71%

Heating 1%

Exports 13%

Industry 8%

Coal used to make coke 7%

Figure 7-3 *Petroleum, a fossil fuel, is transported from the icy frontier through the Alaskan pipeline (left). The petroleum will be converted into oil, gas, and other products, some of which fuel racing cars (right).*

Millions of year ago, layer upon layer of plants and animals died and were buried beneath layers of mud. As the years passed, heat and great pressure turned the mud above to rock and the plant and animal matter below to coal, tar, oil, and gas.

These fossilized remains of plants and animals are made up mostly of compounds of hydrogen and

Figure 7-4 *What is the chemical formula for the hydrocarbon used in bottled gas?*

SOME SIMPLE HYDROCARBONS

Name	Chemical Formula	Use
Methane	CH_4	Major part of natural gas; raw material for many synthetic products
Ethane	C_2H_6	Used to make ethyl alcohol, acetic acid, and other chemicals; refrigerant
Propane	C_3H_8	"Bottled gas" for home heating, portable stoves and heaters; refrigerant
Butane	C_4H_{10}	Used in portable lighters, home heating fuel, portable stoves and heaters
Pentane	C_5H_{12}	Solvent; measuring column in low-temperature thermometers
Hexane	C_6H_{14}	Major component of materials used in certain motor fuels and dry cleaning solvents
Heptane	C_7H_{16}	Main part of turpentine from Jeffrey pine
Octane	C_8H_{18}	Important part of gasoline fuel for cars, trucks, buses, and the like

carbon. Such compounds, called **hydrocarbons,** give fossil fuels their heating value. Kilogram for kilogram, fossil fuels provide more energy than wood or any other type of vegetation. The heating value of a kilogram of coal is more than twice that of a kilogram of dry wood. The heating values of oil and natural gas are more than three times that of wood. In addition, fossil fuels provide more concentrated energy than wood. They are also easier to transport, store, and use.

Despite these advantages, the use of fossil fuels does present problems. Some deposits of coal and oil contain large amounts of sulfur. When high-sulfur fuels are burned, they release dangerous pollutants such as sulfur dioxide into the atmosphere.

One solution to this problem is to use cleaner fuels, such as natural gas and low-sulfur coal and oil. Another solution is to use devices in furnaces and power plants that "scrub" the smoke by removing sulfur and other pollutants from it. And now some energy specialists are showing renewed interest in going back to vegetation once again as a fuel.

Unlike fossil fuels, vegetation is a renewable resource. When a seam of coal has been fully mined or an oil deposit completely pumped dry, the resource is gone forever. But after a forest has been cut down, a new one can be planted.

Another advantage of vegetation is that it can be changed into more convenient fuels such as oil, gas,

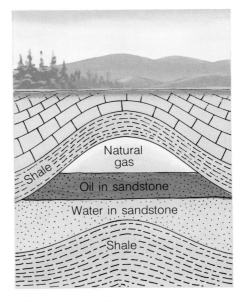

Figure 7-5 *Oil and natural gas are often found in the same areas. Why do you think natural gas is usually found above oil deposits?*

Figure 7-6 *From sugar cane grown in Hawaii (left), tiny pellets of fibrous wastes (center) are formed. These fuel pellets can then be burned in a factory (right).*

and concentrated fuel bricks. Various proposals have been made to farm fast-growing trees, sugar cane, sunflowers, and giant seaweeds as fuel sources. But as long as fossil fuels remain relatively inexpensive and plentiful, it is unlikely that much will be done about energy farming.

SECTION REVIEW

1. Define combustion.
2. List three fossil fuels.
3. Using Figure 7-4, determine the general chemical formula for a hydrocarbon.

Figure 7-7 *At Odeille, France, hundreds of movable mirrors (left) focus the direct light of the sun onto an enormous curved mirror (right). The curved mirror reflects the light onto a single point in a solar furnace. Temperatures of more than 3800° C, hot enough to melt lead, have been produced in Odeille.*

7-2 Solar Energy

Practically all the energy people use comes directly or indirectly from the sun. Energy from the sun, or solar energy, enables plants to grow. So when plants or the fossil remains of plants are burned, energy from the sun is being used indirectly.

Heat from the sun warms some parts of the atmosphere more than others. This causes the air to move around, sometimes with great force. Such air motion is called wind. Since ancient times, people have used the power of the wind to propel ships and to turn great wheels. Today the wind is still used for these purposes, as well as to generate electricity.

Wind power is another example of the indirect use of the sun's energy.

The sun's radiant energy also warms ocean surfaces and sends water vapor into the atmosphere. Then, at another time and place, the water is returned to the earth's surface in the form of rain or snow. On land, a portion of this returning water creates tumbling streams and rushing rivers. So tapping the power of falling and flowing water is another example of the indirect use of solar energy.

Perhaps you are thinking that it would be more efficient to make direct use of the sun's energy than to go through various in-between stages. Well, you are right, but there is a problem with this approach. The effect of the sun's radiant energy on the earth's surface is very spread out. In many regions, haze and cloud cover may block, absorb, and scatter a great deal of solar energy before it reaches the earth's surface. What is more, the sun does not shine on any one part of the earth all the time.

In order to make direct use of the sun's radiant energy, methods to concentrate it, store it, and possibly change it into other forms of energy must be developed.

Solar Heating

When it comes to providing solar energy for the widest possible use, cost and storage are important considerations. Solar heating systems for heating homes, schools, and commercial buildings may be one answer.

In a typical solar system, a large, dark surface area covered with glass or plastic receives and absorbs the sun's radiant energy. Water running through pipes or a flat surface in or beneath this solar collector is warmed by the sun's energy. The warm water in the pipes flows through a storage tank filled with water. Heat is transferred to the storage tank, and the now cool water in the pipes flows back to the solar collector to be reheated by the sun. At the same time, the water in the storage tank that has absorbed the heat from the pipes is pumped throughout the house to provide hot water and heat. You can get a better idea of how a typical solar heating system works by studying Figure 7-8.

Figure 7-8 *Water in the solar panel* (top) *is heated by the sun. The solar heating system* (bottom) *transfers this heat and then uses it to provide hot water and warmth.*

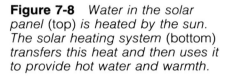

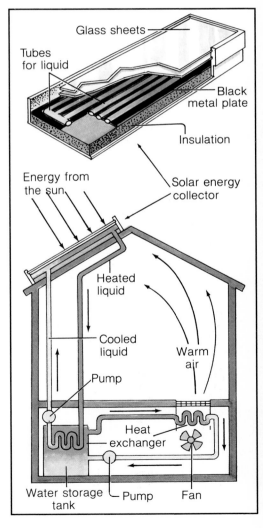

Figure 7-9 *This house is heated entirely by solar heating. Notice the solar panels on the roof.*

Sunlight to Electricity

At this time, solar heating systems represent the most common use of solar energy. But experts say that if the cost of solar cells is sharply reduced, they will be used in many other ways.

A solar cell, also called a **photovoltaic cell,** directly converts light into electricity. Most solar cells are "sandwiches" of very thin layers of silicon and metal. When light strikes the surface of this "sandwich," electrons flow across the layers. This flow of electrons is electric current that can be put to work. Unfortunately, each cell produces only a very small amount of electricity. So huge numbers of cells are needed to produce useful amounts of electricity.

For more than 20 years, solar cells have been used to provide power aboard various spacecraft. In recent years, such cells have been used to provide electric power to various devices, appliances, and vehicles on Earth.

In 1980, an airplane powered by solar cells flew for the first time in California. A year later, another solar-powered plane flew across the English Channel. And in 1983, a solar-powered car, the *Quiet Achiever,* was driven 4130 kilometers across Australia.

The solar cell has come a long way. But in terms of meeting the everyday electric needs of homes, schools, and factories, it still has a long way to go. A single cell can now provide only about one watt of electricity—while the sun shines. That means that

Figure 7-10 *A solar cell, or photovoltaic cell, converts sunlight directly into electricity.*

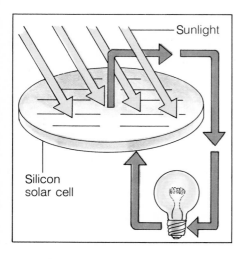

Sunlight

Silicon
solar cell

Figure 7-11 *In 1981, power from solar cells enabled this solar plane to cross the English Channel* (left). *This experimental car is also powered by solar cells* (right).

about 5000 cells and a large storage battery would be needed to provide electricity for an average American home!

Scientists are working hard to increase the electric output of solar cells. They are working even harder to cut the costs of solar cells. And successes are being scored on both efforts. Researchers predict that in the future, the roofs of homes will be covered with solar-cell shingles. These shingles, a little more expensive than the ordinary kind, will provide effective roof protection and at the same time provide electricity for the home.

Looking even farther ahead, the National Aeronautics and Space Administration, or NASA, has come up with the idea of using solar stations in space to provide electricity for people on Earth. Huge collections of solar cells, several kilometers wide and deep, would be assembled in space. A craft linked to each collection of cells would keep the cells facing the sun. With no atmosphere to block the sun's powerful rays, the cells would efficiently generate electricity 24 hours a day, 365 days a year.

At the space station, the electricity would be converted to microwaves, a kind of radio wave, and beamed to Earth. Stations on Earth would receive the microwave energy and change it back to electricity. Such a system is likely to be in place by the year 2000.

Figure 7-12 *Solar power stations of the future will beam energy from space to collecting stations on Earth.*

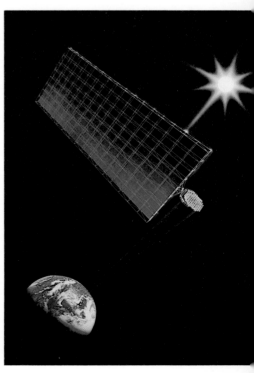

1. What is the primary source of almost all the energy people use?

2. What is a photovoltaic cell?

7-3 Wind and Water

More than 4000 years ago, the Egyptians added sails to oar-powered boats to take advantage of the wind's energy. The ancient Persians used windmills to turn wheels, grind corn, and pump water.

Over the ages, people improved on these devices, and the use of wind energy spread throughout the world. Two hundred years ago, thousands of windmills dotted the landscape of Europe. Thousands of wind-powered ships sailed the world's oceans. The age of wind energy was at its peak.

Within 50 years, however, wind machines on land and sea were rapidly being replaced by coal-fired steam engines. But while the use of wind machines was declining in Europe, it was just starting on the American farm.

Wind Machines

Around 1860, small windmills on tall wooden towers started to appear on farms across America. Lightweight, efficient, relatively inexpensive, and easy to install, these wind machines were used to pump water out of the ground for crops and farm animals. In dry farming regions of the Midwest and Southwest, these wind-powered pumps were vital.

In 1890, a Danish inventor increased the usefulness of these wind machines by developing a windmill that could generate electricity. Wind machines became common sights throughout the land, and American farmers started to enjoy the benefits of electricity.

As a source of electricity, wind generators were not always reliable. They did not work on calm days. And when fierce gales raged, they were easily knocked down or blown apart. So when hydroelectric power plants started supplying electricity to rural

Figure 7-13 *A modern wind generator provides electricity in Hawaii.*

regions, farmers welcomed the change. This electricity was cheaper and more dependable than that produced by the wind. By 1950, most wind generators had been abandoned.

But wind energy was not ignored for long. In 1973, an oil shortage that caused concern about an "energy crisis" sparked new interest in wind generators. Several new designs were developed and put into use.

In designing wind generators, the unpredictability of the wind must be taken into account. If a wind machine is made sensitive enough to respond to the gentlest breeze, what will happen to it in a violent storm? And if it is designed to withstand a fierce gale, will it work when the wind barely blows?

Designers of large wind generators carefully select sites where the wind is strong, yet predictable, most of the time. Then they build the system to suit the site. Such is not the case for small generators intended for use in homes and small towns. Those systems must be developed for a broad range of conditions. Designs for new, small wind generators range from traditional propellerlike rotors to rotors that look like eggbeaters and box kites.

The use of wind energy at sea also seems to be making a comeback. A Japanese shipbuilder launched a sailing tanker in 1980. The ship's sails are made of metal and controlled by computers.

Activity

Windmills

Wind turbines, windmills built to produce electricity, differ in construction from windmills built to pump water or grind grains.

Using books and reference materials in the library, find out more about windmills and wind turbines. Compare their appearance, construction, design, and operation. Present your findings in a report to your class.

Figure 7-14 *Notice the metal sails on this modern Japanese sailing vessel. The sails help to conserve fuel.*

They are used in addition to the ship's engine in order to save fuel. The Soviets have two modern sail-assisted ships. And the United States and West Germany are considering several designs for similar ships.

Energy planners do not expect the wind to become a major source of energy. But they believe that increased use of the wind will save fuel and reduce pollution.

From Water Wheels to Great Dams

Like the wind, water motion was put to work in ancient times. The Persians, Greeks, and Romans used water wheels and mills to move objects and grind corn. In the late 1700s, water wheels provided energy for machine looms to make cloth. But by the 1800s, most water mills had been replaced by steam engines. With Thomas Edison's invention of the light bulb in 1879, the demand for electricity increased tremendously. And so a new age of water-powered energy was born.

Falling or flowing water, a form of mechanical energy, is now used to generate a quarter of the world's electrical energy. Barriers, or dams, built across rivers can hold back millions of tons of water.

Figure 7-15 *Moving water turns the water wheel in this mill where corn was once ground* (left). *Falling water at Hoover Dam hydroelectric plant helps spin a turbine to generate electricity* (right).

176

Some of this trapped water is channeled past the blades of a turbine. The rushing water spins the blades to generate electricity.

There are hundreds of hydroelectric power plants in the world. They are particularly numerous in mountainous countries with heavy rainfall. While new hydroelectric plants are still being built, energy planners point out that there is a limit to the number of rushing rivers available. So it might seem that there is a limit to the use of water energy. But there are other ways to tap the energy of water motion. One of these ways is to harness the energy of ocean tides.

Energy from the Tides

Twice a day, the waters of the oceans rise and fall. These high tides and low tides are caused mainly by the gravitational pull of the moon. If the difference between the high tides and low tides is significant, then this movement of water can be used to generate electricity.

In some coastal areas, the difference between high tides and low tides can be as much as 15 meters. The rising and falling of the ocean tides causes water to flow in and out of bays. A low dam across a bay entrance can temporarily hold back the incoming or outgoing flow of tidal water. The water can then be channeled to flow past turbines to generate electricity. This setup is similar to the operation of a river hydroelectric power plant. But there is a difference. In a river plant, the water always flows in the same direction. In a tidal plant, the water flows in and out. Therefore, the turbines must be able to operate efficiently in both directions. It was not until the 1970s that turbines were perfected for this use.

Tidal power stations now exist in France, Canada, and the U.S.S.R. Although others are being considered for construction in various parts of the world, the number of tidal bays that can be used is limited.

Activity

Timing Tides

At Cape May along the shore of the Atlantic Ocean, there is a high tide every 24 hours and 50 minutes. If this high tide occurs at 6:00 A.M. on Tuesday, at what time will it occur Wednesday? On Thursday?

SECTION REVIEW

1. Why were wind generators not considered reliable energy sources?
2. Name two ways in which the energy of rushing rivers has been harnessed for human use.

Figure 7-16 *Three Mile Island—scene of the first serious accident at a nuclear plant*

Activity

Chernobyl

In 1986, the most serious nuclear accident to date occurred at the Chernobyl nuclear power plant in the Soviet Ukraine. Using reference materials in the library, write a report on the cause of the Chernobyl disaster, its short-term effects, and its potential long-term effects. Describe its impact on the future of nuclear power.

7-4 Nuclear Power

On Wednesday, March 28, 1979, West German scientists and political leaders met in Hannover, Lower Saxony, to talk about plans for the world's biggest nuclear power plant. Most of the people there favored nuclear power. They viewed it as an abundant source of energy that would enable them to conserve coal, oil, and natural gas. While the people in Hannover were talking about a nuclear future, an accident was occurring in faraway Pennsylvania—an accident that would change their plans and cast doubt over the future of nuclear energy.

The Fission Option

At the Three Mile Island nuclear power plant near Harrisburg, Pennsylvania, several water pumps broke down. And without that constant flow of water, the nuclear reactor overheated. The resulting escape of radioactive gases from the plant caused great concern for the safety of people in the area.

Fortunately no one was killed. But many people felt that the Three Mile Island accident could have resulted in disaster. News of the accident spread around the world. Within days, protests in West Germany forced postponement of the nuclear installation in Lower Saxony. In fact, plans for other nuclear plants in various places were postponed or canceled. Safety checks of existing plants were stepped up, and some plants were closed for repairs.

In nuclear power plants, enormous heat is generated through controlled nuclear fission, or splitting of the nuclei, of uranium or plutonium atoms. Thirty years ago, **nuclear fission** was considered the most promising energy source. But even then there were doubts and fears.

One obvious fear of many people is radiation escaping from nuclear power plants. Radiation is dangerous to all forms of life. And there is evidence that radiation has leaked from some plants. Also, evidence indicates that some nuclear plants were not built according to strict construction standards set by the United States government. If nuclear power is to be safe, power plants must follow all construction standards.

Leakage from power plants into the environment is not the only radiation problem. Dangerous nuclear wastes are produced by nuclear power plants. At the present time, no safe way to get rid of these wastes has been found. Such wastes, and the radiation they release, are a health hazard today and could become a serious health hazard to future generations.

Another problem caused by nuclear power plants is **thermal pollution.** Thermal pollution refers to the heating of bodies of water near nuclear power plants caused by the hot water released by such plants. Thermal pollution is a very clear danger to organisms living in such bodies of water, particularly fish.

Scientists are hard at work on solving the problems of nuclear energy. If they are not solved, then the future of nuclear energy as a major source of power is in doubt. If the problems involved with nuclear energy and fission reactors are solved, then nuclear energy may become an extremely important energy source in the years to come.

The Fusion Option

Great energy can be produced by splitting atoms. But even more energy can be produced by causing the nuclei of atoms to come together. **The combining of atomic nuclei is called nuclear fusion.** The process that produces the sun's energy is **nuclear fusion.**

Within the sun and other stars, enormous heat and pressure cause the nuclei of hydrogen atoms to combine and form helium atoms. Tremendous heat is given off, which triggers more fusion.

When a hydrogen bomb explodes, uncontrolled fusion is taking place. To use fusion as a source of energy, it must be tamed. Scientists are working on several approaches. One approach is to produce a superheated stream that contains the nuclei of certain gases—a **plasma**—and squeeze it with magnetic force. Another is to blast pressurized pellets of frozen hydrogen with powerful laser beams.

So far, neither approach has worked. Some people say that fusion is an impossible dream; others insist that fusion is an eventual reality. When it is achieved, fusion will provide people with unlimited, clean, inexpensive energy.

Figure 7-17 *Tiny hydrogen fuel pellets are placed in the chamber of an experimental laser fusion device (top). When the beams are turned on, the pellet reaches temperatures over 70 million° C and explodes in on itself in a kind of fusion (bottom).*

Figure 7-18 *A geyser erupts in Iceland, carrying geothermal energy from deep within the earth.*

Figure 7-19 *This chart shows the sources of energy used in the United States. How much energy is presently obtained from fossil fuels?*

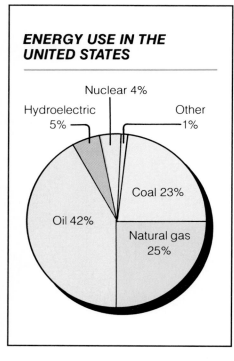

ENERGY USE IN THE UNITED STATES

Nuclear 4%

Hydroelectric 5%

Other 1%

Oil 42%

Coal 23%

Natural gas 25%

7-5 Energy: Today and Tomorrow

Anyone who has watched a volcano erupt realizes that there is tremendous energy locked within the earth. But it is not very practical to consider using the energy of volcanoes. There are easier ways to get at the earth's inner heat, or **geothermal energy.**

Glowing molten rock boils and bubbles within the earth at a temperature around 1800°C. A rocky crust with an average thickness of 64 kilometers separates the earth's surface from this inner fire. However, there are cracks and thin spots in this crust through which heat seeps.

In some of the earth's hot spots, water is heated by contact with lava. And this hot water frequently bursts forth as fountains of steam and boiling water called geysers. Geysers are used in Iceland to heat homes and greenhouses. In Italy, New Zealand, the United States, and the Soviet Union, geysers are spinning turbines and generating electricity.

Geothermal energy is but one of many new and unusual alternative energy resources being considered by scientists—even though there are enough energy resources to meet the world's needs. Why then do people worry so much about finding new energy resources? The answer is twofold.

For one thing, the use of many energy resources pollutes our environment. In particular, the burning of fossil fuels adds a wide variety of pollutants to the environment. These pollutants can cause health problems today. And as they continue to build up, they may cause even more severe health problems for future generations. You will read more about pollution and its relationship to various energy resources in Chapter 11.

There is another important reason to develop new and clean energy sources. Long-range energy planning is vital to future generations. Society cannot simply use up all available energy resources today and not worry about tomorrow. Today's generations must look at energy use—and misuse—with an eye toward the future. If not, future generations may be doomed to a world in which energy is not readily available. And without energy, society as we know it cannot exist.

Scientists keep such concepts in mind when they develop new energy sources. That is why so much time and money is spent on solar energy. For as long as the sun shines, solar energy will be available.

You can be an energy-conscious person. Something as simple as turning off a light when leaving the room conserves energy. **Conserving energy and using energy resources that do not pollute the environment is not just for scientists: It is a job for everyone.**

Activity

Other Energy Sources

Using books and reference materials in the library, prepare a report on one of the following energy sources:

magnetohydrodynamic generators (MHD)

fuel cells

solid wastes

Ocean Thermal Energy Conversion (OTEC)

SECTION REVIEW

1. What is geothermal energy?
2. Why is it vital to seek new energy resources?

Career: *Geophysical Prospector*

HELP WANTED: GEOPHYSICAL PROSPECTOR Requires a bachelor's degree in geophysics and a master's degree in petrology. Job involves locating petroleum deposits.

Petroleum is one of the most valuable natural resources in the world. It is the major energy source for the industrial societies of the world. Petroleum is the key raw material for the manufacture of fuels used for all forms of transportation. It is also the basic raw material used for making rubber, cosmetics, medicines, plastics, and fertilizers.

Petroleum is found beneath every ocean and continent. But before it can be recovered, it must be located. Scientists responsible for locating petroleum reserves are called **geophysical prospectors.** With the use of special instruments—seismographs, magnetometers, and gravimeters, for example—they conduct research studies of rock formations below the surface. The data from these studies are used to prepare contour maps of subsurface features. These maps are then used to determine desirable spots for drilling.

A geophysical prospector also supervises drilling crews, who collect rock and soil samples for chemical analysis. Hydrocarbon content in a sample provides information about the location of petroleum. To learn more about this career, write to the Society of Exploration Geophysicists, P.O. Box 3098, Tulsa, OK 74101.

LABORATORY ACTIVITY

Solar Heating

Purpose

In this activity, you will examine how well solar energy heats various objects.

Materials *(per group)*

Black and white construction paper
2 plastic jars with plastic lids
2 thermometers
Water
Scissors and tape
Clock or watch with a second hand

Procedure

1. Tape two layers of black paper around one jar. Cover the other jar with two layers of white paper.
2. Fill each jar with water at room temperature.
3. Cover the jars with their lids. Using scissors, carefully puncture the center of each lid in order to make a hole large enough to hold a thermometer. **CAUTION:** *Handle the scissors very carefully*.
4. Carefully insert a thermometer through the hole in each lid. Make certain that the bulb is below the surface of the water. **CAUTION:** *Be careful in handling the thermometer.*
5. Place the jars on a sunny windowsill.
6. Record the temperature of each jar every 3 minutes for one hour.
7. Make a bar graph of the time and temperature change.

Observations and Conclusions

1. How effectively did the sun's light energy heat the water in the jars?
2. How did the color of the jar affect the amount of light energy absorbed by the water?

CHAPTER REVIEW

SUMMARY

7-1 Fuels and Their Use

- Fire was one of the first sources of energy harnessed by human beings.

- When a substance combines with oxygen from the air to produce heat and light, combustion occurs.

- For many centuries, vegetation such as wood, dried grass, and leaves was the fuel most commonly used for combustion.

- Today coal, oil, and natural gas—the fossil fuels—have replaced vegetation as fuel sources for industrialized nations.

- Because vegetation produces less pollution than fossil fuels, energy scientists are showing renewed interest in it as an energy source.

- Fossil fuels get their heating value from hydrocarbons, compounds made up of the elements hydrogen and carbon.

7-2 Solar Energy

- Practically all the energy used by people comes directly or indirectly from the sun.

- Examples of energy sources that come indirectly from the sun are vegetation, fossil fuels, wind, and falling or flowing water.

- Solar systems are used for heating homes, schools, and buildings.

- Solar cells, or photovoltaic cells, convert light directly into electricity.

7-3 Wind and Water

- Throughout history, people have harnessed wind energy by using devices such as windmills and the sails of ships.

- Hydroelectric power plants generate electricity from falling or flowing water.

- A new source of energy comes from harnessing ocean tides.

7-4 Nuclear Power

- Nuclear power plants produce electricity by harnessing the heat energy produced by the splitting of uranium and plutonium atoms.

- A potential source of energy in the future is nuclear fusion.

7-5 Energy: Today and Tomorrow

- Geothermal energy is the energy supplied by the earth's inner heat.

- Conserving energy and using energy resources that do not pollute the environment is everyone's responsibility.

VOCABULARY

Define each term in a complete sentence.

combustion	hydrocarbon	nuclear fusion	plasma
fossil fuel	nuclear	photovoltaic cell	thermal pollution
geothermal energy	fission		vegetation

CONTENT REVIEW: MULTIPLE CHOICE

Choose the letter of the answer that best completes each statement.

1. In which of the following ways are fires started in nature?
   a. by lightning   b. by the sun's radiation
   c. by lava   d. by all of these

2. The most widely used method to release stored energy for human benefit is
   a. flowing and falling water.   b. solar radiation.
   c. combustion of fuels.   d. splitting atoms.
3. Which of the following substances is *not* a fossil fuel?
   a. natural gas   b. wood   c. coal   d. oil
4. Kilogram for kilogram, which of these fuels provides the greatest heating value?
   a. wood   b. oil   c. paper   d. coal
5. Sunlight can be converted directly into electricity through the use of a
   a. plasma.   b. windmill generator.   c. photovoltaic cell.   d. hydroelectric plant.
6. Wind generators of the 1800s were *not* a reliable electricity source because
   a. they took too long to build.   b. they worked only with heavy winds.
   c. heavy winds could knock them down.   d. all of these
7. One quarter of the world's electricity is generated by
   a. wind.   b. animal muscle power.
   c. solar radiation   d. falling or flowing water.
8. Hydroelectric power plants generate electricity by harnessing
   a. solar energy.   b. nuclear energy.
   c. mechanical energy.   d. chemical energy.
9. Ocean tides are caused mainly by the gravitational pull of the
   a. moon.   b. sun.   c. earth.   d. solar system.
10. Nuclear fusion occurs naturally within
    a. oceans.   b. volcanoes.   c. geysers.   d. stars.

CONTENT REVIEW: COMPLETION

Fill in the word or words that best complete each statement.

1. _____ is the burning of fuels to produce heat and light.
2. Compounds made of hydrogen and carbon are called _____.
3. One day, satellites in space may convert sunlight to _____, which could be beamed back to Earth and converted into electricity.
4. A solar cell, or _____, converts light directly into electricity.
5. Wind generators are a(n) _____ use of solar radiation.
6. _____ is the splitting of uranium or plutonium atoms.
7. The process in which hydrogen nuclei are joined to form helium is called _____.
8. _____ is caused by hot water that is released from nuclear power plants into nearby lakes and streams.
9. The tremendous heat energy locked within the earth is called _____.
10. Steam from geysers can be used to spin _____ and generate _____.

CONTENT REVIEW: TRUE OR FALSE

Determine whether each statement is true or false. If it is true, write "true." If it is false, change the underlined word or words to make the statement true.

1. Early people used <u>fire</u> to make tools, ornaments, and metal weapons.
2. Kilogram for kilogram, fossil fuels provide <u>less</u> energy than wood.

3. Most of the energy people use comes directly or indirectly from <u>the sun</u>.
4. When <u>high-sulfur</u> fuels are burned, dangerous pollutants are released into the air.
5. Large wind generators are built where the wind is <u>weak</u> but predictable.
6. Hydroelectric plants are built mainly in <u>flat</u> countries with heavy rainfall.
7. In a <u>river</u> power plant, the water generating the electricity flows in two directions.
8. Today, nuclear power plants get energy from nuclear <u>fusion</u>.
9. Nuclear fusion can produce <u>more</u> energy than nuclear fission.
10. Geysers are produced by <u>hydroelectric</u> energy.

CONCEPT REVIEW: SKILL BUILDING

Use the skills you have developed in this chapter to complete each activity.

1. **Making calculations** The population of the United States is approximately 215 million people. For each person, approximately 35 kilograms of fossil fuels are consumed every day. How much fuel is used every day in the United States? Every month? Every year?
2. **Making observations** Over a period of several days, keep a list of the ways in which you use energy produced by fuels. Be sure to identify the type of fuel that produces each type of energy.
3. **Applying concepts** In what ways is solar energy used in your home? Considering the region in which you live, what other forms of solar energy might be appropriate for use in your home?
4. **Making inferences** Most scientists believe that oil and natural gas formed beneath the ocean floor. However, a great amount of oil and natural gas are now found beneath dry land. Explain how this could have occurred.
5. **Relating concepts** Why do you think alternative energy sources such as tidal power, wind energy, and geothermal energy are not used in all parts of the world?
6. **Making maps** Choose geothermal energy or tidal power and find out where in the world these energy resources are being used. Make a map to display these locations.

CONCEPT REVIEW: ESSAY

Discuss each of the following in a brief paragraph.

1. When fossil fuels such as coal and oil burn, they release dangerous pollutants, such as sulfur dioxide, into the atmosphere. Discuss some possible solutions you have to this problem.
2. Energy use per person in the United States is five times as great as the world's average. Discuss some possible ways people can lower their energy appetite without sacrificing comfort.
3. Many states—such as Texas, Louisiana, and Alabama—depend upon oil and natural gas reserves for much of their state's income. What do you think might happen if the oil and gas reserves were depleted? In your answer, consider alternative measures to extend the usability and life of current oil and gas wells.
4. Discuss the advantages and disadvantages of a solar cell.

$\textcircled{8}$ Chemical Technology

CHAPTER SECTIONS

8–1 Fuels from Petroleum

8-2 Petrochemical Products

8-3 Health Chemistry

CHAPTER OBJECTIVES

After completing this chapter, you will be able to:

8-1 Identify the major fractions of petroleum.

8-1 Describe the process of fractional distillation.

8-2 Explain how polymers are formed from monomers.

8-2 Describe the process of polymerization.

8-2 List some important natural and synthetic polymers.

8-3 Relate health chemistry to the development of synthetic membranes, antibiotics, and vaccines.

"Plastic!"

What does that word make you think of? To many people, "plastic" stands for something that is inexpensive, artificial, and "not as good as the real thing." The "real thing" may be metal, glass, wood, wool, clay, cotton, or paper. Plastics are often used as substitutes for all of these materials. And that makes some people unhappy. They complain about a "plastic world" and "plastic values."

But scientists are not at all unhappy about the development of plastics and other new materials. They point out that plastics can be stronger than steel and lighter than paper. They can be more heat-resistant than clay and more flexible than rubber. And they can last for a long time.

Plastics are now used in making planes, trains, cars, and buildings. They are used to make spare parts for the human body. They can be used as superinsulators to block the flow of electricity or as superconductors to speed that flow. Plastic materials help shield' homecoming spacecraft from the enormous heat of reentry into the earth's atmosphere. And inflated plastic bags have even been used to lift a 165-ton sunken schooner to the surface. In the near future, some of the thousands of different synthetic materials called plastics may help people to settle colonies in space and at the bottom of the sea.

Plastic bags help raise a ship

8-1 Fuels from Petroleum

The oil that gushes from deep within the earth is a mixture of chemicals called crude oil, or **petroleum.** Petroleum is usually black or dark brown. But it can be green, red, yellow, or even colorless. Petroleum may flow as easily as water or it may ooze slowly like thick tar. The color and density of petroleum depend on the substances that make it up. By itself, petroleum is almost useless! But the different parts, or **fractions,** of petroleum are among the most useful chemicals in the world.

Petroleum is separated into its useful parts by a process called fractional distillation. The process of **distillation** involves heating a liquid until it vaporizes and then allowing the vapor to cool until it condenses back into a liquid. The different fractions of petroleum have different boiling points. So each fraction vaporizes at a different temperature. The temperature at which a substance boils is the same as the temperature at which it condenses. Thus, each fraction will condense back to a liquid at a different temperature. By drawing off each fraction as it condenses, petroleum can be easily separated into its various parts.

Fractional distillation of petroleum is done in a **fractionating tower.** The process of separating petroleum into its fractions is called refining. At a

Figure 8-1 *Geologists drill through the earth's surface to find crude oil, which is then recovered by devices such as an oil rig* (left).*The first oil well in the United States was drilled in 1859 in Pennsylvania* (right). *What is another term for crude oil?*

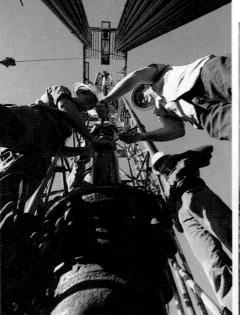

Figure 8-2 *Petroleum is separated into fractions in fractionating columns in an oil refinery* (left). *Each fraction condenses at a different temperature and is drawn off in collecting vessels located at fixed points along the column* (right).

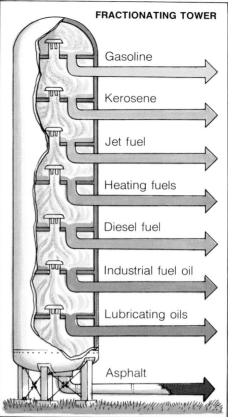

FRACTIONATING TOWER

Gasoline

Kerosene

Jet fuel

Heating fuels

Diesel fuel

Industrial fuel oil

Lubricating oils

Asphalt

Figure 8-3 *This illustration shows the amount, or percent yield, of each fraction that can be obtained from a barrel of crude oil. Which fraction represents the highest percent yield?*

refinery, fractionating towers may rise 30 meters or more. Petroleum is piped into the base of the fractionating tower and heated to about 385°C. At this temperature, which is higher than the boiling points of most of the fractions, the petroleum vaporizes.

Figure 8-2 shows a typical fractionating tower. When the petroleum vaporizes, the fractions rise up the tower. As they rise, they cool and condense. Some fractions condense at high temperatures. These fractions condense near the bottom of the tower and are drawn off to collecting vessels. Other fractions continue to rise in the tower. As they rise, they cool even more before they condense. These fractions are drawn off at higher levels in the tower. As a result of this vaporization–condensation process, the various fractions of petroleum are separated and collected.

You will notice in Figure 8-2 that asphalt is collected at the bottom of the fractionating tower. Asphalt vaporizes at a temperature that exceeds the temperature in the tower. When the other fractions vaporize, asphalt is left behind as a liquid that simply runs out of the bottom of the tower. Which fraction in the tower condenses at the lowest temperature?

PRODUCTS PRODUCED
FROM A BARREL OF CRUDE OIL

	% Yield
Gasolines	46.7
Fuel oil	28.6
Jet fuel	9.1
Petrochemicals and Miscellaneous products	3.8
Coke	3.5
Asphalt and road oil	3.1
Liquified gases	2.9
Lubricants	1.3
Kerosene	0.9
Waxes	0.1

1. What physical property forms the basis of fractional distillation?

2. Why do substances with low boiling points condense near the top of a fractionating tower?

3. How would you separate three substances—A, B, and C—whose boiling points are 50°C, 100°C, and 150°C, respectively?

8-2 Petrochemical Products

Ride a bicycle down your street and you are probably gliding along on a product of petroleum, or a petrochemical product. The rubber in the inner tube is made from petrochemicals. Put on your winter jacket and you are probably keeping yourself warm with a petrochemical product—the lining of your jacket is made from petrochemicals.

Polymer Chemistry

One simple definition of chemistry is the "making and breaking of bonds." In a chemical reaction, the chemical bonds that hold atoms together in molecules are broken. The atoms are rearranged, different bonds are formed, and new molecules are produced. The petrochemical products that are part of your life come from the making and breaking of chemical bonds in petrochemicals. A general term for this process is polymer chemistry. And polymer chemistry involves **polymers** (PAHL-ih-merz).

The term polymer comes from the Greek words *polys*, meaning "many," and *meros*, meaning "parts." The word "parts" refers to a grouping of atoms called a molecular unit. A molecular unit alone is not a polymer. But many molecular units strung together in a series form a unique polymer.

The individual molecular units that form a polymer are called **monomers** (MAHN-uh-merz). You can think of a polymer as a chain of monomers all bonded together one after another. The type of monomers and the length and shape of the polymer chain determine the properties of the polymer.

Figure 8-4 *A polymer is made up of a series of monomers. What factors distinguish one polymer from another?*

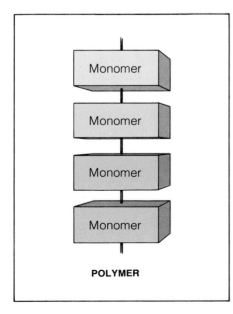

Monomer

Monomer

Monomer

Monomer

POLYMER

Methane

Figure 8-5 *Substances produced from methane include Plexiglas, antifreeze, fire extinguisher foam, and Teflon (top). Ethylene products include plastic laser disks, aspirin, plastic wrap, and synthetic fibers (bottom).*

Ethylene

Figure 8-6 *In the past, rubber was obtained from rubber trees (left). Today, the rubber used in products such as these truck tires is manufactured in factories (right). What type of polymer is rubber obtained from rubber trees? From factories?*

Natural Polymers

Most of the polymers you will read about in this chapter are made from petrochemicals. Some polymers, however, occur in nature. Cotton, silk, wool, and natural rubber are all natural polymers. Cellulose and lignin, important parts of wood, are natural polymers. In fact, all living things contain polymers. Protein, an essential ingredient of living matter, is a polymer. The monomers from which proteins are made are called **amino acids.** Combined in groups of one hundred or more units, amino acid monomers form many of the parts of your body—from hair to heart muscle.

Synthetic Polymers

Although the term polymer may be new to you, the polymers produced from petrochemicals are probably quite familiar. Polymers produced from petrochemicals are called synthetic polymers. Petrochemical products such as rubber and plastic wrap are synthetic polymers. Synthetic polymers are used to make fabrics such as nylon, rayon, orlon, and dacron. Plastics, used in many products from kitchen utensils to rocket engines, are petrochemical products made of polymers. The list goes on and on.

The first polymer was manufactured in 1909. Since then, **polymerization** (puh-lihm-uhr-ih-ZAY-shuhn) has come a long way. **Polymerization is the process of chemically bonding monomers to form polymers.** Most early polymers consisted of fewer

Figure 8-7 *The model is of a polymer that forms the synthetic fiber on the spool* (left). *Bullwinkle, familiar from the Thanksgiving Parade, is made of the first successful synthetic fiber and is coated with the first successful synthetic rubber* (right). *So when you enjoy such parades, thank polymers.*

than two hundred monomers. Today's polymers may contain thousands of monomers. The numerous ways in which these monomers can be linked may be very complex. They include single chains, parallel chains, intertwining chains, spirals, loops, and loops of chains!

Polymer chemistry has produced synthetic materials that are strong, light, heat resistant, flexible, and long lasting. These properties give polymers a wide range of uses. For example, polymers are used as substitutes for human tissue, such as bones and arteries. These polymers must last a lifetime and withstand the wear and tear of constant use. Polymer adhesives, rather than thread, are often used to hold clothes together. Polymers are replacing glass, metal, and paper as containers for food. The cup of hot chocolate you may have held today did not burn your hand because it was made of a white insulating polymer. Polymer materials also are used for rugs, furniture, wall coverings, and curtains. Look around you and see how many polymers you can spot. And remember to thank petroleum for all these useful polymers.

Figure 8-8 *Polymer technology has produced some amazing materials. This sheet of plastic simply bends no matter how hard it is struck by a hammer.*

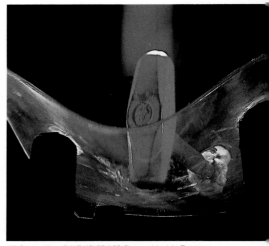

Life Science Library/GIANT MOLECULES, Photograph by John Zimmerman
© 1966 Time, Inc. Time-Life Books, Inc., Publisher.

Career: Patternmaker

On July 4, 1986, a figure that represents freedom to people of the United States and most of the world was honored with a huge birthday party. The figure is the Statue of Liberty. Almost everywhere you looked that day there were replicas of the one hundred-year-old statue. The replicas were cast from almost every material imaginable: chocolate, ice, aluminum, glass, plastic, concrete, plaster, and—like the original statue—copper.

Producing the molds from which these statues were formed kept many **patternmakers** busy for months before the celebration. A patternmaker produces molds for new car parts, new board game pieces, machine parts, and many other products.

Using blueprints that show how the finished product should look, a patternmaker first makes a model of the new product. The model is usually made of clay, wood, or plaster. The model is then pressed into clay, sand, plaster, or other materials to make a hollow mold. The finished piece is then cast, or formed, from this mold.

Frequently, a mold is used to shape new synthetic materials. So a patternmaker must be familiar with the chemical technology that is used to develop new materials. A high school diploma and courses in art, math, mechanical drawing, and metalworking are required to become a patternmaker. Usually a patternmaker learns the skills of the trade through a five-year apprenticeship. For information about a career as a patternmaker, contact the American Foundrymen's Society/Cast Metals Institute, Inc., Golf and Wolf Roads, Des Plaines, IL 60016.

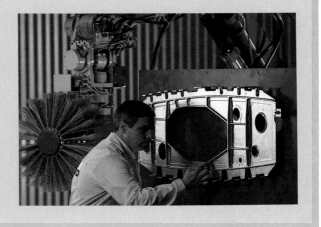

Life Science Library/GIANT MOLECULES. Photograph by Bruce Roberts © 1966 Time, Inc. Time-Life Books, Inc., Publisher.

Polymer materials also can be mixed and matched to produce substances with unusual properties. Different plastics and synthetic fibers are combined to make punctureproof tires and bulletproof vests. Layers of polymer materials can be combined to make waterproof rain gear.

Polymer chemistry also is important in the transportation industry. Each year the number of polymer parts in cars, planes, and trains increases. A plastic car engine has been built and tested. This engine is lighter, more fuel efficient, and more durable than a metal engine.

Figure 8-9 *Synthetic fibers are one of the many products formed from polymers. What is the name of the process of chemically bonding monomers to form polymers?*

Figure 8-10 *The scientist is holding a thin strand of Kevlar, a polymer five times stronger than steel* (right). *Ropes of Kevlar have replaced steel in lines used to hold ships at dock* (left).

Devices that produce electricity also are being improved with polymers. Polymer batteries and solar electric cells will soon be available. These developments are expected to increase the use of solar energy and improve energy conservation. Recently, a new polymer was developed that can conduct electricity almost as well as metals such as copper. One of the scientists who developed this polymer described its possible use "as a lightweight, rechargeable battery about as thick as a sheet of paper." As you can see, polymers made from petroleum are extremely important today. And they will be even more important in the future.

SECTION REVIEW

1. What is the relationship between a monomer and a polymer?
2. List three examples of natural polymers.
3. What is the name of the process in which monomers are chemically bonded to form polymers?
4. What might be some of the economic side effects of increased use of polymers in automobiles?

Activity

Kapton Calculations

A polymer known as Kapton can withstand temperatures as high as 400°C and as low as −233°C. This characteristic makes Kapton ideal for use in rockets. Calculate how many degrees there are in this temperature range.

Figure 8-11 *Just a few drops of polymer adhesive applied between the two steel cylinders under the hook holds up this safe, which has a mass of over 500 kilograms.*

Life Science Library/GIANT MOLECULES. Photograph by John Zimmerman. © 1966 Time, Inc. Time-Life Books, Inc., Publisher.

Bakelite

Bakelite is the name of the first synthetic polymer. Its development is an interesting story. Using books and other reference materials in the library, find out about the discovery of this polymer. Present your findings in a written report. Be sure to include the following information in your report: how, when, and by whom Bakelite was discovered; the characteristics and commercial uses of Bakelite.

8-3   Health Chemistry

Polymer chemistry has had a great impact on human health. Some of the effects have been bad, others good. The making of polymers spills pollutants into the environment. And some of these pollutants are harmful to human health. But scientists point out that the making of polymers may be much less dangerous than the manufacture of certain other chemical substances. And polymer chemistry may offer some solutions to a variety of health problems. **Among the polymers that have been beneficial to human health are synthetic membranes, antibiotics, and vaccines.**

Membrane Science

A biological membrane is a thin, soft, flexible layer of tissue. Such membranes occur in every living thing. Each cell—the basic unit of living matter—is surrounded by a membrane. So are certain groups of cells. So, too, are larger organs.

In the human body, there are membranes within membranes within membranes. Through these membranes, the flow of many chemicals is controlled. For

Figure 8-12 *The doctor is holding up a bit of artificial skin used on burn victims.*

example, some membranes allow harmful chemi to pass out of a cell while keeping needed chemicals inside the cell. Your liver and kidneys contain membranes that do this kind of job. Such biological membranes are natural polymers.

More than 40 years ago, scientists began to wonder whether they could produce synthetic membranes that could imitate the functions of biological ones. In 1944, a **synthetic membrane** that worked like a natural biological membrane made possible the invention of the artificial kidney.

In the human body, two kidneys constantly filter waste materials from the blood. But what would happen if the kidneys stopped doing this vital job? At one time, such a situation would quickly have led to death. Now, however, there are two lifesaving options. A healthy kidney may be transplanted from another person. If that is not possible, an artificial kidney can periodically be used to purify the blood.

The artificial kidney is essentially a large filtering machine. A tube from the machine is inserted into an artery in the patient's arm. Blood flows from the patient into the machine, where it is filtered by a synthetic membrane. Then the purified blood is pumped back into the patient's system.

Since 1944, synthetic membranes have been greatly improved so that they now have a wide variety of uses. Some membranes are used as skin substitutes for people who have been badly burned. Other membranes are the ingredients of artificial spare parts used in the human body. Synthetic membranes are also used to filter pollutants from air and

Figure 8-13 *Polymers are used to build artificial body parts such as this artificial heart* (top), *and this artificial knee joint* (bottom). *What important properties must polymers used in artificial body parts have?*

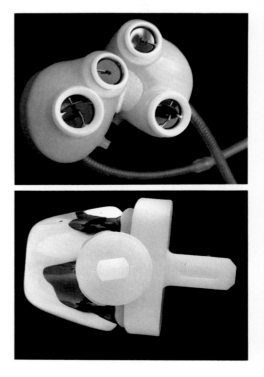

Figure 8-14 *No, the bird is not drowning. It is surrounded by a synthetic membrane that allows oxygen to pass from the water to the bird.*

water, to separate gases, and to turn salt water into fresh water.

A new development is the use of synthetic membranes for the controlled release of medication into the body. A membrane package may be patched onto the skin or implanted in the body to provide delayed release of certain drugs. Some scientists predict that in the future, implanted membranes will be used to filter poisons from the human body.

Antibiotics

The human body is under constant attack by invaders such as bacteria, fungi, and viruses. Fortunately, the body has a defense system. Part of this defense system is the immune system, which produces certain substances that destroy the invaders.

Every once in a while, the body's defense system needs some outside help to fight the invaders. High on the list of defense helpers are **antibiotics.** These chemical substances slow the growth of bacteria and other microorganisms, thus enabling the body to destroy the invaders more easily.

198

Antibiotics are produced by certain microorganisms. These natural antibiotics were the first types discovered and used. Penicillin is one of the most common natural antibiotics. But the use of more and more antibiotics revealed a sometimes serious drawback. Some antibiotics had unwanted side effects. In addition, certain bacteria became resistant to antibiotics. To reduce side effects and produce more effective antibiotics, scientists began making synthetic antibiotics. These synthetic antibiotics can be designed to fight specific disease organisms without producing unwanted side effects.

Vaccines

Antibiotics fight bacteria. But they are not effective against viruses—the smallest invaders. Viruses cause disease by directly attacking cells. While under attack, the body's defense system produces chemicals to fight the particular virus that is attacking. But that process can take days, and in that time a great deal of damage can be done. If, however, the body's defense system has prior warning, it can work faster. This is where **vaccines** come in. At present, most vaccines are made from disease-causing viruses or bacteria that have been treated so that they are unable to cause disease. When a vaccine is injected into a person's body, it causes the person's defense system to produce the substances necessary to fight disease. The body's defenses are now ready to go into action if the disease organisms attack.

A great deal of chemical research is now devoted to analyzing the different materials with which the body naturally defends itself. With knowledge of the composition and structure of these substances, scientists hope to synthesize them and use them to boost the body's natural defenders. In that event, there may no longer be a need for such "old-fashioned" defenders as antibiotics and vaccines.

Figure 8-15 *This scientist is adding bacteria to various tubes to help develop a new vaccine.*

SECTION REVIEW

1. Give two uses of synthetic membranes.
2. What chemicals were developed by scientists to aid the body's natural defense system?
3. What is a vaccine?

LABORATORY ACTIVITY

Comparing Natural and Synthetic Polymers

Purpose

In this activity, you will test natural and synthetic polymers for strength, absorbency, and resistance to chemicals.

Materials (*per group*)

12 Styrofoam cups	Marking pen
Liquid bleach	Scissors
Water	Paper towel
Oil	Rubber gloves
Medicine dropper	Metric ruler

Mild acid (lime juice, vinegar, or lemon juice)

3 samples of natural polymer cloth: wool, cotton, linen

3 samples of synthetic polymer cloth: polyester, nylon, acetate

Procedure

1. Record the color of each of the six different cloth samples.
2. Label six Styrofoam cups with the names of the six cloth samples. Also write the word "bleach" on each of the cups.
3. Using scissors, cut off a 2-cm-square piece from each of the cloth samples and put one in each cup. **CAUTION:** *Handle the scissors with care.*
4. Wearing rubber gloves, carefully pour a small amount of liquid bleach into each cup.
5. Using the other six cups, repeat steps 2 through 4. This time replace the bleach with a mild acid. Be sure to label the cups properly.
6. Set the cups aside for 24 hours. Meanwhile, proceed with steps 7 through 9.

7. Using the remaining samples of cloth, attempt to tear each one. Record your results.
8. Next, place a drop of water on each material. Note whether the water forms beads or is absorbed. Record whether the water is absorbed slowly, moderately, or rapidly.
9. Repeat step 8, but replace the water with a drop of oil.
10. After 24 hours, pour off the liquids in the cups into the sink. Dry the samples with a paper towel.
11. Record any color changes of the samples.

Observations and Conclusions

1. Which material held its color best in bleach?
2. Which materials were least resistant to chemical damage by bleach or mild acid?
3. Which material has the strongest fiber—that is, which is hardest to tear?
4. Which materials are water-repellent?
5. Did any of the materials repel the oil?

CHAPTER REVIEW

SUMMARY

8-1 Fuels from Petroleum

■ Oil found deep within the earth is called crude oil, or petroleum.

■ Petroleum is made up of different parts called fractions.

■ Petroleum is separated into its components through a process called fractional distillation.

■ During fractional distillation, petroleum is heated to a temperature at which most of its fractions vaporize. As the fractions rise up the fractionating tower, they cool and condense at different temperatures. The liquid fractions are drawn off and separated at different levels in the tower.

■ One fraction of petroleum, called asphalt, does not vaporize in a fractionating tower. It remains a liquid and is drawn off at the base.

8-2 Petrochemical Products

■ Substances derived from petroleum are called petrochemicals.

■ Most petrochemical products are polymers.

■ A polymer is a series of molecular units called monomers.

■ The type of monomer and the length and shape of the polymer chain determine the properties of the polymer.

■ The process of chemically combining monomers to make a polymer is called polymerization.

■ Natural polymers include cotton, silk, wool, natural rubber, cellulose, lignin, and protein.

■ Proteins are made of amino acids.

■ Synthetic polymers include rubber, plastics, and fabrics such as nylon, orlon, rayon, and dacron.

■ Polymers are usually strong, lightweight, heat resistant, flexible, and long lasting.

8-3 Health Chemistry

■ Polymers are used in the manufacture of synthetic membranes that can act like the membranes found in living things.

■ Antibiotics are chemical substances designed to help the human body fight disease. Today many antibiotics are synthetic.

■ Vaccines are made from bacteria or viruses that have been treated so that they cannot cause disease. In the future, synthetic vaccines may help reduce unwanted side effects.

VOCABULARY

Define each term in a complete sentence.

amino acid	**fraction**	**petroleum**	**synthetic membrane**
antibiotic	**fractionating tower**	**polymer**	**vaccine**
distillation	**monomer**	**polymerization**	

CONTENT REVIEW: MULTIPLE CHOICE

Choose the letter of the answer that best completes each statement.

1. Crude oil is
   a. a single substance.   b. gasoline.   c. asphalt.   d. a mixture.
2. The physical property used to separate petroleum into its parts is
   a. melting point.   b. boiling point.   c. density.   d. solubility.

3. The highest temperature in a fractionating tower is about 385°C because that is
   a. below the boiling point of most petroleum fractions.
   b. above the boiling point of most petroleum fractions.
   c. equal to the boiling point of most petroleum fractions.
   d. below the melting point of most petroleum fractions.
4. Of the following, the least likely to vaporize in a fractionating tower is
   a. kerosene.   b. gasoline.   c. asphalt.   d. heating fuel.
5. The process of distillation involves
   a. vaporization and condensation.   b. freezing and melting.
   c. vaporization and melting.   d. freezing and condensation.
6. A polymer is made up of a series of
   a. atoms.   b. monomers.   c. fuels.   d. synthetic molecules.
7. An example of a natural polymer is
   a. wool.   b. plastic.   c. crude oil.   d. copper.
8. An example of a synthetic polymer is
   a. natural rubber.   b. protein.   c. rayon.   d. cotton.
9. The process of chemically bonding monomers to form polymers is called
   a. distillation.   b. fractionation.   c. polymerization.   d. refining.
10. Chemical substances that slow the growth of bacteria and other microorganisms are called
   a. adhesives.   b. antibiotics.   c. monomers.   d. synthetic membranes.

CONTENT REVIEW: COMPLETION

Fill in the word or words that best complete each statement.

1. Oil that gushes from deep within the earth is called crude oil, or _____.
2. The process of _____ involves heating a liquid until it vaporizes and then allowing it to cool until it condenses.
3. To separate crude oil into its useful components, a _____ tower is used at a _____.
4. Each fraction of petroleum has a different _____.
5. The natural polymers _____ and _____ are important components of wood.
6. A polymer consists of many _____ bonded together.
7. _____ are products made from petroleum.
8. _____ are the monomers from which proteins are made.
9. _____ is the process in which monomers are chemically bonded to form polymers.
10. _____, which can filter chemicals from various liquids and gases, can now be produced by scientists.

CONTENT REVIEW: TRUE OR FALSE

Determine whether each statement is true or false. If it is true, write "true." If it is false, change the underlined word or words to make the statement true.

1. Petroleum taken directly from the earth is called <u>asphalt</u>.
2. Petroleum can be separated into its different parts, or <u>fractions</u>.

3. The process of separating petroleum into its components is called boiling.
4. Heating a liquid to its boiling point turns it into a vapor.
5. When a vapor evaporates, it changes back to a liquid.
6. A monomer is a long chain of polymers.
7. Silk is an example of natural polymer.
8. Polymerization involves the chemical bonding of monomers into polymers.
9. Plastics are examples of natural polymers.
10. Vaccines are made from disease-causing viruses or bacteria that have been treated to make them harmless.

CONCEPT REVIEW: SKILL BUILDING

Use the skills you have developed in this chapter to complete each activity.

1. **Relating facts** Describe some of the uses of synthetic polymers in your life. Then describe what changes you would have to make in your life style if these polymers were not available.
2. **Applying concepts** Select five objects in your home that are made from naturally occurring substances such as wool or silver. For each object, predict whether a synthetic polymer may be developed to replace the naturally occurring substance. Describe the characteristics each synthetic polymer should have, to make it more suitable than the naturally occurring substance.
3. **Relating cause and effect** Many people use and enjoy the products derived from petroleum. However, some of the chemical processes used to make these products, as well as the burning of petroleum fuels, add to the pollution of the air, land, and water in the United States. So people often must decide whether manufacturing a certain product is worth the damage done to the environment. In other words, people often must make a trade-off between products they use and the effects on the environment. What is your feeling on this issue?
4. **Applying technology** Imagine that you are an engineer whose task is to design a car that is fuel efficient yet meets all of the current standards for safety and durability. What kinds of materials would you consider using? What properties must the materials used in the engine have? How about the materials used in safety belts and seat cushions?
5. **Making graphs** The yield in percent of products that are derived from petroleum is shown in Figure 8-3 on page 189. On a sheet of graph paper, plot the type of product on one axis and the percentage yield of that product on the other axis. What conclusions can you draw from your finished graph?

CONCEPT REVIEW: ESSAY

Discuss each of the following in a brief paragraph.

1. Many people believe the United States has undergone a chemical revolution in the past 30 years. Having read this chapter, explain what the term "chemical revolution" means to you.
2. Describe some of the ways polymer chemistry is used in medicine.

9 Space Technology

CHAPTER SECTIONS

9-1 Rocketry

9-2 Artificial Satellites

9-3 People in Space

9-4 Deep Space Probes

9-5 Space Technology Spinoffs

CHAPTER OBJECTIVES

After completing this chapter, you will be able to:

9-1 Describe the principle by which a reaction engine works.

9-1 Discuss Newton's law of gravitation.

9-1 Define escape velocity.

9-2 Describe the functions of communications satellites, weather satellites, navigational satellites, and scientific satellites.

9-2 Define geosynchronous orbit.

9-3 Discuss the Apollo project.

9-3 Discuss the uses and importance of an orbiting space station.

9-4 Compare the findings of space probes such as *Pioneer*, *Mariner*, *Viking*, and *Voyager*.

9-5 Describe some of the uses of space technology on Earth.

It was April 1985. Onboard the Space Shuttle, the astronauts prepared to launch the *Leasat 3* communications satellite. Despite hopes for a successful mission, things did not go as planned. Although the satellite was released from the shuttle, its engines did not fire up. The satellite was unable to rocket into its intended orbit some 35,000 kilometers above the earth.

The failure to launch *Leasat 3* was a big disappointment to scientists at the National Aeronautics and Space Administration, or NASA. But few of the scientists were willing to give up the project. So in September 1985, when the Space Shuttle *Discovery* was launched, two scientists, James D. van Hoften and William F. Fisher, attempted a daring rescue of the faulty satellite. First they retrieved the satellite with the shuttle's robot arm. Once the satellite was positioned in the shuttle's cargo bay, they began the repair job.

To fix the satellite, van Hoften and Fisher had to replace a defective timing device. The astronauts completed the repair in two days. All that remained to be done was the release of the 5 meter by 5 meter cylindrical satellite. "I'm going to give it a heck of a push," reported van Hoften to mission control at the Johnson Space Center in Houston, Texas. The push worked! The satellite was clear of the shuttle. The crew of the *Discovery* had just completed "the most successful salvage mission in the history of the space program."

The rescue of *Leasat 3* is a good example of how technology is used by modern scientists. In this chapter, you will read more about space technology successes, as well as how technology is also used to study the earth.

Astronaut William F. Fisher repairs the Leasat 3 *communications satellite.*

Figure 9-1 *In a reaction engine such as this rocket, exploding gases forced out of the tail cause an equal and opposite reaction. The rocket shoots forward. The force of this forward movement is called thrust.*

9-1 Rocketry

Blow up a balloon and pinch the nozzle so that no air can escape. Do not tie it. Hold the balloon at arm's length; then let it go. What happens?

When the balloon nozzle is released, air shoots out of it. At the same time, the balloon moves in a direction opposite to the movement of the escaping air. The released balloon is behaving like a rocket.

This example illustrates the idea of a **reaction engine.** Its movement is based on Sir Isaac Newton's third law of motion, which states that every action produces an equal and opposite reaction. The escaping rush of air out of the balloon nozzle causes the balloon to shoot off in the opposite direction. A reaction engine acts in much the same way. **In a reaction engine, such as a rocket, the rearward blast of exploding gases causes the rocket to shoot forward.** The force of this forward movement is called **thrust.**

Dawn of Rocketry

Long before Newton's time, the ancient Chinese, Greeks, and Romans made use of reaction engines. The Greeks and the Romans used steam to move toys. One toy consisted of a kettle on wheels with a basket holding glowing embers beneath it. Heat from the embers caused water in the kettle to boil. As the water boiled, steam hissed out of a horizontal nozzle on the kettle. In reaction to the escape of steam in one direction, the wheeled kettle rolled off in the opposite direction.

The first useful reaction engines were rockets developed by the Chinese around the year 1000. Their first known use was as weapons of war. These early Chinese rockets were long cylinders, probably sections of hollow bamboo, filled with gunpowder. One end of the cylinder was sealed, usually by a metal cap. The other end was open and had a fuse running through it into the gunpowder.

When the gunpowder was ignited, burning gases shot out the open end of the cylinder. In reaction to this movement of gases, the cylinder shot off in the opposite direction.

By the end of the nineteenth century, some scientists began dreaming of using rockets to explore space. But would it be possible to build a rocket large and powerful enough to travel out of the earth's atmosphere? Late in the nineteenth century, a number of scientists studied this question. And at least one of them, a Russian named Konstantin E. Tsiolkovsky (tsyul-KUV-skee), considered it a definite possibility.

As a teenager, Tsiolkovsky had experimented with reaction engines, including types used by ancient Greeks and Romans. Using his lunch money to pay for materials, he had built a carriage powered by a reaction engine. But his experiment did not work. The engine could not develop enough thrust to move the carriage.

From his failure, Tsiolkovsky actually learned a lot about reaction engines. He started thinking about using such engines for space travel. Drawing on the work of Newton and other scientists and mathematicians, Tsiolkovsky worked out mathematical formulas for space flight. He even dreamed of creating human colonies in space. But before such colonies could be built, Tsiolkovsky knew that scientists would have to solve the enormous problems involved in building rockets powerful enough to escape the earth's attractive force.

Figure 9-2 *The action of the rocket's thrusters causes an opposite reaction and the rocket goes forward* (top). *Similar types of thrusters in this manned maneuvering unit (MMU) allow an astronaut to move in any direction in space* (bottom).

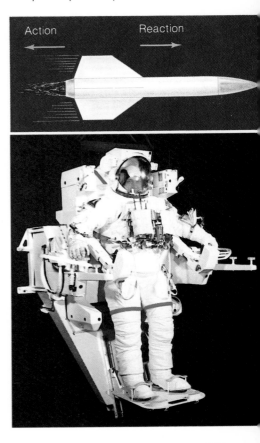

1. Tie each end of a piece of string to a separate rubber band.

2. Tie one end of a second piece of string to a third rubber band.

3. Now tie the free end of the second string to either one of the other rubber bands. You should have two rubber bands attached to a middle rubber band.

4. Pull the two end rubber bands apart and carefully observe the lengths of all three rubber bands.

Explain your observations using Newton's third law of motion.

A key force in all considerations of rocketry and space flight is **gravity.** Gravity is the force of attraction between all objects in the universe. To understand this force, you must first understand another of Newton's ideas.

Gravity—The Universal Attraction

It is often said that Newton discovered gravity when an apple fell from a tree and hit him on the head. But that is just a story. Long before Newton was born, people were aware of the earth's gravity, or the earth's pull on objects above its center. What Newton did was explain how gravity affected all things in the universe.

According to Newton's law of gravitation, all objects exert an attractive force on each other. That is, all objects pull on each other. The earth pulls on the moon, and the moon pulls on the earth. The sun pulls on both the earth and the moon. And though it may seem hard to believe, both the earth and the moon pull on the sun.

Why, then, does the moon not come crashing into the earth? What keeps the earth and moon from falling into the sun? The moon does not crash into the earth because the moon is in constant motion. In fact, without the earth's gravitational pull, the moon would speed off through space and be lost forever.

Figure 9-3 *These two Space Shuttle astronauts are actually orbiting the earth. While in orbit, their outward motion cancels the inward pull of gravity, and the astronauts are weightless.*

But fortunately, the moon's outward thrust is balanced by the earth's inward pull. A balance of forces exists between them.

The moon travels around the earth at an average velocity of 3680 kilometers per hour. If that velocity were much higher, the moon would escape from the earth's gravitational pull. If it were much lower, the moon would tumble out of orbit into the earth.

The same conditions apply to the earth and the other eight planets in our solar system in relation to the sun. Gravitation is the force that holds the solar system together. It is also the force that works against the escape of a space vehicle from the earth.

Escape Velocity

As you just learned, it is possible for an object moving at the right velocity to escape the earth's gravity. What determines the velocity that a vehicle must achieve in order to overcome the gravitational pull of the earth or other object?

The **escape velocity,** as scientists call it, depends on the mass of the planet and the distance of the escaping vehicle from the planet's center. The escape velocity from Earth is 11.2 kilometers per second, or 40,320 kilometers per hour. From the moon, it is just 2.3 kilometers per second. From mighty Jupiter, the escape velocity is 63.4 kilometers per second. And from the sun, it is 616 kilometers per second. Can you relate these differences in escape velocity to the mass of each object?

The first step into space involves escape from the earth. Tsiolkovsky predicted that through the use of a huge reaction engine, a vehicle would someday leave the earth's gravitational field. But he also concluded that a rocket powered by gunpowder or some other solid fuel would not be able to accomplish this feat. Why not?

Solid fuel burns rapidly and explosively. Its pushing force is used up within seconds. Although it provides an enormous early thrust, it cannot maintain that push. As the rocket soars upward, the pull of the earth's gravity would tend to slow its climb and eventually bring it back to the earth.

Consider this situation. You are trying to push a shopping cart up a steep hill. So you stand at the

ESCAPE VELOCITIES

Object	Escape Velocity (km/sec)
Mercury	4.2
Venus	10.3
Earth	11.2
Moon	2.3
Mars	5.0
Jupiter	63.4
Saturn	39.4
Uranus	21.5
Neptune	24.2
Pluto	0.3*
Sun	616
Sirius B	3400*
Neutron star	200,000*

*Estimated

Figure 9-4 *This table shows the escape velocities for the nine planets in our solar system, the sun, and several other stars. Why is the escape velocity of Pluto so much lower than that of the other planets?*

Figure 9-5 *When the force of Earth's gravity (green arrow) is more powerful than the rocket's forward force (red arrow), the rocket soon falls to Earth. If the two forces are equal, the rocket remains in orbit. And if the pull of Earth's gravity is the weaker force, then the rocket will shoot off into space.*

bottom of the hill and with all your might you give the cart an upward push. The cart rolls upward. At first its movement is fast. But then it rapidly slows and finally comes rolling back. Even if you get some friends to help you, it is unlikely that a single push from the bottom of the hill can get the cart going fast enough to go up and over the steep hill. But suppose you run most of the way up with the cart, pushing all the time. Isn't the cart likely to roll over the top when you let go?

A solid fuel gives a rocket an enormous first push. But it does not keep that push going as the rocket climbs through the atmosphere. In order for a rocket to build up enough speed to overcome the earth's downward pull, the rocket must have a fuel that continues to burn and provide thrust through the lower levels of the atmosphere.

Although Tsiolkovsky proposed this idea, he never built such a rocket. But in the 1920s, the American scientist Dr. Robert H. Goddard did. In 1926, Goddard launched a small rocket that combined gasoline with liquid oxygen and burned this mixture. The rocket did not go very far or very fast, but it did prove the point that liquid fuels could be used to provide continuous thrust.

Goddard built bigger and bigger rockets. And he drew up plans for **multistage rockets.** As each stage in such a rocket used up its fuel, the empty fuel container would drop off. Then the next stage would

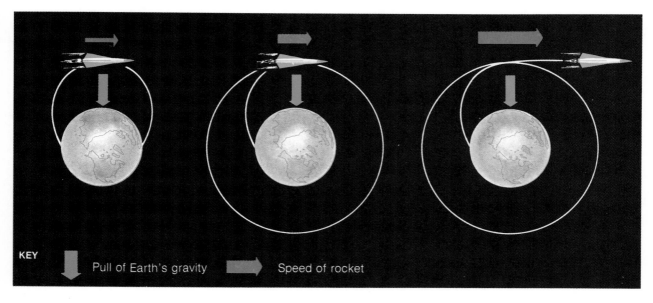

KEY — Pull of Earth's gravity — Speed of rocket

ignite, and its empty fuel container would drop off. In this way, a vehicle could be pushed through the atmosphere and out of the earth's grip. Today's rockets work much the same as Goddard's early rocket. Now, however, the fuel is liquid hydrogen and liquid oxygen.

SECTION REVIEW

1. What is a reaction engine?
2. What is gravity?
3. What is meant by escape velocity?

9-2 Artificial Satellites

The first dramatic step into space was taken on October 4, 1957. On that historic day, a Soviet rocket boosted *Sputnik 1,* the world's first artificial satellite, into orbit. The space age had begun!

Since that day, well over a thousand satellites have been placed in Earth orbit. The world is now ringed with them. And their number increases each year. Like the moon, which is the earth's natural satellite, artificial satellites travel just fast enough so that they neither escape the earth's gravity nor immediately fall back down.

Figure 9-7 *The Navstar satellite helps ships and planes navigate.*

Communications satellites, weather satellites, navigational satellites, and scientific satellites are among the artificial satellites that orbit the earth today. Communications satellites are used to beam television, radio, teletype, and telephone signals from point to point around the globe. Scientific satellites are of two basic types: those used to study the earth and those used to probe the mysteries of space.

From their location in space, instruments on weather satellites track and measure cloud formations, wind patterns, and atmospheric temperature and pressure. This information is beamed down to the earth stations and used to prepare weather forecasts.

Satellites are also used to give navigational assistance to earthbound travelers. For instance, a number of Navstar satellites in orbit about 20,000 kilometers above the earth send precise, continuous navigation signals to ships and planes all over the world.

Communications Satellites

A communications satellite is an electronic relay in the sky. It receives signals from an earth station. It changes the frequency of the signals, amplifies them, and retransmits them to another earth station. Such a satellite can link a single broadcast station to many receiving stations.

Figure 9-8 *The satellite* Leasat 2 *beams telephone and radio messages from one place on Earth to another. What type of satellite is* Leasat 2?

A communications satellite is always placed in **geosynchronous orbit.** A geosynchronous orbit is one in which the satellite moves at a speed that exactly matches the earth's rate of rotation. As a result, the satellite stays in one place above a certain point on the earth's surface. Three such satellites, placed equal distances apart at about 35,900 kilometers above the earth's surface, can relay signals to any place on the earth.

A new development in satellite communications is the Direct Broadcast Satellite, or DBS, service. Like other communications satellites, a DBS receives signals from a ground transmitting station. It processes these signals and rebroadcasts them. But it uses about 40 times as much power as a regular communications satellite to rebroadcast the signals. And instead of transmitting the signals to ground stations, it broadcasts them to a large area where they can be picked up directly by TV sets in people's homes. The DBS service will deliver entertainment and information to remote parts of the world.

Scientific Satellites

All astronomical observatories on the earth face a problem. Views of the sun, stars, planets, comets, galaxies, and other objects in space are partially blocked, changed, and distorted by the earth's magnetic field and by the earth's atmosphere. Air and

Figure 9-9 *This communications satellite was the first satellite released by the Space Shuttle. It is in geosynchronous orbit and remains over the same spot on Earth.*

Figure 9-10 *A scientific satellite took this infrared photograph of Galveston Bay on the Gulf Coast of Texas. The satellite is charting the flow of sediments, located in the pale-blue areas, which stream off the land and are carried away by the Gulf Stream current.*

light pollution have also added to the problem. As a result, much of the universe has been invisible to observers until recently.

Long before *Sputnik*, scientists looked forward to the day when they could observe the earth and parts of the universe from an orbiting satellite. Perhaps then, they believed, they would be able to solve many old mysteries and make new discoveries about the universe. And they were right!

In 1958, the first United States satellite, *Explorer 1*, discovered a huge radiation belt around the earth. Since that time, other scientific satellites have added greatly to knowledge of the universe. One satellite in particular, the heat-sensing Infrared Astronomy Satellite, or IRAS, has solved many mysteries of the universe.

IRAS was launched into orbit on January 25, 1983. One week later, the cover of the satellite's telescope was automatically released. And IRAS began detecting objects in space never before seen: objects invisible to ordinary telescopes.

As the infrared telescope scanned the universe, it detected heat from newborn stars and from stars hidden from view by swirling clouds of stardust. IRAS also discovered evidence of planetary systems forming around some distant stars. Five new comets and a ring of dust around the Andromeda galaxy, a family of stars much like the Milky Way galaxy, were

Figure 9-11 *The Space Telescope will detect objects from deep in space. The image of the object will then be transmitted to an orbiting satellite, and then back to Earth. On Earth, computers will recreate the image, giving scientists a clearer look into space than they can get from Earth's surface.*

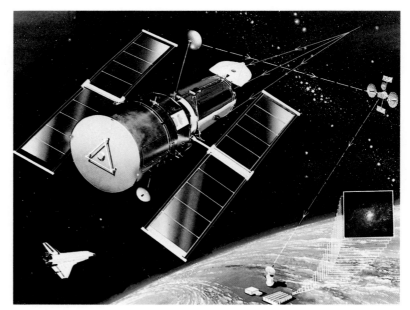

also discovered by IRAS. Some evidence that galaxies, including the Milky Way, have massive black holes at their cores was provided by the IRAS probe into space. A black hole is a collapsed star that is so dense that nothing, neither light nor any other kind of radiation, can escape its grip.

Although IRAS's operating lifetime was limited to 340 days, it provided millions of items of new information about the universe during this time. In the future, most astronomers probably will not be content to remain on Earth while telescopes in space probe the remote corners of the universe. Orbiting observatories where astronomers live and work will soon be commonplace.

Figure 9-12 *More than 250,000 infrared spots detected by IRAS are plotted in this projection of the sky. The Milky Way, our galaxy, is the bright band running through the center of the photograph. In this IRAS shot, the warmest areas appear blue and the coolest are red.*

SECTION REVIEW

1. What are some of the uses of artificial satellites?
2. Why is it important that communications satellites be put into geosynchronous orbit?

9-3 People in Space

"Attention, Earth, here is the cosmonaut." Those words were spoken by Soviet cosmonaut Yuri Gagarin from the spaceship *Vostok* on April 12, 1961. His voyage marked the start of humankind's venture into space. Gagarin orbited the earth once at a height ranging from 181 to 327 kilometers. The total mission lasted one hour and 48 minutes.

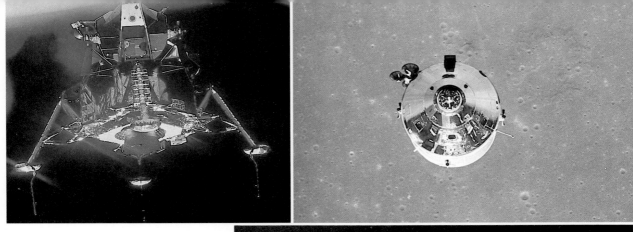

Figure 9-13 *Conquering the moon was a dramatic and technologically complex mission. Here you see the Lunar Lander approaching the moon* (top left). *This shot of the Apollo Command Module, which remained in orbit during the mission, was taken by the crew on the Lunar Lander soon after it separated from the Command Module* (top right). *Hours later, astronauts walked on the moon* (right). *No mission is complete, of course, until the final splashdown, when the astronauts return safely from space* (bottom).

This first earth-orbit mission proved that a person could withstand the shock of being rocketed through the atmosphere. It also demonstrated that a person could function in the weightless condition of spaceflight. And it helped Americans set their sights on a distant target in space—the moon!

To the Moon and Back

In 1961, the United States National Aeronautics and Space Administration, or NASA, started working on the Apollo Project, an effort to put a person on the moon within ten years. Between October 1968 and May 1969, the Apollo Project scored some spectacular achievements. Four Apollo spacecraft escaped the earth's gravity and traveled to the moon, went into orbit around the moon, and safely returned to Earth. But the biggest achievement of all occurred on July 20, 1969. On that day, humans took their first steps on the moon.

While the "parent" *Apollo 11* spacecraft *Columbia* circled the moon, its lunar landing module *Eagle* eased astronauts Neil Armstrong and Edwin Aldrin onto the surface of the moon. "That's one small step for a man, one giant leap for mankind," Armstrong said as he stepped from the lunar module onto the moon's dusty surface.

The two astronauts took close-up photos of the moon's surface and collected samples of lunar rocks and dust. Scientists' understanding of the earth's large natural satellite was greatly increased as a result of this moon mission. In addition, the voyage proved that people could reach new frontiers.

The Apollo moon-landing program ended in 1973. During the life of the program, a total of 12 astronauts explored the moon's surface and conducted many experiments. Much more was learned about the earth's neighbor as a result of this program. And scientists began to develop the technology that would enable people to live in space.

Labs in Orbit

Other ventures into space followed the spectacular moon-landing program. Skylab, a workshop in orbit, was launched in 1973. Visiting crews aboard Skylab made detailed studies of the sun, conducted several health-related experiments, and learned to work in space.

Then, on April 14, 1981, a new kind of space vehicle soared into the sky. It was called *Columbia,* and

Activity

Space Technology Facilities

Space technology facilities are located throughout the world. Some of those run by the United States are listed below. Choose one that sounds interesting to you. Using books and reference materials in the library, find out more about the facility you have chosen. Be sure to include information on where the facility is located, what technological development occurred there, and what plans are being made for future research.

Jet Propulsion Laboratory (JPL)

Goddard Space Flight Center

Ames Research Center

Shuttle Infrared Telescope Facility (SIRTF)

Figure 9-14 *The various phases of a Space Shuttle mission*

it was the first Space Shuttle. A Space Shuttle is an airplanelike vehicle that must be boosted into space by rockets but that can land on earth like a gliding airplane.

Unlike all previous space vehicles, the Space Shuttle can be used over and over again for a variety of missions. On several of its missions, the Space Shuttle has placed satellites in orbit. Space Shuttles have served as high-flying science laboratories. Future Space Shuttles will be used to transport supplies and relief crews to orbiting space stations.

Space Colonies

"We have put men on the moon. Can people live in space? Can permanent communities away from the earth be built and inhabited?" These questions were asked by NASA officials, who later provided a dramatic one-word answer: yes!

Figure 9-15 *The Space Shuttle is carried into space by rockets. How does it return to Earth?*

Career: *Astronaut*

HELP WANTED: ASTRONAUT Requires bachelor's degree in engineering, biological or physical science, or mathematics. Must have at least 1000 hours as pilot in command of a high-performance jet. Must pass strict physical examination. Apply to NASA.

On July 20, 1969, Neil Armstrong stepped onto the moon and sent a message back to the people on earth, "The surface is fine and powdery. . . . I can see the footprints of my boots and the treads in the fine, sandy particles."

Neil Armstrong is an **astronaut.** He was the first person to set foot on the moon. Armstrong, like all the astronauts, worked long and hard to achieve his place in the space program. Astronauts must endure difficult training periods with complex equipment. For example, they must practice moving about in a spaceship environment. They do this by performing daily activities during periods of weightlessness. They become used to working in pressurized spacesuits, and they practice approaching and landing in a special aircraft. Practice sessions are designed to be as close as possible to the real flight, so that the astronauts will be confident and successful in the performance of their duties. It is also the astronauts' responsibility to keep their flying skills sharp and their physical condition excellent.

Men and women who keep physically fit, who enjoy flying, and who have superior academic qualifications in the sciences can make effective astronauts. If becoming an astronaut interests you, write to the Johnson Space Center, National Aeronautics and Space Administration, Houston, TX 77058.

Figure 9-16 *Astronauts on board the Space Shuttle practice techniques that will be used to build large space stations* (right). *Here you see an artist's idea of how a space station may look in the future* (left).

It has already been established that people can go into space, live there for a time, and return safely to Earth. NASA scientists point to the success of the Space Shuttle program as evidence that a permanent orbital space station can be built and supported at this time.

Such a space station could perform the functions of many different satellites. These functions include communications, navigation, weather forecasting, Earth Resource surveys, military observation, and astronomical studies. In time, a permanent orbital station could be expanded to permit the manufacture of certain materials in space and to serve as a base for the exploration of Mars, Venus, and other planets.

Scientists believe that the first orbital space stations may well lead to the building of large self-sufficient settlements in space. Fueled by almost unlimited solar energy and supplied with raw materials from meteoroids, asteroids, moons, and planets, such a settlement could serve as a supply source for the "old world," Planet Earth. It could also serve as a jumping-off point for exploration of new worlds beyond the solar system.

SECTION REVIEW

1. What was the purpose of the Apollo Project?
2. What is a space station?

Figure 9-17 *This photograph of Mars, taken by a Viking lander, shows a red rocky surface and a salmon-colored sky. The sky color is due to dust particles in the thin Martian atmosphere.*

Figure 9-18 *Voyager took photographs of Jupiter and its many moons. Here you see a composite photograph showing the planet Jupiter and its four largest moons.*

9-4 Deep Space Probes

On Monday, June 13, 1983, the space probe *Pioneer 10* became the first human-made object to travel out of the solar system. *Pioneer 10* was launched on March 3, 1972. Although it was intended, along with *Pioneer 11,* to probe the outer planets of the solar system, no one expected it to go beyond the solar system toward the stars.

Pioneers, Vanguards, Explorers, Mariners, Rangers, Vikings, Surveyors, and Voyagers have been the workhorses of the United States' effort to explore the solar system. And their record has been impressive. The first successful probe of Venus was made by *Mariner 2* in 1962. The spacecraft approached to within 35,000 kilometers of the cloud-wrapped planet. Instruments on board *Mariner 2* determined that the surface temperature on Venus is extremely high. They also discovered that, unlike Earth, Venus does not have a magnetic field.

The first successful probe of Mars was made by *Mariner 4* in 1965. Going to within 10,000 kilometers of the red planet, the spacecraft sent back 21 pictures and other data. Two later probes, *Mariner 7* in 1969 and *Mariner 9* in 1971, sent back thousands of pictures of the Martian surface. They also provided the first detailed pictures of Mars's two moons, Phobos and Deimos.

Achievements of *Mariners 7* and *9* paved the way for the successful landings of *Vikings 1* and *2* on Mars in 1975. In addition to taking close-up photos of Martian soil and rocks, experiments aboard the Viking craft tested Martian soil for signs of life. No certain evidence of Martian life was found. But the possibility of it was not ruled out.

Mariner 10 was the first and only spacecraft to fly by Mercury, innermost planet of the solar system. During three passes in 1974, *Mariner 10* mapped volcanoes, valleys, mountains, and plains on the tiny planet.

Outward bound, *Pioneer 10* took a look at the giant planet Jupiter in December 1973 and sent back more than 300 pictures. It also provided data on Jupiter's stormy atmosphere and many moons. These findings were confirmed by the pictures sent back by *Pioneer 11* a short time later.

Six years later, two larger spacecraft, *Voyager 2* and *Voyager 1*, flew by Jupiter and sent back data that revealed surprises about the giant planet. Faint rings of particles and many new moons exist around the planet. Both *Pioneers* and both *Voyagers* examined Saturn and its mysterious rings. *Voyager* photos showed that what were considered a few broad rings are actually thousands of thin ringlets. In 1986, *Voyager 2* passed by Uranus and sent new information about that distant planet back to Earth.

Pioneer 10 is now beyond the solar system. *Pioneer 11* follows, and by the end of the century the *Voyagers* will follow into outer space. In case it should ever be found by people from another world, *Pioneer 10* contains a plaque with a message from the people of Earth. *Pioneer 10* will never return. Neither will *Pioneer 11* or the *Voyagers*. But in the not too distant future it is possible that spacecraft will be sent from Earth to probe beyond the edge of the solar system—and return!

Several scientists are convinced that a spaceship can be designed to make a round trip to the nearest stars. The journey would take many hundreds of years. Such a ship might sail through space powered

Figure 9-19 *Here you see an artist's idea of how* Voyager *appeared as it passed by Saturn and made its way toward the very edge of our solar system and beyond!*

by energy from the sun. Enormous metal-coated plastic sails would unfold in space and "catch" the solar wind, particles moving outward from the sun. This solar wind would move a ship through space at great speed. A model solar sail is scheduled to be boosted into space aboard the French rocket *Ariane* in the late 1980s. If the test is successful, it may lead to great ships sailing to the stars and back.

SECTION REVIEW

1. What mission was the first to probe Venus? Mars?
2. What type of information do the space probes provide to scientists?

9-5 Space Technology Spinoffs

Although the main purpose of the United States space program has been directed outside the planet Earth, many of its achievements have found dramatic uses on Earth. For example, in 1967 NASA scientists and engineers were hard at work hunting for a fabric with which to weave spacesuits. The fabric would have to be strong enough to withstand the extreme temperature variations found in space yet easy to weave.

It was not long before the fabric was invented. Astronauts walking in space and on the moon found themselves dressed properly—and safely—for events in space. Soon after, the same fabric was used to roof a department store in California, an aquatic entertainment center in Florida, and a football stadium in Michigan.

Anyone who runs a long distance, such as a marathon, encounters a risk of overheating. So too does an astronaut exposed to sunlight in space. To reduce the possibility of overheating, space scientists developed various devices to be put into spacesuits. One of these devices is a gel packet that can draw heat away from various parts of the body, thus reducing overheating. These gel packets are now used by marathoners to absorb excess heat from their forehead, neck, and wrists.

Figure 9-20 *The fabric that makes up the roof of the Silverdome in Pontiac, Michigan, was originally developed for astronauts' spacesuits.*

Figure 9-21 *In Alexandria, Virginia, firefighters now use special gear that employs lightweight fire-resistant materials. This gear uses materials first developed for astronaut spacesuits.*

One of the questions that puzzled scientists before men and women were sent soaring into space was how a human being would react to this new environment. To find the answers, scientists designed a series of automatic monitoring devices that would relay to Earth an astronaut's blood pressure, heart rate, and other vital statistics. Such devices are now used by paramedics when they answer emergency calls. These devices provide rapid and accurate information about a patient's condition. Such information can be a matter of life or death.

The message seems clear. A scientific advance—even one intended for use far beyond the frontiers of the earth—may have very practical applications for the billions of people who will rise no farther from the earth's surface than an energetic leap can take them.

SECTION REVIEW

1. Name one practical application of the fabric used for spacesuits.
2. What device has been designed to keep astronauts from overheating when exposed to sunlight in space?
3. How do scientists keep track of an astronaut's vital signs during spaceflight?

LABORATORY ACTIVITY

Making a Model of Hero's Engine

Purpose

In this activity, you will construct a model of a steam-driven reaction engine invented by the ancient Greek scientist Hero of Alexandria. You will explain how the device operates by referring to Newton's third law of motion.

Materials *(per group)*

Hammer	Candle
Nail	Matches
Ring stand with clamp	Thin string or thread
	Safety goggles

Small rectangular metal can with press-on lid, such as a spice can

Procedure

1. Place an unlit candle on the base of a ring stand.
2. Attach the ends of a length of thread to the clamp on the ring stand so that a loop of it hangs about 12 cm above the candle.
3. Use the hammer and nail to punch a hole in the front of the can, near the upper left corner. Turn the can over to punch a hole in the other side of the can, again near the upper left corner. The two holes should be near the top of the can.
4. Pour about 15 mL of water into the can. Hang the can from the bottom of the loop of thread by slipping the loop under the lid and closing the lid. Make sure that the lid fits tightly and that the can hangs straight, with its bottom only a few centimeters above the wick.
5. Light the candle, and record your observations for the next 5 or 10 minutes. **CAUTION:** *Be very careful in doing this, and avoid touching the can, which will become very hot. Keep your face away from the setup. Wear your safety goggles.*

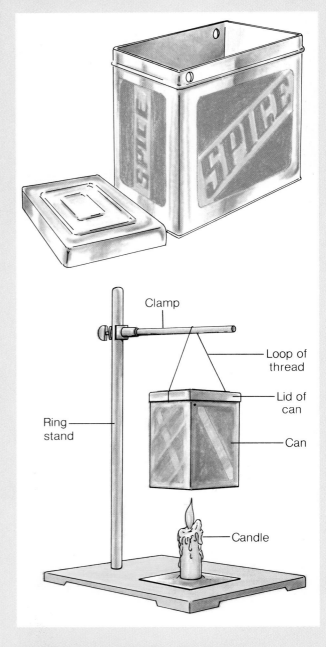

Observations and Conclusions

1. What happened to the water inside the can?
2. Account for the motion of the can, referring to Newton's third law of motion.

CHAPTER REVIEW

SUMMARY

9-1 Rocketry

- A reaction engine operates on the principle that for every action there is an equal and opposite reaction. This is Newton's third law of motion.

- The first useful reaction engines were developed by the Chinese around the year 1000 A.D.

- The rearward rush of exploding gases from a rocket creates a forward force of motion called thrust.

- Gravity is the force of attraction between all objects in the universe.

- Escape velocity is the velocity an object must attain in order to overcome the gravitational pull of another object.

- The escape velocity from an object like a planet or a star is related to the object's mass. The greater the mass, the greater the escape velocity.

- Multistage rockets burning liquid fuel gain enough continuous thrust to escape the earth's gravity.

9-2 Artificial Satellites

- Since 1957, artificial satellites have been sent into orbit for a variety of purposes.

- Communications satellites are used to beam television programs, radio messages, and other types of messages from one point on Earth to another point on Earth.

- Navigation satellites are used to help ships and planes navigate on Earth.

- Weather satellites track conditions on Earth to help forecasters better predict the weather.

- Scientific satellites enable scientists to better observe objects in space, as well as to help gather scientific data about Earth.

- A satellite in geosynchronous orbit moves at the same speed at which the earth rotates.

9-3 People in Space

- In 1969, astronauts Neil Armstrong and Edwin Aldrin made history by being the first people to walk on the moon.

- The Space Shuttle is a reusable spacecraft that is carried into space by rockets and returns to Earth like a glider.

- The National Aeronautics and Space Administration, or NASA, is currently working on launching permanent space stations that will someday house communities of people.

9-4 Deep Space Probes

- Space probes have explored Venus, Mars, Mercury, Jupiter, Saturn, and Uranus.

9-5 Space Technology Spinoffs

- Technology designed to aid the space program has several practical applications.

VOCABULARY

Define the following terms in a complete sentence.

escape velocity   gravity   reaction engine

geosynchronous orbit   multistage rocket   thrust

CONTENT REVIEW: MULTIPLE CHOICE

Choose the letter of the answer that best completes each statement.

1. The force of attraction between objects is
   a. gravity.   b. thrust.   c. escape velocity.   d. weightlessness.

2. Which scientist discovered gravity?
   a. Konstantin E. Tsiolkovsky   b. Dr. Robert H. Goddard
   c. Yuri Gagarin   d. Sir Isaac Newton

3. On which object would it be easiest to escape the pull of gravity?
   a. Earth   b. moon   c. Jupiter   d. sun

4. A communications satellite used to transmit to remote areas on Earth is
   a. *Sputnik 1.*   b. *Apollo 11.*   c. Direct Broadcast Satellite.   d. *Explorer 1.*

5. Which is a scientific satellite used to detect infrared radiation?
   a. *Sputnik 1*   b. *Explorer 1*   c. IRAS   d. all of these

6. Which United States program was the first to put a person on the moon?
   a. spaceship *Vostok*   b. Apollo-Soyuz space mission
   c. Apollo Project   d. Space Truck

7. The space vehicle that can be reused for a variety of missions is
   a. the Space Shuttle.   b. Skylab.   c. *Apollo 18.*   d. *Soyuz 19.*

8. Orbiting space stations will be fueled by
   a. coal.   b. nuclear fusion.   c. nuclear fission.   d. solar energy.

9. *Pioneers 10* and *11* will never return to earth because they
   a. have landed on Saturn.   b. are orbiting Jupiter.
   c. are now beyond the solar system.   d. have burned up during reentry.

10. The use of spacesuit fabric to roof buildings illustrates that
   a. space program devices have practical applications.
   b. space program devices have no practical uses.
   c. the fabric absorbs excess heat.
   d. the fabric is inexpensive.

CONTENT REVIEW: COMPLETION

Fill in the word or words that best complete each statement.

1. _____ is the force that must be overcome to launch rockets into space.

2. According to Newton's _____, every action produces an equal and opposite reaction.

3. The speed that an object must attain to overcome the gravitational pull of a moon, a planet, or a star is called _____.

4. A(n) _____ is the orbit in which a satellite moves at a speed that matches the rate of the earth's rotation.

5. _____ was the first United States scientific satellite.

6. The _____ is Earth's only natural satellite.

7. The IRAS telescope was designed to detect _____ radiation from space.

8. The first Space Shuttle was called the _____.

9. Instruments on board *Mariner* determined that _____ does not have a magnetic field.

10. The Silverdome in Pontiac, Michigan, is an example of _____.

Determine whether each statement is true or false. If it is true, write "true." If it is false, change the underlined word or words to make the statement true.

1. The reaction engine is based on the principle that for every action there is an opposite and <u>greater</u> reaction.
2. The moon's outward thrust is balanced by the earth's <u>gravitational pull</u>.
3. Konstantin <u>Tsiolkovsky</u> formulated the law of gravitation.
4. As the mass of a planet or star increases, the escape velocity from it <u>decreases</u>.
5. Liquid oxygen and liquid <u>hydrogen</u> are the ingredients of liquid rocket fuel.
6. Multistage rockets burn liquid fuel to give <u>continuous thrust</u> to a space vehicle.
7. The earth's natural satellite is <u>Venus</u>.
8. The Apollo spacecraft were designed to explore the <u>moon</u>.
9. The Space Shuttle is launched into space by rockets but can land on Earth the way a glider does.
10. <u>Gel packets</u>, a spinoff from spacesuit development, are used to absorb heat from a runner's forehead, neck, and wrists.

Use the skills you have developed in this chapter to complete each activity.

1. **Making comparisons** Compare the various kinds of artificial satellites.
2. **Making diagrams** Based on what you have read about space stations, draw a space colony as you imagine it might be. Include all the things necessary for life.
3. **Expressing an opinion** Some people think the space program is a waste of money. What do you think? Explain.
4. **Applying concepts** Explain what you think the phrase, "The space program is a down-to-earth success" means.
5. **Making inferences** The chart shows the escape velocities from Earth and from several other objects in space. Determine how many times greater ($+$) or less ($-$) the escape velocities of the other objects are as compared to that of Earth. What can you infer about their relative masses based on their escape velocities?

Object	Escape Velocity (km/sec)
Earth	11.2
Moon	2.3
Sun	616.0
Venus	10.3
Mars	5.0
Jupiter	63.4

6. **Relating concepts** You are on ice skates facing due north on a frozen pond. You are not moving. You throw your backpack to your friend who is also on ice skates and is facing due south. Your friend catches the backpack. Using Newton's laws of motion, determine the direction of motion for (a) you, (b) the backpack, (c) your friend.

Discuss each of the following in a brief paragraph.

1. Explain how balloons and rockets act as examples of reaction engines.
2. Discuss the functions of deep space probes.

10 The Computer Revolution

CHAPTER SECTIONS

10-1 **Computer Technology**

10-2 **Computer Operation**

10-3 **Computer Applications**

CHAPTER OBJECTIVES

After completing this chapter, you will be able to:

10-1 Define a computer.

10-1 Describe the development of the modern computer.

10-1 Relate the discovery of semiconductors to modern computer technology.

10-2 Identify the various components of computer hardware.

10-2 Explain the binary system.

10-2 Represent decimal numbers in the binary system.

10-3 Identify six basic computer applications.

Sooner or later it had to happen. And on Election Day in 1952, it did. Millions of Americans came face to face with the computer age for the first time. Many were shocked by the outcome.

The presidential contest that year was between Dwight D. Eisenhower and Adlai E. Stevenson. As people turned on their television sets early in the evening to learn the early voting returns, they got a surprise. News commentator Walter Cronkite announced that an "electronic brain"—the huge UNIVAC I computer—was going to predict the outcome!

For weeks before the election, computer scientists had put district-by-district results of the presidential elections of 1944 and 1948 into UNIVAC's computer memory. They also programmed the computer—gave it a set of instructions—on how to analyze the early 1952 voting returns by comparing them with the last two election results.

On election evening, after just three million votes were counted, UNIVAC predicted a landslide victory for Eisenhower. No one believed it. Political analysts had predicted a close race. They did not think that the lopsided outcome the computer had predicted was possible. The television news staff, and even the computer scientists, felt that there was a mistake in the computer program. Many television viewers stayed up all night to see the "electronic brain" proved wrong.

But the computer was not wrong. When all the votes were counted, UNIVAC's prediction turned out to be remarkably close to the actual results. People were impressed. The computer age had dawned for most Americans.

A photographer's view of computers

Figure 10-1 *Radar on a spacecraft orbiting Venus was able to penetrate the thick cloud cover to provide this computer-generated image of the Venusian surface. Circle on top is unfinished portion of computer picture.*

10-1 Computer Technology

A computer is an electronic device that performs calculations and processes information. A modern electronic **computer** can do thousands of calculations per second. At equally incredible speed, it can file away billions of bits of information in its memory. Then it can rapidly search through all that information to pick out particular items. It can change numbers to letters to pictures to sounds—and then back to numbers again.

Using these abilities, modern computers are guiding spaceships, navigating boats, diagnosing diseases and prescribing treatment, forecasting weather, and searching for ore. Computers can make robots move, talk, and obey commands. Computers can play games and make music. They even can design new computers!

Computer Development

The starting point of modern computer development is considered to be 1890. In preparation for the United States census that year, Herman Hollerith devised an electromagnetic machine that could

Figure 10-2 *This computerized robot may not be quite ready to run the household, but it can help walk the dog. Amazingly, the computer in this robot would have filled an entire room twenty years ago!*

handle information punched into cards. The holes allowed small electric currents to pass and activate counters. Using this system, Hollerith completed the 1890 census in one-fourth the time it had taken to do the 1880 census! Hollerith's punch card became the symbol of the computer age.

The first American-built computer was developed in 1946 by the United States Army. The Electronic Numerical Integrator and Calculator, or ENIAC, consisted of thousands of electronic tubes and occupied a warehouse. It cost millions of dollars to build and millions of dollars to maintain. It was constantly breaking down and had to be rebuilt each time a new type of calculation was done. ENIAC required great amounts of energy, generated huge amounts of heat, and was very expensive. By today's standards, ENIAC was slow. It could do only 100,000 calculations per second!

The first general purpose computer was introduced in 1951. It was called the Universal Automatic Computer, or UNIVAC. UNIVAC certainly was an improvement over ENIAC, but it was still large, expensive, and slow.

Increased demand for computers encouraged more advanced computer technology. Technical breakthroughs in electronic devices reduced the size and cost of computers. They also increased the efficiency, speed, and uses of computers. And equally important, they brought the computer within everyone's reach.

The future of computers lies in both the very small and the very large. Electronic circuits called **microprocessors** can hold the entire processing capability of a computer on one small chip. At the other extreme, groups of computers are being linked together to form supercomputers.

Figure 10-3 *The uses of computers are many and varied. Computer applications include the identification of worldwide ozone concentrations* (left), *the aerodynamic design of cars* (center), *and the determination of controls and seat positions in automobiles* (right).

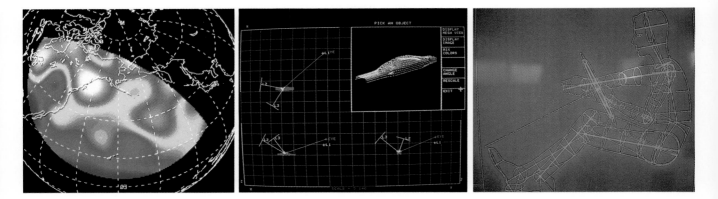

Figure 10-4 *Early computers used large vacuum tubes such as these. Vacuum tubes were neither fast nor reliable.*

Figure 10-5 *A diode is the simplest type of vacuum tube. In a diode, electrons flow from the negatively charged filament to the positively charged plate, creating a one-way flow of electrons. As you can see, a diode is considerably smaller than a vacuum tube.*

The Miracle Chip

The switching circuits of early electronic computers were made up of **vacuum tubes.** Vacuum tubes are one-way valves, or gates, for a flow of electricity. They have positively and negatively charged plates inside a sealed container in which all the air has been removed. A vacuum tube can be made to allow electricity to flow through it, or it can be made to stop the flow. Since the electric flow in the tubes could be on or off, vacuum tubes acted as the switches in the early computers.

However, computer circuits using vacuum tubes were bulky. They required a lot of electric power. And they gave off a lot of heat. What is more, individual vacuum tubes, like light bulbs, were constantly burning out. So it seemed that if computers were to go on using vacuum tubes, they would never be very small, very fast, very cheap, or very reliable.

While designers struggled to improve vacuum tube computers, three scientists at Bell Labs in New Jersey developed a replacement for the vacuum tube. The replacement was the **transistor.** Introduced in 1948, the transistor was based on the discovery of a group of very special materials called **semiconductors.** Semiconductors are materials that are able to conduct electric currents better than insulators but not as well as metals. Devices that use semiconductors are called solid-state devices.

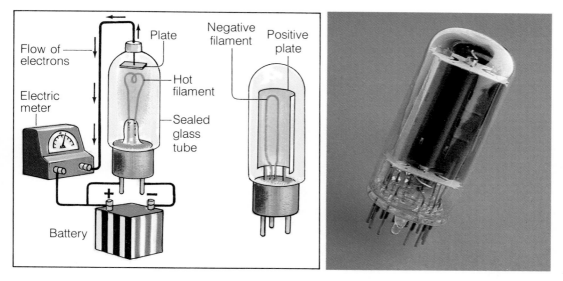

Silicon and germanium, two metalloids, are the most commonly used semiconductors. These elements have crystal structures that cause them to act like vacuum tubes. In these two elements current passes easily in one direction but not in the other.

Solid-state devices have several advantages over vacuum tubes. Using crystals of semiconductors makes solid-state devices much smaller and lighter than vacuum tubes. A tiny piece of semiconductor material can be made into a very small crystal switch. Such a switching device gives off less heat, uses far less power, is more dependable, and lasts longer.

During the 1950s, transistors replaced vacuum tubes in radios, televisions, and computer circuits. The transistors were much smaller than vacuum tubes. Eventually, they also cost much less. They required much less electric power. And because they gave off practically no heat, they could be packed closely together. Transistors were also much more reliable. An electronic circuit as big as a shoe box in the late 1940s was down to the size of a cracker by the late 1950s. But that was just the beginning.

In the early 1960s, several scientists realized that dozens of transistor circuits could be etched, or printed, onto a single plate of silicon. This grouping of circuits on one silicon plate was known as an **integrated circuit.** Today, this kind of integrated circuit is better known as a silicon **chip.** Soon other computer designers found ways to pack more and more circuits onto a single chip. Now a chip no bigger than a postage stamp could contain as many as a million circuits! In fact, the entire processing unit, or "brain," of the computer is often on a single tiny

Figure 10-6 *Transistors come in a variety of shapes and sizes. What advantages does a transistor have over a vacuum tube?*

Figure 10-7 *An integrated circuit, or chip, contains many thousands of transistor circuits in complex combinations on a thin slice of silicon crystal. Here, you see the size of a chip in comparison to the wafer from which it is made (left). This photograph of a computer chip, magnified 175 times by a scanning electron microscope, shows the integrated circuit paths. A human hair is wider than 150 of these paths (right).*

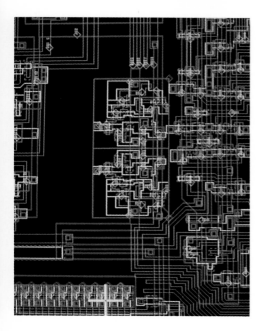

Figure 10-8 *One of the many uses of computers is the design of complex circuitry for future computers.*

Figure 10-9 *Computer hardware includes a central processing unit, main memory, an input device, and an output device. What is the function of each?*

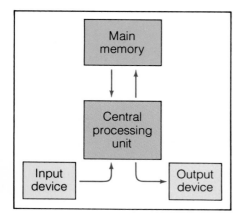

chip. Imagine—as many components as would be found in a dozen TV sets are incorporated in a chip no bigger than your thumbnail!

But computer scientists today are not satisfied. They continue to search for ways to put billions of circuits on a single chip. Such superchips are needed to create the supercomputers of the future. A future supercomputer may be able to do more than 1 trillion counting steps a second. It may also be able to solve several different problems at the same time.

SECTION REVIEW

1. What is a computer?
2. What were some of the problems with ENIAC?
3. What is a vacuum tube? How does it work?
4. What is a semiconductor? Give two examples.
5. What is an integrated circuit?

10-2 Computer Operation

A modern computer is made up of many parts. Some parts put information into the computer, while other parts remove and display it. Some parts control and process information, and other parts store it. And some parts give the computer a set of instructions to follow.

Computer Hardware

Computer **hardware** refers to the physical parts of a computer. **Computer hardware includes a central processing unit, main storage, input devices, and output devices.**

The brain of a computer is the **central processing unit,** or **CPU.** A CPU controls the operation of all the components of a computer. It executes the arithmetic and logic instructions that it receives in the form of a **computer program.** A computer program is a series of instructions that tells the computer how to perform a certain task. A computer program can be written in one of several different computer languages.

The main storage of a computer is often referred to as the **main memory.** The main memory contains data and operating instructions that are processed by the CPU. In the earliest computers, the main memory consisted of thousands of vacuum tubes. Modern computer memory is contained on chips. The most advanced memory chip can store as much information as 1 million vacuum tubes can.

Data are fed to the central processing unit by an **input device.** One common input device is a keyboard. A keyboard looks very much like a typewriter. Using a keyboard, a person can communicate data and instructions directly to a computer. Other input devices include magnetic tape, optical scanners, and disk or diskette drives.

A **disk drive** reads information off a disk or diskette and enters it into the computer's memory or into the CPU. Information from a disk drive can be placed into a computer very quickly.

Information produced by the computer can be removed and stored on a disk. So a disk drive is also an **output device.** An output device receives data from the central processing unit. Output devices include printers, cathode-ray tubes, magnetic-tape drives, and voice synthesizers. Even robots are output devices!

Like a disk drive, a **modem** is an input and output device. A modem changes electronic signals

Figure 10-10 *Various computer parts and peripherals, which are devices that can be connected to a computer, are shown in this illustration.*

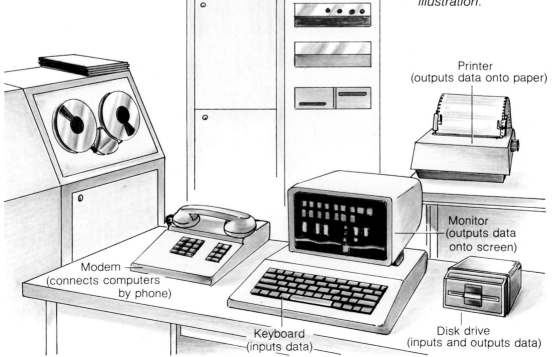

Printer
(outputs data onto paper)

Monitor
(outputs data onto screen)

Modem
(connects computers by phone)

Keyboard
(inputs data)

Disk drive
(inputs and outputs data)

Figure 10-11 *Computers have a wide variety of applications. Computers are used to study body mechanics* (left) *and to produce images of the heart* (right).

from a computer into sounds that can be carried over telephone lines. It also changes the sounds back into computer signals. A modem allows a computer to communicate with other computers, often thousands of kilometers away. As computers link in this way, they form a network in which information can be shared. A modem allows use of this network by accessing information from a central **data bank.** A data bank is a vast collection of information stored in a large computer.

The Binary System

Computer hardware would be useless without **software.** Software is the program or set of programs the computer follows. Software must be precise because a computer cannot think on its own. It can only follow instructions. For example, to add two numbers, a program must tell a computer to get one number from memory, hold it, get the other number from memory, combine the two numbers, and print the answer. After completing that instruction, the computer must be told what to do next.

A computer executes instructions by counting with just two numbers at a time. The numbers are 0 and 1. The system that uses just these two numbers is called the **binary system.** The operation of all computers is based on the binary system.

Computer circuits are composed of electronic devices called diodes. Diodes are gates that are either open or closed to electric current. If the gate is open, current is off. If the gate is closed, current

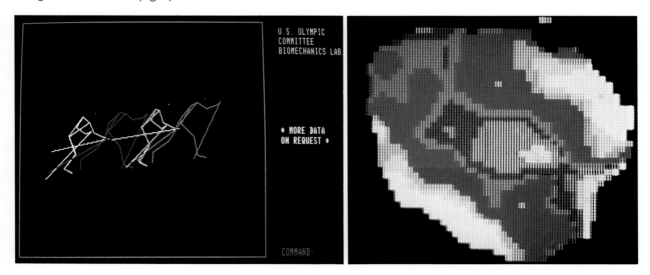

Byte representation	128	64	32	16	8	4	2	1	Numeral
0 0 0 1 0 0 0 1									17
0 1 1 0 1 0 1 0									106
0 0 1 1 0 0 1 1									51
1 1 0 1 1 1 0 0									220

is on. To a computer, 0 is current off and 1 is current on. Each digit, then, acts as a tiny electronic switch, flipping on and off at unbelievable speed.

Each single electronic switch is called a **bit.** A string of bits—usually 8—is called a **byte.** Numbers, letters, and other symbols can be represented as a byte. For example, the letter A is 01000001. The letter K is 11010010. The number 9 is 00001001. See Figure 10-12. What do you think the code for the number 7 is? For the number 83? What is the value of the largest number that can be represented by one byte?

You do not need to be reminded of the importance of computers. You have only to look around you! The uses of computers are many, and their presence is almost universal. Any list of computer applications cannot really be completed today. For by the time today is over, another new application will have been devised.

Figure 10-12 *All computers execute instructions by using the binary system. The off/on positions of these light bulbs correspond to the off/on positions of electronic switches, or bits. What is the name for a string of 8 bits?*

SECTION REVIEW

1. What are the four hardware components of a computer system? What is the function of each?
2. What is a modem? How is it related to a data bank?
3. How is the binary system used by a computer?
4. Show how the following numbers would be represented by a byte: 175, 139, 3, 45, 17.

10-3   Computer Applications

What can you do with a computer? **The most basic applications of a modern computer include: problem solving, simulation, data processing, word processing, computer control, and computer-aided design.** There can be hundreds of variations and combinations of these functions. And each function can be put to many uses.

Problem Solving

Because a computer can process numbers at incredible speed, it can be programmed, or given operating instructions, to count people or votes. Or it can solve the complex math problems involved in spaceflight. This function is the reason computers were developed in the first place.

The "number-crunching" ability of computers allows scientists to quickly try out hundreds of solutions to a particular problem. For example, some labs use computer programs to replace lab animals such as guinea pigs, rabbits, mice, and monkeys in certain experiments. Biological functions of the animals are converted to mathematical equations and programmed into a computer. To find out the effects of a certain condition, such as the safest dosage

Figure 10-13 *The structure of this molecule—an enzyme that helps the body fight cancer—is being studied on the computer screen. Through such studies, scientists hope to develop substances that can aid the enzyme's fight against cancer.*

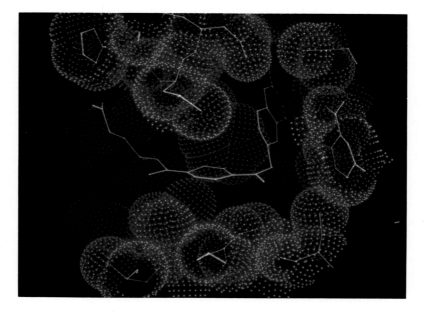

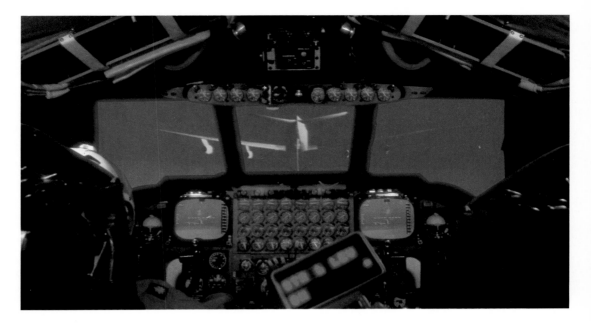

of a new animal medicine, a technician enters numbers representing the condition in the computer. In turn, the computer solves the problem mathematically and provides a result. This process can be done again and again with slight changes in conditions.

The computer approach to this type of research is faster than using lab animals. It is also cheaper. And, of course, it may save the animals' lives.

Simulation

A flashing red light in the space shuttle signals emergency. A control panel light identifies the problem. The automatic latching system for the cargo bay door has malfunctioned. Feeling that the indicator might be wrong, an astronaut quickly types a question into the onboard computer. The computer runs a check of the systems. There is no mistake; the latching system has malfunctioned. What should be done? How serious is the danger?

Fortunately, this is a computer **simulation,** or imitation, of one of the thousands of things that could go wrong on a space mission. Such simulations are important to train astronauts and to help plan space missions and design space systems.

Thousands of different conditions, events, situations, and processes can be simulated by computer programs. So can flights of fancy. All video games

Activity

Computing Speed

Shuffle a deck of playing cards. Have a friend time you as you sort the cards, first into the four suits, and then from the 2 through the ace in each suit. Determine how many "sorts" you made. Remember, each time you place a card somewhere, it is a sort. Calculate how many sorts you made per second.

A bank check-sorting machine can make 1800 sorts a minute. How long would it take this machine to do the same number of sorts you did? How much faster than you is this machine.

are computer simulations. So are many of the computer-assisted instruction programs used in schools and job training courses. Some computer simulation is also used in making movies.

In the future, computer simulations are likely to be used to "explore" the unknown before robots or humans set out on an actual mission. Through the use of simulations, scientists can consider all aspects of a flight to a distant planet or a mining operation on the ocean floor.

Data Processing

Billions of bytes of information, or data, can be stored in a computer's memory and on magnetic disks or tapes used with the computer. A computer can file, rearrange, select, compare, and display vast amounts of data within seconds. This ability makes computers valuable to banks, libraries, and most types of offices. A bank's computer may hold information about millions of individual accounts. Yet it can pick out and display information from any one account within seconds. A police computer can quickly search through thousands of fingerprint pattern types to identify a particular print left at the scene of a crime. And, using computers to predict weather patterns, weather forecasters can provide up-to-the-minute weather reports.

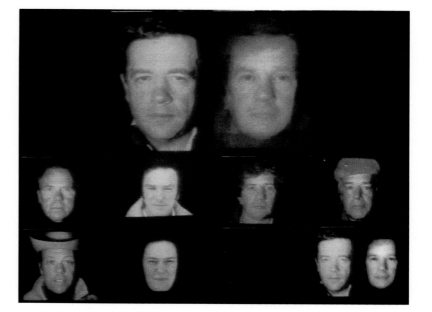

Figure 10-15 *In order to help police identify criminals, this computer identidisc is used to show sample faces to the victim. The victim then picks features from various faces that appear familiar and the computer averages all the features into one face.*

Word Processing

Word processing is a computer function that involves putting words on paper in various desired ways. Of course one can do that with a pencil, pen, or typewriter. But the computer offers many advantages. With a computer, a person can type, review, edit, correct, and, if necessary, rearrange the words before printing them. Not only can the computer help with the editing, it can make spelling corrections. Some computers can even translate the material into a foreign language.

Computer Control

A computer can be programmed to convert words and numbers into mechanical motions, sounds, and light patterns. It can then convert these motions, sounds, and light patterns back into words and numbers. A computer can also record

Career: *Computer Artist*

HELP WANTED: COMPUTER ARTIST Requires college degree in computer programming or computer science. Background in art and design needed. Experience creating art by computer desired. Needed to create scientific illustrations using the computer.

A special science series for educational television was in the works. Before its airing, however, a group of **computer artists** had to spend many hours working at computer terminals. They were busy developing a series of drawings demonstrating the process of evolution. A single cell changed into a fish, then into a frog, into a lower mammal, and finally into a human. This entire sequence was programmed to take place in a matter of seconds.

Computer artists create art on computers. These artists require both a mathematical mind and an artistic eye. Sometimes computer artists program the computer to create images that would be impossible to photograph in real life, such as the structure of molecules.

Computer artists are hired to create special effects for movie studios, to produce scientific and technical graphics, to design commercial products, and to produce artwork for business presentations. If you are interested in this rapidly expanding field, write to the National Computer Graphics Association, 8401 Arlington Boulevard, Fairfax, VA 22031.

Figure 10-16 *These dinosaurs at Epcot Center in Walt Disney World are run by a computer system.*

conditions—such as humidity, pressure, sound, stress, vibration, and temperature—from automatic measuring devices. And if any measurement goes over a set limit, the computer can trigger certain actions. It can turn on, turn off, or change machines.

With these abilities, a computer can make a robot handle things, listen, look, talk, and walk. A computer also can run an entire factory or an amusement park. At Walt Disney World in Florida, computers are used to control animated characters, complex displays, fountains, games, internal environments, lights, rides, and security systems.

Computer-Aided Design

A computer's ability to turn numbers and instructions into graphic pictures—and back again—makes it a useful design tool for architects, artists, engineers, fashion designers, and movie makers. In recent years, computers have been used to help design bridges, nuclear power stations, scientific instruments, space stations, and supersonic aircraft.

There are two basic advantages to computer-aided design. The first is the speed with which an object can be designed. Without a computer, it might take several months to design a car. With a computer, it takes several hours.

The second advantage is that a computer allows a designer to build, experiment with, and improve a

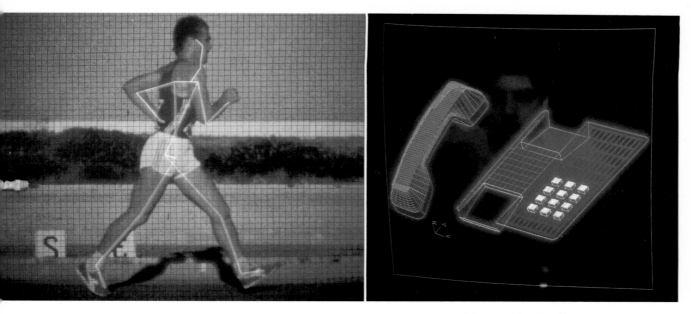

design in order to develop the best product—all on a TV screen! And then the design and all the parts can be quickly, safely, and completely tested!

Figure 10-17 *Computers are used to study body mechanics during exercise* (left) *and to design industrial products such as this new phone system* (right).

The Future of Computers

There are two major goals for future computer development. One involves making computer circuits smaller. The other involves making computer operation more "intelligent."

One approach to making computers smaller requires building three-dimensional cubes instead of flat chips. These cubes could contain billions of circuits. Another approach involves using tiny magnetic bubbles to build computer circuits. An even more unusual proposal includes using organic molecules similar to proteins and fats in computer circuits.

In the effort to make "smarter" computers, designers are trying to imitate human reasoning abilities. This field is called artificial intelligence research. It holds much promise for the future.

Figure 10-18 *This imaginative drawing was done completely on a computer.*

SECTION REVIEW

1. What are the six basic applications of a modern computer?
2. What is a simulation? Describe an example.
3. What are the two major goals for future computer development?

LABORATORY ACTIVITY

The First Calculator: The Abacus

Purpose

In this activity, you will operate an abacus.

Materials *(per group)*

Abacus

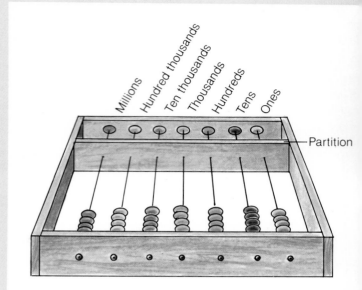

Procedure

1. The columns of beads of the abacus represent, from right to left, units of ones, tens, hundreds, thousands, ten thousands, hundred thousands, and millions.
2. The single bead in the upper section of each column, above the partition, equals five beads in the lower section of that column.
3. Always start from the lower section of the far right, or ones, column.
4. Count to three by sliding three beads up from the lower section of the ones column to the partition.
5. Continue counting to eight. Slide the fourth bead up to the partition. You have run out of beads in this section. Slide all four beads back down and slide the single bead from the upper section of column 1 down to the partition. Remember, the top bead equals five lower beads. Continue counting from six to eight by sliding the beads in the lower section of the ones column up to the partition. Check with your teacher to see that you are using the abacus correctly.
6. Continue counting to twelve. Slide the last bead in the ones column up to the partition. You now have a total of nine. You have run out of beads in the ones column. Slide all

these beads back to their original zero position. Slide one bead in the lower section of the tens column up to the partition. This represents exactly ten. Again continue counting in the ones column until you reach twelve.

Observations and Conclusions

1. Count to each of these numbers on the abacus:
   (a) 16   (b) 287   (c) 5016   (d) 1,816,215
2. How would you find 8 + 7 on the abacus? You would start by counting to eight on the abacus. Then you would continue adding seven more beads. Find the following sums:
   (a) 3 + 4   (b) 7 + 8   (c) 125 + 58

CHAPTER REVIEW

SUMMARY

10-1 Computer Technology

■ A computer is an electronic device that performs calculations and processes information.

■ Early computers were large, expensive, slow, and subject to breakdown.

■ Electronic circuits called microprocessors can hold the entire processing capability of a computer on one small chip.

■ In a vacuum tube, electrons are permitted to move in only one direction.

■ Semiconductors are materials that are able to conduct electric currents better than insulators but not as well as metals.

■ Silicon and germanium are the most commonly used semiconductors.

■ Transistors are smaller than vacuum tubes, cost much less, require less electric power, and are more reliable.

■ A grouping of many transistor circuits on a single silicon plate is known as an integrated circuit.

■ The development of integrated circuits on a silicon chip increased computer power.

10-2 Computer Operation

■ Computer hardware refers to the physical parts of a computer. Computer hardware includes a central processing unit, main storage, input devices, and output devices.

■ The central processing unit, or CPU, is the brain of a computer.

■ The main storage of a computer is often referred to as the main memory.

■ Input devices feed data to the central processing unit.

■ Output devices remove, store, and display information produced by a computer.

■ A modem is a device that allows a computer to communicate with other computers.

■ A data bank is a vast collection of information stored in a large computer.

■ Computer software is a program or set of programs the computer follows.

■ The operation of all computers is based on the binary system.

■ In the binary system, each single electronic switch is called a bit. A string of bits, usually 8, is called a byte.

10-3 Computer Applications

■ The six basic applications of a computer are problem solving, simulation, data processing, word processing, computer control, and computer-aided design.

■ An imitation of conditions, events, situations, and processes is called a simulation.

■ The future goals of computer designers are to build smaller computer circuits and to make computers more "intelligent."

VOCABULARY

Define each term in a complete sentence.

binary system	computer	integrated circuit	semiconductor
bit	computer program	main memory	simulation
byte	data bank	microprocessor	software
central processing unit	disk drive	modem	transistor
chip	hardware	output device	vacuum tube
	input device		

CONTENT REVIEW: MULTIPLE CHOICE

Choose the letter of the answer that best completes each statement.

1. Which of the following devices were used as switches in computers such as ENIAC?
   a. vacuum tubes   b. transistors
   c. integrated circuits   d. silicon chips
2. Which of the following is a semiconductor?
   a. copper   b. plastic   c. silicon   d. oxygen
3. A single chip that functions as the central processing unit in a microcomputer is a
   a. main memory.   b. microprocessor.   c. modem.   d. transistor.
4. The physical parts of a computer are collectively referred to as computer
   a. software.   b. peripherals.   c. programs.   d. hardware.
5. Which of the following is computer software?
   a. printer   b. disk drive   c. program   d. memory
6. A piece of equipment such as a modem or printer is a(n)
   a. microprocessor.   b. central processing unit.
   c. output device.   d. main memory.
7. A computer "talks" to another through a
   a. monitor.   b. modem.   c. printer.   d. peripheral.
8. In the binary system, the number 86 would be represented as
   a. 01100110.   b. 01010110.   c. 10101001.   d. 11010010.
9. A vast collection of information stored in a large computer is called a
   a. data bank.   b. main memory.
   c. microprocessor.   d. silicon chip.
10. Which of the following is not an application of a computer?
   a. store data   b. perform complex calculations
   c. rectify alternating current   d. design new computers

CONTENT REVIEW: COMPLETION

Fill in the word or words that best complete each statement.

1. Transistors are made of materials called _____.
2. The _____ of a computer stores information and computer operating instructions.
3. The part of a computer that resembles a television screen is a(n) _____ device.
4. The brain of a computer is called the _____.
5. The device that allows computers to communicate with one another is a(n) _____.
6. The number system on which the operation of all computers is based is called the _____.
7. Each single electronic switch in a computer is called a(n) _____.
8. There are eight _____ in one byte.
9. A computer imitation of a real-life event is called a(n) _____.
10. The filing, rearranging, selection, and display of large amounts of information is known as _____.

Determine whether each statement is true or false. If it is true, write "true." If it is false, change the underlined word or words to make the statement true.

1. ENIAC was used to count the number of people in the United States.
2. Transistors give off a lot of heat and are bulky to work with.
3. An example of a semiconductor material is silicon.
4. The conductivity of transistors is between that of conductors and insulators.
5. One way of entering information into a computer is through a keyboard.
6. Microprocessors are integrated circuits that can hold the entire processing capability of a computer on one chip.
7. Output devices feed data to a computer.
8. A data bank is a vast collection of information stored in a large computer.
9. A bit is a string of switches connected together.
10. One way to make smaller computers is to use tiny magnetic bubbles as circuits.

CONCEPT REVIEW: SKILL BUILDING

Use the skills you have developed in the chapter to complete each activity.

1. **Making diagrams** Draw a diagram that shows how the four main hardware components of a computer are related.
2. **Classifying computer devices** Many methods of putting data into a computer are similar to methods of getting data out of a computer. Identify each of the following as an input device, an output device, or both: typewriter keyboard, CRT, printer, optical scanner, magnetic tape, disk drive, punch cards, voice synthesizer.
3. **Applying definitions** Write the following numbers in binary form: 19, 57, 1, 95, 161, 129, 255.
4. **Expressing an opinion** Computers are used to develop and distribute vast quantities of information in various data bases. Some of that information may include something about you. For example, if you have ever applied for a passport, ham radio license, or a social security card, you are in a computer data base. Many people do not mind being in a data base they know nothing about. Other people consider it an invasion of privacy. They point to mistakes in data bases that can go uncorrected for years. How do you feel about this topic?
5. **Making predictions** Computers will affect your life when you are an adult. How do you think they will affect you?
6. **Applying concepts** A program is a list of instructions that tells a computer how to perform a task. Write a program that describes the steps involved in your task of waking up and arriving at school for your first class.

CONCEPT REVIEW: ESSAY

Discuss each of the following in a brief paragraph.

1. What is a semiconductor? How is it used to make integrated circuits?
2. Why are semiconductor transistors better than their vacuum-tube ancestors?
3. What is a modem? How is it related to a data bank?
4. Describe two applications of computers.

11 Pollution

CHAPTER SECTIONS

11-1 Pollution—What Is It?
11-2 Water Pollution
11-3 Air Pollution
11-4 Land Pollution

CHAPTER OBJECTIVES

After completing this chapter, you will be able to:

11-1 Define pollution.

11-2 Discuss the importance of water that is free of hazardous pollutants.

11-2 Compare point and nonpoint sources of water pollution.

11-3 Relate the burning of fossil fuels and the use of motor vehicles to air pollution.

11-3 Define smog and explain how a temperature inversion occurs.

11-3 Trace the events that lead to acid rain.

11-3 List several ways of reducing air pollution.

11-4 Define sanitary landfill.

11-4 Relate the importance of recycling to the reduction of land pollution.

The year 1858 was remarkable for London, England. It was a time of enormous progress. But, it was also the year of the "Great Stink"! Beginning in 1847, all the sewage of London was piped into the Thames River. Year by year, as London's population swelled, the river became more and more filthy. Fish no longer lived in parts of its waters. Birds vanished from certain river areas. And with every rise and fall of the tides, slimy garbage was deposited along the river's shores.

As London grew, the pollution of its air and land also increased. Railroad engines, factory smokestacks, and home chimneys pumped increasing amounts of smoke into London's damp air. The increased smoke helped to cause many of the great London fogs of the early 1900s. Such fogs were a threat to health and safety and a scar on London's beauty.

In 1858, as now, pollution often was viewed as the price of progress. But was it a price that had to be paid? Some people said no. They argued that the same knowhow that had created progress could also be used to clean up its waste. And they were right. Today, London's thick "pea-soup" fogs are only memories of the past. Most species of birds have returned to the Thames. And in 1982, for the first time in more than 130 years, salmon were seen swimming in its waters.

Modern London—clean air and water

11-1 Pollution—What Is It?

You probably hear the word **pollution** often. But do you really know what it means? **Pollution is the changing of the environment for the worse, usually due to human activities.**

Let's take a can of soda. To obtain metal for the can, rocks containing the metal must be dug out of the earth. This digging scars the land. Later, a factory may use many chemicals to get the metal out of the rock. Remaining chemicals are often washed away with water. The water may end up in a river or a stream. The chemicals, so useful in the factory, become pollution in the water.

Heat is needed to get the metal out of the rock—and to make the can. So a fuel such as coal or oil must be burned at some point. As a result of burning fuels, smoke, soot, and various gases are released as pollutants into the air.

Even before a fuel is burned, it can indirectly cause pollution. Land, for example, can be destroyed by **strip mining** for coal. In this process, entire hills are cut apart by huge earth-moving machines in search of coal. And at sea, there is the risk of oil spills. Or poisonous wastes can be given off into the air by the making of oil fuels.

Making the soda that goes in the can also produces a flow of wastes onto land, air, and water.

Figure 11-1 *Strip mining for coal can destroy the land from which the coal is removed* (left). *However, the land can be reclaimed and returned back to its natural beauty* (right).

Bringing the can of soda to market in trucks and ships involves the burning of fuel and the creation of air pollutants. But the possibility of pollution does not end here. Eventually, the can of soda ends up in the hands of a consumer. That person drinks its contents and may toss the empty can to the side of the road. There it becomes part of a growing litter of cans, bottles, plastic containers, scraps of rubber, and even discarded machinery. This litter is more than an eyesore and danger to wildlife. It can contribute to the poisoning of soil and water.

Fortunately, there are ways to avoid polluting the environment. So now let's look into the three main types of pollution—water, air, and land pollution—and the ways in which people battle them.

SECTION REVIEW

1. What is pollution?
2. List three ways the making of a can of soda can pollute the environment.

Figure 11-2 *Litter from industry and people can seriously damage the environment.*

Figure 11-3 *In 1978, the Amoco Cadiz oil tanker broke apart near the coast of France, spilling millions of tons of oil into the water.*

11-2 Water Pollution

About 70 percent of the earth's surface is covered by water. Without this water, life on the earth would be impossible. **In order to support life, water must be free of pollutants that can harm or kill living things.** Yet every day such substances find their way into oceans and seas, rivers, lakes, streams, and underground water.

Oceans and Seas

On the stormy evening of March 16, 1978, the oil tanker *Amoco Cadiz* smashed onto hidden, jagged rocks near the coast of Brittany, France. High winds and towering waves pounded the tanker. Soon, the *Amoco Cadiz* ripped apart. Before it finally sank, however, the broken tanker spilled millions of tons of oil into the surrounding sea.

Within days, wind and tides started washing the gooey oil ashore. Kilometers of beautiful coastline

were quickly blackened. Sea plants and animals touched by the oil died. Soon, the terrible smell of oil was joined by that of rotting fish and sea birds.

Safeguarding Sea Water

The wreck of the *Amoco Cadiz* was a terrible environmental tragedy. Yet some valuable clean-up lessons were learned from it. The best way to control oil spills, of course, is to prevent them in the first place. But despite all precautions, occasional oil spills can occur anyway.

There are three basic ways to control oil spilled at sea. An oil spill can be destroyed by fire. It also can be removed from the place where it spilled and gotten rid of somewhere else. Or it can be trapped in the area where it spilled and later removed.

In several earlier oil spills, attempts were made to burn the oil. However, it seemed that burning often added to the problems. Smoke, soot, fumes, and par-

Figure 11-4 *In this photograph, you can see how close the* Amoco Cadiz *was to the French shoreline* (top, right). *Despite all efforts, much of the oil reached the shore, killing wildlife* (bottom, left). *A massive cleanup was then undertaken to save the beach* (bottom, right).

Figure 11-5 *In order to protect the beach, inflatable barriers were set up to keep the oil from the shore (left). Vacuum-type devices were also used to pump some of the oil from the water (right). Neither technique, in this case, worked.*

ticles from the burning oil polluted the air over large areas. In most cases, large amounts of oil still ended up on beaches and in rivers. For these reasons, a decision was made not to try to burn the oil in and around the *Amoco Cadiz* wreck. Instead, all other means of dealing with the oil spill were used.

Ships and boats with pumps rushed to the scene. A floating pipeline and several pumps on shore were also used to draw off oil from the spill. Small tankers at sea and tanker trucks on shore carried the oil to various disposal sites. In this way, large amounts of oil from in and around the *Amoco Cadiz* were removed. In addition, several boats with special equipment tried to skim oil from the sea surface. Unfortunately, the weather was too stormy for the skimming and pumping methods to be completely successful.

As a last line of defense for the Brittany shore areas, various types of floating barriers were used to block the oil from drifting ashore. Some of these barriers were made of plastic foam. Others were tire-like inflatable tubes. But the foam barriers were difficult to move around. And the inflatable barriers were so light that they could not always stand up against the wind and waves. So the floating barriers were only partly successful.

In the end, huge amounts of oil from the *Amoco Cadiz* washed up on Brittany's beaches. There, the oil caused great damage to plant and animal life. Enormous human effort eventually was needed to clean the oil from beaches, rocks, and river inlets.

Today, several new weapons have been developed to fight oil spills at sea. These include the use of high-speed skimmers and "super-sucker" vacuum pumps to get the oil out of the water. For shore defense, plastic foam barriers that can be built on the spot have been developed. Based on experiences with the *Amoco Cadiz* spill, new ways have been found to place those barriers to make the best use of tides and currents. Most oil platforms at sea now have inflatable barriers that rapidly can be put into place around a platform at the first sign of a spill. New types of **absorbents,** or substances that can soak up oil on or near the shore, have been tested. For example, chicken feathers were used to help clean up a recent oil spill on the Mississippi River. And scientists are developing a type of bacteria that "eats" oil droplets and cleans the water.

Rivers, Lakes, Streams, and Ground Water

Not long ago, researchers uncovered a strange and frightening coincidence. People living near large bodies of water in several areas of the country seemed to be getting cancer at a higher rate than normal. What is more, the same could be said for the fish in the rivers and lakes near these areas. Was there a connection?

Scientists tested the water in these areas. The results were shocking. Water tested contained a number of different chemicals known to cause cancer in animals. The chemicals included polychlorinated biphenyls (pahl-ee-KLAWR-uh-nay-tihd by-FEHN-uhlz), or PCBs. Where had the poisonous chemicals come from? In one case, there was evidence that PCBs had been dumped into a large river by an electric company. The dumping had been stopped in 1976. But some experts believe PCBs are still seeping into the river from underground dumping sites. A large oil company was also accused of polluting the river with "oil, chemicals, pollutants, and other wastes."

Rivers are not the only victims of pollution. Lakes and streams have been polluted with sewage and factory wastes. Even ground water, or underground water, which many people use for drinking, has been

Figure 11-6 *In many parts of the country, water supplies have become too polluted for human use.*

WATER POLLUTED UNFIT TO DRINK

M.D.C.

polluted by substances that sink into the ground. Groundwater pollution can happen by accident, such as the cracking of a gasoline storage tank under a service station. Or it can be the result of deliberate acts, such as spreading **pesticides** over the land. Pesticides are chemicals used to kill harmful insects and other pests. But when pesticides are carried by rainwater or wind into rivers and streams, they become water pollutants.

Safeguarding Rivers, Lakes, Streams, and Ground Water

In 1972 and 1973, the United States Congress passed two strict laws to fight water pollution. They were The Clean Water Act of 1972 and The Safe Drinking Water Act of 1973. Both of these laws were intended to stop the flow of untreated wastes into our waterways from **point sources.** Point sources included the sewer pipes of towns, cities, and factories.

Both laws set up rules to greatly reduce water pollution from point sources. Towns and cities were forced to build or improve sewage treatment plants. Such plants clean sewage before it is allowed to run into waterways. Industries also were forced to clean their wastes before releasing them into lakes, streams, and rivers. Most of these actions were successful. Water quality improved.

Activity

A Water Treatment Plant

Arrange a visit to a local water treatment plant. Write a report on how water is treated in your community. Be sure to include answers to the following questions:

1. How is water treated before it is allowed to go to your home?
2. Where does your water supply come from?

Figure 11-7 *Nonpoint sources of pollution include pesticides sprayed on plants that end up in our water supplies (left). Point sources of pollution include untreated sewage released into rivers and streams (right).*

The 1972 and 1973 laws greatly reduced water pollution from point sources. However, the laws did nothing to reduce pollution from **nonpoint sources.** Nonpoint sources of water pollution include solid waste dumps that ooze poisonous liquids and leaking industrial waste ponds. They also include poisonous wastes illegally dumped, and pesticides and fertilizers carried by water from farmlands into rivers.

Unfortunately, the wastes from such nonpoint sources are usually the most hazardous to the environment. And they often are difficult to find and clean up. For example, drums of **toxic,** or dangerous, chemical wastes may lie in solid waste dumps for many years. Often the drums are not marked as containing toxic chemicals such as PCBs. The drums may be buried under other garbage or even underground. Buried, but not necessarily forgotten. For these drums can decay and spill toxic chemicals into the soil and waterways year after year. Such drums can even resurface generations later, causing nightmares for people who must clean up the damage—if it can be cleaned up.

Career: *Inhalation Toxicologist*

HELP WANTED: INHALATION TOXI-COLOGIST Requires M.D. or PhD. Special training will be provided on poisonous air pollutants. Individual needed to study effects of air pollutants on chemical workers.

An investigation was ordered because workers in a chemical plant were getting sick more than normal. Analysis of the air in the plant showed that all the workers were breathing fumes of one particular chemical. Based on this finding, an **inhalation toxicologist,** a specially trained scientist who studies the effects of inhaled poisons, tried to determine whether the fumes were causing the sickness.

An inhalation toxicologist often begins an investigation by studying the ways in which the poisons affect laboratory animals. These findings are then used to determine how the substance might affect humans. The scientist can also test the chemical on human cells grown in the laboratory. Together, all this information could lead to the cause of the outbreak of sickness. Protective measures can then be taken.

Anyone interested in becoming an inhalation toxicologist should be prepared to set out on a long journey of study into the biological or physical sciences. More information on this career can be gathered by writing to the Chemical Industry Institute of Toxicology, P.O. Box 12137, Research Triangle Park, NC 27709.

What is the solution? Obviously, chemical dumps must be checked carefully for leakage. Other sources of pollution must be checked as well. And, whenever possible, hazardous wastes should be disposed of properly at the place where they were created. Such disposal can be difficult and expensive. But proper disposal is far less difficult and costly than removing these wastes from the environment years later.

SECTION REVIEW

1. List three ways to deal with an oil spill on water.
2. What is a pesticide?
3. Name two point sources of pollution. Name two nonpoint sources.

11-3   Air Pollution

The air that makes up the earth's atmosphere is a mix of several gases. These gases include oxygen, nitrogen, carbon dioxide, and water vapor. Air can be polluted by burning fossil fuels such as gasoline, oil, and coal. Clean air is necessary for life. Polluted air is dangerous to life.

When fossil fuels are burned, a brew of pollutants enters the air. These pollutants include nitrogen and sulfur gases and tiny solid particles in smoke. **Much pollution is due to the burning of fossil fuels by industry, but the worst sources of air pollution in the United States are the engines that power motor vehicles.** The gasoline that an engine burns contains hydrocarbons, or compounds of hydrogen and carbon, that break up during burning. Pollution occurs when an engine does not completely burn up the gasoline. Some hydrocarbons escape into the air. At the same time, carbon monoxide, a poisonous gas, enters the atmosphere.

Figure 11-8 *The burning of fossil fuels in cars and industry is a major source of air pollution.*

Smog

Hydrocarbons, carbon monoxide, and several other gases react in sunlight to make a variety of poisonous pollutants. In many areas, the pollutants

257

Figure 11-9 *In a temperature inversion, cool air containing pollutants becomes trapped under a layer of warmer air (left). In this photograph, much of Los Angeles is hidden by the smog due to such a temperature inversion (right).*

Cold, clean air

Warm air

Trapped cool air

Activity

How Acidic Is Your Rain?

Find out whether the rain in your area is acidic.

1. Next time it rains, collect a sample of rainwater in a jar. Label it Sample A.

2. Place some distilled water in another jar and label it Sample B.

3. Obtain some pH paper from your teacher. Your teacher will show you how to use pH paper to test the acidity of each of your water samples. Record your findings.

Was there a difference in acidity levels between the two samples? What could have caused the difference?

form a thick cloud known as **smog.** It contains chemicals that irritate the eyes and make breathing difficult. Smog is especially damaging for people with lung diseases. People can even die if smog is truly bad. Other ingredients in smog kill plants.

Smog can build up heavily over a city because of a flip-flop in layers of air called a **temperature inversion.** Normally, the warm air near the ground rises. The warm air carries pollutants high into the atmosphere, away from people. Sometimes, however, a temperature inversion occurs. A layer of cool air sneaks in under the warm air. The cool layer cannot rise through the warm air above it. The cool air is trapped, along with the pollutants that enter it. Usually, the warming rays of the sun break up the temperature inversion by midday. But sometimes an inversion can last several days or more, causing serious smog-related health problems.

Acid Rain

Factory smokestacks and car exhausts release various pollutants into the atmosphere. Some of these pollutants include sulfur and nitrogen compounds called oxides. In the atmosphere, sulfur oxides can combine with water vapor through a series of complex chemical reactions. The result is tiny bubbles of sulfuric acid. Nitrogen oxides combine in a similar way to form nitric acid bubbles. These bubbles fall to the earth in rain—**acid rain!** And very often the acid rain falls many kilometers from the original source.

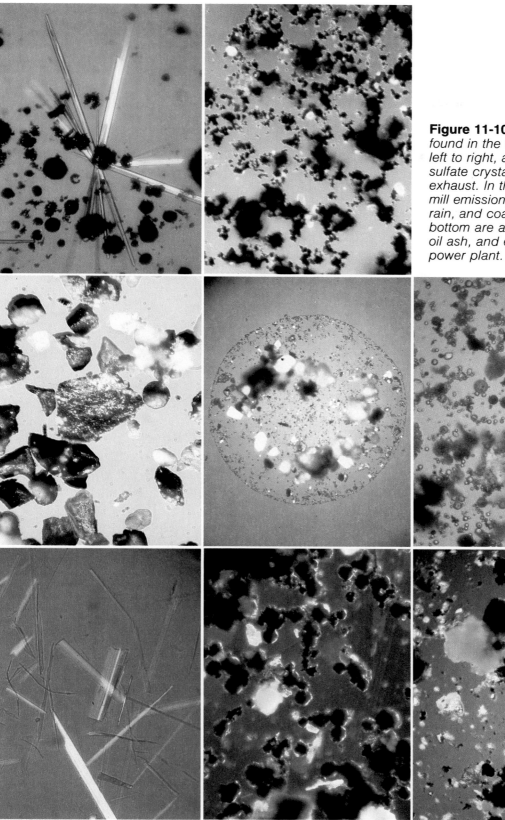

Figure 11-10 *Some pollutants found in the air. Reading from left to right, at the top are sulfate crystals and auto exhaust. In the center are steel-mill emission, a drop of acid rain, and coal ash. At the bottom are asbestos particles, oil ash, and emissions from a power plant.*

Measuring Dust Pollution

Take a clean glass microscope slide. Using a marking pencil, draw a square section on the slide measuring one centimeter by one centimeter. Apply a thin coating of petroleum jelly to the marked area only. Wipe off any jelly outside the square. Place the slide in your classroom, home, or in a safe area outdoors. At the end of three days, examine the slide with a magnifying glass or a microscope. Count the number of particles trapped in the square centimeter. Record this value. Calculate how many particles would have been trapped in a square meter. Record your answer.

Acid rain from air pollution in Germany, France, and Britain is being blamed for killing fish in Swedish lakes and destroying some trees in Swedish forests. Acid rain blown by the wind from industrial areas of the Midwest of the United States is being blamed for the pollution of lakes and forests in Northeast United States and Canada.

Pollution caused by acid rain is a serious problem. Naturally, the best way to control acid rain is to stop releasing sulfur and nitrogen oxides into the air. For example, factories can burn fuels with a very low sulfur content. But such fuels often cost more and are harder to find. So scientists continue to search for other ways to stop acid rain and other forms of air pollution.

Safeguarding the Air

Gases and particles given off when fuels are burned are called **emissions** (ee-MISH-uhnz). In theory, if the burning of fuels such as coal, oil, and natural gas is complete, the only waste products should be carbon dioxide and water vapor. In practice, however, there are always some polluting emissions given off as well. But the polluting emissions can be reduced in various ways.

For example, devices called wet scrubbers frequently are used to "wash" particles and some sulfur oxides out of smokestack fumes. The fumes are made to pass through a blanket of steam. In the process, most of the polluting emissions are dissolved in the steam. Then as the steam cools, the waste products rain down into a special collector.

Emission-cleaning tools are only a few of the many ways scientists are working to help clean up the air. In many ways, the air today is much cleaner than it was a decade ago. But in some ways, it is more polluted. Environmentalists say that to stay ahead of air pollution some pollution laws must be tightened. And emission control technology must be improved. Also alternative sources of cleaner energy, such as electric-powered cars and solar-powered homes and factories, must be further developed.

Alternate sources of energy will never eliminate all possible sources of air pollution. And tools to clean emissions will be of little value if such devices are not used. So it is vital that industry and other air pollution sources make every effort to meet air pollution standards set by our government. Furthermore, a great deal of air pollution can be traced back to people. People, for example, drive the cars that add to air pollution. But this kind of air pollution can be reduced if people make sure their cars are well tuned and their engines and exhaust systems are in good working order.

SECTION REVIEW

1. What are hydrocarbons?
2. What is it called when a layer of cold air is trapped under a layer of warm air?

11-4 Land Pollution

Mountains of garbage in solid waste dumps surround our cities. Most of these dumps are offensive to your eyes and nose. One way to deal with solid waste dumps is to cover them with thick layers of soil. In other words, bury them out of sight. But, buried dumps can still pose problems. Wastes ooze out of them to poison soil and water. Chemicals in them react to produce heat and fumes. A number of dump fires have smoldered underground for years. A few have exploded.

Figure 11-11 *Mountains of garbage* (left) *and leaking chemical drums* (right) *add to land pollution in this country.*

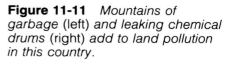

Many of the things you take for granted in your daily life produce pollution or are made from processes that produce pollution. Some examples are central heating, air conditioning, cars, and electricity. Imagine trying to live for a day without using anything that contributes to pollution. Write a 200-word story that describes what such a day would be like. Try to use as many chapter vocabulary words as you can.

Safeguarding the Land

Problems in dumps have led some environmentalists to call for an end to the dumping of solid wastes on the land. Others argue that, if it is done right, the **sanitary landfill** method can be the best way for disposing of solid wastes. In such a sanitary landfill, no hazardous wastes ever would be dumped. All garbage would be compacted or packed into the smallest possible volume. And the garbage would be covered at least once a day with a layer of soil. Built and used properly, sanitary landfills work. But they cannot handle more than a portion of the solid wastes this country produces.

The alternatives to burying garbage include dumping it in the ocean, burning it, or recycling it. At one time, much solid waste was dumped into offshore areas of the ocean. But since this is a cause of ocean pollution, it is being stopped.

Burning garbage in dumps and in the incinerators of apartment buildings, hospitals, and factories also is being halted. The burning was a major source of air pollution. But there is another type of burning increasingly being used. Since the 1960s, several European countries have burned garbage in highly efficient incinerators fitted with emission controls. Some of these efficient incinerators are in use in the United States.

Figure 11-12 *Volunteers at this recycling plant sort out substances that can be reused from those that cannot.*

Recycling, which not only gets rid of wastes but also creates useful materials, is considered the solid waste solution of the future by most environmentalists. A typical recycling plant grinds garbage into a pulp. A magnetic separator pulls iron and steel scrap out of the pulp. That scrap is recycled and used again to make useful products. Then the remaining pulp goes into a sorter. There, light wastes such as paper fibers are separated from the heavy wastes such as glass. Separated wastes are used to produce products ranging from fertilizer to aluminum cans to road-surfacing materials. Recycling plants are expensive. But in time they could pay for themselves while providing one pollution solution.

Pollution and Technology

In the chapters in this unit, you read about the wonders of science and technology. In this chapter, you learned that technology and progress can cost a price. That price can be the pollution of our environment. Perhaps nowhere is this more obvious than in the dangerous radioactive wastes produced in nuclear power plants. Some of these wastes can last thousands of years. What to do with wastes that can outlast their containers—wastes so dangerous they cannot be allowed to enter our water, air, or land uncontrolled—is one of the most serious pollution problems. However, just as technology caused this problem, technology may provide an answer to it and other pollution problems.

Technology alone, however, can do nothing. People must also be involved. For a glass bottle tossed onto the side of the road by a person can remain there unchanged for over a million years, even after radioactive wastes have become safe. Everybody, to a degree, causes pollution. And everybody can help to control its spread. Scientists point out that we have or can develop the technical knowledge to fight all types of pollution. What we need is an awareness of the problem and a will to deal with it.

Figure 11-13 *While these radioactive wastes can be temporarily stored at various disposal sites, a more permanent solution to the problems of radioactive wastes has not yet been devised.*

SECTION REVIEW

1. List four ways to dispose of garbage.
2. Name two metals removed in a recycling plant.

LABORATORY ACTIVITY

Classifying Litter

Purpose

In this activity, you will group litter according to its method of disposal.

Materials *(per group)*

Large plastic bag   Safety gloves

Procedure

1. Collect enough litter around your neighborhood or school to fill a large plastic bag.
2. List all the litter that is combustible, or usually disposed of through burning.
3. List all the litter that can be recycled.
4. List all the litter that decomposes rapidly when buried.
5. Record the total number of pieces of litter.

Observations and Conclusions

1. Calculate the percentage of litter that is combustible.

$$\% \text{ combustible} = \frac{\text{no. of combustible items}}{\text{total items}} \times 100$$

2. Calculate the percentage of litter that can be recycled. Record your calculations on a sheet of notebook paper.
3. Calculate the percentage of litter that decomposes rapidly. Show your calculations on another sheet of notebook paper.
4. Calculate the percentage of litter that will not burn, recycle, or decompose rapidly. What can be done with this litter?
5. Did you find any litter that could be reused without any recycling? List these items.
6. Which litter do you consider the most serious pollution problem?

CHAPTER REVIEW

SUMMARY

11-1 Pollution—What Is It?

- Pollution is the changing of the environment for the worse.

- The manufacturing and use of even a can of soda can lead to pollution of the air, water, and land.

11-2 Water Pollution

- There are three basic ways to deal with an oil spill: burn the oil, remove the oil to some-place else, or contain it in a small area.

- New ways to fight oil spills include high-speed skimmers, super vacuum pumps, plastic foam barriers, and absorbents.

- Rivers, lakes, streams, and ground water become polluted when chemicals seep or are dumped into them.

- Laws have been passed to prevent pollution. The laws are effective with some pollution sources but not with others.

11-3 Air Pollution

- The burning of fossil fuels by industry and cars and trucks is the major source of air pollution.

- Smog is formed when hydrocarbons and carbon monoxide react in sunlight.

- When a temperature inversion occurs, a layer of warm air traps cool air at the surface. The trapped air cannot rise and carry pollution away.

- Some pollutants combine with moisture in the air to form acids. When this moisture falls to earth, it is called acid rain.

- Forests and lakes can be destroyed by acid rain.

- Wet scrubbers and other devices can clean polluting emissions from exhaust fumes and the air.

- Use of low-sulfur fuel and emission controls also reduce air pollution.

11-4 Land Pollution

- Solid waste, or garbage, is often dumped on the land and buried. Poisonous chemicals, however, can seep out of the waste and pollute the land and water, while gas produced by decaying waste can explode and burn.

- Besides being buried, garbage can be dumped in the ocean, burned, or recycled.

- Only recycling, which allows materials to be used again, does not further pollute the environment.

VOCABULARY

Define each term in a complete sentence.

absorbent	**nonpoint source**	**pollution**	**strip mining**
acid rain	**pesticide**	**sanitary landfill**	**temperature inversion**
emission	**point source**	**smog**	**toxic**

CONTENT REVIEW: MULTIPLE CHOICE

Choose the letter of the answer that best completes each statement.

1. Strip mining involves
   a. digging in the earth in search of oil.
   c. cutting apart hills in search of coal.
   b. digging in the earth in search of coal.
   d. cutting through the ocean floor in search of oil.

2. About what percentage of the earth's surface is covered by water?
   a. 50 percent   b. 33 percent
   c. 70 percent   d. 20 percent
3. The best way to deal with oil spills in the first place is to
   a. pump them away.   b. prevent them from happening.
   c. burn them.   d. contain them.
4. A name for any dangerous chemical waste is
   a. absorbent waste.   b. toxic waste.
   c. sanitary waste.   d. nonpoint waste.
5. An example of a point source of water pollution is
   a. a solid waste dump.   b. a town sewer pipe.
   c. oozing poisonous liquids.   d. an industrial waste pond.
6. In a temperature inversion, compared to the air above it, the air on the ground is
   a. cooler.   b. warmer.
   c. the same temperature.   d. lighter.
7. Nitrogen and sulfur oxides may combine with water vapor in the air to form
   a. smog.   b. acid rain.
   c. polluting emissions.   d. solid waste particles.
8. In a wet scrubber, polluting particles are passed through a blanket of
   a. smoke.   b. electric plates.
   c. steam.   d. absorbents.
9. Gases and particles given off when fuels are burned are called
   a. hydrocarbons.   b. smog.   c. emissions.   d. acid rain.
10. Which of these do environmentalists look to as the solid waste solution of the future?
   a. burying solid wastes
   b. burning solid wastes
   c. recycling solid wastes
   d. dumping solid wastes

CONTENT REVIEW: COMPLETION

Fill in the word or words that best complete each statement.

1. _____ is a change for the worse in the environment.

2. About _____ of Earth is covered by land.

3. "Super-sucker" vacuum pumps and skimmers are weapons used to fight _____.

4. _____ are substances used to kill harmful insects.

5. _____ can form when nitrogen and sulfur gases released during the burning of fossil fuels react with water vapor in the atmosphere.

6. Drums of _____, or dangerous, wastes may lie in solid wastes dumps.

7. _____ of pollution include sewer pipes from towns, factories, and cities.

8. In a _____, air near the ground is cooler than the air above it.

9. _____ involves removing and using again various parts of garbage.

10. A sanitary landfill is a good place to dispose of nonhazardous _____ wastes.

CONTENT REVIEW: TRUE OR FALSE

Determine whether each statement is true or false. If it is true, write "true." If it is false, change the underlined word or words to make the statement true.

1. Pollution is caused by <u>natural</u> activity.
2. Cans and bottles are all forms of <u>litter</u>.
3. Dealing with an oil spill by burning it <u>adds more</u> pollution to the environment.
4. Dispersants are substances that <u>soak up oil near the</u> shore.
5. Nonpoint sources are the <u>least</u> dangerous.
6. Thick clouds of pollutants are known as <u>smog</u>.
7. Temperature inversions occur when <u>warm</u> air is trapped under <u>cold</u> air.
8. Burning <u>low-sulfur</u> fuels causes acid rain.
9. <u>Emission</u> controls reduce air pollution.
10. At a recycling plant, solid wastes are <u>carefully buried under a layer of soil</u>.

CONCEPT REVIEW: SKILL BUILDING

Use the skills you have developed in the chapter to complete each activity.

1. **Making predictions** Predict at least one problem that could result from dumping hazardous wastes into the ocean.
2. **Relating cause and effect** Describe how a temperature inversion can make air pollution much worse.
3. **Relating concepts** Explain why land, water, and air pollution cannot really be separated from one another.
4. **Expressing an opinion** Write a brief essay that either supports or refutes the following statement:
   "I think this whole environmental thing has gone too far. Once industrial profits go down because of all this government interference, the country will be worse off than before."
5. **Relating concepts** Write a short report in which you discuss how each of the following groups might react to the problem of acid rain in a certain area:
   a. tourists
   b. owners of industry
   c. wildlife preservationists
   d. people who fish
6. **Relating cause and effect** In what ways does the increasing human population on Earth cause an increase in pollution?
7. **Making predictions** Imagine the time is now 2010. Air pollution has become so bad that Congress has passed a law forbidding the use of automobiles. How do you think your life would be changed by this law?
8. **Developing a model** Plan a new town to replace the town you live in. Consider the placement of industries, shopping malls, parks and recreational facilities, housing developments, farms, and road systems. What would you do in your new town to control pollution?

CONCEPT REVIEW: ESSAY

Discuss each of the following in a brief paragraph.

1. Think about your community. List as many sources of pollution as you can. Make suggestions as to how each source could be eliminated or made less polluting.
2. Describe how a pollutant buried underground in one area might cause pollution many kilometers away from the burial site.

Adventures in Science

Jerrold Petrofsky and His *WALKING* Machine

Dr. Jerrold Petrofsky made news with his device that enable paralyzed people to walk. Here he is shown at a news conference with his first patient, Nan Davis.

AS SHE RODE in the car, Nan Davis thought back pleasantly to the events of her high school graduation. Only a few hours had passed since she had walked down the aisle to receive her diploma. A smile crossed Nan's face. Then, without warning, her car crashed. Nan was left paralyzed from the ribs down. She would never walk again . . . or would she?

The Ohio laboratory of Jerrold Petrofsky looks more like a surplus electronics store than a lab. Located at Wright State University, the lab contains a 75-kilogram computer made mostly of surplus parts connected to other electrical gadgets by a dizzying tangle of wires. At first glance, you might think you had stumbled into the workshop of an amateur inventor. But this is a place where great feats of technology are being performed.

Dr. Jerrold Petrofsky is a biomedical engineer, a scientist who uses engineering to solve problems of medicine and biology. For example, during the early 1980s, Petrofksy invented a computer-controlled mini exercise gym. It was designed to build strength in muscles that had thinned and weakened through lack of use. Through this work, Petrofsky met many physically challenged people whose muscles were not only weak but were paralyzed. Exercise would not be enough to get these people to walk again. But Petrofsky wondered whether a specially designed computer might bring about such a "miracle." He thought it might be possible to construct a computer that would act as a substitute nervous system for paralyzed legs.

Nan Davis, paralyzed in an accident, managed to take six steps down this walkway with the help of a computer and Jerrold Petrofsky's "walking machine."

Working toward this goal, Petrofsky began to experiment with a two-hundred-year-old method of electrically stimulating muscles. This method includes sending a weak electric current to the muscles to make them contract. Muscles react to such electrical signals just as they do to normal nerve impulses from the nervous system. Wires carrying the current can be attached to the skin over the muscles. They can even be put into the muscles themselves.

Petrofsky planned to use a computer to send out a series of rhythmical electrical impulses to leg muscles. But would this make the legs move in a normal way? In other words, would Petrofsky be able to find a way to coordinate the leg movements and ensure balance?

Using surplus parts bought wherever he could find them, as well as some wire that had been left behind by the telephone company, Petrofsky built a computer that could give out 2,000 different commands. It was capable of delivering measured electrical signals to paralyzed leg muscles. It could also receive and process continual signals about the position of a person's feet, legs, and hips.

The First Test

By 1982, Petrofsky was ready for his first experiment. And twenty-two-year-old Nan Davis was to be his first subject.

For the experiment, the laboratory at Wright State University was rigged with a walkway bordered by parallel bars. Nan was outfitted with a jumble of wires that led from the computer to various muscles of her legs. She was also wearing a parachute strap across her chest and shoulders that would support one third of her weight during the experiment.

Now the time had come for the test. Petrofsky turned the computer on and gave it a series of commands. Nan's right leg jerked off the floor and moved forward. Teetering from side to side, she managed to walk six

In order to walk using Dr. Petrofsky's machine, Nan's leg muscles had to be wired to a computer. The computer could make the muscles in her legs respond almost as if they were being controlled by Nan's own nervous system.

steps. These steps took her a total of three meters down the walkway. Although she could not feel her legs moving, the computer made them respond almost as if they were being controlled by Nan's own nervous system.

Nan's historic walk made headlines. But before the technique could have any real-life applications, the bulky computer would have to be replaced by a small one. This could be worn on a belt or put under the skin. Petrofsky thinks that such a feat is very possible. The technology needed to make paralyzed legs walk is much simpler than that needed to send a person to the moon, he emphasized. And that has already been done.

Nan Davis herself admits that she has a long way to go before she can again walk by herself. Computer-assisted walking still cannot help her turn, climb stairs, or sit down. Nevertheless, her first few steps made her certain that it will not be long before the "miracle lab" at Wright State University opens the door to a brighter future for herself and others like her.

Issues in Science

Is the Space Program a Good Buy?

Metal blankets keep New York City marathon runners from cooling down too quickly. The material was first developed for space exploration.

Many people worry about the cost of the space program. They ask, "Are we spending too much money on space? Could the money be better spent elsewhere?"

Of course, the space program costs money. But those in favor of continuing and expanding aerospace technology have some convincing arguments. One of these arguments involves "spinoffs." Spinoffs are products that began as materials in the space program but that turned out to have practical uses on Earth.

You often see space program spinoffs, but you may not recognize them. For example, have you ever seen marathon runners wrapped up in shiny metallic blankets after a race? These blankets keep the runner's body temperature from dropping too low. Made from lightweight, thin fabric covered with a layer of aluminum particles, these blankets were developed from space technology. The

Saudi Arabia's Haj Airport Terminal is the world's largest fabric structure. The fabric was first designed for the United States' space program.

National Air and Space Administration, or NASA, used similar metallic material to bounce radio signals off the *Echo I* communications satellite back in 1960. Since then, NASA has used this material for insulation in space. Uses on Earth include packaging for frozen foods, window shades, and candy wrappers.

There are other spinoffs as well. Liquid hydrogen was first used as a rocket fuel. It is now used in gasoline production; in the making of fertilizers, drugs, and margarine; to strengthen metals, and so on. And new practical uses of space products such as these increase by about 10 percent a year.

Fireproof fabrics developed for spacesuits are now used in fireproof clothing and blankets. The special high-intensity flood lighting designed for the Kennedy Space Center has been adapted to light up such places as Niagara Falls. Noise protection material, originally developed to stop spacecraft from vibrating, is now being used to soundproof buildings. The ability to make miniature parts for spacecraft has led to the development of miniature medical devices. These devices can be put into people's bodies to keep them alive.

People who believe the space program is very worthwhile point to other important facts. For example, they point to the many orbiting communications satellites that allow people all over the world to speak by telephone quickly and easily. Also, such satellites make possible the transmission of live TV pictures and sound from any point on Earth to any other point. Earth-orbiting satellites also keep us informed of changing weather conditions. The list of practical uses is a long one. And not many people argue about the value of these uses. But one part of the space program does spark arguments—exploration of the solar system's planets.

Why Go to the Planets?

Once, a mountain climber was asked a similar question about his desire to climb Mt. Everest, the tallest mountain on Earth. His answer? "Because it is there!"

People have always been fascinated by the unknown. And one of the great challenges that sparks scientific exploration is making the unknown known. Put another way, the planets and their moons and the stars beyond "are there." They hold mysteries, many of which if solved would unravel secrets of our own planet—secrets such as how Earth was born, how it will change, and what is in store for its future. Space scientists argue that such basic information could be very important to survival on Earth. And even if it were not of practical value, isn't the solving of nature's riddles reason enough to travel into space?

Perhaps, some people say. But we have problems on Earth that need solving too—problems of life and death such as poverty and hunger. Isn't space exploration simply too expensive? Wouldn't the money be better spent on Earth?

*F**are to Saturn—$2.00*

People in favor of the space program claim that it is not especially costly. In 1982, less than one percent of the United States' federal budget was spent on space exploration. And the two *Voyager* missions to Saturn cost each American only about $2.00. You probably spend more money than that on pizza in just a few weeks.

Another thing to remember, those in favor of space exploration point out, is that money spent *on* space is not money spent *in* space. The money that is spent goes to people right here on Earth. The space program creates jobs for people. People build the spacecraft. People monitor the spacecraft, give them instructions, and collect the data satellites send back to Earth. Still other people analyze the data. If the space program were discontinued, thousands of people would be forced to find work elsewhere.

Space scientists say that the cost of future space missions could be brought down. They recommend a program of 14 space missions to be launched between 1988 and 2000. This would lower the cost of each mission, the scientists say, since such a schedule would allow missions to be flown closer together. This would save money. Furthermore, the same kind of spacecraft could be used to fly all the missions. This would be less expensive than building different kinds of spacecraft.

This program would give scientists new glimpses of Mars, Venus, Saturn, Uranus, comets, and asteroids. Programs that would follow include: bringing back samples of rock and soil from Mars; exploring the surface of Mars with "rovers," or remote controlled carts; and bringing back a clump of a comet.

Could all of this space exploration lead to practical benefits on Earth? Scientists say that there are many valuable natural resources in space, especially metals of all kinds. But we cannot get at these until we learn how to get around in space. And that is one thing a continued space program will teach us.

Spinoffs, space resources, and the answers to puzzling questions are "products" of space exploration. Are they worth spending money on? What do you think?

Are expensive communications satellites worth the money we spend on them?

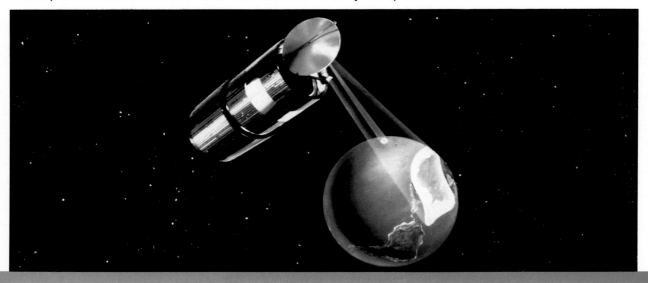

Sailing to the Stars

Tim gulped down his breakfast on Starship *Metropolis* and headed for the space school on Deck 2. He was late. In another ten minutes, the first period bell would ring and the space technology test would begin. Today's test was on the history of starships. Tim was counting on his own experience with space technology to help him pass the test. After all, he had lived on a spaceship all his life.

Tim had been born 14 years before on Starship *Metropolis*. The ship was then in the 15th year of its 40-year voyage to Earth's nearest star, Alpha Centauri. His father and mother had been part of the original crew that had boarded the spaceship on Earth in the year 2079. But for Tim, Earth was almost an unknown planet. Certainly his parents still talked about Earth, and he was mildly curious. But for the most part, it was only the subject of a history course that he would study the following year.

Tim's world was the 2-kilometer-long Starship *Metropolis*. It was made up of 20 circular decks containing 2500 passengers, 20 shops, a hospital, a laser video theater, and 1100 living units. Most living areas were surrounded by constantly rotating cylinders that prevented weightlessness. The rotating cylinders also shielded Tim and the other people on the ship from the dangerous and penetrating radiation of space.

Nuclear Powered Rockets

Tim trotted along the circular corridor of Deck 11. As he ran, he reviewed some of the facts about early space technology. He knew that the first spaceships had been based on engineering principles developed by earth scientists more than a hundred years ago. That time was now known as the "great age of space engines." During this time, the first chemically powered rockets were produced. These rockets were able to escape the pull of Earth's gravity and reach the moon.

However, before the end of the 20th century, most space scientists knew that no spaceship could travel fast enough to reach the distant stars without the use of nuclear fuel. Nuclear fuel is millions of times more powerful than any chemical fuel.

Deuterium, a heavy form of hydrogen, was the first nuclear fuel used in the spaceships of the early twenty-first century. The deuterium atoms were fused, or brought together, in nuclear reactors. This fusion process produced an almost unending flow of energy. Some of the early nuclear spaceships were capable of carrying several million tons of deuterium for long voyages to stars outside the earth's solar system. Others carried less fuel but contained refining equipment. This equipment could get deuterium out of raw materials that the ship stopped to mine on other planets during the space voyage.

By the time Tim reached Deck 5, where the shops were arranged like a shopping mall, he was beginning to feel more confident about the test. If enough of the test questions turned out to be about his own spaceship, he knew he would have no trouble passing.

Inside the Starship *Metropolis* are all the comforts of home.

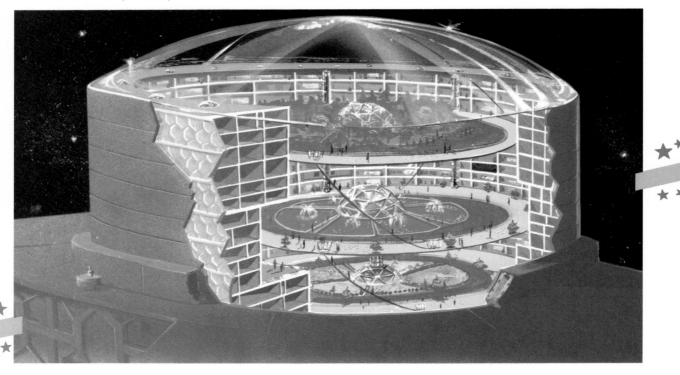

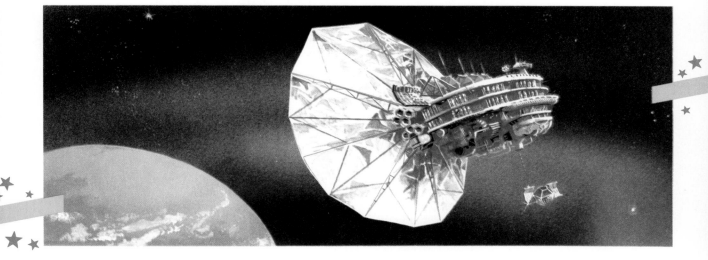

Relying on the light of nearby stars or lasers on Earth,
a light sail propels a starship through space.

The Latest in Starships

Starship *Metropolis* represented one of the most amazing achievements in spaceship technology. It could go anywhere without ever running out of fuel. It would never run out of fuel because it was powered by hydrogen that it picked up from space. At this very moment, the ship was plunging through space at more than one tenth the speed of light. It was attracting hydrogen from space with a magnetic field shaped like an enormous funnel. The magnetic field was thousands of kilometers in diameter. When the ship finally approached the end of its journey, it would be slowed down by reversing its magnetic field to repel, rather than attract, hydrogen.

Between Decks 3 and 2, where the classroom was located, Tim came to a passage without gravity. He dropped into a suction chute and slid into the weightlessness of the passage. There he floated down the passage, using handles on the wall to move himself along. While he glided, he felt a tinge of pride about living on Starship *Metropolis*. It certainly was the latest in spaceship technology. Then he remembered the new starship being designed on Earth, which his teacher had told the class about. The new ship would be propelled by a light sail made of a thin sheet of aluminum that was many kilometers wide. As this ship traveled through space, the sail would gather light energy from a laser on Earth, or light from nearby stars. The light energy would be used to send the ship sailing through space.

Tim reached Deck 2 and cut across the park, which contained full-sized trees and an entire flower garden in bloom. For a moment he was struck by the fact that his entire world, including apartments, a school, and even a park, could be contained in one starship hurtling through space. What would it be like, he wondered, when the journey finally came to an end, and he was able to leave the only world he had ever known?

Tim looked up through the plastic dome of the ship. A very bright yellow star shone in the blackness of space. Alpha Centauri was like a beacon guiding Tim and the Starship *Metropolis* to a new home.

Oceanography

Roaring toward shore, a huge wave curls over and plunges downward. The wave is packed with energy that may have been released into the ocean thousands of kilometers away. For waves are born far out at sea where winds stir up the water. The energy of these winds builds waves.

There is, of course, much more to the sea than foaming waves. Beneath the waves live some of the strangest creatures on earth: fish of all sizes and shapes, giant clams, gigantic squid, and the largest animal ever to inhabit the earth, the blue whale.

This is a world where great "rivers" flow; where mountains rise but never touch the air; where not far beneath the surface there is total blackness—except for the tiny glowing lights of strange animals and the few research vessels that venture deep beneath the waves.

CHAPTERS

12 **Currents and Waves**

13 **The Ocean Floor**

14 **Ocean Life**

A huge ocean wave

12 Currents and Waves

CHAPTER SECTIONS

12-1 Ocean Waves

12-2 Ocean Currents

CHAPTER OBJECTIVES

After completing this chapter, you will be able to:

12-1 Explain what causes waves.

12-1 Identify four characteristics of waves.

12-1 Explain what happens when waves reach the shore.

12-1 Discuss why tsunamis are so dangerous.

12-2 Explain what causes currents.

12-2 Describe the characteristics of surface currents.

12-2 Compare surface currents and deep currents.

On April 1, 1946, a strong earthquake cracked the ocean floor 3500 kilometers north of Oahu, Hawaii. An enormous amount of energy was released. Much of this energy went into producing a series of fast-moving ocean waves. The waves spread out from the center of the earthquake like ripples in a pond. These waves were far apart and hardly noticeable. But the waves were traveling at the speed of a jet plane—about 780 kilometers an hour!

About four hours after the earthquake, these fast-moving waves approached Oahu. In the shallow waters off Oahu the waves bunched together and increased tremendously in height. As the first huge wave neared Oahu, the sound of normal waves breaking on the beach suddenly stopped. The ocean retreated far beyond normal low tide, exposing reefs and stranding fish.

People did not realize what was happening and hurried toward the shore to see. Suddenly, a wall of water rushed over the horizon and roared in. The wave was more than 30 meters high—a terrible wall of destruction.

A half dozen of these huge waves hit the island. One eyewitness said the waves "sounded like dozens of locomotives blowing off steam." What forces create these waves, and ordinary waves as well? You will find the answers as you explore the pages of this chapter.

Destruction caused by a tsunami

12-1 Ocean Waves

What causes the waves that you normally see at the beach? Where do these waves come from? **Waves are pulses of energy that move through the ocean.** If you wiggle your fingers in a still pond of water, you create a series of ripples that spreads out in every direction. The ripples are set in motion by the movement of your fingers. Put another way, the energy of your moving fingers is transferred to the water. The ripples are surface waves, just like ocean waves but much smaller.

Most ocean waves are caused by the energy of moving air, or wind. Ocean waves begin as wind-stirred ripples on the sea's surface. Some of the

Figure 12-1 *The ocean is calm and has very low waves when there is little or no wind (top). But when the energy from strong winds is transferred to the ocean, the water becomes rough and there are high waves (bottom).*

FACTORS THAT AFFECT THE HEIGHT OF SURFACE WAVES

Wind speed (m/sec)	Length of time wind blows (hr)	Distance wind blows over water (km)	Average height of wave (m)
5.1	2.4	18.5	0.27
10.2	10.0	140.0	1.5
15.3	23.0	520.0	4.1
20.4	42.0	1320.0	8.5
25.5	69.0	2570.0	14.8

Figure 12-2 *The factors that affect the height of surface waves are shown in this chart. What happens to the height of a wave as the wind speed increases?*

energy from the wind is transferred to the sea. The waves look like great surges of rapidly moving water. But the water is not moving forward at all. It is actually energy that moves forward through the water producing one wave after another!

The height of surface waves depends on three factors. These factors are the wind's speed, the length of time the wind blows, and the distance the wind blows over the water. As each of these factors increases, the height of the wave increases. See Figure 12-2 . Because the Pacific Ocean has the longest stretch of open water in the world, you might expect that the biggest waves sweep over this area. This should happen because winds can travel the longest distance in the Pacific.

As it turns out, the largest surface wave ever measured in the middle of any ocean occurred in the North Pacific on February 7, 1933. At that time, a wind storm was sweeping over a stretch of water thousands of kilometers long. A ship in the United States Navy, the *U.S.S. Ramapo*, was plowing through the storm when its officers spotted and measured a gigantic wave. It was at least 34 meters high! Such a wave could rise above a ten-story apartment house.

Waves of about 13 to 15 meters high occur in the Atlantic Ocean. Waves are usually not higher because the Atlantic has shorter stretches of open water than the Pacific. So winds do not travel as far.

Activity

Waves and Energy

The following experiment may help you better understand that wave motion is the transfer of energy between two points without the transfer of matter.

Find a length of rope. You and a friend hold either end of the rope. You make waves by shaking your end of the rope. You can see the waves travel down the rope, but obviously the rope itself is not moving from you toward your friend. What is actually traveling down the rope between you and your friend?

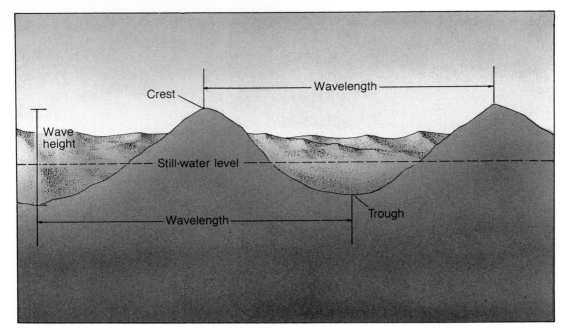

Figure 12-3 *Some characteristics of ocean waves are shown in this diagram. What is the highest point of a wave called?*

Figure 12-4 *This unusual formation is the result of waves crashing against a rocky shoreline and slowly wearing away most of the rocks.*

Characteristics of Waves

Every surface wave has a characteristic crest, trough, wavelength, and wave height. The highest part of a wave is called the **crest.** The lowest part of a wave is called the **trough** (trawf). The horizontal distance between two successive crests or two successive troughs is called the **wavelength.** The vertical distance between a crest and a trough is called the **wave height.** See Figure 12-3. Waves can have various wavelengths and wave heights.

The same pattern of wave motion can occur over and over again at regular intervals of time. The interval of time required for successive crests or troughs to pass a given point is the **wave period.** Changes in the speed of the wind blowing over the waves will change the wave period.

The relationship between the period, speed, and wavelength of a wave can be shown by the following equation:

period of wave (seconds) =

$$\frac{\textbf{wavelength of wave (meters)}}{\textbf{speed of wave (meters per second)}}$$

For example, what is the speed of a wave if the period is 15 seconds and the wavelength is 90 meters? Let X equal wave speed, then

$$15 \text{ seconds} = \frac{90 \text{ meters}}{X \text{ meters per second}}$$

$$X \text{ meters per second} = \frac{90 \text{ meters}}{15 \text{ seconds}}$$

$$X = 6 \text{ meters per second}$$

So, the wave is traveling at 6 meters per second.

Now suppose the wavelength is 100 meters and the speed of a wave is 50 meters per second. What is the period, or time required for successive crests to pass a given point?

Career: *Physical Oceanographer*

HELP WANTED: PHYSICAL OCEANOGRAPHER Master's degree in oceanography and a bachelor's degree in oceanography, physical sciences, or mathematics required. Duties include data collection and analysis. On-the-job-training will be provided.

The sea has always been a source of mystery and fascination. For years, people sailed the seas for purposes of fishing, trade, and transportation. Today many sailors study the sea in the interest of science to gather valuable information. Among these scientific sailors are the **physical oceanographers**.

Physical oceanographers study currents and waves. Their research provides data that aids in managing pollution and in navigating submarines. It also informs the fishing industry about the distribution and abundance of available fish. Study of the interaction between the sea and atmosphere may aid in more accurate weather prediction. Research also includes the study of tsunamis and the ocean bottom and its sediments and composition.

Oceanographers use ships, aircraft, satellites, and underwater craft in their work. They also use a variety of specialized instruments including cameras and sounding devices. Oceanographers often work in on-shore laboratories. Here they can study the actions of waves and tides by reproducing them in large water tanks.

Students who enjoy nature and the outdoors, have a curiosity about the sea, and do well in the study of science may want to learn more about oceanography. To do so, write to the International Oceanographic Foundation, 3979 Rickenbacker Causeway, Virginia Key, Miami, FL 33149.

Figure 12-5 *This photograph, taken near Oahu, Hawaii, is a spectacular example of an ocean wave.*

Out at sea, waves stay about the same distance apart for thousands of kilometers. So wavelength is usually constant. These waves are called **swells**. They are long, wide waves that are not very high.

But waves change as they near shore. The waves slow down as they touch the shallow bottom of the ocean. In addition, the waves get closer and closer together. That is, their wavelength decreases and the wave height increases. At last they crash forward as **breakers** and surge up the beach. The surging water is called the **surf**.

Then the water flows back toward the sea. You can see the water pulling sand, pebbles, and bits of seaweed oceanward. Sometimes this flow of water back out to sea is very strong. It may continue for several kilometers. This retreating water is called an **undertow**. A strong undertow can be very dangerous. Swimmers can be pulled out to sea by a strong undertow.

Tsunamis

As you read in the introduction to this chapter, earthquakes can also cause waves. Earthquakes cause the largest of all ocean waves. These waves are called **tsunamis** (tsoo-NAH-mees). "Tsunami" is a Japanese word meaning "large wave in a harbor."

When an earthquake causes the land to move under an ocean, energy is transferred to the ocean. But this energy, great as it is, is spread out through a

Figure 12-6 *The pattern of a swell as it reaches a sloping beach is shown in this diagram. What happens to the wavelength and the wave height as the wave nears the beach?*

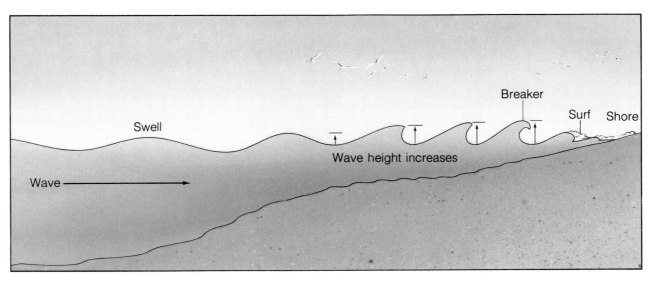

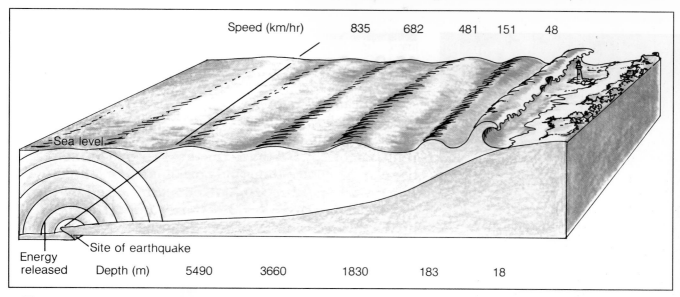

| Speed (km/hr) | | 835 | 682 | 481 | 151 | 48 |

Sea level

Energy released

Site of earthquake

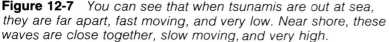

| Depth (m) | | 5490 | 3660 | 1830 | 183 | 18 |

Figure 12-7 *You can see that when tsunamis are out at sea, they are far apart, fast moving, and very low. Near shore, these waves are close together, slow moving, and very high.*

great depth of water. So in deep water, the energy only causes a small wave at the ocean's surface. Each wave may be only about 30 centimeters high. Moreover, its wavelength may be up to 720 kilometers. But as the waves travel toward shore, their wavelengths shorten. The waves are slowed down as the ocean becomes shallower. The waves pile closer together and get very high. The energy that was spread throughout a great depth of water is now concentrated in much less water. This energy produces the huge waves of tsunamis. Tsunamis can reach heights of 35 meters or more when they strike the shore.

As you might expect, tsunamis can cause great damage and loss of life along coastal areas. One of the most famous groups of tsunamis was caused by the volcanic eruption of the island of Krakatoa between Java and Sumatra in 1883. Nine tsunamis that rose up to 40 meters high hit along the Java coast. Nothing was left of the coastal towns and about 36,000 people died.

SECTION REVIEW

1. What causes ocean waves? List the three factors that determine the height of surface waves.
2. List four characteristics of surface waves.

Activity

Waves in Your Bathtub

This activity works best at night with a bright bathroom light turned on.

1. Place about 2 cm of water in your bathtub. Tap the water with the eraser end of a pencil and observe the resulting wave.

2. Tap the water with the pencil laid flat and observe the resulting wave.

3. Place a ruler in the water as a barrier. Position the ruler so it forms a 45-degree angle with the flat pencil.

4. Tap the flat portion of the pencil and observe the resulting wave.

How do the characteristics of the three waves differ?

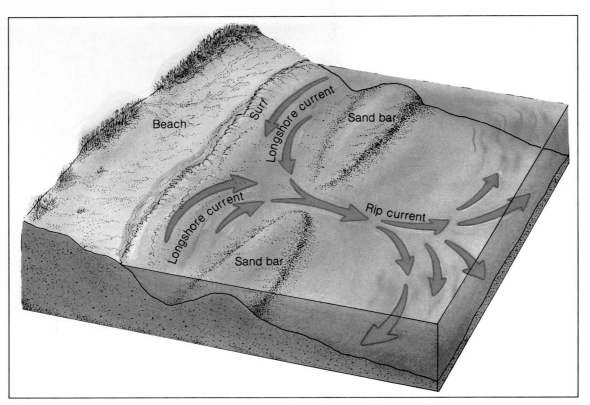

Figure 12-11 *When longshore currents cut through a sand bar, a rip current is formed.*

As longshore currents move parallel to shore, they can pick up large quantities of material, such as sand from the beaches. The sand is deposited in open water close to shore. A long, underwater pile of sand called a sand bar builds up.

Longshore currents can become trapped on the shore side of a sand bar. These currents eventually may cut an opening in the sand bar. The currents then return to the sea in a powerful narrow flow called a **rip current.** See Figure 12-11. A rip current is the type of strong undertow that you read about earlier in this chapter.

Deep Currents

Some currents are caused mainly by differences in water density deep beneath the ocean's surface. The density, or mass per unit volume, is affected by temperature and salinity, or saltiness. Cold water is more dense than warm water. And the saltier the water is, the more dense it is. For example, cold dense water flowing out of the world's polar regions moves downward under less dense warm water. This deep river of water is called a **deep current**.

Cameras lowered to the ocean floor in many places have photographed evidence of these powerful deep currents. The photographs show ripples carved into the sand of the ocean bottom. In places on the floor, heavy clay has been piled into small dunes, as if shaped by winds. These "winds," scientists conclude, must be ocean currents. And to shape and move the heavy clay, these currents must be very strong.

Most deep currents flow in the opposite direction from surface currents. For example, in the summer, the Mediterranean Sea loses more water by evaporation than it gets back as rain. As a result, the salinity of the Mediterranean increases and so does its density. This causes deep currents of dense Mediterranean water to flow out along the ocean floor into the Atlantic Ocean. At the same time, Atlantic Ocean water that is less salty, and thus less dense, flows into the Mediterranean at the ocean's surface.

The densest ocean water in the world lies off the Antarctic coast. This dense, cold Antarctic water sinks to the ocean floor and tends to flow northward through the world's oceans. These deep Antarctic currents travel for thousands of kilometers. At the same time, warm surface currents near the equator tend to flow south toward Antarctica.

As the deep Antarctic currents near the land, the ocean floor rises, forcing these cold currents upward. The rising of deep cold currents to the ocean surface is called **upwelling**. Upwelling is very important because the rising currents carry with them rich foodstuffs that have drifted down to the ocean floor—the remains of dead animals and plants. Wherever these deep currents rise, the sea life is plentiful. For example, deep currents move upward off the coasts of Peru and Chile. There are very important fishing industries in both of these areas.

Figure 12-12 *There is plentiful fishing off the coasts of Peru and Chile. The reason is that in these areas deep Antarctic currents carry water rich in food matter toward the ocean's surface.*

SECTION REVIEW

1. What are the causes of ocean currents?
2. What is the main cause of surface currents? Of deep currents?

LABORATORY ACTIVITY

Observing a Model Thermocline

Purpose

In this activity, you will set up and observe a model of a thermocline—a thin zone of rapid temperature change that occurs within a body of cool water when it is heated from above.

Materials (per group)

2-L plastic soda bottle with top cut off
6 thermometers (100° C)
Light source
Sheet of plastic (transparency or plastic folder)
Clear tape
Safety goggles
Clock or watch with sweep second hand
Graph paper
Colored pencils or crayons

Procedure

1. Put your safety goggles on.
2. Fill a plastic container with water to a height of 16 cm.
3. Tape six thermometers to a plastic sheet so that the top one is just below the surface of the water in the container. The remaining thermometers should be placed so that they record temperatures at depths of 2, 4, 6, 8, and 10 cm below the water's surface. Allow a minute or two for all of the thermometers to reach water temperature. Then record the temperature at each level.
4. Adjust the light source so that it is about 15 cm above the surface of the water and turn it on. Observe and record the temperatures at each level every 2 minutes for a total of 20 minutes.
5. At the end of the 20-minute heating period, turn off the light source.

Observations and Conclusions

1. Make a graph of the temperature at each level versus time. Use a different colored pencil or crayon for each different thermometer. Properly label the temperature curves drawn for each level.
2. On another piece of graph paper, make a second graph. Plot the data for temperature versus depth at the end of the 20-minute heating period only. This graph should show a single curve.
3. At which depth did you observe the greatest range in temperature? In °C, what was the extent of this temperature range? At which depth did you observe the smallest range in temperature? In °C, what was the extent of this temperature range?
4. What is the approximate depth and thickness of the zone in which temperatures changed most rapidly? This represents the location of the thermocline.

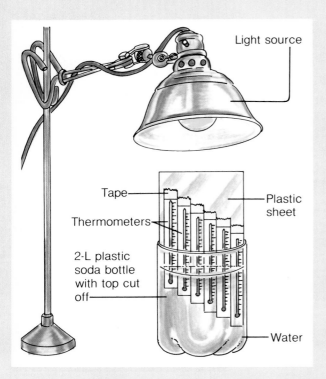

Light source

Tape

Thermometers

2-L plastic soda bottle with top cut off

Plastic sheet

Water

CHAPTER REVIEW

SUMMARY

12-1 Ocean Waves

- Waves are pulses of energy that move through the ocean.

- Most ocean waves are caused by wind.

- The height of surface waves depends on the wind's speed, the length of time the wind blows, and the distance the wind blows over the water.

- Characteristics of waves include crest, trough, wave height, wavelength, and period.

- Tsunamis are the largest of all ocean waves and are usually caused by earthquakes.

12-2 Ocean Currents

- Currents are streams of water in the ocean.

- Ocean currents are caused mainly by wind patterns and differences in water density.

- Currents are located near the surface or deep in the ocean.

- Surface currents are caused mainly by wind patterns.

- Deep currents are caused mainly by density differences in ocean water.

- Most deep currents flow in the opposite direction from surface currents.

VOCABULARY

Define each term in a complete sentence.

breaker

crest

current

deep current

long distance
  surface current

longshore current

rip current

short distance
  surface current

surf

surface current

swell

trough

tsunami

undertow

upwelling

wave

wave height

wavelength

wave period

CONTENT REVIEW: MULTIPLE CHOICE

Choose the letter of the answer that best completes each statement.

1. The height of surface waves in the ocean depends on
   a. wind speed.   b. length of time the wind blows.
   c. distance the wind blows over the water.   d. all of the above.
2. The horizontal distance between two successive crests is called the
   a. period.   b. wavelength.   c. wave height.   d. trough.
3. The time required for successive crests to pass a given point is called the
   a. period.   b. wavelength.   c. wave height.   d. trough.
4. A strong flow of water back toward the sea is called a(n)
   a. swell.   b. breaker.   c. undertow.   d. surf.

5. Tsunamis are
   a. usually caused by earthquakes.   b. usually caused by winds.
   c. dangerous far out at sea.   d. all of the above.

6. Ocean currents can be caused by
   a. wind patterns.   b. differences in water density.
   c. none of the above.   d. both of the above.

7. The Gulf Stream is an example of a
   a. short distance surface current.   b. cold-water current.
   c. long distance surface current.   d. deep current.

8. Longshore currents are examples of
   a. short distance surface currents.   b. rip currents.
   c. long distance surface currents.   d. deep currents.

9. A powerful undertow flowing out to sea through a narrow opening in a sand
   bar is called a
   a. longshore current.   b. swell.   c. rip current.   d. breaker.

10. Deep currents are caused mainly by
   a. winds.   b. differences in water density.
   c. earthquakes.   d. short distance surface currents.

CONTENT REVIEW: COMPLETION

Fill in the word or words that best complete each statement.

1. Waves are pulses of _____ that move through the ocean.

2. Most ocean waves are caused by the energy of _____.

3. The _____ is the highest part of a wave.

4. The vertical distance between a crest and a trough is called the _____.

5. Long, wide waves out at sea that are not very high are called _____.

6. The largest of all ocean waves are known as _____.

7. _____ are the main cause of surface currents.

8. An undertow that flows like a powerful narrow stream is a _____.

9. A current that runs parallel to the shoreline is called a(n) _____ current.

10. Currents caused mainly by density differences are called _____.

CONTENT REVIEW: TRUE OR FALSE

Determine whether each statement is true or false. If it is true, write "true." If it is false, change the underlined word or words to make the statement true.

1. Waves are pulses of <u>energy</u> that move through the ocean.

2. The lowest part of a wave is called the <u>crest</u>.

3. A <u>wavelength</u> is the vertical distance between a crest and a trough.

4. A strong flow of water back out to sea is called a <u>swell</u>.

5. Tsunamis start as <u>small</u> waves far out at sea.

6. <u>Differences in water density</u> are the main cause of surface currents.

292

7. The Gulf Stream is a <u>short</u> distance surface current.

8. A rip current is a <u>short</u> distance surface current.

9. A longshore current flows <u>parallel</u> to the shoreline.

10. Deep currents are caused mainly by <u>winds</u>.

CONCEPT REVIEW: SKILL BUILDING

Use the skills you have developed in the chapter to complete each activity.

1. Interpreting charts List the factors that determine the height of surface waves. Then use Figure 12-2 to explain what happens when each of these factors decreases.

2. Identifying relationships Explain the relationship between the period, speed, and wavelength of a wave. Does the period of a wave increase or decrease when the wavelength and wave speed increase?

3. Making calculations Complete the following table.

Speed *(m/sec)*	Period *(sec)*	Wavelength *(m)*
20		100
	25	60
70		80
50	10	

4. Relating facts Why do you think ocean water near the equator is less dense than ocean water near the poles?

5. Relating cause and effect In 1964, an earthquake hit Alaska. At about the same time, Crescent City, California was damaged by a giant wave. Are these events related? Explain your answer.

6. Interpreting diagrams Use the following diagram to answer these questions:

a. Which wave has the greatest wavelength?

b. Which wave has the greatest wave height?

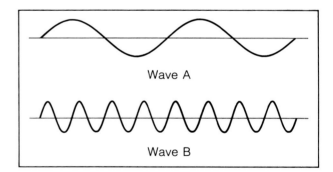

Wave A

Wave B

CONCEPT REVIEW: ESSAY

Discuss each of the following in a brief paragraph.

1. Explain in terms of energy why tsunamis are very small far out at sea and very high near shore.

2. Discuss how surface currents and deep currents can affect ocean life.

3. Describe four characteristics of a wave.

4. Compare surface and deep currents.

5. What is an undertow? Why can it be dangerous for swimmers?

6. Describe the major causes of currents.

7. Compare long distance and short distance surface currents.

8. Explain why areas near upwellings tend to be important fishing areas.

13 The Ocean Floor

CHAPTER SECTIONS

13-1 Continental Margins

13-2 Deep-Sea Basins

CHAPTER OBJECTIVES

After completing this chapter, you will be able to:

13-1 Describe and explain the differences between continental shelves, continental slopes, and submarine canyons.

13-2 Identify the features of the ocean basins.

13-2 Compare seamounts, islands, and tablemounts.

13-2 Compare the three different types of coral reefs.

Alvin is ready to dive. It is hot and muggy inside the little cabin of this submarine. The water rises over the viewports. Dropping at a rate of 30 meters a minute, *Alvin* begins a 2740-meter dive to the bottom of the Atlantic Ocean. The dive will take about an hour and a half.

Twenty seconds pass. The total pressure of the sea on *Alvin's* hull is now nearly 150 tons. And every twenty seconds of the dive the pressure will increase by the same amount.

Within 15 minutes, the bright sunlight at the water's surface fades quickly as if it had never been. All that is left is a faint greenish glow. The sunlit surface layers of the sea, where ships sail and scuba divers explore, makes up only a small percentage of the sea's total depth.

About 75 percent of the world's oceans lie in cold and darkness. The landscape beneath the oceans is as unearthly as the moon's. In this chapter, you will explore this region of the ocean. Your journey begins at the edge of the ocean.

Alvin explores the ocean depths

Figure 13-1 *This one-person research vessel can descend about 610 meters beneath the ocean's surface. The clawlike hands are used to collect underwater specimens.*

13-1 Continental Margins

The **continental margin** is the area where the underwater edges of the continents meet the ocean basin. Although the continental margins form part of the ocean floor, they are more a part of the land than of the sea. **Included in the continental margin are such ocean features as continental shelves, continental slopes, and submarine canyons.**

Continental Shelves

You are about 45 kilometers off the New Jersey coast in a small submarine. Traveling eastward, you are a short distance above the sea floor, which is about 33 meters below the ocean's surface. The part of a continent between the shoreline and the area where the ocean floor begins a steep descent is called the **continental shelf.** The light is dim. Looking upward, you can see why. The water is cloudy. Powerful beams from your searchlights show countless tiny particles slowly floating downward through the sea. These particles of sand, mud, and clay come

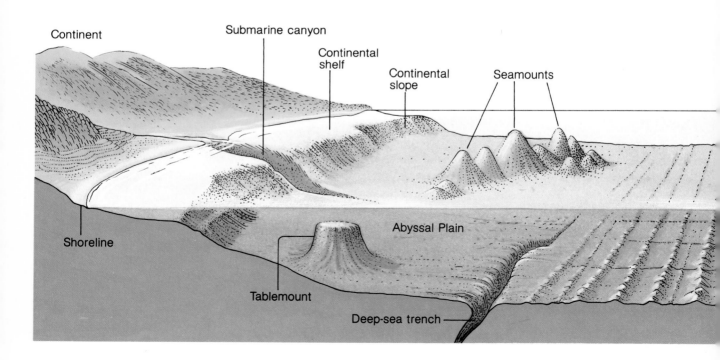

Continent

Submarine canyon

Continental shelf

Continental slope

Seamounts

Shoreline

Tablemount

Abyssal Plain

Deep-sea trench

from the land, carried by the flow of rivers into the ocean. The ocean floor beneath you is covered with layers of the same materials.

Buried in these layers are bones of long extinct animals, remains of stone spears, knives, and axes, and some human skeletons. Similar layers also are found along the continental shelves of other continents around the world.

Scientists believe that about 18,000 years ago the shelves were dry land. The world was colder then. Much of the water that now makes up the ocean was frozen in huge ice caps around the North and South Poles. As a result, sea levels were lower and the shelves were dry land. As the world warmed, the ice melted and sea levels rose, flooding the shelves. Time and again in the earth's history, this cycle has been repeated.

Now lobsters, crabs, and starfish roam this drowned land. Animals that look like plants are rooted to the ocean floor. Fish swim all around.

You travel onward. The shelf begins to slant gently downward. This slant is so gradual that you notice little change. You travel along the continental margin more than five kilometers before your depth increases by even a meter.

Figure 13-2 *In this illustration, you can see the major features of the ocean floor that make up the continental margins and deep-sea basins.*

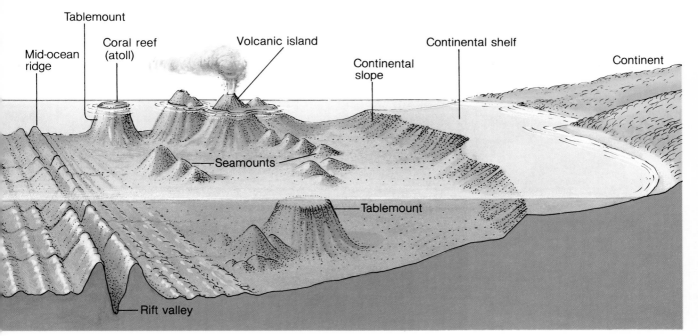

Continental Slopes

The depth increases slowly as you travel farther from shore. Suddenly, you do not see any ocean floor! You are floating over a chasm, almost like a bottomless pit. Below you there seems to be nothing but murky water.

You have traveled over the edge of the continental shelf. The ocean floor plunges down at an average change of about 66 meters per kilometer. This part of the ocean floor is called the **continental slope**. Some slopes are much steeper than others. The continental slope is the boundary between the continents and the varied features of the basin.

Submarine Canyons

You now have traveled to a depth of the ocean where you can "see" better with sound than light. Your special echo-ranger sends out sound waves in all directions and times the return of the echoes. In this way, you can build an "echo-picture" of your surroundings. Suddenly, the echoes show that you are between two steep cliff walls!

You are in a **submarine canyon**. These deep canyons are U- or V-shaped valleys that cut through the continental shelf and slope. This particular canyon is called the Hudson Submarine Canyon. At this point, the floor of the canyon lies 230 meters beneath your ship! The far wall is seven kilometers away, too far to be seen.

Your ship drops further into the canyon. The canyon walls are full of cracks. Lobsters and crabs dart into these cracks as the ship descends. Suddenly, what looks like a solid gray wall looms up in front of you. But it is not solid. It twists and churns like a thick column of smoke, plunging rapidly down the canyon wall.

Once your ship changes direction and rises to safety, you realize that you have seen a powerful **underwater avalanche**. Somewhere above on the canyon rim, a mud slide started the avalanche. Underwater avalanches are made up of swiftly moving rocks and mud that slide down the continental slopes. Perhaps the avalanche was triggered by a minor earthquake or other movement on the slopes.

Figure 13-3 *These divers are swimming toward a submarine canyon cut into the continental shelf.*

A mud slide often begins an underwater avalanche, as tons of mud begin sliding down into the canyon. Such slides reach speeds of nearly 100 kilometers an hour. The sliding, gritty material cuts into the rocks like sandpaper. The mud slide disappears into the depths. But for a long time you can hear it rumbling down the canyon floor to the deep sea.

The undersea avalanche you saw is common along submarine canyons. Avalanches play a major part in carving out these great canyons—some of which are deeper and wider than the Grand Canyon of the Colorado River!

Again you change direction and steer your ship farther into the ocean depths. The continental slope

Career: *Oil-rig Worker*

HELP WANTED: OIL-RIG WORKERS
To join drilling team on off-shore oil rig. High school diploma needed. Vocational training or previous experience a plus. Involves outdoor work requiring strength and stamina.

The oceans are filled with an abundance of plant and animal life. When marine organisms die, they sink into the ocean depths and are gradually covered with layers of soil and rock. Those remains that were deeply buried millions of years ago have since been exposed to great heat and pressure—turning them into fossil fuels. Today these fossil fuels, crude oil and natural gas, provide three-fourths of all the energy used in the United States.

To recover the oil and gas stored beneath the continental shelves, the petroleum industry hires many scientists and nonscientists to locate the fuels and bring them to the surface. A team of **oil-rig workers** is sent by helicopter and boat to the drill site many miles off the coast. They build a drilling rig to support the equipment. Other drill team workers, such as the "roughnecks" and "roustabouts", periodically connect lengths of pipe and apply mud for lubrication during the drilling process.

All the workers on an offshore oil rig work long hours and are on constant call. They may live on the rig for two weeks and then be off for two weeks. Workers must be physically fit, agile, and unafraid of heights.

Oil-rig work is a dangerous and exciting job done in isolated places. Anyone interested should enjoy working outdoors under a variety of weather conditions. Mechanical ability is also needed to work with tools, instruments, and machinery. Wages are high and there is a good chance for advancement, especially for those with math and science ability. To learn more, write to the American Petroleum Institute, 1220 L Street, NW, Washington, DC 20005.

descends in a series of jagged steps stretching down into the deep ocean. You are rapidly approaching the ocean basin.

SECTION REVIEW

1. What is a continental margin?
2. List three features of continental margins.
3. How may submarine canyons form?

Activity

Exploring the Ocean Depths

Darkness and high pressure have been the major problems in underwater exploration. Many different kinds of vehicles have been or will be used for scientific research of the ocean depths. The first deep-sea expedition was conducted by scientists aboard the research ship *Glomar Challenger*. Other vehicles include *Cyana*, *Alvin*, *Deep Tow*, *Epaulard*, *Argo* and *Jason*, and the *Trieste*.

Using reference materials in the library, find out about the journeys taken by these vehicles into the ocean depths. Write a report. Include answers to the following questions:

1. How deep can each vehicle go?
2. Were people on board or were these vehicles guided by remote control?
3. What kinds of experiments did the scientists conduct?
4. What new information did these vehicles discover about the ocean depths?

13-2 Deep-Sea Basins

Ocean basins form the true sea floor. The ocean basin of the North Atlantic extends from the edges of the North American Continental Margin to the edges of the European and North African continental margins. If you think that the bottom of the ocean is flat, you are in for a surprise. The basins are places of great contrast. Their landscapes are awesome. **Basins consist of such features as abyssal plains, oceanic ridges, rift valleys, deep sea trenches, seamounts, tablemounts, islands, and reefs.** You will learn more about these features as your journey continues. As you read the following pages, refer to Figure 13-2 on pages 296 and 297.

Abyssal Plains

Your ship is now traveling along an abyss (uh-BIS). An abyss is a very deep place. Except for the trenches and other valleys, the **abyssal plains** are the deepest parts of the ocean floor. They are between 3000 and 6000 meters deep. About 42 percent of the ocean floor consists of abyssal plains.

The abyssal plains are very flat, featureless areas of the ocean floor. A steady "rain" of solid, finely powdered sediment settled on these plains for millions of years. This sediment covers the rocky bed of the plain like a smooth, flat blanket.

Much of the sediment comes from land. You saw how material from the land is carried by river currents out to sea, where it settles on the continental

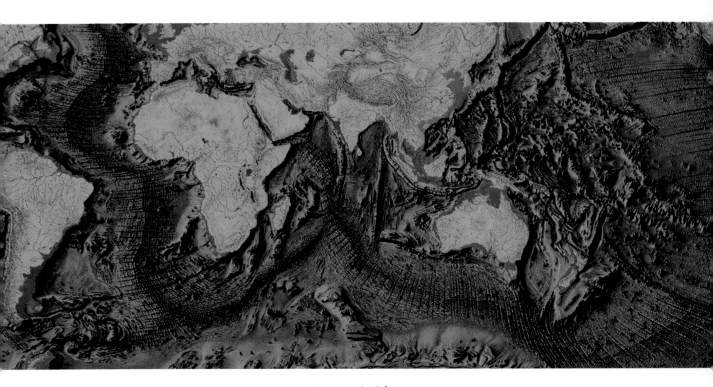

Figure 13-4 *The land beneath the ocean has varied features. This map shows the topography of the ocean floor. What is the flat, featureless part of the ocean floor called?*

shelves. Mud slides carry this material down the slopes and out onto the abyssal plains. Ocean currents that move from the coast out to sea also carry this material.

In some places, the plains are covered with thick layers of ooze. Scientists use that name because the layers are like thick, gooey mud. Bits of ooze seen through a microscope have startlingly beautiful patterns. They are mainly the limestone shells of microscopic sea animals. Such animals have lived near the ocean surface for some 500 million years. By identifying their shells, scientists can tell how old some sediments are.

Oceanic Ridges And Rift Valleys

You continue your journey across the flat abyssal plains. Suddenly, massive objects loom in front of you. What are they? Your echo-ranger, powerful searchlights, and other instruments give you the answer. They are large rows of volcanic mountains.

Figure 13-5 *Your submarine is in a rift valley surrounded by mountains that make up part of the oceanic ridge system. In the central part of the rift valley you can see molten rock that has cooled. This rock will eventually become new ocean floor.*

These usually parallel underwater mountain ranges are called **oceanic ridges**. In the Atlantic Ocean, these volcanic mountains make up the Mid-Atlantic Ridge and are about 1000 kilometers wide. These ridges are only part of the worldwide Mid-Ocean Ridge System, which is about 74,000 kilometers long.

Your instruments indicate that these huge mountains stand hundreds to thousands of meters above the level of the abyssal plains. Many of these mountains are taller and steeper than the volcanic mountains on dry land.

Wanting a closer look, you steer your ship between the rows of parallel mountains. And you see an amazing sight. For running along the ocean floor between these mountains are deep cracks called **rift valleys**. These valleys are about 25 to 50 kilometers wide and are as much as 2 kilometers below the bases of the surrounding mountain peaks.

Your ship moves closer to the rift valley. Now you notice that this is a region of great activity. Molten rock from inside the earth rises up through the valley, spreading out on either side. This material cools and spreads along the sea floor to form new crust. This activity also builds up the mountains.

On land, molten rock erupting from volcanoes cools slowly and spreads over a greater area. But under the sea, molten rock cools more quickly and piles up higher and steeper.

Deep-Sea Trenches

You decide to turn your ship around and head south along the Atlantic coast and back toward the edge of the continental margin. Near Puerto Rico you observe a long, narrow V-shaped crack in the ocean basin. This crack is one of the deepest parts of the ocean and is called a **deep-sea trench.** Your instruments tell you that this trench is more than 8500 meters deep.

These deep-sea trenches are off the edges of some continental margins—not in the center of the oceans. Such trenches run parallel to the coasts of continents. In fact, the trenches belong partly to the margins and partly to the deep sea floor.

The Pacific Ocean has more trenches than the other oceans. The Mariana Trench, near the island of Guam, is about 70 kilometers wide and more than 2550 kilometers long. The Challenger Deep, located in the southwest corner of the Mariana Trench, is the deepest place known on the earth. Challenger Deep is more than 11,000 meters deep. See Figure 13-6 for a list of the major oceanic trenches and their depths.

Seamounts, Islands, and Reefs

It's time to travel back to the ocean's surface. On your way you see some individual volcanic mountains of the mid-ocean ridge system rising more than 1000 meters above the deep-sea floor. These volcanic mountains are called **seamounts** and are found in all the oceans. Nearly all seamounts have steep sides and narrow cone-shaped peaks. The rocks that make up seamounts are typical volcanic rocks. Seamounts

Activity

Ocean Floor Models

Here is a way to make your own model of the ocean floor.

1. Use papier-mâché, plaster, or modeling clay to construct a model of the ocean floor. Include at least one example of each of the features shown in Figure 13-2.

2. Label each feature on your model.

Figure 13-6 *Ocean trenches are the deepest parts of the oceans. According to this table, which is the deepest ocean trench?*

MAJOR OCEAN TRENCHES

Trench	Depth *(meters)*
Pacific Ocean:	
Aleutian	8,100
Kurile	10,542
Japan	9,810
Mariana (Challenger Deep)	11,034
Philippine	10,497
Tonga	10,882
Kermadec	10,800
Peru-Chile	8,055
Mindanao	11,500
Atlantic Ocean	
Puerto Rico	8,648
South Sandwich	8,400

are created as molten rock hardens and piles up higher and higher above the sea floor.

Most undersea seamounts stop erupting before the volcanic mountain reaches the ocean's surface. But sometimes seamounts go on erupting and get higher and higher. Seamount peaks that reach above the ocean's surface become islands.

The birth of a volcanic island is a dramatic event. If you had been a member of the crew of a small fishing boat near Iceland in November of 1963, you would have seen the birth of a volcanic island. Less than two kilometers from the boat, clouds of smoke and steam suddenly spouted up from the sea. Lightning flashed in the sky. By nightfull, the cloud was six kilometers high. During the night, the cloud was almost invisible, but constant lightning flashes marked its place. Next morning the sun shone on the black top of a volcano 10 meters above the ocean's surface. Molten rock streamed down the sides of the new tiny island, hissing as it touched the sea. This island is called Surtsey.

Your ship has reached the ocean's surface. Now you decide to travel to a well-known group of islands, the Hawaiian Islands. The Hawaiian Islands were built by huge undersea volcanoes. Hawaii, the

Figure 13-7 *Great clouds of dense gas and dust poured from Surtsey when it became an island* (left). *The volcanic island of Hawaii continues to grow bigger as a volcano pours out enormous amounts of molten rock* (right).

largest and youngest island of the group, was formed by three volcanoes. Because two of these volcanoes are still active, the island of Hawaii continues to grow. There are no active volcanoes on the other Hawaiian Islands.

The Hawaiian Islands are a chain that extends northwest from the main island of Hawaii. As your ship travels north past these islands, you can see that the islands become more and more worn down. Great volcanic peaks become mere hills. At the northern end of the chain, the islands are just low strips of sand, barely above sea level.

Your ship again dives beneath the ocean's surface, and you see seamounts. The tops of some of these seamounts lie two kilometers beneath the waves. But the searchlights from your ship show you something unusual about some of these seamounts.

Figure 13-8 *The age of the Hawaiian Islands becomes older as you travel toward the northwest. The islands have become worn down to tablemounts and seamounts. Loihi Seamount, off the coast of Hawaii, is slowly growing taller. Loihi will eventually become the newest Hawaiian island.*

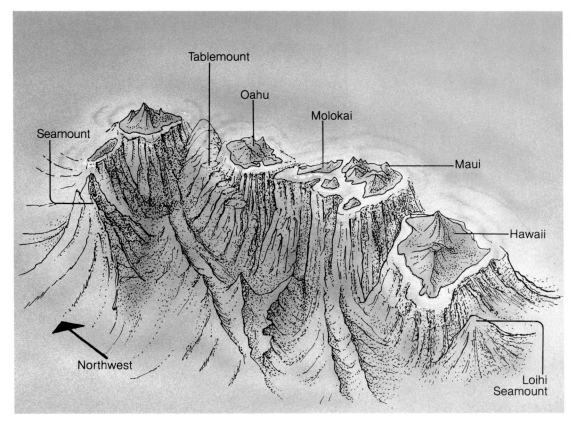

Instead of sharp peaks, these seamounts have flat, broad tops like tables. For this reason, they are called **tablemounts.** They are seamounts with the tops neatly sliced off. But how could that happen?

The Hawaiian Islands suggest an answer. At most, volcanoes are active for only a few million years. After that time, volcanic peaks above water are worn flat by wind, rain, and especially by waves. Tablemounts are the remains of old volcanoes that once were islands but have now sunk beneath the ocean's surface.

Your ship returns to the ocean's surface. The trip is about over and you steer your ship back toward land. Here in the tropical waters, you approach the continental shelf. You again see some volcanic islands. But these islands look different from the other islands you have seen.

Surrounding these islands offshore are large masses and ridges of limestone rock. The limestone structures contain the shells of plants and animals. These structures are called **coral reefs**. Reef-building organisms cannot live in waters colder than 18° C. So such reefs are found only in tropical waters. And reef-building organisms cannot live at depths greater than about 55 meters. Why? These organisms use sunlight to help them make their hard limestone skeletons. And there is not enough sunlight below this depth. Let's visit the three kinds of coral reefs.

Reefs that touch the shoreline of a volcanic island are called **fringing reefs**. See Figure 13-9. The width of fringing reefs may be several hundred meters but generally is less than 30 meters.

Figure 13-9 *In 1842, Charles Darwin, an English naturalist, had a theory about reefs. He stated that an island first develops a fringing reef* (left) *and then a barrier reef* (middle). *Finally an atoll* (right) *forms after the island has been worn away to below the ocean's surface.*

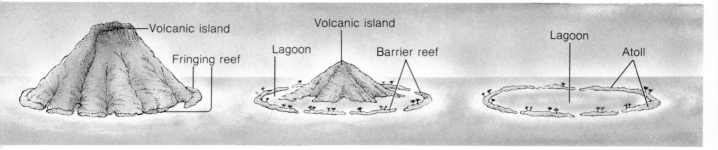

Figure 13-10 *A barrier reef is separated from this island by a lagoon* (left). *An atoll surrounds only a lagoon* (right) *because the island had been worn away and is no longer above the ocean's surface.*

Barrier reefs are separated from the shore by an area of shallow water called a lagoon. See Figures 13-9 and 13-10. Islands with barrier reefs usually have sunk farther into the ocean than islands with fringing reefs. Barrier reefs are generally much larger than fringing reefs. The Great Barrier Reef of Australia is a good example. It is from 40 to 320 kilometers wide and parallels the northeastern coast of Australia for a distance of about 2300 kilometers. Many kinds of plants and animals live along this barrier reef.

In order to visit the third type of reef, you travel farther out to sea. Here is an island that has been worn away and has sunk beneath the waves. What remains is a ring of coral reefs called an **atoll**. See Figures 13-9 and 13-10.

Your trip has taken you from the ocean's surface along continental margins and deep-sea basins to the deepest part of the ocean and back again. In the next chapter, you will discover some of the living things that are found in these ocean places.

SECTION REVIEW

1. List six features of deep-sea basins.
2. Why are abyssal plains so flat?
3. Describe the three types of coral reefs.

LABORATORY ACTIVITY

The Effect of Water Depth on Sediments

Purpose

In this activity, you will find out what effect differences in water depth have on the settling of sediments containing mixed particles.

Materials *(per group)*

Plastic tubes of different lengths containing sediment samples and water

---

Procedure

1. Select one tube from those provided by your teacher.
2. Check to see that each end of the tube is securely capped.
3. Hold the tube by both ends and gently tip it back and forth until the sediment is *thoroughly* mixed throughout the water.
4. Set the tube in an upright position in a place where it will not be disturbed.
5. Repeat steps 1 through 4 for each of the tubes remaining.
6. Carefully observe which type of sediment settles first.

Observations and Conclusions

1. What general statement can you make about the effect that the size of sediment particles has on the order in which sediment settles in a tube?
2. Observe each column carefully. Make a detailed sketch to illustrate the heights of the different layers formed by the settling sediment in the tube containing the shortest column of water.
3. Describe the effect that the length of a water column has on the number and height of layers formed in a sediment sample containing mixed particles.

CHAPTER REVIEW

SUMMARY

13-1 Continental Margins

- Continental margins are areas where the edges of continents meet the ocean basins.
- Continental shelves are shallow, flat tops of continental margins.
- Continental slopes are boundaries between continents and the ocean basin.
- Underwater avalanches help form submarine canyons.

13-2 Deep-Sea Basins

- The ocean basins are the true sea floor.
- Abyssal plains are very flat, featureless areas of the ocean floor.

- Parallel rows of underwater volcanic mountain ranges are called oceanic ridges.
- Molten rock rises through rift valleys to form new ocean floor.
- The deepest parts of the oceans are called deep-sea trenches.
- Seamounts are underwater mountains that usually have narrow cone-shaped peaks.
- Seamount peaks that reach above the ocean's surface become islands.
- Tablemounts are underwater seamounts that have flat, broad tops.
- The three kinds of coral reefs are fringing reefs, barrier reefs, and atolls.

VOCABULARY

Define each term in a complete sentence.

abyssal plain	continental shelf	fringing reef	submarine canyon
atoll	continental slope	oceanic ridge	tablemount
barrier reef	coral reef	rift valley	underwater avalanche
continental margin	deep-sea trench	seamount	

CONTENT REVIEW: MULTIPLE CHOICE

Choose the letter of the answer that best completes each statement.

1. The area where the edge of the continent meets the ocean basin is called the continental
   a. shelf.   b. slope.   c. margin.   d. plain.
2. The area between the shoreline and the steep descent to the ocean floor is called the continental
   a. shelf.   b. slope.   c. canyon.   d. basin.
3. The boundary that exists between a continent and the ocean basin is called the continental
   a. shelf.   b. slope.   c. plain.   d. valley.
4. A U- or V-shaped valley that cuts through a continental shelf and slope is called a
   a. margin.   b. rift valley.
   c. deep-sea trench.   d. submarine canyon.

5. Very flat, featureless areas of the ocean floor covered with ooze are called
a. abyssal plains.   b. continental shelves.
c. oceanic ridges.   d. seamounts.

6. Parallel rows of underwater volcanic mountain ranges are called
a. seamounts.   b. tablemounts.
c. oceanic ridges.   d. continental slopes.

7. Molten rock rises from inside the earth to form new ocean crust through
a. deep-sea trenches.   b. seamounts.
c. submarine canyons.   d. rift valleys.

8. The deepest parts of the ocean are called
a. rift valleys.   b. deep-sea trenches.
c. submarine canyons.   d. abyssal plains.

9. Seamount peaks that reach above the ocean's surface are called
a. tablemounts.   b. islands.   c. atolls.   d. continental shelves.

10. The type of coral reef that forms when an island has sunk beneath the ocean's surface is called a(n)
a. barrier reef.   b. tablemount.   c. fringing reef.   d. atoll.

CONTENT REVIEW: COMPLETION

Fill in the word or words that best complete each statement.

1. The _____ is the area between the shoreline and the steep descent to the ocean floor.

2. _____ play a major part in carving out submarine canyons that cut through the continental shelf and slope.

3. _____ are very flat, featureless areas of the ocean floor covered with ooze.

4. Large underwater mountain ranges that are part of a worldwide system of mountains are called _____.

5. _____ are the deepest parts of the ocean.

6. When molten rock rises up through deep cracks called _____, new ocean floor forms.

7. Seamount peaks that are high enough to reach above the ocean's surface are known as _____.

8. _____ are seamounts that have broad, flat tops.

9. A(n) _____ reef touches the shoreline of a volcanic island.

10. A(n) _____ is a ring of coral reefs that forms when an island has sunk beneath the ocean's surface.

CONTENT REVIEW: TRUE OR FALSE

Determine whether each statement is true or false. If it is true, write "true." If it is false, change the underlined word or words to make the statement true.

1. The continental margins include continental shelves, slopes, and <u>abyssal plains</u>.

2. Very flat, featureless areas of the ocean floor are called <u>oceanic ridges</u>.

3. The <u>continental shelf</u> is the area between the shoreline and the steep descent to the ocean floor.
4. <u>Submarine canyons</u> are deep valleys that cut through the continental shelf and slope.
5. Deep cracks called <u>deep-sea trenches</u> are found between oceanic ridges.
6. The deepest parts of the ocean are called <u>rift valleys</u>.
7. Seamount peaks that reach above the ocean's surface become <u>islands</u>.
8. <u>Tablemounts</u> are seamounts with flat, broad tops.
9. Fringing reefs and <u>atolls</u> surround islands that are above the ocean's surface.
10. A <u>fringing reef</u> is separated from shore by a <u>lagoon</u>.

CONCEPT REVIEW: SKILL BUILDING

Use the skills you have developed in the chapter to complete each activity.

1. **Making comparisons** How is the ocean floor similar to the surface of the earth?
2. **Relating facts** Why are there no coral reefs growing off the coast of Canada?
3. **Making generalizations** An old folktale tells of an island appearing and disappearing in the ocean. Is there any basis for such a tale? Explain your answer.
4. **Applying concepts** Is the ocean floor a stable environment? Explain your answer.
5. **Making calculations** The speed of sound in water is about 1500 m/sec. Use this information to answer the following questions:
   a. Sound waves given off by sonar instruments on board a ship take eight seconds to travel to the ocean floor and back. How deep is the ocean floor?
   b. Suppose it took sound waves four seconds to travel to the ocean floor and back again. How deep would the ocean floor be?
   c. If the depth of the ocean floor is 9000 meters, how long does it take sound waves to travel to the ocean floor?
6. **Making inferences** Scientists have found dust from meteors, or particles from space, in deep-ocean sediments. How do you think this dust may have gotten there?

CONCEPT REVIEW: ESSAY

Discuss each of the following in a brief paragraph.

1. Explain how the different kinds of coral reefs form and how they may change from one kind to another.
2. Compare ocean trenches with rift valleys.
3. Describe the abyssal plains.
4. Explain how submarine canyons may be formed.
5. Describe three features of the continental margin.
6. Compare seamounts and oceanic ridges.
7. Describe the birth of a volcanic island.

14 Ocean Life

CHAPTER SECTIONS

14-1 Life in the Ocean Zones
14-2 Life Around Deep-Sea Vents

CHAPTER OBJECTIVES

*After completing this chapter,
you will be able to:*

14-1 Describe the kinds of life in
the three major ocean life
zones.

14-1 Name and give the location of
the three life zones of the
open sea zone.

14-2 Describe how living things
survive around deep-sea
vents.

14-2 List some of the unusual animals found around deep-sea
vents.

J. D. Starkey, a fisherman aboard a ship in the In-
dian Ocean, dropped a string of light bulbs into the
dark water to attract fish. Sure enough, the water
soon swarmed with fish. Then, all of a sudden, the
fish vanished.

"As I gazed, a circle of green light glowed in my
illumination . . . it was a giant eye looking directly at
me . . . I was gazing at a colossal squid—the body
alone filled my view as far as my sight could penetrate
. . ."

Starkey said that the squid's tentacles were about
as thick as a person's body. He said the eye was about
the size of a dinner plate. And the squid had a par-
rotlike beak as big as a person's hand. Starkey also
saw a funnel-like structure that seemed to sprout
from behind the squid's head. To Starkey, the squid
seemed to swell up, as water shot through the funnel.
Then the squid disappeared into the darkness.

This is only one of many reports describing giant
squid. Many stories have been told about these giants
of the sea grabbing and pulling large ships under the
water. Although these stories may not be true, it is
true that the ocean is filled with many strange and
wondrous creatures.

All squid have large eyes and many tentacles.

14-1   Life in the Ocean Zones

Conditions in the oceans vary widely. There are shallow beach areas that dry out twice a day and then become wet again once the tides change. There are ocean depths where no ray of sunlight ever reaches and where the temperature stays a few degrees above freezing all year round. And in between these extremes is the open sea with a range of environments at different depths. Scientists have explored some of these areas, but much of the ocean still remains unexplored.

Many factors affect the kinds of plant and animal life found in the ocean. Three of these factors are available sunlight, temperature, and pressure. As you go deeper into the ocean, there is less sunlight, lower temperatures, and greater pressure. Organisms that live in the ocean must adapt to the environment in which they live. **The three major environments, or life zones, in the sea are the intertidal zone, the neritic zone, and the open sea zone.**

Intertidal Zone

The region that lies between the low- and high-tide lines is called the **intertidal zone.** This region is the most changeable zone in the sea. Sometimes it is

Figure 14-1 *Living things, such as these coral and fish, must be able to adapt to the particular ocean environment in which they live.*

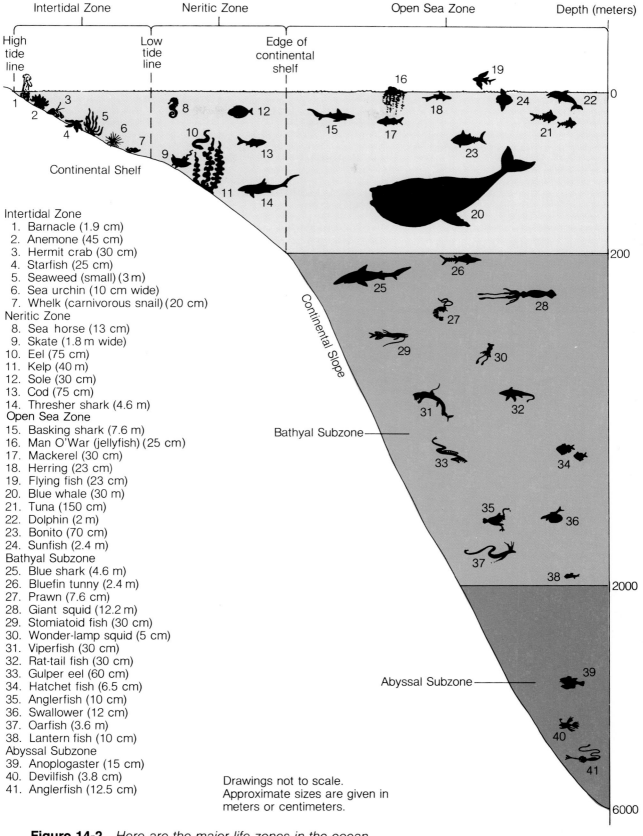

Intertidal Zone — Neritic Zone — Open Sea Zone — Depth (meters)

High tide line
Low tide line
Edge of continental shelf

Continental Shelf

Continental Slope

Bathyal Subzone

Abyssal Subzone

0
200
2000
6000

Intertidal Zone
1. Barnacle (1.9 cm)
2. Anemone (45 cm)
3. Hermit crab (30 cm)
4. Starfish (25 cm)
5. Seaweed (small) (3 m)
6. Sea urchin (10 cm wide)
7. Whelk (carnivorous snail) (20 cm)

Neritic Zone
8. Sea horse (13 cm)
9. Skate (1.8 m wide)
10. Eel (75 cm)
11. Kelp (40 m)
12. Sole (30 cm)
13. Cod (75 cm)
14. Thresher shark (4.6 m)

Open Sea Zone
15. Basking shark (7.6 m)
16. Man O'War (jellyfish) (25 cm)
17. Mackerel (30 cm)
18. Herring (23 cm)
19. Flying fish (23 cm)
20. Blue whale (30 m)
21. Tuna (150 cm)
22. Dolphin (2 m)
23. Bonito (70 cm)
24. Sunfish (2.4 m)

Bathyal Subzone
25. Blue shark (4.6 m)
26. Bluefin tunny (2.4 m)
27. Prawn (7.6 cm)
28. Giant squid (12.2 m)
29. Stomiatoid fish (30 cm)
30. Wonder-lamp squid (5 cm)
31. Viperfish (30 cm)
32. Rat-tail fish (30 cm)
33. Gulper eel (60 cm)
34. Hatchet fish (6.5 cm)
35. Anglerfish (10 cm)
36. Swallower (12 cm)
37. Oarfish (3.6 m)
38. Lantern fish (10 cm)

Abyssal Subzone
39. Anoplogaster (15 cm)
40. Devilfish (3.8 cm)
41. Anglerfish (12.5 cm)

Drawings not to scale.
Approximate sizes are given in meters or centimeters.

Figure 14-2 *Here are the major life zones in the ocean and some of the living things that are usually found in these zones. In which zones would you find plants?*

315

Relating Temperature and Salinity

1. Pour 100 mL of hot tap water into a glass.

2. Add salt, one teaspoonful at a time, to the water. Stir the water after each addition. Stop adding salt when no more can be dissolved. Record the number of teaspoons of salt added.

3. Using 100 mL of cold tap water, repeat steps 1 and 2.

In which glass did more salt dissolve? What is the relationship between temperature and salinity?

Figure 14-3 *These anemones are animals that are adapted to the constant pounding of waves in the intertidal zone.*

ocean. Sometimes it is dry land. These changes happen twice a day as the ocean surges up the beach at high tide and retreats to its lowest point on the beach at low tide. This zone is continually pounded by waves and swept by currents. It is a place where many organisms attach themselves to the sand or rocks or dig into the wet sand for protection. Plants and animals that live in this zone must be able to live without water part of the time. Let's take a look at some of the plants and animals that live in the intertidal zone.

The anemones look like flowers blooming atop a thick stalk. But an anemone is not a plant. It is an animal crowned with tentacles instead of petals. See Figure 14-3. Each tentacle is covered with thousands of poison-containing stinging cells. They enable the anemone to catch and paralyze its prey, including small fish.

Some kinds of anemones grow on rocks exposed to waves and are flat and pancake-shaped. Other kinds of anemones that grow in sheltered places, however, are much taller. What accounts for the difference? A flattened pancake shape resists battering by the waves. Tall anemones would be swept away if they grew in exposed places. Here their tallness would be a disadvantage. But in sheltered places tallness would be an advantage. The tall anemones would more easily catch passing fish.

All living things in an intertidal zone have structures and behaviors suited to their survival in tough surroundings. On rocky shores, there is often a dense growth of seaweed. These plants are anchored to the rocks by leathery structures called holdfasts that act like the roots of a tree. Often the holdfasts cling so tightly to the rocks that even a strong person cannot break their grip. Neither can the waves.

At low tide, the seaweed lies flat against the rocks. Many are covered with a slimy waterproof film that keeps them from drying out during long exposures to the hot sun. If you look closely at the seaweed, you will see that it has many pods, or balloonlike structures. These pods are really air-filled sacs that act as floats. See Figure 14-4.

When the tide comes in, the mass of seaweed rises slowly off the rocks as the floats pull it upward. At last, as the water deepens, the seaweed stands

completely upright. The floats keep the seaweed close to the surface, where it is exposed to the sunlight it needs to survive.

Seaweed is not the only living thing in the intertidal zone that clings to the rocks. Even fish in this zone are rock clingers! Such fish have fins that act as suckers. Using them, the fish cling tightly to rocks. These fish have very small scales or no scales. Large scales would be easily damaged by the pounding of the waves. Instead, the fish have a smooth, slimy skin over which the waves slide smoothly.

Figure 14-4 *During high tide, these air-filled sacs help seaweed stay afloat* (right). *Masses of such seaweed are found in the intertidal zone* (left).

Neritic Zone

The region of the ocean that extends from the low-tide line to the edge of the continental shelf is called the **neritic** (nuh-RIT-ik) **zone.** This zone extends to a depth of about 200 meters.

The neritic zone is home to many different plants and animals. There is plenty of sunlight and the water pressure is low. Also, the temperature remains fairly constant, especially at the deepest depths. Plants in this zone, such as seaweed, are different from similar plants in the intertidal zone. For example, seaweed grows larger in the neritic zone, where the ocean is usually much calmer. Here there are great dense forests of seaweed that may be 60 to 90 meters long. Seaweed stops growing below 200 meters. The reason is that there is not enough sunlight below this depth to enable the seaweed to produce its own food.

Figure 14-5 *Schools of fish such as these snappers are common in the neritic zone (left). This flounder burrows into the continental shelf floor of the neritic zone (right). Its flat shape is almost invisible as it waits for food. This fish can match the color of its surroundings in a few minutes.*

The neritic zone is richer in life than any other ocean zone. Most of the world's great fishing areas are within this zone. The zone is rich in life because here sunlight supports abundant growth of green plants, such as seaweeds and many microscopic plants. Using minerals dissolved in the water and the energy from sunlight, these green plants make food for themselves—and others. Microscopic animals eat the plants and both are eaten by little fish and other small sea animals. They in turn are eaten by larger animals.

Open Sea Zones

The region that includes all the ocean beyond the continental shelves is called the **open sea zone.** This zone has a vast range of depth. It stretches to depths of 3000 to 6000 meters from the sunlit surface to the icy black depths of the abyssal plains. Three subzones, or subdivisions, make up the open sea zone.

PHOTOSYNTHETIC ZONE The subzone of the open sea from the surface to a depth of about 200 meters is where plants receive enough sunlight to make food and continue to grow. This region is called the **photosynthetic** (fo-tuh-sin-THET-ik) **zone.** Photosynthesis is the process by which plants use sunlight to make food. It is the same process green plants in the neritic zone use to make food.

Like the waters above the continental shelves, this zone supports a rich variety of plant life, as well as the animals that feed upon the plants. But in the open sea most of the plants are microscopic one-celled organisms such as diatoms. Diatoms have glassy, transparent walls that are often very beautiful. The walls are riddled with holes so the living cell can take in minerals and gases that are dissolved in the water. The walls are covered with spikes and knobs. These projections increase the surface of the diatoms, which helps them stay afloat. Diatoms alone are so numerous that they make up about 75 percent of the plant food in the oceans.

Diatoms are food for many small sea animals, including the shrimplike krill that are found in all the world's oceans. In cold Antarctic waters, blue whales and other giants of the sea live almost exclusively on krill. And for many fish, such as the tuna, mackerel, smelt, and herring, this zone provides a vast well-stocked cafeteria made up of many different living things. Most of these animals are fast swimmers—for in this cafeteria, if the eaters don't move fast enough, they become the eaten!

BATHYAL ZONE Below the photosynthetic zone lies a subzone that can extend down about 4000 meters. This region is called the **bathyal** (BATH-e-uhl) **zone.**

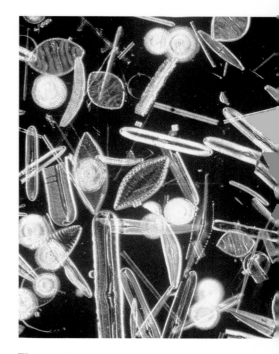

Figure 14-6 *Diatoms, seen here highly magnified, are the basic food plants of the ocean. Their tiny bodies are protected by transparent shells that are rich in proteins and vitamins.*

Figure 14-7 *Sharks are fast and powerful hunters that feed in the open sea and neritic zones.*

Figure 14-8 *This anglerfish can remain almost motionless except for the movement of a flexible spine on top of its head. Attracted by this movement, a fish comes close. The angler opens its huge mouth. The resulting rush of water due to pressure changes forces the fish into the angler's mouth.*

Figure 14-9 *Here are two of the strange creatures that live in the darkness of the abyssal zone. These creatures have common traits such as a fierce-looking appearance, small size, large eyes, large mouth, and large needle-like teeth.*

Photosynthetic plants do not grow in most of the bathyal zone because there is not enough sunlight to support photosynthesis.

Many kinds of animals are found in the very dim light and darkness of this zone, such as whales, sharks, and squid. The squid has a unique adaptation to life in this dim zone. It has the largest eyes of any animal. Each eye is nearly 25 centimeters across. Fish in this zone—such as the anglerfish shown in Figure 14–8, and certain eels—have huge basketlike stomachs that can hold prey larger than the fish themselves! This is another adaptation to life in the bathyal zone.

Food is scarce in the bathyal zone. So animals that eat other animals must be very efficient at catching prey of almost any size whenever it is available. Anglerfish have another fascinating adaptation to darkness. They have organs that give off light. These organs hang in front of the anglers' mouths. The light attracts fish, which are quickly eaten by the angler.

ABYSSAL ZONE Below about 4000 meters is the **abyssal** (uh-BIS-uhl) **zone.** This open sea subzone can plunge to about 6000 meters. It is always dark throughout this zone. Food is found mainly on the flat, abyssal plains. The temperature throughout this zone is just above freezing. And the pressure at its bottom is very high—more than 600 kg/cm^2!

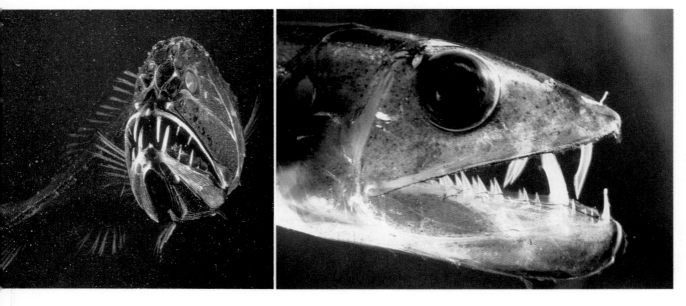

In spite of the unfavorable conditions in this zone, life exists. Most of the animals are small, and many look very strange, as you can see in Figure 14-9. Here bottom-feeders such as rat-tail fish burrow into the abyssal ooze for food. Many of the animals produce their own light. Deep sea crabs and sea spiders prowl along the bottom in search of food.

Life Across the Zones

Although some plants and animals live in only one zone of the sea, others live in more than one zone. For example, the largest group of marine plants and animals, called **plankton** (PLANGK-tuhn), drift and float on or near the ocean's surface across all zones. Plankton are small organisms. Some plankton are even microscopic. Near the shore they live at

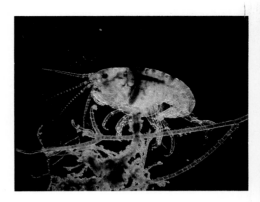

Figure 14-10 *This microscopic animal is an example of plankton. Where in the ocean are plankton found?*

Career: *Biological Oceanographer*

HELP WANTED: BIOLOGICAL OCEANOGRAPHER. Master's degree in oceanography or biology required. Doctoral degree preferred. To conduct laboratory research—both on land and at sea—on the distribution, ecology, and behavior of marine organisms. To plan and participate in research cruises on small ships. Must process and analyze data, and prepare reports for publication.

It was two o'clock A.M. The wind blew cool, salt air into their faces. The sea was rougher than expected. Yet the scientists donned their scuba gear, picked up their cameras—specially equipped with strong lights—and carefully lowered themselves over one side of the ship. It was their goal to take photographs of marine life living in the ocean depths. Such scientists are called **biological oceanographers.**

On this particular expedition, certain marine plants and animals were being studied. The work included collecting samples for identification and analysis in laboratories. Such at sea expeditions may last from weeks to months.

The types of organisms studied by biological oceanographers range from tiny, one-celled plankton to the blue whale, the largest of all

living organisms. During their studies, oceanographers relate organisms to where they live. They examine how physical and chemical factors and the action of other living things affect the way marine plants and animals distribute themselves within a given area.

Biological oceanographers are employed by universities, governments, and industry. To become a biological oceanographer, a person should have an interest in the sea and science. To work at sea, one needs to be physically active, alert, and in excellent health. For more information, write to the International Oceanographic Foundation, 3979 Rickenbacker Causeway, Virginia Key, Miami, FL 33149.

Figure 14-11 *This killer whale (left) is a free swimming or nekton animal. Groups of three to 40 killer whales swim through all the oceans eating many other nekton animals. This toadfish (right) is a bottom dweller or benthos animal. It can match the color of its surroundings as it waits for food.*

Activity

Living and Working Under the Sea

Using reference materials in the library, find information on how people can live and work underwater for long periods of time. Discuss Jacques-Yves Cousteau's seafloor habitat called *Conshelf Three*. This structure supported six men for 22 days in 1965 at a depth of about 100 meters.

Write a short report about this topic and include answers to such questions as the following:

1. What are some of the problems that must be resolved when living and working underwater for long periods of time?

2. What might be some beneficial results of living and working under the sea?

depths to about 1 meter. In the open ocean, they live at depths down to about 200 meters. Examples of plankton are diatoms and krill.

Animals that swim freely in the ocean are called **nekton** (NEK-tahn). The most important of these animals are the fish. There are more than 20,000 different kinds of fish in the ocean. Other nekton include octopuses, squid, whales, dolphins, and seals.

The third group of plants and animals are called **benthos** (BEN-thahs). These organisms live on the ocean bottom from the shallow waters near the shore to the deepest parts of the ocean floor. Examples of these bottom-dwelling organisms are seaweed, barnacles, oysters, snails, sea lilies, starfish, sea anemones, coral, crabs, and toadfish.

SECTION REVIEW

1. List the three major life zones of the ocean.
2. Which is the most changeable zone in the ocean?
3. Which zone has the most kinds of living things?
4. List two nekton and two benthos animals.

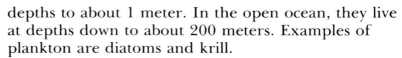

14-2   Life Around Deep-Sea Vents

In 1977, scientists aboard the research submarine *Alvin* found an unknown world filled with living creatures. The submarine was about 2600 meters down on the Pacific Ocean floor near the Galapagos Islands.

The scientists found superheated sea water and minerals pouring out of volcanic vents, or natural chimneys, in the sea floor. One scientist said the area looked like the blast furnaces at a steel mill. The extremely hot water often exceeds 350° C, which is hot enough to melt lead. This water contains many sulfur-rich substances. Under tremendous heat and pressure, these substances are changed into hydrogen sulfide. Hydrogen sulfide is poisonous to most living things.

Yet this place swarms with life! There are giant red-plumed tube worms more than 3.5 meters long, as well as rat-tail fish, anemones, giant clams nearly 30 centimeters long, and white crabs. **The vent creatures do not depend on plants for their food but rather on food produced by bacteria living in the vents.** These bacteria combine hydrogen sulfide, oxygen, and carbon dioxide. During this combining process, energy is released. The process provides the basic source of energy for the living things of the vents. These living things are examples of the only organisms on Earth that do not depend on sunlight as a basic energy source!

SECTION REVIEW

1. List four animals that live around deep-sea vents.
2. Describe the relationship that exists between a deep-sea vent creature, such as a giant clam, and bacteria living in the vents.

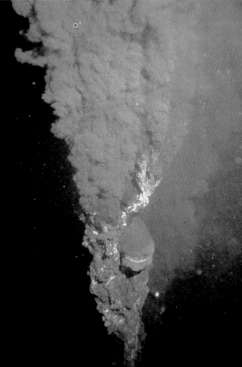

Figure 14-12 *Superheated water and minerals pour out of a natural chimney or volcanic deep-sea vent in the sea floor (right). These giant tube worms (left) live near a vent. Billions of bacteria living inside these worms break down hydrogen sulfide and provide food and energy for themselves and for the worms.*

LABORATORY ACTIVITY

Preparing a Saltwater Aquarium

Purpose

In this activity, you will create an ocean environment in a saltwater aquarium.

Materials *(per class)*

Glass aquarium
Air pump with two air outlets
Airline tubing
Undergravel filter
Aquarium gravel
Natural sea water or synthetic sea salts
   dissolved in water
Live seawater animals

Procedure

1. Place the undergravel filter in the aquarium. Add a 7-8 cm layer of aquarium gravel to cover the filter base plate. Using airline tubing, connect each vertical outlet to one airpump outlet.
2. Either add natural sea water or a mixture using synthetic sea salts. Instructions on how to mix the salts are on the package.

Note: Do not use chlorinated water to make the sea water. If the tap water is chlorinated, allow it to stand in an open container for 24 hours. The tap water will then be dechlorinated and be safe to use.

3. The filtering system needs time for natural bacteria to develop in the system. Sea anemones, snails, hermit crabs or stone crabs should be added to the aquarium first since they help bacteria grow. Fish can be added in two or three weeks. **CAUTION:** *Never clean the gravel in the filter bed or the natural bacteria will be destroyed.*

Observations and Conclusions

1. Observe the behavioral interactions between the sea organisms. Write a brief report on how each living organism contributes to maintaining a balanced ocean environment.

CHAPTER REVIEW

14-1 Life in the Ocean Zones

- The intertidal zone is the region between the low- and high-tide lines.

- The neritic zone is the region that extends from the low-tide line to the edge of the continental shelf.

- The neritic zone has more different kinds of organisms than any other ocean zone.

- The open sea zone includes all the ocean beyond the continental shelves from the ocean's surface to the deepest abyssal plains.

- The open sea zone is made up of three subzones, or subdivisions, called photosynthetic, bathyal, and abyssal.

- Living things that inhabit more than one zone include plankton, nekton, and benthos.

14-2 Life Around Deep-Sea Vents

- Some unusual organisms live around deep-sea vents in the sea floor.

- Living things around these vents use energy released by bacteria instead of the sun's energy.

VOCABULARY

Define each term in a complete sentence.

abyssal zone	**intertidal zone**	**neritic zone**	**photosynthetic zone**
bathyal zone	**nekton**	**open sea zone**	**plankton**
benthos			

CONTENT REVIEW: MULTIPLE CHOICE

Choose the letter of the answer that best completes each statement.

1. The most changeable sea zone is the
   a. nekton.   b. intertidal.
   c. neritic.   d. bathyal.

2. The zone in which seaweed clings to rocks is the
   a. bathyal.   b. plankton.
   c. intertidal.   d. neritic.

3. Most of the world's great fishing areas are found in the zone called
   a. neritic.   b. nekton.
   c. photosynthetic.   d. abyssal.

4. The zone of the open sea from the surface to a depth of about 200 meters is called
   a. bathyal.   b. abyssal.
   c. neritic.   d. photosynthetic.

5. Diatoms are part of the
   a. nekton.   b. plankton.
   c. bathyal.   d. benthos.

6. The temperature is just above freezing and the pressure is very high in which zone?
   a. abyssal   b. bathyal
   c. neritic   d. benthos
7. Fish, squid, and whales are examples of
   a. nekton.   b. plankton.
   c. bathyal.   d. neritic.
8. Starfish, coral, and snails are examples of
   a. nekton.   b. plankton.
   c. photosynthetic.   d. benthos.
9. Superheated water from deep-sea vents is rich in substances containing
   a. nitrogen.   b. ammonia.
   c. sulfur.   d. carbon.
10. Vent animals receive their energy from
   a. abyssal ooze.   b. bacteria.
   c. the sun.   d. green plants.

CONTENT REVIEW: COMPLETION

Fill in the word or words that best complete each statement.

1. Organisms that live in the _____ zone must be able to live without water part of the time.
2. Fish and seaweed cling to rocks in the _____ zone.
3. The _____ zone is where most of the world's great fisheries are found.
4. Diatoms and krill are mainly found in the _____ subzone of the open sea zone.
5. Plants and animals called _____ drift and float with the currents and tides at or near the ocean's surface.
6. Fish swim freely in the ocean and are called _____.
7. Animals that live on the ocean bottom are called_____.
8. Many kinds of nekton are found in the _____ subzone of the open sea zone.
9. Bottom-feeders burrow into the ooze of the _____ subzone of the open sea zone.
10. Certain bacteria combine hydrogen sulfide, oxygen, and carbon dioxide and release _____ to creatures living in deep-sea vents.

CONTENT REVIEW: TRUE OR FALSE

Determine whether each statement is true or false. If it is true, write "true." If it is false, change the underlined word or words to make the statement true.

1. Factors that affect the kinds of organisms found in the ocean include temperature, sunlight, and <u>pressure</u>.
2. The region that extends from the low-tide line to the edge of the continental shelf is called the <u>open sea zone</u>.

3. The region that lies between the low- and high-tide lines is called the intertidal zone.
4. Fish, squid, dolphins, seals, and whales swim freely in the ocean and are called benthos.
5. Green plants receive enough sunlight to make food down to a depth of about 200 meters.
6. The subzones that make up the open sea zone are called photosynthetic, neritic, and abyssal.
7. Nekton drift and float at or near the ocean's surface.
8. Most of the world's great fishing areas are found within the open sea zone.
9. Diatoms and krill are members of the largest group of marine plants and animals and are called plankton.
10. Bacteria release energy that is used by vent creatures.

CONCEPT REVIEW: SKILL BUILDING

Use the skills you have developed in the chapter to complete each activity.

1. **Applying concepts** The neritic zone is richer in life than any other zone. Explain this statement.
2. **Classifying organisms** Classify each of the following organisms as either plankton, nekton, or benthos.

   a. shark
   b. snail
   c. krill
   d. eel
   e. dolphin
   f. tuna
   g. octopus
   h. diatom
   i. starfish
   j. sea turtle
   k. crab
   l. barnacle

3. **Relating concepts** Suppose a scientist took both a horizontal and a vertical sample of ocean life. Which sample would be more varied? Give a logical reason for your answer.
4. **Relating facts** Many deep-sea animals have huge mouths and stomachs that can stretch to enormous sizes. What might be the advantage of such adaptations?
5. **Applying concepts** Within the intertidal zone there are actually four "subzones," each having its characteristic plant and animal life. Based on what you have read about the nature of the intertidal zone, suggest a reason for the existence of these subzones.
6. **Making inferences** Starfish, which live in the intertidal zone, have tiny tube-shaped feet on the undersides of their arms that act like suction cups. Explain why these tube feet are an advantage to the starfish.

CONCEPT REVIEW: ESSAY

Discuss each of the following in a brief paragraph.

1. Discuss how sunlight, temperature, and pressure affect life in the ocean.
2. Compare the intertidal and neritic zones.
3. Describe how plants and animals differ in each of the three subzones of the open sea zone.
4. Compare plankton, nekton, and benthos.
5. What type of adaptations do plants and animals in the intertidal zone have that enable them to survive?
6. Describe how organisms survive around deep-sea vents.
7. Why is it that no plants live in the bathyal and abyssal zones?

Adventures in Science

Robert Ballard...

water—unseen and untouched until September 1, 1985. On that historic day, Robert Ballard and a team of French and American oceanographers found the first piece of wreckage from the *Titanic*.

Robert Ballard, a senior scientist at Woods Hole Oceanographic Institution, is part explorer, part geologist, and part engineer. One of his most important projects was the creation of a vessel that could descend into the underwater depths to locate and photograph objects on the ocean floor.

When Ballard began his research, the Woods Hole Oceanographic Institution already had *Alvin*, a submersible that could explore the ocean bottom. *Alvin* could carry people deep beneath the ocean surface and could collect ocean-floor material with a mechanical arm. According to Ballard, a trip in *Alvin* was like a voyage to the moon. He describes the journey as a trek into a freezing pitch-black "inner-space."

Ballard designed a new submersible, which he named the Argo-Jason. The Argo-Jason can be sent undersea without a crew. It is controlled by a mother ship that re-

She was billed as the largest, most luxurious, and most technologically advanced passenger ship of her day. But even more important was the proud claim of her builders that their masterpiece was unsinkable. So when the ocean liner *Titanic* set out on her maiden voyage from England to New York in April 1912, no one could possibly have foreseen the events of the night of April 15. On that fateful night, the *Titanic* hit an iceberg in the North Atlantic Ocean. Three hours later, the "unsinkable" ship and many of her 1522 passengers had plunged to the bottom of the ocean floor. There the ship remained beneath three kilometers of

...AND THE SEARCH FOR THE TITANIC

mains at the water's surface. The Argo is a long cage equipped with special lights, complex sonar devices, and computer-enhanced underwater cameras. These cameras can take perfect pictures of the underwater world and then send the images to a video screen on the mother ship.

The Argo can also scan sections of the ocean floor. When it detects something of interest, it sends Jason out to investigate. Jason is a smaller robot attached to the Argo by a long "leash." Equipped with mechanical arms, Jason's duty is to collect samples from places along the ocean floor that cannot be reached by the Argo.

Ballard was pleased with the creation of the Argo-Jason, but many other scientists did not believe that his invention would be able to collect ocean-floor samples effectively. So Ballard had to think of a way to prove that the Argo-Jason could indeed work. Thus was born Ballard's search for the *Titanic*, using the Argo-Jason.

Ballard had always been fascinated by the sunken luxury liner. He considered himself an expert on the details of the incident. "I read just about every book or document ever published about the disaster," says Ballard. But even Ballard admitted that the search for the *Titanic* would be difficult. "From the historical data, the best we could do was to reduce the likely site to an area of no less than 388 square kilometers. And when you consider the depth (of the ocean), you'd have to admit that locating the ship makes finding a needle in a haystack seem trivial."

The Argo-Jason made the difference. Within several days, and after a couple of malfunctions, the Argo began scanning the ocean bottom with its cameras. Less than a week later, the Argo found the *Titanic*, and its cameras focused on the ship's boilers. During the next few days, the Argo took hundreds of photographs of the *Titanic*. Dr. Ballard was amazed with the results. Although the ship had been lying 3.2 kilometers below the ocean surface for 73 years, many objects were perfectly preserved.

Dr. Ballard had succeeded twice: he had discovered the resting place of the *Titanic* and he had proved that the submersible Argo-Jason did work. Ballard still had one more wish, however. He wanted to see the *Titanic* with his own eyes. Ten months after the discovery, Dr. Ballard went down to the wreck in the *Alvin*. He carefully examined the inside and outside of the great ship in an attempt to figure out what had gone wrong on that terrible day in 1912. But Ballard, who has asked Congress to declare the *Titanic* an international memorial and protect its burial site, would not touch anything or bring any souvenirs back to the surface. "The quest for the *Titanic* is over," he said. "May she now rest in peace."

Cameras on board the Jason photographed the *Titanic* lying on the ocean floor under 4000 meters of water.

Issues in Science

Are we DESTROYING the GREATEST CREATURES of the SEA?

During the late 1860s, a Norwegian inventor, Svend Foyn, invented a harpoon with a tip that exploded when it hit its target: a whale. This new weapon enabled whalers to kill their prey much faster and easier than ever before. Foyn's harpoon led to the development of modern whaling and the slaughter of the world's whales.

Since the beginning of this century, more than three million whales have been killed. Several species are now endangered. The number of blue whales, the largest living creatures, has dropped from 100,000 to less than 1,000. There are only small numbers of right whales and bowheads left. Many other species also are declining in number.

Most countries that once carried on commercial whaling, including the United States, have long since stopped. But a few, such as Japan and Norway, continue to hunt whales for profit. Whaling nations contend that they do not hunt endangered species, only those species that are still common. Conservationists argue that even whales of common species are dropping too rapidly in number. These people believe that, for several years at least, no whales of any species should be hunted.

Stopping the Slaughter

In response to conservationists, the International Whaling Commission voted in 1982 to ban commercial whaling starting in 1986. Set up to regulate whaling, the commission has members from more than two dozen nations, the United States and whaling countries among them. But the ban does not guarantee that the killing will stop. For one thing, a country can withdraw from the commission at any time and kill all the whales it wants to.

Moreover, within 90 days after the ban was voted upon, Norway, Japan, and other whaling nations filed protests against it with the commission. Under commission rules, this exempts them from the ban.

Even so, however, the nations that protested may choose not to take advantage of their exemption. If they did take advantage of their exemption, their actions could prompt a strong reaction from the United States, which led the campaign for the ban. Both private businesses in the United States and the federal government have been urged by conservationists to boycott products from countries that continue to kill whales. In fact, our government can even place fishing restrictions on nations that break whaling commission rules. These restrictions would apply only in United States waters. Our government can also bar fish imports from nations that ignore the commission.

Japan fishes heavily in United States waters. Norway and Japan sell millions of dollars of fish products to the United States each year. If they do not go along with the whaling ban, they could lose a great deal.

There is a chance, however, that the whaling countries could take a position on the ban that the United States might find hard to criticize. The commission allows certain groups of people, such as Alaskan Eskimos, to hunt a limited number of whales for their own use. The Eskimos, the commission reasons, need whale oil and meat to live.

Japan and Norway contend that many whalers in their countries need to hunt whales commercially to live. Whaling is a tradition for these people just as it is for the Eskimos. Why not, ask the Japanese and Norwegians, give their whalers the same consideration as the Eskimos and let them kill and sell a limited number of whales?

To do so, says environmentalist Allan Thornton, in a report for the conservation group Defenders of Wildlife, would "be a disaster for whale conservation." He warns it would be impossible to police the limits on small-scale commercial whaling. Even hunting by Eskimos, he adds, is endangering some whales. All whaling, not just commercial whaling, needs a second look, according to Thornton.

One job of The International Whaling Commission is to control the killing of whales, such as this minke whale.

An Age That Has Passed

Whaling was once a worldwide business, and brave men in sailing vessels roamed the globe to hunt the huge creatures. Oil from whales was burned in lamps. Whalebone was used in making women's undergarments. The teeth of some whales were used to make piano keys. Today, however, many whale products can be or have been replaced by other materials. But whale meat still has a market, most notably in Japan. So whaling can still be profitable, even if not as profitable as in the past.

Even in Japan, however, whale meat accounts for less than 1 percent of the protein eaten by the Japanese. Echoing conservationists, United States Representative Don Bonker noted in Congress, "There is no reason to continue commercial whaling at any level."

Conservationists view whales as a symbol. If people cannot preserve the largest animals on Earth, they say, there is little hope for any other part of nature.

Whales, moreover, play an important part in keeping the ocean environment balanced.

A humpback whale begins its dive to safety. But if the hunting of whales is not stopped, scenes such as this may not be seen in the future.

The huge blue whale is at the top of an important food chain. If whales vanished, the balance of life in the sea might be forever changed.

The largest whales, such as the blue whale, feed on tiny shrimplike creatures and other small organisms, collectively known as krill. The whales obtain the krill by straining it from the water with huge sievelike structures in their mouths called baleen, or whalebone.

The baleen whales are at the top of an important food chain. They eat krill, which feed on microscopic plants, which in turn convert the sun's energy and sea salts into food. The waste excreted by whales provides nutrients for microscopic plants and other organisms in the water. All in all, the relationship between the whale and the other organisms in the food chain is a neatly balanced natural cycle that constantly renews the food resources of the sea.

If the baleen whales disappear, the cycle will be broken. What will happen then? Scientists are not sure. But there is no doubt that the fragile balance of nature in the ocean would tip—and not in our favor.

CITIES under the SEA

"Oh no," I groaned, "that ends our plans for surfacing."

I gazed sadly at the three-dimensional image that floated in the middle of my room. The picture my holovision produced showed towering waves and sheets of falling rain. The voice of the weather forecaster could be heard describing the violent storm that raged 70 meters above my head. The "weather" where I lived was, of course, perfectly calm. It always was since the effects of storms disappear just a few meters below the sea's surface.

"Off," I said sharply to the control computer, taking my anger and disappointment out on the machine.

"Now what?" I thought. As if in answer to my question, the communications system chimed.

"Yes?" I said as I eagerly turned toward the computer console.

My friend Willie's image appeared on the screen. "I guess we're not going to picnic on an island after all," she said. "Disappointed?"

"Of course. I've been to the surface only a few times. I was really looking forward to today's trip, in spite of what's up there: the danger of sunlight to my skin and eyes, air pollution, storms, hot days and cold ones."

"Well cheer up," Willie quickly replied. "Old Professor Melligrant has another plan in mind. She's going to take us to the site of a wreck. It's many kilometers from here, so we're going to use scooters. Grab your gill and get going!"

Preparing for Travel

With my spirits high at the thought of an adventure, I slipped on my water suit. It felt stiff and warm while I remained in my underwater home. But I knew I'd appreciate its warmth and protection in the cool watery world outside. Then I reached into a drawer for my goggles and the all-important gill. I looked at the thin membrane that would fit comfortably over my nose and mouth. And I marveled that such a small, simple device could enable a person to work and travel for countless hours under water.

The material the gill is made of contains proteins. These proteins separate oxygen from water. And we breathe the oxygen. The gill material is used in many ways throughout our underwater city—in our homes, work stations, and transportation vehicles—to provide oxygen for breathing. Without it, human cities beneath the sea would be impossible.

Dressed in my water suit and holding my gill and goggles, I pressed a button that would call a transporter. Seconds later, a blue lamp glowed above the door. My vehicle had arrived. When the door opened, I stepped into the car and pressed the button that indicated where I wanted to go. Whizzing through the transparent tubes that linked various parts of the underwater city, I could see dozens of other cars moving in one direction or another.

At last my car pulled into the transport station located next to the great dome of our school. Professor Melligrant and nine students were already at the school. Melligrant waved me over.

I couldn't help laughing to myself when I saw John. In addition to the usual gear everyone was wearing for this trip, John was loaded down with camera, lights, sonic probe, and a long-range communicator. The sonic probe, which he held in his hand, gave off sounds that could be heard by fish, but not by humans. It was often used to round up or drive away fish. The long-range communicator would come in handy if our little group of explorers got into trouble far from home.

Professor Melligrant unfolded a large map. As we clustered around, she pointed to the general area of the wreck. We walked to the school's exit chamber, a room that would fill with water when we were ready to go. In the dimness of the exit chamber, our suits glowed. So did the water scooters parked nearby. Both the suits and scooters contain materials that react chemically with sea water and give off light. So it would be easy to spot our band of adventurers in the darkness of the ocean.

Exploring the Depths

When everyone was finally ready, the switches were flipped and water flooded into the exit chamber. We turned on the engines of our scooters and followed Melligrant out into the open ocean. After traveling about one kilometer, the lights of the city's power station came into view. From the ocean floor, the station rises almost to the surface of the water. Here electricity is generated for the entire city. And at a nearby station, some of that electricity is used to separate hydrogen from water. The hydrogen is used as fuel.

Next came the farms. Although we could not see them, we knew that sonic fences surrounded the area. These invisible fences send out sounds that fish can hear. The fish do not pass through these sound fences. And as a result, huge schools of fish remain penned in fish farms. As we passed by, a lone herder waved to us. Just a short distance away, flashing lights indicated the location of thick wire cables. At the top of these cables, which extended to just below the ocean surface, are the huge kelp beds. Kelp, a kind of seaweed, is an important food substance. And kelp farming is a popular occupation.

A few kilometers beyond the kelp farms, we came across the first signs of seabed mining. According to the older inhabitants of our city, the prospect of seabed mining had first brought people to live under the sea. Robot miners, which looked like big horseshoe crabs, slowly moved along the sea floor scooping up lumps of the metals titanium and manganese.

Beyond the mining area were several large canyons, which we speedily crossed. Then, as we approached an extremely wide one, Professor Melligrant's scooter slowed down. She turned to the right and gradually descended. We followed.

The searchlight beam on Professor Melligrant's scooter probed the canyon floor. Then it came to a stop at what looked like a big rock. We had reached the wreck. We parked our scooters around it. Our searchlights brightened the whole area.

Professor Melligrant had never told us exactly what type of ship the wreck was. So I had expected to see the funnels and decks of an old oceanliner. Instead, what I gazed at was part of a sausage-shaped object covered with sea organisms.

Using a portable communicator, Professor Melligrant explained to us that the wreck was a submarine of the twentieth century. In this type of vehicle, people without gills had ventured beneath the surface of the sea.

Unlike other explorers of the deep, the people in this submarine had not come in peace. But that had been long, long ago. Today, the only enemy a person can find under water is a curious shark. And it can quickly be sent swimming away with the silent toot of a sonic probe.

Weather and Climate

On September 21, 1938, unknown to anyone, a killer stalked the northeast coast of the United States. It had been spotted earlier, on September 16. But four days later it had been declared harmless, and now it was all but forgotten. Its path had veered eastward into the Atlantic Ocean—or so the weather forecasters said.

They were wrong!

The killer, a monster hurricane packing winds of 193 kilometers an hour, was headed straight for Long Island, a strip of land east of New York City. At about 3:20 P.M. on the afternoon of September 21, the mighty hurricane came ashore and slashed a trail through New England 525 kilometers long. No one in the path of the "Long Island Express," as the storm came to be known, would ever forget it. And when you have finished this unit, you will know why.

CHAPTERS

15 The Atmosphere

16 Weather

17 Climate

The power of a hurricane wind

15 The Atmosphere

CHAPTER SECTIONS

15-1 The Origin of the Earth's Atmosphere

15-2 The Present Atmosphere

CHAPTER OBJECTIVES

After completing this chapter, you will be able to:

15-1 Describe how the early atmosphere on Earth changed to the present atmosphere.

15-1 Explain the importance of the ozone layer to life on Earth.

15-2 List the four layers of the atmosphere and describe the characteristics of each.

With an earth-shattering boom, a small mountain disappears. In its place, sparks, flames, and dense dust clouds rise into an orange-red sky. Flashes of lightning pierce the clouds.

Suddenly, cracks appear in the solid ground. The cracks spread to reveal a glowing, boiling sea of molten rock. Great slabs of earth break off and bob on this sea of rock, like rafts on a rushing river.

Gases and fumes explode out of the cracks in the ground. Steam hisses from pools among the rocks. These fumes and vapors pour into an atmosphere of deadly gases—an atmosphere that cannot support any known forms of life.

Where is this hot, violent world? Is it a distant planet? In a way, yes. However, this planet is distant not in space but in time!

Earth billions of years ago

Figure 15-1 *Eruptions in Iceland spread molten rock across the earth's surface and release various gases. This is the way the earth may have looked billions of years ago when the atmosphere first formed.*

15-1 The Origin of the Earth's Atmosphere

As you may have guessed, the strange place you just read about is the earth. It is not the earth of today, of course, but a much younger earth. This description is a picture of what many scientists believe our planet was like about four billion years ago.

Matter from that time still exists. Some of it was originally dust that fell out of the earth's atmosphere. By analyzing this dust, scientists can figure out what kind of an atmosphere the earth had about four billion years ago.

The conclusions of the scientists may surprise you. Why? Because that long-ago atmosphere contained two very deadly gases called methane and ammonia. There was also some water in the air. During the next four billion years, this atmosphere changed again and again. As you well know, our air is no longer deadly. In fact, we could not live without it. Here is how scientists believe the changes occurred.

First Changes and the Sun

Dust trapped in the ice of Greenland gives scientists a clue to a change in the earth's atmosphere that occurred about 3.8 billion years ago. Analysis of the dust, which is about 3.8 billion years old, provides evidence of the earth's atmosphere at that time. Although the chemistry and the reasoning are complex, the story probably goes something like this.

Sunlight triggered chemical reactions among the methane, ammonia, and water in the early atmosphere. Through many chemical steps, new materials—such as nitrogen, hydrogen, and carbon dioxide—were formed. The methane and ammonia had vanished. But the water still remained.

Hydrogen escaped into space. Hydrogen is a very lightweight substance, and the earth's gravity could not hold it. What was left? Lots of nitrogen, which still makes up most of the atmosphere; a large amount of carbon dioxide; and some water vapor.

The water vapor, which you might think of as a kind of worldwide haze, quickly turned into liquid, almost as dew does in the morning. It rained. Pools formed, then lakes, seas, and finally the oceans. Above the oceans, new changes were gradually transforming the atmosphere even more.

An Ozone Shield Forms

Sunlight began breaking down water vapor in the upper parts of the earth's atmosphere. The water vapor broke down into oxygen and hydrogen gases. As before, the atoms of hydrogen gas escaped into space. But the oxygen atoms began to combine with each other to form **ozone.** Each molecule of ozone is made up of three oxygen atoms joined together. The end result was a layer of ozone, most of it between 19 and 30 kilometers above the earth's surface.

Figure 15-2 *Scientists collect ice samples from the earth's polar regions. Dust trapped in the ice helps scientists study changes in the earth's early atmosphere.*

Figure 15-3 *The ozone layer absorbs most of the harmful ultraviolet radiation before it reaches the earth's surface. Visible light is not absorbed by the ozone layer.*

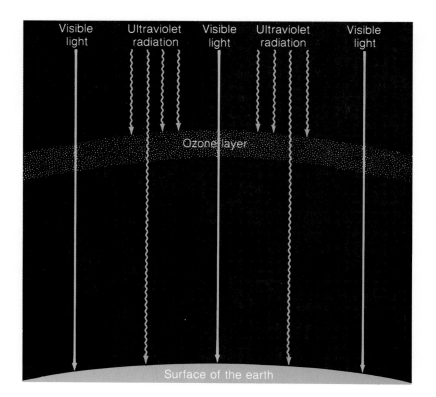

Figure 15-4 *Blue-green algae like these were a simple form of life in the earth's oceans billions of years ago. They produced their own food through photosynthesis, releasing oxygen as a waste product.*

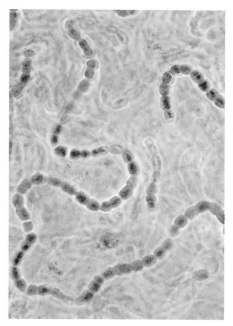

Scientists often refer to the ozone layer as an umbrella for life on Earth. That is because the ozone layer absorbs most of the harmful ultraviolet radiation from the sun. Without the protection of this ozone shield, few living things could survive.

Before the ozone layer formed, the only living things on Earth were microscopic organisms that lived well below the surface of the oceans. The water protected them from most of the ultraviolet radiation. After the development of the ozone layer, certain types of organisms called blue-green algae started appearing on or near the water's surface. These tiny algae could use the energy in sunlight to combine carbon dioxide from the air with water to produce food. This process is called **photosynthesis** (foh-tuh-SIN-thuh-sis).

The algae used the food they made during photosynthesis for growth and development. Fortunately, a waste product of photosynthesis would soon change the planet forever. That waste product was oxygen. Unlike ozone, these oxygen atoms combined in twos and stayed near the bottom of the atmosphere. It would be this oxygen that animals would later breathe.

Figure 15-5 *Many millions of years ago, blue-green algae released oxygen into the atmosphere and oceans. The increase of oxygen allowed more complex plants and eventually animals to develop.*

In the meantime, green plants began to grow on the land as well. And they too released oxygen into the atmosphere while removing carbon dioxide. Through photosynthesis, the oxygen content in the atmosphere greatly increased. Then, around 600 million years ago, the amount of oxygen and the amount of carbon dioxide in the air leveled off. Since that time, the composition of the air has remained about the same.

SECTION REVIEW

1. Name one important clue to the composition of the earth's early atmosphere.
2. List two of the gases that were formed when sunlight broke down ammonia and methane in the atmosphere.
3. Name the process by which green plants use sunlight to produce food.

15-2　The Present Atmosphere

Today, about 78 percent of the earth's atmosphere is nitrogen gas. Another 21 percent or so of the atmosphere is oxygen. There is also some water vapor in the atmosphere. In Figure 15-6 you can see some of the other gases that are found in our

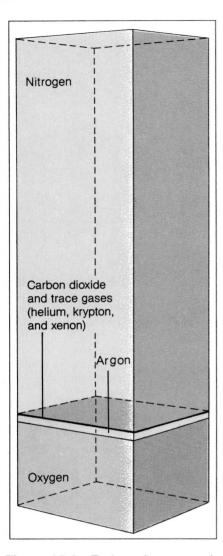

Figure 15-6 *Today, nitrogen and oxygen make up most of the gases in the earth's atmosphere. What other gases are found in the atmosphere?*

atmosphere. As you can tell, the composition of the atmosphere has certainly changed in the past four billion years. The temperature of the atmosphere, as it turns out, has changed as well.

Temperature in the Atmosphere

If you ever climb a very high mountain, you will notice two things. As you go higher, your lungs have to work harder to supply your body with needed oxygen. That is because the air gets thinner, or less dense. It holds less oxygen. For extremely high peaks, such as Mount Everest, climbers usually take along oxygen tanks.

The other thing you will notice as you climb is that the air gets colder. You may have started out in a tropical valley wearing shorts and a light shirt. But by the time you reach an altitude of three kilometers, you are likely to need heavy slacks, a woolen sweater, and, perhaps, a fleece-lined jacket.

Why does the air get colder as one climbs higher? Isn't a person more exposed to the sun's energy on a high mountain than at sea level under the cover of clouds, mist, and fog? Yes! In fact, you are more likely to get sunburned on a high mountain peak than in a deep valley of the same region. But you are also likely to freeze on that mountain at the same time. That is because the thin, dry air of the mountain peak holds much less heat than the denser, damper air of the deep valley.

Figure 15-7 *Climbers need heavy clothing on a high mountain because the air is colder. As they climb ever higher, the air thins and they must use oxygen masks.*

Figure 15-8 *This high-altitude balloon will be used to record temperatures at different heights in the earth's atmosphere.*

Layers of Atmosphere

Up to about 70 years ago, scientists generally believed that the temperature of the atmosphere always decreased with altitude. This belief that the higher you go the colder the air is was based on the experiences of mountain climbers and early balloonists. However, the use of high-altitude balloons and rockets in later years showed that this was true only up to a certain altitude.

Atmospheric research showed that air temperature steadily decreases up to a height of about 10 kilometers, then levels off. At about 20 kilometers, the temperature increases up to a height of about 48 kilometers, then levels off again. At about 54 kilometers the temperature again begins to decrease. It levels off at about 80 kilometers. From about 90 kilometers upward, the temperature increases. These temperature changes led scientists to conclude that the atmosphere was made up of layers, each with a kind of temperature boundary. **Based on temperature differences, scientists divide the atmosphere into four major layers: the troposphere, the stratosphere, the mesosphere, and the thermosphere.**

TROPOSPHERE   The lowest layer of the earth's atmosphere is the **troposphere** (TRAH-puh-sfeer). It is here that almost all the earth's water vapor is found.

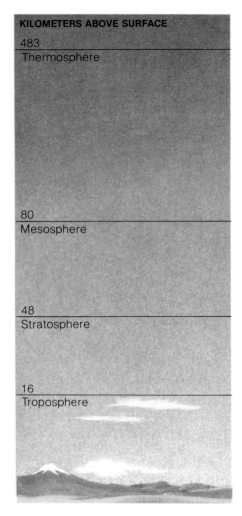

KILOMETERS ABOVE SURFACE
483
Thermosphere
80
Mesosphere
48
Stratosphere
16
Troposphere

Figure 15-9 *The locations of the four major layers of the atmosphere are shown in this diagram. In which layer do you live?*

Water vapor rises into the troposphere when the sun heats water in oceans, lakes, and streams. As the water vapor rises, it begins to cool. Clouds form. In time, the water vapor will return to the earth's surface as rain, snow, sleet, and hail.

The troposphere is also a place where fierce winds blow. Here there is a constant movement of air. This constant movement can create great storms. For this reason, the troposphere is often called the home of weather on the earth.

STRATOSPHERE The next layer is the **stratosphere** (STRAT-uh-sfeer). In the lower part of the stratosphere, air temperature remains constant and very cold, around −60° C. This layer of cold air keeps the warm air of the troposphere from rising. But the air now is forced to move sideways along the boundary between the upper troposphere and the lower stratosphere. This movement creates the jet stream, a fast-moving current of air.

The temperature in the upper portion of the stratosphere is much warmer, around 18° C. That is because the upper part of the ozone layer reacts with ultraviolet radiation and heat is given off. Most of the ozone layer is found in the stratosphere.

MESOSPHERE The upper portion of the ozone layer spills over into the next higher section of the atmosphere—the **mesosphere** (MES-uh-sfeer). Here the sun's radiation breaks down ozone molecules into free oxygen atoms. So here the ozone layer ends.

Figure 15-10 *This colorful sunset is caused by the scattering of sunlight through the atmosphere.*

The temperature in the mesosphere drops steadily as the altitude increases. But the air temperature rises again in the highest section of atmosphere—the **thermosphere** (THER-muh-sfeer).

THERMOSPHERE The thermosphere contains a region known as the **ionosphere.** That is because the sun's radiation causes **ions** to form there. An ion is an atom that has an electric charge. The thermosphere is the earth's outer frontier. It also marks the beginning of outer space.

SECTION REVIEW

1. Name the two most common gases in the earth's present atmosphere.
2. List the four layers of the earth's atmosphere.
3. In which atmospheric layer is most of the ozone layer found?

Activity

Atmospheric Layers

Figure 15-9 shows the layers of the earth's atmosphere and the altitudes at which they begin and end. Using the information in the diagram, calculate the average thickness of each layer.

LABORATORY ACTIVITY

Heat Transfer by Convection

Purpose

In this activity, you will learn how heat energy is transferred by convection.

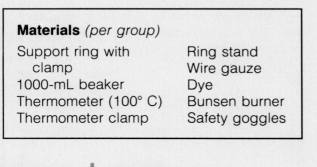

Materials *(per group)*

Support ring with clamp	Ring stand
1000-mL beaker	Wire gauze
Thermometer (100° C)	Dye
Thermometer clamp	Bunsen burner
	Safety goggles

Procedure

1. Attach a support ring to a ring stand and cover the ring with wire gauze.
2. Fill a beaker to 2 cm from its top with cold, clear water. Place the beaker on the ring.
3. Attach a thermometer clamp to the ring stand so that a thermometer can be inserted into the water in the beaker. Allow the setup to remain undisturbed for several minutes.
4. Carefully drop a small amount of dye into the water near the edge of the beaker.
5. Turn on the Bunsen burner. Position it so that the flame is directly under the dye. **CAUTION:** *Be careful in lighting and positioning the burner. Remember to wear your safety goggles.*
6. Observe the pattern of flow (movement) that appears in the water.
7. On paper, sketch a picture of the fluid movement that you observe in the beaker. Use arrows to show the direction of the flow of water.
8. Now place the thermometer in the water near the top of the beaker and record the temperature. Then lower the thermometer to the bottom of the beaker and record the temperature of the water there.

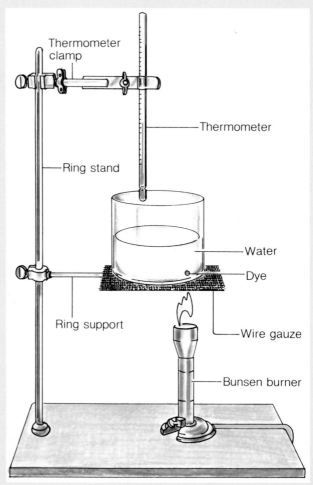

Observations and Conclusions

1. Label on your sketch, in the correct location, the following information: areas of high temperature; areas of low temperature; areas of high density; areas of low density.
2. Does the density of a fluid increase or decrease as temperature increases? As temperature decreases?
3. Based on the relationship you found in question 2, how do you explain the flow of water in the beaker in terms of temperature and density differences?
4. Explain how gravity is involved in the process of convection.

CHAPTER REVIEW

SUMMARY

15-1 The Origin of the Earth's Atmosphere

■ About 3.8 billion years ago, sunlight began to change the atmosphere from ammonia, methane, and water vapor to nitrogen, hydrogen, and carbon dioxide.

■ Sunlight broke down water vapor in the atmosphere into ozone, a form of oxygen.

■ Ozone absorbs harmful ultraviolet radiation from sunlight.

■ Green plants combine carbon dioxide and water to form food in a process known as photosynthesis.

■ A waste product of photosynthesis is oxygen.

15-2 The Present Atmosphere

■ The atmosphere is now composed mainly of about 78 percent nitrogen gas and 21 percent oxygen gas. Traces of other gases make up the remaining 1 percent.

■ Changes in air temperature led scientists to conclude that there are four main layers in the atmosphere.

■ The troposphere is the lowest layer of the atmosphere. Clouds, rain, snow, wind, and storms are found in the troposphere.

■ Above the troposphere is the stratosphere. Most of the ozone layer is in the stratosphere.

■ The jet stream is found between the troposphere and the stratosphere.

■ The mesosphere is found above the stratosphere. The ozone layer ends in the lower mesosphere.

■ The thermosphere is the outermost layer of the atmosphere. It contains a region known as the ionosphere.

VOCABULARY

Define each term in a complete sentence.

ion	**mesosphere**	**photosynthesis**	**thermosphere**
ionosphere	**ozone**	**stratosphere**	**troposphere**

CONTENT REVIEW: MULTIPLE CHOICE

Choose the letter of the answer that best completes each statement.

1. A gas found in the atmosphere of today but not in the early atmosphere is
   a. methane.   b. water vapor.
   c. oxygen.   d. ammonia.
2. A lightweight gas that can easily escape into space is
   a. oxygen.   b. carbon dioxide.
   c. hydrogen.   d. nitrogen.
3. A gas used by green plants to make food is
   a. ammonia.   b. nitrogen.
   c. oxygen.   d. carbon dioxide.
4. Ozone is formed from
   a. carbon dioxide.   b. oxygen.
   c. ammonia.   d. methane.

5. A product of photosynthesis that made possible the atmosphere of today is
   a. oxygen.   b. carbon dioxide.   c. methane.   d. nitrogen.
6. The lowest section of the atmosphere is the
   a. stratosphere.   b. troposphere.
   c. mesosphere.   d. thermosphere.
7. The layer above the stratosphere is the
   a. ionosphere.   b. troposphere.
   c. mesosphere.   d. thermosphere.
8. The thermosphere contains a region known as the
   a. stratosphere.   b. jet stream.   c. ozone layer.   d. ionosphere.
9. The layer of the atmosphere that contains most of the ozone layer is the
   a. stratosphere.   b. ionosphere.
   c. mesosphere.   d. thermosphere.
10. The upper portion of the ozone layer is in the
   a. stratosphere.   b. ionosphere.
   c. mesosphere.   d. thermosphere.

CONTENT REVIEW: COMPLETION

Fill in the word or words that best complete each statement.

1. The atmosphere of four billion years ago contained two deadly gases, _____ and _____.

2. _____ triggered chemical reactions among the substances in the atmosphere of four billion years ago.

3. The atmosphere of today is made up mostly of _____.

4. _____ is the process of combining the sun's energy, carbon dioxide from the air, and water to make food.

5. Almost all of the earth's water vapor is found in the layer of the atmosphere called the _____.

6. The _____ is the layer of the atmosphere that has often been called the home of weather on the earth.

7. Most of the _____ layer is found in the upper part of the stratosphere.

8. The fast-moving current of air between the troposphere and the stratosphere is called the _____.

9. Atoms that have an electric charge are called _____.

10. The outermost layer of the atmosphere is called the _____.

CONTENT REVIEW: TRUE OR FALSE

Determine whether each statement is true or false. If it is true, write "true." If it is false, change the underlined word or words to make the statement true.

1. Methane was part of the earth's atmosphere four billion years ago.

2. The action of electricity changed the gases of the early atmosphere into nitrogen, hydrogen, and carbon dioxide.

3. Water vapor can be broken down into hydrogen and nitrogen.

4. The upper portion of the stratosphere is warmer than the lower portion.

5. The mesosphere is above the ionosphere.

6. A molecule of ozone is made up of <u>three</u> oxygen atoms joined together.
7. Most of the atmosphere today is composed of <u>oxygen</u> gas.
8. As you climb a tall mountain, the air gets <u>warmer</u>.

9. Air on top of a mountain holds <u>less</u> heat than air at the bottom.
10. Constant movement of air creates great storms in the <u>troposphere</u>.

CONCEPT REVIEW: SKILL BUILDING

Use the skills you have developed in the chapter to complete each activity.

1. **Making charts** Using Figure 15-6 on page 344 and information from your text, construct a pie chart showing the percentage of various gases in the atmosphere. Which gas makes up the greatest percentage of the atmosphere? Which gases make up the smallest percentage of the atmosphere?
2. **Making predictions** Recently, scientists have discovered a "hole" in the ozone layer above Antarctica. Predict what might happen to the earth and to the organisms living on the earth if this hole becomes larger.
3. **Sequencing events** Create a series of drawings to illustrate the various steps by which the early atmosphere changed into the atmosphere of today. Be sure to include labels in your drawings.
4. **Relating facts** If you have ever travelled by airplane, you have probably been in a pressurized cabin. Explain why it is necessary for air pressure within a plane to be controlled.

5. **Relating cause and effect** During the past hundred years, and especially during the past thirty years, there has been an increase of carbon dioxide in the atmosphere. Most of this increase is caused by the burning of fossil fuels. At the same time, however, an increasing number of forests around the world are being cut down. How does this destruction of forests affect the amount of carbon dioxide in the atmosphere? What steps can be taken to reverse the trend of increasing carbon dioxide in the atmosphere?
6. **Making graphs** Use what you learned in this chapter to construct a line graph comparing the temperatures found in the four main layers of the atmosphere. You can plot the altitude of each layer on the X-axis and the temperature on the Y-axis. What can you conclude from your graph?

CONCEPT REVIEW: ESSAY

Discuss each of the following in a brief paragraph.

1. Describe the four major layers of the atmosphere. On what basis do scientists classify these layers?
2. What is the ozone layer? Why is it important to life on Earth?
3. Why is sunburn a problem at the top of a mountain where the air is cold and dry?

4. Describe the early atmosphere.
5. Explain how temperature and pressure change as you climb a mountain.
6. Explain why plants and not animals were the first organisms to appear on Earth.

16 Weather

CHAPTER SECTIONS

16-1 Forces That Shape Weather

16-2 Heating the Earth

16-3 Atmospheric Pressure

16-4 Winds

16-5 Moisture in the Air

16-6 Weather Patterns

CHAPTER OBJECTIVES

After completing this chapter, you will be able to:

16-1 Identify the factors that interact to cause weather.

16-2 Discuss the three basic methods of heat transfer.

16-3 Define atmospheric pressure.

16-3 Explain how a barometer can be used to predict weather.

16-4 Compare local and global wind patterns.

16-5 Define humidity.

16-5 Identify three basic types of clouds.

16-6 Compare the four major types of air masses.

16-6 Explain how fronts affect weather patterns.

16-6 Interpret a weather map.

The F8U Crusader jet fighter plane roared smoothly through the air. Its pilot, Colonel William H. Rankin, settled back for what he expected to be a routine flight between Massachusetts and North Carolina. But all thoughts of "routine" would vanish a few hours later over Norfolk, Virginia. There a huge thunderstorm lay in wait for Rankin and his plane.

Rankin spotted the storm ahead and began to climb so as to pass over it. As his jet reached an altitude of 14,325 meters, Rankin was about to breathe a sigh of relief. Then WHAM! Something seemed to pound against the plane. A second later its engine stopped roaring and went dead. Reading his instruments, Rankin realized there was only one thing to do: eject!

With the push of a button, Rankin shot out into the air. When his parachute opened, Rankin found himself on an incredible natural roller coaster. For seconds he would plunge downward. Then fierce updrafts would throw him upward, higher and higher. Then would come a stomach-wrenching drop. He felt like a hailstone being tossed up and down through the angry cloud. And, as any meteorologist will tell you—and as this chapter will reveal—Rankin was acting very much like a hailstone. But fortunately, he did not crash to Earth as fast. After more than half an hour in the air, he finally landed—safe, but battered from an experience he would never forget.

A thunderstorm cloud and rain

Figure 16-1 *Fierce storms can cause much damage. In this photograph, such a storm smashes sections of the boardwalk at Atlantic City, New Jersey.*

16-1 Forces That Shape Weather

When you woke up this morning, did you stop to think about the weather? Was it warm or cold? Windy or calm? Did you take an umbrella with you? Were you able to have your picnic?

Weather affects you daily. It influences you and the world around you. The types of homes people build, the clothes they wear, the crops they grow, the jobs they work at, and the ways they spend their leisure time are all determined by the weather.

Today people have a good understanding of the weather. Weather satellites, computers, and other kinds of weather instruments provide accurate information about weather conditions.

Scientists now know that weather is caused by the interaction of several factors in the earth's atmosphere. **The atmospheric factors that interact to cause weather are heat energy, air pressure, winds, and moisture.**

SECTION REVIEW

1. What atmospheric factors interact to cause weather?
2. List two instruments that scientists use to learn about weather conditions.

16-2 Heating the Earth

Almost all of the earth's energy comes from the sun. This energy is called **radiant energy.** Radiant energy helps warm the earth. The atmosphere also helps warm the earth by absorbing, storing, and recycling the sun's radiant energy.

As the sun's energy reaches the atmosphere, part of it is reflected back into space or scattered throughout the atmosphere. This happens when incoming rays strike water droplets and dust particles in the atmosphere.

Much of the sun's energy is absorbed by the atmosphere. In the upper atmosphere, the ozone layer absorbs ultraviolet rays, one form of radiant energy. Ultraviolet radiation, which causes sunburns, can be dangerous to people if absorbed in large quantities.

Radiant energy that is neither reflected nor absorbed by the atmosphere reaches the earth's surface. Here it is absorbed by the earth and changed into heat. Eventually, this heat energy travels from the earth's surface back out into space, warming the atmosphere in the process.

If the whole atmosphere is warmed by heat rising from the earth, how can the air temperature vary so

Figure 16-2 *The sun's radiant energy helps warm the atmosphere. The atmosphere then warms the earth. What six things happen to the sun's radiant energy according to this diagram?*

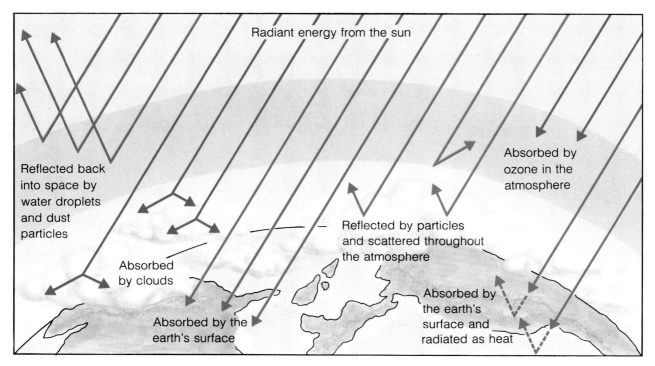

Radiant energy from the sun

Reflected back into space by water droplets and dust particles

Absorbed by clouds

Reflected by particles and scattered throughout the atmosphere

Absorbed by ozone in the atmosphere

Absorbed by the earth's surface

Absorbed by the earth's surface and radiated as heat

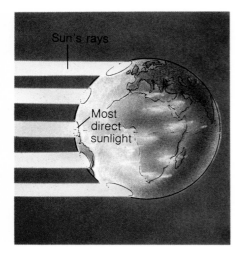

Sun's rays

Most
direct
sunlight

Figure 16-3 *Radiant energy from the sun strikes the earth at different angles, causing uneven heating of the earth's surface. Which area receives the most direct sunlight?*

Activity

Convection Currents

Here is a way for you to see how convection currents form.

1. Pour water into a small beaker until it is almost full.

2. Add two or three drops of food coloring to the surface of the water.

3. Put on safety goggles and light a candle. Put on heat-resistant gloves. Using laboratory tongs, hold the beaker about 10 centimeters above the flame.

What happens to the food coloring? Relate your observations to the way convection currents work in air. At what location on the earth would air constantly be rising because of convection currents?

much from place to place? To help you answer this question, look at Figure 16-3.

The angle at which the sun's rays strike the earth's surface is not the same everywhere on the globe. At the equator, which is an imaginary line that separates the earth into two halves, the sun is nearly overhead. The sun's rays strike the earth at an angle of 90° all year long. The greatest heating occurs when the sun's rays are most direct, or strike the earth at or near an angle of 90°. So areas at or near the equator receive the most radiant energy and have the highest temperatures.

The farther an area is from the equator, the less radiant energy it receives. Why is this so? The angle at which the sun's rays strike the earth is smaller than 90°. The same amount of radiant energy is spread over a wider area. The result is less heat and lower temperatures. As the angle of the sun's rays decreases from 90°, the rays become less direct. The amount of energy received at a location decreases.

Conduction, Convection, and Radiation

The sun's energy that is absorbed by the earth is spread throughout the atmosphere in three basic ways: conduction, convection, and radiation.

Conduction is the direct transfer of heat energy from one substance to another. As air above the earth's surface comes in contact with the warm ground, the air is warmed. So temperatures close to the ground are usually higher than temperatures a few meters above the surface. Soil, water, and air are poor heat conductors. So conduction plays only a minor role in spreading heat energy through land, sea, and atmosphere.

Convection is the transfer of heat in a fluid. Air is a fluid. When air near the earth's surface is heated, it becomes less dense and rises. Cooler, more dense air from above sinks. As it sinks, it is heated by the ground and begins to rise. The process of warm air rising and cool air sinking continues. Convection currents are formed. Convection currents are caused by the unequal heating of the atmosphere. Most of the heat energy in the atmosphere is transferred by convection currents.

Radiation is the transfer of heat energy in the form of waves. When the sun's energy moves by radiation, it does not need the presence of a solid, liquid, or gas. It can travel right through space.

Infrared radiation, or heat energy from the sun, is absorbed by soil, water, plants, and animals on the earth's surface. This absorbed energy is eventually reradiated back into the atmosphere and out into space.

SECTION REVIEW

1. What three things happen to the sun's rays when they reach the atmosphere?
2. What are three ways by which heat energy is spread throughout the atmosphere?
3. What factor causes unequal heating of the earth?

Career: *Weather Observer*

HELP WANTED: WEATHER OBSERVER To assist meteorologist in collection of weather data to be used in forecasting.

Another school day! The sun shines brightly through your bedroom window. You jump up, dress, and head downstairs. What a great day for the ball game! As you enter the kitchen, however, you notice boots and rain gear set by the door for you to wear to school. How can this be, you wonder, as you adjust a curtain to shade the breakfast table. Mom or Dad obviously heard a forecast of rain over the radio. You continue to wonder how anybody can tell that it will rain on a day that starts with the sun out.

Amazingly there are hundreds of **weather observers** located at points all around the world. At the same times each day, four times a day, they cart their data charts out toward an instrument shelter station. The weather data collected at these stations, such as wind speed, wind direction, air pressure, and relative humidity, are radioed or phoned to the National Meteorological Center in Maryland. There the information is fed into large computers that print out maps based on the weather observations. Meteorologists study the weather patterns on these maps before they make their forecast.

The weather predictions made from this information help people plan their outdoor activities. For some businesses it is important to know the weather conditions to prevent added expense. For example, some housing materials may be damaged if they are exposed to rain or snow. If you wish to learn more about weather observing, write to the United States Department of Commerce, NOAA, National Weather Service, Silver Spring, MD 20910.

*Tracking Weather
with a Barometer*

Can you use a barometer to forecast weather?

1. For five days before school, during science class, and after school, use a barometer to measure air pressure. Record these measurements.

2. At the same time, observe and record the weather conditions outside.

3. Make a graph of your pressure measurements.

Does the barometer help you predict the weather? Explain your answer.

Figure 16-4 *When air pressure increases, the column of mercury rises in the barometer tube* (right). *When air pressure decreases, the column of mercury drops in the tube* (left).

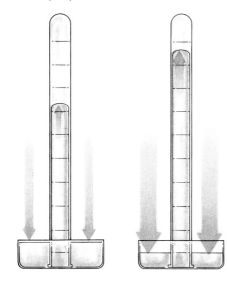

16-3 Atmospheric Pressure

Atmospheric pressure, or air pressure, is a measure of the force created by the weight of air pressing down on each square centimeter of the earth's surface. Scientists use a special instrument to measure **air pressure.** This instrument, a **barometer,** was invented in 1643 by an Italian scientist named Evangelista Torricelli.

Many scientists in the early 1600s thought that atmospheric pressure changes from time to time. But no one was able to prove it. Then Torricelli found a way. He took a narrow glass tube, almost a meter long, with one end sealed. He filled the tube with mercury and put his finger over the open end. He placed the open end of the tube in a basin of mercury, removed his finger, and held the tube upright. The mercury in the tube dropped to a certain point. He marked that point. During the following days, he noted that the column of mercury in the tube rose and fell. He had invented an instrument that could measure the changes in atmospheric pressure.

Torricelli reasoned that the weight of the air pressing down on the mercury in the basin forced the mercury up inside the tube. As the air pressure increased, the mercury rose higher in the tube. And as the air pressure decreased, the mercury in the tube dropped. See Figure 16-4.

Soon scientists realized that barometers could be used to help forecast the weather. Air pressure may become relatively high when large masses of air come together in the upper atmosphere. These air masses press down on the layers of air below. This pressure usually prevents warm, moist air from rising into the upper atmosphere. As a result, clouds do not form. So high pressure usually means fair weather. But there are exceptions.

Air pressure may become relatively low when large masses of air move apart in the upper atmosphere. This reduces pressure on the layers of warm air below. As a result, the warm air rises. If the warm air is moist, clouds will form in the upper atmosphere. These clouds can lead to rain, snow, and other bad weather. But again, there are exceptions.

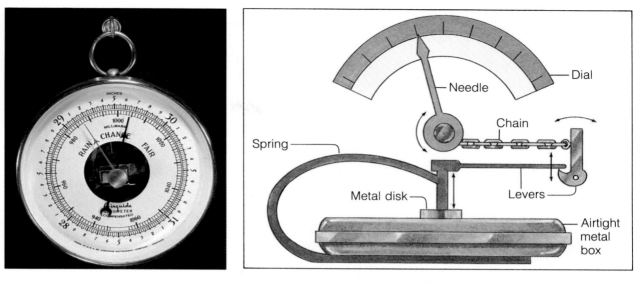

Figure 16-5 *The aneroid barometer, a common type of barometer, consists of an airtight metal box from which most of the air has been removed. A change in air pressure causes the needle to move and indicate the new air pressure.*

SECTION REVIEW

1. What is air pressure?
2. What is the name of the instrument that scientists use to measure air pressure?
3. What type of weather can you usually expect when air pressure is high? When it is low?
4. When does the column of mercury in a barometer rise? When does it drop?

16-4 Winds

When air is heated, its density decreases. The warm air rises and produces an area of low pressure. Cooler, denser air, which produces an area of high pressure, moves in underneath the rising warm air. So air moves from an area of high pressure to an area of low pressure. **Winds** are formed by this movement of air.

There are two general types of winds: local winds and global winds. Local winds are the type you are most familiar with. They blow from any direction and usually cover short distances. Global winds blow from a specific direction and almost always travel longer distances. **Both local winds and global winds are caused by differences in air pressure due to unequal heating of the air.**

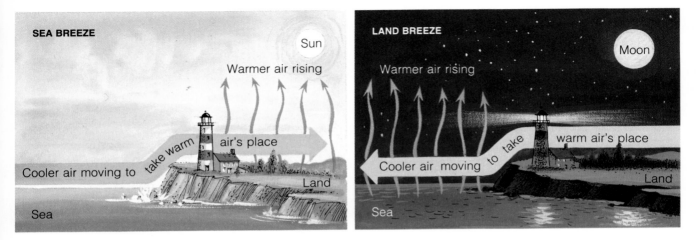

Figure 16-6 *Land and water absorb and lose heat at different rates, causing a sea breeze during the day and a land breeze during the night. Which heats up faster, land or water?*

Activity

Heating the Land and Sea

Which heats up faster, land or sea?

1. Place equal amounts of water and sand in separate beakers.

2. Expose the beakers to sunlight or to a very bright light bulb. Make sure each beaker is the same distance from the light source.

3. Note the temperature of the beakers at regular intervals.

4. Remove the beakers from the source of heat and again note the temperature as each cools.

Which heats up faster? Which cools faster? Which holds its heat longer? Based on your answers, explain why land and sea breezes occur.

Local Winds

During the daytime, the air over a land area is often warmer than the air over a nearby lake or sea. The air is warmer because the land heats up faster than the water. As the air over the land rises, the cooler air over the sea moves inland to take its place. This flow of air from the sea to the land is called a **sea breeze.** See Figure 16-6.

During the night, the land cools off faster than the water. The air over the sea is now warmer than the air over the land. This warm air over the sea rises. The cooler air over the land moves to replace the rising warm air over the sea. A flow of air from the land to the sea, called a **land breeze,** is formed. See Figure 16-6.

The name of a wind will tell you where the wind is coming from. A *land* breeze flows from the land to the sea. You are probably more familiar with winds that have a direction in their names. For instance, a northwest wind flows *from* the northwest. This wind, however, will be moving *toward* the southeast.

A major land and sea breeze is called a **monsoon** (mahn-SOON). A monsoon is a seasonal wind. During part of the year, the wind blows from the continent to the ocean. During the rest of the year, it blows from the ocean to the continent. When the wind blows from the ocean, it brings in warm, moist air. Huge amounts of rain and warm temperatures over land areas result. This rainy season is important to many countries. It supplies fresh water for farming. Many monsoon winds occur on the Asian continent.

Global Winds

Unequal heating of the earth's surface also forms large global wind systems. In areas near the equator, the sun is almost directly overhead for most of the year. The direct rays of the sun heat the earth's surface rapidly. The polar regions receive slanting rays from the sun. The slanting rays do not heat the earth's surface as rapidly as the direct rays do. So temperatures in the polar regions are lower than those in areas near the equator. At the equator, the warm air rises and moves toward the poles. At the poles, cooler air sinks and moves toward the equator. This movement produces a global pattern of air circulation.

Global winds do not move directly from north to south or from south to north, as you might expect. Because the earth rotates, the paths of the winds shift in relation to the earth's surface. All winds in the Northern Hemisphere curve to the right as they move. In the Southern Hemisphere, winds curve to the left. This effect is called the **Coriolis effect.** See Figure 16-7.

The Coriolis effect is the apparent shift in the path of any fluid or object moving above the surface of the earth due to the rotation of the earth. For example, suppose an airplane is traveling south from Pittsburgh, Pennsylvania, to Miami, Florida. If the pilot does not make adjustments for the Coriolis effect, the airplane will land west of the point from which it started. It would appear as if an invisible force were pushing it west.

DOLDRUMS   At the equator, surface winds are very calm. These winds are called the doldrums (DOHL-druhmz). Throughout the year, a belt of air around the equator gets much of the sun's radiant energy. Warm air rises from this belt almost all the time. This warm rising air produces a low-pressure area that extends many kilometers north and south of the equator. Normally, cooler high-pressure air flows into such an area, creating winds. But the cooler air is warmed so rapidly near the equator that the winds that form cannot go into the low-pressure area. Consequently, if there are any winds, they will be weak winds.

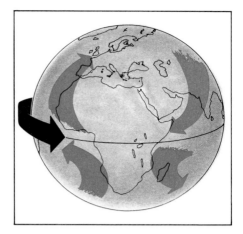

Figure 16-7   *The earth's rotation curves winds to the right in the Northern Hemisphere and to the left in the Southern Hemisphere. This shift in winds is known as the Coriolis effect.*

The Beaufort Scale

Wind speed can be estimated and given a descriptive name by using the Beaufort scale.

1. Use information from reference books to prepare a complete chart of the Beaufort scale.

2. Your chart should have columns for Beaufort numbers, wind speeds in kilometers per hour, and effects of wind speed on land objects.

3. Using the Beaufort scale, record wind speeds in your area each day for ten days. Make two observations a day.

The doldrums can be a problem for sailing ships. Because there may be no winds, the ships can be stuck in the doldrums for many days.

OTHER GLOBAL WINDS   Remember the warm air rising from the equator? In the upper atmosphere, some of this rising air branches off to the north and some branches to the south. Let's follow the northern flow. Keep in mind that similar movements occur in the Southern Hemisphere.

As it cools, the rising air levels off. Following the curve of the earth, it flows northward in the upper atmosphere. The cool air starts to sink at about 20° north latitude. Latitude lines are imaginary circles that run parallel to the equator and measure distance north and south. The equator has a latitude of 0°, while the North Pole has a latitude of 90°.

Pressing down on the atmosphere below, this sinking cool air creates a series of high-pressure areas around the globe. As the air sinks toward land

Figure 16-8 *Global wind patterns are caused by unequal heating of the earth's surface and by the rotation of the earth. Warm air rises. Cold air sinks. And the Coriolis effect bends the winds. What are the three major global winds?*

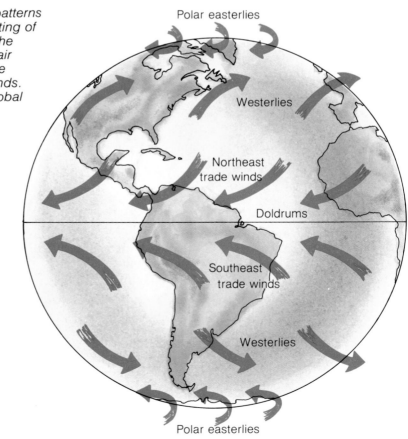

and ocean surfaces, it forces warm air out to the north and south. For a time, the outward-flowing warm air travels close to the earth's surface. It even gets warmer as it moves and eventually rises.

Because of the Coriolis effect, air moving south in the Northern Hemisphere curves to the right, in this case to the southwest. To an observer on the surface, the resulting winds appear to come from the northeast. So they are called the northeast trade winds. Air moving north curves to the northeast. So the resulting winds are called the westerly winds, or prevailing westerlies, named for the general area they come from, the west. See Figure 16-8. In the early days of exploration and settlement, sailing-ship captains relied on the northeast trade winds for quick passages from Europe to the Americas and on the westerlies to return home.

The westerlies influence the movement of most weather systems in North America. Low-pressure storms often occur in the area of the westerlies. And the wind can blow in any direction in such a storm. But the general movement of the wind is from the southwest toward the northeast.

In both hemispheres, the westerlies start rising and cooling between 50° latitude and 60° latitude. Here they meet winds flowing from the cold polar regions. The polar winds flow from east to west and are known as the polar easterlies.

JET STREAMS For centuries, people have been aware of the global winds you just read about. But it was not until the 1940s that another global wind was discovered. This wind is a narrow belt of strong high-speed air called a jet stream.

Scientists now know that jet streams are high-pressure belts of air that are swirled from west to east by the earth's rotation. However, the streams do not flow around the globe in regular bands. They wander up and down as they circle the globe. At times, the jet streams take great detours north and south. The wind speed and depth of jet streams can vary enormously.

The wandering jet streams affect the atmosphere below them. The rush of a jet stream creates waves and eddy currents, swirling motions opposite to the flow of the main stream, in the lower atmosphere.

Figure 16-9 *This device consists of a weather vane, which measures wind direction, and an anemometer, which measures wind speed. Wind speed can be determined by counting the number of times the cups of the anemometer revolve.*

Figure 16-10 *A high-altitude jet stream moves over the Nile Valley and the Red Sea.*

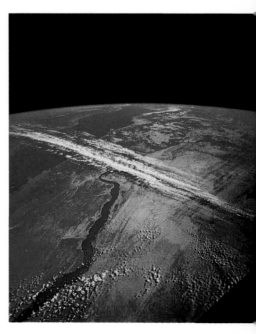

These disturbances can cause air masses in the lower atmosphere to diverge, or spread out. This produces areas of low pressure. And those low-pressure areas may serve as the centers of local storms.

SECTION REVIEW

1. How do local and global winds differ?
2. Describe the Coriolis effect.
3. Name three global winds.

16-5   Moisture in the Air

Heat and wind are shapers and movers of our weather. But atmospheric moisture is its main ingredient. **Moisture in the air is called humidity.** The sun's radiant energy turns liquid water into a gas, or water vapor. This process is called **evaporation.** The atmosphere gains moisture, or **humidity** (hyoo-MIHD-uh-tee), through evaporation.

Of course, the amount of moisture in the air can vary greatly from place to place and from time to time. The amount of moisture in the air is often stated in terms of **relative humidity,** or the percentage of moisture the air holds relative to the amount it can hold at a particular temperature. Warm air can hold more moisture than cold air. If a space holding a kilogram of air could hold 12 grams of water vapor but actually holds 9 grams, the relative humidity is 9/12, or 75 percent. If it held 12 grams, the air would be holding all the moisture it could. The relative humidity would be 100 percent.

Warm, moist air usually rises in the atmosphere. As it rises, it cools. When the air reaches a certain temperature, called the **dew point,** moisture in the air comes together into droplets. This process is called **condensation.** Through condensation, clouds form. The condensed water from these clouds often falls to the earth as rain, sleet, snow, or hail. Water that falls from the atmosphere to the earth is called **precipitation** (prih-sihp-uh-TAY-shuhn).

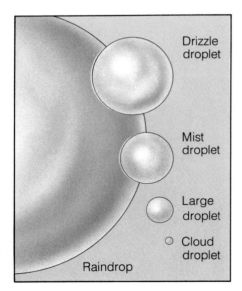

Figure 16-11 *Notice the relative sizes of water droplets in a cloud. When water droplets get large enough, they fall to the earth.*

Drizzle droplet

Mist droplet

Large droplet

Cloud droplet

Raindrop

Clouds

Clouds are classified according to shape and altitude in the atmosphere. There are three main types: **cumulus clouds, stratus clouds,** and **cirrus clouds.**

Cumulus (KYOOM-yuh-luhs) clouds look like piles of cotton balls in the sky. These clouds are very puffy and have flat bottoms. They form at altitudes of 2.4 to 13.5 kilometers.

Cumulus clouds usually indicate fair weather. But sometimes they develop into the larger clouds that produce thunderstorms. These large clouds are called cumulonimbus clouds.

Gray, smooth clouds that cover the sky and block out the sun are called stratus (STRAT-uhs) clouds.

Activity

Fog in a Bottle

Fog is actually stratus clouds that form close to the ground. Here is a way to make your own fog.

1. Fill a narrow-necked bottle with hot water. **CAUTION:** *Do not use water hot enough to cause burns.*

2. Pour out almost all the water, leaving only about 3 centimeters at the bottom.

3. Place an ice cube on the mouth of the bottle.

4. Set up another experiment using cold water instead of hot water in the same type of bottle.

Why does fog form in the bottle with hot water but not in the bottle with cold water? Why is it helpful to set up an experiment with cold water?

Figure 16-12 *Clouds are classified according to their shape and altitude. Cumulus and stratus clouds that develop at altitudes between 2 km and 7 km have the prefix alto- in their names. What prefix is used for these clouds if they are at an altitude above 7 km?*

Figure 16-13 *There are three main types of clouds: fluffy cumulus (top), layered stratus (center), and wispy cirrus (bottom).*

These clouds form at an altitude of about 2.5 kilometers. Light rain and drizzle are usually associated with stratus clouds. Nimbostratus clouds bring rain or snow.

Stratus clouds that form close to the ground are called fog. Ground fog is formed when air above the ground cools rapidly at night. Warmer temperatures during the day cause the fog to disappear.

Very feathery or fibrous clouds are called cirrus (SIR-uhs) clouds. Cirrus clouds form at very high altitudes. They are usually found at altitudes between 6 and 12 kilometers. Cirrus clouds are made of ice crystals. Sometimes these clouds are called mare's tails. You can see cirrus clouds when the weather is fair, but they often indicate rain or snow within several hours.

Storms

A storm is a violent disturbance in the atmosphere. It is marked by sudden changes in air pressure and rapid air movements. A storm may cover a huge area or a very small area.

THUNDERSTORMS Thunderstorms develop from cumulonimbus clouds. These clouds form when there is a rapid upward rush of warm air from very hot areas on the ground and a rapid downward movement of cool air around the warm air. The result is an explosive buildup of dense storm clouds that may reach altitudes of 10 to 15 kilometers.

The top of a cumulonimbus cloud may reach the bottom of the stratosphere. Even on a very warm day, the air may be a chilly $-60°$ C. Water droplets in the upper portions of the cloud freeze into snow and ice crystals. At a certain point, these crystals start falling through the cloud. As they do, they chill the water droplets in the cloud and cause them to form larger drops and fall. The usual result is a downpour of rain accompanied by thunder and lightning.

Lightning is caused by the buildup of a negative electric charge at the bottom of the thundercloud. That means that the molecules there have extra electrons compared to the ground. As the charge builds up, a point is reached at which the air can no longer block the passage of electricity. Then there is an enormous flash of electric energy between the cloud and the ground or from cloud to cloud—lightning!

As the electric energy passes through a section of air, it heats the section, causing a violent outward movement of air. The movement is so sharp and so sudden that it produces a booming sound—thunder!

Sometimes ice crystals falling through a thunderstorm are caught and tossed back up by an updraft of warm air. In the process, water droplets freeze onto the crystals, making them bigger. The crystals may bounce up and down several times in a thundercloud. Eventually they get so big and heavy that they fall to the ground. This form of precipitation is called hail. The crystals are called hailstones.

TORNADOES A more deadly product of a thunderstorm is a tornado. Few thunderstorms actually give rise to tornadoes. But tornadoes are so fierce that they are considered to be major weather hazards.

Under special conditions, a downward funnel of air may spin out of the base of a thundercloud. The area at the bottom of this funnel of swirling air is extremely low in air pressure. When this low-pressure point touches the ground, it acts like a giant vacuum cleaner. Dust, soil, trees, animals, people, cars, and even buildings may be drawn up into it and whirled around. Fortunately, tornadoes usually last no more than a few minutes. But during those few mintues, a tornado can do enormous damage.

Figure 16-14 *These hailstones became large and heavy enough to fall to the ground.*

Figure 16-15 *A tornado lasts only a few minutes, but it is the most violent storm on the earth (left). A tornado over a lake or an ocean is called a waterspout (right).*

HURRICANES In terms of the total energy involved, hurricanes are the greatest storms on the earth. They usually form in late summer or early fall over the warm tropical waters of the Atlantic just north of the equator. At that time, ocean surface temperatures are at their highest. The warm air heats the air above it and creates updrafts of air currents.

In the center of such an updraft, the air pressure is low. In the Northern Hemisphere, this creates a swirling counterclockwise movement of air around the low-pressure center, called a tropical cyclone.

As time passes, more and more warm air may be drawn up through the center of the system. As this air rises, it spreads out, cools, and swirls down and back into the cyclone. The air moves faster and faster as rising warm air adds energy to the system. When the wind speed reaches about 117 kilometers per hour, the storm is considered a hurricane.

A hurricane may cover an area of several hundred square kilometers. Its center is usually calm and cloudless. This calm center is the eye of the storm. Around the eye, fierce winds blow. Hurricane winds are not as strong as tornado winds. But

Figure 16-16 *This photo taken from space shows a hurricane over the Atlantic Ocean (left). The storm has a large circular counterclockwise movement of air surrounding a low pressure center (right).* What is the name of the calm center of a hurricane?

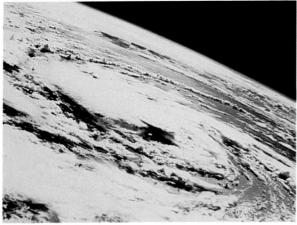

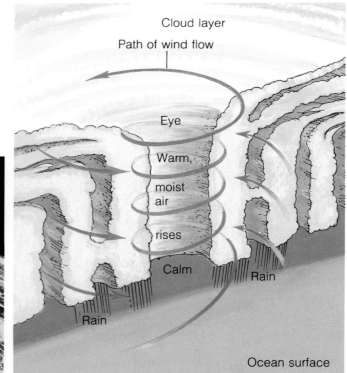

Cloud layer

Path of wind flow

Eye

Warm,

moist

air

rises

Calm

Rain

Rain

Ocean surface

because a hurricane is so large, it packs enormous energy and can do damage over a wide area.

SECTION REVIEW

1. What is humidity? Relative humidity?
2. List four forms of precipitation.
3. How are clouds classified? What are the three main types of clouds?
4. Describe three major types of storms.

16-6 Weather Patterns

Changes in the weather are caused by movements of air called **air masses.** Air masses have the same temperature and humidity throughout. They usually cover thousands of square kilometers. They are classified according to where they form. Some form over continents. Others form over oceans. The amount of moisture in an air mass depends on where the air mass develops. **There are four major types of air masses that affect the weather in the United States: maritime tropical, maritime polar, continental tropical, and continental polar.**

The maritime tropical air mass forms over the ocean near the equator. It holds warm, moist air. In the summer, the maritime tropical air mass brings very hot, humid weather. But if the warm, moist air comes in contact with a cold air mass in the winter, rain or snow will fall.

The maritime polar air mass forms over the Pacific Ocean in both the winter and the summer. It forms over the cold North Atlantic waters in the summer. During the summer, the maritime polar air mass brings cooler temperatures to the eastern states and fog to California and other western states. Heavy snow and very cold temperatures are produced by the maritime polar air mass in the winter.

During the summer, a continental tropical air mass forms over land in Mexico. It brings dry, hot air to the southwestern states. The continental polar air mass forms over land in northern Canada. In the winter, this cold, dry air mass causes very cold temperatures in the United States.

Figure 16-17 *In September 1985, Hurricane Elena struck the southeastern United States. Because of its enormous energy, the hurricane caused tremendous damage.*

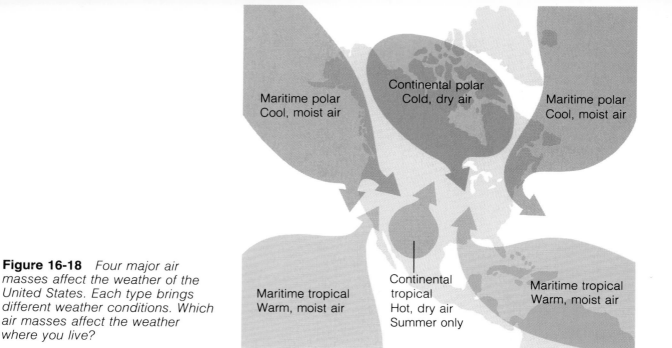

Figure 16-18 *Four major air masses affect the weather of the United States. Each type brings different weather conditions. Which air masses affect the weather where you live?*

Figure 16-19 *A cold front forms when a mass of cold air meets and replaces a mass of warm air, as shown in the illustration (right). Notice the weather symbols showing the edge of the cold front on the satellite weather photograph (left).*

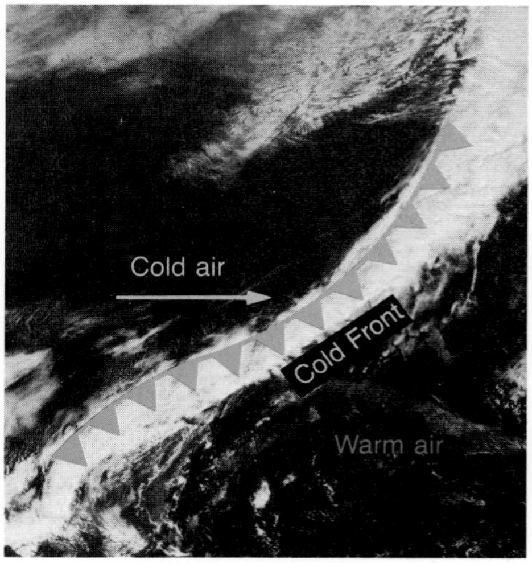

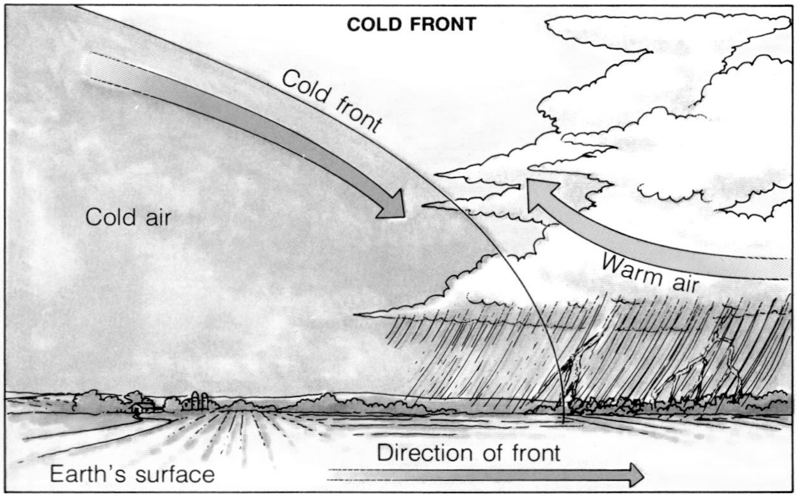

Fronts

When two air masses meet, a **front** forms. A front is the boundary between air masses that have different temperatures and humidity. The weather at a front is usually unsettled and stormy. Four different types of fronts are possible.

A **cold front** forms when a mass of cold air meets and replaces a mass of warm air. See Figure 16-19. The cold air mass forces its way underneath the warm air mass and pushes it upward. Violent storms are associated with a cold front. Fair, cool weather usually follows.

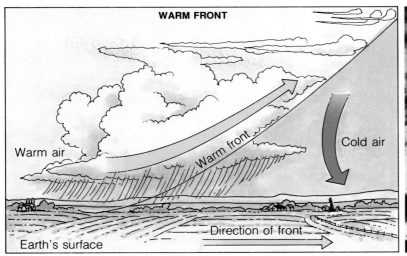

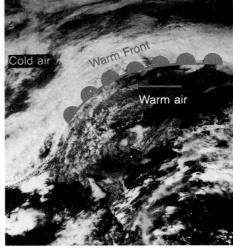

Figure 16-20 *A warm front forms when a mass of warm air overtakes a cold air mass and moves over it, as shown in the illustration (left). Notice the weather symbols showing the edge of the warm front on the satellite weather photograph (right).*

A **warm front** forms when a mass of warm air overtakes a cold air mass and moves over it. See Figure 16-20. Rain and showers usually accompany a warm front. Hot, humid weather usually follows.

A cold front travels faster than a warm front. When a cold front overtakes a warm front, an **occluded front** occurs. See Figure 16-21. The warm air is pushed upward, and the cold air meets cool air. As a result, the occluded front produces less extreme weather than a cold or a warm front. An occluded front may also occur when cool air overtakes a cold front and warm air is pushed upward.

When a warm air mass meets a cold air mass and no movement occurs, a **stationary front** forms. Rain may fall in an area for many days when a stationary front is in place.

Figure 16-21 *An occluded front occurs when a cold front overtakes a warm front, as shown in the illustration (left). Notice the weather symbols showing the occluded front on the satellite weather photograph (right).*

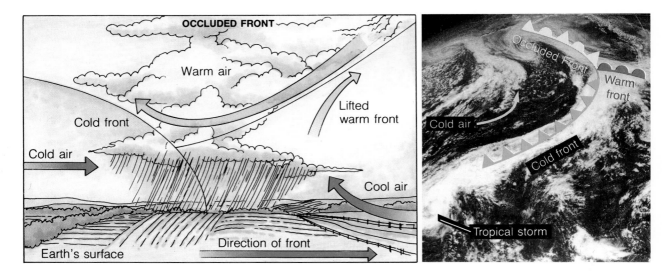

Mapping the Weather

Accurate weather forecasting is made possible by studying such data as temperature, air pressure, precipitation, and winds at several places. Often these data are used to prepare a weather map. The information on weather maps is recorded in the form of numbers, symbols, and lines. See Figure 16-22.

Figure 16-22 *This illustration shows a typical weather map with data from observation stations all over the country. Use the symbol key below the map to determine the weather conditions in your home state on this particular day.*

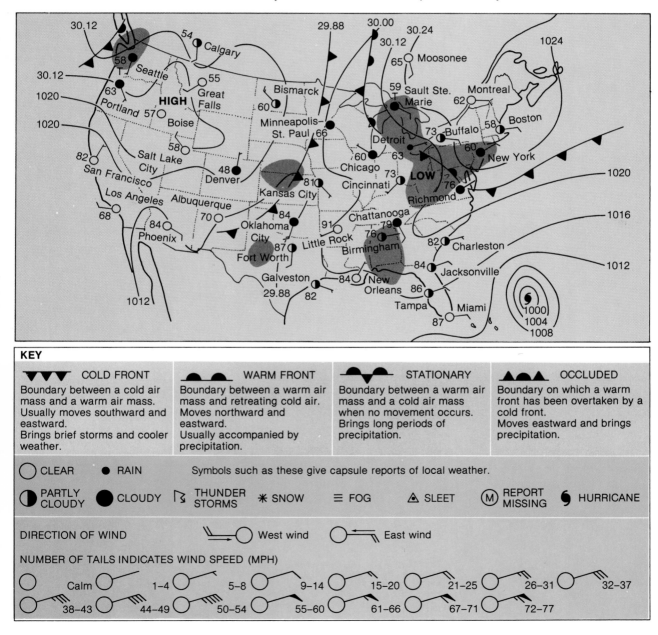

KEY

▼▼▼ COLD FRONT	●▬●▬ WARM FRONT	▬●▬▼ STATIONARY	▲●▲ OCCLUDED
Boundary between a cold air mass and a warm air mass. Usually moves southward and eastward. Brings brief storms and cooler weather.	Boundary between a warm air mass and retreating cold air. Moves northward and eastward. Usually accompanied by precipitation.	Boundary between a warm air mass and a cold air mass when no movement occurs. Brings long periods of precipitation.	Boundary on which a warm front has been overtaken by a cold front. Moves eastward and brings precipitation.

○ CLEAR   ● RAIN   Symbols such as these give capsule reports of local weather.

◐ PARTLY CLOUDY   ● CLOUDY   ↳ THUNDER STORMS   ✳ SNOW   ≡ FOG   △ SLEET   Ⓜ REPORT MISSING   ๑ HURRICANE

DIRECTION OF WIND   ⤸○ West wind   ○⟵ East wind

NUMBER OF TAILS INDICATES WIND SPEED (MPH)

○ Calm   ○— 1–4   ○— 5–8   ○— 9–14   ○— 15–20   ○— 21–25   ○— 26–31   ○— 32–37

○— 38–43   ○— 44–49   ○— 50–54   ○— 55–60   ○— 61–66   ○— 67–71   ○— 72–77

The circles on the weather map represent observation stations in various locations. Figure 16-23 shows data from a particular observation station. Think of the station circle as the point of an arrow. Attached to the station circle is a line, the shaft of an arrow. The wind direction is represented as moving along the arrow's shaft toward the center of the station circle. The wind direction is the direction from which the wind is blowing. In this station circle, the wind is blowing from southwest to northeast. Often there are small lines at the end of the shaft. These lines are symbols for wind speed.

Now look again at the weather map in Figure 16-22. Notice the curved lines running through the map. These lines are called **isobars** (IGH-suh-barz). Isobars are lines joining places on a weather map that have the same atmospheric pressure. The numbers at the ends of these lines are the atmospheric pressure recorded at each observation station along the lines. Atmospheric pressure can be given in inches or millibars of mercury. A millibar equals about 0.03 inch of mercury. In this map, isobars are marked at one end with barometric pressure in inches and at the other end with barometric pressure in millibars. Inches of mercury are usually given to the hundredths place and range from 28.00 to 31.00.

On some weather maps, you may see curved lines called **isotherms** (IGH-suh-thermz). Isotherms are lines connecting locations that have the same temperature. The number on the end of an isotherm indicates the temperature at all points along the isotherm line.

On this map, average daily temperature is given in degrees Fahrenheit next to the station circle. Shaded areas mark precipitation such as rain. Other symbols for sky conditions are explained in the key. These symbols may differ from those used on the simplified weather maps often shown in newspapers.

SECTION REVIEW

1. Name four types of air masses.
2. Describe the four kinds of fronts.
3. What kinds of information can you obtain when you read a weather map?

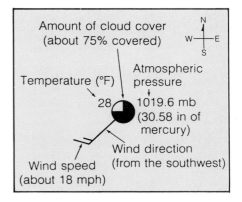

Figure 16-23 *These data indicate the weather readings taken at a weather observation station. Data from thousands of such stations are used by meteorologists to produce detailed weather maps.*

Activity

Predicting and Observing the Weather

How accurate are weather predictions?

1. Each day cut out the weather map from your local newspaper. What type of weather is predicted for your area?

2. Each day write down a brief description of your actual weather conditions.

3. Obtain a copy of the *Farmer's Almanac* and read the weather predictions for those days.

4. How do the long-range *Almanac* predictions compare with the daily weather map predictions and your description of the actual weather?

LABORATORY ACTIVITY

Using a Sling Psychrometer to Determine Relative Humidity

Purpose

In this activity, you will construct a sling psychrometer in order to determine relative humidity.

Materials (per group)

2 metal or plastic-backed thermometers
Wooden dowel (for handle)
Hammer   Two-sided foam tape
2 washers   1 large-headed nail
Thread   Small piece of gauze

Procedure

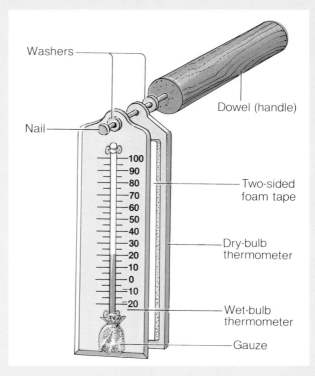

1. Attach two thermometers back to back with two-sided foam tape.
2. Wrap gauze around the bulb of one thermometer. Using thread, tie the gauze to the bulb. This thermometer will now be referred to as the wet-bulb thermometer.
3. Slide the thermometers and washers onto the nail. As shown in the diagram, place a washer in front of each thermometer.
4. Gently hammer the nail into the dowel. See the diagram. **CAUTION:** *Be extremely careful when hammering the nail into the dowel. Do not hit the thermometers with the hammer.*
5. Using a medicine dropper, add a few drops of water to the gauze of the wet-bulb thermometer.
6. Holding the dowel in your hand, slowly whirl the psychrometer. This whirling motion will speed the evaporating process.
7. Periodically check the temperature recording of the wet-bulb thermometer until the temperature has stopped decreasing.
8. When the wet-bulb temperature has stopped decreasing, read both the wet-bulb and the dry-bulb temperatures. Determine the difference between the two temperatures. This value is called the wet-bulb depression.

9. Using the dry-bulb temperature and the difference between the dry-bulb and wet-bulb temperatures, refer to the table provided by your teacher to determine the relative humidity. Note: Add a percent sign to your answer.

EXAMPLE:

Dry-bulb temperature	= 20° C
Wet-bulb temperature	= 12° C
Difference	= 8° C
Relative Humidity	= 37%

Observations and Conclusions

1. Which of the two thermometers measures the temperature of the air?
2. What would the relative humidity be if the two thermometers measured the wet-bulb and the dry-bulb temperatures to be the same? Explain your answer.

CHAPTER REVIEW

SUMMARY

16-1 Forces That Shape Weather

- Weather is caused by the interaction of such factors as heat energy, air pressure, winds, and moisture.

16-2 Heating the Earth

- Almost all of the earth's energy comes from the sun's radiant energy.

- The earth's surface is heated unevenly. The most heating occurs when the sun's rays hit the surface at or near a right angle.

- Heat is spread throughout the atmosphere by conduction, convection, and radiation.

16-3 Atmospheric Pressure

- Scientists use a barometer to measure air pressure.

- High air pressure usually means fair weather. Low air pressure usually means bad weather.

16-4 Winds

- Winds are caused by differences in air pressure due to unequal heating of the air.

- Some examples of local winds are land breezes, sea breezes, and monsoons.

- The Coriolis effect is the curving of all global winds in the Northern Hemisphere to the right and in the Southern Hemisphere to the left as a result of the earth's rotation.

- Global winds include the northeast trade winds, the prevailing westerlies, the polar easterlies, and jet streams.

16-5 Moisture in the Air

- Moisture in the air is called humidity.

- Relative humidity is the percentage of moisture the air holds relative to the amount it can hold at a particular temperature.

- Moisture in the air goes through three processes: evaporation, condensation, and precipitation.

- Clouds are classified according to shape and altitude as cumulus, stratus, or cirrus clouds.

16-6 Weather Patterns

- Large bodies of air with the same temperature and humidity throughout are air masses.

- The boundary between two different air masses is called a front. Cold fronts, warm fronts, occluded fronts, and stationary fronts are the four types.

- Weather maps summarize and organize weather information in the form of numbers, symbols, and lines.

VOCABULARY

Define each term in a complete sentence.

air mass	Coriolis effect	isobar	radiation
air pressure	cumulus cloud	isotherm	relative humidity
barometer	dew point	land breeze	sea breeze
cirrus cloud	evaporation	monsoon	stationary front
cold front	front	occluded front	stratus cloud
condensation	humidity	precipitation	warm front
conduction	infrared radiation	radiant energy	wind
convection			

CONTENT REVIEW: MULTIPLE CHOICE

Choose the letter of the answer that best completes each sentence.

1. An imaginary line that separates the earth into two halves is the
   a. latitude. b. convection. c. equator. d. jet stream.
2. Unequal heating of the air causes
   a. radiation currents. b. convection currents.
   c. precipitation. d. conduction coils.
3. The greatest heating occurs when the sun's rays strike the earth at or near an angle of
   a. 90°. b. 60°. c. 30°. d. 120°.
4. Air pressure is measured with an instrument called a(n)
   a. thermometer. b. barometer. c. anemometer. d. weather vane.
5. A land breeze usually occurs
   a. at night. b. during the day.
   c. in summer only. d. in the morning.
6. Because of the Coriolis effect, air moving south in the Northern Hemisphere will curve to the
   a. northwest. b. southwest. c. southeast. d. northeast.
7. The amount of water vapor in the air is called
   a. humidity. b. dew point. c. precipitation. d. fog.
8. Feathery high-altitude clouds that often indicate rain or snow are called
   a. cirrus clouds. b. cumulus clouds.
   c. stratus clouds. d. nimbostratus clouds.
9. Large bodies of air with the same temperature and humidity throughout are
   a. air masses. b. isobars. c. isotherms. d. air fronts.
10. Curved lines on a weather map connecting locations that have the same barometric pressure are called
    a. isotherms. b. anticyclones. c. isobars. d. cyclones.

CONTENT REVIEW: COMPLETION

Fill in the word or words that best complete each sentence.

1. _____ energy is energy from the sun.
2. Warmer air is usually _____ dense than cooler air.
3. _____ pressure usually indicates fair weather.
4. The center of a hurricane, called the _____, is usually calm and cloudless.
5. The curving of a wind's flow due to the rotation of the earth is known as the _____.
6. The temperature at which air condenses is called the _____.
7. _____ clouds are fairly flat and layered.
8. A(n) _____ breeze flows from the land to the sea.
9. The boundary between air masses with different temperature and humidity is called a(n) _____.
10. When a cold front overtakes a warm front a(n) _____ front occurs.

CONTENT REVIEW: TRUE OR FALSE

Determine whether each statement is true or false. If it is true, write "true." If it is false, change the underlined word or words to make the statement true.

1. The earth's surface is heated evenly.
2. Convection is the direct transfer of heat energy from one substance to another.
3. A sea breeze usually forms during the night.
4. Winds in the Southern Hemisphere curve to the right as they move.
5. The doldrums are calm surface winds at the equator.
6. Cool air is more dense than warm air.
7. The northeast trade winds move from the northeast to the southwest.
8. Water that falls from the atmosphere to the earth is called condensation.
9. Thunderstorms develop from cumulus clouds.
10. A continental tropical air mass forms over the ocean near the equator.

CONCEPT REVIEW: SKILL BUILDING

Use the skills you have developed in the chapter to complete each activity.

1. **Making calculations** Suppose 1 kg of air can hold 15 g of water vapor but actually holds 10 g. What will be the relative humidity?
2. **Relating facts** A weather report often includes a "comfort index." The comfort index includes the effects of temperature and humidity on people. Explain how temperature and humidity affect comfort.
3. **Making predictions** Explain how both the temperature and the amount of water vapor in the air could change and yet the relative humidity could stay the same.
4. **Relating concepts** Suppose you are the captain of a sailing ship. You must go from the east coast of the United States to England and then back again. Describe the route you would take in order to make the best use of the winds. You may want to consult the map on page 362.
5. **Interpreting maps** Use the weather map in Figure 16-22, page 372, to answer the following questions:
   a. Describe the weather conditions in Fort Worth.
   b. What is the wind speed in Denver? In Bismarck? In Boise?
   c. Find the isobar passing through New York. What is the air pressure in New York? What other locations have the same air pressure?
   d. Predict the probable weather conditions in Kansas City the day after this map was issued.

CONCEPT REVIEW: ESSAY

Discuss each of the following in a brief paragraph.

1. Compare conduction, convection, and radiation.
2. How can a barometer be helpful in predicting weather?
3. Relate evaporation, condensation, and precipitation in terms of moisture in the air.
4. Explain the specific movements of the three major global winds in terms of unequal heating and the Coriolis effect.
5. Compare local and global winds.
6. Describe the four major air masses.
7. Describe the four possible types of fronts.

17 Climate

CHAPTER SECTIONS

17-1 The Nature of Climate

**17-2 Climate Regions
of the United States**

17-3 Changes in Climate

CHAPTER OBJECTIVES

*After completing this chapter, you
will be able to:*

17-1 Identify the factors that determine climate.

17-1 Describe the factors that
affect temperature and
precipitation.

17-1 Classify the earth's climate
zones.

17-2 Compare the major climate
regions of the United States.

17-3 Describe how a change in
ocean currents can cause
climate changes.

17-3 Describe ice ages and interglacials and identify their
possible causes.

You are about to embark on an incredible journey—without actually going anywhere. To begin,
imagine you live in the Midwest. That will be easy if
you already do. Now pretend that you happen upon
a time machine. Excited, you step inside and turn a
few dials. Suddenly lights flash and flutter. After a
few seconds, everything returns to normal. You have
arrived! Opening the hatch of the time machine, you
step into the world of 6000 years ago.

The air is warm. But it is also much more humid
than you are used to. Tall grasses are everywhere.
Many different types of flowers add splashes of brilliant colors to the grasslands.

The world you have reached looks and feels more
like a tropical grassland than your midwestern home.
Obviously, the climate of 6000 years ago was very different from the climate of today. What might it be
like at a much earlier time?

Back in the time machine, you set the dial to
16,000 years ago. When you step out of the machine
again, a blast of cold air sets you shivering. Stretching
away to the north is a sheet of endless ice. To the
south, you see a bleak landscape of mossy grassland.
In the distance, a herd of elephantlike woolly mammoths graze on low bushes.

As you head back to the warmth of the time machine you think about how drastically the climate has
changed over the last 20,000 years. What can the future hold in store? Back in the time machine, you set
the dials to 30,000 years in the future and wonder
what type of climate awaits you. . . .

Woolly mammoths in a cold climate

17-1 The Nature of Climate

If you kept a record of the weather for an extended period of time, you would discover some general conditions of temperature and precipitation for your area. Such general conditions are described as the average weather for a region. Scientists call the general conditions of temperature and precipitation for an area **climate.** Every place in the world has its own special climate. For example, the climate of the southwestern United States tends to be warm and dry all year round. The climate of Florida is warm but much wetter.

The climate in any region of the world is determined by two basic factors: temperature and precipitation. Different combinations of temperature and precipitation are used to classify the earth's major climates. Temperature and precipitation are in turn influenced by several factors.

Factors That Affect Temperature

Latitude, altitude, and the nearness of ocean currents are three factors that affect temperatures at a particular location. The extent to which these factors affect climate varies from place to place.

LATITUDE Latitude is a measure of distance north and south of the equator. Areas close to the equator, or 0° latitude, receive direct rays of the sun. Direct rays provide more radiant energy. So these areas

Figure 17-1 *Climate is the characteristics of the weather in an area over a long period of time. In certain climates, winter brings cold temperatures and lots of precipitation* (left). *Summer brings warm, dry conditions that evoke thoughts of the beach* (right).

near the equator have a warm climate. Farther from the equator, the sun's rays are not as direct. Less radiant energy is received by areas farther from the equator. So climates are cooler. In general, the lowest average temperatures occur near the polar regions, where the sun's rays are least direct.

ALTITUDE Altitude is distance above sea level. As altitude increases, the air becomes less dense. This means that there are fewer particles of air and they are spread farther apart. Less dense air cannot hold as much heat. So as altitude increases, the temperature decreases.

OCEAN CURRENTS An ocean current is a stream of water in the ocean that follows a definite path. Some ocean currents are warm water currents. Other ocean currents are cold water currents. See Figure 12-7 on page 287. The surface temperature of water affects the temperature of the air above it. Warm water warms the air. Cold water cools the air. So land areas near warm water currents have warmer temperatures. And land areas near cold water currents have cooler temperatures.

Ocean currents travelling away from the equator, such as the Gulf Stream, are warm water currents. Ocean currents travelling toward the equator, such as the California Current, are cold water currents.

Factors That Affect Precipitation

Two factors that affect precipitation at a particular location are prevailing winds and mountain ranges. As with temperature factors, the effects of precipitation factors vary from place to place.

PREVAILING WINDS A **prevailing wind** is a wind that blows more often from one direction than from any other direction. Prevailing winds have a great influence on the climate of regions in their paths. Different prevailing winds carry different amounts of moisture. The amount of moisture carried by a prevailing wind affects the amount of precipitation a region receives.

Figure 17-2 *Although these two locations have the same latitude, their difference in altitude produces a dramatic difference in climate. In the cool, dry Andes Mountains (top), snow is visible and vegetation is sparse. Thick vegetation is plentiful in the hot, humid Amazon jungle (bottom). What factor other than latitude and altitude affects climate?*

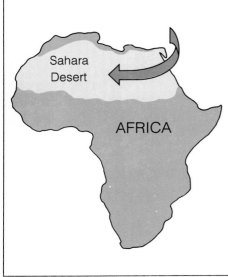

Figure 17-3 *Although the Sahara Desert in Africa is bordered on the west by the Atlantic Ocean, it is one of the driest places on the earth (top). The prevailing winds, which originate far inland, carry very little moisture as they sweep south and then west across the region (bottom).*

Warm air is able to hold more moisture than cold air. As warm air rises, it cools and cannot hold as much moisture. The moisture it can no longer hold falls to the earth as some form of precipitation. Winds formed by rising warm air tend to bring precipitation. Winds formed by sinking cold air become warmer and can then hold more moisture. So winds formed by sinking cold air tend to bring very little precipitation.

The direction from which a prevailing wind blows also affects the amount of moisture it carries. Some prevailing winds blow from land to water. Others blow from water to land. The prevailing winds that blow from water carry more moisture than those from land. So regions in the paths of wind originating over water receive more precipitation.

The combined effect of a prevailing wind's moisture content and direction makes it possible for a desert to exist next to a large body of water. The Sahara Desert in northern Africa is one of the driest places on the earth. Yet it is bordered on the west by the Atlantic Ocean. However, the prevailing winds flowing over this region are from a source of dry sinking air. The prevailing winds are also dry because they originate far inland. So, little precipitation ever reaches the Sahara Desert, even though there is a large source of water nearby.

MOUNTAIN RANGES   The amount of precipitation at a particular location is also affected by mountain ranges. Mountain ranges act as a barrier to prevailing winds. Mountains cause air to rise. See Figure 17-4. As air rises, it cools, and most of the moisture it contains condenses, or becomes a liquid. As a result, there is much precipitation on the **windward side** of the mountain, which is the side facing the wind. The region on the windward side of the mountain has a wet climate.

Conditions are very different on the **leeward side** of the mountain, which is the side facing away from the wind. By the time the prevailing winds reach the top of the mountains, they have lost most of their moisture in the form of precipitation. So relatively dry air moves down the leeward side. As a result, there is very little precipitation on the leeward side of the mountain. The region has a dry climate.

Precipitation

Dry air moving toward desert

Moist air blown from Pacific Ocean

Windward side

Leeward side

Figure 17-4 *There is a rainy climate on the western slopes of the Rocky Mountains because moist air from the Pacific rises, cools, and forms rain clouds. Dry air moving down the eastern slopes results in a desert climate. Which slopes represent the windward side? The leeward side?*

Climate Zones

The earth's climates can be divided into general zones according to average temperatures. These climate zones can be broken down into subzones. And even the subzones have further subdivisions. In fact, scientists often talk of very localized climates called **microclimates.** A microclimate can be as small as your own backyard!

The three major climate zones on the earth are the polar, tropical, and temperate zones. Temperatures in these three zones are determined by the location of the zone and the kind of air masses commonly found there. See Figure 17-5 on page 384.

POLAR ZONES Climates in the **polar zones** are also known as high-latitude or arctic climates. Located above a latitude of 60° north and south, the polar zones include the always frozen icecaps of Greenland in the north and Antarctica in the south. Also included in the polar zones are places where the snow does melt in the cool summer, such as the northern coasts of Canada and Alaska and the southern tip of South America.

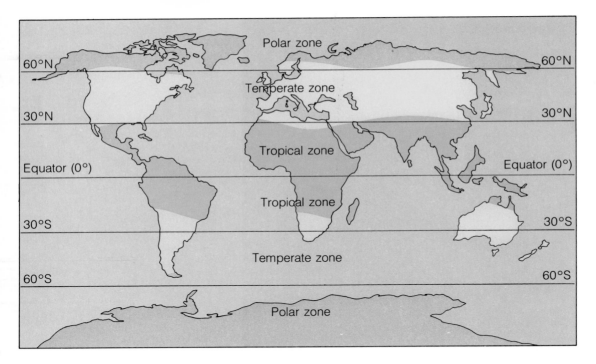

Figure 17-5 *The three major types of climate zones on the earth are shown in this diagram.*

Activity

Radiant Energy and Climate

1. Tape a piece of paper to a wall at waist level.

2. Using one hand, hold a flashlight 25 cm away from the paper.

3. Shine the light at a 5° angle onto the paper. Using your free hand, trace the outline of the circle of light.

4. Repeat steps 2 and 3 using angles of 45° and 90°.

At what angle is the radiant energy most concentrated? Least concentrated? What climate zone is represented by each of the three circles of light?

TEMPERATE ZONES Would it surprise you to learn that the snowy slopes of Utah and the hot desert of Arizona are in the same climate zone? Well, they are both part of the same **temperate zone.** The temperate zones, also called the middle-latitude zones, range from a latitude of 30° to 60° north and south. Temperate zones, quite obviously, cover a huge portion of the globe. So it should no longer surprise you that a temperate zone can range from the cool rain forests of Washington State to the hot rain forests of southeastern China—with a lot of different kinds of climate in between.

TROPICAL ZONES Warm, humid weather is the rule in most areas found in the **tropical zones.** Also called low-latitude zones, the tropical zones stretch up from the equator to a latitude of 30°N and down from the equator to a latitude of 30°S.

SECTION REVIEW

1. What two factors determine climate? What conditions influence these factors?

2. Explain how cold water currents and warm water currents affect the climate of a location.

3. Describe the three major climate zones.

17-2 Climate Regions of the United States

The three climate zones—polar, tropical, and temperate—are all represented in various sections of the United States. Alaska is located in the polar zone. Hawaii and southern Florida are located in the tropical zone. Most of the United States, however, is located in the temperate zone.

Within the temperate zone, there are many different climates. To describe each climate more precisely, scientists have divided the mainland United States into six major climate regions. **The division of the mainland United States into six major climate regions is based on the amount of precipitation and the temperature in each region.** See Figure 17-7. But it is important to remember that even within a particular climate region, variations in precipitation and temperature exist.

Mediterranean Climate Region

The narrow coastal area of California has a **Mediterranean climate.** Cyclones and maritime polar air masses bring heavy precipitation in winter. In

MEDITERRANEAN CLIMATE

	Summer	Winter
Average Temperature: (°C)		
San Francisco	17.3	10.0
Sacramento	24.0	9.0
Average Precipitation: (cm/month)		
San Francisco	0.2	9.8
Sacramento	0.2	8.0

Figure 17-6 *Temperature and precipitation vary in the Mediterranean climate region.*

Figure 17-7 *Climate regions of the United States are shown on this map. The climates do not change suddenly but actually blend into one another.*

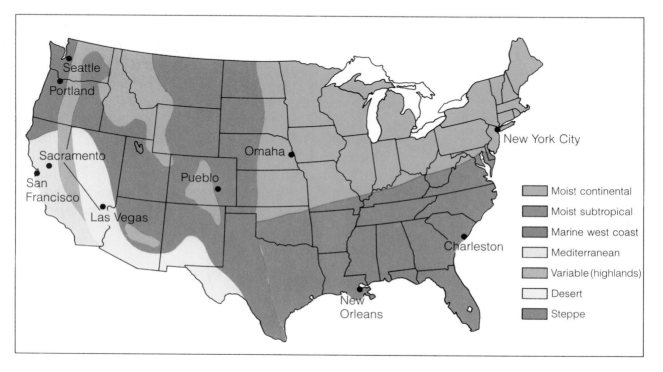

Figure 17-8 *Shrubs and stunted trees are found in the Mediterranean climate (left). Forests of red cedar, spruce, and firs are characteristic of the marine west coast climate (right).*

Figure 17-9 *What variations exist between Portland, Oregon, and Seattle, Washington?*

MARINE WEST COAST CLIMATE	Summer	Winter
Average Temperature: (°C)		
Seattle	17.0	5.3
Portland	18.5	5.0
Average Precipitation: (cm/month)		
Seattle	2.3	11.9
Portland	2.3	15.5

summer, there is almost no rain. Winters are cool. Summer temperatures are slightly higher than winter temperatures. See Figure 17-6 on page 385.

The Mediterranean climate of wet winters and dry summers results in two basic types of vegetation. One type is a dense growth of shrubs and stunted trees. The other type consists of scattered oak and olive trees with a ground cover of grasses.

Marine West Coast Climate Region

The northwest coast of the United States has a **marine west coast climate.** This is a rainy climate because moist air from the Pacific Ocean rises, cools, and releases precipitation on the western slopes of the Cascade Mountains. Cool winters and only slightly warmer summers are characteristic of the marine west coast climate. See Figure 17-9. The temperature range from one season to another is small due to the moderating effect of the nearby Pacific Ocean. Forests of needleleafed trees—such as red cedar, spruce, and firs—are the most common type of vegetation in this climate region.

Moist Continental Climate Region

The portion of the United States extending from the northern Midwest to the North Atlantic coast has

Figure 17-10 *The pine forest in this photograph of Acadia National Park, Maine, is characteristic of the moist continental climate.*

a **moist continental climate.** Continental polar air masses flowing south across the region produce very cold winters. In summer, tropical air masses flowing north across the region produce high temperatures throughout the region.

The region receives a moderate amount of precipitation throughout the year. During the summer, however, there is a marked increase in precipitation for all locations. During the winter, the decrease in precipitation varies from one place to another. See Figure 17-11.

In some sections of the moist continental climate region, forests of broadleafed and needleleafed trees are dominant. In other sections, much of the land is covered with tall grasses.

Moist Subtropical Climate Region

The southeastern United States has a **moist subtropical climate.** Summers are hot in this climate region. The average precipitation in summer is greater than it is in winter. See Figure 17-13 on page 388. The characteristic summer temperatures and precipitation of the moist subtropical region are very similar to those of the tropical zone. So in summer

MOIST CONTINENTAL CLIMATE

	Summer	Winter
Average Temperature: (°C)		
New York City	22.0	−0.3
Omaha	23.7	−4.3
Average Precipitation: (cm/month)		
New York City	10.0	8.4
Omaha	8.7	2.2

Figure 17-11 *The moist continental climates of New York City, New York, and Omaha, Nebraska, show variations in temperature and precipitation.*

Figure 17-12 *Forests of oak, chestnut, and pine trees, such as those of South Carolina, are characteristic of the moist subtropical climate.*

MOIST SUBTROPICAL CLIMATE

	Summer	Winter
Average Temperature: (°C)		
New Orleans	26.3	12.7
Charleston	27.2	11.3
Average Precipitation: (cm/month)		
New Orleans	14.0	10.1
Charleston	15.0	7.6

Figure 17-13 *A moist subtropical climate is found in New Orleans, Louisiana, and in Charleston, South Carolina. Are the variations in temperature and precipitation extreme?*

the climate of the moist subtropical region of the United States is very similar to the climate of the tropical regions of the world. Maritime tropical air masses moving inland from the tropics greatly influence the summer climate.

The similarity between the moist subtropical climate and the tropical climate ends in winter. Although winters are generally cool and mild, the mixing of polar air masses with maritime tropical air masses causes the temperature to occasionally drop below freezing. Severe frosts in the northern areas of the region sometimes occur.

The vegetation of the moist subtropical climate region is forests of broadleafed and needleleafed trees. Oak, chestnut, and pine trees are commonly found in this region.

Desert and Steppe Climate Regions

Located within the western interior of the United States are two regions that have very similar climates. These climates are the **desert climate** and the **steppe climate.** The desert climate region and the steppe climate region begin just east of the west coast mountain ranges and end in the central midwest.

Figure 17-14 *Despite the harsh conditions of the desert climate of the southwestern United States, short trees and flowering cacti grow well here.*

The desert and steppe climate regions receive the lowest amount of precipitation of any climate region of the United States. However, the steppe climate region receives slightly more precipitation than the desert climate region does. See Figure 17-15.

One reason precipitation is so low in these regions is that they are located far from the ocean sources of moist maritime air masses. In addition, high mountain ranges along the regions' western borders block most of the maritime air masses. Winter invasions of dry continental polar air masses further reduce the amount of precipitation.

Despite the harsh conditions of the desert climate, many plants—including cacti, yucca, and short trees—grow well here. The slightly higher precipitation of the steppe climate encourages the growth of short grasses and scattered forests of needleleafed evergreen trees.

DESERT AND STEPPE CLIMATES

	Summer	Winter
Average Temperature: (°C)		
Las Vegas	28.3	8.2
Pueblo	22.5	−0.3
Average Precipitation: (cm/month)		
Las Vegas	10.3	1.4
Pueblo	4.2	1.2

Figure 17-15 *The desert and steppe climates of Las Vegas, Nevada, and Pueblo, Colorado, receive the lowest amount of precipitation of any climate region of the United States. The steppe climate, however, receives slightly more precipitation than the desert climate.*

SECTION REVIEW

1. What are the major climate regions of the United States? What factors do scientists use to determine climate region?
2. Describe the climate in the area in which you live. What causes this climate?

17-3 Changes in Climate

Though weather changes from day to day, climate patterns remain relatively unchanged for many years—but not forever! **Climates do change slowly over time.** The climate of a region can change from that of a lush rain forest to that of a barren icecap within a relatively short span of the earth's history.

What causes climates to change? One factor that can cause a minor climate change is ocean currents. Ocean currents help transfer heat to the atmosphere, a process that generates global winds. The winds, in turn, help move the ocean currents. As you know, ocean and wind currents have a strong influence on climate. Any major change in an ocean current can cause a change in climate.

Career: *Paleoclimatologist*

HELP WANTED: PALEOCLIMATOLOGIST To study the weather and climate from prehistoric times to the present. Graduate and undergraduate degrees must combine paleontology and climatology. Experience in fossil study desirable.

Greenland is commonly known as a very cold place. Much of it is always frozen. Even its warmest region has temperatures rising no higher than 10° C—and that's in July! How is it, then, that fossils of palm and magnolia trees formed 80 million years ago have been discovered in Greenland? The answer must be that the climate of Greenland 80 million years ago was warm and moist. Such a climate could have supported palms and magnolias. And that is, in fact, the case.

Scientists study the fossil record and other natural sources to learn about ancient weather and climate. They are called **paleoclimatologists.** Their work has shown that the earth's history has included a series of ice ages, or cold periods, falling between warm periods.

Paleoclimatologists study various types of records to gain clues about the earth's past climates. One principle they use is that certain conditions, such as temperatures and rainfall, needed by a plant or animal today were also needed by that plant or animal in the past. So fossils from a certain time period can help to indicate what the climate was like at that time. Annual growth rings of living trees and fossil wood can also give clues to climates going back over 8000 years. These scientists know that rainfall, temperature, pressure, and weather patterns influence tree-ring widths in characteristic ways.

Anyone interested in a career in paleoclimatology should enjoy outdoor work, problem solving, and scientific study. For career information about paleoclimatology, write to the American Geological Institute, 5205 Leesburg Pike, Falls Church, VA 22041.

El Niño is a warm water current that flows from west to east across the Pacific Ocean near the equator and down the west coast of South America. It strikes with little warning every two to seven years. El Niño brings with it dramatic changes in world climates. In 1982 and 1983, the strongest El Niño in history caused severe droughts in some regions. Other regions were subjected to unusually heavy rains and flooding. Scientists still do not know just what causes El Niño. But important progress has been made in understanding the interactions of ocean and atmosphere, so accurate predictions of future El Niños may be possible within a few years.

Scientists can better predict future climate changes and their effects on life once they understand the causes of past climate changes. An example of such past climate changes are the **ice ages.** The ice ages are periods of time throughout history when much of the earth's surface was covered with enormous sheets of ice. There is evidence that during the last two million years, there have been at least four major ice ages, or **major glaciations.**

During a major glaciation, the average temperature on the earth was about 6C° below the average temperature today. Glaciations lasted about 100,000 years or more. The times between major glaciations are called **interglacials.** Interglacials are warm periods. During an interglacial, the average temperature was about 3C° higher than the average temperature is today. During the last glaciation, which ended only about 10,000 years ago, a great sheet of ice moved as far south as Iowa and Nebraska. So much water was locked in the ice that average sea level rose about 85 meters when the glacier melted.

The exact causes of ice ages are not known. But many scientists believe that major glaciations are associated with gradual changes in the direction of the earth's axis and in variations in the distance between the earth and the sun.

SECTION REVIEW

1. What is El Niño?
2. Compare the temperature on the earth during a major glaciation to the temperature during an interglacial.

Figure 17-16 *The arrival of El Niño is unpredictable. But it usually results in surprising weather for much of the world. Such weather includes heavy rains and high waves along the California coast* (above), *dust storms in Australia, floods in South America, and a severe water shortage in Africa.*

Activity

El Niño

Using reference materials from the library, find out about El Niño. Be sure to include information about the following topics.

1. What scientists believe may be the causes of El Niño.

2. Some of the worldwide weather changes that result from El Niño.

3. New methods of predicting El Niño.

4. The process of upwelling and its effect on ocean life in an area where it occurs.

5. The effect of El Niño on upwelling.

LABORATORY ACTIVITY

Graphing Climate Characteristics

Purpose
In this activity, you will determine how climate factors are used to classify and compare different places in the world.

Materials (per student)
Graph paper, 2 sheets
Colored pencils, 3 colors

Procedure
1. Using the data in the table for average monthly rainfall in Winnipeg, Canada, construct a graph of the amount of rainfall for each month. Use the vertical axis for amount of rainfall and the horizontal axis for the months.
2. Connect the points on your graph.
3. Using the same colored pencil, construct a separate graph of average temperature for each month in Winnipeg. Use the vertical axis for average temperature and the horizontal axis for the months.
4. Connect the points on your graph.
5. Repeat steps 1 through 4 using the data for Izmir, Turkey, and Ulan Bator, Mongolia. Place the three graphs of precipitation on one sheet of graph paper and the three graphs of temperature on the other sheet. Use a different-colored pencil for each city.

Observations and Conclusions
1. Which city has the highest winter temperatures? The lowest?
2. Which city has the greatest range of temperature from winter to summer? Which has the smallest range?
3. Which city has the driest summer? Which has the wettest?
4. Which city has the driest winter? Which has the wettest?
5. What United States climate region is most similar to the climate of Winnipeg? Izmir? Ulan Bator? Explain your answers.
6. Winnipeg is located in north-central North America. How does its climate differ from that of New York City? Why?
7. Izmir, Turkey, is located on the coast of the warm Mediterranean Sea. Compare its climate to that of San Francisco.

WINNIPEG, CANADA													
Month	J	F	M	A	M	J	J	A	S	O	N	D	Year
Temperature (°C)	−18	−16	−8	3	11	17	20	19	13	6	−5	−13	3
Precipitation (cm)	2.6	2.1	2.7	3	5	8.1	6.9	7	5.5	3.7	2.9	2.2	51.7

IZMIR, TURKEY													
Month	J	F	M	A	M	J	J	A	S	O	N	D	Year
Temperature (°C)	9	9	11	15	20	25	28	27	23	19	14	10	18
Precipitation (cm)	14.1	10	7.2	4.3	3.9	0.8	0.3	0.3	1.1	4.1	9.3	14.1	69.5

ULAN BATOR, MONGOLIA													
Month	J	F	M	A	M	J	J	A	S	O	N	D	Year
Temperature (°C)	−26	−21	−13	−1	6	14	16	14	9	−1	−13	−22	−3
Precipitation (cm)	0.1	0.2	0.3	0.5	1	2.8	7.6	5.1	2.3	0.7	0.4	0.3	21.3

SUMMARY

17-1 The Nature of Climate

- Climate is determined by the two basic factors of temperature and precipitation.

- Temperature is influenced by latitude, altitude, and nearness to ocean currents.

- In general, highest temperatures occur near the equator and lowest temperatures occur near the polar regions.

- Temperature usually decreases as altitude increases.

- Areas located near cold water currents usually have cooler temperatures. Areas located near warm water currents usually have warmer temperatures.

- Precipitation is influenced by prevailing winds and mountain ranges.

- The direction and moisture content of prevailing winds is an important factor in the amount of precipitation an area receives.

- There are usually wet conditions on the windward side of mountains and dry conditions on the leeward side of mountains.

- The three major climate zones on the earth are the polar, tropical, and temperate zones. Most of the United States is located within the temperate zone.

17-2 Climate Regions of the United States

- The United States mainland can be divided into six different climate regions based on the amount of precipitation and the temperature in each region.

- The narrow coastal area of California has a Mediterranean climate.

- The northwest coast of the United States has a marine west coast climate.

- The portion of the United States extending from the northern Midwest to the North Atlantic coast has a moist continental climate.

- The southeastern United States has a moist subtropical climate.

- The western interior of the United States has desert and steppe climates.

17-3 Changes in Climate

- Although climate patterns remain relatively unchanged for many years, climates do change slowly over time.

- El Niño is a warm water current that causes climate changes.

- Major glaciations have occurred alternately with interglacials throughout the history of the earth.

VOCABULARY

Define each term in a complete sentence.

climate
desert climate
El Niño
ice age
interglacial period
leeward side
major glaciation
marine west
  coast climate

Mediterranean
  climate
microclimate
moist continental
  climate
moist subtropical
  climate
polar zone
prevailing wind

steppe climate
temperate zone
tropical zone
windward side

CONTENT REVIEW: MULTIPLE CHOICE

Choose the letter of the answer that best completes each statement.

1. Climate is determined by
a. temperature and pressure. b. precipitation and pressure.
c. temperature and cloud cover. d. temperature and precipitation.

2. The measure of distance north and south of the equator is called
a. altitude. b. climate. c. latitude d. steppes.

3. In general, as altitude increases
a. temperature increases. b. plant life increases.
c. temperature decreases. d. air pressure increases.

4. A factor that affects precipitation at a particular location is
a. altitude. b. ocean currents. c. prevailing winds. d. latitude.

5. The climate zone with the coldest average temperatures is
a. tropical. b. polar. c. marine. d. temperate.

6. The climate zone with the greatest variations is the
a. polar zone. b. temperate zone. c. microclimate. d. tropical zone.

7. The division of the United States mainland into different climate regions is based on
a. temperature and prevailing winds. b. prevailing winds and ocean currents.
c. temperature and precipitation. d. ocean currents and precipitation.

8. Forests of needleleafed trees—such as red cedar, spruce, and firs—are the most common type of vegetation in the
a. marine west coast climate region. b. moist continental climate region.
c. Mediterranean climate region. d. moist subtropical climate region.

9. Which receives the lowest amount of precipitation?
a. Mediterranean climate region b. desert climate region
c. steppe climate region d. marine west coast climate region

10. Ice ages are believed to be associated with changes in the
a. flow of rivers. b. location of continents.
c. earth's orbit and axis. d. ocean and air currents.

CONTENT REVIEW: COMPLETION

Fill in the word or words that best complete each statement.

1. The average weather conditions in one place over a period of a year or longer is called _____.

2. The southeastern United States has a _____ climate region.

3. Two factors that affect precipitation are _____ and _____.

4. Precipitation will usually fall on the _____ side of a mountain.

5. There are _____ major climate zones on the earth.

6. The climate zone with the highest average temperatures is the _____.

7. The United States mainland is divided into _____ climate regions.

8. Three factors that affect temperature are _____, _____, and _____.

9. Cacti are common in the _____ climate region.

10. Short warm periods between major glaciations are called _____.

CONTENT REVIEW: TRUE OR FALSE

Determine whether each statement is true or false. If it is true, write "true." If it is false, change the underlined word or words to make the statement true.

1. Climate is determined by temperature and <u>pressure</u>.
2. In general, areas located farther away from the equator receive a <u>greater</u> amount of solar energy.
3. The influence of <u>prevailing winds</u> helps explain why a desert can border an ocean.
4. Dry climates are usually found on the <u>windward</u> side of a mountain.
5. Major ice ages are called <u>interglacials</u>.
6. The <u>temperate zone</u> extends from the pole to 60° latitude.
7. The <u>marine west coast</u> climate of wet winters and dry summers is found along the California coast.
8. Two climate regions east of the Mississippi River are <u>moist continental</u> and <u>steppe</u>.
9. Climates <u>do not</u> change slowly over time.
10. The localized climate of a backyard is called a <u>microclimate</u>.

CONCEPT REVIEW: SKILL BUILDING

Use the skills you have developed in the chapter to complete each activity.

1. **Making predictions** Suppose a warm ocean current flowing along a coastal area suddenly became a cold ocean current. What would happen to the climate along the coast?
2. **Applying concepts** Explain the following conditions.
   a. A mountain near the equator has snow on its peak throughout the year.
   b. Deserts exist on the eastern side of the Rocky Mountains.
3. **Making comparisons** If you were to take a trip from New York to Louisiana during the summer, what changes in climate would you expect to experience?
4. **Analyzing data** A person travelling up the west coast of the United States from Seattle, Washington, to Juneau, Alaska, notices that even though she has gone 1200 km to the north, the temperature has dropped only 5C°. On the same day, another person is travelling from Seattle due east over the Cascade Mountains to Spokane, Washington, a distance of only 375 km. This person also observes a temperature drop of 5C°. Explain why the temperature drop travelling 1200 km north was not greater than the temperature drop travelling 375 km due east.

CONCEPT REVIEW: ESSAY

Discuss each of the following in a brief paragraph.

1. Explain how a large body of water such as an ocean can keep a nearby landmass cool in summer and warm in winter.
2. Explain how prevailing winds and mountain ranges affect precipitation.
3. Compare tropical, temperate, and polar climate zones.
4. Describe the six climate regions of the United States.
5. How does El Niño affect climate?
6. Using examples, describe the ways latitude, altitude, and ocean currents affect temperature.
7. What may have caused the ice ages?

Adventures in Science

JOANNE SIMPSON'S STORMY STRUGGLE

Joanne Simpson spent the year 1943 contributing to the American effort in World War II by teaching weather forecasting to air force personnel. At the same time, she was fighting a more personal battle. Simpson, who had graduated from the University of Chicago, wanted to return there to earn additional degrees in meteorology. Her efforts, however, were met with much opposition from professors at the University. They told Simpson that the idea of a woman meteorologist was a "lost cause." The concept of a female scientist, they claimed, was a "contradiction in terms," and "there was no point" in her trying to get an advanced degree. Yet, in 1949, the determined Simpson became the first American woman to receive a Ph.D. in meteorology.

Simpson's interest in meteorology began when she was a young girl. Her father was a journalist who wrote about aviation, and she sometimes went flying with him. During her teen years, Simpson spent summers as an assistant to the director of aviation for the state of Massachusetts. She also began to take flying lessons.

In 1940 Simpson enrolled at the University of Chicago. She was introduced to meteorology while training for her pilot's license. The ability to read and understand a weather map as well as knowledge of weather patterns and the atmosphere are important to flying. Simpson was so fascinated by the subject that she signed up for a course at the University.

After receiving her undergraduate degree and teaching military personnel for a year, Simpson decided to continue her studies in meteorology. At first none of the faculty at the University of Chicago would support her venture. But Simpson, a very determined young scientist, eventually won the support of Herbert Riehl. He agreed to supervise her research project, which involved the study of cumulus clouds—their interaction with the environment and their relationship to tropical waves.

Woods Hole, Massachusetts, a small town at the southwest tip of Cape Cod, provided an ideal natural environment for Simpson's research on cumulus clouds. Simpson studied at both Woods Hole and the University of Chicago before receiving her Ph.D. in meteorology in 1949.

Simpson's interesting and dynamic career has included teaching at several universities—among them, the University of California at Los Angeles and the University of Virginia. In 1979, she was invited to head the Severe Storms Branch of the Goddard Laboratory for Atmospheric Sciences. This laboratory is part of the National Aeronautics and Space Administration (NASA).

Dr. Simpson enjoys a challenge, so for her NASA is a perfect place to be. She continues to study the formation and development of cumulus clouds. And she is currently working on a new weather satellite that will provide accurate measurements of the rainfall in tropical ocean areas. The sat-

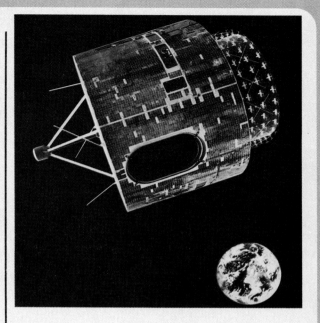

From information gathered by weather satellites, meteorologists like Joanne Simpson hope to learn more about various atmospheric conditions.

ellite, which is scheduled to be launched in 1994, should give meteorologists a better understanding of various changes in climate. These discoveries could enable scientists to make more accurate and longer range weather forecasts.

In the last 40 years, Simpson has published 115 scientific research papers, won numerous awards and honors, traveled across the globe, and served on many scientific councils and committees. The honors that have given her the greatest personal satisfaction are the Meisinger Award, given to her in 1962 for her work on cumulus clouds; NASA's Exceptional Scientific Achievement Medal; and the Carl-Gustav Rossby Research Medal, the American Meteorological Society's highest award. Simpson's courage and determination have earned her the respect of her colleagues and the public. She has truly paved the way for a generation of women meteorologists.

Skyfire & Stormfury:

MISSIONS IMPOSSIBLE?

Swinging northwards out of the Uinta Mountains in northeast Utah, the Bear River makes a sudden U-turn in southern Idaho. From there the river plunges southward like a blue arrow aimed at Great Salt Lake in Utah. On the way, the river and its offshoots carry water to hundreds of farms. The river fills reservoirs where people sail, water-ski, fish, and hunt. Its rushing waters also provide power for five hydroelectric plants. Electricity from these plants lights homes and runs factories.

Clearly, the Bear River is a key to the health of the whole area through which it flows. The water that the Bear River carries makes the region healthy. Where does this water come from? Originally, from the sky. And most of it comes in the form of winter snows, which melt in the spring. The more snow, the more water. And nature usually provides the right amount of snow.

But "usually" is not good enough for the local electric company. Officials of the company would be much happier if they could increase snowfall and thus provide the Bear River with more water. From this increased supply of water would come more electricity for the people of the area. These officials seem to have a good argument. Of all the moisture that crosses the United States from west to east, only about 5 percent falls from the sky as rain or snow. So why not increase that percentage, if possible?

To do this, scientists would have to find a way to control the weather around the Bear River. Can this be done? During the past 30 years or so, scientists working for the electric company have made various attempts. But before you learn how successful the scientists have been at taming "Mother Nature," journey back to a seemingly ordinary day in 1946.

Notice how this airplane is releasing silver iodide crystals from the back of the wing as it flies through the clouds. Cloud seeding is a common method of producing rain in areas that need precipitation during dry periods. ▼

The date was December 20. The place was northern New York State, not far from the city of Schenectady. The residents were delighted with their weather forecast: "fair and warmer." But that prediction would not come true.

High in the air, a small plane soared through the clouds. In the plane sat Vincent Schaefer. For several years, this scientist had been studying how moisture in clouds turns to snow and ice. His laboratory experiments had identified tiny particles as triggers in the formation of ice crystals, snowflakes, and raindrops. In nature, these particles might be dust or newly formed crystals of ice. What would happen, Schaefer had wondered, if such particles were sprinkled on an otherwise "quiet" cloud?

Using an ordinary home freezer, Schaefer had made his own miniclouds and sprinkled them with all sorts of particles—salt, talcum powder, sugar, soap powder, ground-up carbon, even dust from volcanoes. But nothing had happened.

Next, Schaefer had loaded the freezer with dry ice This frozen form of carbon dioxide had a temperature of $-78.5\,°C$. To Schaefer's surprise, the inside of the freezer had begun to sparkle with thousands of tiny ice crystals. Growing larger and larger, the crystals had finally become snowflakes! Would the same thing happen in a real cloud?

There was only one way to find out. So on December 20, 1946, Schaefer sprinkled a cloud with dry ice. Soon the cloud was producing huge amounts of snow; over sixteen centimeters blanketed the roads and homes below. Cars could not move. People could not get to and from work. These were the first hints that meddling with the weather could cause trouble.

But many scientists believed that the benefits of weather control would far outweigh the drawbacks. What could be more important, they argued, than knocking out a devastating hurricane, a crop-destroying hailstorm, or a lightning storm that could set fire to valuable forests? So the search for ways to control the weather began.

On August 18, 1969, a squadron of planes took off from an airport in Puerto Rico. Five of the planes carried very unusual bombs. Eight other planes tagged along to measure the effects of the bombs. Oddly, the bombs did not carry high explosives. Nor was their target some enemy airfield or ship.

The target was one of the most powerful and destructive forces on earth—a hurricane! Its name was Debbie. And the flight was part of an experiment designed to find out whether hurricanes could be weakened. This experiment and others like it were part of project Stormfury.

The planes flew into Debbie's 180-kilometer-per-hour winds at an altitude of more than 10,000 meters. The bombs were set loose. As they tumbled into the clouds and exploded, tiny particles of a substance called silver iodide shot out in all directions.

As had happened in Schaefer's pioneering experiments, water in Debbie's towering clouds turned to ice around the particles. And as any scientist will tell you, when a liquid turns to a solid, heat is given off! It was this heat that the Stormfury scientists hoped would weaken Debbie's fierce winds. What did the planes measuring the winds find? After the fifth day of silver iodide treatment, Debbie's winds had dropped from 180 to 126 kilometers per hour!

In the next few years, other experiments of this kind were performed. But none turned out to be as successful as the experiment with Hurricane Debbie. And there was another problem. Not enough hurricanes occurred near the eastern and southern coasts of the United States to experiment on. But there were many such storms in the Pacific Ocean. These storms, called typhoons, often crashed into the coasts of Japan and China, causing great damage and loss of life. Certainly the Japanese and Chinese would welcome Project Stormfury to the Pacific Ocean.

But such was not the case! As the Japanese pointed out, almost half of their water came from typhoon rains. So what was "bad" weather in the United States was not at all "bad" in Japan.

More than 10,000 forest fires a year are thought to be caused by lightning. Since the 1960s, various attempts have been made to "short-circuit" the electricity in thunderstorms so that fewer lightning bolts hit the ground. One experiment, called Project Skyfire, was conducted over the forests of Montana. The results of Project Skyfire were hard to figure out. No one knew for sure whether the experiment had proved anything.

Other experiments with different kinds of weather were performed. A region in northeast Colorado called "Hail Alley" came in for special treatment. As you might guess, in this region hailstorms occur frequently. These storms often destroy farm crops. Some scientists thought that if silver iodide crystals were sprinkled into hail clouds, more hailstones would form. But, the scientists hoped, these hailstones would be smaller and less damaging. Unfortunately, the experiment did not work.

Nevertheless, the search for ways to control the weather goes on. And so does the argument that one person's good weather may be another's bad weather. For example, rain in a farm area could be very helpful. But in a vacation spot, rain might mean disaster to business. Too much rain could cause floods. But too little rain could bring severe droughts.

Tomorrow's Climate:
THE HEAT'S ON!

The sightseeing boat glides quietly through the empty streets of the once busy city. Tourists lean against the boat's rail and gaze at partly submerged office buildings, museums, monuments, and sports stadiums. The tour guide's voice comes over the speaker loud and clear.

"All you can see of City Hall is the old TV antenna on your left. Up ahead is Ruth Stadium, where our local baseball team won the World Series of 2018. You could play water polo in it today, if you wanted to."

A man looking out at the lonely concrete structures shakes his head and mops sweat from his brow. The temperature is very warm, as it is all year round. Hard to believe, he thinks, that just one hundred years ago a January day like this would have been icy cold.

Is this scene only fantasy? Perhaps. But it may someday be fact. Your great-grandchild might be that man riding on the sightseeing boat. And your town or city might be the one partly covered by water. For events are taking place in the earth's atmosphere that could soon—very soon—change our planet's climate. As an official of the United States Environmental Protection Agency declared in the autumn of 1983, "Changes will be here by the years 1990 to 2000."

What are these changes? What will be their effects on our planet? And what is causing them?

The man on the sightseeing boat has provided an answer to the first question: unusual heat! The average temperature of the earth is going up. Scientists estimate that by the year 2040, the earth will have warmed up about 2° C. And by the year 2100, people may be living on a planet that is 5° C warmer than it is today.

Too Hot to Handle?

So what? you may be thinking. After all, the temperature where you live probably varies right now. From winter to summer, the temperature may change some 20, 30, or 40 degrees. But these seasonal changes do not affect the entire earth's average temperature. And a change of 5° C in this *average* temperature is really significant.

To get an idea of how dramatic this change is, consider these two facts: In the past 1000 years, the earth's average temperature has changed only 2° C. And in the past one million years, the change has been between 6° C and 7° C. These larger changes, scientists tell us, are enough to trigger ice ages or bring them to an end. It all depends on whether the change causes warmer or colder conditions.

Herein lies the answer to the next question: How will the change in temperature affect us? Remember, it is the *average* temperature that may change 5° C over the next 100 years or so. This means some places will warm up more while other places warm up less. It turns out that the polar regions of the world are expected to warm up a great deal more than other areas.

Water, Water, Everywhere?

Again, you might wonder what this temperature change means. How could a rise in temperature create the submerged city you read about at the beginning of this article? There is a huge sheet of ice that covers the Antarctic continent. In places, the ice sheet is thousands of meters thick. That ice could melt if the temperature changes you've read about took place. Then water levels in the oceans would rise as much as seven or eight meters!

Such a rise in water level would change the map of the world. If sea levels rose only five meters, eleven million people in the United States alone would find their homes under water. But this would be only one effect of higher world temperatures.

Warmer temperatures in the western parts of the United States would reduce rainfall. And increased evaporation of water from

If higher world temperatures melted the polar ice cap, scenes such as this might become common in all coastal areas. Millions of lives and homes could be destroyed by walls of rising ocean water.

A worldwide rise in temperature could cause serious problems for both country and city dwellers. If too many farms were to dry up because of a water shortage, where would food be grown?

streams and rivers would signal disaster to farmers. A United States Government report states: "The impact would be especially severe in the Missouri, Rio Grande, Upper Colorado, and Lower Colorado regions." Here farms might have to be abandoned because of a lack of water.

In other places, more rain would fall and growing seasons would be longer. But this effect would not be as good as it at first seems. For some scientists warn that long, hot, wet seasons would spark an insect population explosion. Valuable food crops would be gobbled up by millions of insect pests.

Clearly, a rise in temperature would cause many serious problems. By now you are probably wondering what is turning on the heat in the earth's atmosphere. The answer is the sun!

A Burning Question

This may seem strange to you. After all, the sun has been with us for a long time. Yet this warming up of the earth is fairly new. So something besides the sun must be at work. But what is this "something"?

For every person on the earth, about four tons of this "something" is pumped into the atmosphere every year. And by the year 2100, the amount will be four times as great. Yet just a few hundred years ago, there was much less of this "something" streaming into the air. How can the increase in this substance be explained? What did people start doing a few hundred years ago that they are now doing at a faster rate?

The answer is burning fossil fuels such as coal, oil, gasoline, and natural gas. When these fuels burn, they produce energy needed to run factories, generate electricity, warm homes and offices, and move cars, trucks, and buses. But when these fuels burn, they also produce a gas called carbon dioxide, CO_2. And carbon dioxide is the "something" that is helping to warm the earth.

An Invisible Blanket

Carbon dioxide has a very special property— one that is at the heart of the heat problem! In the atmosphere, CO_2 acts like an invisible blanket. It lets sunlight pass through to the earth's surface. The sunlight heats the earth. Normally, a good portion of this heat radiates back into space. And our planet stays comfortably cool. But a thick CO_2 blanket does not let the heat escape. The heat is trapped under the blanket. And temperatures slowly rise.

Scientists call this process the "greenhouse effect" because the CO_2 acts like the glass in an ordinary greenhouse. If you have ever been in a greenhouse, you have felt the effect of this action. The inside of the greenhouse is warm—even on a cold winter day!

A Ray of Hope

Can anything be done to reverse the earth's greenhouse effect? Not much, say scientists. We depend too much on fossil fuels for our energy needs. Then what can we do? Get ready, is the answer. Make plans to hold back the sea. Move people from threatened areas to safe ones. Find ways to keep water flowing to places that become dry. And continue to search for new ways to reduce the effects of the coming global heat wave. If these efforts are successful, sightseeing boats of the future will still be sailing around cities rather than through them.

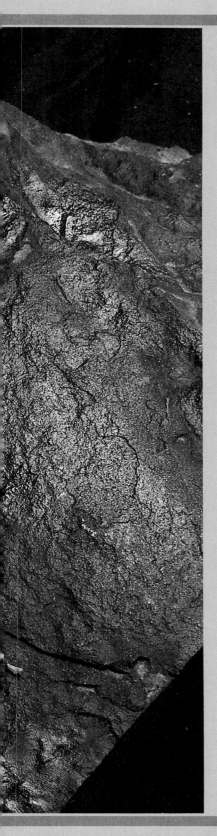

Heredity and Adaptation

Several years ago in the small town of Post, Texas, a group of scientists worked to uncover the bones of an ancient baby dinosaur. When they at last completed their task, however, the scientists were very surprised to see that the bones they had uncovered were not from a baby dinosaur at all!

At first, the scientists were not sure what they had found. The uncovered bones had a variety of unusual characteristics. They were hollow, and some formed a well-developed wishbone. The breastbone had a keel, which is a ridgelike part that anchors the muscles a bird uses for flight. When they observed the bones under a microscope, the scientists spotted tiny bumps where feathers were once attached. From this evidence, the scientists concluded that the bones must have belonged to a bird and not to a baby dinosaur, as originally thought.

The organism whose bones had been uncovered was quickly named *Protoavis,* or "first bird." *Protoavis* lived more than 225 million years ago. Some of its characteristics were common in dinosaurs of that time. Other characteristics are common in birds of today. Because of this combination of dinosaurlike and birdlike characteristics, scientists have suggested that dinosaurs may be the distant ancestors of modern birds.

In this unit, you will learn why organisms have certain characteristics and how they pass on these characteristics to their offspring. You will also discover how organisms change over time. In other words, you will learn about heredity and adaptation.

CHAPTERS

18   Genetics

19   Human Genetics

20   Changes in Living Things Over Time

21   The Path to Modern Humans

Fossilized bones of Protoavis, *or "first bird"*

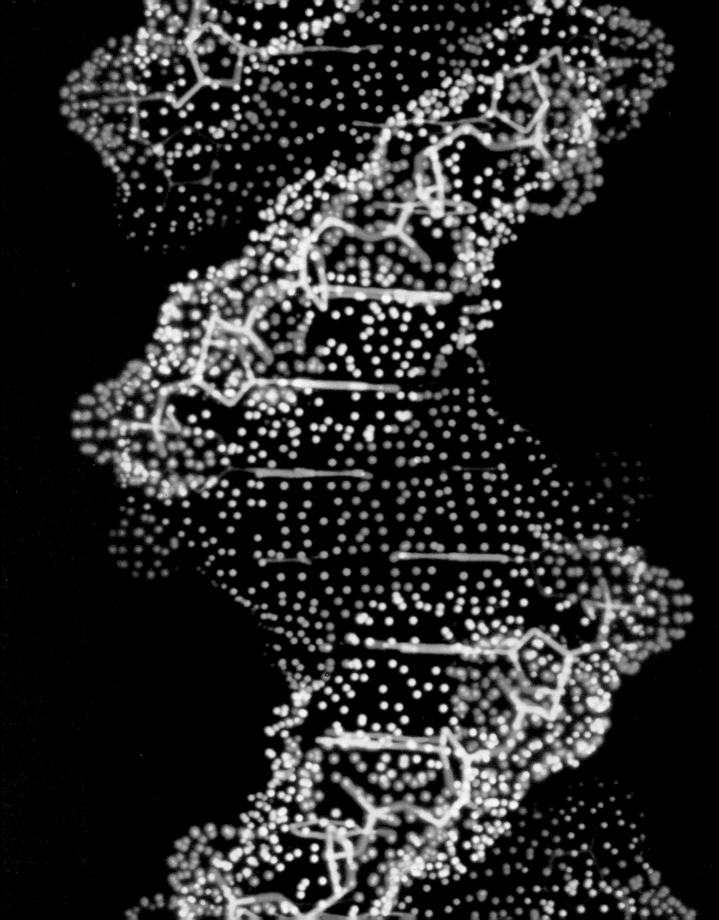

18 Genetics

CHAPTER SECTIONS

18-1 History of Genetics

18-2 Modern Genetics

CHAPTER OBJECTIVES

After completing this chapter, you will be able to:

18-1 Define genetics.

18-1 Explain the terms dominant and recessive.

18-1 State the law of segregation and the law of independent assortment.

18-1 Use Punnett squares to predict the results of crosses.

18-2 Explain the concept of incomplete dominance.

18-2 Describe the chromosome theory and relate it to sex determination and mutations.

Like a strange galaxy in outer space, the atoms of a computerized model of a DNA molecule sparkle against a black background. In many ways, the DNA molecule is similar to a galaxy. Both are made up of many parts. One helps explain the nature of the universe. The other helps explain the nature of life.

Hidden in the structure of the DNA molecule are chemical instructions that shape every living thing. Because no two living things hold the same instructions, all living things are different.

Scientists have unraveled the way in which the instructions in DNA pass from one generation to the next. Using this knowledge, scientists called genetic engineers have been able to change the instructions of some DNA molecules. By doing so, the scientists have produced forms of life that have never before existed—forms of life that will help human beings in ways never dreamed of.

Computer-generated DNA molecule

18-1   History of Genetics

"We wish to suggest a structure for the salt of deoxyribose nucleic acid." So began a letter from two scientists in 1953 to a scientific journal. What followed in this letter was a description of the spiral-shaped structure that would help unlock the deepest secrets of **genetics**—the secret of life itself. **Genetics is the study of heredity, or the passing on of characteristics from an organism to its offspring.**

The spiral-shaped structure written about in the letter was deoxyribonucleic (dee-ahk-si-righ-boh-noo-KLE-ik) acid or, **DNA.** DNA is the basic substance of heredity. Sometimes DNA is called the "code of life." DNA is called this because it contains all the information needed to make and to control every part of an organism.

The two scientists who wrote the letter about DNA were James Watson, an American biologist, and Francis Crick, a British biologist. In 1962, they were awarded the Nobel Prize for physiology or medicine for their work on the structure of DNA. Many scientists believe that the discovery of the structure of DNA was the most important biological event of this century. Research into DNA has led to improved breeds of plants and animals and more efficient ways of producing certain medicines. It has also taken a step toward early detection and prevention of some inherited disorders.

Figure 18-1   *Notice how this young snow monkey has traits that are similar to its mother. The passing of traits from parent to offspring is called heredity.*

The Work of Gregor Mendel

In order to understand how DNA was discovered, you must go back in time to a small monastery in Czechoslovakia 100 years ago. As you approach the monastery, you see a monk bending over some pea plants. Who is this person? What is he doing? The person is Gregor Mendel, an Austrian monk and biologist.

Mendel experimented with garden pea plants to see if there was a pattern in the way they inherited characteristics. Why did Mendel choose pea plants for his experiments? The pea plants grew quickly. Many generations could be observed in a fairly short time. And the plants could be crossed, or bred, easily.

The flowers of pea plants contain stamens, which are the male reproductive structures. Stamens produce pollen, which contain sperm cells. The flowers also contain the female reproductive structure, called the pistil, which produces the egg. When the pollen lands on the top of the pistil of a flower, pollination occurs. Seeds for the next generation of plants are produced through pollination. See Figure 18-2.

Figure 18-2 *Gregor Mendel experimented with pea plants because their life cycles, from flower to new plant, occur very quickly. This enabled Mendel to study several generations and many offspring during a short period of time.*

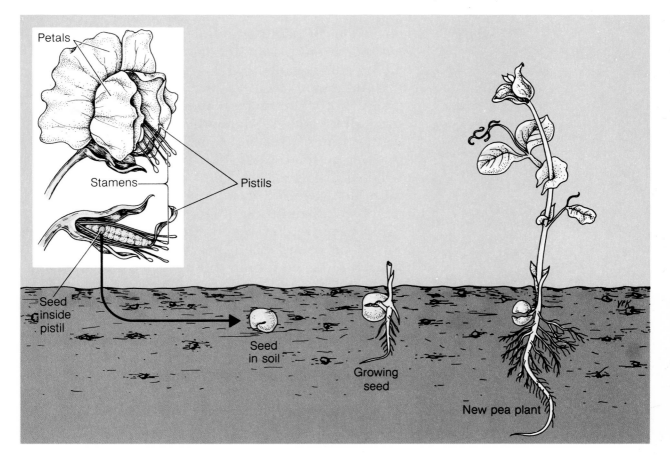

Petals

Stamens

Pistils

Seed inside pistil

Seed in soil

Growing seed

New pea plant

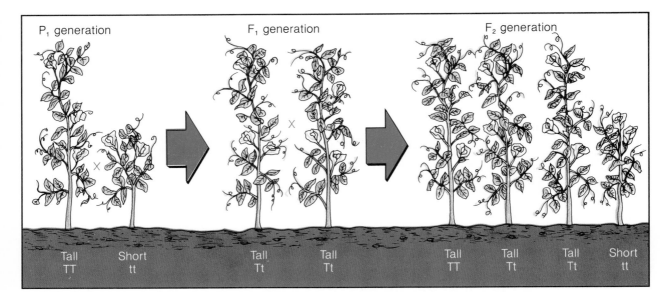

Figure 18-3 *Mendel experimented by crossing tall and short pea plants. He discovered that the offspring in the first, or F₁, generation were all tall, while those in the second, or F₂, generation were tall and short.*

Mendel's Experiments

Mendel discovered that if he planted seeds from pea plants with short stems, only short-stemmed plants grew. The next generation of these plants was also short stemmed. This result was what he, and everyone else at that time, expected. The new generations of plants from one parent always resembled the parent plant. Mendel called these plants true-breeding plants.

Did the seeds from tall pea plants give the same results? Not all the time. Some tall pea plants produced all tall plants, while other tall pea plants produced mostly tall and some short pea plants. However, in the case of short pea plants, they produced *only* short plants. These results made Mendel realize that there were two kinds of tall plants, the true-breeders and those that did not breed true.

But what would happen, Mendel wondered, if he took pollen from a plant that produced only tall plants and dusted it onto the pistil of a short plant? Mendel tried it and called these first two plants the parental generation, or P₁. He discovered that all the plants in the next generation, the first filial (FI-li-uhl) generation, or F₁, were tall! It was as if the trait for shortness that had existed in one of the parent plants had disappeared completely!

What happened next was even more of a mystery. Mendel covered the tall plants of the F₁ generation and allowed them to pollinate themselves. That is, the pollen of a flower was allowed to fall on the pistil of the *same* flower. Mendel expected that the tall plants would again produce only tall plants. Instead, some of the plants of the second filial generation, or F_2, were tall and some were short. The trait for shortness seemed to have reappeared!

By keeping careful records of his work, Mendel reasoned that the tall plants of the F_1 generation did not breed true. These plants had to contain factors for both tallness and shortness. When both factors were present, only tallness showed. Today, these factors, or units of heredity, are called **genes.**

From his observations, Mendel knew that the plants produced by crossing two plants of opposite traits, shortness and tallness, showed the tallness trait. The "stronger" trait is called **dominant.** The trait that seemed to disappear, or be the "weaker" trait, is called **recessive.**

Today, scientists use symbols to represent different forms of a trait. Dominant genes are represented by capital letters. For example, tallness in pea plants is written as "T." Recessive genes are represented by small letters. Shortness in pea plants is written as "t."

Activity

Genetic Scientists

Listed below are some people you may like to know more about. The library has many resources to help you find out about these people. Find out what each of them had to say about hereditary factors and genetics. Present your findings in a written report.

Rosalind Franklin
James D. Watson
Martha Chase
Jacques Monod
Barbara McClintock

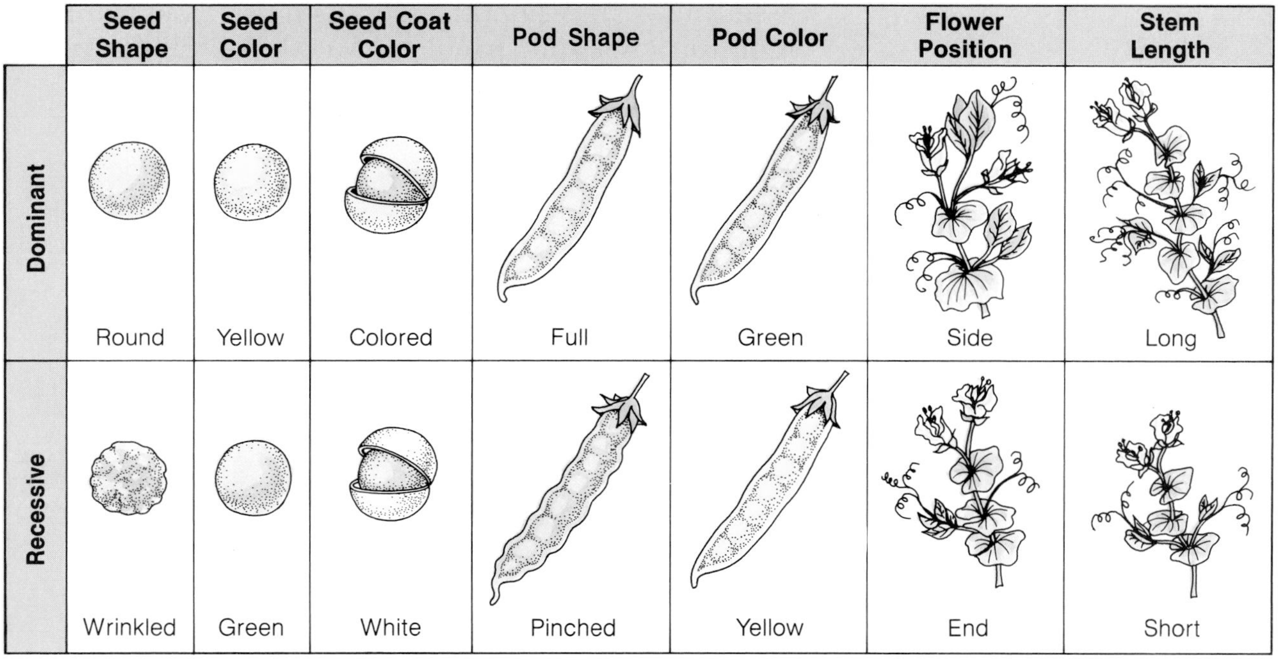
Seed Shape
Seed Color
Seed Coat Color
Pod Shape
Pod Color
Flower Position
Stem Length
Dominant
Round
Yellow
Colored
Full
Green
Side
Long
Recessive
Wrinkled
Green
White
Pinched
Yellow
End
Short

Figure 18-4 *The chart shows the seven characteristics that Mendel studied in pea plants. Each characteristic has a dominant and a recessive gene.*

In this activity, you will use coins to observe the results of a hybrid cross.

1. Obtain two coins.

2. Cut four squares of masking tape that are equal in size. The squares should not hang over the edges of the coins.

3. Place the letter R on one side of the coin and the letter r on the other side.

4. Repeat step 3 for the second coin.

5. Toss both coins 100 times. Record the genetic makeup for each toss.

What are the possible gene combinations? What is the ratio of the gene combinations?

Laws of Genetics

Mendel studied not only the height of pea plants, he studied other traits. These traits were seed shape, seed color, seed coat color, pod shape, pod color, and flower position. In every case, crossing two true-breeding plants with opposite traits did not result in mixtures of the trait. For example, Figure 18-5 shows a cross between a plant with round seeds (RR) and a plant with wrinkled seeds (rr). The type of seeds that are produced in the F_1 generation are all round. Why? The gene for roundness, R, masks or hides the gene for wrinkledness. Therefore, all the seeds are round. What happens when the F_1 generation pollinates itself? In this case, most of the seeds are round and some are wrinkled. The recessive trait for wrinkled seeds reappears.

Today, scientists call organisms that have genes that are alike for a particular trait, such as RR or rr, purebred. An organism that has genes that are different for a trait (Rr) is called a **hybrid** (HIGH-brid). Looking back, you can see that Mendel's parental generation of pea plants was purebred. The plants in the F_1 generation were hybrid plants. They were produced from the crossing of two purebred plants with different traits.

LAW OF SEGREGATION By examining his observations and results, Mendel formed a **hypothesis** (high-PAH-thuh-sis). A hypothesis is a suggested explanation for a scientific problem. Mendel's hypothesis was

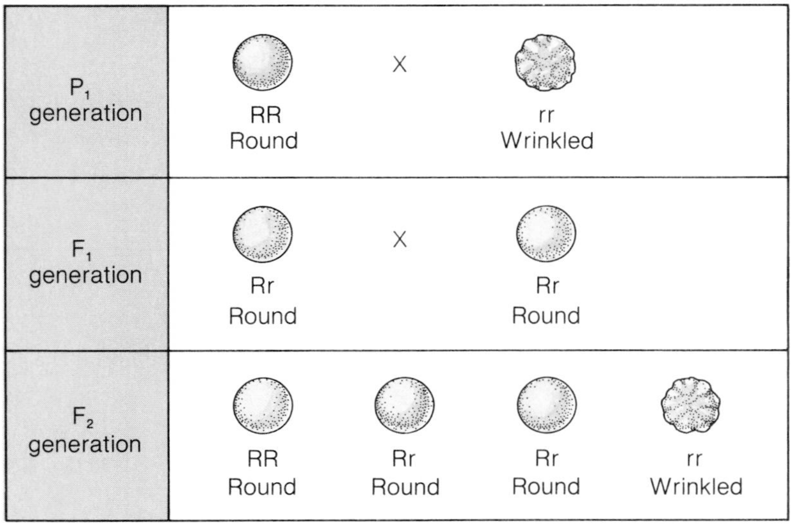

Figure 18-5 *When Mendel crossed a purebred round-seeded plant with a purebred wrinkled-seeded plant, he discovered that the wrinkled trait seemed to disappear in the F_1 generation. However, the trait reappeared in the F_2 generation. This trait is recessive.*

P_1 generation	RR Round	X	rr Wrinkled	
F_1 generation	Rr Round	X	Rr Round	
F_2 generation	RR Round	Rr Round	Rr Round	rr Wrinkled

that each pea plant parent has a pair of factors. To-day, this pair of factors is called a gene pair. Mendel further reasoned that each parent could contribute only one of these factors to each pea plant in the next generation. In that way, the next generation also had a gene pair for each trait, one gene from each parent.

Now Mendel could account for the fact that a pea plant with green seeds can develop from a cross between parents with yellow seeds. Mendel reasoned that the factors for the green color must be present in the parents. For example, a parent with the Yy factors would have yellow seeds but would also be carrying the recessive factor (y) for green seeds. The green seed trait would be hidden in the parent but could be passed on. Look at Figure 18-6. What are the possible gene pairs for seed color of the cross between two hybrid plants with yellow seeds?

Scientists now know that genes, or Mendel's factors, for different traits are found on **chromosomes**. Chromosomes are rod-shaped structures found in the nucleus of cells. The chromosomes carry the genes that determine the traits of pea plants, or any other living things.

Chromosomes are found in pairs within the nucleus. In general, for any particular trait, one gene contributed by a parent is on one of the paired chromosomes. The other gene for that trait from the other parent is on the opposite chromosome. Of course, if each parent contributed all its chromosomes and genes to an offspring, then the offspring would have twice the number of chromosomes as its parents. This does not happen because of a process called **meiosis** (migh-OH-sis).

The process of meiosis produces the sex cells, either sperm or egg cells. As a result of meiosis, the number of chromosomes carried by each sex cell is exactly half the normal number of chromosomes found in the parent. When sex cells combine to form the offspring, each sex cell contributes half the normal number of chromosomes. In the end, the offspring gets the normal number of chromosomes, half from each parent.

You can see in Figure 18-7 how meiosis works. In this example, each parent cell has four chromosomes,

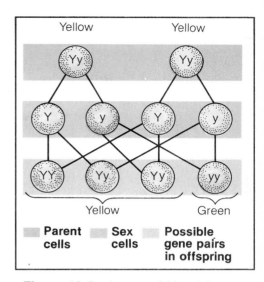

Figure 18-6 *In one of Mendel's experiments, he discovered that a pea plant with green seeds can develop from a cross between parents with yellow seeds. To explain this, he reasoned that the gene for green color (y) must be present in the parents.*

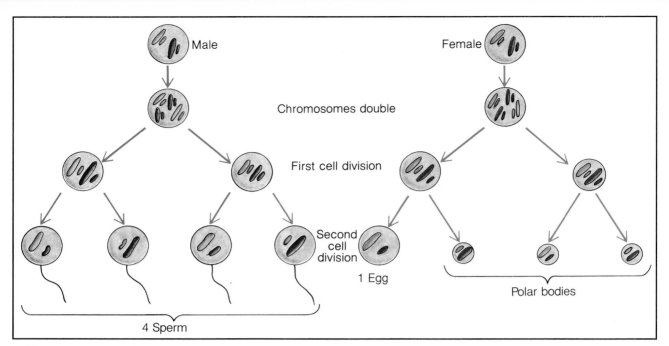

Figure 18-7 *During meiosis, a cell undergoes two divisions resulting in cells that have half the normal number of chromosomes. The sex cells, egg and sperm, are formed by meiosis. The polar bodies disintegrate, leaving only one egg cell.*

Figure 18-8 *When sex cells form during meiosis, gene pairs segregate, or separate. During sexual reproduction, the sex cells unite to form a zygote that contains a gene pair, or one gene from each parent.*

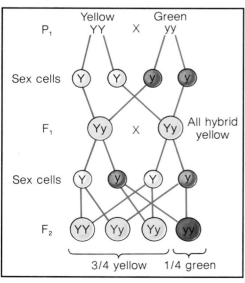

which come in two pairs. First the chromosomes in the cell double, producing eight chromosomes. Then the cell divides. During this cell division, the chromosomes separate and are equally distributed. So the two cells formed by this cell division each have four chromosomes. Next, these cells divide again. So the resulting cells each now have two chromosomes. That is, the last group of cells produced by meiosis each have half the number of chromosomes as the original parent cell. In the process, the chromosomes have been segregated. This is known as the **law of segregation**.

Notice in Figure 18-8 that one half of the sex cells of a pea plant with a yellow/green (Yy) gene pair for gene color have a gene for yellow (Y). The other half of the sex cells carry a gene for green (y). During sexual reproduction, a male and a female sex cell unite to form a zygote (ZIGH-goht), or fertilized egg. In each zygote, the gene pair, one gene from each parent, is formed again. When these offspring plants develop and produce sex cells, their gene pairs separate again.

LAW OF INDEPENDENT ASSORTMENT Mendel also crossed pea plants that differed from one another by two or more characteristics. Based on Mendel's results the **law of independent assortment** was formed.

This law states that each gene pair is inherited independently of all other traits. For example, when a tall plant with yellow seeds forms sex cells the genes for stem length separate independently from the genes for seed color. See Figure 18-9.

The seven pairs of genes that Mendel studied separated independently because they were on different chromosomes. If the genes had all been on the same chromosomes, however, they would not have separated independently.

Probability

Suppose you flipped a coin. What are the chances that it will land heads up? If you said a 50 percent chance, you are correct! You, like Gregor Mendel, used the laws of probability. Probability is the chance that something will or will not happen. Probabilities are usually written as a fraction or a percentage. For example, the chance that a sex cell will receive a Y gene from a Yy parent is ½, or 50 percent.

In probability, the results of one chance event do not affect the results of the next. Each event happens independently. For example, if you toss a coin 10 times, and it lands heads up each time, the probability of it landing heads up on the next flip is still ½, or 50 percent. The first 10 flips do not influence the result of the eleventh flip.

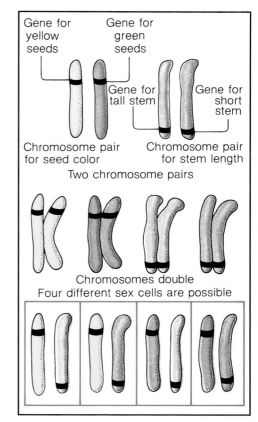

Figure 18-9 *During meiosis, the chromosomes double and then separate. Different gene pairs on different chromosomes separate independently. This is known as the law of independent assortment.*

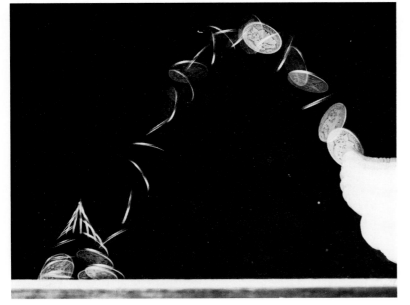

Figure 18-10 *According to the law of probability, a coin will land heads up 50 percent of the time and tails up 50 percent of the time.*

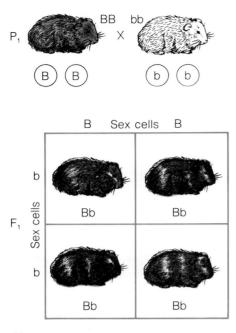

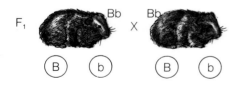

Figure 18-11 *Punnett squares can be used to show the results of crosses. What is the phenotype of the guinea pig offspring?*

Figure 18-12 *In a cross between two hybrid black-haired guinea pigs, what percentage of the offspring will be of the same genotype as the parents?*

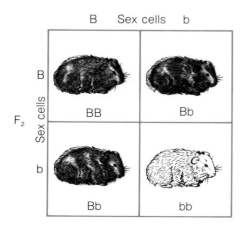

PUNNETT SQUARES In addition to probability, scientists use a special chart to show possible combinations of the cross between two organisms. This chart is called a Punnett square. It was developed by Reginald C. Punnett, an English geneticist.

Let's see how a Punnett square works. Look at the Punnett square in Figure 18-11. It shows a cross between two guinea pigs. Each of the genes in the two female sex cells is listed along the top. The genes in the male sex cells are listed along the left side. Remember that when male and female sex cells join, a zygote forms. Each box in the chart represents a *possible* zygote.

Notice in Figure 18-11 that in the P_1 generation, the female has both genes for black hair. The male has both genes for white hair. As a result, all of the F_1 generation are hybrid black (Bb). If you were to look at these hybrid black-haired guinea pigs, you would not be able to tell the difference between them and purebred black-haired guinea pigs. Both of their **phenotypes** (FEE-nuh-tighps), or visible characteristics, are the same. Phenotype refers to visible characteristics. However, their **genotypes** (JEN-uh-tighps) are different. A genotype is the actual gene makeup. For example, a purebred black-haired guinea pig has the genotype BB, while a hybrid black-haired guinea pig has the genotype Bb, even though they both have black hair.

Figure 18-12 shows a cross between two of the hybrid black-haired guinea pigs from the F_1 generation. The results of the F_1 cross, or the F_2 generation, are ¼ purebred black, ½ hybrid black, and ¼ purebred white.

SECTION REVIEW

1. What spiral-shaped structure is the basic substance of heredity?
2. What is an organism called if it has genes that are different from each other?
3. Which law of genetics states that each gene pair is inherited independently of all other traits?
4. What is probability?
5. Use a Punnett square to predict the outcome of a cross between a hybrid black guinea pig and a white guinea pig.

18-2 Modern Genetics

Mendel kept records and carefully wrote up the results of his experiments. Though he tried to make his work known in the early 1860s, it remained ignored and unnoticed until 1900. Then, three different scientists accidentally came across Mendel's papers. Separately, each of these scientists had been working out their own laws of inheritance. They were amazed to find out that their laws had been worked out by Mendel over 30 years earlier!

Since the time of Mendel, scientists have learned more about genetics. **Among the important genetic concepts that have been developed are incomplete dominance, the chromosome theory, mutations, sex determination, and genetic engineering.**

CAREER: *Plant Breeder*

HELP WANTED: PLANT BREEDER
Master's degree in plant genetics required. Doctorate a plus. Involves field and laboratory work.

Shotgun and tripod in hand the young scientist trudges far into the redwood forest. Upon discovery of the tallest, strongest, and healthiest-looking tree, the scientist positions the gun in the tripod. Lying on her back on the forest floor, she aims for a tree branch 30 meters above. She pulls the trigger and, within seconds, several small branches come tumbling down. To ensure a safe trip to the laboratory, the branches are wrapped in plastic. At the lab, they are carefully planted.

Weeks later, after the branches have rooted, the **plant breeder** will perform experiments that may change the size, the shape, or even the life span of future forests. A plant breeder is a scientist who tries to improve plants through genetic methods. Not only do plant breeders try to improve forests, they also try to develop new crop plants with more desirable traits.

Plant breeders are employed by colleges and universities, government agencies, lumber and pharmaceutical industries, and seed and food companies. If you have an interest in plants, you may want to learn more about a career in plant breeding. If so, write to the U.S. Department of Agriculture, Science and Education, 6505 Belcrest Road, Hyattsville, MD 20782.

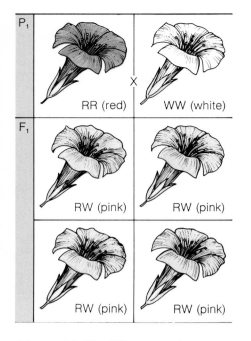

Figure 18-13 *When a red gene and a white gene are present in a four o'clock flower, a pink flower results.*

Incomplete Dominance

One scientist who took Mendel's work a step further was the German botanist Karl Correns. He discovered that in some gene pairs the genes are neither dominant nor recessive. Instead, these genes show **incomplete dominance.** Correns worked with four o'clock flowers. He discovered that when he crossed purebred red four o'clock flowers (RR) with purebred white four o'clock flowers (WW), the result was all pink four o'clock flowers (RW). See Figure 18-13. Notice that the symbols for the gene pairs for red, white, and pink are all capital letters. This is because no one gene is dominant over the others.

Incomplete dominance also occurs in animals. In Andalusian (an-duh-LOO-zhuhn) fowl, a kind of chicken, neither black nor white feathers are dominant. When a gene for black feathers and a gene for white feathers are present, the fowl appears to have black feathers with tiny white dots. This gives the fowl's feathers a blue-gray color. Shorthorn cattle show incomplete dominance too. A shorthorn with a gene for red hair and a gene for white hair is roan, or reddish-brown in color.

Activity

Incomplete Dominance

Use coins to simulate a cross between two RW plants.

1. Obtain two coins.

2. Cut four squares of masking tape that are equal in size and fit on the coins.

3. Place the letter R on one side of a coin and the letter W on the other side.

4. Repeat this procedure for the second coin.

5. Toss both coins 100 times, recording the genotype for each toss.

What is the percentage of occurrence for each genotype? Construct a Punnett square showing this cross.

The Chromosome Theory

At about the same time Correns was doing his work, Walter Sutton, a 25-year-old American graduate student, suggested that Mendel's factors might be chromosomes. Sutton made this observation after studying meiosis in grasshopper cells. Grasshoppers have 12 pairs of chromosomes, or 24 chromosomes. Sutton noticed that individual sex cells contained one chromosome from each pair, or 12 chromosomes. Sutton also saw that after the male and female sex cells united, the zygote that was formed had 12 pairs, or the original number of chromosomes. In other words, the offspring had exactly the same number of chromosomes as each of its parents.

From his work, Sutton concluded that chromosomes carried the hereditary factors from one generation to the next. And these factors accounted for the traits of an organism. It is amazing that Mendel was able to do all of his work without even knowing about chromosomes!

Mutations and Sex Determination

In 1886, while out on a walk, Hugo De Vries (duh-VREES), a Dutch botanist, made an accidental discovery that would go beyond Mendel's work. De Vries came across a group of American evening primroses. As with Mendel's pea plants, some primroses were very different from others. De Vries bred the primroses and got results similar to the results of Mendel's work with pea plants. But he also found that every once in a while, a new variety of primrose would grow—a variety that could not be accounted for by genetic laws. De Vries called these sudden changes in characteristics **mutations**. A mutation is caused by a change in genes or chromosomes.

If a mutation occurs in a body cell, the mutation affects only the organism that carries it. But if a mutation occurs in a sex cell, then that mutation can be passed on to the next generation. The mutation may then cause a change in the characteristics of the next generation.

Mutations may occur spontaneously, or they may be caused by factors in the environment such as radiation or certain chemicals. In fact, scientists have used radiation to sterilize insect pests so that they could not reproduce. An example of this method was used in California to control an invasion of the Mediterranean fruit fly, or Medfly.

Most mutations are harmful, that is, they reduce an organism's chances for survival or reproduction. For example, sickle-cell anemia is a serious blood disease caused by a mutation in a gene. Sickle-cell anemia results in blood cells that are shaped like a sickle or half circle. People who have sickle-cell anemia have difficulty obtaining enough oxygen. This happens because the sickle-shaped cell cannot carry enough oxygen to the rest of the body. The sickle-shaped cells may clump and clog tiny blood vessels.

Some mutations are helpful and cause desirable traits in living things. For example, when mutations occur spontaneously or are induced by scientists in crop plants, the crops may become more useful to people. A gene mutation in potatoes has produced a new variety of potato, called the Katahdin potato. This potato is resistant to diseases that attack other potatoes. Also, the new potato looks and tastes better than other types of potatoes.

Figure 18-14 *Sudden changes in the characteristics of an organism are known as mutations, or changes in genes or chromosomes. One mutation caused the fruit fly (top) to grow legs instead of antennae on its head. Another mutation caused the koala (bottom) to have albinism, a condition in which not enough colored pigment is produced. Are these mutations helpful or harmful?*

419

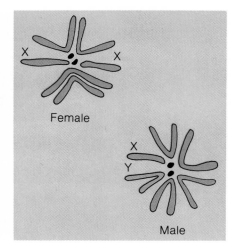

Figure 18-15 *A fruit fly has four pairs of chromosomes. A female fruit fly has two X chromosomes, while a male fruit fly has one X and one Y chromosome.*

Activity

Improvements Through Breeding

Using reference materials in the library, investigate how people have selectively bred plants and animals. What improvements have breeders made in the following plants and animals?

dairy cows	cats
pigs	wheat
chickens	corn
horses	grape-fruit
dogs	cotton

It may seem as if mutations produce only helpful or harmful traits. This is not so. Many mutations are neutral and do not produce any obvious changes. Still other mutations are lethal, or deadly, and result in the death of an organism.

In 1907, American zoologist Thomas Hunt Morgan began his own study in genetics. Morgan experimented with tiny insects called fruit flies. He chose fruit flies for three reasons. First, they are easy to raise. Second, they produce new generations very quickly. And third, their few chromosomes are easy to study.

Morgan quickly discovered something peculiar about the four pairs of chromosomes that each fruit fly had. In females, the chromosomes of each pair were the same shape. In males, however, the chromosomes of one pair were not the same shape. One chromosome, which Morgan called the X chromosome, was rod shaped. The other chromosome in the pair, which Morgan called the Y chromosome, was shaped like a hook.

Through a number of experiments, Morgan discovered that the X and Y chromosomes determined the sex of an organism. Any organism that has two X chromosomes is a female. Any organism that has one X and one Y chromosome is a male. These chromosomes are called **sex chromosomes.** All other chromosomes are "body" chromosomes.

Figure 18-16 *You can see from the drawings of the male and female fruit flies that they have some physical differences. The Punnett square shows the probability of the sex of an offspring.*

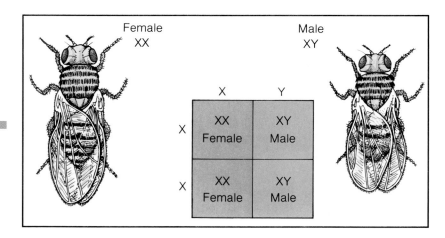

Other Discoveries

Between 1943 and 1952, scientists working with viruses and bacteria proved beyond a shadow of a doubt that DNA is the substance out of which genes are made. Scientists also determined that chromosomes are long strands of DNA.

The brief letter from Watson and Crick, which was discussed at the beginning of this chapter, explained the structure of DNA with such accuracy that by 1961 scientists were able to crack the entire genetic code. In fact, the complete genetic makeup of many forms of life is already on record in several enormous computers in the United States! One day scientists may be able to map and store a record of the genes of an endangered species such as the giant panda. Later, if the species becomes extinct, its genes could be duplicated in order to save the species.

The genetic code contains the instructions that determine how all cells develop. Cracking the code has led to one of the most important activities in modern biology—genetic engineering. Through genetic engineering, scientists have learned to cut apart the DNA molecules that make up chromosomes and to add entirely new parts of genes. These changed chromosomes can then be put into living cells, which changes the genetic makeup of the cell. Using this method, bacteria cells have been changed into living factories that produce large quantities of substances previously only made by human cells. These substances include insulin, interferon, and human growth hormone. Genetic engineering is discussed further in Chapter 19.

SECTION REVIEW

1. What is it called when the genes in some gene pairs are neither dominant nor recessive?
2. How are chromosomes involved in heredity?
3. In genetics, what are sudden changes in characteristics caused by an accidental change in a gene called?
4. What are the two types of sex chromosomes?
5. What process involves the adding of new gene parts into living cells?

Figure 18-17 *The science of genetics has come a long way since the time of Mendel. Today new types of wheat plants (top) have been developed from the crossing of two similar plants. In laboratories, scientists have developed new techniques that enable them to isolate strands of DNA (bottom).*

LABORATORY ACTIVITY

Observing the Growth of Mutant Corn Seeds

Purpose

In this activity, you will study the effect that a mutation has on the growth of corn plants.

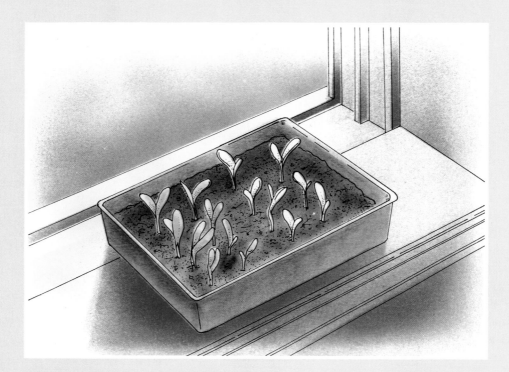

Materials (per group)

10 albino corn seeds
10 normal corn seeds
Flower box
Potting soil

Procedure

1. Fill a flower box with potting soil.
2. Plant each seed about 1 cm below the soil's surface. The seeds should also be spaced at least 1 cm from each other.
3. Place the flower box on a table near the window or on a windowsill where it will get sunlight. Keep the soil moist. Note the length of time it takes for the albino and normal corn seeds to sprout.
4. After the seeds have sprouted, continue to water the corn plants. Observe their growth every few days.

Observations and Conclusions

1. Do the mutant albino seeds sprout as well as the normal seeds? Explain your answer.
2. What happened to the albino plants? Why?

CHAPTER REVIEW

SUMMARY

18-1 History of Genetics

- Genetics is the study of the passing on of characteristics from an organism to its off-spring.

- DNA is the spiral-shaped structure that is the basic substance of heredity.

- Gregor Mendel's work provided the basis for the modern laws of heredity.

- Mendel crossed purebred plants with other purebred plants that had different traits. These plants were the parental generation, or P_1. The trait that appeared in the first, or F_1, generation was called dominant. The trait that disappeared in this generation but reappeared in the second, F_2, generation was called recessive.

- The "stronger" trait is called dominant, while the "weaker" trait is called recessive.

- A purebred trait has genes, or units of heredity, that are alike (TT,tt).

- A hybrid has genes that are different for a trait (Tt).

- According to the law of segregation, one gene from each gene pair goes to each sex cell.

- The law of independent assortment states that each gene pair is inherited independently of all other traits.

- Probability is the chance that something will or will not happen. In probability, the results of one chance event do not affect the results of the next.

- Punnett squares show the possible combinations resulting from a cross between two organisms.

- A phenotype is a visible characteristic, while a genotype is the gene makeup.

18-2 Modern Genetics

- In some gene pairs, niether gene is dominant or recessive. This is known as incomplete dominance.

- Walter Sutton determined that chromosomes carry the hereditary traits.

- A mutation is a sudden change caused by an accidental change in a gene.

- Thomas Hunt Morgan discovered the existence of sex chromosomes. An organism that has two X chromosomes is a female and an organism that has one X and one Y chromosome is a male.

- In genetic engineering, parts of the DNA molecules that make up chromosomes are removed and new parts of genes are added into the chromosomes. They can then be put into living cells, which changes the genetic makeup of the cell.

VOCABULARY

Define each term in a complete sentence.

chromosome	genetics	incomplete dominance	mutation
DNA	genotype	law of independent assortment	phenotype
dominant	hybrid	law of segregation	recessive
gene	hypothesis	meiosis	sex chromosome

CONTENT REVIEW: MULTIPLE CHOICE

Choose the letter of the answer that best completes each statement.

1. The female reproductive structure in garden pea plants is the
   a. pistil.   b. stamen.   c. petal.   d. pollen.
2. If purebred tall plants are crossed with purebred short plants, all of the off-spring will be
   a. TT.   b. Tt.   c. tt.   d. none of these.
3. Hereditary factors that are passed from parent to offspring are found in
   a. mutations.   b. phenotypes.   c. Punnet squares.   d. sex cells.
4. Which have the same phenotypes?
   a. BB and bb   b. Bb and bb   c. BB and Bb   d. all of these
5. In a gene pair, when one gene is neither dominant nor recessive, it is called
   a. segregation.   b. independent assortment.
   c. mutation.   d. incomplete dominance.
6. The cross between two pink four o'clock flowers will produce
   a. ½ pink; ½ white.   b. ½ red; ½ white.
   c. ¼ red; ½ pink; ¼ white.   d. all pink.
7. Hugo De Vries discovered
   a. DNA.   b. genes.   c. mutations.   d. chromosomes.
8. Fruit flies are easy to study because they
   a. are easy to raise.   b. reproduce rapidly.
   c. both a and b   d. neither a nor b
9. How many pairs of chromosomes does a fruit fly have?
   a. 4   b. 12   c. 23   d. 14
10. Who discovered the existence of sex chromosomes?
   a. Gregor Mendel   b. Thomas Hunt Morgan
   c. Walter Sutton   d. Hugo De Vries

CONTENT REVIEW: COMPLETION

Fill in the word or words that best complete each statement.

1. James Watson and Francis Crick discovered the spiral-shaped structure of _____.
2. The male reproductive structure in garden pea plants is the _____.
3. The _____ is the basic unit of heredity.
4. The chance that something will or will not happen is called _____.
5. A(n) _____ is a special chart that shows the possible combinations resulting from a cross of two organisms.
6. The phenotype of a hybrid tall pea plant is _____.
7. The genotype of a purebred tall pea plant is _____.
8. A(n) _____ is a sudden change caused by an accidental change in a gene.
9. The X or Y chromosome is called a(n) _____.
10. The adding of new gene parts into living cells is called _____.

CONTENT REVIEW: TRUE OR FALSE

Determine whether each statement is true or false. If it is true, write "true." If it is false, change the underlined word or words to make the statement true.

1. Modern laws of heredity were established by the work of <u>Walter Sutton</u>.
2. In the genotype Yy, y is the <u>dominant</u> gene.
3. The weaker trait is called the <u>dominant</u> trait.
4. The genotype for a hybrid tall pea plant is <u>TT</u>.
5. A suggested explanation for a scientific problem is a <u>hypothesis</u>.
6. The rod-shaped structures in the nucleus of a cell that carry the code for inherited traits are <u>chromosomes</u>.
7. Sex cells form during the process of <u>meiosis</u>.
8. The law of <u>segregation</u> states that the genes for each gene pair separate during gamete formation.
9. The sperm is an example of a <u>zygote</u>.
10. In fruit flies, an XX zygote is <u>female</u>.

CONCEPT REVIEW: SKILL BUILDING

Use the skills you have developed in the chapter to complete each activity.

1. **Relating facts** Can a short-stemmed pea plant ever be a hybrid? Explain.
2. **Making predictions** A family has four daughters. What is the probability that a fifth child will be a female? Does the fact that the family has four daughters increase their probability of having another daughter? Explain your answer.
3. **Relating concepts** Explain why mutations that do not occur in sex cells are not passed on to future generations.
4. **Making diagrams** Use a Punnett square to show the genotypes of the F₁ generation when a hybrid black (Bb) rabbit is crossed with a purebred brown (bb) rabbit.
5. **Making inferences** If the gene for freckles (F) is dominant over the genes for no freckles (f), what are the possible genotypes of the parents of a child who does not have freckles?
6. **Applying concepts** Short stems (t) are recessive to tall stems (T) in pea plants. Two hybrid pea plants (Tt × Tt) are crossed. One hundred seeds from the two plants are collected and planted. How many of the plants in the next generation can be expected to have tall stems?
7. **Relating facts** A body cell of a mouse has 40 chromosomes. How many chromosomes did the mouse receive from each of its parents? How many chromosomes would one of the mouse's sex cells have?

CONCEPT REVIEW: ESSAY

Discuss each of the following in a brief paragraph.

1. Explain how traits are passed on from one generation to another.
2. Compare dominant and recessive traits.
3. What is the difference between a hybrid organism and a purebred organism?
4. Describe the process of meiosis.
5. Use an example to explain the law of segregation. Then use an example to explain the law of independent assortment.
6. Compare genotypes and phenotypes.
7. Explain how chromosomes determine the sex of an organism.

19 Human Genetics

CHAPTER SECTIONS

19-1 Inheritance in Humans

19-2 New Developments in Human Genetics

CHAPTER OBJECTIVES

After completing this chapter, you will be able to:

19-1 Explain how the basic principles of genetics can be applied to human heredity.

19-1 Relate multiple alleles to the inheritance of human blood groups.

19-1 Identify several inherited diseases.

19-1 Explain sex-linked traits and nondisjunction.

19-2 Define genetic engineering.

19-2 Describe the steps that produce recombinant DNA.

19-2 Discuss four applications of genetic engineering.

If someone told you scientists could make people sprout feathers and robins grow hair, you would probably laugh out loud. When you stopped laughing, you might patiently explain why such events could not possibly take place. "The genes of birds and the genes of people are different," you might say. "And it's genes that determine what a living thing looks like. People don't have genes for feathers. And birds don't have genes for hair."

What if someone told you that the drop of clear liquid pictured on the opposite page was a human chemical made by bacteria? You might think such a statement was even sillier than the one about feathered people and hairy birds. Yet that drop of liquid *is* a human chemical. And it *was* made by bacteria. What is more, to some people it is a life-saving human chemical. How did scientists get bacteria to make it? The answer begins on the next page.

Human insulin produced by bacteria

19-1 Inheritance in Humans

Human beings, like all living things, are what they are because of the genes they inherit from their parents. These genes—and there are about 100,000 of them—are located on the 46 chromosomes in the nucleus of almost every body cell. An exception is the sex cells, which have half the number of chromosomes. The 46 chromosomes consist of 23 pairs. Each pair has matching genes for a particular trait such as eye color, hair color, and earlobe shape.

Because a person gets one matching chromosome from each parent, the person gets matching genes from each parent as well. For example, you received genes for eye color from each of your parents. The way these genes combined in turn determined your eye color.

Another way of expressing what genes do is through body chemistry. Genes tell body cells what chemicals to make and how to make them. These chemicals are proteins. Special proteins called enzymes are responsible for making the pigment, or coloring material, in your eyes.

Other proteins include the red pigment in your blood, which is called hemoglobin. Still another protein is a hormone, or body regulator, called insulin. Each of these proteins plays a key role in human

Figure 19-1 *As is true of all living things, these students inherited their characteristics from their parents.*

health. And each is the object of ongoing research breakthroughs in genetics. **Scientists now know that some of the basic principles of genetics can be applied to human heredity.**

Multiple Alleles

In Chapter 18 you learned that a trait, like the color of a flower, is determined by how a pair of genes act. You learned that one gene in the pair may be dominant or recessive. And the same can be said of the other gene in the pair.

In human beings, some traits are not so easily determined. Skin color, for example, is determined by a blending of four pairs of genes. Various combinations of these eight individual genes can produce all the skin colors of people. Each member of a pair of genes is called an **allele.** In many flowers, there are only two alleles for flower color. In human skin, there are eight alleles for color. So scientists say that the trait of human skin color is determined by **multiple alleles,** or more than two alleles.

The four major human blood groups are also determined by multiple alleles. These groups are called A, B, AB, and O. Scientists know blood groups are determined by multiple alleles because there is no way a single pair of alleles can produce four different characteristics.

Both the allele for group A blood and that for group B blood are dominant. When this combination is inherited—an A from one parent and a B from the other—the child will have AB blood. The O allele, however, is recessive. So a person who inherits an O and an A allele will have group A blood. A person who inherits an O and a B will have group B blood. What two alleles must a person inherit to have group O blood?

Inherited Diseases

Sometimes the structure of an inherited gene contains an error. If the gene controls the production of an important protein, like hemoglobin, the hemoglobin will also have an error in its structure. In such a case, the hemoglobin may not do its job well. This is an example of what scientists call an **inherited disease**.

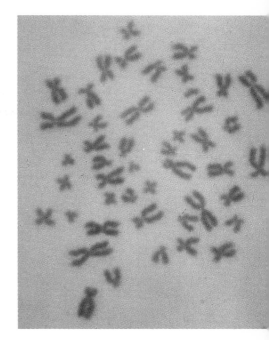

Figure 19-2 *In this photograph, you can see some of the 23 chromosome pairs that are found in human cells.*

Figure 19-3 *Your blood group is determined by multiple alleles. What combination of alleles must a person inherit to have group B blood?*

BLOOD GROUP ALLELES

Blood groups	Combination of Alleles
A	AA or AO
B	BB or BO
AB	AB
O	OO

Career: *Genetic Counselor*

Human genetics is one of the fastest changing fields in medical science today. This is because the knowledge of genetic diseases has advanced so rapidly in the last 10 years. Although there is still more to be discovered, much information has been learned about genetic disorders, such as Down's syndrome and sickle-cell anemia.

Unfortunately, although there are doctors who specialize in genetic disorders, they often do not have enough time to explain to patients and family members about a genetic disorder. Instead, **genetic counselors** provide this information. Genetic counselors talk with parents who are concerned that they might be carrying genes for a disease or trait that they could pass on to their children.

Most jobs for genetic counselors are found in medical centers and teaching hospitals. In addition to providing support services to families, counselors also become resource people for the public or do research in the field of medical genetics. Those interested in this fascinating and rewarding career can write to the March of Dimes, Birth Defects Foundation, 1275 Mamaroneck Avenue, White Plains, NY 10605.

Although some inherited diseases can be treated, until recently there was no hope of actually curing them. Because to cure an inherited disease meant correcting the error in a gene. And no one knew how to do this. Then, in early 1982, a group of scientists at the University of California at San Francisco performed the first successful "operation" on a damaged human gene.

The gene is responsible for making a part of the human hemoglobin molecule. When this gene is damaged, the part never gets made. In human beings, this causes a very serious inherited blood disease called **beta thalassemia** (thal-uh-SEE-mee-uh). The scientists in California reasoned that if they could repair the gene, it would produce regular hemoglobin. The gene then could be put into blood-forming cells in a person with beta thalassemia. A person might be cured of the disease through this procedure.

Using a special technique, the scientists were able to repair the damaged gene. But would it produce normal parts for a molecule of human hemoglobin? To answer this question, the scientists put the repaired gene into selected frog cells. Scientists then analyzed what the cells produced. Sure enough, one of the products was a perfect part for human hemoglobin. But the scientists said that it was a long way from being successful with frog cells to curing a human disease. Nevertheless, the first step was taken toward such a cure.

Another widespread inherited blood disorder is **sickle-cell anemia**. This disorder occurs when a person inherits a damaged gene for the manufacture of hemoglobin from each parent. These genes are recessive and, among other things, cause red blood cells to become sickle shaped. See Figure 19-4. Sickle-shaped red blood cells can block up tiny blood vessels, which can cause damage to body tissues. Also, sickle-shaped cells cannot transport oxygen nearly as well as regular red blood cells.

Like beta thalassemia, sickle-cell anemia might be curable if the damaged genes that cause it could be repaired. In the early 1980s, scientists discovered a chemical that could slightly change the structure of

Activity

Human Genetic Disorders

Using reference materials in the library, find out about Klinefelter's syndrome, Turner's syndrome, phenylketonuria, and Tay-Sachs disease. Write a report on these disorders.

In your report, include how these genes are inherited, the symptoms of the disorder, and the treatment that is available for the disorder. Include a drawing on posterboard to show how each disorder is inherited.

Figure 19-4 *The normal donutlike shape of red blood cells* (left) *becomes sickle shaped* (right) *in people who suffer from sickle-cell anemia. These electron micrographs have been magnified 5555 times.*

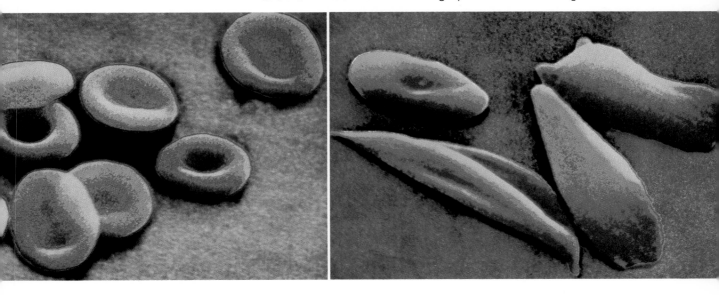

Spread of Hemophilia

Using reference materials in the library, find out about the presence of hemophilia in the descendants of Queen Victoria in England. On posterboard, draw a family tree that traces the spread of hemophilia through the royal families of Europe.

Figure 19-5 *In male pattern baldness, hair loss results from the combination of an inherited trait and the effects of a male hormone.*

genes. It was just this structure that needed to be changed to get people with sickle-cell anemia and those with beta thalassemia to produce greater amounts of regular hemoglobin. In December of 1982, scientists at three different hospitals in the United States did just that. They reported that they had given the chemical to three patients with sickle-cell anemia and three patients with beta thalassemia. Every patient's condition improved. But again, the scientists cautioned that more tests would have to be performed before the chemical could be tried with large groups of patients. Then, if the tests proved successful, these diseases would be curable.

Sex-Linked Traits

You will remember from Chapter 18 that X and Y chromosomes are sex chromosomes. The X and Y chromosomes are the only chromosome pair that do not always match each other. All body cells of normal human males carry one X chromosome and one Y chromosome. Females have two matching X chromosomes, or XX.

X chromosomes also carry genes for traits other than sex. However, Y chromosomes carry few if any genes other than those for maleness. Therefore, any gene—even a recessive gene—carried on an X chromosome will produce a trait in a male who inherits the gene. That is because there is no matching gene on the Y chromosome. Such traits are known as **sex-linked traits** because they are passed from parent to child on a sex chromosome, the X chromosome. Because a female has two X chromosomes, a recessive gene on one X chromosome can be masked, or hidden, by a dominant gene on the other X chromosome.

An example of a sex-linked recessive trait is **hemophilia** (hee-muh-FI-li-uh). Hemophilia is an inherited disease that causes the blood to clot slowly or not at all. This disease was very common in the royal families of Europe. During the nineteenth century, Queen Victoria of England had a son and three grandsons with hemophilia. At least two of her daughters and four of her granddaughters carried the gene for hemophilia on one X chromosome. But they did not have the disease because they carried a

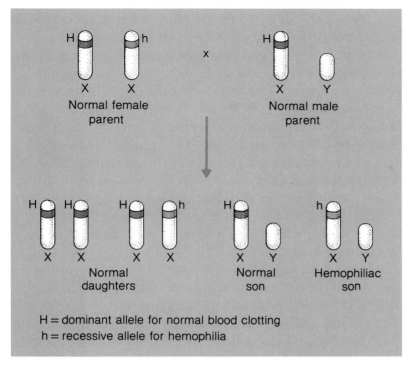

Figure 19-6 *There is a 25-percent chance that a female who carries a gene for hemophilia and a normal male will have a male child with hemophilia.*

regular gene on their other X chromosome. Hemophilia spread through the royal families in Europe as Victoria's descendants married other royalty and passed the hemophilia gene on.

Colorblindness is another sex-linked recessive trait. For this reason, there are more males who are colorblind than there are females. A female has to inherit *two* recessive genes for colorblindness. A male has to inherit *one* such gene. The most common type of colorblindness involves difficulty in distinguishing between the colors red and green.

Nondisjunction

As you remember from Chapter 18, meiosis is the process through which sex cells are formed. During meiosis, chromosome pairs usually separate, but in rare cases a pair may remain joined. This failure of chromosomes to separate is known as **nondisjunction** (nahn-dis-JUNK-shuhn). When this happens, body cells inherit either extra chromosomes or fewer chromosomes than is normal.

Figure 19-7 *In addition to hemophilia, colorblindness is another sex-linked trait. Very few females are colorblind because a female has two X chromosomes. So a recessive gene on one X chromosome can be hidden by a dominant gene on the other X chromosome.*

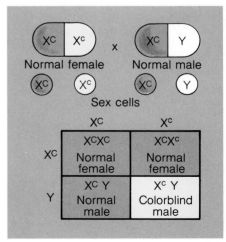

433

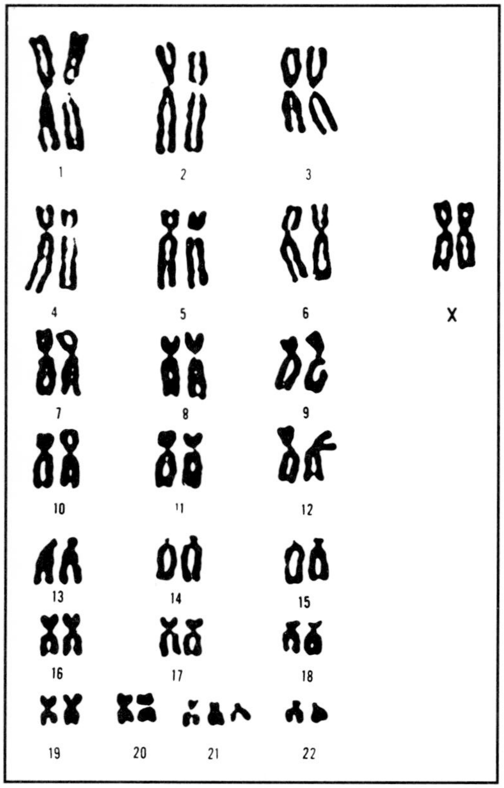

Look carefully at Figure 19-8. This is an example of a human karyotype. A karyotype shows the size, number, and shape of chromosomes in an organism. How many chromosomes are there? If you said 47, you are correct. The extra chromosome is found in what would normally be the twenty-first *pair*. Such a group of three chromosomes is called a trisomy (tri-SOH-mee). When the twenty-first pair of chromosomes becomes a trisomy, a condition called **Down's syndrome** results. People with Down's syndrome may have various physical problems and some degree of mental retardation. However, many people with Down's syndrome hold jobs and provide important contributions to society.

Is there a way of determining before a child is born whether it will have Down's syndrome or another inherited problem? There are a number of ways. One, called **amniocentesis** (am-nee-oh-sen-TEE-sis), involves taking a little bit of fluid out of the sac that surrounds a baby while it is still in its mother. This fluid contains some of the baby's cells. Using special techniques, doctors and scientists can examine the chromosomes of the cells. By doing this they can, for example, discover whether an unborn child does or does not have Down's syndrome. Various other tests can reveal the presence of a wide variety of inherited disorders. Scientists hope that such tests will eventually lead to the treatment of some disorders before babies are born.

Figure 19-8 *Down's syndrome, or trisomy-21, is a condition in which all the body cells have an extra twenty-first chromosome. What is the total number of chromosomes in the body cells of a person with Down's syndrome?*

Figure 19-9 *Although people with Down's syndrome are physically challenged, many can still lead full, active lives.*

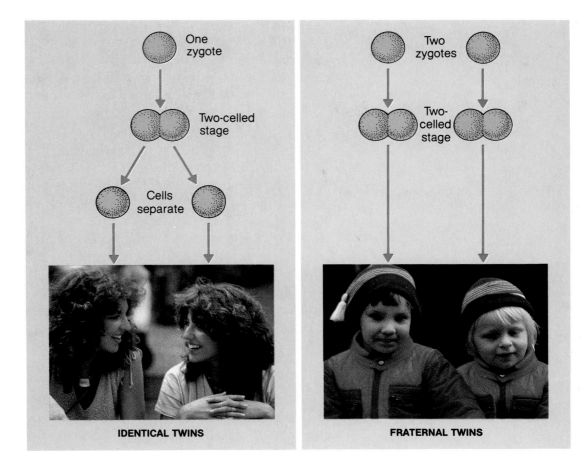

IDENTICAL TWINS

FRATERNAL TWINS

Figure 19-10 *Because identical twins develop from the division of one zygote, they have the exact same chromosomes and are always of the same sex. Fraternal twins develop from two different zygotes and, therefore, do not have to be of the same sex.*

Heredity and Environment

Most people would readily agree that such physical characteristics as straight or curly hair or skin and eye color are inherited. But what about such physical characteristics as muscle tone or height? It is very likely that a tendency to firm muscle tone is inherited. At the same time, exercise or lack of it can mean the difference between firmer or softer muscle. Height is also an inherited trait. But people only grow to their full height when they receive a proper diet. And diet is a factor that is always determined by the environment.

The roles of heredity and environment are easier to evaluate in organisms that have the same or similar heredity. To do this in humans, scientists often study identical twins. Identical twins are genetically identical. Fraternal twins are not genetically identical. Therefore, most differences between identical twins are the result of environmental factors.

Recent studies of identical twins who were separated at birth or at an early age suggest that more of human behavior may be inherited than was previously thought. Surprisingly, some of the twins studied were found to have very similar behavior.

SECTION REVIEW

1. What are the members of a gene pair called?
2. Name the multiple alleles that determine blood groups.
3. What are two sex-linked diseases?
4. What is one way of determining if an unborn child will have Down's syndrome?

19-2 New Developments in Human Genetics

During the mid-1970s, scientists discovered how to transfer DNA from the cells of one organism to the cells of another organism. The new piece of combined DNA is known as **recombinant DNA,** and the technique is called **genetic engineering.**

Genetic engineering is the process in which genes, or parts of DNA, from one organism are transferred into another organism. A common example of genetic engineering is the transfer of DNA from a complex organism, such as a human, into a simpler organism, such as a bacterium. As the bacterium reproduces, copies of the recombinant DNA are passed on from one generation to the next.

Making Recombinant DNA

Scientists use a special process to make recombinant DNA. Let's use human and bacterial DNA as examples to illustrate this process. Some bacterial DNA comes in the form of a ring called a **plasmid.** You might think of this as an unbroken circle of rope. Using special techniques, a scientist snips open the "rope." The scientist then removes a short piece of DNA from a human cell. You might think of this as a short length of rope. The scientist "ties" this

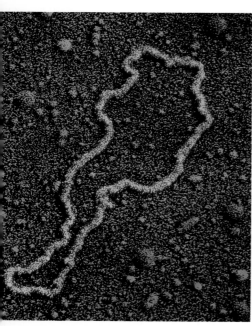

Figure 19-11 *This electron micrograph of a plasmid, or ringlike form of DNA, contains more bits of information than a home computer.*

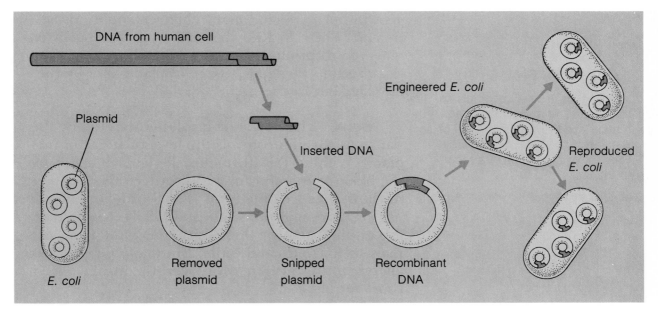

Figure 19-12 *During the formation of recombinant DNA, a plasmid from a bacterium, such as E. coli, is snipped open. A short piece is then removed from the DNA of a human cell. This piece is inserted into the snipped plasmid. And the plasmid is placed back into the bacterium.*

length of "rope" to the cut ends of the bacterial DNA. Now the bacterial DNA forms a circle again. But this DNA circle has something new in it: directions for making a human protein!

Finally, the scientist puts this combined DNA back into the bacterial cell. What happens now? If all goes well, the bacterium *and all its offspring* will produce the human protein that the piece of human DNA holds instructions for.

Products of Recombinant DNA

Scientists use recombinant DNA to turn certain bacteria and yeast cells into "factories" that make human protein. The organisms are grown in huge containers where they produce large amounts of human proteins. Many of these proteins are needed to treat human disorders. Before genetic engineering, proteins such as the following were very hard or impossible to make.

HUMAN GROWTH HORMONE Human growth hormone is a chemical messenger produced in the brain that controls growth. A lack of this hormone prevents people from growing normally. Until 1981, children who did not have enough human growth hormone were given injections of the hormone. However, there was only a limited supply of human growth hormone and many children could not be treated. Then, in 1982, bacteria were genetically engineered to produce human growth hormone. Soon, this precious hormone will be available, not by the milliliter but by the barrel!

INSULIN The hormone insulin is secreted by the pancreas. Insulin controls the level of sugar in the blood. Without this hormone, the level of sugar in the blood rises and causes a disorder called diabetes mellitus. The treatment for this disorder can involve one or more injections of insulin daily. In the past, the insulin used for these injections came from animals such as pigs and cattle. But many people were allergic to this insulin. Moreover, the insulin was in short supply.

Then a few years ago, human insulin was produced by genetically engineered bacteria. In 1980, a person suffering from diabetes was successfully injected with bacterially produced insulin for the first time! Scientists expect that this insulin will be plentiful, will not cause allergies, and will be inexpensive. By the way, that drop of clear fluid in the picture at the beginning of this chapter is bacterially produced human insulin.

Figure 19-13 *This 800-liter container is used to manufacture large amounts of recombinant DNA. The DNA is used to make the hepatitis B vaccine.*

Figure 19-14 *These two flasks contain blood cells that are used to produce interferon. The white balls act as insulators.*

INTERFERON　Another human substance produced by bacteria through recombinant DNA is interferon. Interferon is normally produced by human body cells and helps cells fight viruses that enter the body.

How does interferon fight viruses? When a virus enters a cell, the cell produces interferon. Interferon then leaves the infected cell and "alerts" the surrounding cells to produce their own antiviral chemicals. For a long time, scientists believed that interferon could be used to treat many viral infections of human beings and, perhaps, even cancer. But there was not enough interferon available to test this idea. However, scientists are now able to produce interferon from genetically engineered bacteria. And many experiments are underway to discover whether interferon can be used as a new weapon against human diseases.

SECTION REVIEW

1. What technique transfers parts of DNA?
2. What is the ringlike form of DNA called?
3. Name three human substances that are genetically engineered by bacteria.

LABORATORY ACTIVITY

Dominant and Recessive Traits

Purpose

In this activity, you will examine the phenotype, or visible characteristics, of dominant and recessive human genes.

Trait	Number of Students in Class	Number of Students Demonstrating Trait	Number of Students Not Demonstrating Trait	Percentage Demonstrating Trait	Percentage Not Demonstrating Trait
Tongue: roll					
Hair color: dark					
Handedness: right					
Earlobe: attached					
Widow's peak: none					

Procedure

1. On a sheet of paper, copy the chart shown. The dominant traits are the ability to roll your tongue into a U shape, dark hair, and right-handedness. Earlobes attached directly to the side of your head and lack of a widow's peak are recessive traits. A widow's peak is a hairline that forms a distinct point in the center of the forehead.
2. Count the total number of students present in the class. Record this number in the appropriate column.
3. Count the number of your classmates that demonstrate or do not demonstrate each trait listed. Fill in the numbers for each trait on your chart.

4. To determine the percentage of students demonstrating each trait, divide the number who have the trait by the total number of students in your class and multiply by 100.
5. Determine the percentage of students not demonstrating each trait. Fill in the percentages on your chart.

Observations and Conclusions

1. Which traits are most common in your class? Least common?
2. Do any students have traits that are intermediate between the dominant and recessive trait? If so, how do you account for these intermediate traits?

CHAPTER REVIEW

SUMMARY

19-1 Inheritance in Humans

■ Human beings have genes, which are located on the 46 chromosomes. There are 23 pairs of chromosomes found in the nucleus of all human body cells, except the sex cells.

■ Genes tell body cells what chemicals to make and how to make them.

■ In human beings, each member of a gene pair is called an allele.

■ Many human traits such as skin color and blood groups are controlled by multiple alleles, or more than two alleles.

■ Beta thalassemia and sickle-cell anemia are inherited blood diseases. They are caused by a damaged gene that is responsible for making hemoglobin.

■ Any gene, even a recessive gene, carried on the X chromosome will produce a trait in a male who inherits the gene. This is known as a sex-linked trait.

■ Hemophilia and colorblindness are examples of sex-linked traits. Hemophilia is a disease that causes the blood to clot slowly or not at all. Colorblindness is a disorder that involves difficulty in distinguishing between certain colors.

■ Nondisjunction of the twenty-first chromosome pair causes Down's syndrome.

■ Some inherited disorders, such as Down's syndrome, can be detected before a child is born. In amniocentesis, fluid containing a baby's cells is removed from the sac that surrounds a baby while it is still in its mother. The cell's chromosomes are then examined for any abnormality.

■ Scientists often study identical twins to try to find out the roles of heredity and environment in human development.

19-2 New Developments in Human Genetics

■ In recombinant DNA, parts of DNA are transferred from one organism to another. As the organism reproduces, so does the recombined DNA, passing new genetic information to its offspring.

■ Genetic engineering is the technique of recombining DNA.

■ The ringlike shape of DNA in some bacteria is called a plasmid.

■ Using recombinant DNA techniques, scientists have been able to get certain bacteria and yeast cells to produce such human proteins as human growth hormone, insulin, and interferon. Before genetic engineering, these proteins were very hard or impossible to make.

VOCABULARY

Define each term in a complete sentence.

allele
amniocentesis
beta thalassemia
colorblindness
Down's syndrome

genetic engineering
hemophilia
inherited disease
multiple allele
nondisjunction

plasmid
recombinant DNA
sex-linked trait
sickle-cell anemia

CONTENT REVIEW: MULTIPLE CHOICE

Choose the letter of the answer that best completes each statement.

1. How many pairs of chromosomes do most human body cells contain?
   a. 46   b. 36   c. 18   d. 23

2. A hereditary disease in which the red blood cells are crescent-shaped is
   a. hemophilia.   b. colorblindness.
   c. sickle-cell anemia.   d. beta thalassemia.

3. In humans, which chromosome combination is that of a female?
   a. XX   b. YY   c. XY   d. any of these

4. What is the probability that a human will be a male?
   a. 1/1   b. 1/2   c. 1/4   d. 1/8

5. Which chromosome carries the gene for colorblindness in humans?
   a. X   b. Y   c. 15th   d. 21st

6. What is the total number of chromsomes in a body cell of a person with Down's syndrome?
   a. 22   b. 23   c. 46   d. 47

7. Some genetic diseases can be detected before a baby is born by
   a. genetic engineering.   b. amniocentesis.
   c. nondisjunction.   d. recombinant DNA.

8. Bacteria that produce human insulin were developed by
   a. nondisjunction.   b. genetic engineering.
   c. amniocentesis.   d. multiple allele.

9. A protein produced by cells that have been attacked by a virus is called
   a. insulin.   b. interferon.
   c. human growth hormone.   d. hemoglobin.

10. Which substance is *not* being produced by genetic engineering?
   a. insulin   b. interferon
   c. hemoglobin   d. human growth hormone

CONTENT REVIEW: COMPLETION

Fill in the word or words that best complete each statement.

1. In humans, there are _____ pairs of chromsomes.

2. If a person inherits an A allele and an O allele, he or she will have group _____ blood.

3. The ringlike form of DNA is called a(n) _____.

4. An organism with two X chromosomes is a _____.

5. Colorblindness and _____ are examples of sex-linked diseases.

6. The failure of a gene to separate during meiosis is _____.

7. The condition caused by the presence of an extra chromsome on the twenty-first pair is known as _____.

8. Studies of identical twins who have been raised separately have been used to compare the effects of heredity and _____.

9. _____ is a genetic disease that causes red blood cells to be crescent shaped.

10. The hormone that controls the level of sugar in the blood is _____.

442

CONTENT REVIEW: TRUE OR FALSE

Determine whether each statement is true or false. If it is true, write "true." If it is false, change the underlined word or words to make the statement true.

1. An <u>allele</u> is a gene for a single trait.
2. The inheritance of blood groups is controlled by <u>double</u> alleles.
3. Hemophilia is an example of a <u>sex-linked</u> disease.
4. In humans, hemophilia is linked to the <u>Y</u> chromosome.
5. The failure of chromosomes to separate during meiosis is <u>recombinant DNA</u>.
6. A <u>karyotype</u> shows the size, number, and shape of chromosomes in an organism.
7. Colorblindness is most common in <u>males</u>.
8. In <u>nondisjunction</u>, some of the fluid that surrounds a developing baby is removed and examined.
9. The transferred parts of DNA that joined to the DNA of a receiving organism are known as <u>recombinant DNA</u>.
10. Insulin, <u>interferon</u>, and human growth hormone are human substances that can be produced by <u>genetic engineering</u>.

CONCEPT REVIEW: SKILL BUILDING

Use the skills you have developed in the chapter to complete each activity.

1. **Making predictions** Mrs. Booth has the genotype BB for blood group. Mr. Booth has the genotype AO. Predict the possible blood groups of their children.
2. **Sequencing events** In the diagram below, the steps used to make recombinant DNA are represented. However, the sequence in the diagram is wrong. What is the proper order for the steps? Describe what is happening in each step.

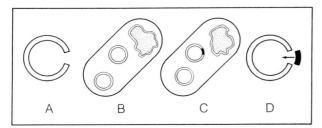

3. **Relating facts** In many parts of the world, people are not allowed to marry close relatives. Relate this fact to the inheritance of genetic diseases.
4. **Relating concepts** Explain why it is difficult for researchers to determine whether a personality trait such as shyness can be inherited.
5. **Applying concepts** Many people are concerned about the introduction of new organisms into the environment through genetic engineering. These people believe that the organisms may prove harmful to the environment or to other living things. What guidelines would you develop concerning the introduction of genetically engineered organisms into the environment?

CONCEPT REVIEW: ESSAY

Discuss each of the following in a brief paragraph.

1. Explain how blood group is determined in humans.
2. Describe two inherited blood diseases.
3. Use an example to explain how a sex-linked trait is inherited.
4. How can an inherited trait be affected by a person's environment? Give an example.
5. Describe three applications of recombinant DNA technology.

20 Changes in Living Things Over Time

CHAPTER SECTIONS

20-1 Change Over Time
20-2 Natural Selection
20-3 Migration and Isolation
20-4 Change: Rapid or Slow?

CHAPTER OBJECTIVES

After completing this chapter, you will be able to:

20-1 Define evolution.

20-1 Describe both anatomical and fossil evidence of evolution.

20-2 Explain how natural selection can lead to new and varied species.

20-2 Describe the effects of over-production and variation on natural selection.

20-3 Explain how migration and isolation affect evolution.

20-4 Explain how evolution can occur slowly or in relatively rapid bursts.

In 1802, a Massachusetts farm boy named Pliny Moody came upon something quite amazing. While on a quiet walk in the Connecticut River Valley, Moody discovered what appeared to be the footprints of a giant bird set in sandstone. But no one had ever seen a bird with such large feet. Many years later the tracks were scientifically identified. They were made by a small dinosaur, a group of reptiles that lived about 200 million years ago.

Two hundred million years may seem like an eternity to you. But it is really a small amount of time when compared to the total age of Earth. Scientists estimate Earth to be about 4.6 billion years old. During Earth's long history, both the planet and the organisms on it have gone through considerable changes.

Perhaps all the events that have occurred on Earth over such an unimaginable span of time can be better understood if they are viewed as having taken place in the span of a year. Using this time scale, each day would represent 12.3 million years. Starting from January, the first forms of life on Earth would not have appeared until early May. The dinosaur whose prints were found by Pliny Moody would not have arrived until early December. Mammals would not have existed until mid-December. And humans as they now look would have made their first appearance on Earth one hour before midnight, on the last day of the year!

Earth 200 million years ago

20-1 Change Over Time

The quagga vanished from its home in South Africa about 100 years ago. Descriptions of the animal paint a strange picture. The quagga had stripes like a zebra. But the stripes covered only its head, neck, and the front part of its body. Was this animal closely related to the zebra? Or was it a completely different kind of creature?

Scientists often asked these and similar questions about other animals and plants that appeared to be closely related. The scientists knew that in one way or another all living things are related to each other. But which are more closely related and which are only distantly related?

Today, scientists believe that a process known as **evolution** holds the key to these answers. **Evolution is a change in a species over time.** The word "evolution" comes from Latin and means "to unfold or open out." A scientific way to say the same thing is

Figure 20-1 *The quagga is a South African mammal that became extinct about 100 years ago. Notice the stripes on its head, neck, and front part of its body.*

descent with modification. "Descent" means to come from something that lived before. And "modification" means a change. So in simple terms, evolution means that all living things that ever inhabited Earth are changed forms of living things that came before.

There is a tremendous amount of scientific evidence to support the idea of evolution. You will be able to examine this evidence for yourself in the pages of this chapter. This evidence has allowed scientists to develop the *theory of evolution.* A scientific theory is a very powerful and useful idea. It is an explanation of facts and observations. Moreover, it is an explanation that has been tested many times by many scientists. If a scientific theory fails a test, the theory is modified or discarded. Scientific theories also let scientists make predictions of future events. If these predictions come true, the theory passes a key test.

What does all this have to do with the relationship between quaggas and zebras? Among other things, the theory of evolution predicts that the more closely related two living things are, the more similar the structure of their DNA molecules will be. In 1984, Dr. Allan Wilson of the University of California at Berkeley analyzed DNA taken from the muscle tissue attached to the preserved skin of a quagga. The skin had been stored for more than a hundred years in a German museum. Dr. Wilson also analyzed DNA taken from a modern-day plains zebra. He found that the structure of the DNA in the two samples was 95 percent identical! Dr. Wilson was then able to conclude that the quagga and the plains zebra were indeed close relatives who shared a common ancestor about 3 million years ago. Thus, both the quagga and the plains zebra are examples of evolution, or descent with modification, from an animal that lived during an earlier time.

How did these animals change? And why do some animals survive while others die off? During the history of life on this planet, chance mutations of genes produce new or slightly modified living things. Most of these new living things cannot compete with other organisms and soon die off. However, some new life forms do not die off. Instead, these life forms survive and reproduce because they just happen to meet the demands of their environment

Figure 20-2 *This photograph shows a plains zebra that lives in South Africa. How is a zebra similar to a quagga?*

Activity

Dating Fossils

The most accurate means of dating fossils was developed after scientists discovered that certain elements undergo a process known as radioactive decay. During radioactive decay, the atoms of an element break apart at a fixed rate. Using library and other reference materials, write a short report on the various ways radioactive decay can be used to date fossils. Be sure to include the term half-life in your report. Also include the types of radioactive elements that are the most accurate indicators of fossil ages.

447

Figure 20-3 *This drawing shows a variety of organisms that inhabited Earth thousands of years ago. As their environments changed, many of them could not survive and became extinct.*

better than other organisms. Because of this process, many living things that inhabit our planet today did not exist millions of years ago.

Anatomical Evidence of Change

Chemical similarities in DNA molecules are only one kind of evidence of evolution. Seven years after Pliny Moody discovered the "big bird" footprints, a biologist in France named Jean-Baptiste de Lamarck began to develop some theories about evolution.

In his book *Philosophie zoologique*, Lamarck suggested that species that now seem very different can be proven by close study to have developed from the same ancestors. All forms of life could be organized into one vast "family tree," he thought. All of Lamarck's theories were based on the evidence of

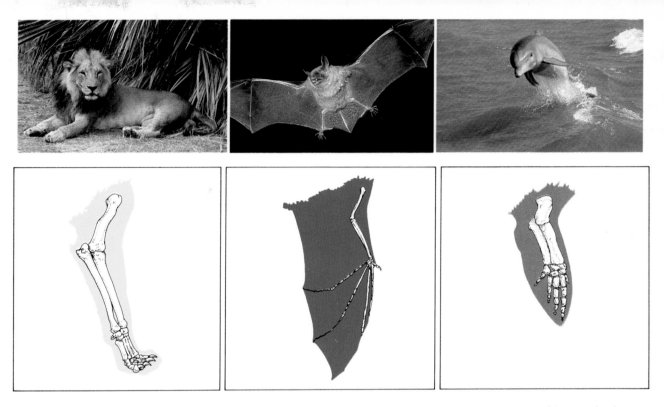

Figure 20-4 *Notice that the arrangement and number of bones in the forelegs of the lion* (left), *bat* (center), *and dolphin* (right) *are similiar. These parts are said to be homologous.*

anatomy, which is the study of the physical structure of living things.

In Figure 20-4, look at the bones of a lion's foreleg, a bat's wing, and a dolphin's flipper. Like Lamarck, can you see any similarities in the shape and arrangement of the bones of these animals? When body parts and organs are similar in *structure*, they are said to be **homologous** (hom-MAH-luh-guhs). Although certain parts of Lamarck's theories have been disproven, his idea that animals that have homologous structures are closely related still seems true.

Fossil Evidence of Change

Believe it or not, whales or their whalelike ancestors once walked! The evidence that these huge mammals once lumbered across land lies in the fact that they possess the bone structure of long lost hind legs. However, such anatomical evidence alone could not have convinced the majority of scientists that whales once walked, if it were not for the added evidence of **fossils**.

Figure 20-5 *Fossils are remains or imprints of plants or animals that lived many years ago. The imprint of the leaves of the maidenhair tree is an example of a fossil.*

Fossils are the imprints or remains of plants or animals that existed in the past. In 1983, fossil hunters found a buried skull belonging to an animal that had lived more than 50 million years ago. The skull was very similar to that of a whale. But the bony structure that allowed the animal to hear could not have worked underwater. Scientists believe that this whalelike skull belonged to a land-living ancestor of today's whales. Similar kinds of fossil evidence allow scientists to trace the evolution of many of the world's living things.

Reading the Fossil Record

A ride on muleback into the Grand Canyon is a descent to a time 2 billion years ago. The canyon is the deepest visible crack in the earth's land surface. Its stacked layers of **sedimentary rock** tell the history of life on Earth. Sedimentary rock is a type of rock formed from layers of mud and sand that harden slowly over time. Even the canyon's topmost sedimentary rock layer is 200 million years old. By the time you reach the layer at the bottom, you are looking at rocks that were formed 2 billion years ago. Many of the layers of these rocks hold the fossils of plants and animals that lived when the layers were first formed.

Clearly, the lower layers are older than the upper layers. So the fossils found in the upper layers are of plants and animals that lived more recently. Using this knowledge, scientists have studied fossils in various rock layers all over the world to reconstruct the story of life on this planet. All the fossil evidence scientists have collected forms what is known as the **fossil record.** The fossil record is the most complete biological record of life on Earth.

Here is an example of how scientists read the fossil record. Some years ago in the Mississippi River Valley scientists found the fossil bones of a leg and a foot of an unknown animal. The fossils were in a deposit of sedimentary rock. From the bones, scientists discovered that the animal had four toes on each of its front feet. Moreover, the toes were spread apart.

The discovery of other fossils in the same sedimentary layer helped scientists piece together what the entire animal probably looked like. It was about

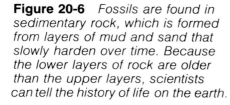

Figure 20-6 *Fossils are found in sedimentary rock, which is formed from layers of mud and sand that slowly harden over time. Because the lower layers of rock are older than the upper layers, scientists can tell the history of life on the earth.*

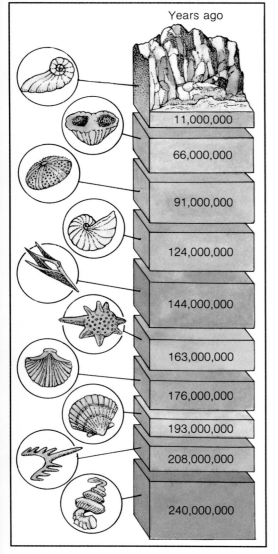

Years ago

11,000,000

66,000,000

91,000,000

124,000,000

144,000,000

163,000,000

176,000,000

193,000,000

208,000,000

240,000,000

Figure 20-7 Eohippus, *or "early horse," lived about 50 million years ago. Notice the four toes on its forelegs and the three toes on its hindlegs.*

the size of a modern-day cat. But except for its small size, short teeth, and four toes, it looked a lot like a horse. Scientists named it *Eohippus*, meaning "dawn horse," or "early horse." Using special techniques, the scientists were able to measure the age of the rock layer in which *Eohippus* was found. The rock layer was about 50 million years old and, therefore, so was *Eohippus*.

From the fossils of plants and animals found in the same layer of sedimentary rock as *Eohippus*, scientists also were able to tell what the Mississippi River Valley may have been like when *Eohippus* lived. Most of the other fossils found in the *Eohippus* layer resemble plants and animals that live in warm, wet climates today. This is evidence that *Eohippus* probably lived in a tropical climate, surrounded by swamps and mud.

Spread-apart toes are very useful for walking on soft mud. They spread an animal's mass over a large area, almost like snowshoes or skis. The structure of *Eohippus's* foot was well suited to the kind of surroundings in which it lived.

Today's horse spends most of its life on dry, hard ground. Its single hard hoof lessens the shock of walking more than four spread toes could ever do. The modern horse also has larger teeth than *Eohippus*. As a result, it can chew the tough, dry grasses of the prairie.

Figure 20-8 *The process by which many different species develop from a common ancestor such as the cotylosaur, is called adaptive radiation.*

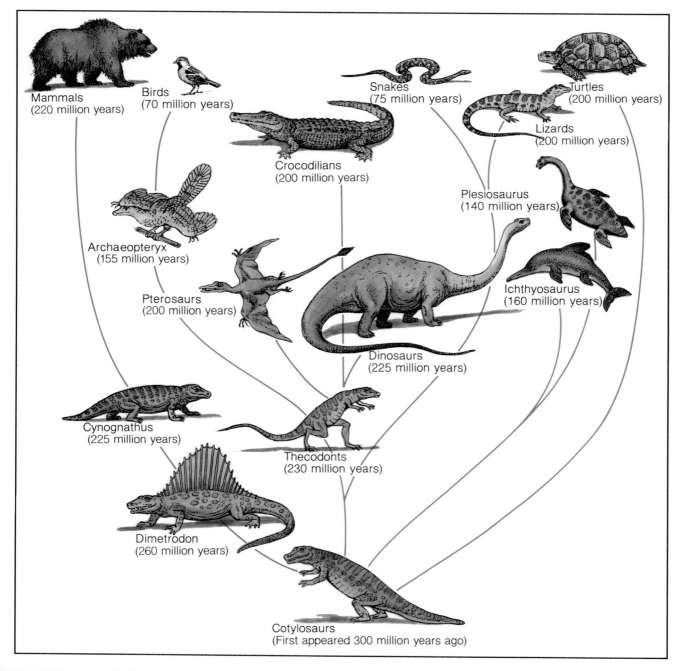

Mammals
(220 million years)

Birds
(70 million years)

Snakes
(75 million years)

Turtles
(200 million years)

Crocodilians
(200 million years)

Lizards
(200 million years)

Archaeopteryx
(155 million years)

Plesiosaurus
(140 million years)

Pterosaurs
(200 million years)

Ichthyosaurus
(160 million years)

Dinosaurs
(225 million years)

Cynognathus
(225 million years)

Thecodonts
(230 million years)

Dimetrodon
(260 million years)

Cotylosaurs
(First appeared 300 million years ago)

Scientists conclude that the fossils of *Eohippus* and other plants and animals are evidence that generations of species go through changes. A plant or animal with a new kind of trait may first come into being, perhaps as a result of a mutation. If the change happens to make it easier for the organism to survive in its surroundings, then it will have a chance to pass this new trait on to its offspring.

A change that increases an organism's chances of survival is known as an **adaptation.** The feet of *Eohippus* were well adapted to walking on soft, wet ground, but not to walking on hard earth. Perhaps a change in the climate of the Mississippi River Valley millions of years ago dried up the land. If so, animals with hooves would have been better adapted to the land than was *Eohippus*. *Eohippus* may have become **extinct,** or died out, because of this. Over large spans of time, so many small adaptations may occur that a species will no longer resemble its ancient ancestors. Such major adaptations require many generations. Gradually, a new species forms.

SECTION REVIEW

1. Name the theory that describes change in a species over time.
2. List two kinds of evidence of evolution.
3. What is an adaptation?
4. What term is used to describe a species that no longer exists?

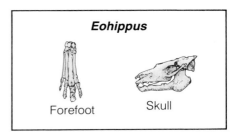

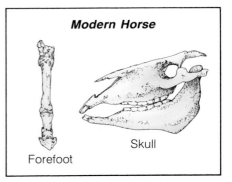

Figure 20-9 *By comparing the bones of* Eohippus *(top) to the bones of a modern horse (center), scientists have learned how the horse has evolved over the last 50 million years.* Eohippus *looked very different from the kind of horse you see today (bottom).*

20-2 Natural Selection

The Galapagos Islands rise out of the Pacific Ocean about 1000 kilometers from the west coast of South America. The islands received their name from the giant Galapagos tortoises that live there. The tortoises' long necks, wrinkled skin, and mud-caked shells make them look like prehistoric creatures. Sharing the islands with the tortoises are many other animals, including penguins, long-necked diving birds called cormorants, and large, crested lizards called iguanas.

The most striking thing about the animals of Galapagos is the ways in which they differ from related species on the mainland of South America. For example, the iguanas on Galapagos have extra large claws that allow them to keep their grip on slippery rocks, where they feed on seaweed. On the mainland, the same animals have smaller claws. Smaller claws allow the mainland iguanas to climb trees, where they feed on leaves.

In 1832, a young British student named Charles Darwin set sail for a five-year voyage at sea on a ship called the *Beagle*. Serving as the ship's naturalist, Darwin studied animals and plants at every stop the ship made. When Darwin arrived at the Galapagos, he soon noticed many of the differences between island and mainland creatures. As he compared the animals on the mainland to those on the islands, he realized something very special. It appeared that each animal was perfectly adapted to survival in its particular environment. Darwin took many notes on his observations. For the next 20 years he tried to find an underlying theory that could explain his observations. Then, in 1858, Darwin and another British biologist named Alfred Wallace presented a new and exciting concept—the theory of evolution.

Figure 20-10 *The most interesting thing about the animals of the Galapagos Islands is the ways in which they differ from related species on the mainland of South America. These tortoises (left) inhabit the Galapagos Islands, while this tortoise (right) is from the mainland.*

Figure 20-11 *Compare a typical iguana* (left) *from the South American mainland to the marine iguana from the Galapagos* (right).

This theory was enlarged by Darwin in a book entitled *Origin of Species.* In this book, Darwin presented one entirely new idea—the concept of **natural selection.** Darwin used this concept to explain the theory of evolution. **Natural selection is the survival and reproduction of those organisms best adapted to their surroundings.** To understand natural selection, you must first learn about the role of overproduction in nature.

Overproduction and Natural Selection

Anyone who carefully observes nature will notice that many species seem to produce more offspring than can be supported by the environment. Every year, for example, dandelions grow seeds with sails that form into a white puff on the stem. The wind blows the seeds through the air. Most land in places where conditions are wrong for new dandelion growth. Only a few seeds land in a place with the right soil, light, and water conditions. These seeds grow into new dandelion plants. Through overproduction, nature assures that at least some seeds will survive to continue the species.

Activity

Survival of the Fittest

Scatter a box of red and green toothpicks in an area of your lawn or schoolyard. Then have a friend pick up the toothpicks one at a time. Which color toothpicks did your friend spot first? Why? How does this relate to the idea of natural selection?

Figure 20-12 *Although members of species are enough alike to mate, normally no two are exactly the same. Notice the variations in the people and in the dogs.*

Sometimes overproduction of offspring results in competition for food or shelter among the different members of a species. In the case of tadpoles, which hatch from frog eggs, competition can be fierce. The food supply in a pond often is not large enough for every tadpole to survive. Only those strong enough to obtain food and fast enough to avoid enemies will live. These animals will reproduce. The others die.

The process in which only the best-adapted members of a species survive is sometimes called "survival of the fittest." In a sense, the fittest animals are selected, or chosen, by their surroundings to survive. This is basically what Darwin meant by natural selection—nature "selects" the fittest.

Variation and Natural Selection

Although all members of a species are enough alike to mate, no two normally are exactly the same. Put another way, even members of the same species have small **variations**. For example, some polar bears have thicker coats of fur than others. This thicker fur gives them more protection against the cold. Such polar bears are fitter and more likely to survive and pass on this characteristic.

In the same way, members of the same plant species may show minor variations in the length and thickness of roots. Plants with deep root systems can reach deep underground water more easily and will have a better chance for survival than plants with shorter roots. So plants with deep roots are likely to be "selected" by nature and pass on their traits to the generations that follow. On the other hand, plants with shallow root systems would have a better chance for survival in an area in which most water was close to the surface. As you can see, variations among the members of a species are another reason natural selection can lead to new species over long periods of time.

Minor variations in a species are common. Sometimes, however, a mutation can cause a change in an organism's characteristics that is far from minor. For example, most scientists believe that as a result of a series of mutations, certain small carnivorous dinosaurs evolved into the ancient forerunners of modern birds.

In Chapter 18, you learned that helpful mutations better enable an organism to survive and reproduce. For example, in White Sands National Monument in New Mexico, the sand dunes are white. White mice live on these dunes. The light color of the mice was the result of a helpful mutation. Because the mice blend in better with their environment, they are less likely to be eaten by predators. If a mutation occurred that darkened some of the mice, they would not be able to blend in with their surroundings. The darker color would be the result of a harmful mutation. In this case, natural selection would "weed out" the mice with the harmful mutation. As generations of mice reproduced, the darker mice, along with their harmful mutation, would be eliminated from the species. The light-colored mice with the helpful mutation would survive and multiply.

Mirrors of Change

In some ways, living things become a mirror of the changes in their surroundings. The British peppered moth is a recent example of this process. In the 1850s, most of the peppered moths near Manchester, England, were gray in color. Only a few black moths existed. Since the gray moths were almost the same color as the tree trunks they lived on, they were nearly invisible to the birds that hunted them for food. Most of the black moths were spotted by the birds and were eaten. The species as a whole survived because of the gray moths. Then changes in environmental conditions had a drastic effect on the moths that lived in the area.

As more factories were built in the area, soot from the chimneys blackened the tree trunks. The gray moths could then be seen against the tree trunks. More and more gray moths were eaten by the birds. The few surviving black moths, however, now blended in with the tree trunks and survived. These moths produced more black offspring. In time, practically all peppered moths were black. Again the species as a whole survived. The tale of the peppered moths shows how natural selection was able to turn an unusual trait into a common one in a relatively short amount of time.

Activity

Handy Variations

1. Measure the length of one hand of each of your classmates. Measure from the tip of the longest finger to the wrist. Record your results.

2. Make a graph that shows the relationship between the length of each student's hand and the number of students.

What conclusions can you make about variations in hand length? In what situations might large hands have been an advantage for prehistoric people? A disadvantage?

Figure 20-13 *As the trees in Manchester, England, became blackened by soot, black moths became harder to see.*

1. How did Charles Darwin's theory of evolution come about?
2. What concept is often phrased as "survival of the fittest?"
3. What term is used to describe the slight differences in all members of a species?

20-3 Migration and Isolation

Seventy million years ago, the now icy continent of Antarctica was covered with dense forests. A warm sea teeming with swimming reptiles lapped Antarctica's shores. Through recent fossil finds, scientists also know that a kind of animal known as a marsupial lived in the forests of Antarctica. Marsupials are animals that carry their young in a pouch.

Over the years, other fossil discoveries revealed that the very earliest marsupials lived in North America. And today most of the modern species of

Figure 20-14 *The mountain opossum* (left) *and the kangaroo* (right) *are two of the many marsupials that are found only on the island-continent of Australia.*

marsupials live in Australia. This evidence has led to the conclusion that marsupials somehow gradually **migrated**, or moved away from their original homes to new places. This was possible because Antarctica, South America, and Australia were joined together at the time.

As a result of migration, there is only one species of marsupial left in North America—the opossum. On the other hand, there are over 100 species of marsupials living in Australia today. So migration can be an important factor in determining where organisms live and evolve.

In addition to migration, isolation can have an effect on evolution. Australia also offers a good example of **isolation.** Isolation results when members of a species or a group of species are separated from the rest of their kind for long periods of time.

Career: *Museum Curator*

HELP WANTED: MUSEUM CURATOR, GEOLOGY. Master's degree in geology with a specialization in paleontology required. Three years work experience in a museum, in an educational institution, or in a research organization.

As more students became attracted to the field of geology, it was necessary for the university to expand its geology department. So a new **museum curator** was hired. The responsibilities of the new curator were to clean, sort, identify, label, and number all items in the museum's collection.

Museum curators are specialists in a subject area that relates to their museum's collection. They are responsible for the care of all items belonging to the museum. Curators are also responsible for correctly interpreting and identifying those items.

Other tasks of curators include suggesting which items the museum should obtain, deciding which items should be removed from the collection, classifying the items already in the collection, and determining whether an item is genuine. They must also research the museum holdings and publish the results of that research. Curators have managerial duties and are responsible for seeing that museum holdings are displayed in a creative, educational way.

Anyone interested in a career as a museum curator should develop good communication skills and a sound knowledge of the type of collection he or she wishes to oversee. For more information, write to the Museum Reference Center, Smithsonian Institution Libraries, Washington, DC 20560.

Figure 20-15 *Like Australia, the Hawaiian Islands are isolated from other large landmasses. As a result, many species found here occur nowhere else in the world. This unusual silversword plant grows only at Haleakala Crater, on the Island of Maui.*

For example, many millions of years ago the continent of Australia broke away from the land masses of South America and Antarctica. The life forms on Australia were separated from other members of their species. So those particular organisms had millions of years to evolve on their own through natural selection. The result of this isolation is an island-continent that holds many plant and animal species found nowhere else in the world.

SECTION REVIEW

1. What word describes the movement of organisms from one place to another?
2. What concept best explains the cause of so many unusual species of organisms in Australia?

20-4 Change: Rapid or Slow?

Advances in the field of genetics have allowed scientists to take a closer look at evolution. Genetic analysis has also provided answers to some of the questions left open by Darwin's theories.

As a way of comparing different life forms, genetic analysis is often more accurate than anatomical evidence. Homologous structures may point out similarities between two organisms, but such appearances often can be misleading. They may be just a matter of coincidence. Comparing the DNA structure of two life forms, as Allan Wilson did with the quagga and mountain zebra, is a much more foolproof way of determining how they are related.

Using such genetic comparisons, scientists have come up with some surprising findings. Studies have shown, for example, that DNA from human beings is almost 98 percent identical to DNA from chimpanzees. In the past, people did not think that human beings and chimpanzees were so close to each other on the evolutionary tree.

Other studies have shown that some widely different mammals possess some of the same genes. In 1982, it was discovered that pigs carry a gene found

Figure 20-16 *By genetically comparing the DNA from two different animals, scientists have shown that animals, such as the pig (left) and the mouse (right), possess some of the same genes and may have a common ancestor*

earlier in a species of mice. Scientists suspect that the gene was originally carried from one kind of animal to another by a virus that had infected both.

The possibility of widespread gene transfer by viruses has been used to develop one explanation of sudden changes in a species. And it has shed some doubt on Darwin's theory that all evolution occurs gradually over long stretches of time. As a matter of fact, recent theories based on the fossil record do support the idea that Earth has known periods of rapid evolutionary change. "Rapid," of course, does not mean in a second, minute, hour, or day. It means *thousands of years*. When you consider that Earth is 4.6 billion years old, a few thousand years—or even tens of thousands of years—is really a short span of time.

Today, most scientists conclude that the gradual evolution Darwin described has often been combined with relatively fast changes in a species. This combination has led to all the plants and animals living on Earth at this time.

SECTION REVIEW

1. Is anatomical evidence or genetic analysis a more accurate method of comparing different species? Explain.
2. Explain how genetic comparisons are made.

LABORATORY ACTIVITY

Making a Fossil Imprint

Purpose

In this activity, you will create a fossil imprint and then make a cast of the imprint.

Materials *(per group)*

Modeling clay	Water
Plaster	Seashell or bone
Petroleum jelly	Plastic container

Procedure

1. Coat the outside of a seashell or bone with petroleum jelly.
2. Gently press your shell or bone into a lump of clay until most of it is surrounded by the clay.
3. Carefully remove the shell or bone so that you have a sharp impression of the object in the clay. You now have a fossil imprint of the object.
4. Coat the impression you made in the clay with an even layer of petroleum jelly.
5. Use your plastic container to mix water with plaster until you have a thick paste. Add just a little water at a time.
6. Pour the plaster mixture into the impression. Allow it to dry for about 30 minutes.
7. Carefully peel away the clay from the plaster. You now have a cast of the original seashell or bone.

Observations and Conclusions

1. Place your cast and the shell or bone used to make your mold on the table with those of your classmates. Try to match the original objects and their casts. What are the differences between the molds and the casts? Can a cast be made naturally?
2. Suppose one of the casts looked like nothing you had ever seen before. How would you decide what kind of animal or plant had made the fossil imprint? Would it help to know where the imprint had been found?
3. What type of environment do you think is most suitable for the formation of fossils?
4. Why is it difficult to find a fossil of an entire organism?

CHAPTER REVIEW

SUMMARY

20-1 Change Over Time

- Evolution is a change in a species over a period of time.

- Homologous structures provide evidence that various living things may share a common ancestor.

- Scientists use a wide variety of fossils to gain information about organisms from the distant past.

- Sedimentary rock is a type of rock formed from layers of mud and sand that harden slowly over time. Many of these rock layers hold the fossils of living things.

- Through the fossil record, scientists can show that species have changed over the years.

- An adaptation is any change that increases a species chances of survival.

20-2 Natural Selection

- Overproduction in nature leads to competition within a species for food, water, and shelter. Only the organisms most able to compete survive.

- Natural selection refers to the process in which the most able or fit organisms survive while the least fit die off.

- Every member of a species has some variations. Natural selection, over time, allows those organisms with variations that make them most fit to survive.

20-3 Migration and Isolation

- Migration refers to the movement of members of a species from one place to another.

- Isolation refers to a situation in which some members of a species are separated from the rest of their species for long periods of time.

- Both migration and isolation are processes that help determine which organisms live and evolve in a particular area.

20-4 Change: Rapid or Slow?

- Today, scientists can use genetic analysis to determine how closely related different species are.

- Genetic analysis is often more accurate than anatomical evidence. Comparing the DNA of two life forms is a much more foolproof way of determining how closely related they are.

- Most scientists now believe that evolution can take place during periods of rapid change as well as gradually.

VOCABULARY

Define each term in a complete sentence.

adaptation	**extinct**	**homologous**	**natural selection**
anatomy	**fossil**	**isolation**	**sedimentary rock**
evolution	**fossil record**	**migrate**	**variation**

CONTENT REVIEW: MULTIPLE CHOICE

Choose the letter of the answer that best completes each statement.

1. A term that can be described as descent with modification is
   a. natural selection.   b. evolution.   c. isolation.   d. migration.

2. The quagga is thought to be closely related to the
a. *eohippus.*   b. horse.   c. zebra.   d. rhino.

3. A bat's wing bones and a lion's leg bones are examples of
a. variation.   b. homologous structures.   c. natural selection.   d. migratory effects.

4. Rock that forms from layers of mud and sand that harden slowly is called
a. sedimentary rock.   b. igneous rock.   c. metamorphic rock.   d. all of these.

5. A change that increases an organism's chances for survival is a(n)
a. mutation.   b. isolation.   c. adaptation.   d. reproduction.

6. When a species no longer exists, it is
a. isolated.   b. extinct.   c. fossilized.   d. naturally selected.

7. Another way to say "survival of the fittest" is
a. natural selection.   b. competition.   c. natural variation.   d. isolation.

8. Small differences among members of a species are called
a. genes.   b. variations.   c. natural selection.   d. homologous structures.

9. When some members of a species are separated from the rest of their kind for a long period of time the result is
a. isolation.   b. variation.   c. mutation.   d. competition.

10. "Rapid" evolution means evolution that occurs over
a. years.   b. hundreds of years.   c. thousands of years.   d. millions of years.

CONTENT REVIEW: COMPLETION

Fill in the word or words that best complete each statement.

1. _____ is a theory that explains changes in life forms over periods of time.

2. When body parts and organs are similar in structure, they are _____.

3. _____ are the remains of once living organisms.

4. The stacked layers of rocks in the Grand Canyon are _____ rock.

5. The _____ includes all the evidence scientists have gathered from fossils.

6. _____ was the "dawn horse."

7. A change that increases an organism's chances for survival is a(n) _____.

8. *Eohippus* is a species that died out, or became _____.

9. Sometimes overproduction of young results in _____ among members of a species.

10. Marsupials _____, or moved, from North America to Australia.

CONTENT REVIEW: TRUE OR FALSE

Determine whether each statement is true or false. If it is true, write "true." If it is false, change the underlined word or words to make the statement true.

1. <u>Natural selection</u> can be defined as descent with modification.

2. The theory that explains changes in life forms is known as the theory of <u>evolution</u>.

3. <u>Physiology</u> is the study of the physical structure of living things.

4. Homologous organs are organs that have similar <u>functions</u>.

5. <u>Fossils</u> are the imprints or remains of once living things.

6. The <u>fossil record</u> is the most complete biological record of life on earth.

7. *Eohippus* had <u>four</u> toes on each front leg.
8. One of Darwin's most important contributions to the theory of evolution was his concept of <u>natural selection</u>.
9. Most species produce <u>fewer</u> young than the environment can support.
10. <u>Very few</u> members of a species show variations.

CONCEPT REVIEW: SKILL BUILDING

Use the skills you have developed in the chapter to complete each activity.

1. **Making generalizations** Why are people usually unable to see the effects of evolution during their lives?
2. **Applying definitions** Which of the following are fossils?
   a. a footprint of a dinosaur in rock
   b. a footprint of a person in cement
   c. an imprint of an oyster shell in a rock
   d. an oyster shell found on a beach
3. **Making comparisons** Would you expect there to be more similarities between the DNA of a cat and a lion or a cat and a dog? Explain.
4. **Relating concepts** Certain snails that live in woods and in grasses are eaten by birds. The snails that live in grasses are yellow. The snails that live on the woodland floor are dark colored. Explain how the snails have become adapted to their environments through natural selection.
5. **Applying definitions** Are the wing of a bat and the wing of a butterfly homologous structures? Explain.
6. **Making observations** Observe an animal in your classroom, home, or a pet store. List five characteristics of the animal, such as hair color or size. Then list possible variations for each characteristic. Finally, explain how each variation might make an animal more "fit" for survival in its natural environment.
7. **Making inferences** Recently, there has been an increase in the number of white peppered moths near Manchester, England. Suggest a possible reason for this change.
8. **Relating facts** Fossils of organisms that lived in oceans have been found on the tops of mountains. Explain how this can be possible.
9. **Making predictions** Predict how fossils could provide the evidence necessary to prove that evolution occurred either slowly or relatively rapidly.

CONCEPT REVIEW: ESSAY

Discuss each of the following in a brief paragraph.

1. Explain why overproduction plays an important role in nature.
2. Explain what it means to say living things are mirrors of change.
3. List two differences between *Eohippus* and the modern horse. Provide an explanation for each difference.
4. Use an example to explain the concept of natural selection.
5. Explain how sedimentary rock layers provide information about the history of life on Earth.
6. Compare migration and isolation.
7. Explain why genetic analysis, such as comparison of DNA, often is a more accurate method of comparing organisms than anatomical evidence.

21 The Path to Modern Humans

CHAPTER SECTIONS

21-1 The Search for Human Ancestors

21-2 The First Humans

21-3 The Wise Humans

CHAPTER OBJECTIVES

After completing this chapter, you will be able to:

21-1 Describe the characteristics of primates.

21-1 Discuss some of the differences between modern humans and early primates.

21-2 Describe some fossil and chemical evidence that enables scientists to study the course of human evolution.

21-2 Discuss some of the earliest primates to be considered "humans."

21-3 Relate Neanderthals and Cro-Magnons to the development of modern humans.

21-3 Discuss the importance of language to human evolution.

Kilometer after kilometer of scorching sand under a blazing sun—this is the Sahara desert of today. It is one of the driest areas on the face of this planet.

Hundreds of thousands of years ago, this same area contained lush valleys teeming with life. Here a network of waterways brought water to some of the early ancestors of humans. Because early humans once lived here, scientists now hope to learn more about human origins by studying riverbeds buried beneath the sand.

For a quarter of a million years, these buried riverbeds lay hidden. No one even knew they existed. Then, in 1982, a Space Shuttle flying over the Sahara brought back radar photographs that revealed mysteries hidden beneath the sand. Using the photographs as a guide, scientists dug up stone axes made 250,000 years ago by the peoples who had lived on the banks of the now buried rivers. Although evidence of life during this period had been found before, it was not until the discovery of the riverbeds that scientists understood how early humans had been able to survive in an area that is so dry today.

During the past few years, radar photography and other new techniques have helped unlock the secrets of our evolutionary past. Each day brings scientists closer to a time when the path to modern humans will be traced to its beginnings.

Radar photograph of the Sahara Desert

21-1 The Search for Human Ancestors

The search is on. It is taking place in the deserts of Africa and in the research laboratories of universities, in caves in China and in museums in Egypt. All over the world, scientists are busy looking for the first ancestors of humans.

Each new fossil find and each new research paper becomes the subject of a new storm of controversy. Just when scientists think that years of study and debate have brought them a step closer to human origins, a new piece of bone or a new theory turns up. A fresh shadow of doubt is cast on our knowledge of how humans evolved.

In 1984, some of the world's leading experts on the subject of human evolution came to New York City to face the issue head on. They had agreed to examine and discuss some of the earliest human or humanlike fossils that have ever been found. The fossil bones were flown to New York from museums all over the world. This gathering of bones marked the first time so many fossils could be studied together in one place.

Figure 21-1 *Primates are an order of mammals that includes humans, apes, monkeys, and about 200 other species of living things. The mountain gorilla* (left) *and the tree shrew* (right) *are examples of primates.*

Primates

The issue the scientists at the conference hoped to settle was: According to the theory of evolution, when did humans begin to evolve along different paths from other **primates**? Primates are an order of mammals that includes humans, as well as apes, monkeys, and about 200 other species of living things. **Humans share some important anatomical features with the other primates.** For example, almost all primates, including humans, have flexible hands. Their thumbs are able to move toward and touch their other fingers. This is called an opposable thumb. It allows primates to grasp objects, both large and small.

Humans and other modern primates also share **stereoscopic** (stai-ri-uh-SKAHP-ik), or three-dimensional, **vision.** Their eyes are located at the front of their heads rather than at the sides. This placement allows their brains to combine the separate image from each eye into one three-dimensional picture. And it also creates the perception of depth and allows primates to judge distances.

A New Kind of Primate

Here is a scene that may have occurred some 50 million years ago. Whalelike creatures walk on land. Horses are tiny animals with four-toed front feet. And a new kind of primate is beginning to fill the forests of the world: a primate that lives by sight rather than smell. These creatures spend almost their entire lives in the trees. Their sharp vision allows them to judge distances as they leap from tree to tree. Because they have flexible hands with opposable thumbs, they can easily hold onto branches. These swift, graceful creatures are so successful at finding food and avoiding enemies that their numbers swell rapidly. Today their descendants—monkeys, apes, and humans—are found all over the world.

Despite their success in the trees, some of these primates eventually left their tree life and began to live on the ground. No one is sure why they did. But it seems clear that the same qualities that made their life in the trees successful were also useful on the ground. Their sharp vision, for example, helped them avoid enemies and locate food. Their flexible

Figure 21-2 *Like most primates, the gibbon has an opposable thumb on each hand. This type of thumb enables primates to grasp objects.*

Activity

Opposable Thumbs

The ability to touch the thumb to the other fingers of the hand—often referred to as the opposable thumb—is an extremely important adaptation of primates. To find out how important, try going through a day without using either thumb. In a very short time, you may find out how differently human society might have developed without an opposable thumb.

---

primate hands would have been useful on the ground as well. However, these primates used their hands in the task of walking. Many millions of years would pass before a primate evolved that walked upright as humans do. In fact, exactly when this adaptation to two-legged walking occurred among primates was the subject of the conference that took place in New York in 1984.

Human Primates

The human primates who gathered in New York to discuss their own ancestors were themselves excellent examples of their species. One quick look at these primates, who referred to themselves as "scientists," was enough to reveal most of the features that make humans different from all other primates. For one thing, they walked to the conference table on two legs instead of four. This erect posture was made possible by arches that helped their feet support the entire weight of their body. In addition, their pelvises, or hip bones, were wider than those of all other primate species. This adaptation distributed the human's body weight evenly over both legs and made two-legged walking easier.

Walking on two legs left the humans' hands free for other tasks. Their hands had thumbs and fingers that could work together in very refined ways. Free, flexible hands allowed them to use tools such as pens, pointers, notebooks, and telephones. When the human primates opened their mouths to make noise, small teeth that were not as sharp as those of other primates could be seen.

Perhaps the most striking thing about the primates at the New York conference was their behavior. Other species of primates that are closely related to humans, such as chimpanzees and gorillas, can be taught to use simple tools. These primates can also communicate needs or threats to one another by making sounds. But the human primates far surpassed even the chimps in their ability to communicate. They were able to organize a variety of sounds into meaningful groups of symbols to create language. They had even developed a complex system of marks known as writing to represent the language whose sounds they made.

Figure 21-3 *Like humans, some primates, such as the chimpanzee, use tools. This chimpanzee is using a stick to dig for termites.*

1. List three types of primates.
2. What type of vision allows primates to have depth perception?
3. What is the advantage of an opposable thumb?

21-2 The First Humans

Common characteristics of humans and modern primates such as apes, along with fossil and genetic evidence, support the theory that humans and apes both evolved from a common ancestor. However, evolutionary theory does not in any way state that humans evolved from the apes living on Earth today. Rather, evolutionary theory simply states that at one time a creature left the trees and began to live on the ground. Over a great many years, this early creature evolved into other creatures that took different evolutionary paths. One path split off very early and led to monkeys. Other paths split off much later and led to apes such as chimpanzees, gorillas, and orangutans. And, one path eventually led to humans.

The point at which humans separated from the evolutionary development of other primates used to be called the "missing link." "Link" because it linked humans with early primates. And "missing" because the first human ancestor has not actually been discovered. In fact, there is a great deal of controversy as to what creature might be the "missing link."

Some Possible Human Ancestors

In 1977, a team of American and French scientists discovered a humanlike fossil in Africa that they named *Australopithecus afarensis* (aw-stray-loh-PITH-uh-kuhs af-er-EN-sis). They nicknamed it "Lucy," after the Beatles' song "Lucy in the Sky with Diamonds." The age of this fossil is estimated at about 3.5 million years. Some scientists immediately proclaimed Lucy as the missing link. Others disagreed just as quickly. Whether or not Lucy *is* one of the earliest human ancestors is still open to question. From the

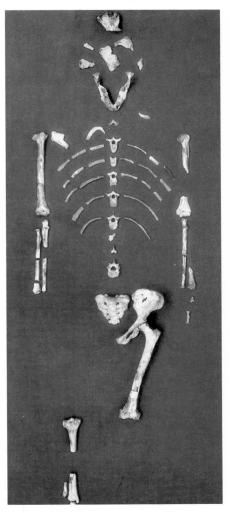

Figure 21-4 *This skeleton of Australopithecus afarensis was nicknamed "Lucy" by its discoverers. After examining this incomplete skeleton, some scientists concluded that Lucy could walk on two legs.*

CAREER: *Physical Anthropologist*

HELP WANTED: PHYSICAL ANTHRO-POLOGIST. Doctoral degree in physical anthropology required. Teaching experience in a college or university expected. Needed to conduct research and field work in an academic environment.

Scientists who research the physical differences between humans and the ways these differences affect human culture, heredity, and environment are called **physical anthropologists.** Their major concern is the biological nature of humans. By tracing the history and adaptation of human groups, anthropologists learn more about how humans differ. Physical anthropologists also study human evolution.

Physical anthropologists gather information from the fossil record, from the remains of populations, and from observations of nonhuman primates. They can reconstruct human life histories from collections of bones. A human skeleton provides the anthropologist with information about the person's gender, race, physical stature, age at death, facial features, diet, past diseases, and injuries.

Most physical anthropologists have teaching positions in colleges and universities. Others have positions working in museums. Anyone considering this career should begin with a pre-med program in college or with any program having courses in biology, physiology, chemistry, and anatomy. For more information, write to the American Association of Physical Anthropologists, 1703 New Hampshire Avenue, NW, Washington, DC 20009.

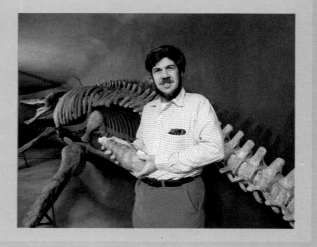

Figure 21-5 *This artist's conception shows how Lucy and others like her might have lived.*

other bones found with Lucy, some scientists have concluded that she could walk on two legs. Others say that her hands show that she was adapted to life mainly in the trees. Tree life, of course, would disqualify her as the first human ancestor.

Until the discovery of Lucy in 1977, a much younger fossil species named *Australopithecus africanus* (aw-stary-loh-PITH-thuh-kuhs af-ri-KAN-uhs), or "southern ape of Africa," was hailed as the first human ancestor. Most fossil specimens of *A. africanus* are only 3 million to 2 million years old. They show a blending of apelike and humanlike characteristics that include small teeth, signs of upright posture, and a brain whose size lies somewhere between that of apes and humans. Is Lucy the earliest ancestor of humans or is *A. africanus*? Might an even younger fossil qualify instead, or perhaps an older fossil? Could the true missing link still be hidden somewhere in the earth's soil? The debate and search continue.

Fossil Evidence Versus Chemical Evidence

Until about 1970, most evidence for human evolution had come from fossils. From fossils, most scientists estimated that apes and humans had begun to take separate evolutionary paths more than 14 million years ago.

In the 1970s, new laboratory evidence began to contradict this concept. Scientists had developed a new method of measuring the differences between the proteins of different species. The scientists also had developed a scale that could be used to estimate the rate of change in proteins over time. This scale of protein change was referred to as a **molecular clock.**

For example, the scientists compared the protein structures of hemoglobin, the red pigment in blood, of various modern primates, including humans. Human and chimp hemoglobin had exactly the same sequence of 287 amino acids, which are the building blocks of proteins. But the hemoglobin of humans and gorillas differed in the position of two amino acids. This evidence led scientists to conclude that gorillas took a separate evolutionary path before the paths of chimps and humans separated.

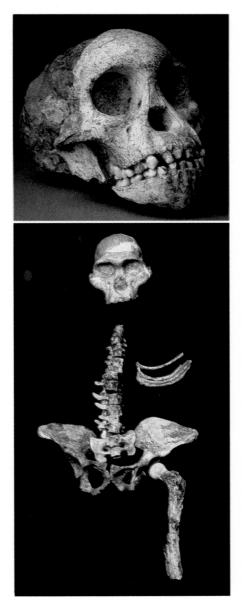

Figure 21-6 *Some scientists believe that* Australopithecus africanus, *whose fossil remains were discovered in 1924, is an ancestor of modern humans. The skull* (top) *is that of a child about five years old. The incomplete skeleton* (bottom) *belongs to a female.*

Activity

A Modern Culture

Prepare a presentation that contains some objects that represent the culture in which you live. Choose objects that would help a scientist 10,000 years from now understand the important views of your culture.

When did the gorilla path split off? Scientists who developed the molecular clock say that each change in the hemoglobin molecule would have happened every 3 to 4 million years. So gorillas would have taken a separate path 6 to 8 million years ago. Chimps and humans would have taken separate paths more recently. This suggested split was much more recent than the 14-million-year date given by fossil evidence.

By the time the New York conference of scientists ended, fossil evidence supporters and biochemical evidence supporters were less at odds with one another. In fact, the data on both sides now seemed to support the idea that the final split between humans and apes actually had occurred more recently than had once been thought. Today, many scientists estimate that this split in evolutionary paths took place as recently as 2 million years ago.

Humans as Toolmakers

The very first species of primate actually to be given the name "human" was also the maker of the first tools. *Homo habilis* (HA-bil-is), which means "skillful man," lived about 2 million years ago. Their fossils were first discovered in 1960 in East Africa by British scientists Mary and Louis Leakey.

Fossils indicate that *H. habilis* had hands capable of performing the same delicate tasks that the hands of modern humans can perform. Because they walked upright, their hands were left free to make simple tools from chipped stone.

Figure 21-7 *The first species of primates that were given the name "human" lived about two million years ago.* Homo habilis, *as they were called, were the first tool makers.*

Homo Erectus

The next humans scientists know about lived in caves, which kept them safe from animals and bad weather. Inside the cave, these humans used fire to provide heat and light. However, these primitive people did not know how to build fires. Instead, they waited until lightning happened to set fire to a nearby bush. Then they carefully brought the fire back to their home. With the fire, they cooked the meat of animals and roasted nuts and seeds.

Scientists have found many of the stone tools of these people. By examining the tools, the scientists have been able to make a good guess as to how the tools were made. Holding a small piece of sandstone in one hand, the primitive humans would strike it against a flat rock again and again, chipping small pieces off the sandstone. These pieces were gathered up. And, if they happened to be the right size, they were rubbed into blades and points that were used to build weapons for hunting small game.

This is just about all scientists know about the life of an early human primate called *Homo erectus* (e-REK-tuhs), who lived from about 1.6 to 0.5 million years ago. The first *H. erectus* fossils were found on

Figure 21-8 *This skull of* Homo habilis *was found in Kenya and is about 1.8 million years old.*

Figure 21-9 Homo erectus, *an early human primate, lived from about 1.6 to 0.5 million years ago. This group of primates was the first to control fire.*

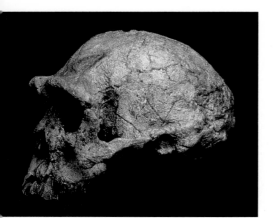

Figure 21-10 *This skull, found in Kenya, is the oldest and most complete fossil remain of* Homo erectus. *Notice its large brain case.*

the island of Java in Southeast Asia. *H. erectus* had thicker bones than modern humans, a sloped forehead, and a very large jaw, which would have been needed to chew some of the tough foods they ate. No one knows precisely what became of them. But most scientists believe that about 300,000 years ago another species of human appeared.

After 100,000 more years, this successful new species had spread to certain parts of Europe and Asia. Their jaws were smaller and their bones thinner than those of *H. erectus*. Because they had larger brain cases, scientists named the species *Homo sapiens* (SAY-pi-ens), or "wise man."

SECTION REVIEW

1. What scale is used to study human and ape evolution using changes in protein structure?
2. What is the first species of primate to be given the name "human"?

Figure 21-11 *This Neanderthal skull is between 35,000 and 53,000 years old and was found in France. The pattern of wear on the teeth shows that this person probably used its teeth for more than eating, perhaps for softening hides.*

21-3　The Wise Humans

What made *H. sapiens* wiser than the species of human primates that had come before? A close look at the life of a **Neanderthal** (nee-AN-der-thawl) may answer this question. Neanderthals were an early type of *H. sapiens* that lived in Europe and Asia from about 100,000 years ago to about 35,000 years ago. They were named after the Neander Valley in Germany, where their bones were first discovered in 1856. Although they stood on two legs as modern humans do, their bones were heavier than those of modern humans and they were shorter. An average Neanderthal was only about 150 centimeters tall.

Neanderthals lived in caves when they were available, but probably kept moving from place to place in search of game. When they camped out in the open, they probably built temporary huts by stretching animal skins over a framework of bones. The burnt wood found in Neanderthal camps suggests that they were experts at controlling fire. They may even have known how to start a fire with flint.

More impressive than the Neanderthals' ability to hunt, fish, cook, or make tools is the fact that they must have been the first primates to act according to beliefs and feelings about the nature of the world. The Neanderthals buried their dead. Like the ancient Egyptians, who lived many thousands of years later, Neanderthals buried their dead with the tools, herbs, or animal bones that had been important to them in life. Sometimes the Neanderthals arranged animal bones around the graves in patterns that suggest religious rituals.

Neanderthals were far more advanced than earlier humans. However, in biological terms, they were not a successful species. For, in time, all the Neanderthals died off.

Figure 21-12 *Neanderthals are the oldest known human primates definitely known to have buried their dead with objects, such as tools, herbs, or animal bones.*

The Cro-Magnons

There is no clear explanation for the disappearance of the first "wise humans." One possible explanation is that the Neanderthals were eliminated by a more modern form of *H. sapiens* that had developed even more successful survival skills. This new culture could have been the **Cro-Magnons** (kroh-MAG-nahnz), a prehistoric people who began replacing Neanderthals about 40,000 years ago.

Figure 21-13 *The red line on this chart represents the path of human evolution from a common ancestor. The dotted blue lines show the possible fossil relatives of modern peoples. According to the chart, what makes modern people different from their ancestors?*

The first meeting between the Neanderthal and Cro-Magnon peoples, if it ever occurred, must have been a strange experience for both. In many ways, the Cro-Magnons resembled modern humans. They had long faces, straight, high foreheads, and small teeth. Although their bones were thinner than those of the Neanderthals, they were probably very muscular. Some were taller than 180 centimeters, much taller than the average Neanderthal.

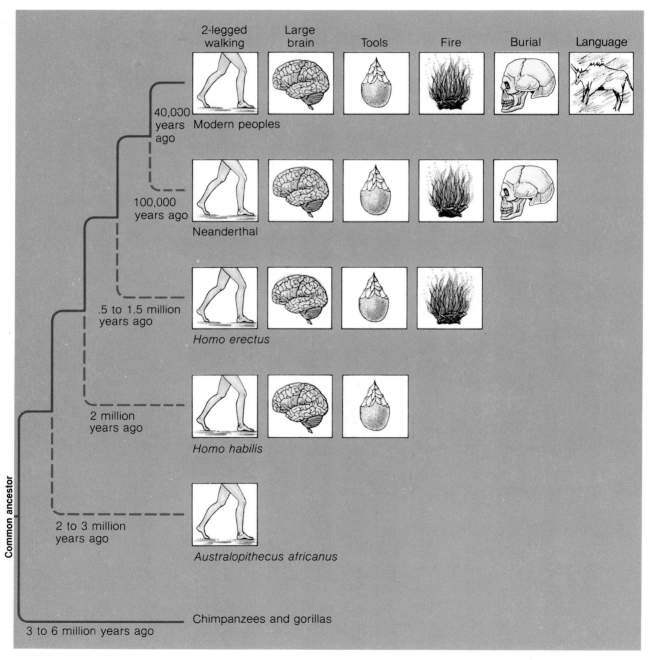

The Cro-Magnon toolmaking skills far surpassed anything ever seen before. Their long, sharp spears, long-bladed knives, and stone-slingers would have terrified the Neanderthals. In a battle between the two, the Neanderthals, with their relatively crude weapons, would not have stood a chance. Forced into more isolated groups by the powerful and more capable Cro-Magnons, the Neanderthal culture may have eventually died out. More likely, however, the two groups mated and blended with each other. **The blending of Neanderthal and Cro-Magnon genes and cultures could have led to modern humans.**

Language and Communication

Scientists have carefully studied evidence that might provide clues to Cro-Magnon life. Such evidence indicates that Cro-Magnons worked together to make tools, build shelters, and hunt. To do so, they probably spoke to each other. But since they did not leave written records, no one has any idea what their language may have been like.

Whatever it may have been like, its importance for the future development of humans right up to today cannot be underestimated. Language is used to spread ideas. Although many animals communicate by sounds, humans are the only known animals to have developed a complicated communication system capable of transferring much of what goes on in one person's mind to that of another.

Language can be thought of as a final step in the evolution of the modern *H. sapiens.* Largely because of language, human primates have developed a totally new characteristic: the ability to describe, or examine, one's own existence. As far as we know, humans are the only animals capable of talking about themselves, and of peering back down the long path of history to their own beginnings.

SECTION REVIEW

1. What evidence indicates that Neanderthals were skilled in building fires?
2. What group of prehistoric people began replacing the Neanderthals?

Figure 21-14 *The Cro-Magnons developed various forms of art and produced cave drawings like this one in Spain.*

Activity

Communication

Sign language is a system of hand signs that a person may use in order to communicate. Look up some words or phrases in sign language and show them to the class.

LABORATORY ACTIVITY

Animals of the Future

Purpose

In this activity, you will design an animal to live on the earth 10,000 years from now.

Materials *(per group)*

Drawing paper
Colored pencils, crayons, magic
   markers, or paints

Procedure

1. Describe the earth as you think it will be 10,000 years from now. Focus on your state or some other location of your choice, and predict what the environment will be like in 10,000 years. Describe such things as climate, geographic features, composition of the air, type of vegetation, and available natural resources.

2. After you have created this future world, design one or more animals adapted to live in this environment. Make drawings of these animals, including some of your new environment in the background. Name your animals.

Observations and Conclusions

1. What features of each animal make it well adapted to its environment?

2. Which of today's animals are probable ancestors of your new animals?

CHAPTER REVIEW

SUMMARY

21-1 The Search for Human Ancestors

■ Primates are an order of mammals that includes humans, as well as apes, monkeys, and about 200 other species of living things.

■ Two important characteristics primates share are stereoscopic vision and flexible hands with thumbs.

■ At some point in time, perhaps some 50 million years ago, scientists believe some primates left the trees and began to lead a life on the ground.

21-2 The First Humans

■ According to the theory of evolution, the order of primates split and separated into different evolutionary paths. One path led to monkeys. Another led to apes such as chimpanzees, gorillas, and orangutans. Still another path led to humans.

■ Chemical and fossil evidence indicates that the split between apes and humans may have occurred 2 million years ago.

■ The first species of primate to be given the name "human" is *Homo habilis*.

21-3 The Wise Humans

■ The wisest species in the primate order is *Homo sapiens*. The first *H. sapiens* were Neanderthals. Neanderthals lived about 35,000 to 100,000 years ago.

■ In time, Neanderthals disappeared. Cro-Magnon people took their place, perhaps beginning an evolutionary path that has led to modern humans.

■ Evidence indicates that Cro-Magnons worked together. To do so, they probably spoke to each other.

VOCABULARY

Define each term in a complete sentence.

Cro-Magnon
molecular clock

Neanderthal
primate

stereoscopic vision

CONTENT REVIEW: MULTIPLE CHOICE

Choose the letter of the answer that best completes each statement.

1. What order includes humans, apes, and monkeys?
   a. mammals   b. vertebrates   c. primates   d. *Homo sapiens*

2. Which of these is *not* a characteristic of all primates?
   a. stereoscopic vision   b. flexible hands
   c. two-legged walking   d. wider hip bones

3. A characteristic humans have that all other primates do not have is
   a. sharp vision.   b. stereoscopic vision.
   c. two-legged walking.   d. opposable thumbs.

4. The molecular clock is used to study changes in
   a. proteins.   b. bones.   c. muscle tissue.   d. brain size.

5. Mary and Louis Leakey discovered
   a. *Homo habilis.*   b. Neanderthal.
   c. *Homo sapiens.*   d. Cro-Magnon.

6. The humans who first skillfully made tools were
   a. *Australopithecus africanus.*   b. *Homo sapiens.*
   c. *Homo habilis.*   d. *Homo erectus.*
7. The first people to be called *Homo sapiens* were
   a. Cro-Magnon.   b. Neanderthal.
   c. *Homo habilis.*   d. *Australopithecus africanus.*
8. The first people known to bury their dead were
   a. *Homo habilis.*   b. *Homo erectus.*   c. Neanderthal.   d. Cro-Magnon.
9. Humans expert at controlling fire include
   a. Neanderthals.   b. *Homo habilis.*
   c. *Homo erectus.*   d. *Australopithecus africanus.*
10. The first humans who are believed to have used language were
    a. *Homo habilis.*   b. Neanderthal.   c. *Homo erectus.*   d. Cro-Magnon.

CONTENT REVIEW: COMPLETION

Fill in the word or words that best complete each statement.

1. _____ are an order of animals that includes humans and apes.
2. A primate's _____ can touch all its other fingers.
3. The hip bones, or _____, of humans are wider than those of other primates.
4. Gorillas and chimpanzees are primates that are included among the _____.
5. The first fossils of the human species _____ were found on the island of Java.
6. A scale of protein change used to study evolution is the _____.
7. *Homo habilis* was the first primate to be given the name _____.
8. _____ was both apelike and humanlike with characteristics that include small teeth, upright posture, and a relatively large brain.
9. The _____ were the first humans to bury their dead.
10. Humans who first appeared around 40,000 years ago are the _____.

CONTENT REVIEW: TRUE OR FALSE

Determine whether each statement is true or false. If it is true, write "true." If it is false, change the underlined word or words to make the statement true.

1. Stereoscopic vision provides an organism with the ability to judge distances.
2. Evolutionary theory does not state that humans evolved from apes.
3. The fossil that came to be called Lucy is about 14 million years old.
4. According to the molecular clock, the evolutionary path of gorillas split off before those of humans and chimpanzees.
5. Neanderthal fossils were first discovered in southern Spain.
6. *Homo habilis* means wise man.
7. Neanderthal may have been the first primates to act according to their beliefs about the nature of the world.
8. One possible reason for the disappearance of Neanderthals is that they were wiped out by Cro-Magnons.
9. The Cro-Magnons were shorter than the Neanderthals.
10. The first humans to have developed a language were probably the Cro-Magnons.

Use the skills you have developed in the chapter to complete each activity.

1. **Relating concepts** People often say that evolution means that humans evolved from monkeys and apes. Explain why such a statement is not an accurate representation of the evolutionary theory.

2. **Relating facts** Explain how the characteristics of primates made them successful at living in trees.

3. **Making comparisons** What advantages does a primate with the ability to walk on two legs have over a primate that must walk on four legs?

4. **Relating concepts** How is the ability to learn language related to the development of human civilizations?

5. **Applying concepts** Do you think evolution has stopped on this planet? Do you think evolution will ever stop? Explain your answers.

6. **Interpreting graphs** Another characteristic that distinguishes humans from other primates is the length of time parents care for their young. The graph illustrates the length of time needed for three different species of primates to reach adulthood. Use the graph to answer the following questions.
   a. Which organism has the shortest pre-adult stage? The longest?
   b. How is the length of the pre-adult stage related to the intelligence of each primate species?

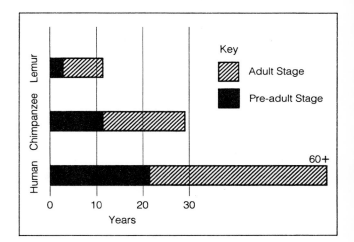

Discuss each of the following in a brief paragraph.

1. Describe the characteristics of primates. Explain how humans are different from other primates.
2. Explain what is meant by evolutionary theory.
3. What is meant by the term "missing link"?
4. Compare *Australopithecus afarensis* with *Australopithecus africanus.*
5. Explain how protein structures are used to measure differences between species. Include a definition of molecular clock in your explanation.
6. Compare *Homo habilis* and *Homo erectus.*
7. Explain why in biological terms Neanderthal was not a successful species.
8. Explain how a blending of Neanderthals and Cro-Magnons could have led to modern humans.
9. Discuss the benefits that result from the ability to use language.

Barbara McClintock:
She Discovered "Jumping" Genes

A very happy Dr. McClintock holds a sample of the corn that helped her win a Nobel Prize.

The news headline for October 10, 1983 read "Biologist Wins Nobel in Medicine." Eighty-one-year-old Barbara McClintock had just won the world's greatest scientific award. She received the award for her discovery that genes can move from one spot to another on a chromosome, or even from one chromosome to another. Many people felt that the award was long overdue. For Barbara McClintock had made the discovery thirty years earlier.

It had taken the scientific world that long to realize the importance of McClintock's research. In 1951, when Dr. McClintock first reported her discovery, she was met with silence. Her fellow scientists either did not understand, or would not believe, that genes do not always remain in a fixed spot on a chromosome.

When McClintock began her research, scientists did not have the knowledge or equipment to unravel the chemical make-up of genes. To determine how genes work in plants, McClintock decided to examine changes in the outward appearance of plants. McClintock used the maize plant to study the color variations in kernels. Maize is another name for corn.

Dr. McClintock's early research during the 1920s and 1930s proved that genes determine a maize plant's characteristics, such as color. In further studies during the winter of 1944-45, she observed a pattern of color spots on some corn kernels that was unlike anything she had seen before. Dr. McClintock wondered how this could be explained.

To find the explanation, McClintock studied the color patterns of kernels in many generations of corn. Using a microscope, she studied certain genes on the chromosome of each plant. These genes controlled changes in the color of kernels. She tried to match the

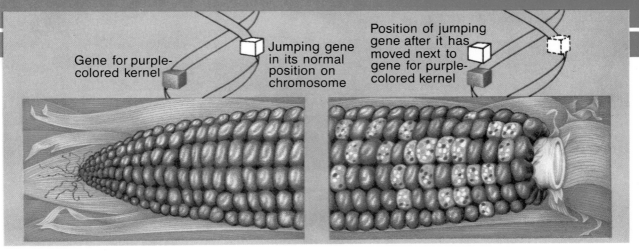

Gene for purple-colored kernel

Jumping gene in its normal position on chromosome

Position of jumping gene after it has moved next to gene for purple-colored kernel

A gene can move on its chromosome and cause a kernel's color to change.

color of the kernels with the position of these genes on their chromosomes.

Some genes, she found, moved! And when these genes moved, they caused the spot patterns of the corn kernels to change. How did the jumping genes do this?

When a jumping gene moved, it landed next to genes that controlled kernel color. The jumping gene then affected the action of these coloring genes. For example, let's say the nearby genes caused a kernel to be purple. The jumping gene interfered with the action of the "purple kernel" genes. This resulted in changes in the color of the corn kernel. The kernel was now speckled purple, pink, and white.

This discovery of jumping genes did not fit in with older scientific ideas about genes. Scientists believed that genes stayed in one place on the strands of chromosomes. It was as if the genes were beads on a necklace. But McClintock discovered that some genes, at least, could move on the chromosomes. When the genes did this, mutations, or changes, were caused in the organisms.

Despite the fact that her findings at the time were ignored, McClintock continued her work. Her confidence was unshakeable. As she said, "If you know you are on the right track, if you have this inner knowledge, then nobody can turn you off . . . regardless of what they say."

Finally, during the late 1960s, researchers began to find jumping genes in other organisms, such as bacteria. Passed on to new generations of bacteria, some jumping genes could give disease-causing bacteria the ability to resist antibiotic medicines.

Jumping genes in the one-celled parasite that causes African sleeping sickness help the parasite to overcome a person's natural resistance to the disease. More recent studies seem to show that moveable genes may also create changes in normal cells that turn them into cancer cells.

Such findings prompted scientists at last to recognize the importance of McClintock's earlier discovery. As Dr. James Watson, one of the discoverers of the structure of DNA, said, "It's really that science has caught up with Barbara."

By the 1970s, Barbara McClintock had become something of a scientific hero. Yet she continued her quiet life at the research center at Cold Spring Harbor on Long Island, New York. Slim and spry, only a little more than five feet tall, she lives alone near the laboratory building that is now named after her.

When she heard that she had won the Nobel Prize, Barbara McClintock said: "The prize is such an extraordinary honor. It might seem unfair, however, to reward a person for having so much pleasure over the years, asking the maize plant to solve specific problems and then watching its responses."

Issues in Science

The African Black rhinoceros has been brought to near extinction by hunters. Will its fate be that of the dinosaur, who mysteriously disappeared millions of years ago?

EXTINCTION?
are we speeding up

Conservationists disagree on whether many species of plants and animals are becoming extinct, or dying out, as part of the natural order of things. Some feel that people are making the environment unfit for certain plants and animals.

About 70 million years ago, the last dinosaur to roam the earth took its final breath and died. What kind of dinosaur was this lone survivor? Perhaps it was the mighty *Tyrannosaurus*, a fierce flesh eater. Or maybe it was the three-horned *Triceratops*, a powerful plant eater. Possibly it was one of the many smaller types of dinosaur that skittered over the landscape on long hind legs. No one knows what kind of dinosaur was the last to look upon the earth. Its identity will forever remain a mystery. But one fact is clear. With the death of the last one, dinosaurs became extinct and would not be seen again.

You may hear the word "extinction" often these days. Many types of plants and animals have vanished in recent times. Many more are on the brink of disappearing. Since the year 1600, about 1000 kinds of mammals, birds, and other vertebrates, or animals with backbones, have become extinct. Extinction has always been a fact of life. But has this process been speeded up by the interference of people? Are living things dying off at an unnaturally fast rate?

A report from the Florida Conservation Foundation states that "extinction is the ultimate fate of all species." However, the report goes on to say that "the modern rate of extinction is not natural." If this is true, what has caused the rapid disappearance of so many organisms? And why are thousands more on the endangered species list?

One possible answer has been suggested by S. Dillon Ripley, secretary of the Smithsonian Institution. Ripley, like many conservationists, feels that certain organisms are in danger because of "man and his intrusion into their fragile environments."

Some scientists disagree with this position on people's role in the extinction process. Dr. John J. McKetta, a chemical engineering professor at the University of Texas, wrote that "it is possible that . . . man may hasten the disappearance of certain species. However, the evidence indicates that he has very little to do with it."

Few conservationists would agree with McKetta's view. But many admit that some species are so primitive that they are easy targets for extinction. This may be the opinion of James Fischer, Noel Simon, and Jack Vincent, three noted conservationists. They have written that "in any period, including the present, there are doomed species: naturally doomed species bound to disappear."

It cannot be argued that the types of organisms that survive are those that adapt best to the changing conditions of the environment. The surroundings in which an organism lives change all the time. Some changes are big, others small. Some changes happen quickly, others slowly. Many of these changes are natural. Mountains rise up, and old mountains crumble. Ponds dry up. Floods cover forest areas. New species appear and compete with the old for food and space.

But conservationists are concerned that when people tamper with an environment, many plants and animals cannot adjust. Although they may be able to adapt to natural changes, certain organisms just cannot keep pace with the changes caused by humans.

The African black rhinoceros is an example of an animal threatened with extinction by humans. Huge and powerful, the rhino has few natural enemies. It is adapted to living on vast plains, eating the tough plants that grow there. But the rhino is a slow-witted creature and is easy prey for human hunters. Despite the laws that are supposed to protect rhinos, hunters kill the animals for their horns. Rhino horns bring high prices in parts of the world where they are used in primitive medicines. As a result, the rhinoceros is on the brink of extinction.

Similarly, the grizzly bear is a fierce animal with few enemies in the wild. For hundreds of years, grizzlies roamed the vast North American wilderness. But as farms, ranches, and towns began to replace wilderness, grizzlies began to decrease in numbers. Those that remained live much closer to people. And grizzlies and people do not mix well. Grizzlies seldom attack people or livestock. But when they do, they are usually hunted down and destroyed. Grizzly bears could be headed for extinction.

Both rhinos and grizzlies are what scientists call highly specialized creatures. This means that they have adapted to very special conditions. When people disturb these conditions—by shrinking the wilderness, for example—these animals find it difficult to exist.

Some animals, on the other hand, are not specialized. They are suited to living under many different kinds of conditions. The raccoon is one of these animals. Raccoons are adapted to the wild. But they also manage to survive well in cities. Instead of eating natural food, they feed on garbage. If they cannot find dens in hollow trees and logs, they make their homes in attics, abandoned buildings, and garages. Raccoons in Cincinnati, Ohio, even learned to use an underpass to cross a busy highway. While some animals have dwindled in number, raccoons are as abundant as ever.

Animals that can adapt to various conditions are more likely to survive in a changing environment. Raccoons, for example, are country animals that easily adapt to city life.

Some scientists think that eventually only very adaptable species such as the raccoon will be able to survive in a world changed by people. Will new species develop that are more adaptable to the modern world? Have the rhino and the grizzly outlived their time? Conservationists suggest that if the changes caused by people drive wild creatures out of existence, the environment itself is not healthy. In the long run, a sick environment endangers the human species. Only time will tell whether or not people are endangered by an environment of their own making.

Futures in Science

EVOLUTION ON VIVARIUM

The rules of evolution, if followed elsewhere in space, may have produced living things undreamed of on Earth.

FROM: Dr. Toshi Kanamoto, Bio-Ship 80
TO: Dr. Peter Harrington, Command Station 40, Earth
RE: Life on Planet Vivarium

Greetings, Pete. We are now orbiting the planet Vivarium and are T minus 3 hours 20 minutes to landing. In just three more hours, we'll strap ourselves into our deceleration chairs. Then, if all goes well, we should be the first Earthlings to touch down on Vivarium.

You can imagine the excitement I feel. According to the data we received from the last exploratory satellite, the atmosphere of Vivarium is rich in oxygen. In fact, there is more than enough oxygen to sustain life as we know it on Earth.

Dr. Susan Haley, our ship's anthropologist, and Captain Jasper Fernandez, our commander, are angry with me. I just showed them the photograph I had been holding of the ET, or extraterrestrial life form. The photo was taken on Vivarium by the satellite we sent out six months ago. Both feel it was wrong of me to keep the photo a secret until now. But I knew the photo would create a storm of controversy among the three of us. I just wanted to avoid spending ten days in space arguing over what the photo tells us. But I'm afraid Haley and Fernandez disagree with my reasoning.

The photo of the ET shows what looks like the head of a land creature, at the edge of a lake. The head is shaped something like an ant's. Fernandez, Haley, and I immediately agreed that its black, smooth 'skin' is probably an exoskeleton, or outer skeleton. This would be similar to the exoskeletons of some of Earth's insects.

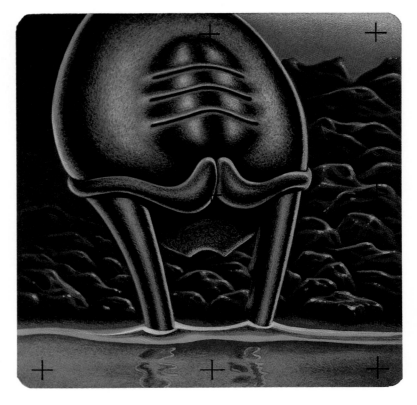

Haley and Fernandez next began to discuss the three slits on the surface of the creature's head, above the mouth. Fernandez insisted that all three openings were breathing holes. They would allow the creature to take advantage of the rich oxygen content of Vivarium's atmosphere. Haley argued that the slits were sense organs, probably eyes. She contended that eyes would be an important adaptation to the rocky, lake-filled terrain of Vivarium.

I suggested that we consider some other senses that might be adaptations on Vivarium. Haley and Fernandez looked at me curiously. Finally Fernandez said, "Go on."

"Well, we know that each hemisphere of Vivarium is in semidarkness part of each year," I reasoned. "Could the creature have evolved a way of seeing by means of heat waves, rather than light waves, to help it live in the dark?"

Haley and Fernandez were impressed with my hypothesis and urged me to continue.

"Let's not forget about the radioactive ores our satellite discovered on Vivarium. Maybe the creature has evolved a sense that is like a biological Geiger counter. This sense would warn the creature whenever it came close to dangerous concentrations of radioactivity."

"Those are two strong possibilities," said Haley. She began scanning the photograph closely. "I wonder how big the ET is. If this is only the head, the entire creature may be three times this size."

Fernandez and I tripled the head proportions, took the scale of the photograph into account, and figured that the creature was 20 times larger than any insect on Earth. But Haley insisted that our calculations had to be wrong. She wanted to know how such a gigantic creature could support its own mass. It would be impossible for an exoskeleton to withstand so much stress. "At any rate," she said, "the creature would need elephant-sized, rather than insect-sized, legs to support such a mass."

Before Haley could continue, Fernandez remainded her of an important difference between Vivarium and Earth. The surface gravity of Vivarium is only one-quarter that of Earth's. This would allow for the evolution of a creature with a more massive body and thinner legs.

"All right," said Haley, "but you've got to admit, such a bulky creature would need at least six legs for balance. We have to picture it making its way over the rocky, uneven terrain of Vivarium in near darkness."

"Why stop at six legs?" I said. "And why consider only legs?" Again the two looked at me expectantly.

"According to the data brought back by our satellite," I went on, "the craters and canyons of Vivarium are covered with a thin film of water at least part of the year. Perhaps the wet, slippery rocks of this planet require the creature to have suction cups instead of legs and feet. Perhaps the creature's body is covered with suction cups so it could move even if it rolled over."

By the time our discussion drew to a close, it was clear to me that we can only make educated guesses about evolution on other planets. The guesses, of course, would be based on our knowledge of the environment of the planet. We had turned the ET into a creature that was the size of an elephant and had a head and outer skeleton that were similar to an ant. It had suction cups covering its body, and the ability to sense changes in heat and radiation levels.

I left Haley and Fernandez arguing about the creature's probable lung capacity. I was glad that I had decided to delay the battle over the ET. As it was, our discussion had taken up the last three hours of the voyage.

Well, Pete, I'm afraid I must sign off now. I can hear the first landing rockets firing. I want to get all of our ET discussion on paper before touchdown. Vivarium may very well prove to be the testing ground for a great many of our hypotheses about evolution on other planets. If everything goes as I expect it will, my next letter should make some very exciting reading.

Ecology

Dr. Archie Carr called it "the lost year mystery." The mystery had nothing to do with a crime. No murder or robbery had been committed. But something far more puzzling had occurred. An entire group of sea turtles had disappeared!

Actually, the disappearance was only temporary. But that made it all the more curious to Dr. Carr. He had been trying to solve the mystery for more than 30 years. The turtle eggs hatched in the sands of beaches along the east coasts of North and South America. The tiny turtles, no larger than your hand, then scurried into the sea—and vanished for one year!

Where did the turtles go? What did they eat? How did they survive? These were all questions that sparked Dr. Carr's curiosity. In 1983, he found the answers.

The tiny turtles hide in tangles of seaweed that float across the surface of the sea. There they feed on small shrimp, little crabs, and jellyfish until they are large enough to survive in the open sea on their own. Eventually, the turtles grow in weight to about five times what you weigh.

CHAPTERS

22   **Biomes**

23   **Pathways in Nature**

24   **Conservation of Natural Resources**

Green sea turtle

22 Biomes

CHAPTER SECTIONS

22-1 Biogeography

22-2 The Tundra

22-3 Forests

22-4 Grasslands

22-5 Deserts

CHAPTER OBJECTIVES

After completing this chapter, you will be able to:

22-1 Describe the ways in which plants and animals disperse from one area to another.

22-1 List six major land biomes and explain how biomes are classified.

22-2 Describe the tundra.

22-3 Compare the three forest biomes.

22-4 Describe the grassland.

22-5 Compare hot deserts and cool deserts.

Night closes in quickly on the plains of East Africa, as if a great, black curtain suddenly has been drawn over the land. The scattered trees and wild animals that dot the plains by day disappear in the darkness. By their sounds, however, the animals reveal they still are there.

If you were camped in a tent for the night, you might hear zebras snorting nearby. Antelopes called wildebeests, or gnus, would stir and shuffle as they settled down. And perhaps lions would begin to roar.

Lions' roaring starts as a series of grunts, faster and faster, each louder than the one before. It might make you think of a giant engine warming up. Within moments, the sound builds into one like thunder. The wild music of lions roaring in the night probably would send chills down your spine.

Lions, zebras, and wildebeests do not live everywhere in Africa. They inhabit only open country, such as plains, with few or no trees and plenty of grass. In the jungle, which has many trees and is too shady for much grass to grow, you would find another mixture of creatures. As you will discover, the animal and plant populations are not the same from place to place. They vary because various areas of the world have different climates.

Waterhole in African plain

22-1 Biogeography

The study of where plants and animals live throughout the world—their distribution—is called **biogeography.** Biogeographers, then, are interested in **ecology,** or the study of the relationships between plants, animals, and their environment.

What types of animals live in an area depends largely on what plants grow there. Zebras, for instance, eat mostly grass. They would have a difficult time finding enough food in the jungle. But grassy plains are a good **habitat,** or living place, for zebras. Plains also are a good habitat for lions. Why? Lions hunt plant eaters, such as zebras, for food.

Plant life, in turn, is determined mainly by climate. Trees, for example, grow tall and thick where it is warm and rainy, especially if the days are long throughout the year. Fewer trees grow in cold, dry climates, where winter with its short days comes early and stays late.

Figure 22-1 *Water provides a habitat for many organisms, such as this beaver.*

Dispersal of Plants and Animals

Biogeographers also study why plants and animals spread to different areas. The movement of living things from one place to another is **dispersal.** Plants and animals disperse in many ways. During prehistoric times, for example, the horse evolved in North America. Eventually the level of the sea dropped, and a bridge of land appeared between Alaska and Siberia, in Asia. Horses soon moved westward across this natural land bridge. As ages passed, horses dispersed all across northern Asia into Europe.

Sometimes plants and animals disperse with help—from wind, water, and even people. Certain lizards, for example, have spread from island to island on floating branches in a process called rafting. Some seeds, such as the coconut, reach new places by floating on the water. Other seeds are carried on the wind. Often animals are brought to new homes by other creatures. Fish eggs may be carried on the feet of ducks and other water birds. Insects may ride in the fur of mammals.

Figure 22-2 *Animals and plants disperse in many ways. The lizard (left) floats from island to island on things such as plants, while dandelion seeds (right) are dispersed by the wind.*

People have also been responsible for the dispersal of animals and plants. About a hundred years ago, a bird lover released some European birds called starlings in New York City. As a result, starlings spread across the country.

During the 1800s, ships bound for the Hawaiian Islands carried water in large barrels for their crews. Before the ships left their home ports, mosquitoes laid eggs in the water. The eggs hatched during the voyage. When the ships arrived in Hawaii, they introduced mosquitoes to the islands. The insects carried an organism that causes a serious bird disease called avian malaria. When mosquitoes bit the Hawaiian birds, they transmitted the organism, causing the death of many birds.

Not all plants and animals carried to new homes by people cause harm. For example corn, tomatoes, and squash were found by European explorers in the Americas. These plants were taken to many parts of the world, where they are now important crops. Water buffaloes from southern Asia were brought to Europe and South America, where they became useful work animals.

Barriers

After the prehistoric horses crossed from North America to Asia, the sea level rose again and covered the land bridge they had traveled. The sea became a

Figure 22-3 *Many objects and conditions provide barriers against dispersal. Among these barriers are mountains, cold temperatures, and increasing altitude.*

natural fence, or barrier, that kept the horses from moving back and forth between the two continents. Eventually, horses became extinct in North America, not to return until European explorers arrived with them about 500 years ago.

Water is one of many barriers in nature that can prevent plants and animals from dispersing. What becomes a barrier for one animal, however, may be easy to cross for others. For example, water is a highway for fish.

Other barriers include mountains, deep valleys, and objects built by people. A dam on a river, for instance, can stop the dispersal of fish. And, a range of mountains can block the dispersal of seeds by the wind.

A mountain too steep or water too wide for an organism to cross is an example of a physical barrier. Barriers also can be ecological. When a habitat does not meet the needs of certain plants and animals, it is an ecological barrier. In recent years the Virginia opossum has spread from the south into the northeastern United States. During cold winters, opossums in northern states suffer frostbite on their hairless ears and tails. It is a sign they have met an ecological barrier—cold climate—that probably will keep them from going much farther north.

Activity

Aquatic Biomes

Biomes also exist in the earth's waters. These aquatic biomes may be in fresh water or salt water. Using reference books in the library, research and report on the plants, animals, and living conditions in one of the earth's aquatic biomes.

Biomes of the World

The climate and the plants and animals living in an area give that area its own special character. The scenery, or landscape, of a grassland, for instance, is quite different from that of a forest. Of course, sometimes it is a bit difficult to tell where one landscape ends and another begins. In East Africa, for example, many grasslands are savannas, flat lands dotted with trees. When are there enough trees on a savanna to make it a forest and not a grassland? Settling such questions is a task for biogeographers.

To bring some order to the variety of landscapes on our planet, scientists have grouped landscapes

Figure 22-4 *According to this chart on biomes, which biome is most likely to contain buffaloes?*

BIOME CHARACTERISTICS

Biome	Average Annual Rainfall (cm)	Climate	Common Plants	Common Animals	
Tundra	20	Extremely cold and dry; permafrost	Lichens, shrubs, and grasslike plants	Arctic foxes, polar bears, caribou, wolves, and migratory birds	
Tropical rain forest	More than 200	Warm and wet all year	Broadleaf evergreens, palms, tree ferns, and climbing vines	Bats, lizards, snakes, monkeys, and colorful birds	
Coniferous forest	More than 50	Cool and moist on mountains; mild winters and heavy rainfalls in coastal areas	Conifers such as cedars, hemlocks, pines, and redwood	Bears, mountain lions, wolves, birds, and elks	
Deciduous forest	More than 75	Moist with cold winters and warm summers	Broadleaf deciduous trees such as elms, maples, and oaks	Raccoons, squirrels, small birds, and deer	
Grasslands	25–75	Mild temperatures and subhumid	Grasses and herbaceous plants	Antelopes, buffaloes, wolves, and coyotes	
Desert	Less than 25	Extremely dry	Cacti, fleshy plants, grasses, and small-leaved shrubs	Lizards, snakes, and small rodents such as wood rats and kangaroo rats	

Activity

Microbiomes

Select a small portion of land about 2 meters square in your neighborhood. Once a week visit your "microbiome" and take notes on the kinds of plants and animals that live in this small area. Pay particular attention to the movements of organisms into and out of your microbiome during various seasons. Also, try to keep a diary of the climate conditions in your microbiome.

with similar climates, plants, and animals into divisions called **biomes.** Biome divisions are merely a system to help scientists describe the natural world. As you might expect, not all scientists divide the world into the same kinds and numbers of biomes. However, as a rule, at least six land biomes are accepted by most scientists. **The six major land biomes are tundra, coniferous forest, deciduous forest, tropical rain forest, grassland, and desert.**

SECTION REVIEW

1. What is a habitat?
2. List three ways plants and animals may disperse from one place to another.
3. What is a biome?

22-2 The Tundra

Imagine you are going on a trip through the world's biomes. Your first stop is the tundra, which rims the Arctic Ocean all around the North Pole. You set up camp near the sea in Canada's Northwest Territories. It is winter, and despite your heavy clothing, the wind cuts to the bone. **The climate of the tundra is very cold and dry.** It is, in fact, like a cold desert. The temperature rarely rises above freezing. And during most years, less than 25 centimeters of rain and snow fall on the tundra.

Figure 22-5 *The tundra is a large biome that borders the Arctic Ocean and surrounds the North Pole. In the winter, caribou travel the tundra in search of food* (left). *In the summer, flowers and short shrubs dot the tundra's landscape* (right).

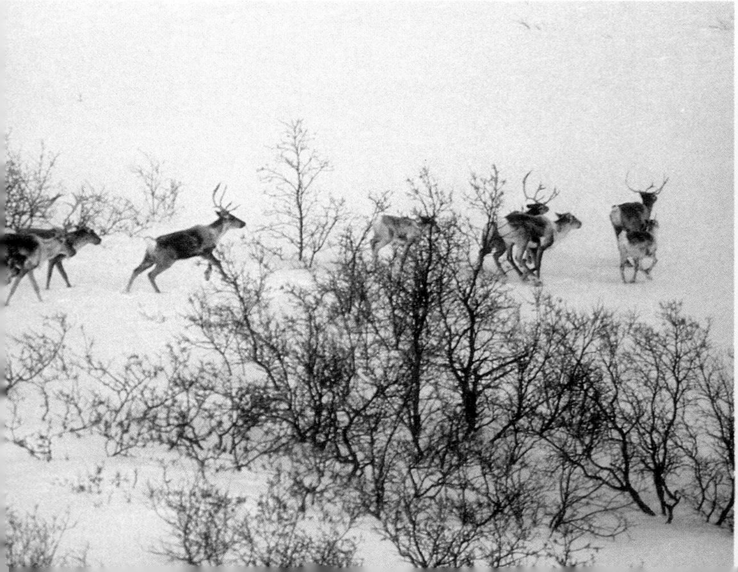

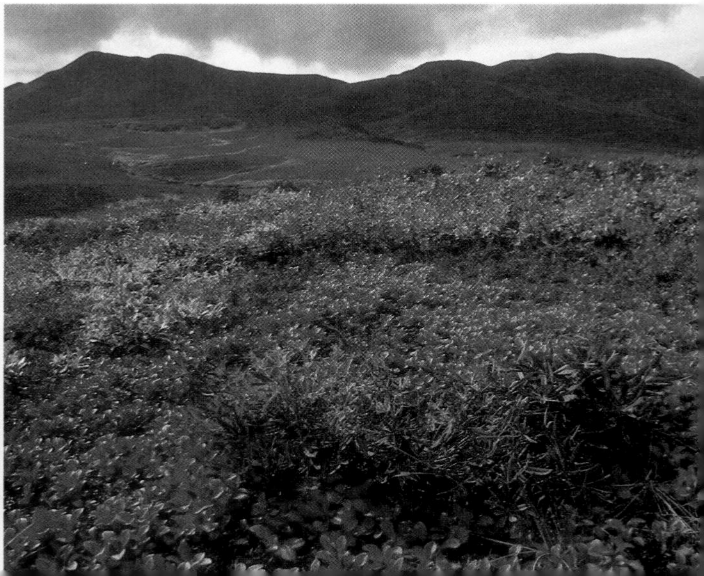

Most water on the tundra is locked in ice within the soil. Even in spring and summer, only three months long together, the soil stays permanently frozen up to about a finger's length of the surface. The frozen soil is called **permafrost.** Permafrost, along with fierce tundra winds, prevents large trees from rooting. The few trees that do grow are dwarf birches and willows less than knee high.

Among the most common tundra plants are lichens. They cover rocks and bare ground like a carpet. Lichens are a main food of caribou, a type of reindeer. During winter, the caribou go where snow is thinnest, so they can find lichens easily. Or else they travel in herds to the forests south of the tundra. Wolves often follow close behind, picking off the old and weak caribou.

As you leave your camp, you see great, shaggy beasts with drooping horns pawing through the snow to eat dwarf willows. They are musk oxen. Under their long outer coat is another coat of fine hair, which insulates them from the cold.

Many small animals inhabit the tundra too. Among the most common are lemmings, rodents that look like meadow mice. When winter approaches, the claws of some kinds of lemmings grow thick and broad, helping them burrow in the snow, ice, and frozen soil.

You stay on the tundra until spring. As the surface soil melts, pools of water form. Clouds of mosquitoes gather about them. Unless you wear netting over your face, they make you miserable. With spring, the tough grasses and small flowers of the tundra burst into life. The sky is filled with birds. Vast flocks of ducks, geese, and shore birds, such as sandpipers, migrate from the south to nest on the tundra. Weasels and arctic foxes hunt the young birds in their nests. Ground squirrels, which hibernated in burrows for the cold months, awaken. The days are long and sunny, but on some nights, it is frosty. The frost is a hint that on the tundra winter is never very far off.

Figure 22-6 *A ptarmigan is a type of bird found in the uppermost part of the Northern Hemisphere. In the winter, the feathers of the ptarmigan are white like the snow* (top). *In the summer, the feathers are reddish brown and black* (bottom).

SECTION REVIEW

1. Describe the tundra climate.
2. What is permafrost?

22-3 Forests

After leaving the tundra, you head south toward the world's forest biomes. **The three major forest biomes are coniferous forest, deciduous forest, and tropical rain forest.**

Coniferous Forests

The northernmost forest, the coniferous forest, is a belt across Canada, Alaska, northern Asia, and northern Europe. Fingers of this forest reach south along the high slopes of mountains such as the Rockies, where the climate is colder than in the lands below. Coniferous forests contain trees called conifers, or evergreens, which produce their seeds in cones.

Sometimes called the "great north woods," the coniferous forest has fewer types of trees than those in warmer regions. Not many kinds of trees can stand the cold northern winters as well as firs, spruces, pines, and other conifers. Their needles, for instance, have a waxy covering that protects them from freezing. Because of the cold, fallen branches, needles, and dead animals do not decay as fast as in warmer regions. Since the decay of plant and animal remains is one of the main factors in producing fertile soil, the soil of the coniferous forest is not

Figure 22-7 *Conifers are cone-bearing trees. They have needlelike leaves that remain on the trees all year round.*

Figure 22-8 *A mother moose and her twins wade through a pond in a coniferous forest.*

particularly rich. Poor soil is another reason that many kinds of trees are unable to grow there.

Together with poor soil, shade from the thick conifer branches keeps many plants from growing on the ground. You find that as you hike through the north woods you hardly ever have to hack through underbrush.

It happens to be late spring, however, so the going still is not easy. The ground is spongy and soggy, and pools of water dot the forest floor. Unlike permafrost, soil in the coniferous forest thaws completely in spring, making some parts of it like a swamp. Indeed, these areas are often called taiga, a Russian word meaning "swamp forest." The taiga not only includes these areas but also the entire northernmost region of the forest.

Near a lake, you see a huge moose, shoulder deep in water. It dips its head and comes up with a mouthful of juicy plants from the bottom. The lake has been formed behind a dam of sticks and logs, built by beavers along a stream. Perhaps, as you move along, you see a Canadian lynx hunting a snowshoe hare. Or one of the many members of the weasel family—perhaps a marten—hunting red squirrels. Some animals found on the tundra also inhabit the coniferous forest, as you find when at night you hear the howling of a wolf pack.

Bird songs awaken you in the morning. Warblers, which leave for the south in the autumn, twitter. Gray jays, which stay all year round, scold. A reddish bird with a bill that is crisscrossed lands on a pine

Figure 22-9 *The crossbill has a beak it uses to pry the scales of a pine cone apart to get to the seeds.*

Figure 22-10 *Before deciduous trees shed their leaves in the autumn, they change color from green to brilliant shades of red, yellow, and orange.*

Figure 22-11 *Like all deer, the white-tailed deer, an inhabitant of deciduous forests in North America, has keen senses of hearing and smell to alert it to danger.*

cone. It is a crossbill, specially adapted to feeding on pines. In a moment, you see how. It pries the scales of the pine cone apart with its bill and takes out a seed with its tongue. Another bird of the biome, the spruce grouse, feeds on needles and buds of spruce and other conifers.

Deciduous Forests

Heading south from the coniferous biome, you reach a deciduous forest. This forest starts around the border of the northeastern United States and Canada. It covers the eastern United States. Other deciduous forests grow throughout most of Europe and eastern Asia. Deciduous trees, such as oaks and maples, shed their leaves in the autumn. New leaves grow back in the spring.

Deciduous forests grow where there is at least 75 centimeters of rain a year. Summers are warm, and winters are cold, but not as cold as in the northern coniferous forests. You wander through oaks, maples, beeches, and hickories. A thick carpet of dead leaves rustles underfoot. The decaying leaves help make the forest soil richer than that of the coniferous forest. Hordes of insects, spiders, snails, and worms live on the forest floor. During the early spring, when the new leaves still are not fully grown, the forest floor is brightly lit by the sun. Wildflowers and ferns grow almost everywhere.

An occasional mouse scurries across the forest floor. Many more small mammals are out of sight under the leaves. A gray squirrel watches you, then disappears in the branches. Suddenly, up ahead, you hear a stir in the brush and see a flash of white. A white-tailed deer has spotted you and dashed away, showing the snowy underside of its tail.

By the side of a small stream, you spy a print in the mud. It looks almost like a small human hand. The print was made by a raccoon searching for frogs during the night. Thrushes, woodpeckers, and blue jays flit back and forth between the trees. A relative of the spruce grouse, the ruffed grouse, rests in a brush tangle and watches you pass. Under a rotting log, you find a spotted salamander, jet black with big yellow spots. A black snake slithers away as it senses your approach.

By winter, many of the birds migrate south. Snakes and frogs hibernate. Raccoons, which grow fat in autumn, spend the coldest weather sleeping in dens. However, they do come out during warm spells. The trees in winter are bare and rattle in the wind. But when spring comes, the leaves will bud and birds will return. The forest will come to life once again.

Figure 22-12 *Deciduous forests provide food for many different animals. A raccoon (left) eats berries and other parts of plants, while a mole (right) looks for insects on the forest floor.*

Tropical Rain Forests

Now your travels bring you farther south, all the way to the Amazon River of South America. You camp there in the tropical rain forest. This biome also is found in central Africa, southern Asia, and even a bit of Australia.

You discover the rain forest is rightly named. It rains for at least a short while almost every day. Rain forests get at least 200 centimeters of rain yearly. The climate is like summer year round, so plants can grow for all 12 months.

After only a few minutes, your clothes are soaking with dampness and perspiration. The air is muggy and still, although not as hot as you expected. It hardly ever gets warmer in the jungle than on a scorching summer day in Chicago or New York City. Why? The answer is overhead, where the tops of trees 35 meters or taller meet to form a green roof,

Figure 22-13 *The warm, moist climate of rain forests is ideal for the growth of a wide variety of plants.*

Figure 22-14 *The tropical rain forest has a greater number and variety of animal life than any other biome. The sulfur-breasted toucan* (top left), *the uakari* (top right), *the cloudforest tree snail* (bottom left), *and the red and blue arrowpoison frog* (bottom right) *are examples of some of the animals that live in the tropical rain forest.*

or **canopy.** The light below the canopy "is strange, dim, and green," wrote explorer and zoologist Ivan Sanderson. The only places where enough light gets through the canopy to allow plants to grow on the ground are where people or fires have made clearings and along river banks.

Most plant life grows in the sunlit canopy. Vines called lianas, some thicker than your leg and more than 50 meters long, snake through the branches. Orchids and ferns perch on branches and in tree hollows. Rain forests have more varied plant life than any other land biome. The jungle you are visiting has more than 40,000 plant species.

Animal life of the rain forest is also marvelously varied. However, many of the jungle's creatures are out of your sight. Atop the tallest trees, poking here and there above the canopy, sit harpy eagles. Their keen eyes search the canopy below for monkeys and other prey. The canopy is full of parrots, toucans, and hundreds of other kinds of birds. At night bats flit among the trees.

Wild cats called ocelots and boa constrictor snakes climb into the lower trees that grow just under the canopy to hunt birds and monkeys. If you are quiet, you may see a tapir on the ground. The Amazon's big cat, the jaguar, is very secretive. But as you explore, you think you hear one roaring far off. Underfoot, the soil is full of insects and other small creatures—centipedes, spiders, ants, and beetles. From the tops of the biggest trees to the soil, the jungle is like an animal apartment house.

SECTION REVIEW

1. Name the three forest biomes.
2. What trees produce their seeds in cones?
3. What is a taiga?
4. What type of trees are oaks and maples?
5. What keeps light from reaching the rain forest's floor?

Activity

Comparing Forest Biomes

How do the three forest biomes differ from one another?

Divide a large piece of poster board into three sections. In each section create a scene from one of the three forest biomes. You can use crayons, magazine photographs, or any other materials you find useful. Be sure that each forest scene contains plants and animals found in that biome.

Career: Biogeographer

HELP WANTED: BIOGEOGRAPHER
To study the influence of certain human activities on plant and animal life. Bachelor's degree in geography and master's degree in geography or biological sciences required. Doctoral degree in biogeography highly desirable. Research results will be published.

Students who wake up and go to school in other parts of the world know the animals and plants that live in their region, but those living things may not resemble the ones in your area at all. Palm trees are found only in certain warm areas, cacti only in deserts, and redwoods only in California. Except for the ones in zoos, koalas live only in Australia and giraffes live only in Africa. Scientists who study the way in which plants and animals are scattered throughout the world are called **biogeographers.** Their research helps us to understand why organisms live where they do.

Biogeographers know about botany, zoology, meteorology, politics, and other areas of

study. Since writing research papers is part of their job, good communication skills are needed. If you enjoy reading, studying, and doing research, you may consider biogeography as a career. To learn more about this diversified field, write to the Association of American Geographers, Biogeography Specialty Group, 1710 Sixteenth Street N.W., Washington, DC 20009.

22-4 Grasslands

From the Amazon rain forest, you travel across the Atlantic Ocean until you reach the grasslands of East Africa. **In a grassland biome, between 25 and 75 centimeters of rain fall yearly. Grasses are the main group of plants.** Africa has the largest grasslands in the world, although other large grasslands are found in western North America, central Asia, South America, and near the coasts of Australia. In Africa and other tropical areas, grasslands are also known as savannas.

Your camp is in a field of grass occasionally dotted with thorny trees called acacias (uh-KAY-shuhz). There are few trees in the grasslands because of the low rainfall. Fires, which often rage over grasslands, prevent widespread tree growth too.

The animals that roam grasslands also keep trees from spreading by eating new shoots before they grow too large. Even large trees are not safe, as you realize when you see a herd of elephants tearing up acacias and feeding on their leaves.

Grass, on the other hand, can take trampling and low rainfall yet still grow thickly. That is why grasslands can feed the vast herds of big plant eaters, such as the zebras and antelope you see around you.

Figure 22-15 *Grassland biomes in different parts of the world are called by different names. This drawing shows the types of plants and animals that inhabit the veldts, or grasslands in Africa.*

Vulture

Lion   Hyena Baboon Zebra

These animals in turn are the food of lions, African wild dogs, and cheetahs.

Many mice, rats, and other small animals also inhabit grasslands, eating seeds, sprouts, and insects. Snakes prowl the ground hunting these creatures. As you walk about your camp at night, you must take care not to step on a puff adder or other poisonous snake as it searches for prey.

The smaller creatures, including snakes, are the food of the keen-eyed hawks and eagles that continually sail over the savanna or perch in the acacias. Vultures circle in the sky, ready to feed on the remains of kills by lions.

Different types of plant eaters and meat eaters live on grasslands in other parts of the world. Elk and bison, for example, are large plant eaters of North American grasslands. They are hunted by wolves and cougars. Much of North America's grasslands, however, has been turned to farms and

Giraffe

African elephant

Cape buffalo

Eland

Rhinoceros

Figure 22-16 *Bison, which once roamed American grasslands in great numbers, still exist in the nation's national parks.*

ranches, and the big wild animals are gone. Increasingly, the same thing is happening in Africa and other parts of the world.

SECTION REVIEW

1. In what part of the world is the largest grassland biome found?
2. What are three factors that prevent trees from overrunning grasslands?

22-5 Deserts

North of the savannas, the grasslands in Africa become increasingly dry. Eventually you come to the Sahara Desert, which covers almost all of North Africa. **A desert biome is an area that receives less than 25 centimeters of rainfall a year.** Other desert biomes are in western North America, western Asia, the center of Australia, and along the west coast of South America.

A desert can be hot or cool. The Sahara is a hot desert, scorching by day, chilly at night. In a cool

desert, such as the Gobi desert in northern China, there is also a great difference between daytime and nighttime temperatures. But in a cool desert, winter temperatures may drop below freezing.

As you walk through the desert, you notice that the plants in the desert are adapted to the lack of rainfall. Many have wide-spread roots near the surface. This enables them to absorb water quickly before the water evaporates. Plants, such as cactus, have thick fleshy stalks that help them store water.

You look hard but see few animals in the Sahara. Even so, they are there. By day, creatures such as lizards and rodents often escape the heat in underground burrows. Night brings them to the surface searching for food.

Like the plants, desert animals must live on as little water as possible. Most of the water used by desert creatures comes from seeds and other food. And desert animals lose almost no water in their wastes. Only in these ways can they survive in a world where rain hardly ever falls.

SECTION REVIEW

1. Describe the characteristics of deserts.
2. Compare hot and cool deserts.

Figure 22-17 *The Sahara Desert is a hot desert, scorching by day and chilly by night* (left). *Temperatures in the Gobi Desert, a cool desert, may drop below freezing on a winter night* (right).

Figure 22-18 *After a rainfall, colorful flowers cover parts of the desert.*

LABORATORY ACTIVITY

Building a Biome

Purpose

In this activity, you will make model biomes and see how well different plants grow in each biome.

Materials *(per group)*

1 2-L cardboard milk carton
Sandy soil or potting soil
Seeds: 5 lima beans, 30 rye grass,
   10 impatiens

Clear plastic wrap	Index card
Scissors	Tape
Lamp	Timer

Procedure

1. Your teacher will assign your group one of the following biomes: desert, grassland, rain forest, or deciduous forest.
2. Cut the entire front wall from a milk carton. Staple the spout closed. **CAUTION:** *Be careful in handling the scissors.*
3. Fill the carton with soil to within 3 cm of the top. Note: If you have been assigned the desert biome, use sandy soil.
4. At one end of the carton, plant impatiens seeds. In the middle of the carton, plant beans 3 cm deep. Scatter rye at the other end of the carton.
5. On your index card, write the names of your group, the seeds, and the type of biome. Tape the index card to the side of the carton.
6. Water the seeds well. Cover the open part of the carton with plastic wrap.
7. Put the carton in a warm place where it will remain undisturbed. Observe the carton every day.
8. After the seeds have sprouted, and depending upon which biome your group has, give it the following amounts of light and water.

Desert: little water, 5–6 hrs. light
Grassland: medium water, 5–6 hrs. light
Deciduous forest: medium water, 1–2 hrs. light
Rain forest: much water, no direct light

"Much water": Keep soil surface wet.
"Medium water": Let surface dry, then add water.
"Little water": Let soil dry to a depth of 2.5 cm.

9. Observe the biomes of the other groups.

Observations and Conclusions

1. After the seeds have sprouted and have grown for a week, describe the growth in each biome.
2. In which biome did most of the seeds grow best?
3. In which biome did the grass seeds grow best? The beans? The impatiens? Explain your results.
4. Which plants grew well in more than one biome?
5. How do beans react to little light?
6. Why did the seeds need water when they were planted?

CHAPTER REVIEW

SUMMARY

22-1 Biogeography

■ Biogeographers study the distribution of plants and animals around the world.

■ The movement of plants and animals from one place to another is called dispersal.

■ Physical or ecological barriers can prevent the dispersal of living things.

■ Scientists have organized the earth's landscapes with similar climates, plants, and animals into divisions called biomes.

22-2 The Tundra

■ The tundra, a northern biome, is cold most of the year.

■ The frozen soil of the tundra is called permafrost.

■ Animals that cannot survive the long tundra winter must migrate farther south to warmer climates.

22-3 Forests

■ Coniferous forests contain mainly conifer trees, or trees that produce their seeds in cones.

■ The soil of the coniferous forest is not very fertile, and many kinds of trees and plants are unable to grow there.

■ Deciduous forests contain mainly deciduous trees, or trees that shed their leaves seasonally.

■ The soil of the deciduous forest is more fertile than that of coniferous forests.

■ The tall canopy of the tropical rain forest prevents much sunlight from reaching the forest floor.

■ Tropical rain forests contain more kinds of plants and animals than any other biome.

22-4 Grasslands

■ Low rainfall and grazing animals prevent trees from overgrowing grasslands.

■ The thick grasses in grasslands provide food for plant-eating animals. These animals, in turn, are hunted by meat-eating animals.

22-5 Deserts

■ Rainfall in deserts is often les than 25 centimeters per year.

■ By conserving water, desert plants and animals have adapted to life in the desert.

VOCABULARY

Define each term in a complete sentence.

biogeography	**canopy**	**ecology**	**permafrost**
biome	**dispersal**	**habitat**	

CONTENT REVIEW: MULTIPLE CHOICE

Choose the letter of the answer that best completes each statement.

1. The study of the relationship between plants, animals, and their environment is called
   a. dispersal.   b. biogeography.   c. ecology.   d. habitat.

2. Plants and animals may disperse with the help of
   a. wind.   b. water.
   c. other organisms.   d. all of these.

3. Which of these is *not* a physical barrier?
   a. a wide river.   b. a steep cliff
   c. a cold climate   d. a dam

4. Landscapes with similar plants, animals, and climates are grouped into divisions called
   a. biomes.   b. habitats.
   c. barriers.   d. forests.

5. In what biome do a wide variety of ducks nest during the short summer?
   a. tropical rain forest   b. coniferous forest
   c. desert   d. tundra

6. Which of these are *not* deciduous trees?
   a. maples   b. pines   c. oaks   d. beeches

7. The amount of rain that falls in a rain forest each year is about
   a. 25 centimeters.   b. 100 centimeters.
   c. 200 centimeters.   d. 1000 centimeters.

8. The green roof formed by rain forest trees is called the
   a. tree line.   b. canopy.
   c. liana.   d. taiga.

9. Because desert plants have widespreading roots near the surface, they
   a. survive strong winds.
   b. absorb water quickly after it rains.
   c. absorb water deep below the ground.
   d. protect themselves from burrowing animals.

10. Which of these biomes receives the most rainfall each year?
   a. desert   b. coniferous forest
   c. tundra   d. deciduous forest

CONTENT REVIEW: COMPLETION

Fill in the word or words that best complete each statement.

1. Grassy plains are a good living place, or _____, for zebras.

2. The process by which an animal can float from one island to another on a branch is called _____.

3. In East Africa, many grasslands, called _____, have scattered trees.

4. Scientists have grouped landscapes with similar climates, plants, and animals into divisions called _____.

5. _____ is the frozen soil of the tundra.

6. The main food of caribou in the tundra is _____.

7. Because dead plants and animals do not quickly _____ in coniferous forests, the soil is not particularly fertile.

8. _____ is a word that means "swamp forest."

9. The biome that has the most varied plant and animal life is the _____.

10. Much of the North American grasslands has been turned into _____.

CONTENT REVIEW: TRUE OR FALSE

Determine whether each statement is true or false. If it is true, write "true." If it is false, change the underlined word or words to make the statement true.

1. <u>Biogeographers</u> study the distribution of plants and animals throughout the world.
2. A tall mountain is an <u>ecological</u> barrier.
3. The tundra gets <u>more</u> than 25 centimeters of rain and snow each year.
4. In the tundra, <u>musk oxen</u> follow the trail of caribou as they migrate south in the winter.
5. The <u>deciduous</u> forest is the northernmost forest biome.
6. <u>Conifers</u> are trees that produce seeds in cones.
7. Deciduous trees shed their leaves in the <u>spring</u>.
8. <u>A great deal</u> of sunlight reaches the floor of a tropical rain forest.
9. The largest grasslands in the world are in <u>the United States</u>.
10. Desert plants in different deserts usually appear very <u>different from</u> one another.

CONCEPT REVIEW: SKILL BUILDING

Use the skills you have developed in the chapter to complete each activity.

1. **Making generalizations** Why is it difficult to tell exactly where one biome ends and another begins?
2. **Classifying biomes** In which biome or biomes would each of the following organisms be found?
   a. fir tree
   b. oak tree
   c. cactus
   d. zebra
   e. caribou
   f. moose
   g. liana
   h. monkey
   i. acacia tree
   j. raccoon
   k. musk ox
   l. parrot
3. **Making inferences** What characteristics would you expect animals that stay on the tundra all year long to have?
4. **Applying concepts** Why do you think there are no tall trees in the desert?
5. **Relating facts** The tropical rain forest has a greater variety of species than any other biome. What characteristics of the tropical rain forest could account for this?
6. **Relating concepts** As you climb a mountain, you may walk through several biomes. Explain how this is possible.
7. **Relating cause and effect** How would lions be affected if a disease killed all the zebras and antelopes on the African grasslands?
8. **Making predictions** The Arctic tundra has come to be valued for its natural resources, such as oil and gas. It has also become a vacation spot for fishing and hunting. Predict how development might affect the tundra biome.

CONCEPT REVIEW: ESSAY

Discuss each of the following in a brief paragraph.

1. Briefly describe each of the six major land biomes.
2. Explain why some people call the tundra biome a cold desert.
3. Describe how the tropical rain forest is like an animal apartment house.
4. Compare physical barriers with ecological barriers.
5. How do scientists classify landscapes into biomes?

23 Pathways in Nature

CHAPTER SECTIONS

23-1 Rhythms and Cycles
23-2 Chemical Cycles
23-3 Ecological Succession

CHAPTER OBJECTIVES

After completing this chapter, you will be able to:

23-1 List the factors that affect the rhythms or cycles of living things.

23-1 Identify some examples of daily, lunar, and annual rhythms.

23-2 Describe how chemicals such as nitrogen, water, oxygen, and carbon dioxide are recycled in the environment.

23-3 Describe the process of ecological succession.

From a sea darkened by night, the surf crashes on a beach south of Los Angeles, California. The waves surge up the beach, then slide back into the ocean in a swirl of foam. As each wave retreats, small, silvery fish appear as if by magic out of the foam. Their slender bodies carpet the smooth, wet sand.

Squirming and flopping, the fish work their way up the beach until they are just out of reach of the waves. Some of them dig into the sand tail first, leaving only their heads above the surface. Others crowd around them. Those in the sand are females; the rest are males. The fish are mating and burying their eggs in the sand. When they finish, they wriggle back into the waves and are swept back to sea.

The fish are grunion. Of all the fish in the sea, only grunion lay their eggs on land. Grunion deposit their eggs at places on the beach reached only a few times each month by the highest tides. For two weeks, the eggs are safe from the waves. By the time the tides are high again and the waves reach the eggs, the young grunion are ready to hatch. As the waves swirl the eggs from the sand, the tiny grunion pop out and are carried to the ocean. The process repeats itself year after year, generation after generation—an age-old cycle that ties the survival of a tiny fish to the movements of the sea, the earth, and the moon. In the following pages, you will learn more about the other types of cycles in nature.

Grunion on a California beach

23-1 Rhythms and Cycles

The timing of the grunion's reproductive behavior to match the tides demonstrates an important fact. **Many activities of both animals and plants are in harmony with certain natural cycles, such as shifting tides, passage of day into night, and changing seasons.** These cycles occur without fail and have a regular rhythm. A vast number of biological processes in living things are in step with such rhythms.

Scientists do not fully understand how animals and plants keep in rhythm with these cycles. But scientists do have a name for the mysterious inner timer. It is called a **biological clock.** Many different conditions in the environment may set and control the biological clocks of living things. For example, when the days grow longer and there is more light during the spring, certain chemicals build up in the bodies of many birds that have wintered in southern regions. As their bodies react to the chemicals, the birds grow restless. Finally, they fly north, nest, and rear young.

Often several environmental changes combine to trigger complex behavior such as nesting and mating. The Chinese alligator, cousin of the American species, nests only after the spring has brought long days, rising temperatures, and higher river water levels because of heavy spring rains.

Figure 23-1 *Animals follow a variety of natural cycles. About once a year, salmon travel upstream to spawn* (left). *At low tide, these fiddler crabs climb out of their burrows in the sand* (right).

Daily Rhythms

Hardly a day goes by when you cannot experience for yourself the working of a biological clock. For example, whether or not a real clock is at your side, you wake up in the morning and become sleepy at night. Morning wakefulness and evening sleepiness are examples of behavior tied to the 24-hour day-night cycle. But there are other, less obvious changes that occur. If your temperature was taken at regular intervals, you would discover that your body temperature is usually lowest in the early morning hours and highest in the early evening hours. Your blood pressure follows a similar pattern.

Most animals undergo similar rhythms. Such animals, active mainly by day, are called **diurnal** (digh-ER-nuhl) **animals.** However, animals active at night, or **nocturnal** (nahk-TER-nuhl) **animals,** have reverse rhythms. These differing rhythms make it possible for nocturnal creatures to share the same habitat with diurnal ones. In the South American jungle, for example, squirrel monkeys and Amazon parrots are active and search for food during daylight. Other monkey species and great horned owls feed and hunt at night. Since nocturnal and diurnal animals are not active at the same time, they do not interfere with one another.

Lunar Rhythms

As the strange case of the grunion illustrates, many organisms are influenced by the rhythms of the tides. Tides are caused mostly by the gravitational pull of the moon on the earth's oceans. Since the word "lunar" refers to the moon, these rhythms are often called lunar rhythms.

There are two kinds of lunar rhythms. One is a two-week cycle, during which tides gradually become greater, peak, then decrease. The other is a 24-hour cycle, during which two high tides and two low tides occur. Most water creatures near the shore are affected by the daily rise and fall of the tides. When the tide flows in, for example, barnacles, mussels, and clams open their shells to feed. At low tide, they clamp their shells tight.

The reproduction of the grunion is in rhythm not only with the two-week cycle of the tides but also

Figure 23-2 *Most animals are active during the day or at night. The ring-tailed lemur (top) is diurnal, or active during the day. The ruffed lemur (bottom) is nocturnal, or active during the night.*

with their daily rise and fall. Off southern California, where the grunion live, one of the two high tides that occur every 24 hours is higher than the other. The grunion mate after the higher of the two tides has peaked and begins to drop. If the grunion were to put their eggs in the sand before the higher tide peaked, the tide would wash them away. Because the higher of these tides is at night, the grunion always visit the beach after dark.

Annual Rhythms

Hidden in the sand of the beach, the grunion eggs are safe from fish and other creatures that would eat them in the sea. Adult grunion mate each spring and summer. Such a yearly cycle is called an annual rhythm. What advantage is this to the grunion? When the eggs hatch, the sea is warm and full of food for the young grunion.

Many other organisms reproduce only at certain times of the year, when conditions are best for the young to survive. For example, antelope on the plains of Africa give birth to their young just after the rainy season, when the grass has grown tall and thick. At that time of year, there is plenty of food for both adults and young.

The seasonal migration of birds between southern wintering grounds and northern breeding grounds is another kind of annual rhythm. Of course, birds are not the only animals that migrate. Gray whales, for example, bear their young in bays along Mexico in winter and feed in Arctic waters during the summer. However, all migrating animals share one thing in common. They move from a hostile environment to one that is more beneficial.

Figure 23-3 *Adult barnacles (bottom) attach themselves to objects, such as rocks. As the tide comes in, it brings along tiny plants and animals. Barnacles (top) feed on the tiny plants and animals strained from the water.*

Some animals have a special way of dealing with a hostile environment. As winter approaches, the internal processes of these animals slow down until their body activities almost stop. This process is called **hibernation.** In the cold of winter, for example, frogs dig into the mud at the bottom of a lake to hibernate. In the dry, hot season, the African lungfish does something similar to hibernation. However, this process of adapting to dry, hot weather has a different name. It is called **estivation** (es-tuh-VAY-shuhn). Estivation and hibernation are further examples of annual cycles in nature.

For some organisms, the annual cycle spans life and death. Plants called annuals, such as the marigold, start from seeds in spring, mature and bear seeds by fall, and die in winter. The next spring another generation sprouts from the seeds, ready to begin the cycle again.

Figure 23-4 *Like grunion, other organisms reproduce at special times of the year. The African springbuck gives birth to its young after the rainy season.*

SECTION REVIEW

1. List some factors that affect the rhythms and cycles of living things.
2. What is a diurnal animal?
3. What animals hibernate? Estivate? Why?

23-2 Chemical Cycles

Every day since the earth first formed, the sun's energy has poured onto our planet. For the past three billion years or so, some of that sunlight has

Figure 23-5 *Some plants, such as these marigolds, are called annuals. Annuals grow from seeds in spring, mature and bear seeds in autumn, and die in winter.*

been used by green plants to help them produce food. Each day the plants use some of the sun's energy. And each day the sun replaces that energy.

Without sunlight, living things could not survive. However, there are other things in the environment that living things also need. You, for example, require oxygen and water. You also need food. Food, air, and water are made up of chemicals found in the natural world. Most of these chemicals were formed when Earth was young. But unlike the sun's energy, great amounts of new chemicals are not added to the environment each day. Unlike energy, however, chemicals can be recycled, or reused. **Chemicals, such as nitrogen, water, oxygen, and carbon dioxide, flow in cycles through living and nonliving parts of the environment.** So the air you breathe may once have filled the lungs of Alexander the Great, who had conquered the civilized world by 320 B.C. The water you drink may have been tasted by Joan of Arc, whose bravery inspired the French in 1429.

The Nitrogen Cycle

About 79 percent of the atmosphere is made up of "free" nitrogen, or nitrogen that is not combined with other elements. Almost all living things need nitrogen to help build proteins and certain other body chemicals. However, in spite of being surrounded by nitrogen gas, most organisms cannot use this free nitrogen in the air. Most living things can use only nitrogen that is combined with other elements in compounds. But how are these compounds made? Among the "factories" for making nitrogen compounds are tiny, one-celled bacteria.

A few kinds of bacteria can take nitrogen directly from the air and form nitrogen compounds. This process is called **nitrogen fixation.** Some of these nitrogen-fixing bacteria live in soil. Others grow on the roots of plants known as legumes (LEG-yoomz), including beans, peas, and peanuts. The bacteria supply the plants with usable nitrogen.

Bacteria build nitrogen compounds in another important way. When plants and animals die and decay, nitrogen in the decaying matter may be combined with hydrogen, oxygen, and other elements.

Figure 23-6 *The tiny, round structures on the roots of this pea plant contain nitrogen-fixing bacteria. These bacteria take nitrogen from the air and form nitrogen compounds needed by the plant.*

This manufacturing job is done by several different bacteria. One family of compounds formed in this way consists of nitrogen compounds called nitrates. Nitrates can be taken directly from the soil by plants.

The formation of nitrogen compounds by bacteria is only the first step in what is known as the nitrogen cycle. Plants use the nitrogen compounds to make food. Animals may then eat the plants—or other animals that have eaten plants. When the plants and animals die, the nitrogen compounds return to the soil. Nitrogen can go back and forth between the soil and plants and animals many times before reentering the atmosphere. Eventually, however, bacteria called denitrifying bacteria break down nitrogen compounds such as nitrates. In the process, free nitrogen is released into the air. The cycle is then complete.

Career: Forester

HELP WANTED: FORESTER Bachelor's degree in forestry or related field such as forest economics, wildlife management, natural resources, or ecology required. Advanced degree desirable. Must work well with people and be able to express oneself clearly. May involve travel by plane, helicopter, or four-wheel-drive vehicles to out-of-the-way places.

Campers and picnickers are some of the people who enjoy forest recreation areas and their wildlife inhabitants. Most people probably do not realize, however, that these areas were planned and developed by **foresters.** Foresters carefully study a possible recreation area to be sure that such items as cooking equipment, picnic tables, utility sources, and roads do not disturb the ecological balance of the forest. Other activities of foresters range from managing forest timberland—which provides wood for lumber, paper, and other products—to clearing away tree branches allowing sunlight to reach the ground cover.

Foresters work with government agencies, in private industry helping to develop products from trees, and with owners of timberland to better forestry and logging practices. Those interested in pursuing a forestry career can get a start by studying chemistry, physics, math, earth science, and biological science in high school. Summer job experience in forest and conservation work is also helpful. Forestry applicants should enjoy working outdoors, be physically fit, and work well with people. For further information, write to the Society of American Foresters, Wild Acres, 5400 Grosvenor Lane, Bethesda, MD 20814.

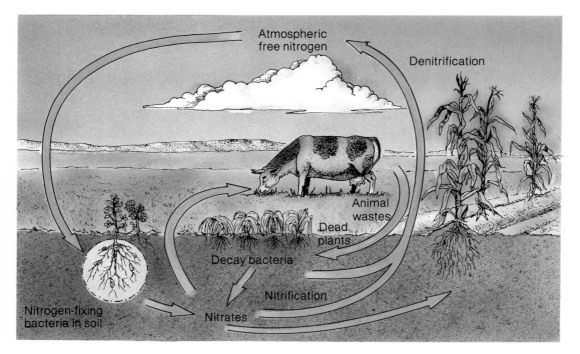

Figure 23-7 *In the nitrogen cycle, nitrogen passes from the atmosphere to living things and then back to the atmosphere.*

The Water Cycle

For many of the world's cultures, water has long symbolized life. Countries with water prospered. Water, then—particularly knowing where it was and where it would be—was a key to success. It soon became apparent to people many thousands of years ago that there is a natural cycle to the flow of water on this planet. It is a cycle people still rely on today.

Water circulates continually between the atmosphere and the surface of the earth. Most of the water on the earth is found in lakes, streams, and especially oceans. Surface water in these lakes, streams, and oceans is heated by the sun and turns to a vapor, or gas. This process is called **evaporation.** The water vapor then rises up into the air. In the upper atmosphere, water vapor cools and changes into liquid droplets. It is these droplets that form clouds. Eventually, the droplets fall back to the surface as rain and snow, or precipitation.

Most precipitation falls directly back into the oceans, lakes, and streams. Some strikes the surface of the land and then flows into these bodies of water. In either case, water that evaporated into the air has returned to the surface of the earth, only to begin the cycle over again.

Not all water, of course, goes directly back into rivers and oceans. Some is taken in by living things. But here the cycle continues. Plants may take in liquid water through their roots, but they also release some water vapor through their leaves. Animals drink water, but they also give water back to the environment when they breathe and in their wastes.

The Oxygen/Carbon Dioxide Cycle

Like all animals, you need oxygen to live. The atmosphere, which is 20 percent oxygen, supplies you and other air-breathing animals with this vital gas. Oxygen that has dissolved from the atmosphere into the water is breathed by fish and other aquatic animals. Clearly, animals would have used up the available oxygen supply in the atmosphere millions of years ago if something did not return the oxygen to the atmosphere. But what could that something be?

Consider this: When you inhale, you take in oxygen. When you exhale, you release the waste gas carbon dioxide. If something used carbon dioxide and released oxygen, it would be the perfect organism to balance your use of oxygen. That something, as you probably know, is green plants. Green plants use carbon dioxide gas from the atmosphere, water from the soil, and the energy of sunlight to make

Activity

Precipitation

Place a small plastic container near your home where it will not be disturbed. Make sure there are no trees or buildings overhead, for you will use the container to collect rain and snow, or precipitation. Each evening pour the contents of the container into a graduated cylinder. Then return the container to the place where you first left it. Measure and record how many milliliters of precipitation fell each day.

Repeat this procedure each day for the first seven days of each month during the school year. Using colored pencils for each month, construct a graph of your measurements.

Figure 23-8 *The circulation of water from the atmosphere to the earth and back to the atmosphere is called the water cycle.*

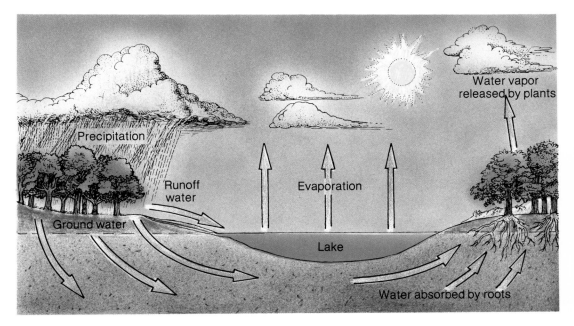

525

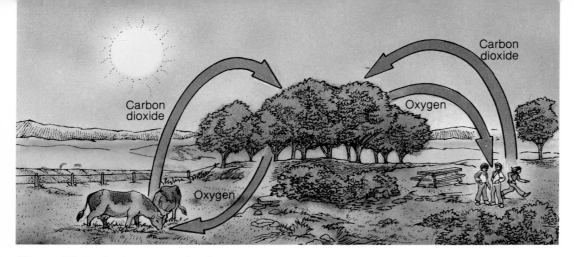

Figure 23-9 *In the oxygen/carbon dioxide cycle, photosynthesis and respiration are the major processes that circulate oxygen and carbon dioxide through the ecosystem.*

food. This process is called **photosynthesis.** During photosynthesis, plants break down water molecules into hydrogen and oxygen atoms. Oxygen from land plants escapes into the atmosphere. Oxygen from aquatic plants escapes into the water and atmosphere. This trade between plants and animals is the key to the oxygen/carbon dioxide cycle.

SECTION REVIEW

1. What substances in the environment are recycled, or reused?
2. What living things perform photosynthesis?

23-3   Ecological Succession

Not all changes in nature occur in cycles. Some changes that occur appear to be a one-way street, at least in the lifetime of a human. Such changes occur in an area where one living thing follows, or succeeds, another living thing over time. **The process of gradual change within a particular place is called ecological succession.**

The process of **ecological succession** can totally change what a place looks like. For example, what may be solid ground under your feet right now may once have been a pond swarming with fish. Here is how the transformation would have occurred.

Heavy rains fall, deep snow melts, or a tiny stream takes a different course. The water travels over the land and settles in low places. If the water does not drain away or evaporate, a pond forms.

At first, the pond is empty of living things. Then a water bird pays a visit. It stays for a while, finds nothing to eat, and flies off. But it may leave behind something special—fertilized fish eggs and water plant seeds washed from its feet. The fish eggs have hitched a ride from some distant lake. Another visitor arrives. It is the wind, which deposits the seeds of land plants around the pond.

As time passes, the fish and plants grow and reproduce. The early generations die, and their remains sink to the bottom of the pond. A fertile mud begins to form there. More time passes. Many rains fall, washing soil into the pond. The pond gets shallower and shallower. Now new organisms can get a foothold. Reeds and cattails start growing around the edges of the pond.

Meanwhile, down at the pond's bottom the mud has grown so rich that water plants can grow in ever-increasing numbers. As they grow, they use up great quantities of oxygen. Fish, which need oxygen, begin to die. The plants take over the pond, growing all across it. The last fish vanish but other animals find the new environment ideal. These new inhabitants are air-breathing frogs and turtles.

Eventually only patches of open water are left. The pond has become a marsh. Like the pond, the marsh keeps filling. It becomes dry land. Rabbits and deer roam where fish and frogs once lived. Bushes take root and then trees. What began as a pond has become a forest.

Succession takes a long time. To go from tiny pond to forest can take more than a century. Outside forces, however, can speed up or slow succession. Fire can burn a developing forest and set it back. Floods can fill a dying pond with water again. But, sooner or later, succession will change the face of the land.

SECTION REVIEW

1. In what process does one living thing follow another in a particular place?
2. How do thickly growing water plants in ponds contribute to the death of fish?

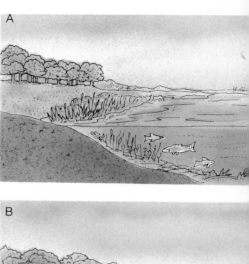

Figure 23-10 *During the succession of a lake, the kinds of plants and animals change as well as the lake's physical appearance.*

LABORATORY ACTIVITY

Going in Cycles

Purpose

In this activity, you will study the life cycle of a housefly and write your own definition of a cycle in nature.

Materials *(per group)*

Magnifying glass   Elastic band
Cotton ball   Water
Glass jar
Piece of gauze cloth large enough to
    cover the top of the glass jar
20 mL of bran flakes
10 mL of diluted canned milk
Paper towel
Houseflies
Metal bottle cap

Gauze cloth
Elastic band
Cotton ball
Bran flakes and milk
Metal bottle cap
Paper towel

Procedure

1. To make a fly cage, place a paper towel in the bottom of a glass jar. Put 20 mL of bran flakes and 10 mL of diluted canned milk on the towel.
2. Wet a cotton ball with water and stick it in the metal bottle cap. Put the bottle cap, with the cotton ball facing up, into the glass jar.
3. Put the flies your teacher gives you into the cage. Stretch the gauze cloth over the mouth of the jar and hold it in place with the elastic band.
4. Using the magnifying glass, check to be sure there is at least one female fly. Female flies have pointed tails and small eyes. Males have rounded tails and large eyes.
5. When eggs appear, release your adult flies outdoors. Fly eggs are small, white, and shaped like sausages.

Observations and Conclusions

1. Each day, check the jar and write a description of what you see.
2. For how many days do you see eggs?
3. Larvae come from the eggs. Draw a larva. For how many days do you see larvae?
4. A larva becomes a pupa. Draw a pupa. For how many days do you see pupae?
5. What does a pupa become?
6. Put young adult flies into a new cage. What stage in the life cycle will you see next?
7. You have observed the life cycle of an insect. You have also read about cycles such as the nitrogen and water cycles. Now write your own definition of a cycle.

CHAPTER REVIEW

SUMMARY

23-1 Rhythms and Cycles

■ The sense of timing that enables plants and animals to keep their lives in rhythm with natural cycles is called a biological clock.

■ Animals active mainly by day are called diurnal animals. Animals active mainly at night are called nocturnal animals.

■ Many animals, such as barnacles, are influenced by the rhythms of the tides.

■ The annual rhythms of some organisms allow them to reproduce only at specific times of the year.

■ The process in which body activities almost stop is called hibernation when it occurs during cold weather and estivation when it occurs during hot weather.

23-2 Chemical Cycles

■ Most chemicals in matter can be recycled and used by living things over and over again.

■ Nitrogen-fixing bacteria take free nitrogen in the air and place it in nitrogen compounds used by plants to make food.

■ Water circulates endlessly between the atmosphere and the surface of the earth.

■ Animals breathe in oxygen and release carbon dioxide. Plants take in carbon dioxide and release oxygen. In this way, the oxygen/carbon dioxide cycle is maintained.

23-3 Ecological Succession

■ Sometimes organisms entering an environment change that environment. This leads to changes in the species living in that environment, as well as to physical changes in the environment. Long-term changes in conditions and species in an area are known as ecological succession.

■ Ecological succession usually takes a long time, often spanning centuries.

VOCABULARY

Define each term in a complete sentence.

biological clock	estivation	hibernation	nocturnal animal
diurnal animal	evaporation	nitrogen fixation	photosynthesis
ecological succession			

CONTENT REVIEW: MULTIPLE CHOICE

Choose the letter of the answer that best completes each statement.

1. Biological clocks can be set by a
   a. change in temperature.   b. change in rainfall.
   c. change in amount of daylight.   d. all of these.
2. Which of these is *not* a cycle in nature?
   a. shifting tides   b. ecological succession
   c. change from day to night   d. changing seasons
3. Waking in the morning and sleeping at night is an example of
   a. annual rhythm.   b. lunar rhythm.
   c. daily rhythm.   d. all of these.

4. Which of the following is a nocturnal animal?
a. squirrel monkey   b. Amazon parrot
c. great horned owl   d. all of these

5. How many high tides and low tides are there each day?
a. one   b. two   c. four   d. eight

6. Which of these are *not* normally affected by the rise and fall of tides?
a. barnacles   b. sharks   c. clams   d. grunion

7. Migration of birds is an example of a(n)
a. annual rhythm.   b. tidal rhythm.
c. daily rhythm.   d. lunar rhythm.

8. About 79 percent of the atmosphere is made up of
a. oxygen.   b. carbon dioxide.   c. nitrogen.   d. water vapor.

9. During photosynthesis, plants break down water into
a. hydrogen and oxygen atoms.   b. oxygen and carbon atoms.
c. hydrogen and carbon atoms.   d. nitrogen and oxygen atoms.

10. Which of these do plants use to produce food?
a. carbon dioxide   b. water   c. sunlight   d. all of these

CONTENT REVIEW: COMPLETION

Fill in the word or words that best complete each statement.

1. The name of the inner clock that allows an organism to stay in tune with natural rhythms is its _____.

2. Animals that are active at night are called _____.

3. _____ are caused mainly by the gravitational pull of the moon on the earth's bodies of water.

4. Frogs often dig into the mud of lakes in the winter as part of the process called _____.

5. _____ have young in bays along Mexico in winter and feed in Arctic waters in summer.

6. _____ take free nitrogen from the air and combine it with other elements to produce nitrogen compounds.

7. _____ is a process in which liquid water changes to water vapor.

8. Green plants produce food in a process called _____.

9. Animals would have used up the available oxygen supply in the atmosphere if it were not for the activities of living things called _____.

10. The gradual change in a particular area from one group of living things to another is called _____.

CONTENT REVIEW: TRUE OR FALSE

Determine whether each statement is true or false. If it is true, write "true." If it is false, change the underlined word or words to make the statement true.

1. <u>Very few</u> conditions in the environment may influence the biological clocks of various organisms.

2. Chinese alligators nest only in the spring when river levels are at their <u>lowest</u>.

3. <u>Diurnal animals</u> are active mainly by day.

4. Tidal rhythms are often called <u>solar</u> rhythms.
5. Grunion always mate after the <u>lowest</u> of the tides has peaked.
6. Antelope on the African plains give birth to their young just <u>before</u> the rainy season.
7. During the hot, dry summer the process of slowing down body activities is known as <u>hibernation</u>.
8. Most chemicals on the earth <u>cannot</u> be recycled, or reused.
9. <u>Denitrifying bacteria</u> break down nitrogen compounds and return nitrogen gas to the atmosphere.
10. The atmosphere is made up of <u>40 percent</u> oxygen.

CONCEPT REVIEW: SKILL BUILDING

Use the skills you have developed in the chapter to complete each activity.

1. **Relating cause and effect** Recently there has been great concern that by burning fossil fuels such as coal and oil people are adding a lot of carbon dioxide to the atmosphere. In addition, people are destroying forests at a rapid rate. How could this affect the oxygen/carbon dioxide cycle?
2. **Expressing an opinion** Most people do not think they are influenced by lunar rhythms. However, not all people agree. What do you think about the idea that people are affected by the rise and fall of tides?
3. **Applying concepts** Twice a year you change the time on your clocks. In the spring, you move your clocks ahead one hour. In the fall, you move your clocks back one hour. Do these actions have any effect on your biological clock? Explain your answer.
4. **Relating facts** Explain why most people are unaware of ecological succession even though it may be occurring all around them.
5. **Applying concepts** Explain how chemicals in your food today may have been part of a dinosaur.
6. **Sequencing events** Trace the path of water in the water cycle.
7. **Relating concepts** Like all living things, humans have an internal biological clock. This clock is tied to a 24-hour day–night cycle. Explain how you can upset your biological clock.
8. **Applying formulas** During the process of photosynthesis, carbon dioxide (CO_2), water (H_2O), and energy from sunlight produce oxygen (O_2) and a food called glucose ($C_6H_{12}O_6$). Using this information, write a word equation and a chemical equation for photosynthesis.

CONCEPT REVIEW: ESSAY

Discuss each of the following in a brief paragraph.

1. Explain how nocturnal animals and diurnal animals can share the same environment in harmony.
2. Describe the nitrogen cycle.
3. How does precipitation differ from evaporation? How is it the same?
4. Compare hibernation and estivation.
5. What is nitrogen fixation? Which living things perform this process?
6. Explain the process of photosynthesis.
7. What is a biological clock? Give an example of a biological clock.

24 Conservation of Natural Resources

CHAPTER SECTIONS

24-1 Nonliving Resources
24-2 Living Resources

CHAPTER OBJECTIVES

After completing this chapter,
you will be able to:

24-1 Classify living and nonliving natural resources.

24-1 List various farming methods used to conserve our soil resources.

24-2 Explain how people have caused the extinction and near extinction of various plant and animal species.

24-2 Describe a goal of conservation efforts.

At dawn, the Bialowieza Forest in Poland is cloaked in fog and mist. A herd of shaggy, horned animals slips out of the trees as silently as the fog. Half-hidden in the mist, the animals look like ghosts—and, in a way, they are.

The animals are European bison. The European bison is a relative of the American buffalo, which is pictured on the opposite page. European bison are survivors from the past. Prehistoric people hunted them, as did the kings and nobles of the Middle Ages. Over time, so many bison were killed that their numbers dwindled. Making matters worse, the forests in which they lived gradually disappeared as people cut down trees to be used for lumber.

By the beginning of this century, European bison remained only in a few remote spots such as the Bialowieza Forest. When World War I raged across Europe, most of the wild bison perished.

A few of the animals survived in zoos. Others lived on animal preserves, where they were safeguarded. The bison reproduced until their numbers increased to the point that some could be released in the wild again. In 1952, bison were set free in the Bialowieza Forest. This particular herd has grown. Bison have also been released in a few other places in Europe.

Saving the European bison, a type of natural resource, is an outstanding example of conservation. In the following pages, you will find out more about the earth's natural resources. You will also learn how people can destroy or protect these natural resources.

American buffalo grazing

Figure 24-1 *To conserve plant life, people plant new trees* (left) *to replace mature trees that have been cut down* (right).

24-1 Nonliving Resources

The aim of **conservation** is to protect the environment. Conservation is the wise use of natural resources, so that they will not be used up too soon or used in a way that will damage the environment. **Natural resources** are materials produced by the environment and used by people. Conservation involves planning for the future.

Scientists divide natural resources into two kinds, living and nonliving. **Plants and animals are the earth's living natural resources. Nonliving resources include water and soil, as well as minerals and fossil fuels such as coal and oil.**

Water

Water! No living thing, neither plant nor animal, can survive without this precious liquid. Yet for people, water is even more than something to drink. People use water for bathing, cooking, growing crops, and in industry. However, as human populations increase, agriculture and industry need more and more water—often more water than is readily available. Also, while some parts of the world have adequate water supplies, other parts of the world are dry. In 1983, for example, there was widespread flooding in the United States due to heavy rains and snowfalls. At the very same time, in parts of Africa there had been no rain for more than seven years.

As time goes on, more and more water on the earth is becoming unusable. One obvious reason is water pollution. But there are less obvious reasons as well. In many places, the environment has been changed by the actions of people so that less water is available than in the past. In the Andes Mountains of South America, for example, farmers have cleared many of the forests off steep slopes. Forests and other vegetation slow water runoff. When rain falls on slopes that no longer have forests, the runoff rushes down in floods and sweeps into rivers. Eventually, the fresh water enters the salty oceans.

What can be done about our dwindling water supplies? One solution is to replant vegetation on barren slopes. Another solution is to build dams for water storage. Although dams work, they can create another problem. Once the land is flooded behind a dam, it no longer is available for the animals and plants that lived there.

In their search for water, people often drill for new sources of **ground water.** Ground water is water found below the surface of the earth. Half of the drinking water in the United States comes from the ground. More than 300 billion liters of ground water are taken out of the ground daily in this country, mostly for factories and farms. Ground water is the

Figure 24-2 *Rain does not fall evenly over the earth. At times, some areas may get too much rain* (left), *while other areas may get too little rain* (right).

Erosion

If the world loses 1.8 billion kilograms of soil to erosion each year, how many kilograms of soil are lost after 3.5 years?

Figure 24-3 *These people in Nepal have stripped a mountainside of trees to obtain much needed firewood. But in doing so, they are also speeding up the erosion of the mountain soil.*

most important source of fresh water in places such as the western United States and northern Africa, which have little surface water in lakes and rivers.

It takes a few hundred years for a large amount of ground water to accumulate. In many areas, ground water is being used up faster than it is being replaced. As a result, the level of ground water drops and eventually streams and lakes may dry up.

Even though scientists find new sources of water, the total amount of water available is limited. As populations continue to grow and their water needs increase, the best way to ensure the world's water supply is to conserve water. Treatment of sewage before it is released into rivers helps to avoid pollution and to conserve water. Planning for water use by industries and farms cuts down waste. Maintaining watersheds, or areas with trees and other plants, helps to store ground water and keep the soil from washing away. Also, people can manage their own water use more wisely, particularly during times of water shortages.

Soil

The carrying of soil from one place to another by water and wind is called **erosion.** Erosion is a natural process, but people have quickened its pace. Each year, the world loses more than 1.8 billion kilograms of soil to erosion. Most of the soil is the rich, upper layer called **topsoil,** which crops need to grow. Across the world, topsoil is being lost at a yearly rate of up to 10 times the rate at which new soil forms.

Much of the erosion results from people removing vegetation from the land in an uncontrolled manner. Forests, for example, may be completely cut to make room for farms or for timber and firewood. In addition, people in many developing countries depend on wood for heat and cooking. For example, in parts of the Himalayan Mountains of Asia, families may spend a fourth of their day searching for firewood. Today, many areas of these remote, high mountains have been stripped bare of forests. As a result, during the seasonal heavy rains called monsoons, torrents of water race down the mountainsides, carrying off the fertile topsoil.

Erosion is at its worst in developing countries because farmers lack the knowledge and means for wise agricultural practices. The stripping of trees and other vegetation from the land has spread out of control. Much of the vegetation is removed not by people but by their grazing livestock, such as cattle. Cattle in many parts of Africa have overgrazed grassy plains. Without grass, whose spreading roots help hold soil down, the wind can blow off the topsoil. No other plants then grow, and once-rich areas turn to desert.

Developed countries, however, also have erosion problems. Topsoil has been lost in parts of western North America overgrazed by cattle and sheep. To avoid future soil loss, farmers now leave rows of trees called windbreaks between their fields. The windbreaks help prevent wind from carrying away topsoil.

Erosion is not the only danger to soil. Nutrients needed by plants can be washed away by water through a process called **depletion.** Depletion also occurs when one type of crop is grown on soil for too long. Corn, for example, removes important nitrates from the soil. In Chapter 23, you read about the importance of nitrates in the soil. If corn is grown in the same soil for many years in a row, the nitrates in the soil will be used up.

Fertilizers can return depleted nutrients to the soil. Alternating crops each year on the same land, a method known as **crop rotation,** can also return nutrients. This involves planting a nitrate-using crop, such as corn, one year and a nitrate-producing crop, such as clover, the next year.

Several other methods of farming can prevent the loss of soil. Plowing a slope in vertical rows up and down its incline causes erosion. A better method, called **contour farming,** is to plow horizontally across the face of a slope. Another method of conserving soil is to make a series of level plots in steplike fashion on the slope. This method is called **terracing.** Contour farming and terracing slow runoff and allow water to soak into the soil.

Fields of corn and other grains often lose soil because the plants are spaced far apart, leaving bare soil in between. A method of avoiding this problem

Figure 24-4 *These screens have been placed over the river bank to control the erosion of soil.*

Figure 24-5 *One method used by farmers to conserve soil is called terracing. This method involves making a series of level steplike plots on a slope to slow water runoff.*

is **strip cropping.** In strip cropping, farmers plant low strips of cover crops that hold down the soil between strips of grain crops.

SECTION REVIEW

1. Into what two divisions do scientists divide our natural resources? Give an example of each.
2. What is water called when it is found below the earth's surface?
3. What two methods can farmers use to slow water runoff?

24-2 Living Resources

Since life began on the earth, countless species of plants and animals have appeared. Some still remain today, but untold numbers have become extinct, or died off. **Extinction,** the process by which a species passes out of existence, is a natural part of our planet's history. Species can become extinct because they cannot adjust to changes in the earth's environment. The environment is always changing. Streams shift course. Mountain chains rise. Climates become warmer or colder.

Species change too. Organisms with new traits can appear. These traits may then be passed on to offspring. If new traits help a species adjust to environmental change, the species survives. If not, it can become extinct. The race to survive often means adapting to environmental change.

Throughout most of the earth's history, the race to survive occurred at a slow pace. Great natural changes, such as shifting climates, usually happen over long periods of time. So it may take hundreds, thousands, or millions of years for a species to vanish. Today, however, people and their activities have increased the pace. Some alterations people made in the environment caused it to change so rapidly that many species have not been able to keep up. These species have become extinct.

An important goal of conservation is to help protect those species of plants and animals that are in danger of becoming extinct. Because extinction is a natural process, not all species can be saved. So scientists involved in conservation often concentrate on those species that are in danger mainly due to the actions of people.

Plants

More than 300 species of plants in the United States alone have become extinct since the Europeans first came to the Americas. Worldwide, a tenth

Activity

The Dodo

The dodo bird was a most unusual animal. Unfortunately, all the world's dodos have become extinct. Using reference books in the library, report on the fascinating story of the dodo and how it came to be extinct.

Figure 24-6 *Over the course of history, the climate on Earth has changed many times. On the left are the lush forests of Greenland many millions of years ago. On the right is Greenland as it appears today.*

Figure 24-7 *An area in this rain forest is being cleared for the growing of crops. As a result, many plant and animal habitats are destroyed.*

Figure 24-8 *These oconee bells grow in shady areas. If trees shading the flowers were cut down, the oconee bells might soon become extinct.*

of the plants known to science are in danger of extinction. Combined, this means 20,000 different kinds of plants are close to disappearing. Vegetation in general is suffering in many parts of the world. Erosion and overgrazing in the Middle East, for instance, have turned forests into bare ground.

The most dangerous threat to living things is the destruction of their habitat. This destruction can happen when people clear land for farms, cities, and other large communities. For example, when Europeans first arrived, forests covered most of the eastern half of the United States. Almost all the original forest was cleared to make room for farms and towns and to harvest timber.

Today the largest forests on the earth, the tropical rain forests, are being destroyed for the same reasons. Scientists fear that half of all tropical forests will be gone by the end of this century. When the forest trees are cut, not only are the trees lost, but the thousands of other plants that live on or among the trees also vanish.

Sometimes, if a species of plant only lives in a small area, it does not take a big change to destroy the species. Oconee bells—little white flowers that grow only in a few shady woodlands of Georgia, Virginia, and the Carolinas—must have shade to survive. Cutting down just a few trees around an area where oconee bells grow would spell the end for the flowers there.

There are more than a thousand species of plants that are found only in Hawaii. Almost half are in danger of extinction. One of the main reasons for this threat is that plants and animals from the United States mainland have been brought to Hawaii. Goats brought from other areas, for example, run wild in many parts of Hawaii. They have eaten vast numbers of wild plants. A geranium that grows as big as a tree, which lives only on one volcano in Hawaii, has almost been eaten into extinction by the goats. Elsewhere, blackberries brought from Europe have crowded out many Hawaiian plants.

The threats to a species can come from many sources. The giant saguaro is a cactus that can grow 15 meters high. It grows only in the Sonora Desert of northwestern Mexico, southwestern Arizona, and southeastern California. Cattle have trampled many young saguaros. Vehicles have crushed them as well. Other saguaros have been uprooted and taken for house plants. Resorts for tourists and housing developments have been built on the desert where the saguaros grow. People even have chopped them up for fun. For all these reasons, scientists fear saguaros will become extinct.

In the long run, the threat to plants is a threat to people as well. Throughout history, about 3000 kinds of plants have been used for food. Today most food comes from about 15 kinds of plants, chiefly grains. These grains all descended from wild plants. If wild plants are destroyed, scientists wonder where

Activity

The Greenhouse Effect

The world's trees remove a vast amount of carbon dioxide gas from the air during photosynthesis. When forests are cut down, the amount of carbon dioxide in the air increases. Burning fossil fuels also adds carbon dioxide to the air.

Using reference books and magazines from the library, research the process called the greenhouse effect. This effect is caused by carbon dioxide in the air. Find out how increasing carbon dioxide levels in the air can result in changes in climate and the effects such changes could have on plants and wildlife.

Figure 24-9 *People have hunted whales for centuries. Today, many species of whales are extinct or endangered.*

Figure 24-10 *Hunting some animals, such as the black rhinoceros, is outlawed in order to prevent these animals from becoming extinct.*

Figure 24-11 *As these elephants pass through the dense African bush, they may come upon a farmland clearing and trample it. To protect their farms, farmers may kill the elephants, which may eventually lead to the animals' extinction.*

the new food sources of the future may come from. Also, many medicines come from plants. Some scientists suggest that perhaps 50,000 kinds of medicines and other useful chemicals are still found in plants. Each time a species of plant vanishes, the odds of finding a new source of food or medicine go down.

Wildlife

The destruction of plants also has a direct impact on wildlife, or animals. When tropical forests are cleared, for example, wildlife living in them, such as jaguars and parrots, lose their habitat and can quickly become extinct. Like plants, wild animals have been destroyed because people used them thoughtlessly and wastefully. In colonial times, a bird called the passenger pigeon was so numerous in eastern North America its flocks darkened the skies. There may have been two billion of these birds. People felt there were so many they could shoot all they wanted for food. By the beginning of this century, the passenger pigeon was extinct.

Uncontrolled hunting threatens several animal species today. Although the black rhinoceros is protected by law in many African countries, people still kill it, not for food but for its horn. A powder made from the rhino horn is incorrectly considered to have medicinal properties in parts of Asia, where people pay high prices for it. Some Africans kill rhinos and sell the horns to earn money.

Human populations are growing rapidly in Africa, which causes another problem for large animals such as rhinos and elephants. People farm in areas where these animals live. Farmers do not want the animals eating crops and trampling the land. So the farmers kill the animals or ask their governments to remove the animals.

Sometimes what seem like harmless actions by people mean trouble for wildlife. Farmers in southern Florida are draining marshes to grow more crops. The marshes contain snails eaten by a hawk-like bird known as the Everglades kite. As the marshes vanish, so does the kite's food. The Everglades kite is close to extinction.

Another example of people accidentally causing a species to die off occurred about a century ago. A lighthouse keeper on an island off New Zealand had a pet cat. One day the cat appeared carrying a small dead bird. As weeks passed, it killed more birds of the same kind. Scientists eventually discovered that the bird was a new species of wren. By the time they knew this, however, the cat had killed every one and the species had become extinct.

Saving Plants and Wildlife

Just as human activities have hurt plants and wildlife, people can take action to save them. Government agencies and many organizations are devoted to conserving living things. One organization has suggested a "World Conservation Strategy." This strategy is a plan to help countries develop and use their natural resources wisely. The organization seeks ways through which development of farms and industries will not wipe out plants and animals. As

Career: *Conservationist*

HELP WANTED: CONSERVATIONIST
Bachelor's degree in the biological sciences or in natural resources required. To work as part of a conservation field force in the scientific management of national forest land. Involves outdoor work and research.

At one time, prairie chickens lived throughout the North American prairies. Since then, however, the prairies have been farmed with corn and wheat. The farming deprived the prairie chickens of a place to live, thus greatly reducing their numbers.

The people who see to it that the use of natural resources causes the least possible harm to the environment are called **conservationists.** Their major concern is to keep advanced technology from depleting or damaging resources such as coal, oil, water, air, and living things. As part of their conservation activities, they may seek solutions to problems caused by poisonous pesticides, insect and disease control, and illegal hunting of endangered wildlife.

There are many varied positions in the field of conservation. One might work as a soil scientist, range manager, wildlife manager, or researcher. A conservationist might be involved in water and land management, improving habitats, surveys, or research. People who become conservationists have an interest in nature and have a desire to be part of a program that cares for natural resources. For more information about this rewarding field, write to the Forest Service, U.S. Department of Agriculture, P.O. Box 2417, Washington, DC 20013.

Figure 24-12 *A wide variety of animals, including giraffes, are protected on this African game preserve.*

Figure 24-13 *At one time, the Peregrine falcon was close to extinction in the United States. Today, through the actions of conservationists, Peregrine falcons once more soar through the skies.*

part of the strategy for Indonesia, for instance, some of the money from cutting timber in tropical forests will be used to plant new trees. Programs are underway in Africa to bring more tourists to the area so that they can marvel at its wildlife. In this way, Africans can earn money through the tourist industry. Then they will want to leave some wildlife habitats undisturbed.

Preserving habitats is the most important step in saving plants and animals. Many countries have set up parks and preserves that cannot be developed by industry. In 1976, for instance, Costa Rican officials set aside over 500 square kilometers of rain forest as a preserve. As a result, many rare plants and animals live and thrive in the forest.

Another method of conservation is to limit the number of plants and animals that people may use so there are enough left to reproduce. Limitations are the reason for hunting and fishing laws that specify the size and number of the catch. As long as hunting and fishing are controlled, they do not threaten the future of species. Control means the laws must be enforced. In Arizona, for example, state wardens, called cactus cops, are assigned to make sure people do not uproot rare cacti.

Rare species, of course, must be completely protected. Sometimes, however, a rare species increases so that it can be used by people once again. During the 1960s, laws were enacted to protect the American alligator. The alligator was decreasing in numbers because too many had been killed for hides and their wetlands habitat had been destroyed. Under protection, alligators increased in number, and in some places they can be hunted for their hides again.

Educating people about the values of plants and wildlife also is an important part of conservation. Recently, desert tribes in Israel, for example, killed wild goats called ibexes. The government explained to the tribes that if they killed too many goats, the goats would disappear. The government paid the desert people to watch after the ibexes. Within a few years, Israel had large numbers of ibexes. Moreover, leopards suddenly returned. The ibex is an important food source for leopards.

As the case of the European bison mentioned in the beginning of this chapter proves, animals that

Figure 24-14 *Hunters once brought both the Israeli ibex (left) and the American wild turkey (right) close to extinction. Today, careful wildlife management has greatly increased their numbers.*

have disappeared from the wild can be bred in captivity and then released. When in the 1960s an antelope called the Arabian oryx (AWR-iks) seemed doomed in the wild, conservationists captured some and sent them to zoos in the United States. The zoos bred the antelopes, and 10 years later some were set free where they once had roamed.

Such success stories show that conservation works. Indeed, while many plants and wildlife are in danger today, many more have been saved from extinction.

All such conservation efforts require the cooperation of people. At the same time, conservation will not work unless the needs of people are taken into consideration. The World Conservation Strategy recognizes that the requirements of plants and animals must be balanced with those of people. "Development and conservation are equally necessary for our survival," states this international document. Since it was introduced in 1980, the strategy has been adopted as a framework for conservation in dozens of countries. If it works, worries about endangered plants and wildlife could be a thing of the past.

Figure 24-15 *An Arabian oryx thrives in Phoenix, Arizona. By breeding the oryx in American zoos, conservationists were later able to return the oryxes to their natural habitats.*

SECTION REVIEW

1. What is the process by which a species passes out of existence?
2. What two factors led to bare ground in the Middle East where forests once grew?
3. What is the most important step in saving plants and wildlife?

LABORATORY ACTIVITY

Making a Landfill

Purpose

In this activity, you will build your own landfill. You will then be able to observe how a variety of materials are recycled in soil.

Materials *(per group)*

4-L glass jar with lid
Topsoil (enough to fill the jar one-third to one-half full)
Water
Litter
Glass-marking pencil

Procedure

1. After eating your lunch collect all your litter. Some examples of litter include orange peels, milk containers, plastic wrap, and pieces of bread.
2. Bring the litter into your classroom and make a list of the items.
3. Cover the bottom of a glass jar with soil.
4. Place the items on the soil in the jar, close to the glass.
5. Using a glass-marking pencil, circle the location of each item on the outside of the jar.
6. Add another layer of soil on top of the litter.
7. Add more litter. Again, mark each item's location on the outside of the jar and add more soil so that the objects are covered.
8. Water the soil in the jar lightly. Place the lid on the jar.
9. Predict whether each item will decompose. Observe your landfill every week for a month.

Observations and Conclusions

1. Describe each item in the landfill after one day, a week, two weeks, and a month.
2. Which items decompose fastest? What will these items become?
3. What things do not seem to change?
4. If you had sterilized the soil, jar, and items beforehand, would the materials have decomposed? Why?
5. Compare your prediction with your actual results.

CHAPTER REVIEW

SUMMARY

24-1 Nonliving Resources

- Conservation is a plan for the wise use of the earth's natural resources. Nonliving natural resources include water, soil, minerals, and fossil fuels.

- In many places, the clearing of forests to provide firewood has led to the runoff of great quantities of water where once the water was absorbed by the soil.

- About half the drinking water in the United States comes from ground water.

- The wise management of water is a task for scientists, farmers, industry, and all other people as well.

- The removal of soil by wind and water is called erosion.

- Poor farming techniques have led to the erosion of a great deal of rich topsoil throughout the world.

- Proper farming methods such as crop rotation, contour farming, and strip cropping can help conserve our soil resources.

24-2 Living Resources

- When an entire species dies off, it is said to be extinct.

- When the environment changes, some species die off while others may thrive.

- Worldwide, a tenth of the plants known to science are in danger of extinction. This means 20,000 different kinds of plants are close to disappearing.

- Many plants and wildlife are in danger of becoming extinct due to people's actions.

- People are responsible for saving many plants and wildlife that once were in danger of becoming extinct.

VOCABULARY

Define each of the following in a complete sentence.

conservation	**ground water**
contour farming	**natural resource**
crop rotation	**strip cropping**
depletion	**terracing**
erosion	**topsoil**
extinction	

CONTENT REVIEW: MULTIPLE CHOICE

Choose the letter of the answer that best completes each statement.

1. Living natural resources do *not* include
   a. people.   b. plants.
   c. soil.   d. animals.
2. Nonliving natural resources include
   a. minerals.   b. water.
   c. fossil fuels.   d. all of these.

3. What percentage of drinking water is supplied by ground water in the United States?
   a. 25 percent   b. 50 percent
   c. 75 percent   d. 100 percent

4. The carrying of soil from one place to another by wind or water is called
   a. flooding.   b. erosion.
   c. terracing.   d. runoff.

5. The rich upper layer of soil is called
   a. subsoil.   b. fertilizer.
   c. topsoil.   d. a watershed.

6. When nutrients are washed out of the soil, the process is called
   a. erosion.   b. crop rotation.
   c. depletion.   d. fertilization.

7. Planting a different crop every few years is called
   a. terracing.   b. contour farming.
   c. strip cropping.   d. crop rotation.

8. Plowing horizontally across the face of a slope is called
   a. terracing.   b. contour farming.
   c. strip cropping.   d. crop rotation.

9. The wise use of natural resources is known as
   a. conservation.   b. depletion.
   c. erosion.   d. extinction.

10. Which soil conservation method involves making a series of steplike plots on a slope?
   a. terracing   b. contour farming
   c. strip cropping   d. crop rotation

CONTENT REVIEW: COMPLETION

Fill in the word or words that best complete each statement.

1. _____ is the wise use of the earth's natural resources.

2. _____ are materials produced by the environment and used by people.

3. Farmers often clear vegetation off steep slopes in order to increase water _____.

4. A method in which vegetation is replanted to slow the loss of rainwater is called creating a(n) _____.

5. A method in which crops are planted in horizontal rows along the sides of a hill is called _____.

6. The process in which nutrients needed by plants are washed away by water is _____.

7. _____ is water found below the surface of the earth.

8. _____ are added to the soil by crops such as clover.

9. The process by which a species of plant or animal passes out of existence is known as _____.

10. _____ is the carrying of soil from one place to another by wind and water.

CONTENT REVIEW: TRUE OR FALSE

Determine whether each statement is true or false. If it is true, write "true." If it is false, change the underlined word or words to make the statement true.

1. Supplies of water are distributed <u>equally</u> throughout the world.
2. Ground water is an important source of water in places like the <u>eastern</u> United States, where there is little surface water.
3. Stripping trees off mountains <u>increases</u> erosion.
4. Mountains suffer most from erosion when slopes <u>are not too</u> steep.
5. Planting in a series of level plots on a hill is called <u>contour farming</u>.
6. When <u>almost all</u> of a species has died off, the species is said to be extinct.
7. <u>Terracing</u>, a soil conservation method, involves making a series of level steplike plots on a slope.
8. <u>Draining marshes</u> in the Florida Everglades has caused the near extinction of the Everglades kite.
9. Conservationists <u>are</u> concerned with the needs of people and the preservation of plants and wildlife.
10. <u>Conservation</u> is the process by which a species of plant or animal passes out of existence.

CONCEPT REVIEW: SKILL BUILDING

Use the skills you have developed in the chapter to complete each activity.

1. **Relating cause and effect** "Conservation of nonliving resources is the first step in conservation of living resources." Explain what this statement means.
2. **Relating facts** Identify the natural resource that is being conserved for each of the following.
   a. reduced-flow shower heads
   b. national parks
   c. water treatment plants
   d. controlled hunting
3. **Making calculations** A leaky faucet loses 50 drops of water every minute. How many drops would be lost in a hour? In a day? In a month?
4. **Applying concepts** Extinction is a natural process. What does this statement mean to you?
5. **Applying definitions** Are people natural resources? Explain your answer.
6. **Applying concepts** Why is it an advantage for a farmer to use soil conservation methods?
7. **Making predictions** Predict how an increase in population will affect the soil in an area.

CONCEPT REVIEW: ESSAY

Discuss each of the following in a brief paragraph.

1. Compare living and nonliving natural resources. Give an example of each.
2. Discuss two water conservation methods.
3. What is the effect of an increasing population on the water supply?
4. List and describe four methods used by farmers to conserve soil.
5. What is extinction? Give two examples of living things that have become extinct.
6. Discuss some methods of saving wildlife from extinction.
7. Explain what the World Conservation Strategy is.

Adventures in Science

AGENT X:
Animal Smugglers Beware!

Parrots are beautiful and popular pets in the United States. So the smuggling of these birds into our country can be a very profitable business. Because many parrots are very rare and others carry diseases, customs and wildlife agents try to stop the smuggling.

Leaving their van parked nearby, two men walked quietly toward a large warehouse in Laredo, Texas, near the border with Mexico. One of the men was square-shouldered and had dark hair and a gray-streaked beard. His companion, younger and slimmer, had long, sandy hair and a beard of the same color. Both men looked tough and determined. And they each carried a gun. The older man had his gun hidden inside his jacket; the other man had his in his boot.

The pair, carrying $4000 in $100 bills, entered the warehouse and talked for some minutes with the owner. They claimed to be interested in buying merchandise they believed the owner had stored in the building. The owner pointed the visitors in the direction of a small room.

As one of the visitors opened the door, loud, squawking noises could be heard. The visitors knew immediately that they had found the "goods." For inside a cage were 11 brightly colored parrots. In another room were an additional 11 parrots, stuffed into two sacks made of netting.

"Keep the noise down," snapped the warehouse owner, worried that the parrots would squawk even louder if further disturbed.

The warehouse owner had reason to worry. He was committing a serious crime! The parrots he was selling had been brought into the country illegally. They had been smuggled across the border from Mexico into the United States. Selling the parrots was against the law, and the owner knew it. So did the visitors. But they had nothing to fear because they were United States government agents. They were working undercover to stop the illegal trade in smuggled parrots.

PROTECTING THE ENDANGERED AND DANGEROUS

Parrots are popular pets in this country. They can often sell for hundreds or even thousands of dollars each. Several types of parrots, however, are in danger of becoming extinct. To keep these parrots from dying out completely, federal laws against importing or selling them have been passed.

But even those parrots that can be brought into the country are carefully screened by the government. For parrots can carry diseases. One such disease is Newcastle disease, which can spread easily to chickens. Over the years farmers have lost millions of chickens and millions of dollars because of Newcastle disease. Parrots can also infect humans with a disease known as psittacosis, which is pronounced as if the "p" weren't there. Psittacosis can cause high fever and pneumonia. So Federal Customs officials carefully check any parrot arriving in this country to make sure it is not a protected type or a diseased parrot.

Agents of the United States Customs Service and the United States Fish and Wildlife Service stand watch to protect wildlife.

FIGHTING WILDLIFE CRIME

The two undercover agents, whose names must remain secret for their safety, had been tipped off about the parrots being sold illegally. So they posed as customers who wanted to buy some parrots. Once the agents were sure they had their man, however, they pulled out their badges and arrested the owner. Now there would be one fewer supplier of illegal parrots!

The older agent works for the United States Customs Service. It is his job to prevent the smuggling of a wide variety of goods, including animals. The younger man, who goes by the name "X," is a special agent for the United States Fish and Wildlife Service, a division of the Department of the Interior. His job is to enforce those laws designed to conserve wildlife.

Like many other agents of the Fish and Wildlife Service, "X" has college degrees in both law and biology. He is an effective undercover agent because he is a good actor and can assume many disguises. Wearing old clothes and driving a dirty, beat-up car, "X" easily blends in with the street scene. But "X" is a tough man, as are many of the criminals he is trailing. It is quite common for these smugglers to bring in more than parrots. Their goods often include drugs.

The United States Government hopes to protect endangered parrots by forbidding their sale. If such parrots cannot be sold, people will stop taking them out of their natural habitat. So while Agent "X" is working on the Texas border, he is also helping to protect parrots that live in forests far away.

"X" takes his work very seriously, for wildlife crime is a very serious matter. Those people who commit wildlife crimes do not always see it that way. They often do not believe that what they are doing is wrong because it involves only animals. However, when they meet up with Agent "X" and are led off to jail in handcuffs, the truth is apparent. In the eyes of the law, they are criminals. And they will be justly punished—thanks to the efforts of people like Agent "X."

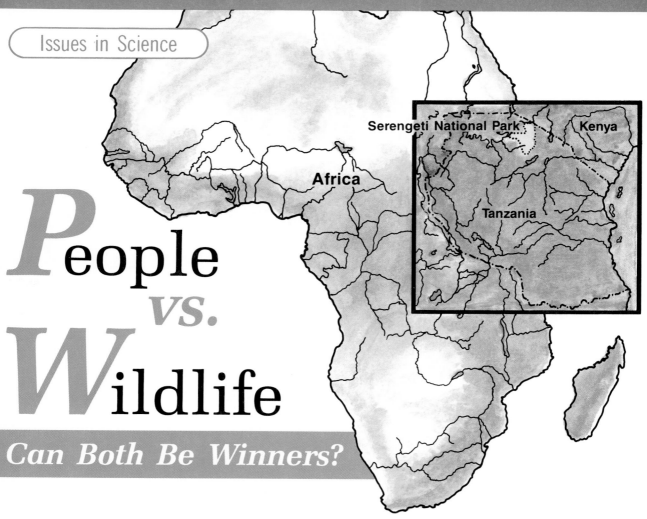

Issues in Science

People
vs.
Wildlife

Can Both Be Winners?

The rainy season has come to the Serengeti Plain of Tanzania, in East Africa. Land that was parched during the dry season is now green with grass. As far as the eye can see, large, gray antelopes, with long tails and curving horns, feed on the new grass. More than 1.5 million of these antelopes, called wildebeests, gather on the Serengeti Plain during the wet season. With them are vast numbers of other animals such as zebras, gazelles, buffaloes, elephants, wild dogs, wart hogs, lions, and cheetahs. Nowhere else on the earth do so many large animals gather in one place.

Most of the Serengeti Plain lies within Tanzania's Serengeti National Park. The park covers 5600 square miles and stretches from Tanzania to Kenya, Tanzania's neighbor to the north. Many conservationists consider the Serengeti the most important wildlife refuge in the world. They hope that Tanzania will protect the wildlife of the Serengeti, whatever the cost. Conservationists feel that the Serengeti belongs not only to Tanzania but also to the world.

So far, Tanzania has done a good job of preserving the Serengeti and its wildlife. The Serengeti National Park is devoted exclusively to wildlife. Neither farming nor ranching is permitted there. Rangers patrol the park to make sure these rules are obeyed and that the animals are safe. Scientists also keep an eye on the animals and their habitat to make sure nature stays in balance.

But many Tanzanians do without such things as food, clothing, and fuel. The country is running out of money because it has to import these items at great cost. Tanzania needs to develop its own agriculture, energy resources, and industry. How can Tanzania afford to give land to wildlife that is needed to better the lives of its people?

Many developing countries face the same question. They have beautiful animals and wildlife areas as well as serious poverty, hunger, and disease. These nations may one day be forced to choose between protecting their wildlife or helping their people.

Kenya's large game reserves provide a safe home for many of Africa's threatened species of animals. Kenya's reserves help the country by bringing in money from tourism.

Helping Pay the Way

A growing number of conservationists feel that less developed countries will be able to continue to conserve wildlife only with the help of more developed countries. Speaking about an important game preserve in his country, Kenyan conservationist Richard Leakey said, "It is part of the world's wildlife heritage so the world must help Kenya pay for it."

A similar view has been expressed by the African Wildlife Foundation, a conservation organization in Washington, D.C. A spokesperson for the foundation said, "There is no hope for the survival of the wild places of Africa until they come to be seen not only as part of the whole world's heritage but its responsibility as well."

Conservation organizations in western countries are helping developing countries save wildlife by providing money and vehicles for rangers to use to patrol park land. The organizations are also helping to train people from developing countries to become scientists, wildlife managers, and game wardens.

Even with this help, however, developing countries do not find it easy to set land aside just for wildlife. Because human populations continue to grow very fast in

Seen from above, this herd of wildebeests on the Serengeti Plain during the wet season seems to stretch in all directions.

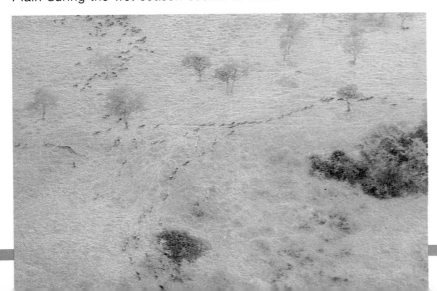

most developing countries, more people need more land on which to live and grow food. If people give up land to wildlife, they expect something in return.

"Wildlife should be a source of prestige, profit, and protein," said Tanzania's President Julius Nyerere. Certainly, by saving great wildlife areas, developing nations gain the respect of other nations. They can also gain profits from tourism. And, perhaps they can use at least some of the animals to feed their people.

Profits and Protein

Probably no other country makes as much profit on wildlife as Kenya. Kenya has many fine wildlife parks and preserves. In fact, wildlife refuges account for six percent of the country's land. Tourists from all over the world flock to Kenya's wildlife refuges. The country takes in more money from tourism that from any other source.

Some conservationists, such as Tanzania's President Nyerere, suggest that by using wildlife to fight hunger, the people will see wildlife as an important natural resource. Norman Myers, a wildlife consultant who has worked in Africa for many years, has suggested that African governments kill antelopes and other abundant animals in parks and refuges to provide meat for people. Using some of the more common animals for food, he said, would save these animals from overcrowding and help people at the same time.

During the 1960s, the Ugandan government killed a number of elephants and hippos. These animals had become too numerous in some of Uganda's national parks. The meat was given to people who lived nearby, and it fed many families for a long time.

Often, however, the wildlife that could be used for food lives far from people. The expense of refrigerating the meat and shipping it to market would make this plan impractical, says Dr. A.R.E. Sinclair. Sinclair is a scientist from the University of British Columbia, who has studied the Serengeti wildebeest. Sinclair also has pointed out the great expense of sending out teams of hunters to kill the animals. Moreover, he adds, there is the expense of the veterinarians. Veterinarians must accompany hunters to inspect meat for disease before it can be eaten by people.

Another argument against using wildlife for food was cited by Nehemiah K. arap Rotich, an official of the East African Wildlife Society, headquartered in Kenya. "If people... get used to seeing antelope in groceries, pretty soon there will be more poachers [illegal hunters] than ever out shooting them in the parks at night," he said. And that might lead to the end of the antelope.

Whether or not wildlife should be used for profit and food remains a big question. But most conservationists agree that if wildlife in developing countries is important to everyone, then people around the world will have to carry the burden of saving the animals.

Elephants like these thrive in Uganda's national parks. In fact, in the 1960s, the elephants had become so numerous that Uganda's parkland could not support them.

WHAT WILL BECOME OF AFRICA'S ANIMALS?

The sun is not yet up. In the kitchen of a comfortable home on the outskirts of a medium-sized city, a man is brewing coffee. Looking at a calendar, he checks the date—January 24, 2050. Although it is still cool outside, the man wears short pants and a short-sleeved shirt. He expects another scorching day here in East Africa.

Just as dawn breaks the man jumps into a vehicle and drives away from the city. On each side of the road sprawl rich farms with vast, neatly cultivated fields of crops. Within 20 minutes, he pulls up to a gate, where a guard greets him. His workday has begun.

This man is a game warden at a large national park and wildlife sanctuary.

At the same time every morning, the warden makes the rounds to see how the wild animals in the park are doing. The road over which he drives is paved with blacktop. The warden wonders how it must have been back in the 1990s, when wardens drove battered cars over roads that were nothing more than dirt tracks.

At that time, the park was far away from any farms and cities. All around it stretched grassy plains. Wild animals wandered freely in and outside of the park. In 2010, however,

the land near the park was set aside for farming. The population of the country had grown so large that all the fertile land was needed to produce food. Only the parks were left wild. "At least," the warden thinks to himself, "my country saved the parks." In a country nearby, the need for food had been so great that even the national parks were turned into farms.

As the warden reaches the park's western boundary, he stops to check the condition of a high wire fence that encloses it. The fence was built 20 years earlier to stop animals from wandering off park property onto farmland. Elephants, buffaloes, antelopes, and zebras were eating the farmers' crops. Lions were killing livestock and threatening people. When the farmers complained, the fence was put up.

The fence was not strong enough to stop the elephants, however. They broke through the fence and kept destroying crops. In the end, there was only one solution to the problem. The elephants had to go. Most were killed, but some young ones were caught and shipped to a special park far away from both farms and cities. It is one of the few parks that are big enough to contain such large, far-roaming animals. Only these parks still have elephants and, for that matter, lions. Even with fences separating them, people do not want to live next door to animals as dangerous as lions. So lions are permitted only in the most distant parks.

Keeping Animals Alive

Back in his vehicle, the warden drives through a broad valley. On all sides are antelopes and zebras, even a few buffaloes. The warden stops at a large concrete drinking tub. He switches on a pump and watches the tub fill with water. It is the dry season in East Africa, and the natural watering holes in the park have dried up. Water must be pumped out of the ground for the animals to drink. Before the fence went up, they could leave the park during the dry season to drink at rivers out on

the plains. But the animals no longer have that freedom, so the warden must provide water for them.

As the warden continues his rounds, he meets two of his park rangers. They are counting the number of wildebeests, a type of antelope, in a herd. Years ago, more than a million wildebeests visited the park each year in the wet season. When the park land dried out and the grass turned brown in the dry season, the wildebeests would leave. They would travel to an area 160 kilometers away to find water and green grass to eat. But that area was finally taken over by farms and villages. Because they no longer had a place to go in the dry season, most of the wildebeests died. The government's conservation department rounded up the rest of the wildebeests and drove them back to the park. They can survive in the park because of the drinking tubs. But the small amount of grass left on the land during the dry season can support few wildebeests.

Wildebeests travel the African countryside in search of green grass to eat. During the dry seasons, the wildebeest must be able to leave an area with dried grass for an area with moist grass. If the human population continues to grow, however, the wildebeest will be unable to roam great distances. What will the consequences be?

So the number of wildebeests must be kept below 20,000 or they will starve. That is why the rangers keep count. Once the herd grows larger than 20,000, the warden and his rangers have to kill some of the older animals to keep the size of the herd down. The meat is given to the farmers living just outside the park.

The warden looks over the wildebeest herd with pride. True, it is not nearly as impressive as the herds that used to roam 40 to 50 years ago, he thinks. But still people have a chance to see the animals. The warden remembers how, on a trip to the United States, he visited a national park in the western part of that country. He saw shaggy American bison walking around in the park. Two centuries had passed since the bison wandered freely far and wide, but in the parks they had been preserved. It is the same with his country's wildebeests.

Twilight Thoughts

Late in the day, the warden pauses at a rocky hillside. For a moment, he glimpses a flash of yellow fur with black spots. Then it is gone. "A leopard," he whispers to himself. It has been a year since he has seen one, although he knows that at least six leopards inhabit the park.

Leopards, unlike lions, are meat eaters that seem able to survive near large numbers of people. Leopards move about mostly at night and are loners. Lions are active partly in daylight and live in groups. It takes the meat of many large animals, such as wildebeests and zebras, to feed a group of lions. But a leopard can live very well on smaller prey, such as baboons.

Driving home, the warden thinks about how wonderful it is to be able to see leopards prowl and zebras roam. He cannot help thinking that if his country had fewer people, there could be more wildlife parks. "But," he reminds himself, "we've done our best."

For Further Reading

If you have an interest in a specific area of General Science or simply want to know more about the topics you are studying, one of the following books may open the door to an exciting learning adventure.

Chapter 1: Exploring Energy

Ruchlis, H. *Discovering Scientific Method.* New York: Harper and Row.

Woods, H., and G. Woods. *The Book of the Unknown.* New York: Random House.

Chapter 2: Heat Energy

Cobb, V. *Heat.* New York: Watts.

Stone, A., and B. Siegel. *The Heat's On.* Englewood Cliffs, NJ: Prentice-Hall.

Chapter 3: Electricity and Magnetism

Lieberg, O. S. *Wonders of Magnets and Magnetism.* New York: Dodd, Mead.

Math, I. *Wires and Watts: Understanding and Using Electricity.* New York: Scribner's.

Chapter 4: Sound

Stevens, S. S., and F. Warshofsky. *Sound and Hearing.* New York: Time-Life.

Wicks, K. *Sound and Recording.* New York: Warwick.

Chapter 5: Light

Maurer, A. *Lasers: Light Wave of the Future.* New York: Arco.

Ubell, E. *The World of Candle and Color.* New York: Atheneum.

Chapter 6: Nuclear Energy

Asimov, I. *How Did We Find Out About Nuclear Power?* New York: Walker.

Fermi, L. *The Story of Atomic Energy.* New York: Random House.

Chapter 7: Energy Resources

Satchwell, J. *Future Sources.* New York: Watts.

Spetgang, T., and M. Wells. *The Children's Solar Energy Book Even Grown-ups Can Understand.* New York: Sterling.

Chapter 8: Chemical Technology

Cobb, V. *The Secret Life of Hardware: A Science Experiment Book.* New York: Lippincott.

Davis, B., and S. Whitefield. *The Coal Question.* New York: Watts.

Chapter 9: Space Technology

Fields, A. *Satellites.* New York: Watts.

Lampton, C. *Space Science.* New York: Watts.

Chapter 10: The Computer Revolution

Henson, H. *Robots.* New York: Warwick.

Knight, D. *Robotics: Past, Present & Future.* New York: Morrow.

Chapter 11: Pollution

Carson, R. *Silent Spring.* New York: Fawcett.

Chapter 12: Currents and Waves

Engel, L., and The Editors of Time-Life Books. *Life Nature Library: The Sea.* Alexandria, VA: Time-Life Books.

Sackett, R., and The Editors of Time-Life Books. *Planet Earth: Edge of the Sea.* Alexandria, VA: Time-Life Books.

Chapter 13: The Ocean Floor

Limburg, P., and J. B. Sweeney. *102 Questions and Answers About the Sea.* New York: Julian Messner.

Whipple, A.B.C., and The Editors of Time-Life Books. *Planet Earth: Restless Oceans.* Alexandria, VA: Time-Life Books.

Chapter 14: Ocean Life

Myers, A. *Sea Creatures Do Amazing Things.* New York: Random House.

Chapter 15: The Atmosphere

Brewer, A., and N. Garland. *Exploring and Understanding Air.* Westchester, IL: Benefic Press.

Chandler, T. *The Air Around Us.* New York: Natural History Press.

Chapter 16: Weather

Alth, M., and C. Alth. *Disastrous Hurricanes and Tornadoes.* New York: Watts.

Brandt, K. *What Makes It Rain? The Story of a Raindrop.* Mahwah, NJ: Troll.

Chapter 17: Climate

Lydolph, P. E. *The Climate of the Earth.* Totowa, NJ: Rowman & Allanheld.

Pringle, L. *Frost Hollows and Other Microclimates.* New York: Morrow.

Chapter 18: Genetics

Gonick, L. and M. Wheelis. *The Cartoon Guide to Genetics.* New York: Harper & Row.

Keller, D. *Sex and the Single Cell.* New York: Bobbs-Merrill.

Chapter 19: Human Genetics

Cole, J., and M. Edmondson. *Twins: The Story of Multiple Births.* New York: Morrow.

Pomerantz, C. *Why You Look Like You, Whereas I Tend to Look More Like Me.* New York: W. R. Scott.

Chapter 20: Changes in Living Things Over Time

British Museum of Natural History. *Origin of Species.* London: British Museum.

Ward, P. *The Adventures of Charles Darwin.* New York: Cambridge University Press.

Chapter 21: The Path to Modern Humans

British Museum of Natural History. *Man's Place in Evolution.* London: British Museum of Natural History and Cambridge: Press Syndicate of the University of Cambridge.

Chapter 22: Biomes

Page, J. *Arid Lands.* Alexandria, VA: Time–Life Books.

The Editors of Time–Life Books. *Grasslands and Tundra.* Alexandria, VA: Time–Life Books.

Chapter 23: Pathways in Nature

Jacobs, F. *Bermuda Petrel: The Bird That Would Not Die.* New York: Morrow.

Riedman, S. *Biological Clocks.* New York: Crowell.

Chapter 24: Conservation of Natural Resources

Grove, N. *Wild Lands for Wildlife: America's National Refuges.* Washington, DC: National Geographic Society.

Pringle, L. *Water: The Next Great Resource Battle.* New York: Macmillan.

Appendix A   THE METRIC SYSTEM

The metric system of measurement is used by scientists throughout the world. It is based on units of ten. Each unit is ten times larger or ten times smaller than the next unit. The most commonly used units of the metric system are given below. After you have finished reading about the metric system, try to put it to use. How tall are you in metrics? What is your mass? What is your body temperature in degrees Celsius?

COMMONLY USED METRIC UNITS

Length   The distance from one point to another

meter (m)

(a meter is slightly longer than a yard)

1 meter = 1000 millimeters (mm)

1 meter = 100 centimeters (cm)

1000 meters = 1 kilometer (km)

Volume   The amount of space an object takes up

liter (L)

(a liter is slightly larger than a quart)

1 liter = 1000 milliliters (mL)

Mass   The amount of matter in an object

gram (g)

(a gram has a mass equal to about one paper clip)

1000 grams = 1 kilogram (kg)

Temperature   The measure of hotness or coldness

degrees Celsius (°C)   0 °C = freezing point of water

100 °C = boiling point of water

METRIC–ENGLISH EQUIVALENTS

2.54 centimeters (cm) = 1 inch (in.)
1 meter (m) = 39.37 inches (in.)
1 kilometer (km) = 0.62 miles (mi)
1 liter (L) = 1.06 quarts (qt)
250 milliliters (mL) = 1 cup (c)
1 kilogram (kg) = 2.2 pounds (lb)
28.3 grams (g) = 1 ounce (oz)
°C = 5/9 × (°F − 32)

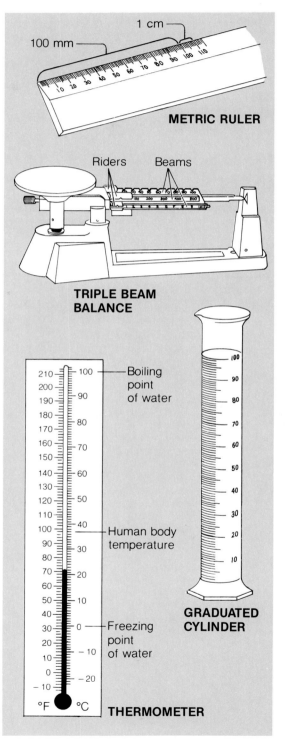

METRIC RULER

TRIPLE BEAM BALANCE

GRADUATED CYLINDER

THERMOMETER

absolute zero: lowest temperature that anything can reach

absorbent: substance that can soak up oil on or near the shore

abyssal plain: flat, featureless area of the ocean floor

abyssal (uh-BIS-uhl) **zone:** ocean life subzone extending from about 4000 meters to about 6000 meters

acid rain: rain containing nitric acid and sulfuric acid, which are formed in a series of chemical reactions between water vapor and the oxides of nitrogen and sulfur—both pollutants

adaptation: change that increases an organism's chances of survival

air mass: large body of air that has the same temperature and humidity throughout

air pressure: pressure exerted on the earth by gravity pulling the air toward the earth's surface

allele: each member of a pair of genes

alpha decay: decay process in which the nucleus of a radioactive atom releases 2 protons and 2 neutrons, resulting in the formation of a different element

alternating current: electric current in which electrons move back and forth, reversing their direction regularly

amino acid: basic unit, or monomer, of a protein

amniocentesis (am-nee-oh-sen-TEE-sis): process of removing fluid from sac surrounding a developing baby

ampere: unit in which current is expressed; the amount of current that flows past a point per second

amplitude (AM-pli-tyood): maximum distance the vibrating molecules of a medium are moved from their rest position by the energy of a wave

anatomy: study of the physical structure of living things

antibiotic: chemical substance that slows the growth of bacteria and other microorganisms in the human body

astronomy: study of planets, stars, and other objects beyond the earth

atoll: ring of coral reefs around a submerged island

atom: smallest part of an element that has all the properties of that element

atomic number: number of protons in the nucleus of an atom

barometer: instrument for measuring air pressure

barrier reef: coral reef separated from the shore of an island by a lagoon

bathyal (BATH-e-uhl) **zone:** ocean life subzone extending from below the photosynthetic subzone to a depth of about 4000 meters

battery: combination of two or more electrochemical cells

benthos (BEN-thahs): plants and animals that live on the ocean floor

beta decay: decay process in which an electron is released from the nucleus of a radioactive atom, resulting in a different element with the same mass number

beta thallassemia (thall-uh-SEE-mee-uh): inherited blood disease

bimetallic strip: strip consisting of two different metals that expand at different rates, causing the strip to bend

binary system: number system that uses only the numbers 0 and 1, on which computer operation is based

biogeography: study of where plants and animals live throughout the world

biological clock: inner "timer" that controls natural cycles

biome: division of landscape with similar climate, plants, and animals

bit: single electronic switch in a computer

botany: study of plants

breaker: wave that crashes on a beach

byte: string of switches, usually 8, connected together in a computer

calorie: amount of heat needed to raise the temperature of one gram of liquid water one degree Celsius; the basic unit in measuring heat energy

canopy: roof formed by tall trees in a forest

Celsius: temperature scale used in the metric system on which water freezes at 0° and boils at 100°

central processing unit (CPU): "brain" of a computer

chain reaction: continuous series of fission reactions

chemistry: study of the makeup of substances and how they change and combine

chip: silicon plate on which a grouping of circuits is placed

chromosome: rod-shaped cell structure that carries the code for inherited traits

circuit breaker: switch that flips open when the current flow becomes too high, thus breaking the circuit and stopping the flow of electricity

cirrus cloud: feathery or fibrous cloud found at very high altitudes

climate: average weather in a particular place over a long period of time

climate zone: wide area within certain latitudes that generally has similar weather conditions

cold front: boundary formed when a cold air mass slides under a warm air mass and pushes the warm air along

colorblindness: sex-linked trait that causes the inability to distinguish between certain colors

combustion: process in which a substance heated above a certain temperature combines with oxygen from the air and gives off heat and light; burning

compression (kuhm-PRESH-uhn): part of a longitudinal wave in which the molecules of the medium are crowded together

computer: electronic device that performs calculations and processes information

computer program: series of instructions that tells a computer how to perform a certain task

concave lens: lens that is thicker at the edges than at the center and bends light so that it spreads out

concave mirror: mirror with surfaces that curve inward

condensation: changing of a gas into a liquid

conduction (kuhn-DUHK-shuhn): process in which heat is transferred through a substance, or from one substance to another, by direct contact of one molecule with another

conductor: material that permits electrons to move easily

conservation: wise use of natural resources so that they will not be used up too soon or used in a way that will damage the environment

constructive interference: combining of sound waves in such a way that compressions due to one wave meet compressions due to other waves, producing a sound of greater intensity

continental margin: area where the underwater edges of a continent meet the ocean basin

continental shelf: part of a continent between the shoreline and where the ocean floor begins a steep descent

continental slope: part of the ocean floor that is the boundary between the continents and the ocean basin

contour farming: farming method in which a slope is plowed horizontally across the face to avoid erosion

control: experiment run in exactly the same way as the experiment with the variable but with the variable left out

convection (kuhn-VEK-shuhn): process in which molecules of liquids or gases move in currents, transferring heat as they move; movement of gases or liquids caused by differences in temperature and density

convex lens: lens that is thicker at the center than at the edges and bends light so that the rays come toward the center

convex mirror: mirror with surfaces that curve outward

coral reef: limestone rock structure containing the shells of plants and animals

Coriolis effect: apparent shift in the path of any fluid or object moving above the earth's surface caused by the rotation of the earth

crest: highest part of a wave

Cro-Magnon (kroh-MAG-nahn): type of *Homo sapiens* that appeared about 40,000 years ago

crop rotation: farming method of alternating the growth of different crops each year on the same land

cumulus cloud: puffy white pillowlike cloud with flat bottom that usually indicates fair weather

current: stream of moving water below the ocean's surface

data: recorded observations and measurements

data bank: vast collection of information stored in a large computer

decibel: unit for measuring intensity of a sound

deep current: current that flows deep beneath the ocean's surface and is caused mainly by differences in water density

deep-sea trench: long, narrow V-shaped crack in the ocean basin

density: measurement of the amount of mass in a given volume of an object; mass per unit volume

depletion: process in which plant nutrients are removed from the soil

desert climate: climate that receives the lowest amount of precipitation of any climate region

destructive interference: combining of sound waves in such a way that compressions due to one wave meet rarefactions due to other waves, producing a sound of lesser intensity

dew point: temperature at which moisture in the air condenses into droplets

diffuse (di-FYOOS) **reflection:** reflection produced by the scattering of reflected light from an uneven surface

direct current: electric current in which electrons always flow in the same direction

disk drive: device that reads information off a disk and enters it into the computer's memory

dispersal: movement of living things from one place to another

distillation: process that involves heating a liquid until it vaporizes and then allowing the vapor to cool until it condenses back into a liquid

diurnal (digh-ER-nuhl) **animal:** animal active mainly during the day

DNA (deoxyribonucleic (dee-AHK-si-righ-boh-noo-KLE-ik) acid): spiral-shaped substance that is the basic substance of heredity

dominant: stronger trait in genetics

Doppler effect: change in the pitch of a sound due to the motion of either the sound source or the listener

Down's syndrome: condition that results when the twenty-first pair of chromosomes has an extra chromosome

dry cell: type of electrochemical cell that serves as an "electron pump"

ecological succession: process in which one organism follows, or succeeds, another in a particular place as time passes

ecology: study of the relationship between plants, animals, and their environment

electric charge: positive or negative condition of a particle due to unequal numbers of protons and electrons in the atom

electric circuit: closed path for the flow of electrons

electric current: flow of electrons through a wire

electric discharge: loss of static electricity as electric charges move off an object

electric field: region surrounding a charged particle in which an electric force affecting other charged particles is noticeable

electricity: energy associated with electrons that have moved from one place to another

electric power: measure of the rate at which electricity does work or provides energy

electrochemical cell: cell in which chemical energy produced by a chemical reaction is changed into electric energy

electromagnetic spectrum: arrangement of different forms of light in order of increasing frequency and decreasing wavelength

electromagnetic wave: transverse wave that does not need a medium to travel and whose speed in a vacuum is 300,000 kilometers per second

electromagnetism: relationship between electricity and magnetism

electron: negatively charged particle found outside the nucleus of an atom

electron cloud: region around the nucleus of an atom in which electrons travel

electron microscope: microscope that uses a beam of electrons to magnify objects

electroscope: instrument, consisting of a metal rod with two thin metal leaves at one end, used to detect radioactivity; instrument that can detect an electric charge

El Niño: a warm water current that flows from west to east across the Pacific Ocean near the equator and down the west coast of South America; strikes with little warning every two to seven years and brings with it dramatic changes in world climate

emission (ee-MISH-uhn): gases and particles given off when fuels are burned

erosion: process of carrying away soil and rock by wind and water

escape velocity: velocity that a space vehicle must achieve to overcome the gravitational pull of the earth

estivation (es-tuh-VAY-shuhn): process of adapting to dry, hot weather by slowing down activities

evaporation: process in which radiant heat from the sun turns liquid water into a gas

evolution: change in a species over time; descent with modification

extinct: having died out

extinction: process by which a species passes out of existence

farsightedness: condition in which a person's eyeball is too short so the image is focused behind the retina; corrected with a convex lens

fiber optics: branch of optics dealing with the transfer of light through long, thin, flexible fibers of glass or plastic called optical fibers

fission (FISH-uhn): splitting of an atomic nucleus into two smaller nuclei of roughly equal mass

fluorescent (floo-RES-uhnt): producing light by bombarding with electrons the molecules of a gas kept at low pressure in a tube

force of attraction: force that pulls objects together

force of repulsion: force that pushes objects apart

fossil: imprint or remains of an organism that existed in the past

fossil fuel: fuel, such as coal, oil, and natural gas, that formed from layers of dead plants and animals exposed to extreme heat and pressure

fossil record: all the fossil evidence scientists have collected

fraction: petroleum part with its own boiling point

fractionating tower: place where fractional distillation of petroleum takes place

frequency (FREE-kwen-see): number of complete wave vibrations, or cycles, per unit time; number of crests or troughs produced per unit time

fringing reef: coral reef that touches the shoreline of a volcanic island

front: boundary between a mass of warm air and a mass of cold air

fundamental tone: lowest pitched sound that can be made when a string vibrates as a whole

fuse: devise containing a thin metal strip that melts and breaks the flow of electricity if the current becomes too high

gamma decay: decay process in which a radioactive nucleus releases energy in the form of gamma rays

gene: basic unit of heredity

genetic engineering: a technology in which specific genes are added or removed from an organism

genetics: study of characteristics passed from an organism to its offspring

genotype (JEN-uh-tighp): actual gene makeup of trait

geosynchronous orbit: orbit in which a satellite moves at a speed that exactly matches the earth's rate of rotation

geothermal energy: the earth's inner heat

gravity: force of attraction between objects

ground water: water found below the surface of the earth

habitat: place in which an organism lives

half-life: amount of time it takes for half the atoms in a sample of radioactive element to decay

hardware: physical parts of a computer

hemophilia (hee-muh-FI-li-uh): inherited disease that causes the blood to clot slowly or not at all

hertz: unit used to measure wave frequency; equal to one cycle per second

hibernation: inactive state in the winter during which all body activities slow down

holography: technology that uses light to produce a three-dimensional image of a scene

homologous (hom-MAH-luh-guhs): similar in structure

humidity: water vapor, or moisture, in the air

hybrid (HIGH-brid): organism with genes that are different for a trait

hydrocarbon: compound formed from hydrogen and carbon

hypothesis: (high-PAH-thuh-sis): suggested explanation for a scientific problem

ice age: periods throughout history when much of the earth's surface has been covered with enormous sheets of ice

illuminated (i-LOO-muh-nayt-ed): made visible by the bouncing off of light

incandescent (in-kuhn-DES-uhnt): glowing because of intense heat

incomplete dominance: condition that occurs when a gene is neither dominant nor recessive

induction: method of charging an object with static electricity that involves a rearrangement of electric charges

infrared radiation: invisible heat energy from the sun

inherited disease: disease passed from parents to offspring

input device: device used for feeding data into the central processing unit of a computer; keyboard, magnetic tape, optical scanner, disk or diskette drive

insulation: substance used to reduce heat transfer that occurs by conduction

insulator: material that does not conduct electricity well

integrated circuit: circuit that combines many diodes and transistors on a thin slice of silicon crystal

intensity: loudness of a sound

interference: combining of compressions and rarefactions of sound waves produced at the same time by different sources

interglacial: period between ice ages

intertidal zone: ocean life zone that lies between the low and high tide lines

ion: electrically charged atom

ionosphere: lower part of the thermosphere that contains electrically charged particles

iris: colored area of the eye surrounding the pupil; controls the amount of light that enters the eye

isobar (IGH-suh-bahr): line on a weather map connecting locations that have the same barometric pressure

isolation: separation of some members of a species or group of species from the rest of their kind for long periods of time

isotherm (IGH-suh-therm): line on a weather map connecting locations that have the same temperature

isotope (IGH-suh-tohp): atom of an element that has the same number of protons but a different number of neutrons than another atom of the same element

Kelvin scale: metric temperature scale on which 0° represents absolute zero, the boiling point of water is 373°, and the freezing point of water is 273°

kilogram: basic unit of mass in the metric system

kinetic energy: energy of motion

land breeze: flow of air from land to sea at night

laser: device that concentrates light into a narrow, intense beam

law: scientific theory that has been tested many times and is generally accepted as true

law of conservation of energy: law that states that energy can be neither created nor destroyed but can only change form

law of independent assortment: law stating that each gene pair is inherited independently of all other traits

law of segregation: law stating that chromosomes separate during meiosis

leeward side: the side of a mountain that faces away from the wind

lens: any transparent material that refracts light

liter: basic unit of volume in the metric system

long distance surface current: current that flows near the ocean's surface for thousands of kilometers

longitudinal (lawn-juh-TOOD-uhn-uhl) **wave:** wave in which the molecules of the medium move back and forth parallel to the direction in which the wave moves

longshore current: short distance surface current that tends to flow parallel to the shoreline

luminous (LOO-muh-nuhs): giving off its own light

magnetic field: region in which magnetic forces can act

magnetism: force of attraction or repulsion due to the arrangement of electrons

main memory: part of a computer that stores information and all the operating instructions for the computer

major glaciation (GLAY-she-ay-shuhn): ice age

marine west coast climate: rainy climate with cool winters and only slightly warmer summers

mass: amount of matter in an object

mass number: total number of neutrons and protons in the nucleus of an atom

Mediterranean climate: climate with cool wet winters and only slightly warmer but dry summers

medium: any substance that transmits sound

meiosis: (migh-OH-sis): process that results in cells with only half the normal number of chromosomes

mesosphere (MES-uh-sfeer): coldest layer of the atmosphere

meter: basic unit of length in the metric system

metric system: common system of scientific measurement

microclimate: localized climate, such as a backyard

microprocessor: one-chip central processing unit that controls and processes any information in a computer

microscope: instrument that uses light and lenses to magnify objects

migrate: to move away from

modem: computer peripheral that changes electronic signals from a computer into sounds that can be carried over regular telephone lines

moist continental climate: climate with very cold winters and very hot summers

moist subtropical climate: climate with cool mild winters and hot moist summers

molecular clock: scale used to estimate the rate of change in proteins over time

molecule: smallest part of a substance that has all the properties of that substance; made up of two or more atoms chemically bonded

monomer (MAH-nuh-mer): individual molecular unit linked with other units to form a polymer

monsoon: local wind that brings a rainy season to many countries

multiple allele: two or more alleles that combine to determine a certain characteristic

multistage rocket: rocket with many stages that ignite, one at a time, and drop off their fuel containers when they are empty

mutation: sudden change in characteristics caused by an accidental change in a gene

natural frequency: object's frequency of vibration

natural resource: material produced by the environment and used by people

natural selection: process in which only the best-adapted members of a species survive

Neanderthal (nee-AN-der-thawl): early type of *Homo sapiens* that lived from about 100,000 years ago to about 35,000 years ago

nearsightedness: condition in which a person's eyeball is too long so the image is focused in front of the retina; corrected with a concave lens

negative terminal: post of a dry cell that has an excess of electrons

nekton (NEK-tahn): animal that swims freely in the ocean

neon: gas used in the production of light because it glows when electricity passes through it

neritic (nuh-RIT-ik) **zone:** ocean life zone that extends from the low-tide line to the edge of the continental shelf

neutron: neutral subatomic particle located in the nucleus of an atom

nitrogen fixation: process by which some bacteria change nitrogen from the air into nitrogen compounds

nocturnal (nahk-TER-nuhl) **animal:** animal active mainly at night

nondisjunction (nahn-dis-JUNK-shuhn): failure of chromosomes to separate during meiosis

nonpoint source: unexpected source of water pollution that is difficult to regulate, such as leakage from waste dumps or poisonous wastes illegally dumped

Northern Hemisphere: half of the world above the equator

north magnetic pole: end of a magnet that always points north

nuclear energy: energy in the nucleus of an atom that works against the force of repulsion and binds protons together

nuclear fission: splitting of the nuclei of uranium or plutonium atoms to produce energy

nuclear fusion: combining of the nuclei of atoms to produce tremendous amounts of energy

nuclear reactor: device in which controlled fission reactions can be produced

occluded front: type of front that occurs when a cold front overtakes a warm front, pushes it upward, and meets cool air

oceanic ridge: underwater mountain range

ohm: unit of resistance

opaque (oh-PAYK): not transmitting light

open sea zone: ocean life zone that includes all the ocean beyond the continental shelves

output device: device that receives data from the central processing unit of a computer, such as a printer, cathode-ray tube, magnetic tape drive, or voice synthesizer

overtone: note produced when sections of a string vibrate faster than the string as a whole, thereby producing sounds that are higher pitched than the fundamental tone

ozone: molecule made up of 3 atoms of oxygen

parallel circuit: electric circuit with more than one path for the flow of electrons

permafrost: permanently frozen soil in the tundra

pesticide: chemical used to kill harmful insects and other pests

petroleum: crude oil

phenotype (FEE-nuh-tighp): visible characteristic of an organism

phosphor: substance that absorbs ultraviolet rays and changes them into visible light

photoelectric effect: production of an electric current when photons of certain frequencies of light have enough energy to knock electrons out of atoms of a metal plate

photon: tiny packet of energy released by an electron

photosynthesis (foh-tuh-SIN-thuh-sis): process in which green plants use the sun's energy to combine carbon dioxide from the air with water to produce food

photosynthetic (foh-tuh-sin-THET-ik) **zone:** ocean life subzone that extends from the surface to a depth of about 200 meters

photovoltaic cell: solar cell that converts light directly into electricity

physics: study of forms of energy

pitch: how high or low a sound is determined by the frequency of the sound

plane mirror: mirror with a perfectly flat surface

plankton (PLANGK-tuhn): small plants and animals that drift and float on or near the ocean's surface

plasma: superheated stream of nuclei of certain gases

plasmid: bacterial DNA in the form of a ring

point source: expected source of water pollution that can be regulated, such as a sewer pipe of a town, city, or factory

polar zone: major climate zone located above a latitude of 60° north and south

pole: end of a magnet

pollution: changing of the environment for the worse

polymer (PAH-li-mer): large chain of molecular units called monomers

polymerization (pah-li-muh-ri-ZAY-shuhn): process of chemically bonding monomers to form polymers

positive terminal: post of a dry cell that has a shortage of electrons

potential energy: stored energy

precipitation: water that falls from clouds in the form of rain, snow, sleet, or hail

prevailing wind: wind that blows more often from one direction than from any other direction

primate: order of mammals that includes humans, apes, and monkeys

prism (PRIZ-'m): piece of glass that bends light so that it forms the visible spectrum

proton: positively charged subatomic particle located in the nucleus of an atom

pupil: opening in the eye through which light enters

quality: property of a tone determined by its overtones; timbre

quark: basic particle of which all subatomic nuclear particles are made

radiant energy: visible and invisible energy from the sun that moves in waves, such as light and heat

radiation: transfer of heat energy through space

radioactive: giving off radiation

radioactive decay: spontaneous breakdown of an unstable atomic nucleus, releasing subatomic particles and energy

radioactivity: release of energy and matter that results from changes in the nucleus of an atom

rarefaction (rayr-uh-FAK-shuhn): part of a longitudinal wave in which the molecules of the medium are farther apart than they are normally

reaction engine: engine based on the law of motion that states that every action produces an equal and opposite reaction

recessive: weaker trait in genetics

recombinant DNA: new piece of DNA produced by combining parts of separate DNA strands

reflection (re-FLEK-shuhn): bouncing back of light from a surface

refraction (re-FRAK-shuhn): bending of light as it passes from one medium to another

regular reflection: reflection from a smooth surface with little scattering of the reflected light

relative humidity: percentage of moisture the air holds relative to the amount it can hold at a particular temperature

resistance: opposition to the flow of electricity

resonance: ability of an object to vibrate by absorbing energy of its own natural frequency

retina: part of the eye made up of light-sensitive nerves that transfer the image to the brain

rift valley: valley that runs the length of a mid-ocean ridge through which molten rock from inside the earth rises up to form new ocean floor

rip current: powerful narrow flow of water back out to sea; type of strong undertow

sanitary landfill: method for the disposal of solid wastes in which no hazardous wastes are included and the garbage is compacted into the smallest possible volume and covered at least once a day with a layer of soil

scientific method: basic steps taken in solving a problem or uncovering scientific facts

sea breeze: flow of air from sea to land during the daytime

seamount: underwater volcanic mountain

sedimentary rock: type of rock formed from layers of mud and sand that harden slowly over time

semiconductor: substance that can be made to conduct electricity or not conduct electricity by reversing the direction electricity flows through it; used to make a transistor

series circuit: electric circuit with only one path for the flow of electrons

sex chromosome: chromosome that determines the gender of an organism

sex-linked trait: characteristic passed from parent to child on a sex chromosome

short distance surface current: current that flows near the ocean's surface for short distances

sickle-cell anemia: inherited blood disease that causes red blood cells to become sickle shaped

simulation: imitation of an actual event by a computer

smog: thick cloud of pollutants

software: programs a computer follows

sound wave: periodic series of compressions and rarefactions

Southern Hemisphere: half of the world below the equator

south magnetic pole: end of a magnet that always points south

specific heat: number of calories needed to raise the temperature of one gram of a substance one degree Celsius

spectroscope (SPEK-truh-skohp): instrument that breaks up light into its particular colors

spectrum: band of colors

static electricity: buildup of electric charges on objects; stationary electricity

stationary front: type of front that forms when a mass of warm air meets a mass of cold air and no movement occurs

steppe climate: climate that receives only slightly more precipitation than does the desert climate

stereoscopic (stai-ri-uh-SKAHP-ik) **vision:** ability of the brain to combine the separate image from each eye into one three-dimensional picture

stratosphere (STRAT-uh-sfeer): layer of the earth's atmosphere where jet streams and the ozone layer are found

stratus cloud: fairly flat layered cloud usually associated with light rain and drizzle

strip cropping: farming method in which low strips of vegetation are grown between grain plants to hold down the soil

strip mining: process in which entire hills are cut apart by large earthmoving machines in search of coal

strong force: force in the nucleus of an atom that balances the electromagnetic force of repulsion among protons

subatomic particle: proton, neutron, or electron

submarine canyon: U- or V-shaped valley that cuts through the continental shelf and slope

surf: surging water on a beach caused by breakers

surface current: current caused mainly by wind patterns

swell: long, wide wave that is not very high and usually is found far out at sea

synthetic membrane: artificial membrane made of synthetic polymers that works like a natural biological membrane

tablemount: seamount with a broad, flat top

temperate zone: major climate zone located between the latitudes of 30° and 60° north and south

temperature: measure of the average kinetic energy of molecules

temperature inversion: atmospheric condition in which a layer of cool air containing pollutants is trapped under a layer of warm air

terracing: soil conservation method in which a slope is made into a series of level plots in steplike fashion to avoid water runoff and erosion

theory: most logical explanation of events that occur in nature

thermal pollution: damage to the environment by waste heat that causes an unnatural rise in temperature of air or in bodies of water such as lakes and streams

thermometer: instrument for measuring temperature

thermosphere (THER-muh-sfeer): highest layer of the earth's atmosphere where the air is very thin and the temperature is high

thermostat (THER-muh-stat): device that helps control the temperature of an indoor area or of an appliance

thrust: force of forward movement of a vehicle by rearward blast of exploding gases

timbre (TAM-buhr): quality of sound that distinguishes one voice or muscial instrument from another; determined by overtones

topsoil: rich upper layer of the soil

toxic: poisonous

transistor: small electronic device that has replaced the vacuum tube in radios, televisions, and computer circuits

translucent (trans-LOO-suhnt): letting light pass but scattering it so that objects lack detail

transmutation (tranz-myoo-TAY-shuhn): process by which the nucleus of an atom changes so that a new element forms

transparent: easily transmitting light rays

transverse wave: wave in which the wave energy is at right angles to the electric and magnetic fields generated by moving photons of energy

tropical cyclone: low pressure area containing warm air, with winds that spiral counterclockwise around and into the center

volt: unit of voltage

voltage: measure of the energy available to move electrons

warm front: boundary formed when a warm air mass slides over a cool air mass and pushes the cold air along

watt: unit in which electric power is measured

wave: disturbance in a medium; pulses of energy that move through the water

wave height: vertical distance between a crest and a trough

wavelength: horizontal distance between two successive crests or two successive troughs

wave period: interval of time required for successive crests or troughs to pass a given point

weight: measure of the attraction between two objects due to gravity

wind: convection current of air

windward side: the side of a mountain that faces toward the wind

work: force acting on an object and causing it to move

zoology: study of animals

Index

A

Absolute zero, 38
Absorbents, pollution and, 254
Absorption of light, 118, 128
Abyssal plains, 300–301
Abyssal zone, 320–21
AC. *See* Alternating current.
Acid rain, 258, 260
Adaptation and evolution, 453
Air density, 381
Air mass, 369
Air pollution
   acid rain, 258, 260
   methods for cleaning, 260–61
   smog, 257–58
Air pressure, 358
Aldrin, Edwin, 217
Alleles, multiple, 429
Alpha decay, 144
Alternating current (AC) , 66
Altitude, climate and, 381
Alvin, 322
Amino acids, 192
Ammeter, 63
Ammonia, 341
Amniocentesis, 434
Amoco Cadiz, 251–54
Ampere, 63
Amplitude of a wave, 92
Anatomy, 448–49
Anemones, 316
Angstrom, 20
Annual rhythms, 520–21
Antibiotics, 198–99
Apollo 11, 216
Apollo Project, 216
Ariane, 222
Armstrong, Neii, 217
Artificial intelligence research,
   243
Artificial satellites, 211–15
Artificial transmutation, 145–46
Astronomy, 18
Atmosphere, 339–47

formation of the ozone shield,
   341–43
layers of, 345–47
origin of the earth's, 340–43
present, 343–47
temperature in, 344
Atmosphere, layers of
   ionosphere, 347
   mesosphere, 346–47
   stratosphere, 346
   thermosphere, 347
   troposphere, 345–46
Atmospheric pressure, 358
Atoll, 307
Atom
   atomic number, 140–42
   definition, 54–55
   isotopes and, 142
   nucleus of, 55
   strong force and, 139–40
   structure of, 138–42
   subatomic particles of, 55,
      138–39
Atomic number, 140–41
Australopithecus africanus, 473
Avalanches, underwater, 298–99

B

Bacteria, oil spills and, 254
Barometer, 358
Barrier reefs, 307
Barrier, floating
   for oil spills, 253
Barriers and dispersal of plants
   and animals, 497–98
Bathyal zone, 319–20
Batteries, 65
Benthos, 322
Beta decay, 144–45
Beta thalassemia, 430–31
Bimetallic strip, 39
Binary system, 236–37
Biogeography, 496–500
   barriers, 497–98

biomes of the world, 499–500
   definition, 496
   dispersal of plants and animals,
      496–97
Biological clock, 518
Biomes, 495–511
   biogeography, 496–500
   characteristics of, 499
   definition, 499–500
   of the world, 499–500
Biomes, types of
   deserts, 510–11
   forests, 502–507
   grasslands, 508–10
   tundra, 500–501
Bit, 237
Black hole, 215
Botany, 18
Breakers, 284
Byte, 238

C

Caloric, theory of, 34
Calorie, 41
Canopy, 505–506
Cells
   dry, 64–65
   electrochemical, 64
   photovoltaic, 172
   solar, 172–73
Celsius degrees, conversion to
      Kelvin degrees, 38
Celsius scale, 23
Centimeter, 20
Central processing unit (CPU),
   234–35
Chain reaction, 147
Challenger Deep, 303
Charge and force of subatomic
      particles, 58
Chemical cycle, 521–22
Chemical technology, 187–99
   health chemistry, 196–99
   polymer chemistry, 190–95

Chemistry
  definition, 18, 190
  health, 196–99
  polymer, 190–95
Chip, silicon, 233–35
Chromosomes, 413, 428, 432–34
Chromosome theory, 418
Circuit breakers, 71
Circuits, electric, 67–69
  closed and opened, 68
  fuses, 70–71
  overloading and, 70
  series and parallel, 69
Cirrus cloud(s), 366
Clean Water Act of 1972, 255
Climate, 379–91
  altitude and, 381
  changes in, 390–91
  climate zones and, 383–84
  definition, 380
  El Niño and effects on, 391
  latitude and, 380–81
  nature of, 380–84
  oceans and currents and, 381
  precipitation and, 381–82
  regions, 385–89
  temperature and, 380–81
Climate zones, 383–84
  polar, 383
  temperate, 384
  tropical, 384
Clouds, 365–66
Cold front, 370
Color and light
  absorption and, 128
  of opaque objects, 127–28
  of the sky, 129
  of transparent objects, 128
Colorblindness, 433
Columbia, 216, 217–18
Combustion, 166–70
Communication of early
  humans, 479
Communications satellites,
  212–13
Compression, 87–88
Computer(s), 229–43
  development of, 230–34
  future of, 243
  operation of, 234–37,
  parts of, 231–33, 234–36
  technology, 230–34
  vacuum tubes and, 232–33
Computer-aided design, 242
Computer applications, 238–43
  computer control, 241–42
  data processing, 240
  problem solving, 238–39
  simulation, 239–40
  word processing, 241
Computer control, 241–42
Concave lenses, 125
Concave mirrors, 121–22

Condensation, 364
Conduction, 35, 58, 356
Conductor, electric, 58, 195
Cones, eyesight and, 126
Coniferous forests, 502–504
Conservation of natural
  resources, 533–45
  living resources, 538–45
  nonliving resources, 534–38
  plants, 539–45
  soil, 536–38
  water, 534–36
  wildlife, 542–45
Constructive interference, 102
Continental margins, 296–99
  definition, 296
  submarine canyons, 298–300
Continental shelves, 296–97
Continental slopes, 298
Contour farming, 537
Control experiment, 17
Control rods in a nuclear reactor,
  149
Convection, 36, 356
Convex lenses, 125
Convex mirrors, 122–23
Cooling systems, 47
Coral reefs, 306
  atoll, 307
  barrier, 307
  fringing, 306, 307
Coriolis effect, 361, 363
Correns, Karl, 418
Crest of a wave, 92, 282
Crick, Francis, 408, 421
Cro-Magnons, 477–79
Crop rotation, 537
Cumulonimbus cloud(s), 365, 366
Cumulus cloud(s), 365
Current, electric, 63
  alternating, 66
  direct, 66
  direction of, 65–66
  how to produce, 64–65
Currents, ocean, 286–89
  causes, 286, 288
  deep, 288–89
  effect on climate, 381
  El Niño, 391
  longshore, 287–88
  rip, 288
  surface, 286–88
Cycles of living things, 521–26
  chemical, 521–22
  nitrogen, 522–23
  oxygen/carbon dioxide, 525–26
  water, 524–25
Cyclones, 368

D

Daily rhythms, 519
Dams, 176–77

Darwin, Charles, 454–55, 460–61
Data, 17
Data bank, 236
Data processing, 240
DC. *See* Direct current.
Decay, radioactive
  alpha, 144, 145
  beta, 144–45
  gamma, 145
Decibels, 97
Deciduous forests, 504–505
Deep currents, 288–89
Deep-sea basins
  abyssal plains, 300–301
  islands, 304–305
  oceanic ridges, 301–302
  reefs, 306–307
  rift valleys, 302–303
  seamounts, 303–306
  trenches, 303
Deep-sea trenches, 303
Deep-sea vents, life around,
  322–23
Density, 22–23
Deoxyribonucleic acid (DNA), 460
  definition, 408
  discovery of, 421
  recombinant, 436–39
Depletion, 537
Desert climate, 388–89
Deserts, 510–11
Design, computer-aided, 242–43
Destructive interference, 102–103
De Vries, Hugo, 419
Dew point, 364
Diatoms, 319, 322
Diffuse reflection, 120
Direct Broadcast Satellite (DBS),
  213
Direct current (DC), 66
Diseases
  beta thalassemia, 430–31
  colorblindness, 433
  Down's syndrome, 434
  hemophilia, 432–33
  inherited, 429–32
  sickle-cell anemia, 431–32
Disk drive, 235
Dispersal, 496–97
Distillation, 188–89
Diurnal animals, 519
DNA. *See* Deoxyribonucleic acid.
Doldrums, 361–62
Dominant trait, 411
Doppler effect, 95
Down's syndrome, 434
Dry cells, 64–65

E

Eagle, 216
Earthquakes and waves, 284–85
Earth science, 18

Echo-ranger, 301
Ecological barrier, 498
Ecological succession, 526–27
Ecology, 496
  biomes, 495–511
  conservation, 533–45
  definition, 496
  ecological succession, 526–27
  rhythms and cycles, 518–26
Eddy currents, 363–64
Electric charge
  atoms, 55
  charge and force, 56–58
  conductors and insulators, 58–59
  discharge, 61
  electric push, 61–62
  static electricity, 58–61
  subatomic particles and, 55–56
Electric circuits, 67–71
  circuit breakers, 71
  closed and opened, 68
  fuses, 70–71
  overloading and, 70
  series and parallel, 69
Electric current, 63, 64–65
Electric field, 56–57
Electricity, 53, 57–71
  atoms, 54–55
  charge and force in, 56–58
  circuits, 67–71
  conductors and insulators, 58–59
  converting sunlight into, 172–73
  current direction, 65–66
  definition, 57
  electric charge, 54–62
  flow of, 63–67
  how to produce a current,
    64–65
  from magnetism, 76–79
  magnetism from, 74–76
  resistance and, 63–64
  safety and, 70–71
  static, 57–62
  subatomic particles, 55–56
Electric power, 66–67
  equation for, 67
Electrochemical cells, 64
Electromagnetic spectrum,
    112–15
Electromagnetic waves, 111–12
Electromagnetism, 75
Electron cloud, 138
Electronic Numerical Integrator
    and Calculator (ENIAC), 231
Electron microscope, 25–26
Electrons, 55
  how they move, 61–62, 138
Electroscope, 59–60
El Niño, 391
Emissions, 260
ENIAC. See Electronic Numerical
    Integrator and Calculator.
Energy

conversions, 43
electricity and magnetism,
    53–79
geothermal, 180
heat, 33–47
kinetic, 37–38
law of conservation of, 43
light, 109–31
nuclear, 137–49, 178–79
potential, 42
radiant, 355–56
solar, 170–74
sound, 85–103
Energy resources, 165
  fuels and use, 166–70
  geothermal energy, 180
  hydrogen, 179
  nuclear power, 178–80
  solar energy, 170–74
  wind and water, 174–77
Environment, effects on heredity,
    435–36
Eohippus, 450–53
Equator, 356
Erosion, 536–37
Escape velocity, 209–11
Estivation, 521
Evaporation, 364, 524
Evolution, 445–61
  anatomical evidence of, 448–49
  definition, 446
  fossil evidence of, 449–53
  Lamarck and, 448–49
  migration and isolation, 458–60
  natural selection, 455–57
  rate of change, 460–61
  theory of, 447, 454–55
Evolution, human, 467–79
  the first humans, 471–76
  fossil evidence versus chemical
    evidence, 473–74
  homo erectus, 475–76
  homo sapiens, 476–79
  language and communication,
    479
  primates and, 469–70
  search for human ancestors,
    468–70
Experiment
  control, 17
  how to perform, 16–17
Explorer I, 214
Extinction, 453, 538–45
Eye, of a storm, 368
Eyesight, 125–26

F

Facts, 14
Farsightedness, 126
Fiber optics, 130–31
Fire, combustion and, 166–67
Fire, used for oil spills, 252–53

Fish
  in abyssal zone, 321
  in bathyal zone, 320
  in deep-sea vents, 323
  in intertidal zone, 317
  in neritic zone, 318
  in photosynthetic zone, 319
Fission, 147, 178–79
Flow of electricity
  direction of current, 65–66
  electric current, 63
  electric power, 66–67
  how to produce a current,
    64–65
  resistance, 63–64
Fluorescent light, 117
Food calories, 41
Force
  of attraction, 55
  charge and, 55–57
  definition, 55
  of repulsion, 55
  strong, 139–40
Forests
  coniferous, 502–504
  deciduous, 504–505
  tropical rain, 505–507
Fossil fuels, 167–70
  definition, 167–69
  disadvantage of, 169
  heating value of, 169
  types of, 167
Fossil record, 450
Fossils, 449–53
  definition, 449–50
  how to read a fossil record,
    450–53
  human evolution and, 473–74
Fraction, 188
Fractionating tower, 188–89
Franklin, Benjamin, 60
Frequency of a wave
  how to determine, 93
  natural, 98
Fringing reef(s), 306
Fronts, weather, 370–71
Fuel
  fossil, 167–70
  petroleum, 188–89
  nuclear, 148
  vegetation as, 167, 169–70
Fundamental tone, 101
Fuses, 70–71
Fusion, 179

G

Gagarin, Yuri, 215
Galvanometer, 63
Gamma decay, 145
Gamma rays, 115
Gases in the earth's atmosphere,
    340–41

Gel packets, for spacesuits, 222
Gene(s), 411, 413, 428, 429–33, 460–61
Genetic engineering, 421, 436–39
Genetics, 407–21
  definition, 408
  Gregor Mendel and, 409–15
  history of, 408–16
  human, 428–39
  laws of, 412–15
  modern, 417–21
  new developments in, 436–39
  See also Heredity.
Genotype, 416
Geosynchronous orbit, 213
Geothermal energy, 180
Geysers, 180
Glaciations, major, 391
Global winds, 361–64
  doldrums, 361–62
  northeast trade winds, 363
  polar easterlies, 363
  westerlies, 363
Goddard, Robert H., 210
Gram, 22
Grasslands, 508–10
Gravity, 22, 208–209
Ground water, 535–36
  and pollution, 254–57

H

Habitat, 496
Hail, 367
Half-life of an element, 144
Hardware, computer, 234–37
Health chemistry
  antibiotics, 198
  membrane science, 196–98
  vaccines, 199
Heat, difference between
  temperature and, 41
Heat, measuring, 40–43
Heat, specific, 41
Heat, potential energy, 41–43
Heat energy, 33–47
  heating and refrigeration
    methods, 44–47
  molecules and motion, 34–37
  temperature and, 37–43
  weather and, 355–58
Heating the earth, 355–57
Heat transfer, types of
  conduction, 35, 356–57
  convection, 36, 356
  radiation, 37, 356
Hemophilia, 432–33
Heredity, 408
  alleles and, 429
  diseases and, 429–32
  environment and, 435–36
  in humans, 428–36
  nondisjunction, 433–34

sex-linked traits and, 432–33
  See also Genetics.
Hertz (Hz), 93
Hibernation, 521
Hologram, 131
Holography, 131
Homo erectus, 475–76
Homo habilis, 474
Homologous, 449, 460
Homo sapiens, 476–79
  Cro-Magnons, 477–79
  definition, 476
  Neanderthals, 476–77
Human growth hormone (HGH),
  437–38
Humans
  Australopithecus africanus, 473
  first, 471–76
  homo erectus, 475–76
  homo sapiens, 476–79
  language and communication
    of, 479
  Lucy, 471–73
  primates and, 469–70
  as toolmakers, 474
  wise, 476–79
Humidity, 364
Hurricanes, 368–69
Hybrid, 412
Hydrocarbons, 168–69, 257
Hydroelectric power plants, 177
Hypothesis, 16, 412–13

I

Ice age, 391
Illuminated objects, 117
Incandescent lights, 117
Incinerators, 262
Incomplete dominance, 418
Induction, 59, 61
Information, gathering of, 16
Infrared Astronomy Satellite
  (IRAS), 214–15
Infrared light, 37, 113–14
Infrared radiation, 357
Inherited diseases, 429–33
Input device, 235
Insulation, 45–46
Insulators and electricity, 58–59
Insulin, 438
Intensity of sound, 96–97
Interference of sound, 101–102
  constructive, 102
  destructive, 102
Interferon, 439
Interglacials, 391
Intertidal zone, 314–17
Invisible spectrum, 113–15
Ion, 347
Ionosphere, 347
IRAS. *See* Infrared Astronomy
  Satellite.

Iris, 126
Island, birth of, 304–305
Isobar, 373
Isolation and migration, 458–60
Isotherm, 373
Isotopes, 142

J

Jet stream, 346, 363–64
Joule, James Prescott, 34–35

K

Karyotype, 434
Kelvin degrees, conversion to
  Celsius degrees, 38
Kelvin scale, 38
Kilocalories, 41
Kilogram, 21
Kilometer, 20
Kilowatt, 67
Kinetic energy, 37–38
Krill, 319, 322

L

Laboratories in orbit, 217–18
Lakes and water pollution,
  254–57
Lamarck, Jean-Baptiste de,
  448–49
Land breeze, 360
Land pollution, 261–63
  methods of cleaning, 262–63
Language of early humans, 479
Lasers, 25, 131
Latitude, and climate 380–81
Law, 14
  of conservation of energy, 43
  of gravitation, 208
  of independent assortment,
    414–15
  of motion, third, 206
  of probability, 415
  of segregation, 412–14
Leakey, Louis, 474
Leakey, Mary, 474
Leeward side, 382
Length, measurements of, 20
Lenses
  concave, 125
  convex, 125
  definition, 124
  microscope, 25
Life science, 18
Light
  absorption of, 118, 128
  color of, 127–29
  definition, 110–16
  fluorescent, 117
  how to produce, 117–18
  incandescent, 117

infrared, 37, 113–14
neon, 117–18
as a particle or wave, 115–16
reflection of, 118, 119–23
refraction of, 123–27
sources of, 116–19
technology and, 129–31
transmittal of, 118
ultraviolet, 114
Light energy, 110–11
Lightning, 60–62, 167, 366–67
Lightning rods, 61–62
Light waves. *See* Waves,
  electromagnetic.
Liter, 21
Living resources, conservation of,
  538–45
  plants, 539–42
  wildlife, 542–45
Local winds
  land breeze, 360
  monsoon, 360
  sea breeze, 360
Long distance surface currents,
  286–87
Longitudinal waves, 88
Longshore current, 287–88
Lucy, early human ancestor,
  471–73
Luminous objects, 116–17
Lunar rhythms, 519–20

M

McCandless, Bruce, 163
Magnetic field, 72–73
Magnetic forces, 72–73
Magnetism, 53
  definition, 71
  electricity from, 76–79
  from electricity, 74–76
  explanation of, 73–74
  field of, 72–73
  forces of, 72–73
Magnets, types of, 74
Mariana Trench, 303
Marine west coast climate, 386
Mariner 2, 220
Mariner 4, 220
Mariner 7, 220
Mariner 9, 220
Mariner 10, 220
Mass, 21–23
Mass and weight measurements,
  21–23
Mass number, 142
Measurements, scientific
  commonly used metric units,
    20
  length, 20
  mass and weight, 21–23
  metric system, 19–23
  temperature, 23

volume, 21
Mediterranean climate, 385–86
Medium, 87, 89–90
Meiosis, 413–14
Membrane science, 196–98
  biological, 196–97
  synthetic, 197–98
Memory, main, 235–36
Mendel, Gregor, 409–15
Mendel's laws
  law of independent assortment,
    414–15
  law of segregation, 412–14
Mesosphere, 346–47
Meter, 20
Methane, 340–41
Metric system, 19–23
Microclimate, 383
Microprocessor, 231
Microscope, 25
  electron, 26
  optical, 25–26
Microwaves, 114
Migration and isolation, 458–60
Milligram, 22
Milliliter, 21
Millimeter, 20
Mirrors
  concave, 121–22
  convex, 122–23
  plane, 120–21
Missing link, the first humans
  and, 471
Modem, 235–36
Moderator, 148
Moist continental climate, 386–87
Moist subtropical climate, 387–88
Moisture in the air, 364–69
  clouds and, 365–66
  condensation, 364
  dew point, 364
  relative humidity, 364
  storms and, 366–69
Molecular clock, 473
Molecules, 35
Molecules and motion, 34–37, 86
  caloric theory, 34
  heat transfer, 35–37
Monomers, 190–93
Monsoon, 360
Moon, exploration of, 216–17
Morgan, Thomas Hunt, 420
Motion
  molecules and, 34–37
  sound and, 86
Multiple allele(s), 429
Multistage rocket(s), 210–11
Music
  difference between noise and,
    103
  how to make, 99–100
Mutations and sex determination,
  419–20

N

National Aeronautics and Space
  Administration (NASA), 173,
  216
Natural frequency, of sound, 98
Natural magnets, 74
Natural resources, conservation
  of, 534
  soil, 536–38
  water, 534–36
Natural selection, 453–58
  changes in conditions and, 457
  overproduction and, 455–56
  variation and, 456–57
Navstar satellites, 212
Neanderthal, 476–77
Nearsightedness, 126
Negative terminal, 64–65
Nekton, 322
Neon light, 117–18
Neritic zone, 317–18
Neutrons, 55
Newton, Sir Isaac, 206, 208
Newton's law of gravitation, 208
Nimbostratus clouds, 366
Nitrogen cycle, 522–23
Nitrogen fixation, 522
Nocturnal animals, 519
Noise, 102–103
Nondisjunction, 433–34
Nonpoint sources, pollution and,
  256
Northeast trade winds, 363
North magnetic pole, 72
Nuclear energy, 137–49
  definition, 140
  nuclear power, 146–49, 178–79
  structure of the atom, 138–42
  transmutation of elements,
    142–46
Nuclear fission, 147, 178–79
Nuclear fuel, 148
Nuclear fusion, 179
Nuclear power, 146
  fission, 147, 178–80
  fusion, 179
Nuclear radiation, 144
Nuclear reactor, 148–49
Nucleus of an atom, 55

O

Occluded front, 370
Ocean currents. *See* Currents,
  ocean.
Ocean floor, 295–307
  continental margins, 296–300
  deep-sea basins, 300–307
Oceanic ridges, 301–302
Ocean life, 313–23
  across the zones, 321–22
  around deep-sea vents, 322–23

in the intertidal ocean zone, 314–17
in the neritic ocean zone, 317–18
in the open sea zones, 318–21
Oceanography
currents and waves, 279–89
ocean floor, 295–307
ocean life, 313–23
Oceans and seas and water pollution, 251–54
Ocean waves. *See* Waves, ocean.
Ocean zones
intertidal, 314–16
neritic, 317–18
open sea zones, 318–21
Ohm, 63
Ohm's law, 64
Oil spills, how to deal with, 251–54
Ooze, on abyssal plains, 301
Opaque material and light, 118–19
Open sea zones, 318–21
abyssal zone, 320–21
bathyal zone, 319–20
definition, 318
photosynthetic zone, 318–19
Origin of Species, The, 455
Overtones, 101
Oxygen/carbon dioxide cycle, 525–26
Ozone shield, formation of, 341–43

P

Parallel circuit, 69
Particle accelerator, 137, 138, 146
PCBs. *See* Polychlorinated biphenyls.
Period of a wave, 282–83
Permafrost, 501
Permanent magnets, 74
Pesticides, pollution and, 255
Petrochemical products, 190–95
Petroleum
fractions, 188–89
fractional distillation, 188–89
fractionating tower, 188–89
fuels, 188–89
petrochemicals, 190–95
Phenotype, 416
Philosophie zoologique, 448
Phosphors, 117
Photoelectric effect, 115
Photon, light and, 110–11
Photosynthesis, 342–43, 525–26
Photosynthetic zone, 318–19
Photovoltaic cell, 172
Physical science, 18
Physics, 18
Pioneer 10, 220, 221
Pioneer 11, 220, 221

Pitch of sound, 94–96
Doppler effect, 95
radar and, 95–96
Plane mirror, 120–21
Plankton, 321–22
Plants, conservation of, 539–42, 543–45
Plasma, fusion and, 179
Plasmid, 436
Plastics, 192
Poincaré, Jules Henry, 14
Point sources, pollution and, 255
Polar easterlies, 363
Polar zones, 383
Poles, magnetic, 72
Pollution, 179, 180, 249, 250–63
air, 257–61
land, 261–63
technology and, 263
thermal, 179
water, 251–57
Polychlorinated biphenyls (PCBs), 254
Polymer chemistry, 190–95
Polymerization, 192–93
Polymers, 190–95
chemistry, 190
definition, 190
how they are used, 192–95
natural, 192
synthetic, 192–95
Positive terminal, 64–65
Potential energy, 41–43
Precipitation, 364, 381–82
Prevailing wind, 381–82
Primates
definition, 469–70
human, 470
Printer, for computers, 235
Prism, 124
Probability, genetics and, 415
Problem solving, computers and, 238–39
Properties of sound, 93–98
Protons, 55
strong force and, 139–40
Pumps, vacuum for oil spills, 254
Punnett, Reginald C., 416
Punnett square, 416
Pupil, 126

Q

Quality of sound, 100–101
Quarks, 139
Quiet Achiever, 172

R

Radar, 95–96
Radiant energy, 355–56
Radiation, 37, 178–79, 357
infrared, 356

Radioactive decay, 143–45
Radioactive elements, 143–44
Radioactive wastes, 263
Radioactivity, 145
definition, 29
Radio waves, 114
Rarefaction, 88
Reaction engine, 206
Recessive trait, 411
Recombinant DNA, 436–39
how to make, 436–37
products of, 437–39
Recycling of wastes, 263
Reefs
barrier, 307
coral, 306
fringing, 306
Reflection of light, 118, 119–23
definition, 120
kinds of, 120
mirrors for, 120–23
Refraction of light, 123–26
bending and separating and, 123–24
definition, 123
how you see, 125–26
lenses and, 124–25
Refrigeration methods, 44–47
cooling systems, 47
insulation, 45–46
Refrigerator, how it works, 47
Regular reflection, 120
Relative humidity, 364
Resistance, 63–64
Resonance of sound, 98–99
Retina, 126
Rhythms of living things
annual, 520–21
biological clock and, 518
daily, 519
lunar, 519–20
Rift valleys, 302–303
Rip current, 288
Rivers and water pollution, 254–57
Rocketry
escape velocity, 209–11
gravity, 208–209
history of, 206–208
multistage, 210–11
Rumford, Count (Benjamin Thompson), 34

S

Safe Drinking Water Act of 1973, 255
Safety
in the laboratory, 26–27
using electricity, 70
Sandbar, creation of, 288
Sanitary landfill, 262
Satellites, artificial

communications, 212–13
DBS, 213
Explorer I, 214
IRAS, 214–15
Navstar, 212
scientific, 212, 213–15
Sputnik I, 211
uses for, 212, 219
weather, 212
Science
    branches of, 18
    definition, 14–19
Scientific measurements, 19–23
Scientific methods
    basic parts of, 14–18
    experimenting, 16–17
    forming a hypothesis, 16
    gathering information on the
        problem, 16
    recording and analyzing data,
        17–18
    stating a conclusion, 18
    stating the problem, 15
Sea breeze, 360
Seamounts, 303–306
Seaweeds
    in intertidal zone, 316–17
    in neritic zone, 317
Sedimentary rock, 450
Semiconductors, 232–33
Series circuit, 69
Sex chromosomes, 420
Sex determination, mutations
        and, 419–20
Sex-linked traits, 432–33
Short distance surface currents,
        287
Sickle-cell anemia, 431–32
Simulation, 239–40
Skimmers, for oil spills, 253, 254
Skylab, 217
Smog, 257–58
Soil, conservation of, 536–38
Solar cell, 172–73
Solar energy, 170–74
Solar-powered vehicles, 172
Sound(s), 85
    characteristics of waves, 91–93
    combining, 101–103
    intensity of, 96–97
    pitch, 94–96
    properties of, 93–98
    quality of, 100–101
    speed of, 90–91
    wave interactions, 98–103
    waves, 86–91
Sound waves. *See* Waves, sound.
South magnetic pole, 72
Space, people in, 215–19
    colonies, 218–19
    labs in orbit, 217–18
    to the moon, 216–17
Space colonies, 218–19

Space probes, 220–22
Space Shuttle, 218
Spacesuits, 222
Space technology, 205
    artificial satellites, 211–15
    people in space, 215–19
    rocketry, 206–11
    space probes, 220–22
    spinoffs of, 222–23
Specific heat, 41
Spectroscope, 24
Spectrum
    definition, 24
    invisible, 113–15
    visible, 113–15
Sputnik I, 211
Squid, giant, 313
Static electricity
    definition, 57
    discharge of, 58–61
    lightning as, 60–61
Stationary front, 370
Steppe climate, 388–89
Stereoscopic vision, 469
Storms, 366–69
    definition, 366
    hail, 367
    hurricanes, 368–69
    thunderstorms, 366–67
    tornadoes, 367
Stratosphere, 346
Stratus clouds, 365–66
Streams, and water pollution,
        254–57
Strip cropping, 537–38
Strip mining, 250
Strong force, 139–40
Subatomic particles, 55–56,
        138–39
Submarine canyons, 298–300
Sunlight
    converting into electricity,
        172–73
    formation of the earth's atmos-
        phere and, 341
Supercomputer, 231, 234
Surf, 284
Surface currents, 286–88
Sutton, Walter, 418
Swells, 284
Synthetic membrane, 197–98

T

Tablemounts, 306
Temperate zones, 384, 385
Temperature
    in the atmosphere, 344
    definition, 37–38
    how to measure, 38
    metric system, 23
Temperature and heat, 37–43,
        380–81

difference between heat and
        temperature, 41
    kinetic energy, 37–38
    measuring heat, 40–43
    measuring temperature, 38
    thermal expansion, 38–40
Temperature inversion, 258
Terracing, 537
Theory, 14
Thermal expansion, 38–40
Thermal pollution, 179
Thermometers, 38
Thermosphere, 347
Thermostats, 39–40
Third law of motion, 206
Thompson, Benjamin, 34
Three Mile Island, 178
Thrust, 206
Thunder, 367
Thunderstorms, 366–67
Tidal power stations, 177
Tides, 177
Timbre, 100
Tones
    fundamental, 101
    overtones, 101
Tools used by a scientist, 23–26
    electron microscope, 25–26
    laser, 25
    spectroscope, 24
Topsoil, 536
Tornadoes, 367
Toxic wastes, 256
Transistor, computers and,
        232–33
Translucent material and light,
        118
Transmutation of elements
    alpha decay, 144, 145
    artificial, 145–46
    beta decay, 144–45
    definition, 143
    gamma decay, 145
    radioactive decay, 143–45
Transparent material and light,
        118
Transverse waves, 111–12
Trenches, deep-sea, 303
Tropical cyclone, 368
Tropical rain forest, 505–507
Tropical zones, 384
Troposphere, 345–46
Trough of a wave, 92, 282
Tsiolkovsky, Konstantin E., 207,
        209, 210
Tsunamis, 284–85
Tundra, 500–501

U

Ultrasonic waves, 94–95
Ultraviolet waves, 114
Undertow, 284

Underwater avalanche, 298–99
Universal Automatic Computer
 (UNIVAC I), 231
Upwelling, 289

V

Vaccines, 199
Vacuum tubes and computers,
 232–33
Variable, 17
Variation and natural selection,
 456–57
Vegetation
 advantages of using, 169–70
 as fuel, 167
Velocity, escape, 209–11
Vibrations in a medium, 86–87
Viking 1, 220
Viking 2, 220
Visible spectrum, 113–15
Voltage, 62
Voltmeter, 62
Volts, 62
Volume, measurements of, 21
Vostok, 215
Voyager 1, 221
Voyager 2, 221

W

Wallace, Alfred, 454
Warm front, 370
Waste dumps, 261
Water conservation of, 534–36
Water cycle, 524–25
Water pollution, 251–57
 laws to fight, 255, 256
 oceans and seas and, 251–54
 rivers, lakes, streams, and
  ground water and, 254–57
Water power, 176–77
Water wheels, 176–77

Watson, James, 408, 421
Watts, 67
Wave(s)
 amplitude, 92
 characteristics of, 91–93,
  282–84
 electromagnetic, 111–12
 frequency, 93
 gamma rays, 115
 light, 111, 115–16
 micro, 114
 radio, 114
 shape, 92
 transverse, 111–12
 ultraviolet, 114
 wavelength, 92–93
 X-rays, 114–15
Wave height, 282
Wavelength, 92–93, 282–83
Wave period, 282
Waves, ocean, 279, 280–85
 characteristics of, 282–84
 tsunamis, 284–85
 what causes, 280–81
 what determines height of, 281
Waves, sound, 86–93
 amplitude of, 92
 best medium for, 89–90
 characteristics of, 91–93
 crest of, 92
 definition, 88
 frequency of, 93
 how to create, 87–88
 interactions of, 98–103
 length of, 92–93
 shape of, 92
 speed of, 90–91
 trough of, 92
 ultrasonic, 94–93
 vibrations in a medium,
  86–87
Weather, 353–73
 forces that shape, 334–59

 mapping, 372–73
 moisture in the air, 364–69
 patterns, 369–73
 wind, 359–64
Weather satellites, 212
Weight, 21–22
Westerlies, 363
Wet scrubbers, 260
Wildlife, conservation of,
 542–45
Wilson, Allan, 447, 460
Wind(s), 359–64
 Coriolis effect, 361, 363
 definition, 360
 doldrums, 361–62
 global, 361–64
 jet stream, 363–64
 land breeze, 360
 local, 360
 monsoon, 360
 northeast trade winds, 363
 polar, 363
 sea breeze, 360
 westerlies, 363
Wind generators, 174–75
Wind machines, 174–76
Windows, double-pane, 45–46
Wind power, 170–71, 174–76
Windward side, 382
Wise humans, 476–79
Word processing, 241
Work, 37

X

X-rays, 114–15

Z

Zones, climate, 383–84
Zoology, 18

Photograph Credits

1, P. Runyon/*The Image Bank;* **2,** top Bill Pierce/*Sygma;* bottom left, Kenneth W. Fink/*Bruce Coleman;* bottom right, Omni Photo Communications; **5,** top, Anthony Howarth/*Woodfin Camp;* bottom, Ken Karp; **6,** top, © William Jones Warren/*West Light;* bottom, NASA; **7,** top, Joel Gordon; bottom, Norman Tomalin/*Bruce Coleman;* **8,** top, NASA; bottom, Prof. S. Cohen/*Photo Researchers;* **9,** top, Margo Crabtree; bottom, Gordon Langeburg/*Bruce Coleman;* **10,** P. Runyon/*The Image Bank;* **12,** © Don Landwehrle/*The Image Bank;* **14,** © Michael P. Weinstein/*Click*/Chicago; **15,** J. DiMaggio/J. Kalish/© *Peter Arnold;* **16,** both, Lockheed Missiles and Space Co.; **17,** Melchior DiGiacomo/*The Image Bank;* **18,** Dr. Gary Settles/*Photo Researchers;* **19,** left, © Chesher/*Photo Researchers;* right, M. Freeman/*Bruce Coleman;* **21,** Ken Karp; **23,** Jeff Rotman; **24,** Ken Karp; **25,** top right, © Fundamental Photographs; bottom left, Peter Cunningham/*The Image Bank;* bottom right, © Anthony Howarth/*Woodfin Camp;* **26,** IBM; **28,** Ken Karp; **32,** © Norman Benton/*Peter Arnold;* **34,** Eric Simmons/*The Image Bank;* **36,** J. Alex Langley/*dpi;* **37,** Wil Blanche/*dpi;* **38,** Werner Wolff/*Black Star;* **39,** Ken Karp; **40,** © Damnoen Klong/Joseph B. Brignolo/*The Image Bank;* **42,** © John McGrail/*Wheeler Pictures;* **43,** NASA; **46,** top, VANSCAN/*Daedalus Enterprises;* bottom, © Dan McCoy/*Rainbow;* **47,** C. Bonington/*Daily Telegraph Magazine*/*Woodfin Camp;* **54,** Michael Philip Manheim; **59,** Ken Karp; **60,** Comstock; **61,** © Gary Ladd; **62,** top, Culver Pictures; bottom, I. Kennedy/*International Stock Photo;* **64,** Ken Karp; **65,** Ken Karp; **66,** left, © Michael Melford/*Wheeler Pictures;* right, Henry Grossman/*dpi;* **67,** Ken Karp; **68,** John V. A. F. Neal/*International Stock Photo;* **69,** © Thomas Braise/*Stock Market;* **71,** Ken Karp; **72,** Japanese National Railways; **73,** Richard Megna/*Fundamental Photographs;* **75,** left, Ken Karp; right, © Phil Degginger/*Bruce Coleman;* **77,** © Judith Aronson/*Peter Arnold;* **79,** top left, © David P. Mitchell/© *Photo Unique;* top right, © Robert Frerck/*Odyssey Prod.;* bottom, © Joe Bator/*The Stock Market;* **84,** © Michael Melford/*Wheeler Pictures;* **86,** left, Richard Steedman/*The Stock Market;* right, NASA; **87,** top, Ken Karp; bottom, Dotte Larsen/*Bruce Coleman;* **90,** © Sepp Seitz/*Woodfin Camp;* **94,** © Toni Angermayer/*Photo Researchers;* **97,** Fundamental Photographs; **99,** © Michael Melford/*Wheeler Pictures;* **100,** top, © Robert Frerck; bottom, © Margaret McCarthy/*Peter Arnold;* **108,** © William James Warren/*West Light;* **110,** Kelly Langley/*dpi;* **114,** © Dan McCoy/*Rainbow;* **115,** Howard Sochurek/*Woodfin Camp;* **117,** top, Ken Karp; bottom, P. A. Hinchcliffe/*Bruce Coleman;* **118,** Bill Binzen/*The Image Bank;* **119,** top, Ken Karp; bottom, © Charles E. Dorris/*Photo Unique;* **121,** Ron Watts/© *Black Star;* **122,** © Richard Megna/*Fundamental Photographs;* **123,** *Fundamental Photographs;* **124,** © Galen Rowell/*Peter Arnold;* **125,** top left, top right, Fundamental Photographs; bottom, Breck P. Kent/*Earth Sciences;* **126,** © Lennart Nilsson/*Behold Man*/Little, Brown & Co., Boston, **127,** Ken Karp; **128,** David Kingdon/*Black Star;* **129,** © Farrell Grehan/*Photo Researchers;* **130,** © Nancy Safford/*Woodfin Camp;* **131,** top, © Peter B. Kaplan/*The Stock Market;* bottom, © Nancy Safford/*Woodfin Camp;* **136,** © Dan McCoy/*Rainbow;* **138,** Ken Karp; **139,** © Dan McCoy/*Rainbow;* **140,** © Manuel Rodriguez; **143,** Brookhaven National Laboratory; **144,** Oak Ridge National Laboratory; **145,** top, Dan McCoy/*Rainbow;* bottom left, John Pawloski/*Tom Stack;* bottom right, Robert Carr/*Bruce Coleman;* **146,** top left, Fermi National Accelerator Laboratory; top right, Hank Morgan/*Photo Researchers;* bottom, Los Alamos Scientific Laboratory; **148,** © Dan McCoy/*Black Star;* **149,** top, Los Alamos National Laboratory; bottom, DOE; **154,** Homer Sykes/*Woodfin Camp;* **155,** Julian Calder/*Woodfin Camp;* **156,** left, Lenore Weber/*OPC;* right, C. C. Lockwood/*Earth Scenes;* **157,** Breck P. Kent/*Earth Scenes;* **158,** U. of California/*Lawrence Berkley Lab;* **162,** NASA; **164,** Granger Collection; **166,** Ken Sakamoto/*Black Star;* **168,** left, Ira Block/*Woodfin Camp;* right, Kalish/DiMaggio/*Peter Arnold;* **169,** © Paul Chesley/*Photographers Aspen;* **170,** Mark Antman/*Image Works;* **172,** Bruce Wellman/*Picture Group;* **173,** top left, Randa Bishop/*Woodfin Camp;* top right, Steve Smith/*Gamma Liaison;* bottom, NASA; **174,** © Paul Chesley/*Photographers Aspen;* **175,** Eiji Miyazawa/*Black Star;* **176,** left, The Stock Market; right, Judy Flay Derman/*Stock Market;* **178,** Michael Abramson/*Liaison Agency;* **179,** U. of Rochester; **180,** Klaus D. Francke/*Stock Market;* **181,** Steven Kaufman/*Peter Arnold;* **182,** Rodney Jones; **188,** left, J. Alex Langley/*dpi;* right, North Wind Picture Archives; **189,** Don Landwehrle/*The Image Bank;* **191,** clockwise, Jim Merithew/*Picture Group;* Michael Furman/*Stock Market;* Ken Karp; Seth H. Goltzer/*Stock Market;* Ken Karp; bottom clockwise, Vince Streano/*Stock Market,* © Joel Gordon; Ken Karp; © Joel Gordon; © Ted Horowitz/*Stock Market;* **192,** left, William E. Ferguson; right, Hal Yaeger/*dpi;* **193,** left, E. I. DuPont de Nemours & Co.; right, Shreiber/*Liaison Agency;* **194,** top, Palmer/Kane/*The Stock Market;* bottom, Life Science Library/GIANT MOLECULES, photograph by Bruce Roberts © 1966 Time, Inc. Time-Life Books, Inc. Publisher; **195,** top left, top right, E. I. DuPont de Nemours & Co.; **196,** Life Science Library/GIANT MOLECULES, photograph by John Zimmerman © 1966 Time, Inc. Time-Life Books, Inc. Publisher; **197,** all, Dan McCoy/*Rainbow;* **198,** Life Science Library/GIANT MOLECULES, photograph by John Zimmerman © 1966 Time, Inc. Time-Life Books, Inc., Publisher; **199,** © Roy Morsch/*Stock Market;* **204,** NASA; **206,** NASA; **207,** NASA; **208,** NASA; **211,** NASA; **212,** NASA;**213,** NASA; **214,** NASA; **215,** NASA; **216,** NASA; **217,** NASA; **218,** NASA; **219,** both, NASA; **220,** NASA; **221,** NASA; **222,** NASA; **223,** NASA; **228,** © Joel Gordon; **230,** top, NASA; bottom, Ed Kashi/*Liaison Agency;* **231,** left, NASA/*Science Source*/*Photo Researchers;* center, Hank Morgan/*Photo Researchers;* right, George Halling/*Photo Researchers;* **232,** top, IBM; bottom, Ken Karp; **233,** Ken Karp; bottom left, Joel Gordon; bottom right, Alfred Pasieka/*Taurus Photos;* **234,** C. Mula & Haramaty/*Phototake;* **236,** left, Dan McCoy/*Rainbow;* right, *Photo Researchers;* **238,** University of California; **239,** © George Haling/*Wheeler Photos;* **240,** M.I.T.; **241,** © John Zoiner/*Peter Arnold;* **242,** © Michael Melford/*Wheeler Pictures;* **243,** top left, Chuck O'Rear/*West Light*/*Woodfin Camp;* top right, © Sepp Seitz/*Woodfin Camp;* bottom, Ch. Vioujard/*Gamma Liaison;* **248,** © Luis Villota/*The Stock Market;* **250,** Wally McNamee/*Woodfin Camp;* **251,** top, © Michael Patrick/*Picture Group;* bottom, © Martin Rogers/*Woodfin Camp;* **252,** top, © Martin Rogers/*Woodfin Camp;* bottom left, © Martin Rogers/*Woodfin Camp;* bottom right, ©Mark Antman/*The Image Works;* **253,** left, © B. Gilbert Uzam—*Gamma/Liaison;* right, © Laurent Maous—*Gamma/Liaison;* **254,** © Fredrik D. Bodin/*Picture Group;* **255,** left, © Sisse Brimberg/*Woodfin Camp;* right, Dave Healey/*Liaison;* **256,** © George Fisher/Vision/*Woodfin Camp;* **257,** Yoram Lehmann/*Peter Arnold;* **258,** © Jeff Hunter/*The Image Bank;* **259,** all photos: Roger Cheng/*Atmosphere Research;* **261,** left, © Judy Aronson/*Peter Arnold;* right, © Michael Melford/*Wheeler Pictures;* **262,** © Peter Tenzer/*Wheeler Pictures;* **263,** © James Mason/*Black Star;* **264,** *dpi*/Wil Blanche; **268,** top, Carl Skalak/© *Discover* magazine, 1/83. Time, Inc., bottom, Carl Skalak/© *Discover* magazine, 1/83. Time, Inc.; **269,** Carl Skalak © *Discover* magazine 1/83. Time, Inc.; **270,** Bob Strauss/*Woodfin Camp;* **271,** Robert Azzi/*Woodfin Camp;* **272,** Western Union Corp.; **276,** © Michael Melford/*Wheeler Pictures;* **278,** © Kyodo News; **280,** top, Stephen J. Krasemann/*DRK Photo;* bottom, Tom Stack; **282,** Breck P. Kent; **283,** H. C. McComas/*Woods Hole Oceanographic Institution;* **284,** © Don King/*The Image Bank;* **286,** © James H. Butler; **287,** NOAA/NESDIS/NCDC/SDSD/U.S. Dept. of Commerce; **289,** © Josephus Daniels/*The Image Bank;* **294,** © National Geographic Society by Alvin Chandler & Emory Kristoff; **296,** © James M. King; **298,** © David L. Shogren/*Tom Stack;* **299,** Steve Krasemann/*DRK Photo;* **301,** "Carte du Fond des Oceans" by Tanguy de Remur/© Hachette-Guides Bleus; **304,** left, Dr. Harold Simon/*Tom Stack;* right, © Ken Sakamoto/*Black Star;* **307,** left, Nicholas Devore/*Bruce Coleman;* right, © Adam Woolfitt/*Woodfin Camp;* **312,** Jeff Foott/*Bruce Coleman;* **314,** R. L. Sefton/*Bruce Coleman;* **316,** © Breck P. Kent; **317,** right, Gordon S. Smith/*Photo Researchers;* left, Buff Corsi/*Tom Stack;* **318,** left, Ed Robinson/*Tom Stack;* right, Breck P. Kent; **319,** top, © Walker/*Photo Researchers;* bottom, Ron and Valerie Taylor/*Bruce Coleman;* **320,** all, Bruce H. Robison; **321,** top, Kim Taylor/*Bruce Coleman;* bottom, © David L. Shogren/*Tom Stack;* **322,** left, Norman Tomalin/*Bruce Coleman;* right © Breck P. Kent; **323,** right, Robert Ballard/*Woods Hole Oceanographic Institution;* left, Jack Donnelly/*Woods Hole Oceanographic Institution;* **324,** Grant Heilman/*Runk Schoenberger;* **328,** Woods Hole Oceanographic Institution; **329,** top, Sygma; bottom, Woods Hole Oceanographic Institution/*Sygma;* **331,** G. Williamson/*Bruce Coleman;* **332,** top, American Museum of Natural History; bottom, Richard Kolar/*Animals Animals;* **336,** Herman Kokojan/*Black Star;* **340,** © Mats Wibe Lund/*Icelandic Photo;* **341,** Thomas Nebbia/*dpi;* **342,** © Eric Grave/*Photo Researchers;* **343,** Field Museum of Natural History; **344,** Keith Gunnar/*Bruce Coleman;* **345,** Steve Northrup/*Black Star;* **346,** © John McGrail/*Wheeler Pictures;* **347,** © Michael Melford/*Wheeler Pictures;* **352,** © F. Myer/*The Image Bank;* **354,** © Dan Miller/*Woodfin Camp;* **357,** © Michael Melford/*The Image Bank;* **359,** Runk Schoenberger/*Grant Heilman;* **363,** top, Gene Moore; bottom, NASA; **366,** top, John S. Shelton; center, John S. Shelton; bottom, S. J. Kraseman/© *Peter Arnold;* **367,** top, John Running/*Black Star;* bottom left, Everett C. Johnson/*Leo de Wys;* bottom right, *dpi;* **368,** NOAA; **369,** © Randy Taylor/*Sygma;* **370,** NOAA/NESDIS; **371,** top, NOAA/NESDIS: bottom, NOAA/NESDIS: **380,** Patti McConville/*The Image Bank;* right, © Obremski/*The Image Bank;* **381,** top, D. Fishman/*Click*/Chicago; bottom, Jadwiga Lopez/*Click*/Chicago; **382,** Geoff Juckes/*The Stock Market;* **386,** left, Jack Wilburn/*Earth Scenes;* right, © P. A. Whalley/*Photo Researchers;* **387,** © Edward Bower/*The Image Bank;* **388,** Z. Leszczynski/*Earth Scenes;* **389,** Stephen J. Krasemann/*Peter Arnold;* **390,** Breck P. Kent/*Earth Scenes;* **391,** Craig Aurness/*Woodfin Camp;* **396,** left, Joanne Simpson; right, David W. Hamilton/*The Image Bank;* **397,** NASA; **398,** Utah Power and Light Co.; **399,** *dpi;* **400,** NOAA; **402,** left, Baron Wolman/*Woodfin Camp;* right, Jack Parsons/*OPC;* **404,** Barbara Laing, *Picture Group;* **406,** NIH/*Photo Researchers;* **408,** E. Miyazawa/*Black Star;* **415,** H. E. Edgerton/*M.I.T.;* **417,** © Charles West/*Stock Market;* **419,** right, © Breck P. Kent; left, Tom Kaufman/*photo by R. Turner;* **421,** top left, W. H. Hodge/© Peter Arnold; top right, © Douglas Kirkland/*Woodfin Camp;* bottom, © Dennis Brack/*Black Star;* **426,** Eli Lilly Company; **428,** © Richard Hutchings/*Photo Researchers;* **429,** Dan McCoy/*Rainbow;* **430,** © Robert McElroy/*Woodfin Camp;* **431,** Bill Longcore/*Photo Researchers;* **432,** Sonya Jacobs/*The Stock Market;* **434,** top, © Leonard Lessin/*Photo Researchers;* bottom, © Linda K. Moore/*dpi;* **435,** left, © Ellis Hernig/*The Image Bank;* right, © Bo Zaunders/*Stock Market;* **436,** S. Cohen/*Photo Researchers;* **438,** © Hank Morgan/*Photo Researchers;* **439,** John McGrail/*Wheeler Pictures;* **447,** Breck P. Kent; **449,** left, *Breck P. Kent;* center, © Hans Pfletschinger/*Peter Arnold;* right, Stephen J. Krasemann/*DRK Photo;* bottom, Jane Burton/*Bruce Coleman;* **453,** © Werner H. Müller/*Peter Arnold;* **454,** both, Laura Riley/*Bruce Coleman;* **455,** left, © M.P.L. Fogden/*Bruce Coleman;* right, © Christopher Crowley/*Tom Stack;* **456,** left, James H. Karales/© *Peter Arnold;* right, © William Hubbell/*Woodfin Camp;* **457,** © Breck P. Kent; **458,** left, © Breck P. Kent; right, © Breck P. Kent; **459,** © George Dodge/*dpi;* **460,** Werner Stoy/Camera Hawaii/*Bruce Coleman;* **461,** left, © Julie Habel/*West Light;* right, © Breck P. Kent; **462,** E. R. Degginger/*Earth Scenes;* **466,** NASA; **468,** left, © Buff Corsi/*Tom Stack;* right, Stouffer Enterprises/*Animals Animals;* **469,** © Tom McHugh/*Photo Researchers;* **470,** Warren & Genny Garst/*Tom Stack;* **471,** Cleveland Museum of Natural History; **472,** © Wally McNamee/*Woodfin Camp;* **473,** top, bottom, © Margo Crabtree; **475,** © Margo Crabtree; **476,** both, © Margo Crabtree; **479,** © Tom McHugh/*Photo Researchers;* **484,** Nik Kleinberg/*Picture Group* **486,** *Bruce Coleman;* **488,** Breck P. Kent/*Animals Animals;* **492,** Bill Wood/*Bruce Coleman;* **494,** John S. Flannery/*Bruce Coleman;* **496,** Rod Allin/*Tom Stack;* **497,** left, Zig Leszczynsky/*Animals Animals;* right, Manuel Rodriguez; **498,** John Johnson/*DRK Photo;* **500,** left, Jim Brandenburg/*Woodfin Camp;* right, Stephen Krasemann/*DRK Photo;* **501,** both, Stephen Krasemann/*DRK Photo;* **502,** right, John Shaw/*Tom Stack;* left, Tom Bean/*DRK Photo;* **503,** top, Stephen Krasemann/*DRK Photo;* bottom, Wayne Lankinen/*Bruce Coleman;* **504,** top, Manuel Rodriguez; bottom, John Shaw/*Tom Stack;* **505,** left, James H. Karales /*Peter Arnold;* right, J. MacGregor/*Peter Arnold;* bottom, Loren McIntyre/*Woodfin Camp;* **506,** top left, E. R. Degginger/*Animals Animals;* top right, Nadine Orabona/*Tom Stack;* bottom left, Richard K. LaVal/*Animals Animals;* bottom right, Michael Fogden/*Animals Animals;* **507,** Stephen Krasemann/*DRK Photo;* **510,** Lynn M. Stone/*Bruce Coleman;* **511,** top left, *dpi;* top right, © Bruno J. Zehnder/*Peter Arnold;* bottom, Stephen Krasemann/*DRK Photo;* **512,** Rodney Jones; **516,** Jeff Foott/*Bruce Coleman;* **518,** right, Fred Whitehead/*Animals Animals;* left, Stouffer Productions, Ltd./*Animals Animals;* **519,** top, Mickey Gibson/*Animals Animals;* bottom, Gary Milburn/*Tom Stack;* **520,** top, Tom Stack/*Tom Stack;* bottom, Anne Wertheim/*Animals Animals;* **521,** top, Jen and Des Bartlett/*Bruce Coleman;* bottom, Lee Foster/*Bruce Coleman;* **522,** Breck P. Kent/*Earth Scenes;* **523,** Erich Hartmann/*Magnum;* **532,** Brian Milne/*Animals Animals;* **534,** right, Milton Rand/*Tom Stack;* left, Erich Hartmann/*Magnum;* **535,** left, Mike Maple/*Woodfin Camp;* right, Victor Englebert/*Photo Researchers;* **536,** Steven C. Kaufman/*Peter Arnold;* **537,** Keith Gunnar/*Bruce Coleman;* **538,** Mike Yamashita/*Woodfin Camp;* **539,** Steve Krasemann/*DRK Photo;* **540,** top, Fiona Sunquist/*Tom Stack;* bottom, E. R. Degginger/*Earth Scenes;* **541,** Nancy Simmerman/*Bruce Coleman;* **542,** top, Peter Davey/*Bruce Coleman;* bottom, Anthony Bannister/*Animals Animals;* **543,** Lowell Georgia/*Photo Researchers;* **544,** top, *Animals Animals;* bottom, Gordon Langsburg/*Bruce Coleman;* **545,** top right, Leonard Lee Rue III/*Animals Animals;* left, David de Vries/*Bruce Coleman;* bottom, Mark Sherman/*Bruce Coleman;* **546,** Ken Karp; **550,** Lola B. Graham/*Photo Researchers;* **551,** Robert W. Young/*dpi;* **553,** top, J. Alex Langley/*dpi;* bottom, Cannon-Benaventre/*Anthro-Photo;* **554,** J. Alex Langley/*dpi;* **557,** DeVore/*Anthro-Photo.*

Text illustrations by Lee Ames & Zak Ltd. with special acknowledgement to David Christensen. Gazette art by Phil Carver & Friends, Inc.